2

BLACK AMERICAN WRITERS
Bibliographical Essays

Volume 1   *THE BEGINNINGS THROUGH*
    THE HARLEM RENAISSANCE
    AND LANGSTON HUGHES

Black American Writers:
Bibliographical Essays,

Volume 1 *THE BEGINNINGS*
THROUGH THE HARLEM
RENAISSANCE AND
LANGSTON HUGHES

Edited by
M. THOMAS INGE
MAURICE DUKE
JACKSON R. BRYER

New York   *St. Martin's Press*

Library of Congress Catalog Card Number: 77–85987
Copyright © 1978 by St. Martin's Press, Inc.
All Rights Reserved.
Manufactured in the United States of America.
2109
fedcb
For information, write St. Martin's Press, Inc.,
175 Fifth Avenue, New York, N. Y. 10010

cover design: Mies Hora

ISBN: 0-312-08260-6

PREFACE

The last two decades have witnessed a great proliferation of scholarship devoted to the history and culture of Afro-Americans. And out of this increasing recognition of the contribution of blacks to the development of this nation has come a significant reassessment of the aesthetic and humanistic achievements of black writers.

Black American Writers: Bibliographical Essays is intended as an appraisal of the best biographical and critical writings about America's seminal black writers, as well as an identification of manuscript and special resources for continued study. It is also intended to give an overview of the current state of scholarly recognition of the lives and careers of these authors and an appreciation of their works.

The coverage is intentionally selective, both in the figures involved and the material examined in each chapter. Yet we feel that, within our self-imposed chronological limit, no major Afro-American literary figure has been overlooked. Volume 1 covers the early black writers of the eighteenth century, the slave narratives, the early modern writers, the Harlem Renaissance, and Langston Hughes. Volume 2 focuses on four major twentieth-century black writers: Richard Wright, Ralph Ellison, James Baldwin, and Amiri Baraka (LeRoi Jones). A bibliographical survey of the great number of black American writers who have come to prominence since Wright, Ellison, Baldwin, and Baraka would require another volume or volumes and, given the rich and vigorous production of black writers today and the continual emergence of new figures, would perhaps be premature.

Our hope is that the bibliographical essays in these volumes, all by specialists on their topics, will aid and encourage further study of black American writers and literature.

M. Thomas Inge
Maurice Duke
Jackson R. Bryer

KEY TO JOURNAL
ABBREVIATIONS

ABC	American Book Collector	*EH*	Eastern Horizon (Hong Kong)
AH	American Heritage	*EJ*	English Journal
AHR	American Historical Review	*EngR*	English Record
AI	American Imago	*ETJ*	Educational Theatre Journal
AJS	American Journal of Sociology	*EvR*	Evergreen Review
AL	American Literature	*Expl*	Explicator
ALR	American Literary Realism, 1870–1910	*FourQ*	Four Quarters
		GaR	Georgia Review
AmerS	American Studies	*GC*	Graduate Comment
AQ	American Quarterly	*HC*	Hollins Critic
AR	Antioch Review	*IJAS*	Indian Journal of American Studies
ArQ	Arkansas Quarterly	*JAF*	Journal of American Folklore
ASch	American Scholar		
ASoc	Arts in Society	*JAH*	Journal of American History
AtM	Atlantic Monthly		
BALF	Black American Literature Forum	*JAmS*	Journal of American Studies
BARev	Black Academy Review	*JBlS*	Journal of Black Studies
BB	Bulletin of Bibliography	*JBP*	Journal of Black Poetry
BlackBB	Black Books Bulletin	*JEGP*	Journal of English and Germanic Philology
BlackD	Black Dialogue		
BlackR	Black Review	*JHR*	Journal of Human Relations
BlackSch	Black Scholar		
BlackW	Black World	*JML*	Journal of Modern Literature
CathW	Catholic World		
CE	College English	*JNE*	Journal of Negro Education
ChiR	Chicago Review		
CLAJ	College Language Association Journal	*JNH*	Journal of Negro History
ColQ	Colorado Quarterly	*JNT*	Journal of Narrative Technique
ConL	Contemporary Literature	*JPC*	Journal of Popular Culture
CP	Concerning Poetry	*JSH*	Journal of Southern History
Crit	Critique		
DAI	Dissertation Abstracts International	*KanQ*	Kansas Quarterly
DB	Down Beat	*KR*	Kenyon Review
EA	Etudes Anglaises	*L&I*	Literature and Ideology
EAL	Early American Literature	*LanM*	Langues Modernes
		LJ	Library Journal

MarkhamR	Markham Review	*S&S*	Science and Society
MASJ	Midcontinent American	*SAQ*	South Atlantic Quarterly
	Studies Journal	*SatR*	Saturday Review
MD	Modern Drama	*SBL*	Studies in Black
MFS	Modern Fiction Studies		Literature
MidwestJ	Midwest Journal	*SCR*	South Carolina Review
MinnR	Minnesota Review	*SEP*	Saturday Evening Post
MissQ	Mississippi Quarterly	*SF*	Social Forces
ModQ	Modern Quarterly	*SFQ*	Southern Folklore
MQ	Midwest Quarterly		Quarterly
MQR	Michigan Quarterly	*SHR*	Southern Humanities
	Review		Review
MR	Massachusetts Review	*SLJ*	Southern Literary
N&Q	Notes and Queries		Journal
NALF	Negro American	*SNL*	Satire Newsletter
	Literature Forum	*SNNTS*	Studies in the Novel
NAR	North American Review		(North Texas State
NConL	Notes on Contemporary		University)
	Literature	*SR*	Sewanee Review
ND	Negro Digest	*SSF*	Studies in Short Fiction
NEQ	New England Quarterly	*SWR*	Southwest Review
NewL	New Letters	*TAY*	Twice-A-Year
NHB	Negro History Bulletin	*TDR*	The Drama Review
NL	New Leader		(Formerly Tulane
NR	New Republic		Drama Review)
NY	New Yorker	*TQ*	Texas Quarterly
NYHTBW	New York Herald	*TSLL*	Texas Studies in
	Tribune Book Week		Language and
NYRB	New York Review of		Literature
	Books	*UKCR*	University of Kansas
NYTBR	New York Times Book		City Review
	Review	*UR*	University Review
PBSA	Papers of the	*VQR*	Virginia Quarterly
	Bibliographical Society		Review
	of America	*WHR*	Western Humanities
PMLA	Publications of the		Review
	Modern Language	*WLB*	Wilson Library Bulletin
	Association of America	*WSCL*	Wisconsin Studies in
PoeS	Poe Studies		Contemporary
PR	Partisan Review		Literature
PubW	Publishers Weekly	*WWR*	Walt Whitman Review
QJS	Quarterly Journal of	*XUS*	Xavier University
	Speech		Studies
QQ	Queen's Quarterly	*YR*	Yale Review
QRL	Quarterly Review of	*YULG*	Yale University Library
	Literature		Gazette
RAL	Research in African	*ZAA*	Zeitschrift für Anglistik
	Literature		und Amerikanistik (East
RALS	Resources for American		Berlin)
	Literary Study		

CONTENTS

BLACK AMERICAN WRITERS
Bibliographical Essays

*Volume 1   THE BEGINNINGS THROUGH
    THE HARLEM RENAISSANCE
    AND LANGSTON HUGHES*

EARLY WRITERS:
Jupiter Hammon, Phillis Wheatley, and Benjamin Banneker

JEROME KLINKOWITZ

Jupiter Hammon

Jupiter Hammon (1711–c. 1786) lived most of his life as a slave of the Lloyd family on their Long Island, New York, estate. Hammon's literary talents, which found expression in poems of religious exhortation, were encouraged by the Lloyds, and earned him the stature of a preacher and leader among his fellow slaves. Because Hammon's poem "An Evening Thought" was published in 1761, he is generally regarded as America's first black poet, though this rank is determined by formal publication within the structures of genteel white society. Hammon remains noteworthy as a figure whose writing technique served the demands of poetic art as well as those of his religious faith. What earlier critics saw as crudeness, contemporary scholars have come to regard as evidence of folk poetry struggling against the stricter forms of religious verse.

BIBLIOGRAPHY

A complete descriptive bibliography of the works of Jupiter Hammon is provided by Oscar Wegelin in *Jupiter Hammon: American Negro Poet* (New York: Charles F. Heartman, 1915). Wegelin's compilation is also the most accessible, as it is available in reprint editions (Plainview, N. Y.: Books for Libraries, 1969 and 1970), and, in addition, is incorporated in an anthology by Stanley Austin Ransom, Jr., *America's First Negro Poet: The Complete Works of Jupiter Hammon of Long Island* (Port Washington, N. Y.: Kennikat Press, 1970).

EDITIONS

Ransom's anthology reprints nearly all of Hammon's poetry and prose, except for "An Essay on the Ten Virgins." Wegelin's volume includes

1

the same poetry, as well as excerpts from Hammon's "An Address to the Negroes in the State of New York." Of the current anthologies, Dorothy B. Porter provides the best representation of Hammon's poetry and prose, reprinting "An Evening Thought," "An Address to Miss Phillis Wheatly [*sic*]," and the full "An Address to the Negroes in the State of New York" in *Early Negro Writing, 1760–1847* (Boston: Beacon, 1971). Four facsimiles are available on Readex Microprint in the Early American Imprint Series from the American Antiquarian Society: "An Address to the Negroes in the State of New York by Jupiter Hammon, Servant of John Lloyd, Jun., Esq., of the Manor of Queen's Village, Long-Island" (New York: Printed by Carroll and Patterson, 1787); "An Essay on the Ten Virgins" (Hartford, Conn.: Printed by Hudson and Goodwin, 1779); *An Evening's Improvement* (Hartford, Conn.: n.p., 1783); *A Winter Piece* (Hartford, Conn.: For the Author, 1782).

MANUSCRIPTS AND LETTERS

The only catalogued item in Hammon's own hand is his inscription in the original edition of *A Winter Piece,* "For The Rev'd William Lockwood, from His firend [*sic*] & humble Serv't, The Author," preserved in the Library of the Connecticut Historical Society in Hartford. Hammon was not included in the original survey for *American Literary Manuscripts,* edited by Joseph Jones (Austin: University of Texas Press, 1960), but his name was added to the author list compiled in 1970 for the second edition of this work, which is edited by J. Albert Robbins (Athens: University of Georgia Press, 1977).

BIOGRAPHY

The main source for nearly all biographical information on Jupiter Hammon is Oscar Wegelin's *Jupiter Hammon: American Negro Poet.* Wegelin traces Hammon's life beginning with a letter written in 1730 that makes reference to Hammon as a child, but admits that "none of his [Hammon's] contemporaries seemed to have left behind anything which would throw any light upon his life." Therefore Wegelin was forced to piece together his portrait of the writer from what Hammon revealed about himself in "An Address to the Negroes in New York State," and from the tenor of Hammon's other writings. From these Wegelin concludes that Hammon was "a preacher among his people." A history of his publications is provided, along with a statement contrasting Hammon's career with that of Phillis Wheatley: "He, a slave faithfully serving both his Heavenly and earthly Masters, probably almost unknown outside of a small circle in which he moved, while she, the child of fortune, was petted by all with whom she came in contact."

Benjamin Brawley offers a sketch of Hammon, following the details set forth by Wegelin, in *The Negro in Literature and Art in the United States* (New York: Duffield, 1929). In his *Early Negro American Writers* (Chapel Hill: University of North Carolina Press, 1935), Brawley expands his commentary to include Hammon's life as a slave, the importance of the Methodist Wesleyan revival (a popularly based protest against the alleged apathy of the Anglican church) in Hammon's times, and a list of Hammon's works and their publishing history. Brawley's *The Negro Genius* (New York: Dodd, Mead, 1937) reemphasizes Hammon's condition as a slave, and notes his importance in preceding Wheatley as a published poet. Beatrice Lagone draws on both Wegelin and Brawley in her essay, "Jupiter Hammon, America's First Negro Poet" (*ND*, April 1964), stressing the "highly religious nature" of his life and works.

Although the bulk of material presented by Stanley Austin Ransom, Jr., in the introduction to *America's First Negro Poet: The Complete Works of Jupiter Hammon of Long Island* is derived from Wegelin, some new information gleaned from histories of Long Island is added. Ransom incorporates the findings of Charles A. Vertanes, first published as "Jupiter Hammon: Early Negro Poet of L. I." (*Nassau County Historical Journal*, Winter 1957), regarding Hammon's schooling from Nehemiah Bull and his reading of Burkitt and Bishop Beverage in his master's library. Reported also are the speculations of Jacqueline Overton, in *Long Island's Story*, 2nd edition (Port Washington, N. Y.: Ira J. Friedman, 1961), that "in 1782 Hammon composed a set of verses, not yet found and possibly not published, to celebrate the visit of young Prince William Henry, later King William IV, to Lloyd Manor House." In a headnote to Ransom's volume, the publishers add that Lillian Koppel, a graduate student in the American Studies class of Professor Louis Lomax of Hofstra University, had discovered the exact birthdate of Jupiter Hammon. Previously speculated to be approximately 1720, Koppel establishes the date as October 11, 1711, "and it appears in Henry Lloyd's handwriting in a list of birthdates of slaves." Lloyd's ledger, which includes the list, is part of the archives of the Long Island Historical Society.

CRITICISM

Critical reactions to the work of Jupiter Hammon begin with Oscar Wegelin's essay, "Was Phillis Wheatley America's First Negro Poet?" (*Literary Collector*, August 1904), which was expanded (with evidence to support the historical assertions) in Wegelin's *Jupiter Hammon: American Negro Poet*. By locating a copy of "An Evening Thought" published in 1761, a decade before Wheatley's first published work, Wegelin establishes Hammon's precedence as America's first published Negro poet. He then adds that Hammon's verse is flawed and tedious, and suffers by comparison with the work of Wheatley. Wegelin's general assessment was that Hammon's verse "is saturated with a religious feeling not always well expressed, as he did not possess the ability to use the right word at the proper time." Hammon's repetition of certain words, especially "salvation" and "death," mark his religious emphasis; but, as was representative of the times, that religion was narrow and superstitious. Although he ultimately admires Hammon's work in view of the debilitating conditions in which the poet lived, Wegelin regrets the proselytizing zeal of the poetry to the exclusion of any comment about events in Hammon's own life and times during and after the War of Independence.

In *The Book of American Negro Poetry* (New York: Harcourt, Brace, 1931), James Weldon Johnson agrees that Hammon's poetry consisted almost entirely of religious exhortations. The religious influence, however, is seen by Vernon Loggins as being far more complex in his pioneering work, *The Negro Author: His Development in America* (New York: Columbia University Press, 1931). Loggins establishes such influences as the Bible, hymn books, "and possibly such pious poems as Michael Wigglesworth's *The Day of Doom.*" He admits that Hammon's work may have appeared crude at the time that it was written and published, but that now, having some knowledge of Negro folk poetry, one can have "high regard for the strength of wild and native religious feeling in what he wrote, a strength which he achieved without conscious effort." Loggins cites the "strange notions" recurrent in Hammon's verse, and how "his mystic Negro mind played with these notions." Admiration is expressed for Hammon's instinct for music. While some of his metrics are derived from Wesleyan hymns, "his method of composition must have been that of the unknown makers of the spirituals." Hammon would cast a spell by repeating single words that have a haunting sound, such as "salvation." The poet created strange rhymes and unexpected turns of thought, both of which suggest "the bold extravagance of the spiritual." Especially noteworthy are Hammon's syncopated rhythms. But his work was not naively primitive: instead his most representative work shows a "balanced structure of ideas." Loggins concludes that Hammon fell into disregard and eventual oblivion because of his conciliatory attitude toward slavery. These considerations of Hammon's art are voiced again in Jean Wagner's monumental *Black Poets of the United States*, translated by Kenneth Douglas (Urbana: University of Illinois Press, 1973). There Hammon is praised for the bold syncopations in his poetry, which was designed "to be heard rather than read." Wagner praises "An Evening Thought" for its position at "a halfway stage between the guileless art of the unknown composers of spirituals and the already much wordier manner of the black popular preacher." In a brief essay titled "Jupiter Hammon's Poetic Exhortations" (*CLAJ*, September 1974), R. Roderick Palmer compares Hammon's techniques as a poet to those of King David in the Psalms, noting that each advocated "such moral qualities as patience, devotion to duty, obedience to authority, avoidance of violence, and other similar conduct." These exhortations, Palmer insists, helped create a climate for practical Christianity which in turn led to the concept of racial equality.

Benjamin Brawley presents similar appraisals of Hammon in *The Negro Genius* (New York: Dodd, Mead, 1937), and *Early Negro American Writers* (Chapel Hill: University of North Carolina Press, 1937). He notes Hammon's habit of repeating favorite words, and says that "An Address to the Negroes in the State of New York" shows Hammon "as feeling it his personal duty to bear slavery with patience but as strongly opposed to the system and insistent that young Negroes be manumitted." Hammon's work, despite its obvious flaws and suggestions of editorial assistance, possesses a unique "strong style." Brawley concludes that Hammon "was content to express his pious musing in such forms as he knew, and he at least has the virtue of earnestness."

A more negative response to Hammon's work is found in Sterling Brown's *Negro Poetry and Drama* (New York: Associates in Negro Folk Education, 1937). Hammon's poems, Brown asserts, are merely crude doggerel, inferior even by the standards of the time, being "largely exclamations of Methodist piety in the diction and rhythm of Wesley and Watts." In their single and cumulative effects, Hammon's poems "show how a Negro slave had been won over to the passive resignation of Christianity. Without any changing to speak of, Hammon gave back what he had been taught by kindly disposed masters." J. Saunders Redding's *To Make a Poet Black* (Chapel Hill: University of North Carolina Press, 1939) is only slightly less pejorative, but with some characterization of Hammon's method along the lines suggested by Loggins. Redding emphasizes the author's role as a preacher, composing poems "in which the homely thoughts of a very religious man are expressed in limping doggerel. Now and then his lines have a lyric swing that seems to mark them as having been chanted spontaneously in the sermons he preached." In this latter respect Redding finds "An Evening Thought" to be among the best of Hammon's writing. Although "An Address to the Negroes in the State of New York" reveals a "workaday character" missing from Hammon's poetry, it is nevertheless typical of the thought of slaves, since it fails to be "bitterly reproachful of bondage." Redding charges Hammon with being too obedient both to God and to his human master.

Benjamin Quarles uses a historical perspective to praise Hammon's "Address," arguing in *The Negro in the American Revolution* (Chapel Hill: University of North Carolina Press, 1961) that Hammon "summed up the feelings of many Negroes—their high hopes as the war ended and their sense of some disappointment during the years that immediately followed." Quarles believes that Hammon found himself a victim of the times, since "with the removal of the British threat to American liberties, the generous idealism of the Revolution had abated." Stanley Austin Ransom, Jr., argues the case for Hammon's "Address" in *America's First Negro Poet: The Complete Works of Jupiter Hammon of Long Island,* maintaining that the author was "an advocate of liberty for his race, even though he himself did not wish to be free" because of his inability to care for himself at such an advanced age. On the other side, Jean Wagner's *Black Poets of the United States* concludes its statement on Hammon with the regret that his work takes a position so "conciliatory" toward slavery.

Phillis Wheatley

The life of Phillis Wheatley (c. 1753–1784) approaches legendary status among early black American writers. She was purchased near Boston harbor as a child by the merchant John Wheatley, whose family recognized and encouraged Phillis's precocious genius. Her poetry, written in the fashionable style of such English poets as Alexander Pope and Thomas Gray, praised her masters, their society, and their Christian religion. In 1773 her *Poems on Various Subjects, Religious and Moral* was published in London, where she was received as an anthropological curiosity and as an example of the benefits accorded African slaves by American civilization. Following the deaths of her master and mistress (who had freed her), Phillis Wheatley married, left the realm of polite society, and eventually died in poverty.

BIBLIOGRAPHY

Dorothy B. Porter's "Early American Negro Writings: A Bibliographical Study" (*PBSA,* 3rd Quarter 1945) is the standard authority on the publication of Wheatley's poems. Porter incorporates the findings of Charles F. Heartman, as first published in *Phillis Wheatley, a Critical Attempt and a Bibliography of her Writings* (New York: Charles F. Heartman, 1915; rpt. Coral Gables, Fla.: Mnemosyne, 1969), which describes her separate publications and collections from 1770 through 1915, with notes on memoirs about her and a list of secondary sources.

EDITIONS

The definitive edition of Wheatley's writings is *The Poems of Phillis Wheatley,* edited by Julian D. Mason, Jr., (Chapel Hill: University of North Carolina Press, 1966). Mason bases the first part of his text on the 1773 edition of Wheatley's *Poems on Various Subjects, Religious and Moral* (London: A. Bell, 1773), and then reprints her uncollected poems and a proposal made in 1779 for a second Wheatley volume which was never assembled. Four earlier editions of Wheatley's poems remain in print: *Memoir and Poems of Phillis Wheatley, a Native African and a Slave. Also, Poems by a Slave (George Moses Horton)* (Boston: Isaac Knapp, 1838; rpt. Coral Gables, Fla.: Mnemosyne, 1969); William G. Allen, *Wheatley, Banneker, and Horton* (Boston: Daniel Laing, Jr., 1849); Charles F. Heartman, *Phillis Wheatley (Phillis Peters): Poems and Letters* (New York: Charles F. Heartman, 1915; rpt. Coral Gables, Fla.: Mnemosyne, 1969); G. Herbert Renfro, *Life and Works of Phillis Wheatley* (Washington, D. C.: R. L. Pendleton, 1916; rpt. Plainview, N. Y.: Books for Libraries, 1969 and 1970). Eight facsimiles are available on Readex Microprint in the Early American Imprint Series from the American Antiquarian Society (which lists the author as Phillis Wheatley Peters): "An Elegiac Poem, on the Death of That Celebrated Divine, and Eminent Servant of Jesus Christ, the Late Reverend and Pious George Whitfield" (Boston: Ezekiel Russell, 1770); subsequent editions are Boston: Ezekiel Russell and John Boyles, 1770; Philadelphia: William Goddard, 1770; and New York: Samuel Inslee and Anthony Car, 1770); "An Elegy, Sacred to the Memory of That Great Divine, The Reverend and Learned Dr. Samuel Cooper" (Boston: Ezekiel Russell, 1784); *Poems on Various Subjects, Religious and Moral* (n.p.: Joseph Crukshank, 1786); "To the Reverend Mr. Pitkin, on the Death of His Lady" (Boston, June 16, 1772); *Poems on Various Subjects, Religious and Moral* (Albany, N. Y.: Reprinted from the London edition for Thomas Spencer, Book-Seller, Market Street, 1793).

There are two supplements to the work of Julian Mason, Jr. In "Some Unpublished Poems of Phillis Wheatley" (*NEQ,* June 1970), Robert C. Kunico describes five manuscript poems discovered in the Library Company of Philadelphia and in the Historical Society of Pennsylvania. Four were not published in the 1773 London edition of Wheatley's work (because of their interest in American independence, Kunico speculates) nor were they included in the second part of Mason's collection. The four poems are "America," "Atheism," "To the Honble. Commodore Hood on His Pardoning a Deserter," and "On the Death of Mr. Snider Murder'd by Richardson." Carl Bridenbaugh reprints "On Messrs. HUSSEY and COFFIN" (which first appeared in the *Newport Mercury,* December 21, 1767, but which was not included in Mason) as "The Earliest Published Poem of Phillis Wheatley" (*NEQ,* December 1969).

MANUSCRIPTS AND LETTERS

Phillis Wheatley's manuscripts are housed at Harvard University, the Massachusetts Historical Society Library in Boston, the American Antiquarian Society at Worcester, Massachusetts, Bowdoin College, Dartmouth College, the Historical Society of Pennsylvania in Philadelphia, and the Library Company of Philadelphia. Her letters may be found at the Boston Public Library, Harvard University, the Massachusetts Historical Society Library in Boston, Duke University, Haverford College, the Historical Society of Pennsylvania in Philadelphia, and the Archives of Churchill College, Cambridge, England (among the papers of the Countess of Huntingdon).

Wheatley's letters were first published in *Proceedings of the Massachusetts Historical Society* (November 1863), and then reprinted by Charles Deane in *Letters of Phillis Wheatley* (Boston: J. Wilson and Sons, 1864), by Charles F. Heartman in *Phillis Wheatley (Phillis Peters): Poems and Letters,* and by G. Herbert Renfro in *Life and Works of Phillis Wheatley.* Julian D. Mason, Jr., reprints these letters and adds three others, newly discovered, in *The Poems of Phillis Wheatley,* including one first published by Benjamin Brawley in "A Phillis Wheatley Letter" (*JNH*, October 1949). Sara Dunlap Jackson supplements Mason's work by publishing for the first time three letters from Phillis Wheatley to the Countess of Huntingdon in "Letters of Phillis Wheatley and Susanna Wheatley" (*JNH*, April 1972). Four additional letters written by Wheatley to the English philanthropist John Thorton between 1772 and 1774 are discussed by Kenneth Silverman in "Four New Letters by Phillis Wheatley" (*EAL*, Winter 1974).

BIOGRAPHY

Other than Bishop Henri Gregoire's sketch of Wheatley in *An Enquiry concerning the Intellectual and Moral Faculties and Literature of Negroes; Followed with an Account of the Life and Works of Fifteen Negroes and Mulattoes,* translated by D. B. Warden (Brooklyn, N. Y.: Thomas Kirk, 1810), where Gregoire regrets Jefferson's deprecation of Wheatley in his *Notes on Virginia,* the first substantial biographies of Phillis Wheatley are two almost identical memoirs published in the volume *Memoir and Poems of Phillis Wheatley, A Native African and a Slave. Also, Poems by a Slave* (George Moses Horton) and William G. Allen's edition, *Wheatley, Banneker, and Horton* (Boston: Daniel Laing, Jr., 1849). These two memoirs, sometimes mistakenly ascribed to Benjamin Bussey Thatcher, were established by Charles Deane in 1863 to have been written by Margaretta Matilda Odell, who used information supplied by descendants of the original Wheatley family (*Proceedings of the Massachusetts Historical Society,* November 1863; reprinted by Charles Deane in *Letters of Phillis Wheatley*). Thatcher's own *Memoir of Phillis Wheatley, a native African and a slave* (Boston: G. W. Light, 1834; rpt. New York: Moore and Payne, 1834) is based entirely on Odell's work, which described the conditions of Wheatley's slavery, her education, the development of her poetical talents, her literary career, and her decline after her marriage. Further details about the Wheatley family are supplied in Nathaniel B. Shurtleff's footnote to the publication of Wheatley's letters, both in the *Proceedings of the Massachusetts Historical Society* and in Deane's volume.

Except for Benjamin Quarles's note in *The Negro in the American Revolution* (Chapel Hill: University of North Carolina Press, 1961) that Benjamin Franklin met with Wheatley during her visit to England in 1773, no new evidence about the life of Phillis Wheatley has been published since these early biographies. However, subsequent sketches have drawn varying conclusions. John R. Slattery, in "Phillis Wheatley, The Negro Poetess" (*CathW*, July 1884), expressed astonishment at Wheatley's achievement, not because of her race (as had been the case in previous biographies), but rather because of her age and sex. In *Phillis Wheatley, A Critical Attempt and a Bibliography of her Writings*, Charles F. Heartman emphasizes that his unique point of view is innocent of racial concerns, but then argues that "the sensitiveness, the warmth of feeling which so clearly shows itself in her letters and is easily traced in her poems, was probably brought forth by these tragic circumstances," namely, her abduction from Africa and her life as a slave in America. Anticipating the claims of later biographers, Heartman argues against Wheatley's subservience in verse, and stresses that her American patriotism was stronger than any loyalty she may have felt to England, since her poem to George Washington is a stronger work than the verses she directed to King George III.

The essentials of Wheatley's personal life and career as a poet are repeated by Arthur A. Schomburg in "Appreciation," printed with Heartman's *Phillis Wheatley (Phillis Peters): Poems and Letters*, by G. Herbert Renfro in *Life and Works of Phillis Wheatley*, and by Vernon Loggins in *The Negro Author, His Development in America* (New York: Columbia University Press, 1931). The most complete survey of earlier sources appears in *The Poems of Phillis Wheatley*, edited by Julian D. Mason, Jr.

Briefer but historically accurate summaries of Wheatley's life are "The First Negro Poet of America" by Emily Foster Happer (*Literary Collector*, July 1904), and those included by Benjamin Brawley in his works *The Negro in Literature and Art in the United States* (New York: Duffield & Co., 1929), *Early Negro American Writers* (Chapel Hill: University of North Carolina Press, 1935), *The Negro Genius* (New York: Dodd, Mead, 1937), and *Negro Builders and Heroes* (Chapel Hill: University of North Carolina Press, 1937). Two short popular sketches are Wilfred Holmes's "Phillis Wheatley" (*NHB*, February 1943), and Glenn S. Weight's "Anniversary of Phillis Wheatley Remains an Inspiration to All" (*NHB*, January 1962).

A new perspective on Wheatley's identity as a black woman in eighteenth-century America is provided by Merle A. Richmond in her comprehensive study, *Bid the Vassal Soar: Interpretive Essays on the Life and Poetry of Phillis Wheatley and George Moses Horton* (Washington, D. C.: Howard University Press, 1974).

Of works for younger readers, only Langston Hughes, in *Famous American Negroes* (New York: Dodd, Mead, 1954), limits his remarks to established facts. Arthur Huff Fauset's *For Freedom, a Biographical Story of the American Negro* (Philadelphia: Franklin, 1927) heavily romanticizes Wheatley's abduction, sale, and life with the Wheatley family. Shirley Graham's *The Story of Phillis Wheatley* (New York: Messner, 1949) is largely fictionalized, but in no way violates the general context established by earlier biographers. In *Puritan Promenade* (Boston: Houghton Mifflin, 1964), Martha Bacon uses a few facts to draw what Julian D. Mason, Jr., (in *The Poems of Phillis Wheatley*) describes as "highly questionable conclusions": that Wheatley was deeply scarred by her slavery, that she had reached "the nadir of the human condition" in her life with the Wheatley family, and that consequently her degradation was reflected in the servile verse she wrote in compliance to the demands of Boston society. Bacon also attacks the "negative effects" of the evangelist Jonathan Edwards "on all of New England" and the debilitating influence of the Methodist revival of Whitefield and the Wesleys on Phillis Wheatley.

CRITICISM

Phillis Wheatley's poetry was not subjected to substantial literary analysis until the twentieth century. In an essay, "The Reputation of Phillis Wheatley, Poet," prefacing *The Poems of Phillis Wheatley,* which he edited, Julian D. Mason, Jr., provides a thorough account of contemporary reviews and of Wheatley's fame through the subsequent reprintings of her work during the 1830s and the latter part of the nineteenth century. Mason credits some of her reputation in the pre-Abolitionist decades to the fact that her poetry revealed

> an absence of abolition sentiment . . . at a time when generally few works by Negro authors were being reviewed by major American magazines. After all, the work reviewed presented posthumously the poems of a female Negro author with some reputation, whose views generally were not in conflict with those of conservative minds, while her deeds and demonstrated intellect appealed to the more liberal minds of the time.

Arthur Schomburg's "Appreciation," in *Phillis Wheatley (Phillis Peters): Poems and Letters,* edited by Charles F. Heartman, sets the tone for critiques of Wheatley in this century by remarking that

> her poetry was a poetry of the eighteenth century, when [Alexander] Pope and [Thomas] Gray reigned supreme; and that her poetry compared favorably with the other American poetry of her age is by no means to her

discredit. There was no great American poetry in the eighteenth century, and Phillis Wheatley's poetry was as good as the best American poetry of her age.

Schomburg adds that Wheatley wrote before "the mighty outburst of the human spirit" which gave rise to Romanticism in Germany and in England, an observation repeated by James Weldon Johnson in *The Book of American Negro Poetry* (New York: Harcourt, Brace, 1931) with the regret that "had she come under the influence of Wordsworth, Byron or Keats or Shelley," as only her early death prevented her from doing, "she would have done greater work." Johnson agrees that Wheatley's poems are superior in technique to those of Urian Oakes and Anne Bradstreet, but he faults her lack of social protest, and complains that she shows no evidence of even her own condition. Vernon Loggins, in *The Negro Author, His Development in America,* extends this basic analysis. Wheatley's poetry "is noteworthy as an accomplishment in imitation. Her work is sophisticated rather than primitive, artificial rather than spontaneous, polished rather than crude. With the exception of certain specific passages in which the author identified herself, it contains nothing which marks it as the work of a member of the African race." For Loggins the major interest is her curious manner of composition. He finds most of her poetry "occasional," using impersonal feeling, hyperbole, elaborate ornamentation, overuse of personification, pompous diction, and the artificiality proper to neoclassical standards. The one aspect of her own personality revealed in the poetry is her capacity for intense religious faith, which Loggins sees as the motive for her work. Her literary influences were the Bible, tales from classical mythology, Alexander Pope's *Homer,* and the works of Thomas Gray; her most successful poetic device is the "strong rise, marked caesura, and hasten fall" of Pope's line. Following Schomburg and Johnson, Loggins regrets the dominating influence on Wheatley of Pope and the New England elegists, since her attention to "the more subtle sounds of words" promised a better career.

Loggins's sentiments are voiced again by Benjamin Brawley, in *The Negro in Literature and Art in the United States* and in *Early Negro American Writers.* Brawley adds that Wheatley's work was influenced not only by Pope, but also by "the precision that she gained from direct acquaintance with the great Latin authors." He praises her use of diction and control of the couplet form. But he regrets the dominance of religion and the impersonality of the school of Pope in her life, and supposes that her work would have developed its full lyric potential if she had lived forty years later under the sway of the Romantics. Sterling Brown's *Negro Poetry and Drama* (New York: Associates in Negro Folk Education, 1937) criticizes Wheatley's "correct drawing room usage," and accuses her of neglecting the "real griefs" which she witnessed or experienced herself. Brown cites her mastery of the couplet, while adding, "but where Pope was intellectual and satiric, Phillis Wheatley was, as might have been expected, shyly imitative." He censures her for making no mention of the enslavement of blacks. In *The Negro Caravan* (New York: Dryden, 1941) Brown is joined by Arthur P. Davis and Ulysses Lee in accusing Wheatley of ignoring slavery, noting that in only one poem did she express any resentment of her condition, and then in a fairly detached manner. Her dislike for self-revelation was compatible with Pope's form, but the authors believe that she was more shy than Pope or especially than Philip Freneau and John Trumbull.

A later essay summing up the criticisms of Brawley and Brown is William H. Robinson's "Phillis Wheatley: Colonial Quandary" (*CLAJ*, September 1965). Robinson is troubled by Wheatley's "divided, even distorted loyalties, and her curious silence on the most vital issue of her time—human freedom." He notes that she ignored critical historical events which she must have witnessed in Boston and during her trip to England, and suspects that she celebrated and was celebrated by royalists and slaveholders. In the end, Robinson blames her "lofty detachment" for the shortcomings of her verse. The strongest statement of this thesis, however, remains that of J. Saunders Redding, who, in *To Make a Poet Black* (Chapel Hill: University of North Carolina Press, 1939), wonders "to what degree she felt the full significance" of being a Negro poet, since "she stood far outside the institution [slavery] that was responsible for her." Redding adds that the Calvinism to which the poet was exposed may have been a factor in her detachment. (This point is made again by Martha Bacon in *Puritan Promenade*.) Redding repeats that the most debilitating factor in Wheatley's work is her inattention to slavery, and concludes that "it is this negative, bloodless, unracial quality in Phillis Wheatley that makes her seem superficial, especially to members of our race." Martha Bacon's judgment is more severe: "Little can be done with the poetry that Phillis Wheatley left to posterity save to lay it decently to rest. It is time-serving and inadequate, the legitimate result of the tractarians and egotists who called it forth and fostered it."

A line of more favorable commentaries on Wheatley's art begins with Richard Wright's introduction to St. Clair Drake and Horace R. Cayton's *Black Metropolis: A Study of Negro Life in a Northern City* (New York: Harcourt, Brace & World, 1945). Wright uses Wheatley as a benchmark "to show how a gradual estrangement has occurred in the Negro over a period of 160 years, an estrangement from complete identification with the nation to atomized and despairing rebellion." The poetry of Phillis Wheatley "records the feelings of a Negro reacting not as a Negro, but as a human being." In his highly significant "Personal Elements in the Poetry of Phillis Wheatley" (*Phylon,* Summer 1953),

Arthur P. Davis argues against the interpretations of Johnson, Loggins, and his own earlier *Negro Caravan* commentary that Wheatley was too highly objective, too closely neoclassic, and too impersonal. Davis now notes that Wheatley placed an emphasis on being an "Afric" poet, using her race and position as a frame of reference and expressing admiration for Terence as a fellow "Afric." Davis claims that it was the influence of New England Christian values rather than her own native disposition that made her seem to feel superior to her African heritage. As part of her concern with excellence as a poet she developed an awareness of her own handicaps that was overlooked by earlier commentators. Jean Wagner draws heavily on Davis's critique in *Black Poets of the United States,* translated by Kenneth Douglas (Urbana: University of Illinois Press, 1973). "Beneath the reserve that is natural to her," Wagner argues, "there come to unambiguous expression the convictions of an already developed racial consciousness and the exigencies of a religious faith that was enlightened and well balanced." Her poem "On Being Brought from Africa to America" would demonstrate "the grief separating her from the servile simplicities of a Hammon."

The most complete and balanced criticism of Phillis Wheatley's work is by Julian D. Mason, Jr., in his essays prefacing *The Poems of Phillis Wheatley.* He sees her elegies as being representative of her role as "a kind of poet laureate to whom many of the domestic circles of Boston turned for occasional verse." To Mason, Wheatley was not a great poet; instead, "her primary endeavor was to put into rhythmical, poetic forms those thoughts which came to her or which were brought to her attention by the small crises and significant experiences of the people of Boston as they met life and death from day to day." He labels her as "primarily an occasional poet, one interested in the clever crafting of verse," where the task is not to innovate but to take a given topic and fit it skillfully to an existing pattern. By these standards, Mason argues, "she was a better craftsman of verse than most of the others attempting the same type of thing in America in the 1770's." Pope was an appropriate model, and his Homer provided a "tug" on her impressionable mind. Of particular note is her use of invocation and the Miltonic blend of Christian and classical imagery. "Phillis Wheatley was not the wasp that Pope was," Mason advises, "but tended to be more compatible with Milton's Christian classicism and its view of life." He sees a great deal of ambivalence in her awareness of race, on the one hand viewing Western Africa "as a place of peace, beauty, and plenty," while on the other accepting missionary propaganda. Her work is distinguished by a fine use of the heroic couplet, emphasizing the caesura over other devices such as alliteration and onomatopoeia. Mason judges Wheatley's career with a view to the uses other critics made of her: "In part because she was young, in part because she was female, and in part because she was a Negro and nominally a slave, her work has too often been overpraised. On the other hand, she has also been too often dealt with unfairly or not at all because of this overpraising and what engendered it."

In the 1970s a number of significant critical studies appeared that use a sharp contemporary awareness to consider Wheatley's work in its larger cultural context. R. Lynn Matson's "Phillis Wheatley—Soul Sister?" (*Phylon*, Fall 1972) argues that "though Phillis Wheatley may not have been a black nationalist (and of course such a stand would have been impossible considering the time and her position), nonetheless she was very race conscious, aware of her position as a slave, and not at all 'smug' in this position (as comparatively desirable as it may have been) in the Wheatley household." Matson's claim rests on the development of escape themes in Wheatley's poetry, especially her "escapist view of death and Christianity." Comparisons with manuscript versions of her poems show that her more emphatic escapist pronouncements were toned down for publication.

The first quarterly number of the *Jackson State Review* (1974) reprints the papers and proceedings of "The Phillis Wheatley Poetry Festival" at the Jackson State College campus in Mississippi, where a special Wheatley collection is being established. Papers by Paula Giddings and Dorothy B. Porter summarize the critical and bibliographical problems, while presentations by Margaret G. Burroughs and Alice Walker consider the relevance of an eighteenth-century black New England poet for black women writing in the South today. The tenor of this conference, which featured twenty women poets (including Nikki Giovanni, Alice Walker, June Jordan, and Audre Lorde), is described by Carole A. Parks in "Phillis Wheatley Comes Home" (*BlackW*, February 1974). The stated purpose of the conference, Parks reports, was to change the "one-dimensional portrayal in textbooks" of Wheatley as "a cultural orphan freakishly adept at parroting her white 'benefactors.' " A separate essay by Donatus I. Nwoga, "Humanitarianism and the Criticism of African Literature" (*RAL*, 2nd Quarter, 1972) also helps to correct this stereotype by showing how "discussions on the political and moral implications of slavery toward the end of the Eighteenth Century supplied the framework for the contemporary appraisal of the creative writing" by such figures as Wheatley. The theoretical debate over whether or not Africans were inherently inferior to Europeans led either to derogation of creative work on its own terms, or to praise for its conformity to European models. Therefore, Nwoga insists, "This a priori approach invalidated much . . . literary criticism" and fashioned the critical stereotypes we live with today.

Most representative of the new trend in Wheatley scholarship is Merle A. Richmond's *Bid the Vassal Soar: Interpretive Essays on the Life and Poetry of Phillis Wheatley and George Moses Horton* (Washington, D. C.: Howard University Press, 1974). Richmond begins her analysis by juxtaposing Phillis Wheatley and her poetic subject George Washington as "the most renowned slave and the most highly esteemed slaveowner of 1776." According to Richmond, the key to Wheatley's poetry is her attempt to define her own identity between these polar opposites (slave and slaveowner) in Revolutionary America. Richmond argues that Wheatley was "at least equal, and most often superior, to the Boston Brahmins in conversation and intellectual accomplishment"—particularly in relation to the women of the Wheatley household who educated her. For this reason, and not simply because of racial restriction, she could feel at home neither with "white masters nor with black slaves." Her imitation of Pope, Richmond believes, excluded his strongest element—satire—because "for a black poet whites were above the shaft of satire—just as blacks were beneath it." Richmond's study is written with an explicit thesis, that of considering Wheatley's work as having been written by a black in a world dominated by whites, and by a woman in a world dominated by men. It is to Richmond's credit that from this perspective Wheatley's career and the critical reaction to it are clarified.

Benjamin Banneker

Benjamin Banneker (1731–1806) was born a free man in the colony of Maryland. Although he supported himself as a farmer, Banneker showed a great talent for mathematics, and in his spare time constructed a clock, and made astronomical calculations for a series of almanacs, which he published at some profit from 1792 to 1802. He is also noteworthy for his correspondence with Thomas Jefferson and for his work as a surveyor during the planning of Washington, D. C.

BIBLIOGRAPHY

In "Early American Negro Writings: A Bibliographical Study" (*PBSA*, 3rd Quarter, 1945), Dorothy B. Porter provides a checklist of nineteen issues of Banneker's almanacs. This list is expanded to twenty-eight, and a comprehensive annotated secondary bibliography is included, at the end of Silvio A. Bedini's *The Life of Benjamin Banneker* (New York: Scribners, 1972).

EDITIONS

Two of Banneker's almanacs are reprinted in their entirety by Maxwell Whiteman (Philadelphia: Historic Publications, Afro–American History Series, 1969) as *Banneker's Almanack and Ephemeris for the Year of Our*

Lord 1793; Being the First After Bissextile or Leap Year; and Banneker's Almanac, for the Year 1795: Being the Third after Leap Year.

MANUSCRIPTS AND LETTERS

Although Banneker was not included in the original survey for *American Literary Manuscripts*, edited by Joseph Jones (Austin: University of Texas Press, 1960), his name has been added to the second edition of this work, which is edited by J. Albert Robbins (Athens: University of Georgia Press, 1977). To this date the only catalogued Banneker item is his letter to Thomas Jefferson, kept with Jefferson's papers in the Library of Congress. Banneker's chief biographer, Silvio A. Bedini, remarked in *The Life of Benjamin Banneker* that "never had the tangible memorabilia of a man's life vanished so completely as had Banneker's"; he adds that the most important manuscript items, Banneker's journal and commonplace book, remain in the private collection of Dr. Robert Tyson Fitzhugh, a descendant of the original Ellicott family who were Banneker's neighbors and chief patrons. Bedini found other materials in the Historical Society of Pennsylvania Library in Philadelphia, but complains of their uncatalogued state. Banneker's exchange of letters with Jefferson was published in 1792 by Daniel Lawrence in Philadelphia, and later reprinted (*JNH*, January 1918). Both letters are reprinted in full by Bedini, and by Dorothy B. Porter in *Early Negro Writing, 1760–1837* (Boston: Beacon, 1971).

BIOGRAPHY

Banneker's life and achievements were the subject of some abolitionist and political commentary (the latter addressed against Jefferson) in the 1790s and early 1800s. Accurate summaries of these largely inconsequential accounts may be found in the bibliography appended to Bedini's *The Life of Benjamin Banneker*. The first serious biographical attempt is Bishop Henri Gregoire's *An Enquiry concerning the Intellectual and Moral Faculties and Literature of Negroes; Followed with an Account of the Life and Works of Fifteen Negroes and Mulattoes*, translated by D. B. Warren (Brooklyn, N. Y.: Thomas Kirk, 1810). Gregoire describes Banneker's almanacs of 1794 and 1795 but not their history, and mentions only Jefferson's side of their correspondence.

All authoritative biographies of Benjamin Banneker are based on four sources. The first is Rachel Mason's *Selections from the Letters and Manuscripts of the Late Susanna Mason; With a Brief Memoir of Her Life, By Her Daughter* (Philadelphia: Rackliff and Jones, 1836), which includes a firsthand account of a visit to Banneker's home in 1796. At a monthly meeting of the Maryland Historical Society on May 1, 1845, John H. B. Latrobe presented his "Memoir of Benjamin Banneker," which was subsequently published in the *Maryland Colonization Journal* (May 1845), and again as a separate book (Baltimore: John D. Toy, 1845), and finally condensed in William G. Allen's *Wheatley, Banneker, and Horton* (Boston: Daniel Laing, 1849; rpt. Plainview, N. Y.: Books for Libraries, 1970). Latrobe drew on data authenticated by Ellicott family sources to sketch the life and achievements of Banneker. In 1854, before the same group, J. Saurin Norris presented *A Sketch of the Life of Benjamin Banneker; From Notes Taken in 1836* (Baltimore: John D. Toy, n.d.). Norris drew upon the notes of an Ellicott descendant, Martha E. Tyson, who had interviewed acquaintances of Banneker's and others who had known the Ellicott family. Bedini describes it as "one of the most valuable original sources on Banneker," and it is heavily quoted by subsequent researchers. Thirty years later Martha E. Tyson's complete work was published as *Banneker, the Afric–American Astronomer. From the Posthumous Papers of Martha E. Tyson, Edited by Her Daughter* (Philadelphia: Friends' Book Association, 1884). According to Bedini, "this account of Banneker is the most extensive and authoritative of all the published sources on the subject." It is an amplification of Norris's use of her work in 1854, to which were added data collected from surviving contemporaries who had known Banneker.

The authoritative modern biography is Bedini's, which presents a full examination of colonial conditions, especially in tidewater Maryland, for indentured and transported servants (such as Banneker's grandmother Molly Welsh) and for freed slaves (such as Banneker's grandfather Bannka, an African prince). He details Molly Welsh's influence on Banneker's education, and describes Banneker's life as a tobacco farmer and the importance of this experience to his eventual career as a maker of almanacs. The role of the Ellicott family is fully explored, and several myths about Banneker's involvement in the American War of Independence (he was actually untouched by it) are put to rest. For the publishing history of the almanacs, Bedini is careful to establish Banneker's motives as being quite apart from abolitionist propaganda, but he describes the extent to which such motives on the part of others influenced the success of his volume. Bedini provides an accurate account of Banneker's role in the survey of Washington, D. C. (again disposing of several myths), establishing that it was more important as an interruption of Banneker's work on his first almanac than what others have made of it. Banneker's motives in writing to Jefferson are carefully examined in the light of the full evidence of his life, Bedini arguing that Banneker was more interested in the publication and success of his almanac than in the racial significance of his act. Two useful supplements to Bedini's work are his own *Early American Scientific Instruments and Their Makers* (Washington, D. C.: Government Printing Office, 1964), which describes Banneker's scientific career in more technical terms, and Henry J. Jackson's essay, "Negro Membership in the Society of Friends" (*JNH*, April 1936), which establishes that Banneker was never a member of the Society, but attended their meetings at Ellicott's Lower Mills.

There are several short biographical sketches of Banneker that draw upon Tyson and Latrobe and are careful to remain within the bounds of established fact. These include two early essays by Moncure D. Conway, "Banneker, the Black Astronomer" (*Southern Literary Messenger,* July 1856) and "Benjamin, the Negro Astronomer" (*AtM*, January 1863); George W. Williams's *History of the Negro Race in America from 1619–1880* (New York: Putnam, 1883); John R. Slattery's "Benjamin Banneker, the Negro Astronomer" (*CathW*, December 1883); William J. Simmons's *Men of Mark: Eminent, Progressive and Rising* (Cleveland: George M. Rewell, 1887); John W. Cromwell's *The Negro in American History* (Washington, D. C.: The American Negro Academy, 1914); Henry E. Baker's "Benjamin Banneker, the Negro Mathematician and Astronomer" (*JNH,* April 1918); Vernon Loggins's *The Negro Author: His Development in America* (New York: Columbia University Press, 1931); Benjamin Brawley's *Early Negro American Writers* (Chapel Hill: University of North Carolina Press, 1935) and *Negro Builders and Heroes* (Chapel Hill: University of North Carolina Press, 1937); Saul K. Padover's "Benjamin Banneker: Unschooled Wizard" (*NR*, February 2, 1948); William B. Settle's "The Real Benjamin Banneker" (*NHB*, January, February, March, April 1953); and Lerone Bennett, Jr.'s *Before the Mayflower: A History of the Negro in America, 1619–1962* (Chicago: Johnson, 1962).

The specifics of the Banneker–Jefferson relationship are discussed by John Dos Passos in *The Head and Heart of Thomas Jefferson* (Garden City, N. Y.: Doubleday, 1954); by Benjamin Quarles in *The Negro in the American Revolution* (Chapel Hill: University of North Carolina Press, 1961); and by Winthrop D. Jordan *White over Black: American Attitudes Toward the Negro, 1550–1812* (Chapel Hill: University of North Carolina Press, 1968). In *From Slavery to Freedom* (New York: Knopf, 1967), John Hope Franklin details the use of Banneker's achievement in the abolition movement.

Myths about Banneker's career begin with a preface by Daniel Murray, "A Paper Read Before the Banneker Association of Washington," which appeared in Will W. Allen's volume *Banneker, the Afro–American Astronomer* (Washington, D. C.: n.p., 1921; rpt. Plainview, N. Y.: Books for Libraries, 1971). Allen describes his own work as a "compilation" of details from Tyson and Baker, and it is an accurate summary of Banneker's life and career. But Murray's preface makes the unsupported claim that Banneker recalled the architect L'Enfant's plans for Washington, D. C., after the Frenchman had deserted his commission. This same misinformation is repeated by Thomas H. Johnson in "The Story of Benjamin Banneker: A Negro History Play for Radio" (*NHB*, April 1952), by C. L. Lewis in "The Man Who Saved Washington" (*ND*, February 1966), by Otto Lindenmeyer in *Black History: Lost, Stolen, or Strayed* (New York: Avon, 1970), and by William Loren Katz in *Eyewitness: The Negro in American History* (New York: Pitman, 1967), who adds several inaccuracies regarding the construction of Banneker's clock, his relationship with Jefferson, and the magnitude of his role in the survey of Washington, D. C. In John W. Caughey, John Hope Franklin, and Ernest R. May's *Land of the Free, A History of the United States* (New York: Benziger, 1966) Banneker is listed incorrectly as a commissioner for the survey, while Lydia Maria Child's *The Freedmen's Book* (Boston: Ticknor and Fields, 1865) makes the unsubstantiated claim that Jefferson invited Banneker to visit him at Monticello. Lerone J. Bennett, Jr., in "Pioneers in Protest: Benjamin Banneker" (*Ebony*, March 1964), insists that Banneker's sentiments were largely abolitionist in seeking to publish his almanac.

Three fictionalized but essentially accurate accounts of Banneker's life written for younger readers are Silas X. Floyd's *The New Floyd's Flowers, Short Stories for Colored People Old and Young* (Washington, D. C.: Austin Jenkins, 1905); Elizabeth Ross Haynes's *Unsung Heroes* (New York: Dubois and Dill, 1921); and Shirley Graham's *Your Most Humble Servant* (New York: Messner, 1949). In *For Freedom: A Biographical Story of the American Negro* (Philadelphia: Franklin, 1929), Arthur Huff Fauset presents a heavily romanticized picture of Banneker's role in the survey of Washington, and claims an abolitionist motive for his almanacs.

CRITICISM

Vernon Loggins, in *The Negro Author: His Development in America* (New York: Columbia University Press, 1931), uses Banneker's work as evidence that "there is no doubt that there were Negroes in America in 1788 with the intellectual capacity to produce respectable essays." Loggins has further praise for Banneker's ingenious mind. Silvio A. Bedini's *The Life of Benjamin Banneker* puts Banneker's achievement in the context of almanac publication in America, finding it significant that Banneker's efforts came at a period when almanacs were emphasizing national events, local causes, and specialized interests; although abolition was not Banneker's motive, his almanacs rode the tide of such sentiment until it temporarily subsided in the 1800s. Bedini argues that Banneker did not select the literary content of his almanacs, and did not write "A Plan Of a *Peace Office* for the United States" as other commentators believe, but rather was printing an essay written by Benjamin Rush. Bedini does suggest, however, that "Epitaph on a Watchmaker" was very likely Banneker's own composition, and presents analyses of other compositions from Banneker's journal and his common-place book (especially his recorded dreams).

More limited commentaries on Banneker's almanacs may be found in E. Franklin Frazier's *The Negro in the United States* (New York: Macmillan, 1957) and Robb Sagendorph's *America and Her Almanacs, Wit, Wisdom, and Weather 1639–1970* (Boston: Little, Brown, 1970). Confusion over Banneker's authorship of the "peace office" plan undercuts Jesse Zimmerman's essay, "A Secretary of Peace" (*The Crisis,* April 1950), and obscures Benjamin Brawley's critique of Banneker in his three major works, *Early Negro American Writers* (Chapel Hill: University of North Carolina Press, 1935), *Negro Builders and Heroes* (Chapel Hill: University of North Carolina Press, 1937), and *The Negro Genius* (New York: Dodd, Mead, 1937). Brawley had used Banneker's supposed composition of the peace plan as evidence of his intellectual kinship with William Godwin, Thomas Paine, Richard Price, and Mary Wollstonecraft, and as proof of his being "generally in line with the most advanced humanitarianism of the age."

Bedini's work is obviously the pioneering study of Banneker. Having sorted out the facts of his life, established the conditions under which his almanacs were published and the author's intention for them, and revealing the wealth of material in his journal and commonplace book, Bedini has made possible a full and authoritative examination of Banneker's importance in the literary history of America, although this is something that no critic has yet attempted.

SLAVE NARRATIVES

Ruth Miller
peter J. Katopes

In an essay entitled "The Negro Contribution to American Letters" (in *The American Negro Reference Book,* edited by John P. Davis [Englewood Cliffs, N. J.: Prentice-Hall, 1966]), Arna Bontemps suggested that readers examine slave narratives of the nineteenth century if they wish to discover the source of the writing style of Richard Wright, Ralph Ellison, and James Baldwin. Slave narratives in their turn have their roots in Puritan writings, particularly in journals, diaries, autobiographies, and narrations, all designed to record the Puritan experience of the "walk with God." Slave narratives use a similar form to record the flight to freedom; they are chronological in structure, episodic, and provide little, if any, transition. Events are drawn from common experience; incidents that dismay or horrify or repel are frequently recounted with a lack of passion usually associated with literature designed to demonstrate the truth. There are auction blocks, lashings, escapes, and recaptures; there are tears and prayers and exhortations; there are special providences recorded, coincidences, suspenseful moments in flight, tricks to outwit captors, all of this presented in a tone that is pervasively sober. If there is a preponderance of gloom, there is also optimism; despair mingles with joy. And the overriding purpose of the narrative is to activate the will of the reader to abolish first the slave trade and finally slavery.

Thus a powerful tool for antebellum abolitionists was provided by the slaves themselves. Such personal testimony and vivid description of the daily horror and degradation of slave life was sure to fire the hearts of a northern audience already disposed to condemn slavery on moral grounds. And slave narratives made money for their writers as well as for the abolitionist movement. Public imagination was stirred by the picaresque adventures of slaves as they employed guile, deception, and cunning to make their way to freedom.

Unfortunately, there was a negative aspect to the rhetorical and commercial success of these narratives, for not only did editors take the liberty of expanding and altering what were purported to be authentic personal documents, they also sometimes created bogus slave tales.

While some former slaves, notably William Wells Brown and Frederick Douglass, were skilled in the use of vivid language and recorded their own stories, others were encouraged or forced to relate their stories to more skillful writers, who actually put the words on paper, in order to get their tales into print. Because many of those who transcribed the tales were passionate abolitionists and highly conscious of the potential rhetorical impact of these narratives, they felt justified in editing or embellishing the slave's account.

The researcher must therefore be wary, especially when examining slave narratives published between the years 1835 and 1860. Although several of these accounts, like Richard Hildreth's *Memoir of Archy Moore* (1836) or Emily Catherine Pierson's *Jamie Parker, The Fugitive* (1851), have been declared spurious, there is disagreement regarding the authenticity of too many others, notably *Fifty Years in Chains; or, The Life of an American Slave* (1859) and *The Narrative of Lunsford Lane* (1848), two very well-known and frequently cited works.

Bibliographies

Bibliographers attempting to compile lists of slave narratives have been hampered by three major difficulties: locating the materials, defining the form, and determining an appropriate time span. Despite the renewal of interest in all phases of black American literature, locating early published materials remains difficult. Most early manuscripts were published in London, and copies of the original printed text are frequently all that are available to American scholars. There is much uncertainty about how to classify slave narratives, because although many reveal enough of an author's life to be called autobiographies, too often we are confronted with brief accounts of an escape from bondage, with little more than a few fragments of subsequent experience put together for a quick conclusion. A third, and perhaps less serious, problem is the issue of chronological boundaries. The first slave narratives can be traced to the early eighteenth century, but more recent ones have been collected firsthand by researchers interviewing former slaves during the 1930s. Most bibliographies do not represent the entire spectrum.

Marion W. Starling's unpublished dissertation, "The Black Slave Narrative: Its Place In American Literary History" (New York University, 1948) includes a bibliography. This dissertation, which is available on microfilm, cites locations of library holdings of the slave narratives, as well as significant secondary sources, but Starling's research ends in 1946. Publication of an updated version of this bibliography would be useful to scholars of early black American literature.

A comprehensive listing of slave narratives appears in Charles H.

Nichols's *Many Thousand Gone: The Ex-Slaves' Account of Their Bondage and Freedom* (Leiden, the Netherlands: E.J. Brill, 1963; rpt. Bloomington: Indiana University Press, 1974). Nichols lists, without annotation, approximately 80 eighteenth- and nineteenth-century slave narratives, 120 secondary works related to the general topic of slavery, 17 novels which deal with slavery, some 25 books which contain short collected narratives, and approximately 45 articles and pamphlets on slavery.

The bibliography appended to Stanley Feldstein's *Once A Slave: The Slaves' View of Slavery* (New York: Morrow, 1971) lists without annotation over 125 narratives dating from 1704 to the 1940s, with the larger number of entries dating from 1830 to 1860. Also listed are approximately forty-five books containing slave narratives and eighteen antislavery newspapers and periodicals.

Monroe N. Work's massive compilation, *A Bibliography of the Negro in Africa and America* (New York: Wilson, 1928; rpt. New York: Octagon, 1965, 1970) contains references to almost every aspect of Negro life from ancient times to about 1928. Work's listing includes over sixty slave narratives dating from 1734 to 1925. Of particular value in this bibliography is Work's practice of identifying the race of an author.

Louis Kaplan's *A Bibliography of American Autobiography* (Madison: University of Wisconsin Press, 1961) annotates over fifty narratives. Each entry includes the author, date of birth, full title, most easily located edition, place of publication, publisher and date, pagination, and the name of a library in which a copy can be found. The annotations contain information about the author's occupation, dwelling, and, in some cases, comments on the authenticity of the narrative. Kaplan appends a subject index which cross-references the authors by occupation, geographical area, chronological period, and by significant historical events in which they participated. Excluded from this listing are narratives which merely relate "episodic accounts" of the author's escape from slavery. For some unknown reason, one of the best-known narratives, *Narrative of William Wells Brown,* does not appear.

Russell C. Brignano's helpful *Black Americans in Autobiography: An Annotated Bibliography of Autobiographies and Autobiographical Books Written Since the Civil War* (Durham, N. C.: Duke University Press, 1974) includes over forty narratives. Brignano divides his work into three sections. The first is an annotated listing of volumes that describe "appreciable spans" of an author's life. The second lists diaries, travelogues, collections of essays and letters, and eyewitness accounts of public events. The final section is an unannotated checklist of autobiographical works written before the Civil War, but reprinted or published for the first time since 1945. Each section is arranged alphabetically by author, and each entry includes the dates of the author's birth and death, title and subtitle of the work, symbols for up to ten library locations of copies, information about forewords, introductions, illustrations, afterwords, notes, bibliographies and indexes, publisher, place and year of publication, pagination, and, of particular value, references to reprint editions. The annotation provides some basic information about the author's life. Following the compilation are three indexes: the first lists occupations and professions cited in the annotations; the second lists geographic locations and educational institutions cited; and the third contains the titles mentioned in all three sections of the text. All this expands Brignano's earlier checklist, "Autobiographical Books by Black Americans: A Bibliography of Works Written Since the Civil War" (*NALF,* Winter 1973).

The bibliography appended to Vernon Loggins's *The Negro Author: His Development in America to 1900* (New York: Columbia University Press, 1931; rpt. Port Washington, N. Y.: Kennikat Press, 1964) is arranged in eight major sections according to period and genre. Within each section are subsections classifying authors by location, political activity, or writing mode (prose, poetry, etc.). If one does not know beforehand what one wishes to read about, this kind of format can be troublesome. Loggins includes over fifty narratives in his bibliography, giving the full title and original date of publication. Also of help in this list is the identification of a number of white writers who produced fictional slave narratives.

Dorothy B. Porter's pioneer effort, "Early American Negro Writings: A Bibliographical Study" (*PBSA,* 3rd Quarter, 1941), attempts to list all known published material written or compiled by black Americans before 1835. Authors of broadsides or books are listed alphabetically, and each entry includes the original date of publication, as well as library locations of copies, when known. Excluded are works published after 1835. Porter's listing includes ten slave narratives, the earliest of which is by Briton Hammon published in 1760. Despite Porter's claim to comprehensiveness, among the narratives missing from the bibliography are Robert Voorhis's *Life and Adventures of Robert, the Hermit of Massachusetts, who has lived fourteen years in a cave, secluded from human society. Taken from his own mouth, Providence, 1829;* Nat Turner's *Confessions* (1831); and *The Anecdotes and Memoirs of William Boen* (1834). Introducing the compilation is an informative essay in which Porter describes some of the difficulties she encountered in putting the bibliography together. Such questions as the determination of the author's race, the location of the materials, and authenticity were difficult to resolve.

Dorothy B. Porter brought out two other comprehensive bibliographies: *A Working Bibliography on the Negro in the United States* (New York: Xerox Corporation, 1969), and *The Negro in the United States: A Selected Bibliography* (Washington, D.C.: Library of Congress, 1970). *A Working Bibliography* lists about twenty slave narratives, some with very brief descriptive annotations. The listing is alphabetical by author, and each entry includes the title, publisher, place and date of publication, pagination, and the price of paperback and hardcover editions. Obviously, the prices named are no longer accurate, but they do indicate the cost of a good edition. *The Negro in the United States* lists fifteen slave narratives, ten of which already appear in *A Working Bibliography*. Entries are the same, but Library of Congress numbers are substituted for price listings, thereby saving time at the card catalogue. The selections in this compilation were derived from a survey of requests for specific works at libraries having significant collections of black literature, a rather unscholarly reason for inclusion. Neither of Porter's listings includes the narrative of William Wells Brown.

Of limited value for the study of the slave narrative is Mary Sue Carlock's "American Autobiographies, 1840–1870: A Bibliography" (*BB*, May–August 1961). Carlock excludes journals, diaries, and travelogues, as well as autobiographies which did not appear in print prior to 1870. In order to achieve her aim—to define the genre of autobiography—she includes only those narratives in which the authors "attempted to indicate a cause-and-effect relationship between their early and later years." Consequently, the narratives of William Wells Brown, Frederick Douglass, and Solomon Northup are included, but other valuable narratives, such as those of Henry Bibb and William and Ellen Craft, are omitted. The entries are alphabetical by author and include publisher, place and date of original publication, and brief annotation. Unfortunately, the annotations do not comment on the reliability or authenticity of the narratives. Thus the inclusion of items of doubtful reliability can be troublesome for an unwary researcher.

Obviously, there is still a need for a comprehensive, annotated bibliography of black slave narratives.

Editions

The revivial of interest in early black American literature has prompted the appearance of several reprints of individual narratives, as well as a number of collections and anthologies, in both paperback and hardcover format. Here is a representative listing of good editions reprinting individual narratives, as well as a more complete compilation of significant collections and anthologies.

Arno Press and the New York Times have reprinted the following: in 1968, *The Narrative of Sojourner Truth* (1878) and Elizabeth Keckley's *Behind the Scenes* (1868); in 1969, *The Narratives of the Sufferings of Lewis and Milton Clarke* (1846); and in 1970, *Running a Thousand Miles for Freedom: Or, the Escape of William and Ellen Craft from Slavery* (1860).

In 1969 Mnemosyne Press reprinted the Crafts' *Running a Thousand*

Miles for Freedom (1860), *The Narrative and Writings of Andrew Jackson* (1847), Harriet Brent Jacobs's *Incidents in the Life of a Slave Girl* (1862), *The Life of James Mars, a Slave* (1864), and Henry Clay Bruce's *The New Man* (1895).

Negro Universities Press (Westport, Connecticut) has reprinted the narratives of Gustavus Vassa (Olaudah Equiano) (1790), Jermain Wesley Loguen (1859), Austin Steward (1857), Bruce (1895) and James W. C. Pennington (1849).

The more popular slave narratives appear in several editions. Josiah Henson's story has been reprinted by Corinth Books, Addison-Wesley, Gregg, and Afro-Am Publishing Co., and Solomon Northup's by Louisiana State University Press, Dover, and The Scholarly Press. (Full titles may be found in the checklist at the end of this chapter.)

New editions of individual narratives appear frequently, and students should have little difficulty obtaining texts.

There are also a growing number of collections and anthologies available. *Five Slave Narratives: A Compendium* (New York: Arno Press and The New York Times, 1968), edited by William Loren Katz, collects the narratives of William Wells Brown, Moses Grandy, Lunsford Lane, James W. C. Pennington, and Jacob Stroyer, all relatively short and readable. One note of caution, however. Despite Katz's comment to the contrary, *The Narrative of Lunsford Lane* is still of doubtful authenticity.

Puttin' On Ole Massa: The Slave Narratives of Henry Bibb, William Wells Brown, and Solomon Northup (New York: Harper & Row, 1968), edited by Gilbert Osofsky, is particularly valuable for Osofsky's introductory essay, "Puttin' on Ole Massa: The Significance of Slave Narratives." Osofsky challenges such historians as Ulrich B. Phillips, who have tended to discount the historical validity of the slave narrative because of certain stylistic inconsistencies, such as contradiction and hyperbole. Osofsky emphasizes the slave writer's shrewdness, using the contents of the narratives as documentation, and insists that whatever the stylistic flaws, the overall picture of slavery revealed in these tales remains consistent from narrative to narrative. He suggests that for this reason the slave narrative cannot be ignored as a historical document "if a balanced account of the history of slavery in the United States is to be written." Also of value in this essay are Osofsky's discussion of how the slaves had to use pretense as a "sharp-edged tool of self-defense," and his analysis of the central themes found in the slave narratives.

Great Slave Narratives (Boston: Beacon, 1969), edited and introduced by Arna Bontemps, reprints the narratives of Gustavus Vassa, James W. C. Pennington, and William and Ellen Craft. Bontemps's introduction, "The Slave Narrative: An American Genre," points out that the slave narratives for the first time offered the public a chance to view slavery from the victim's perspective. He also suggests that subsequent

American authors, both white and black, were influenced by the auto-biographical style of the slave narratives, citing Mark Twain and Herman Melville as examples of white authors in this tradition.

Bontemps has also edited a collection of lesser-known narratives, *Five Black Lives: The Autobiographies of Venture Smith, James Mars, William Grimes, the Rev. G. W. Offley, James L. Smith* (Middletown, Conn.: Wesleyan University Press, 1971). These narratives are all reprinted from their original versions except for Venture Smith's. Bontemps selected the 1896 edition of Smith's story rather than the original, published almost one hundred years earlier, because it contains additional materials collected from the memories of Smith's family, friends, and neighbors, thus offering facts about him not revealed in the original.

Four Fugitive Slave Narratives (Reading, Mass.: Addison-Wesley, 1969), under the general editorship of Robin W. Winks, reprints the narratives of Josiah Henson, William Wells Brown, and Austin Steward. Reprinted also is Benjamin Drew's *The Refugee: A Northside View of Slavery*, which was first published in 1855, and contains over one hundred excerpts and sketches from the slaves themselves on various aspects of slave society. Each selection in *Four Fugitive Slave Narratives* is preceded by a critical introduction, and each is also available separately in paperback.

John F. Bayliss's *Black Slave Narratives* (New York: Macmillan, 1970) uses excerpts from various narratives to portray the different aspects of slavery, beginning with the slave's journey from Africa and concluding with the ultimate escape to the North. In Bayliss's excellent introduction to the volume, he discusses a number of anthologies and critical works dealing with the slave narrative. He also analyzes general research problems. Each chapter begins with a short biographical note that includes publication data, and goes on to present a different aspect of the slave experience. The chapter titles are "The Africans," "Master and Slave," "Slaveholder Brutality," "The Family," "The Women," "Superstition," "Adventure," "Revolt," and "Escape."

Similar in format to Bayliss's collection is Abraham Chapman's *Steal Away: Stories of the Runaway Slaves* (New York: Praeger, 1971). In part one, entitled "Memories of Africa and the Slave Ships," Chapman includes, in addition to excerpts from Vassa, selections from such lesser-known narrators as Cugoana, Armstrong, Archer, and Baquaqua. Also of interest in the section is his inclusion of the complete "Petition of Belinda, An African" (1787). Part two, "Slave Life and Stealing Away," includes selections from the narratives of Steward, Peter Randolph, Thomas Jones, Josiah Henson, and others. The final part, "History in Fiction," reprints the entire text of Frederick Douglass's "The Heroic Slave." Each selection includes an introductory note which gives the full title of the work excerpted, the original date of publication, and some biographical data.

A collection of twentieth-century slave narratives is *The American Slave: A Composite Autobiography* (Westport, Conn.: Greenwood, 1972) under the general editorship of George P. Rawick. This nineteen-volume compilation reprints material found in *Slave Narratives: A Folk History of Slavery in the United States from Interviews with Former Slaves* (available on microfilm), collected by the Federal Writers' Project (FWP) between 1936 and 1938. These interviews were conducted in seventeen states and more than two thousand former slaves contributed their memories to the collection. Also included in this work are two volumes of interviews with former slaves that were collected at Fisk University during the 1920s.

B. A. Botkin's *Lay My Burden Down: A Folk History of Slavery* (Chicago: University of Chicago Press, 1945) selects and integrates excerpts and complete shorter narratives from the FWP collection, preserving the original dialectic vagaries of the narratives.

Norman R. Yetman, on the other hand, in his *Voices From Slavery* (New York: Holt, Rinehart & Winston, 1970), has attempted to make the FWP collection more available, and so has included only complete narratives in his collection. Unlike Botkin, Yetman has engaged in some "minor editing, designed to improve readability and continuity." A great deal of this editing consists of standardizing the spelling of dialect in the narratives, which may make some readers feel they are missing some of the flavor of the original. In order to make his anthology financially as well as physically practical, Yetman has restricted his selections to about one hundred authors who were at least thirteen years old at the time of the Emancipation. Appended to this collection is Yetman's article describing the FWP project, "The Background of the Slave Narrative Collection."

Blackamerican Literature, 1760–Present (Beverly Hills, Cal.: Glencoe, 1971), edited by Ruth Miller and with a foreword by John Hope Franklin, includes excerpts from several slave narratives, beginning with Briton Hammon and concluding with Moses Roper. Preceding each of the six divisions of the book is a "time line" that offers a chronological list of significant historical events from the period covered by each chapter. Miller also appends a short but helpful bibliography of primary and secondary sources.

Of interest also, and available on microcards from The Lost Cause Press, Louisville, Kentucky, are the 2,500 pamphlets and books from the collection of antislavery propaganda in the Oberlin College library.

Manuscripts and Letters

Original manuscripts of eighteenth- and nineteenth-century slave narratives are very hard to come by, if indeed they exist at all, but original published editions are generally accessible. The following dictionary catalogs of major collections of Negro literature, all of which were published by G. K. Hall of Boston, should be consulted to determine holdings: *The Dictionary Catalog of the Schomburg Collection of Negro Literature and History, the New York Public Library* (1962), with two supplements (1967 and 1972); *The Dictionary Catalog of the Jesse E. Moorland Collection of Negro Life and History, Howard University Libraries, Washington, D.C.* (1970); *The Dictionary Catalog of the Arthur B. Spingarn Collection of Negro Authors, Howard University Library, Washington, D.C.* (1970); and *The Dictionary Catalog of the Negro Collection of the Fisk University Library, Nashville, Tennessee* (1973).

The largest collection of twentieth-century slave narratives is in the Rare Book Division of the Slave Narrative Collection of The Federal Writers' Project at the Library of Congress in Washington, D.C. This collection consists of over ten thousand typewritten pages transcribing interviews conducted during the 1930s by the FWP with former slaves, their relatives, and their friends. The collection is not indexed and does not circulate. However, the manuscripts are available for in-library study and they have been microfilmed.

Holograph letters of former slaves are scattered throughout the country, with no single significant collection in existence. The student wishing to locate some of these letters will find Walter Schatz's *Directory of Afro–American Resources* (New York: Bowker, 1970) helpful, despite several inaccurate and misleading entries.

Biography

The best biographical materials available on slaves and former slaves are, of course, the narratives themselves. Indeed, except for biographies of slave narrators famous for other accomplishments, such as William Wells Brown and Frederick Douglass, there are few reliable full-length biographies on the market. *The Dictionary of American Biography* (New York: Scribners, 1944–1973) offers biographical sketches of Richard Allen, Josiah Henson, Jermain Wesley Loguen, James W. C. Pennington, Harriet Tubman, and Samuel Ringold Ward. *Historical Negro Biographies* by Wilhelmina S. Robinson (New York: Publisher's Co., 1968) includes short sketches of Allen, Absalom Jones, Vassa, the Crafts, Henson, Loguen, Pennington, Sojourner Truth, Tubman, Turner, and Ward.

Particularly helpful is *God's Image in Ebony: Being a Series of Biographical Sketches, Facts, Anecdotes, Etc., Demonstrative of The Mental Powers and Intellectual Capacities of the Negro Race,* edited by H. G. Adams and published in London in 1854. This collection, available on microcard from The Lost Cause Press in Louisville, Kentucky, is dedicated to

Harriet Beecher Stowe and includes sketches of a number of obscure and well-known slaves and former slaves.

Criticism

Until recent times, critics treated slave narratives as mere rhetoric rather than as literature with artistic value. Early critics challenged the narrator's reliability and the accuracy with which he or she portrayed slave society, and were less concerned with aesthetic considerations such as theme, style, attitudes, language, and literary influence. Considering the volatile political atmosphere surrounding the Civil War era, and the long-standing stereotypes of both slave and master that were accepted well into the twentieth century, critical preoccupation with rhetoric and authenticity perhaps was not so strange.

Ephraim Peabody's significant article, "Narratives of Fugitive Slaves" (*Christian Examiner,* July 1849), applauds the great rhetorical value of these accounts of slavery told, for the first time, from the victim's perspective. However, Peabody goes on to suggest that it is this unique perspective which impairs the narrator's objective portrayal of the slave master. While accepting the general truth of the narratives, he has "no doubt that they convey an altogether erroneous idea of the general character of the masters." The impact of Peabody's assessment is more powerful when one remembers that the *Christian Examiner,* although opposed to the radical abolitionist line of men like William Lloyd Garrison, was nonetheless firmly committed to an antislavery philosophy. By casting doubt upon the narrator's reliability, Peabody foreshadowed a serious problem which still exists today.

Twentieth-century critics were not immediately disposed to take the narratives seriously as literature. In the opinion of John Herbert Nelson, they were seldom works of art. In *The Negro Character in American Literature* (College Park, Md.: McGrath Publishing Co., 1926), Nelson chooses rather to attack the accuracy of the writers' portrayal of the southern slave. By claiming that the fugitive authors were unrepresentative of their race because only "the ablest, shrewdest, in other words, the most exceptional," made their way North, and declaring them to be "scarcely Negroes at all, but men European in mental heritage, in emotional quality, in spirit and temper," Nelson undermines the historical validity of the narrative with his suggestion that these men were exceptions and unrepresentative of the "happy-go-lucky, ignorant, coon-hunting, fun-loving field hand who, more than any other class of slave, typified the great mass of Black men in the South."

Even the first legitimate modern attempt at a literary study of the slave narrative, Vernon Loggins's *The Negro Author: His Development in America to 1900* (New York: Columbia University Press, 1931; rpt. Port

Washington, N.Y.: Kennikat Press, 1964), concludes that the "most significant statement regarding biographies of obscure Negroes . . . is that they were commercially successful." This does not take us much beyond Peabody's assessment of eighty years before. Although he surveys a number of narratives and suggests that Vassa's is of the "spontaneous variety one associates with Bunyan or Defoe," a great deal of his critical commentary is limited to observations like "crude, but honest," "colorless," and "interesting." Valuable, however, is Loggins's discussion of the white writers who wrote slave narratives in order to cash in on the commercial market. He analyzes the problems caused by these amanuenses, and identifies a number of bogus narratives, notably *The Autobiography of a Female Slave* (1857), Kate E. Pickard's fictional story of Peter Still and his wife, "Vina" (1856), and the *Life and Adventures of Zamba* (1847). But on the whole Loggins's treatment of the slave narrative is historical rather than literary.

A more recent and useful study is *Many Thousand Gone: The Ex-Slaves' Account of Their Bondage and Freedom* by Charles H. Nichols, Jr. (Leiden, the Netherlands: E. J. Brill, 1963; rpt. Bloomington: Indiana University Press, 1974). Using excerpts from the narratives as a major source of documentation, Nichols tells the story of slavery by proceeding chronologically, beginning with the departure from Africa, ending with the recent past, and focusing all the while on the issue of bondage and the bondsman's response to enslavement. Kenneth Stampp's generally favorable review of Nichols's study (*AHR,* April 1964) suggests that the critical handling of the narratives is perhaps not as disciplined as it might be. Again, it seems that the question of the historical validity of the narratives is the central issue.

Somewhat similar in format to Nichols's work is Stanley Feldstein's *Once A Slave: The Slaves' View of Slavery* (New York: Morrow, 1971). Feldstein also uses the slave narratives as a means of documenting the conditions of slavery. Unfortunately, some of his sources are known to be bogus narratives, yet he does not identify them as such. He quotes several times from Pickard's *The Kidnapped and the Ransomed. Being the Personal Recollections of Peter Still and his Wife "Vina" After Forty Years of Slavery* (1856), and from the *Life and Adventures of Zamba, an African Negro King, and His Experiences of Slavery in South Carolina, Written by Himself* (1847). Both are of doubtful authenticity.

A particularly valuable analysis of the themes and structure of the slave narrative is in Stephen Butterfield's *Black Autobiography in America* (Amherst: University of Massachusetts Press, 1974). Butterfield devotes the entire first section (four chapters) of his study to a discussion of the slave narrative. In chapter one, he deals with the narrator's point of view, suggesting that the slave writers were concerned with creating personas which would reflect their own moral values, and in so doing demonstrate their humanity. Butterfield further suggests that the narrative moves "away from the limbo of anonymity, toward definite goals and values other than those of the slaveholder." He describes the writer's struggles to achieve self-definition and also notes how slaves often used guile as a means of dealing with the violence of their masters, thereby confirming Osofsky's contention, as mentioned above. Chapter two, which includes material from Butterfield's earlier study, "The Use of Language in the Slave Narratives" (*NALF*, Fall 1972), analyzes the influence of white sources (the Bible and abolitionist rhetoric) and black sources (sermons and religious culture) on the language of the slave narrative. Chapter three expands this analysis to examine how white literary materials were assimilated by slave writers and adapted to their own needs. Chapter four discusses Frederick Douglass's narrative as the "finest example of the slave autobiography as a literary art form."

A short but valuable study can be found in J. Noel Heermance's *William Wells Brown and Clotelle: A Portrait of the Artist in the First Negro Novel* (Hamden, Conn.: Archon Books, 1969). Like Butterfield, Heermance discusses point of view and emphasizes the slave writer's use of concrete language, enumeration of detail, and development of dramatic structure. Using the narratives of Lewis and Milton Clarke and Henry Bibb as examples, he demonstrates how the powerful rhetorical impact of the narrative resulted from a mingling of indirect dramatization and the direct polemic of abolitionist oratory. Also interesting in this study is Heermance's examination of the similarities between the slave narratives and the so-called white narratives. Using *The Trial and Imprisonment of Jonathon Walker, at Pensacola, Florida, For Aiding Slaves to Escape From Bondage* (1845), he suggests the common format, details, and approaches of the two kinds of narratives.

An important article dealing with the content of the slave narrative is "Slave Narratives and the Plantation Legend," by Charles H. Nichols, Jr. (*Phylon*, Fall 1949), in which he challenges the portrayal of the "plantation myth" by southern writers from John Pendleton Kennedy to Margaret Mitchell, and demonstrates how the realism of the slave narrative explodes this myth.

"Ante-Bellum Slave Narratives: Their Place in American Literary History" (*SBL*, Autumn 1973), by Edward Margolies, argues that the plantation tradition developed as a response to the propaganda of the slave narrative. He also places the slave narrative within the tradition of American romantic literature, pointing out that the slave goes North seeking freedom and identity much as other fictional characters, Natty Bumppo in particular, moved West for similar reasons. Margolies also criticizes the narrative, citing its "florid asides, turgid rhetoric, and pious sermons that often interrupt the telling of these tales and serve to dampen their natural ardor."

John W. Blassingame's "Black Autobiographies as History and Literature" (*BlackSch*, December–January 1973–1974) examines the importance of the slave narrative in initiating the tradition of black autobiography, which has been the single most important vehicle for the exposition of black cultural development. Also significant is his discussion of the "alien-and-exile theme" in the slave narrative and how it has reappeared throughout subsequent black American literature.

" 'Goodbye to Sambo'—The Contribution of Black Slave Narratives to the Abolition Movement" (*NALF*, Fall 1972), by Paul D. Johnson, discusses how the narratives revealed new images and imaginative patterns of the Negro as an individual, of the society to which he did not belong, and of his future.

"Who Read the Slave Narratives?" (*Phylon*, Summer 1959), by Charles H. Nichols, Jr., summarizes the importance of the slave narrative in the pre-Civil War period and its relation to recent historical and literary works. He also examines the use modern historians have made of the narratives as source documents.

William W. Nichols discusses the dismissal of the slave narratives as valid historical documents in "Slave Narratives: Dismissed Evidence in the Writing of Southern History" (*Phylon*, Winter 1971). He cites the necessity for the identification of reliable texts as an important first step in verifying their legitimacy, and further suggests that the contents of the slave narrative could eventually effect a reappraisal of the significance of violence in the South. Similarly, Rafael L. Cortada's "The Slave Narratives: Living Indictments of American Historiography" (*Current Bibliography on African Affairs*, November 1971) challenges the traditional practice of dismissing the slave narratives as historical evidence merely because of their stylistic inconsistencies, and Randall M. Miller reaffirms the historical value of the slave narratives in "When Lions Write History: Slave Testimony and the History of American Slavery" (*Research Studies*, March 1976).

A Checklist of Slave Narratives

Unless otherwise noted, these narratives must be presumed to be reliable, at least until evidence to the contrary is produced. In each case the edition cited is the earliest version discovered by the compilers. Subsequent editions of some narratives have also been cited when they reflect significant changes in title or pagination, or to indicate the contemporary popularity of a particular narrative. Modern reprints have not been included.

Aaron. See *The light and truth of slavery.*
Adams, John Quincy. *Narrative of the life of John Quincy Adams, when in*

slavery, and now as a freeman. Harrisburg, Pa.: Sieg, Printer, 1874. 64 pp.

Albert, Mrs. Octavia Victoria (Rogers). *The house of bondage; or, Charlotte Brooks and other slaves, original and life-like, as they appeared in their old plantation and city slave life; together with pen-pictures of the peculiar institution, with sights and insights into their new relations as freedmen, freemen, and citizens, by Mrs. Octavia V. Rogers Albert, with an introduction by Rev. Bishop Willard F. Mallalieu, D. D.* New York: Hunt & Eaton; Cincinnati: Cranston & Stowe, 1890. 161 pp.

Alexander, Archer. See Eliot, William Greenleaf.

Allen, Richard. *The life experience and gospel labors of the Rt. Rev. Richard Allen, to which is annexed the rise and progress of the African Methodist Episcopal church in the United States of America. Containing a narrative of the yellow fever in the year of Our Lord 1793. With an address to the people of color in the United States. Written by himself and published by his request.* (N.p., n.d.) Reissued in Philadelphia by the A.M.E. Book Concern in 1887. 69 pp.

———— and Absalom Jones. *A narrative of the proceedings of the black people during the late awful calamity in Philadelphia, in the year 1793: and a refutation of some censures, thrown upon them in some late publications.* Philadelphia: Printed for the authors, by William W. Woodward, at Franklin's Head, No. 41, Chestnut-Street, 1794. 28 pp.

American slavery as it is. See Weld, Theodore D.

Anderson, John. See Twelvetrees, Harper.

Anderson, Robert. *From slavery to affluence; memoirs of Robert Anderson, ex-slave.* Hemingford, Neb.: The Hemingford Ledger, c. 1927. 59 pp.

Anderson, Thomas. *Interesting account of Thomas Anderson, a slave, "Taken from his own lips."* Dictated to J. P. Clark. N.p., 1854.

Armstrong, Orland Kay. *Old massa's people; the old slaves tell their story.* Indianapolis, Ind.: Bobbs-Merrill, 1931. 357 pp.

Arthur. *The Life, and dying speech of Arthur, a Negro man; who was executed at Worcester, October 20, 1768 for a rape committed on the body of one Deborah Metcalfe. Worcester Gaol, October 18, 1768.* Boston: Printed and sold in Milk Street, 1768.

Asa-Asa. See Prince, Mary.

Aunt Sally. *Aunt Sally; or, the cross the way of freedom. A narrative of the slave-life and purchase of the mother of Rev. Isaac Williams, of Detroit, Michigan.* Cincinnati: American Reform Tract and Book Society, 1858. 216 pp.

Ball, Charles. See Fisher.

Banks, J. H. See Pennington, James William Charles.

Bayley, Solomon. *A Narrative of some remarkable Incidents in the Life of Solomon Bayley, formerly a slave in the State of Delaware, North America. Written by himself and published for his benefit. To which are prefixed a few remarks by Robert Hurnard.* London: Harvey & Darton, 1825. 48 pp.

Bibb, Henry. *Narrative of the life and adventures of Henry Bibb, an American slave, written by himself with an introduction by Lucius C. Matlack.* New York: The Author, 1849. 204 pp.

Black, Leonard. *The life and sufferings of Leonard Black, a fugitive from slavery. Written by himself.* New Bedford, Mass.: B. Lindsey, 1847. 48 pp.

————. *The life and sufferings of Leonard Black, a fugitive from slavery. Written by himself.* New Bedford, Mass.: B. Lindsey, 1847. 61 pp.

Bluett, Thomas. *Some memoirs of the life of Job, the son of Solomon the high priest of Boonda in Africa; who was a slave about two years in Maryland; and afterwards being brought to England, was set free, and sent to his native land in the year 1734.* London: Printed for R. Ford, 1734. 63 pp.

Boen, William. *Anecdotes and memoirs of William Boen, a coloured man, who lived and died near Mount Holly, New Jersey. To which is added, the testimony of Friends of Mount Holly Monthly meeting concerning him.* Philadelphia: Printed by John Richards, 1834. 18 pp.

Botkin, B. A., ed. *Lay my burden down; a folk history of slavery.* Chicago: University of Chicago Press, 1945. 285 pp.

Bradford, Sarah. *Scenes in the Life of Harriet Tubman.* Auburn, New York: W. J. Moses, Printer, 1869. 132 pp.

Brent, Linda. See Jacobs, Harriet.

Brooks, Charlotte. See Albert, Octavia Victoria (Rogers).

Brown, Henry "Box." See Stearns, Charles.

————. *Narrative of the Life of Henry "Box" Brown.* Manchester, 1851. 61 pp.

Brown, John. See Chamerovzov, L. A.

Brown, William J. *The life of William J. Brown, of Providence, R. I. With personal recollections of incidents in Rhode Island.* Providence, R.I.: Angell & Co., Printers, 1883. 230 pp.

Brown, William Wells. *Narrative of William W. Brown, a fugitive slave. Written by himself.* Boston: The Anti-Slavery Office, 1847. 110 pp. (Also 1848, 144 pp.)

————. *Narrative of William W. Brown, an American slave. Written by himself.* London: C. Gilpin, 1849. 168 pp.

Bruce, Henry Clay. *The new man. Twenty-nine years a slave. Twenty-nine years a free man. Recollections of Henry Clay Bruce.* York, Pa.: n.p., 1895. 176 pp.

Bruner, Peter. *A slave's adventures toward freedom; not fiction, but the true story of a struggle.* Oxford, Ohio (1919?). 54 pp.

Burton, Annie L. *Memories of childhood's slavery days.* Boston: Ross Publishing Company, 1909. 97 pp.

Campbell, Israel. *An Autobiography. Bond and free; or, yearnings for freedom, from my Green brier house. Being the story of my life in bondage, and my life in freedom.* Philadelphia: Published by the author, 1861. 320 pp.

Chamerovzov, L. A. ed. *Slave life in Georgia: a narrative of the life, sufferings, and escape of John Brown, a fugitive slave, now in England.* London: W. M. Watts, 1855. 250 pp.

(Child) Francis, L. M. *I. T. Hopper; a true life.* London, 1842.

Child, L(ydia) Maria. *Isaac T. Hopper: A True Life.* Boston: John P. Jewett & Co., 1853.

Clarke, Lewis Garrard. *Narrative of the sufferings of Lewis Clarke, during a captivity of more than twenty-five years, among the Algerines of Kentucky, one of the so called Christian states of North America. Dictated by himself.* Boston: David H. Ela, Printer, 1845. 108 pp.

—— and Milton Clarke. *Narratives of the sufferings of Lewis and Milton Clarke, sons of a soldier of the revolution, during a captivity of more than twenty years among the slaveholders of Kentucky, one of the so called Christian states of North America. Dictated by themselves.* Boston: B. Marsh, 1846. 144 pp.

Coombs, Isaac. See Daggett, David.

Cooper, Thomas. *Narrative of the life of Thomas Cooper.* New York: Isaac T. Hopper, 1832. 36 pp.

Craft, Ellen. See Craft, William.

Craft, William. *Running a thousand miles for freedom; or The Escape of William and Ellen Craft from slavery. (With a portrait of Ellen Craft).* London: William Tweedie, 1860. 111 pp.

Cugoano, Ottobah. *Narrative of the enslavement of Ottobah Cugoano, a native of Africa; published by himself, in the year 1807.*

Daggett, David. *The life and adventures of Joseph Mountain, a Negro, who was executed at New-Haven on the 20th of October, 1790, for a rape committed May last. To which are added, the Adventures of Isaac Coombs.* Philadelphia: Printed and sold by William Woodhouse, 1790.

——. *The life and extraordinary adventures of Joseph Mountain, a Negro, who was executed at New-Haven, on the 20th ult. for a rape committed in May last.* Philadelphia: Printed by John Dunlap and David C. Claypoole. Sold by the Hawkers. 1790.

——. *Sketches of the life of Joseph Mountain, a Negro, who was executed at New-Haven, on the 20th day of October instant, for a rape, committed on the 26th day of May last, to be sold at this office. The writer of this history has directed that the money arising from the sales thereof, after deducting the expense of printing, etc. be given to the unhappy girl whose life is rendered wretched by the crime of the malefactor.* New-Haven: Printed and sold by T. and S. Green, 1790. 20 pp.

Davis, Noah. *A narrative of the life of Rev. Noah Davis, a colored man. Written by himself, at the age of fifty-four. Printed solely for the author's benefit.* Baltimore: J. F. Weishampel, 1859. 86 pp.

Dinah. See Simpson, John Hawkins.

Douglass, Frederick. *Narrative of the life of Frederick Douglass, an American slave. Written by himself.* Boston: Anti-Slavery Office, 1845. 125 pp.

———. *Narrative of the life of Frederick Douglass, an American slave. Written by himself.* Dublin: Webb and Chapman, 1845. 128 pp.

———. *Narrative of the life of Frederick Douglass, an American slave. Written by himself.* 2nd Dublin ed. Dublin: Webb and Chapman, 1846. 122 pp.

———. *Narrative of the life of Frederick Douglass, an American slave. Written by himself.* 3rd English ed. Wortley, neer [*sic*] Leeds: Printed by Joseph Barker, 1846. 170 pp.

———. *Narrative of the life of Frederick Douglass, an American slave. Written by himself.* Boston: Anti-Slavery office, 1847. 114 pp.

———. *My Bondage and My Freedom. Part I—Life as a slave. Part II—Life as a freeman. With an introduction.* By Dr. James M'Cune Smith. New York and Auburn: Miller, Orton & Mulligan, 1855. 464 pp.

———. *The heroic slave; a thrilling narrative of the adventures of Madison Washington, in pursuit of liberty.* (n.p.), 1863. 31 pp.

———. *Life and times of Frederick Douglass, Written by himself. His early life as a slave, his escape from bondage, and his complete history to the present time, including his connection with the anti-slavery movement. With an introduction by Mr. George L. Ruffin.* Hartford, Conn.: Park Publishing Co., 1881. 516 pp.

———. *Life and times of Frederick Douglass, Written by himself. His early life as a slave, his escape from bondage, and his complete history to the present time, including his connection with the anti-slavery movement. With an introduction by Mr. George L. Ruffin.* Hartford, Conn.: Park Publishing Co.; Cleveland: G. M. Rewell & Co., 1881. 618 pp.

———. *The life and times of Frederick Douglass, from 1817 to 1822, written by himself. With an introduction by the Right Hon. John Bright. Edited by John Lobb.* London: Christian Age Office, 1882. 454 pp.

———. *Life and times of Frederick Douglass written by himself. His early life as a slave, his escape from bondage, and his complete history to the present time, including his connection with the anti-slavery movement, with an introduction by Mr. George L. Ruffin.* New rev. ed. Boston: DeWolfe, Fiske & Co., c. 1892. 752 pp.

Drew, Benjamin. *A north-side view of slavery. The refugee: or, The narratives of fugitive slaves in Canada. Related by themselves, with an account of the history and condition of the coloured population of Upper Canada.* Boston: J. P. Jewett and Co.; New York: Sheldon, Lamport and Blakeman, 1856. 387 pp.

Drums and shadows; survival studies among the Georgia coastal Negroes by the Savannah unit, Georgia writers' project, Work projects administration. Athens: University of Georgia Press, 1940. 274 pp.

DuBois, Silvia. See Larison, C. W.

Dungy, J. A. *A narrative of the Rev. John Dungy, who was born a slave. Written by his daughter.* Rochester, N.Y.: Printed for the publisher, 1866. 10 pp.

Elder, Orville. *Samuel Hall, 47 years a slave. A brief story of his life before and after freedom came to him.* Washington, Iowa: Journal print, 1912. 41 pp.

Eldridge, Elleanor. *Memoirs of Elleanor Eldridge.* Providence, R.I.: B. T. Albro, Printer, 1838. 128 pp.

Eliot, William Greenleaf. *The story of Archer Alexander; from slavery to freedom. March 30, 1863.* Boston: Cupples, Upham and Co., c. 1885. 123 pp.

Equiano, Olaudah. *The interesting narrative of the life of Olaudah Equiano, or Gustavus Vassa, the African. Written by himself. Vol. I. Five lines of scriptural text from Isaiah XII. 2,4.* London: Printed for and Sold by the Author, No. 10, Union-Street, Middlesex Hospital; and may be had of all the Booksellers in Town and Country. Entered at Stationers' Hall, 1789. 2 vols.

————. *The Interesting Narrative of the Life of Olaudah Equiano or Gustavus Vassa, the African.* London: 1790. 359 pp.

————. *The interesting narrative of the life of Olaudah Equiano, or Gustavus Vassa, the African, written by himself.* 1st American ed. New York: Printed and sold by W. Durell at his book-store and printing office, No. 19, Q Street, 1791. 2 vols. in 1.

Fedric, Francis. *Life and sufferings of F. F., while in slavery. A true tale, etc.* Birmingham, 1859.

————. *Slave life in Virginia and Kentucky; or Fifty years of slavery in the southern states of America. By Francis Fedric, an escaped slave, with preface by the Rev. Charles Lee.* London: Wertheim, Macintosh, and Hunt, 1863. 115 pp.

Fisher. *Slavery in the United States; a narrative of the life and adventures of Charles Ball, a black man, who lived forty years in Maryland, South Carolina and Georgia, as a slave.* Lewistown, Pa.: J. W. Shugert, 1836. Prepared by Mr. Fisher from the verbal narrative of Ball, a slave. 400 pp. (Of doubtful authenticity.)

————. *Slavery in the United States: a narrative of the life and adventures of Charles Ball, a black man, who lived forty years in Maryland, South Carolina and Georgia, as a slave.* New York: J. S. Taylor, 1837. Prepared by Mr. Fisher from the verbal narrative of Ball. (Of doubtful authenticity.)

————. *Slavery in the United States. A narrative of the life and adventures of Charles Ball, a black man, who lived forty years in Maryland, South Carolina and Georgia, as a slave.* Pittsburgh, Pa.: J. T. Shryock, 1853. Prepared by Mr. Fisher from the verbal narrative of Ball. 446 pp. (Of doubtful authenticity.)

————. *Fifty years in chains; or, The life of an American slave.* New York:

H. Dayton; Indianapolis, Ind.: Dayton & Asher, 1858. Prepared by Mr. Fisher from the verbal narrative of Ball, a slave. 430 pp. (Of doubtful authenticity.)

Frederick, Francis. *Autobiography of Rev. Francis Frederick, of Virginia.* Baltimore: J. W. Woods, printer, 1869. (Chapters two through five are a narrative of the author's life as a slave in Kentucky.)

Gilbert, Olive. *Narrative of Sojourner Truth, a northern slave, emancipated from bodily servitude by the state of New York, in 1828.* Boston: The Author, 1850. 144 pp. (Sojourner Truth was also known as Isabella.)

Grandy, Moses. *Narrative of the life of Moses Grandy; late a slave in the United States of America. 1st American from the last London ed.* Boston: O. Johnson, 1844. 45 pp.

Green, Jacob. *Narrative of the life of J. D. Green, a runaway slave, from Kentucky, containing an account of his three escapes, in 1839, 1846 & 1848.* Huddersfield: Printed by Henry Fielding, Kirkgate, 1863. 42 pp.

Green, William. *Narrative of events in the life of W. G. (formerly a slave). Written by himself.* Springfield, 1853. 23 pp.

Griffiths, Mattie. *Autobiography of a female slave.* Redfield, New York, 1857. 401 pp. (Fiction.)

Grimes, William. *Life of William Grimes, the runaway slave. Written by himself.* New York, 1825. 68 pp.

———. *Life of William Grimes, the runaway slave. Written by himself.* New Haven: The Author, 1855. 93 pp.

Gronniosaw, James Albert Ukawsaw. *A narrative of the most remarkable Particulars in the Life of James Albert Ukawsaw Gronniosaw, an African Prince, as related by himself. With a preface by W. Shirley.* Bath: S. Hazard (1770?). 49 pp.

———. *A narrative of the most remarkable particulars in the life of James Albert Ukawsaw Gronniosaw, an African Prince, as related by himself.* Leeds: Printed by Davies and Booth, at the Stanhope Press, Vicar-Lane, 1814. 32 pp.

Hall, Samuel. See Elder, Orville.

Hammon, Briton. *Narrative of the uncommon suffering and surprizing deliverance of Briton Hammon, a Negro man-servant to General Winslow, of Marshfield, who returned to Boston, after having been absent almost thirteen years. Containing an account of the many hardships he underwent . . . how he was cast away in the Capes of Florida . . . inhuman barbarity of the Indians.* Boston: Printed by Green & Russell, 1760. 14 pp.

Hammon, Jupiter. *An address to the Negroes of the state of New York. By Jupiter Hammon, servant of John Lloyd, jun. esq. of the manor of Queen's Village, Long Island.* New York: Published by Samuel Wood, No. 363 Pearl-Street, 1806. 22 pp. (This is not actually a narrative, but it is interesting for its pious acceptance of enslavement.)

Hawkins, William George. *Lunsford Lane; or Another helper from North Carolina.* Boston: Crosby & Nichols, 1863. 305 pp. (Of doubtful authenticity.)

Hayden, William. *Narrative of William Hayden, containing a faithful account of his travels for a number of years, whilst a slave in the South. Written by himself.* Cincinnati, Ohio, 1846. 156 pp.

Henson, Josiah. *The life of Josiah Henson, formerly a slave, now an inhabitant of Canada, as narrated by himself.* Boston: A. D. Phelps, 1849. 76 pp.

————. *Truth stranger than fiction. Father Henson's story of his own life. With an introduction by Mrs. H. B. Stowe.* Boston: J. P. Jewett and Co., 1858. 212 pp.

————. *"Uncle Tom's story of his life." An autobiography of the Rev. Josiah Henson (Mrs. Harriet Beecher Stowe's "Uncle Tom"). From 1789 to 1876. With a preface by Mrs. Harriet Beecher Stowe and an introductory note by George Sturge and S. Morley. Edited by John Lobb.* London: Christian Age Office, 1876. 231 pp.

————. *"Truth is stranger than than fiction." An autobiography of the Rev. Josiah Henson (Mrs. Harriet Beecher Stowe's "Uncle Tom"), from 1789 to 1879. With a preface by Mrs. Harriet Beecher Stowe, introductory notes by Wendell Phillips and John G. Whittier, and an appendix on the exodus, by Bishop Gilbert Haven.* Boston: B. B. Russell & Co., 1879.

Hildreth, Richard. *The slave; or, Memoirs of Archy Moore.* Boston: J. H. Eastburn, Printer, 1836. 2 vols. (Fiction.)

Hopper, Isaac. See Child, L(ydia) Maria.

Hughes, Louis. *Thirty years a slave. From bondage to freedom. The institution of slavery as seen on the plantation and in the home of the planter. Autobiography of Louis Hughes.* Milwaukee: H. E. Haferkorn, 1897. 210 pp.

Isabella. See Gilbert, Olive.

Jackson, Andrew. *Narrative and writings of Andrew Jackson, of Kentucky; containing an account of his birth, and twenty-six years of his life while a slave; his escape; five years of freedom, together with anecdotes relating to slavery; journal of one year's travels, sketches, etc. Narrated by himself; written by a friend.* Syracuse, N.Y.: *Daily* and *Weekly Star* Office, 1847. 120 pp.

Jacobs, Harriet (Linda Brent). *Incidents in the life of a slave girl. Written by herself. Edited by L. Maria Child.* Boston: Published for the author, 1861. 306 pp.

————. *The deeper wrong; Or, Incidents in the life of a slave girl. Written by herself. Edited by L. Maria Child.* London: W. Tweedie, 1862. 306 pp.

Joanna. *Joanna; or, the Female Slave. A West Indian tale, founded on Stedman's Narrative of an Expedition against the revolted Negroes of Surinam.* London, 1824.

————. *Narrative of Joanna; an emancipated slave of Surinam. (From John*

Gabriel Stedman's Narrative of a five year expedition against the revolted Negroes of Surinam.) Boston: I. Knapp, 1838. 64 pp.

Job, the son of Solomon. See Bluett, Thomas.

Johnson, Thomas L. *Africa for Christ. Twenty-eight years a slave.* London: Yates & Co., 1882. 72 pp.

————. *Twenty-eight years a slave; or the story of my life in three continents, by Thomas L. Johnson.* Bournemouth: W. Mate and Sons, Ltd., 1909. 266 pp.

Johnstone, Abraham. *The address of Abraham Johnstone, a black man, who was hanged at Woodbury, in the county of Glocester, and state of New Jersey, on Saturday the 8th day of July last; to the people of colour. To which is added his dying confession or declaration also, a copy of a letter to his wife, written the day previous to his execution.* Philadelphia: Printed for the purchasers, 1797. 47 pp.

Jones, Thomas H. *The experience of Thomas Jones who was a slave for forty-three years. Written by a friend, as given to him by Brother Jones.* Boston: Printed by D. Laing, 1850. 47 pp.

————. *Experience and personal narrative of Uncle Tom Jones: who was for forty years a slave. Also the surprising adventures of Wild Tom, a fugitive Negro from South Carolina.* New York, 1854.

————. *The Experience of T. Jones, who was a Slave for forty-three years. Written by a friend.* Springfield, 1854.

————. *Experience and personal narrative of Uncle Tom Jones: who was for forty years a slave. Also the surprising adventures of Wild Tom, of the island retreat, a fugitive Negro from South Carolina.* Boston: J. E. Farwell & Co., 1855. 56 pp.

————. *The experience of Thomas H. Jones, who was a slave for forty-three years. Written by a friend, as related to him by Brother Jones.* New Bedford, Mass.: E. Anthony & Sons, Printers, 1871. 46 pp.

————. *The experience of Thomas H. Jones, who was a slave for forty-three years. Written by a friend, as related to him by Brother Jones.* Boston: A. T. Bliss & Co., 1880. 83 pp.

Keckley, Elizabeth. *Behind the scenes; or, Thirty years a slave, and four years in the White House.* New York: G. W. Carleton, c. 1868. 371 pp.

Lane, Lunsford. *The narrative of Lunsford Lane, formerly of Raleigh, embracing an account of his early life, the redemption by purchase of himself and family from slavery, and his banishment from the place of his birth for the crime of wearing a colored skin. Published by himself.* Boston: J. G. Torrey, printer, 1842. 54 pp. (Of doubtful authenticity.) See also Hawkins, William George.

Larison, C. W. *Silvia Dubois (now 116 years old) a biografy of the slav who whipt her mistress and gand her fredom.* Ringos, N.J.: C. W. Larison, 1883. 124 pp.

Lewis, Joseph Vance. *Out of the ditch; a true story of an ex-slave.* Houston, Texas: Rein & Sons Co., Printers, c. 1910. 154 pp.

The light and truth of slavery. Aaron's history. Worcester, Mass.: Printed for Aaron, 1843. 48 pp.

Loguen, Jermain Wesley. *The Rev. J. W. Loguen, as a slave and as a freeman. A narrative of real life.* Syracuse, N.Y.: J. G. K. Truair & Co., Stereotypers and Printers, 1859. 444 pp.

Maquama. *Slavery illustrated; in the histories of Zangara and Maquama, two Negroes stolen from Africa, and sold into slavery. Related by themselves.* Manchester, England: W. Irwin; London: Simpkin Marshall, 1849. 36 pp.

Marrant, John. *A narrative of the Lord's wonderful dealings with John Marrant, a Black.* London, 1785. 24 pp.

————. *A narrative of the Lord's wonderful dealings with John Marrant, a black, (now going to preach the gospel in Nova-Scotia). Born in New-York, in North America. Taken down from his own relation, arranged, corrected, and published, by the Rev. Mr. Aldridge.* London: Printed and sold by Gilbert Plummer, 1785. 40 pp.

Mars, James. *Life of James Mars, a slave born and sold in Connecticut. Written by himself.* Hartford, Conn.: Press of Case Lockwood & Co., 1864. 32 pp.

Mason, Isaac. *Life of Isaac Mason as a slave.* Worcester, Mass., 1893. 74 pp.

Mattison, H. *Louisa Picquet, the octoroon; or, Inside views of southern domestic life.* New York: The Author, 1861. 60 pp.

Meachum, John B. *An address to the colored citizens of the United States. By John B. Meachum, pastor of the African Baptist church. St. Louis, Mo.* Philadelphia: Printed for the author, by King and Barid, 1846. 62 pp.

Moore, Archy. See Hildreth, Richard.

Mountain, Joseph. See Daggett, David.

The Negro in Virginia, compiled by workers of the Writers' program of the Work Projects Administration in the state of Virginia. Sponsored by the Hampton Institute. New York: Hastings House, 1940. 380 pp.

Neilson, Peter. *The life and adventures of Zamba, an African Negro King, and his experiences of slavery in South Carolina. Written by himself. Corrected and arranged by P. Neilson.* London: Smith, Elder and Co., 1847. 258 pp. (Fiction.)

Northup, Solomon. *Twelve Years a slave. Narrative of Solomon Northup, a citizen of New-York, kidnapped in Washington city in 1841, and rescued in 1853, from a cotton plantation near the Red River, in Louisiana.* Auburn, N.Y.: Derby and Miller; Buffalo, N.Y.: Derby, Orton and Mulligan, 1853. 336 pp.

Offley, Greenburg. *A narrative of the life and labors of the Rev. G. W. Offley, a colored man, and local preacher, who lived twenty-seven years at the South and twenty-four at the North.* Hartford, Conn., 1860. 52 pp.

Parker, Allen. *Recollections of slavery times.* Worcester, Mass.: Chas. W. Burbank and Co., 1895. 96 pp.

Parker, Jamie. See Pierson, Emily Catherine.

Parker, William. "The Freedman's Story." *Atlantic Monthly,* 17 (February 1866), 152–160; 17 (March 1866), 276–295.

Pennington, James William Charles. *The fugitive blacksmith; or, Events in the history of James W. C. Pennington, pastor of a Presbyterian church, New York, formerly a slave in the state of Maryland, United States.* 2nd ed. London: C. Gilpin, 1849. 87 pp.

———. *A narrative of events of the life of J. H. Banks, an escaped slave, from the cotton state, Alabama, in America. Written, with introduction, by J. W. C. Pennington.* Liverpool, England: M. Rouke, 1861. 92 pp.

Pickard, Kate E. *The kidnapped and the ransomed. Being the personal recollections of Peter Still and his wife "Vina," after forty years of slavery. With an introduction by Rev. Samuel J. May; and an appendix by William H. Furness.* Syracuse, N.Y.: W. T. Hamilton; New York: Miller, Orton and Mulligan, c. 1856. 409 pp. (Fiction.)

Picquet, Louisa. See Mattison, H.

Pierson, Emily Catherine. *Jamie Parker, the fugitive.* Hartford, Conn.: Brockett, Fuller and Co., 1851. 192 pp. (Fiction.)

Platt, Rev. S. H. *The martyrs and the fugitive; or, A narrative of the captivity, sufferings, and death of an African family, and the slavery and escape of their son. Published for the benefit of the fugitive.* New York: Printed by D. Fanshaw, 1859. 95 pp.

Prince, Mary. *The history of Mary Prince, a West Indian slave. Related by herself. With a supplement by the editor. To which is added, the Narrative of Asa-Asa, a captured African.* London: F. Westley & A. H. Davis, 1831. 44 pp.

Randolph, Peter. *Sketches of slave life: or, Illustrations of the "peculiar institution" by Peter Randolph, an emancipated slave.* Boston: The Author, 1855. 35 pp.

———. *From slave cabin to the pulpit. The autobiography of Rev. Peter Randolph; the southern question illustrated and sketches of slave life.* Boston: James H. Earle, 1893. 220 pp.

Redpath, James. *The Roving Editor: or, Talks with slaves in the southern states.* New York: A. B. Burdick, 1859. 349 pp.

Roberts, James B. *The narrative of James Roberts, soldier in the Revolutionary War and at the Battle of New Orleans.* Chicago: Printed for the author, 1858. Hattiesburg, Miss.: The Book Farm, 1945. 32 pp.

Robinson, W. *From Log Cabin to the Pulpit; or fifteen years in slavery.* Eau Claire, Wis.: James H. Tifft, 1913. 200 pp.

Roper, Moses. *A Narrative of the adventures and escape of Moses Roper from American Slavery; with a preface, by the Rev. T. Price, D.D.* London: 1837. 108 pp.

Simpson, John Hawkins. *Horrors of the Virginia slave trade and of the slave-rearing plantations. The true story of Dinah, an escaped Virginian slave, now in London, on whose body are eleven scars left by tortures which were inflicted by her master, her own father. Together with extracts from the laws of Virginia, showing that against these barbarities the law gives not the smallest protection to the slave, but the reverse.* London: A. W. Bennett, 1863. 64 pp.

Singleton, William Henry. *Recollections of my slavery days.* Peekskill, N.Y.: Highland Democrat Co. Print, c. 1922.

Slave narratives: a folk history of slavery in the United States from interview with former slaves, typewritten records prepared by the Federal Writers Project, assembled by the Library of Congress Project, Works Project Administration, for the District of Columbia, in 17 vols., 1936, 1938.

Smith, Harry. *Fifty years of slavery in the United States of America.* Grand Rapids, Mich.: West Michigan Print. Co., 1891. 183 pp.

Smith, James Lindsay. *Autobiography of James L. Smith, including also, reminiscences of slave life, recollections of the war, education of freedmen, causes of the exodus, etc.* Norwich, Conn.: Press of the Bulletin Co., 1881. 150 pp.

Smith, Venture. *A narrative of the life and adventures of Venture, a native of Africa, but resident above sixty years in the United States of America. Related by himself.* New London, Conn.: Printed by C. Holt, at the Bee-Office, 1798. 32 pp.

Spear, Chloe. *Memoir of Mrs. Chloe Spear, a native of Africa, who was enslaved in childhood, and died in Boston, January 3, 1815, aged 65 years. By a lady of Boston.* Boston: J. Loring, 1832. 108 pp.

Stearns, Charles. *Narrative of Henry Box Brown, who escaped from slavery enclosed in a box 3 feet long and 2 wide. Written from a statement of facts made by himself. With remarks upon the remedy for slavery.* Boston: Brown & Stearns, 1849. 90 pp.

Steward, Austin. *Twenty-two years a slave, and forty years a freeman; embracing a correspondence of several years, while president of Wilberforce Colony, London, Canada West.* Rochester, N.Y.: W. Alling, 1857. 360 pp.

Stewart, John. *The missionary pioneer, or, A brief memoir of the life, labours, and death of John Stewart, (man of colour) founder, under God of the mission among the Wyandotts at Upper Sandusky, Ohio.* New York: Joseph Mitchell, printed by J. C. Totten, 1827. 96 pp.

Still, Peter and "Vina." See Pickard, Kate E.

Strickland, S. *Negro slavery described by a Negro: being the narrative of Ashton Warner, a native of St. Vincent's. With an appendix concerning the testimony of four Christian ministers recently returned from the colonies on the system of slavery as it now exists.* London: Samuel Maunder, 1831. 144 pp.

Stroyer, Jacob. *My life in the South.* Salem, Mass.: Salem Observer Book and Job Print, 1889. 83 pp.

"Tales of Oppression." See Child, L(ydia) Maria.

Thompson, John. *The life of John Thompson, a fugitive slave; containing his history of 25 years in bondage, and his providential escape. Written by himself.* Worcester, Mass.: John Thompson, 1856. 143 pp.

Tilmon, Levin. *A brief miscellaneous narrative of the more early part of the life of L. Tilmon, pastor of a Methodist Congregational church in the city of New York. Written by Himself.* Jersey City, N.J.: W. W. & L. A. Pratt, Printers, 1853. 97 pp.

Truth, Sojourner. See Gilbert, Olive.

Tubman, Harriet. See Bradford, Sarah.

Turner, Nat. *The confession, trial and execution of Nat Turner, the Negro Insurrectionist; also a list of persons murdered in the insurrection in Southampton County, Virginia, on the 21st and 22nd of August, 1831, with introductory remarks by T. R. Gray.* Petersburg, Va.: J. B. Ege, Printer, 1881. 23 pp.

Twelvetrees, Harper, ed. *The story of the life of John Anderson, the Fugitive Slave. Ed. by Harper Twelvetrees, M. A. chairman of the John Anderson Committee.* London: W. Tweedie, 1863. 182 pp.

Vassa, Gustavus. See Equiano, Olaudah.

Veney, Bethany. *The Narrative of Bethany Veney, a slave woman. With introduction by Rev. Bishop Mallalieu, and commendatory notices from Rev. V. A. Cooper and Rev. Erastus Spaulding.* Worcester, Mass., 1889. 46 pp.

Voorhis, Robert. *Life and adventures of Robert, the hermit of Massachusetts, who has lived 14 years in a cave, secluded from human society. Comprising, an account of his birth, parentage, sufferings, and providential escape from unjust and cruel bondage in early life—and his reasons for becoming a recluse. Taken from his own mouth, and published for his benefit.* Providence, R.I.: Printed for H. Trumbull, 1829. 36 pp.

Ward, Samuel Ringgold. *Autobiography of a Fugitive Negro; his anti-slavery labors in the United States, Canada and England.* London: J. Snow, 1855. 412 pp.

Warner, Ashton. See Strickland, S.

Washington, Booker T. *Up From Slavery, an Autobiography, by Booker T. Washington.* New York: A. L. Burt Co., 1901. 330 pp.

Washington, Madison. See Douglass, Frederick.

Watkins, James. *Struggles for freedom; or the life of James Watkins, formerly a slave in Maryland, U.S.; in which is detailed a graphic account of his extraordinary escape from slavery, notices of the fugitive slave law, the sentiments of American divines on the subject of slavery, etc.* Manchester: Printed for James Watkins, 1860. 19th edition. 104 pp.

Weld, Theodore D. *American slavery as it is; testimony of a thousand witnesses.* New York: American Anti-Slavery Society, 1839. 224 pp.

White, George. *A brief account of the life, experiences, travels, and gospel labours of George White, an African; written by himself and revised by a friend.* New York: John C. Totten, 1810. 60 pp.

White, William S. *The African preacher; an authentic narrative.* Philadelphia: Presbyterian Board of Publication, c. 1849. 139 pp.

Wild Tom. See Jones, Thomas H.

Wilkerson, James. *Wilkerson's history of his travels and labors, in the United States, as a missionary, in particular, that of the Union Seminary, located in Franklin Co., Ohio, since he purchased his liberty in New Orleans, La., etc.* Columbus, Ohio, 1861. 43 pp.

Williams, James. *A Narrative of events, since the first of August, 1834, by James Williams, an apprenticed labourer in Jamaica.* London: Sold by W. Ball, 1837. 23 pp.

————. *Narrative of James Williams, An American slave who was for several years a driver on a cotton plantation in Alabama.* New York: American Anti-Slavery Society; Boston: I. Knapp, 1838. 108 pp. (This narrative, which had been dictated to John Greenleaf Whittier, was subsequently proven to be unreliable and was withdrawn by the American Anti-Slavery Society.)

Zamba. See Neilson, Peter.

Zangara. See Maquama.

THE POLEMICISTS:
David Walker, Frederick Douglass, Booker T. Washington, and W. E. B. Du Bois

W. Burghardt Turner

The prevailing conditions of the nineteenth century, and the crushing force and dehumanizing effects of chattel slavery, produced a cadre of American writers, black and white, who denounced the social and economic aberration which engulfed them. From among these rose four of the most outstanding polemicists of that century: David Walker (1785–1830), Frederick Douglass (1817–1895), Booker T. Washington (1856–1915), and W. E. B. Du Bois (1868–1963). No two of these were of the same mold, yet they overlapped in style as well as in time. Though their polemics responded to the conditions of the nineteenth century, their lives span the life of the American nation from the birth of David Walker in 1785 to the death of W. E. B. Du Bois in 1963.

There are remarkable parallels in the lives of these four Afro-American leaders. Each was a prominent orator, each was a writer associated with newspaper publishing, each faced opposition or resistance from within the Afro-American community, and each was an innovator who helped set the pace for the era that followed. As opportunities for public exposure to and publication of the work of these four polemicists has increased from the early nineteenth century to the second half of the twentieth century, public awareness of their outstanding achievements has grown and continues to grow.

Margaret Just Butcher, in *The Negro in American Culture* (New York: Knopf, 1956), dealt with the problem of racism. It was part of her main thesis that "American slavery introduced into the very heart of American society a crucial dilemma [of prejudice against blacks]" which has influenced conditions ever since. Most Afro-Americans of genius have used their talents to attack this dilemma and seek its dissolution. August Meier, in "The Paradox of W. E. B. Du Bois," in *Negro Thought in*

America, 1880–1915 (Ann Arbor: University of Michigan Press, 1964), reprinted in *W. E. B. Du Bois: A Profile* edited by Rayford W. Logan (New York: Hill & Wang, 1971), has aptly noted: "If, of the great trio of Negro Leaders, Frederick Douglass best expressed the aspirations toward full citizenship and assimilation, and Booker T. Washington the interest in economic advancement, it was Du Bois who most explicitly revealed the impact of oppression and of the American creed in creating ambivalent loyalties toward race and nation in the minds of American Negroes." Throughout the literature we find the linking of these three great names in various comparisons. Occasionally there is the inclusion of David Walker as the predecessor of the giants, but this is seldom more than a mere acknowledgement of his powerful *Appeal*. The literature on this quartet of polemicists has been increasing rapidly in the wake of aroused interest in the Afro-American.

Bibliographies

Students of the civil rights struggle of the nineteenth and early twentieth centuries have been hampered by the lack of effective research tools. Bibliographies on Walker, Douglass, Washington, and Du Bois have been notably scarce, and almost no analytical bibliographies exist. There are, however, several good general bibliographies. Most students with an interest in Afro-American history are familiar with the classic reference work compiled by Monroe N. Work, *Bibliography of the Negro in America and Africa* (New York: Wilson, 1928). This bibliography, reprinted by Octagon Books in 1965, is most helpful on the literature prior to 1928. However, as yet no one has updated it. Other general bibliographies which contain listings on the four polemicists include Dorothy B. Porter's *The Negro in the United States: A Selected Bibliography* (Washington, D.C.: Library of Congress, 1970) and *Blacks in America* (Garden City, N.Y.: Doubleday, 1971) compiled by James M. McPherson and others. Both of these have helpful annotations and topical groupings. Additional sources are: *The Negro in America: A Bibliography* (Cambridge, Mass.: Harvard University Press, 1970), compiled by Elizabeth W. Miller and Mary L. Fisher, which is very inadequate regarding these four men; Erwin K. Welsch's *The Negro in the United States: A Research Guide* (Bloomington: Indiana University Press, 1966); Darwin T. Turner's *Afro-American Writers* (New York: Appleton, 1970); Theressa Gunnels Rush, Carol Fairbanks Myers, and Esther Spring Arata's *Black American Writers Past and Present* (Metuchen, N.J.: Scarecrow, 1975); and Russell C. Brignano's *Black Americans in Autobiography* (Durham, N.C.: Duke University Press, 1974).

One should not overlook the helpful dictionary catalogs of the Library of Congress and some of the major library collections. Of particular value are those listing card catalogs of the Schomburg, Fisk University, and Howard University libraries, published by G. K. Hall of Boston: *Dictionary Catalog of the Schomburg Collection of Negro Literature and History, The New York Public Library* (1962) with a first supplement (1967) and a second supplement (1972); *Dictionary Catalog of the Jesse E. Moorland Collection of Negro Life and History, Howard University Libraries, Washington, D.C.* (1970); *Dictionary Catalog of the Arthur B. Spingarn Collection of Negro Authors, Howard University Library, Washington, D.C.* (1970); and *Dictionary Catalog of the Negro Collection of the Fisk University Library, Nashville, Tennessee* (1973).

Most of the recent periodical literature by and about Afro-Americans has been indexed in a succession of publications, the most recent being *Index to Periodical Articles By and About Negroes, Cumulation 1960–1970* (Boston: G. K. Hall, 1971), prepared by the staff of Hallie Q. Brown Memorial Library, Central State University, Wilberforce, Ohio, and of the Schomburg Collection of Negro Literature and History of The New York Public Library. This index was originally undertaken by the Hallie Q. Brown Memorial Library to replace the *Guide to Negro Periodical Literature,* which was issued quarterly. The first forty quarterly issues of the index have been cumulated and published under the title *Index to Selected Periodicals, Decennial Cumulation, 1950–1959* (Boston: G. K. Hall, 1962). The publisher is now issuing enlarged annual editions with expanded indexing. Many of these articles have been abstracted and collected in *Afro-American History: A Bibliography* (Santa Barbara, Calif.: ABC-Clio, 1974), edited by Dwight L. Smith with an introduction by Benjamin Quarles. This is a selection of abstracts from *America: History and Life* (ten vols., 1964–1972) that can be referred to for more recent writings.

Another specialized bibliography is the Race Relations Information Center's *Directory of Afro-American Resources* (New York: Bowker, 1970), edited by Walter Schatz. It describes 5,365 collections of mainly primary source materials in libraries and organizations throughout the country.

The search for specific bibliographic materials is more difficult. The absence of any bibliographies on Walker is primarily because of the scarcity of literature about him. Almost all references to him are very brief paragraphs, biographical sketches, or excerpts from the *Appeal,* as will be noted below.

Frederick Douglass's career accumulated a considerable body of literature, and recent attention has added greatly to it. The most extensive listing is the hardest to find—Historical Records Survey's *Calendar of Writings of Frederick Douglass in the Frederick Douglass Memorial Home, Anacostia, D.C.* (Washington, D.C.: District of Columbia—Historical Records Survey, Division of Professional and Service Projects, WPA, December 1940), with a foreword by Carter G. Woodson. The entire collection of materials has been made available on microfilm by the Library of Congress.

The only other lengthy Douglass bibliographies of substance are in the biography *Frederick Douglass* by Benjamin Quarles (Washington, D.C.: Associated Publishers, 1948; rpt. New York: Atheneum, 1968) and *Frederick Douglass: The Colored Orator.* (New York: Funk & Wagnalls, 1891, revised 1895) by Frederick Holland. Holland includes in an appendix a list of publications by Frederick Douglass which is interesting but incomplete. Quarles has the most balanced and scholarly bibliography. It is a good listing of material about Douglass but does not have much on works by him. There was no attempt to update this listing for the reprinting of this excellent biography in 1968. The 1962 Macmillan edition of Douglass's autobiography *Life and Times* has a good annotated bibliography which, by its lucid tone and scholarly quality, appears to have been written by Rayford W. Logan, who wrote the introduction to that edition.

What other scholars have neglected to do has been ably compensated for by Philip S. Foner's superb collection, *The Life and Writings of Frederick Douglass* (New York: International Publishers, 1950–1975). Although his five volumes do not contain a bibliography, his table of contents can serve this purpose. However, there is no inclusion of writings about Douglass. Also missing are citations of Douglass's book-length writings. It is hoped that John W. Blassingame's forthcoming study of the Douglass papers will produce a complete annotated bibliography of literature by and about Douglass. The voluminous writings of Booker T. Washington have been listed by Daniel T. Williams in *Eight Negro Bibliographies* (Millwood, N.Y.: Kraus Reprint, 1970), by far the most complete bibliography of Washington's published works. The listing is fifty-five pages long and includes a chronology, biographical notes, a list of major speeches and addresses, and a list of Sunday evening talks to students and faculty members of Tuskegee Institute, in addition to a list of publications by and about Washington. This is a most helpful tool for anyone studying Washington. However, it lacks full citations of publishers, does not list the numerous editions, and has no annotations. Help is provided by brief annotations in Karl Wallace's contribution to William N. Brigance's *History and Criticism of American Public Address* (New York: Russell & Russell, 1960), and by the bibliographies in Samuel R. Spencer's *Booker T. Washington and the Negro's Place in American Life* (Boston: Little, Brown, 1955) and *Booker T. Washington and His Critics: The Problem of Negro Leadership,* edited by Hugh Hawkins (Lexington, Mass.: Heath, 1962). Louis R. Harlan, in *The Booker T. Washington Papers* (Urbana: University of Illinois Press, 1972, 1974, 1975), gives a bibliography of works referred to in volumes 2, 3, and 4. The most voluminous compilation is the 105-page United States Library of Congress Manuscript Division listing, *Booker T. Washington: A Register of His Papers in the Library of Congress,* which was prepared in 1958 and is available on microfilm.

Dr. Du Bois was well known as a writer, but one could only guess at the magnitude of his work until Herbert Aptheker published his magnificent *Annotated Bibliography of the Published Works of W. E. B. Du Bois* (Millwood, N.Y.: Kraus-Thompson Organization, 1973) which in 563 pages annotates 1,975 published items. These include periodicals, newspapers, pamphlets, and books by Du Bois. In spite of the length of the sixty-one-page index, it does not include titles of essays, editorials, and the like, making it very difficult to find an item if the source or the date of publication is unknown. Similarly, the absence of any topical groupings or cross-references is a shortcoming, as there is no way to identify autobiographical writings or topics. Moreover, the volume does not indicate the existence of archival collections of Du Bois's materials nor does it list the many reprints of his writings. A good, although less complete, bibliography of Du Bois's publications had previously been provided by Julius Lester in *The Seventh Son: The Thought and Writings of W. E. B. Du Bois* (New York: Random House, 1971).

As yet there is no analytical bibliography of writings about Du Bois. *Dr. W. E. B. Du Bois: A Bibliography,* compiled in 1964 by S. I. A. Kotei, Ghana Library Board, Padmore Research Library on African Affairs (Accra, Ghana) is the only one which includes an extensive list of materials about Du Bois. However, it has been criticized because of its errors and omissions. Rayford W. Logan has helped fill the void of works commenting on Du Bois in a part of his astute twenty-five-page bibliographical note in *W. E. B. Du Bois: Profile* (New York: Hill & Wang, 1971).

There are several other short, incomplete bibliographies in published biographies. The most comprehensive list of Du Bois's writings is in Meyer Weinberg's collection, *W. E. B. Du Bois: A Reader* (New York: Harper & Row, 1970). Elliot Rudwick included a more limited bibliography in *W. E. B. Du Bois: Propagandist of the Negro Protest* (New York: Atheneum, 1972).

The need for a more comprehensive, if not definitive, bibliography of the writings, both autobiographical and critical, remains.

Manuscripts and Letters

The collections of manuscripts by the four polemicists are varied and extensive, except in the case of David Walker, for whom there is very little to report. There are no known manuscript copies of his *Appeal.* Although Walker appears to have corresponded with several people, such as the editors of *Freedom's Journal,* no letters or other papers have as yet turned up.

The papers of Frederick Douglass are in better shape. The largest collection is at the Library of Congress. This collection formerly was housed at the Douglass home at Anacostia. It contains about 1,000 letters to and from Douglass, along with many other documents, such as deeds, bond holdings, and insurance policies. The collection also includes many of his published works. The more than 15,000 items have been reproduced on microfilm by the Library of Congress. The Howard University Founders Library has in its Moorland Negro Collection about 300 Douglass items, including correspondence. Another large archival collection which includes Douglass material is in the Boston Public Library. Similarly helpful are the Gerrit Smith papers at the Syracuse University Library; these are particularly valuable because of Douglass's long and close relationship with Smith. Also valuable, though covering a shorter period, are the Stanton manuscripts in the Library of Congress, and Goodell Scrapbooks relating to slavery in the Oberlin University Library. Additional holdings are at the libraries of the University of Rochester and Duke University. The Harvard University Library has items in various collections.

The vast majority of the Douglass papers, aside from his three autobiographies and the four newspapers he edited, have been brought together in the five volumes of *The Life and Writings of Frederick Douglass,* edited by Philip S. Foner. They contain all of Douglass's speeches and letters that were available as of 1950.

The largest amount of Washington correspondence and other files are in the Manuscript Division of the Library of Congress. Louis R. Harlan notes that they hold approximately a million items. Included are some of the most important as well as the most trivial personal and Tuskegee communications and school records. In the Tuskegee archives there are large and important holdings of Washington papers which Walter Schatz indicates amounts to forty-two boxes of correspondence, manuscripts, and other papers. There is also an important collection in the Collis P. Huntington Memorial Library at Hampton Institute. Louis R. Harlan, Washington's main biographer and the director of the Booker T. Washington Papers Project, has brought together a large body of material at the University of Maryland Department of History, but the collection currently is not open to researchers. Additional materials may be found at the Booker T. Washington National Monument at Hardy, West Virginia.

A large selection of the Washington papers may be found in *The Booker T. Washington Papers,* Vol. 2, 1860–1889; Vol. 3, 1889–1895; Vol. 4, 1895–1898; and Vol. 5, 1899–1900, edited by Louis R. Harlan. It is expected that the complete publication of the papers will comprise fifteen volumes. John H. Bracey, Jr. (*The New York Times,* March 4, 1973) suggests that the publication of the Washington papers will allow us a greater understanding of Washington than we could get from the public image. He expects that Washington's life "may offer more to blacks during this period of growing white indifference to black aspirations, and growing repression of attempts to move to meet their needs, than those of the leading purveyors of rhetoric who pass for black leaders in our day." A statement on the importance and value of the papers is found in an article by the editors, Louis R. Harlan and Raymond W. Smock, in "The Booker T. Washington Papers" (*Maryland Historian,* Spring 1975). They emphasize the need to make available in printed form the long-neglected papers of Afro-American personalities, which are now relegated to the less-accessible form of microfilm.

The principal collection of Du Bois papers had been kept intact by Dr. Du Bois himself, who, according to Herbert Aptheker, his friend and admirer, "began systematically to preserve his papers and letters before he had reached his twentieth year, a habit he maintained until his death at ninety-five. He saved literally everything. . . . " Most of these were included in the papers that he entrusted to Aptheker to organize for publication. These have recently been acquired from his widow, Shirley Graham Du Bois, by the University of Massachusetts. They are being organized by Dr. Aptheker and will be published in a series that may reach forty volumes. The first part has been published under the editorship of Dr. Aptheker as *The Correspondence of W. E. B. Du Bois,* 1877–1934 (Amherst: University of Massachusetts Press, 1973 [Vol. 1, 1877–1934]; 1976 [Vol. 2, 1934–1944]).

There is a valuable collection of Du Bois papers at the Fisk University Library in Nashville, Tennessee, that includes correspondence, notebooks, and manuscripts. Among the manuscripts is the unfinished and unpublished study of the Afro-American soldier in World War I, which Du Bois announced and outlined in the pages of *The Crisis.* Additional significant materials may be found in various collections in the Yale University and Harvard University libraries. The Schomburg Collection of the New York Public Library (135th Street Branch) has material on each of these men. From time to time additional unpublished manuscripts are discovered in the files of other individuals. Two such recent finds are "W. E. B. Du Bois' Impressions of Woodrow Wilson," by Kenneth M. Glazer, (*JNH,* October 1973) and "W. E. B. Du Bois' Confrontation with White Liberalism During the Progressive Era" (*Phylon,* Fall 1974), by William M. Tuttle, Jr., which was the transcript of an interview in the Ray Stannard Baker files in the Manuscript Division of the Library of Congress.

For a basic statement, one should consider the superb work of John Hope Franklin, *From Slavery to Freedom* (New York: Knopf, 1947; 4th ed., New York: Vintage, 1974). Although he does not provide needed footnotes, his excellent bibliographical notes are helpful and specific. The incomparable research of Gunnar Mydral and a team of top-ranking social scientists produced *An American Dilemma* (New York: Harper & Bros., 1944), which has had numerous editions since that first publication. It is a reference work which would be hard to exhaust. Its 48 pages of reference titles and 328 pages of footnotes will meet the needs of all but the most thorough researchers. E. Franklin Frazier, one of the outstanding scholars who contributed to *An American Dilemma*, has provided his own work in *The Negro in the United States* (New York: Macmillan, 1949), which presents the material from the perspective of the sociologist. It is considered controversial by some. There are important interpretive statements on Douglass, Washington, and Du Bois in August Meier and Elliot M. Rudwick's *From Plantation to Ghetto* (New York: Hill & Wang, 1966). For a lighter and livelier statement, see J. Saunders Redding's *They Came in Chains* (Philadelphia: Lippincott, 1950).

Two other works that extoll the achievements of blacks are *The Black Response to America: Men, Ideals, and Organizations from Frederick Douglass to the NAACP* (Reading, Mass.: Addison-Wesley, 1970) by Robert L. Factor, and *The Long Struggle for Black Power* (New York: Scribners, 1971) by Edward Peeks. Both have extensive discussions of the roles of Douglass, Washington, and Du Bois. A very different type of treatment can be found in Arna Bontemps's *100 Years of Negro Freedom* (New York: Dodd, Mead, 1961). Bontemps uses his literary skills effectively to interweave biographical stories about these great polemicists, giving analyses as he entertains.

David Walker

WRITINGS

David Walker, the son of a slave father and a free mother, was born after his father's death. According to Henry Highland Garnet, Walker was born in Wilmington, North Carolina, in 1785. After he moved to Boston he became an active abolitionist. In 1827 he became the Boston agent and contributor for *Freedom's Journal* and later for its successor, *Rights of All*. These were the first Afro-American newspapers in the country. In 1829 Walker published the first edition of *Walker's Appeal, in Four Articles, together with a Preamble, to the Coloured Citizens of the World, but in particular, and very expressly, to Those of the United States of America*. A copy of this first edition is in the Arthur B. Spingarn collection at the Howard University Library in Washington, D. C. In the next year he issued two revised and enlarged editions; the last was published in 1830 and contained some eighty-eight pages. He published all three editions at his own expense, thereby setting an example which many other Afro-American writers would follow when confronted by a reluctant and resistant publishing world.

The next appearance of *Walker's Appeal* came through the action of a younger Afro-American abolitionist who had been strongly influenced by it. In 1848 Henry Highland Garnet reprinted the full text of the second edition along with a biographical sketch of Walker and a modified version of an address which Garnet had delivered at the National Convention of Colored Citizens held at Buffalo in 1843. The 1848 publication carried the title *Walker's Appeal with a Brief Sketch of his Life and also Garnet's Address to the Slaves of the United States of America* (New York: J. H. Tobitt, 1848). Evidence seems to indicate that part of the money for this publication came from the then little-known John Brown.

This volume not only helped to revive knowledge of Walker, but helped to preserve knowledge of him for future generations. Walker died in 1830, the same year as the publication of his third edition, and there is no evidence that anyone had undertaken to continue its circulation. The State Convention of Colored Citizens of Ohio in 1849 voted to buy and distribute 500 copies of Garnet's pamphlet containing the full text of the *Appeal*. However, there is some question as to whether this resolution was ever implemented. In spite of this, Garnet asserted that Walker's memory was held in "very high esteem."

In spite of the high esteem and the general desire to preserve his *Appeal,* that momentous document disappeared from publication lists after 1848 until it was revived by Herbert Aptheker, who republished the entire third edition in his *"One Continual Cry": David Walker's Appeal to the Colored Citizens of the World (1829–1830)* (New York: Humanities, 1965). In it he also republished the biographical sketch by Garnet.

In the same year that Aptheker's volume appeared, Charles M. Wiltse edited the third edition of *David Walker's Appeal in Four Articles: Together with a Preamble to the Coloured Citizens of the World, but in particular, and very expressly, to those of the United States of America* (New York: Hill & Wang, 1965). This was followed shortly by the reprinting of Garnet's volume under the editorship of William L. Katz (New York: Arno Press and The New York Times, 1969). To introduce these two early abolitionist militants, Katz asserts, "Those who think Black Militancy started with Stokeley Carmichael and Rap Brown should read the works of David Walker and Henry Highland Garnet."

In recent years the complete text was included in two collections of documents. The first was a reprinting of the complete second edition edited by George Ducas and Charles Van Doren, *Great Documents in Black History* (New York: Praeger, 1970) with an introduction by C. Eric

Lincoln. The most recent reprint is in Sterling Stuckey's *The Ideological Origins of Black Nationalism* (Boston: Beacon, 1972), which used the third edition. Excerpts from the *Appeal* are commonplace. One of the earliest was in Du Bois's *Gift of Black Folk* (Boston: Stratford, 1924). Benjamin Brawley had selections from each of the four articles of the *Appeal* in his *Early Negro American Writers* (Chapel Hill: University of North Carolina Press, 1935; rpt. Plainview, N.Y.: Books for Libraries, 1968).

BIOGRAPHICAL INFORMATION

Biographical information about Walker is scarce. There are no biographies of him, he wrote no autobiography, and there are no substantive writings by his associates. The principal source to which most writers turn is the short sketch by Henry Highland Garnet, which he published as a part of his 1848 pamphlet. Aptheker says this is "the fullest work directly dealing with the life of David Walker." Other information about Walker may be drawn from personal references in the pages of the *Appeal* and its footnotes. This was skillfully and effectively done by Lerone Bennett in *Pioneers in Protest* (Chicago: Johnson, 1968). In his lively and provocative style he has dubbed Walker "The Fanon of the Nineteenth Century," fashioning a full chapter out of very little material. Along with a biographical sketch he has given an analysis of the *Appeal.*

Although many books and articles mention Walker, few have studied him in depth. *Freedom's Journal* has several references to Walker and his activities. His business advertisements appear in *Freedom's Journal* and in *Rights of All.* Reactions to the *Appeal* were printed in Lundy's *Genius of Universal Emancipation* and *The Liberator.* Material from both of these newspapers is reprinted in *Documents of Upheaval* (New York: Hill & Wang, 1966), edited by Truman Nelson. Nelson found Lundy's pacifist attitude was "typical of the liberal position on Negro violence." Garrison was much less negative, though he was ambivalent, for while he "deprecated its spirit," he found the *Appeal* to be "one of the most remarkable productions of the age" and reminded the American people that it was not for them "to denounce it as bloody or monstrous." He rejected any notion that Walker did not actually write the pamphlet and added, "no white man could have written in language so natural and enthusiastic." Other excerpts from *The Liberator* are found in Bradford Chambers's *Chronicles of Negro Protest* (New York: Parents' Magazine Press, 1968) which has some commentary and several letters to the editor. Carter G. Woodson has included two letters and some commentary in *The Mind of the Negro as Reflected in Letters Written During the Crisis 1800–1860* (Washington, D.C.: Associated Publishers, 1926).

One of the letters contains information concerning Walker's death. George W. Williams has included the important correspondence from H. G. Otis, mayor of Boston, to the governor of Virginia and the mayor of Savannah, Georgia, in the appendix of his *History of the Negro Race in America* (New York: Putnam, 1883). They had asked Otis to take legal action against Walker and suppress the distribution of the *Appeal,* which he declined to do.

Other than the *Appeal,* the only known literary product of Walker was his address to the General Colored Association in Boston, which was published in *Freedom's Journal* (December 19, 1828). It lacks the flair and fervor of the *Appeal* and is concerned mainly with racial unity and the need for organization. It has been reprinted in *Black Nationalism in America* (Indianapolis, Ind.: Bobbs-Merrill, 1970), edited by John H. Bracey, Jr., August Meier, and Elliott Rudwick, and also in the *Voice of Black Rhetoric* (Boston: Allyn & Bacon, 1971), edited by Arthur L. Smith and Stephen Robb. Although Smith and Robb state that Walker often wrote articles for *Freedom's Journal,* a search of its files fails to reveal any articles attributed to him.

An early assemblage of the facts concerning the effects of the issuance of the *Appeal* was made by Wendell Phillips Garrison and Francis Jackson Garrison in *William Lloyd Garrison 1805–1879, The Story of His Life Told by His Children* (New York: Century, 1885). They show not only Garrison's attitude, but also notices in the southern press, legal and legislative action, and correspondence.

The published views of contemporary Afro-Americans indicate support for the publication of the *Appeal.* The earliest known biographical sketch of Walker appeared in Robert B. Lewis's *Light and Truth* (Boston: 1836). This book was published first by Lewis, and later reprinted in Boston by a Committee of Colored Gentlemen in 1844. Lewis says, "His celebrated appeal in behalf of his brethren is highly esteemed by wise men: he was a man of strong mind and great talents." Walker is also cited in William C. Nell's *The Colored Patriots of the American Revolution* (Boston: Robert F. Wallcut, 1855; rpt. New York: Arno Press, 1968). Nell observed that the *Appeal* was "ably written, very impassioned and well adapted to its purpose." We learn from Samuel J. May of the jailing of "the Rev. messrs Worcester and Butler, missionaries to the Cherokees . . . for having one of Walker's pamphlets," in *Some Recollections of Our Antislavery Conflict* (Boston: Fields, Osgood, 1869; rpt. New York: Arno Press, 1968).

There are many references to Walker in the general histories of Afro-Americans, but few contain any significant information. Nicholas Halasz, in *The Rattling Chains: Slave Unrest and Revolt in the Antebellum South* (New York: David McKay, 1966), has devoted a chapter to Walker and the *Appeal.* It is written in an engaging journalistic style but

Halasz is careless at times with the facts. Benjamin Brawley, in *A Social History of the American Negro* (New York: Macmillan, 1921; rpt. New York: Collier, 1970), helps broaden our understanding of the man and the times. Even more helpful for a view of Boston during Walker's time is John Daniels's *In Freedom's Birthplace* (Boston: Houghton Mifflin, 1941; rpt. New York: Negro Universities Press, 1968). Another general view is offered by Leon Litwack in *North of Slavery* (Chicago: University of Chicago Press, 1961). The scarcity of longer works on Walker indicates the need for more research in this area.

CRITICAL ANALYSIS

There are few published articles on Walker and the *Appeal*. "David Walker and Malcolm: Brothers in Radical Thought" by William Seraile (*BlackW*, October 1972) is narrow in its research and perspective. By far the best piece of research on the effect of the *Appeal* is Clement Eaton's "A Dangerous Pamphlet in the Old South" (*JSH*, August 1936). He has focused on the "frightened" and "alarmed" reactions in the South and uses newspaper accounts, letters, and legislative records for his sources. Eaton's scholarly article is one of the few sources cited frequently by other writers. His work has proved a reliable source of information. Additional insight on the reaction of the South and the method of distribution of the *Appeal* is given in a documentary article by William H. Pease and Jane H. Pease (*JNH*, July 1974). Herein we have the "Testimony and Confession" and the indictment of a white seaman, Edward Smith, who had brought some of the pamphlets to Charleston and given them to Afro-Americans.

Perhaps the most revealing article is Donald M. Jacobs's "David Walker: Boston Race Leader, 1825–1830" (*Essex Institute Historical Collections*, January 1971). Jacobs has examined the Boston press and public records about Walker to see "the role that citizen David Walker played in Boston among his fellow blacks during the last five years of his life." He gives considerable attention to Walker's relationship with *Freedom's Journal* and raises the question of his correct date of birth. He concludes that "the book is not yet closed on David Walker. We have several answers, but many questions still remain, and it will take a good deal more research before the picture of this important black leader will be historically complete."

Frederick Douglass

A symbol of what the slave could become, Frederick Douglass was himself a convincing polemic against the slave system. "The very look and bearing of Douglass," wrote James Russell Lowell, "are an irresistible logic against the oppression of his race." Something of what Douglass accomplished on the platform and in print has been indicated by James M. McPherson in his introduction to the Atheneum reprint of the biography by Benjamin Quarles (cited below): "Without a day of formal schooling, he developed into a writer of vigorous prose and an orator whose sense of timing, intimacy, wit and pathos was unexcelled even in that age of oratorical giants." Evidently, the lack of schooling gave Douglass some insecurity in his early years. His first article for publication was "The Folly of our Opponents," which appeared in *The Liberty Bell* by Friends of Freedom (Boston: Massachusetts Anti-Slavery Fair, 1845). At that time, Douglass felt he was "ill prepared" and stated, "I felt exceedingly strange in my own eyes, as I sat writing."

AUTOBIOGRAPHIES

The "one continual cry" that David Walker expected to be "raised in all parts of the confederacy," and which he did raise, was ably picked up by Frederick Douglass when he mounted the speaker's rostrum in 1841. His oratory raised abolitionism to new heights through his first-hand accounts of the malevolence and dehumanization of slavery. He was soon forced to prove his authenticity by skeptics, who more and more came to doubt that he had ever been a slave. This he did when he wrote his first autobiography, *Narrative of the Life of Frederick Douglass, an American Slave* (Boston: Boston Anti-Slavery Society, 1845). This early slave narrative was an eminent success and, like Walker's *Appeal*, it was a historic act as well as a piece of literature.

The first edition of the *Narrative* included a letter by Wendell Phillips and a prefatory statement by William Lloyd Garrison. This publication increased the danger of Douglass's recapture and re-enslavement by his former master. This peril seemed so great that Wendell Phillips advised that the manuscript be thrown into the fire. Four editions of the *Narrative* were published in the United States before the year had passed, and issues followed in 1846, 1847, and 1849. A series of *Extracts from the Narrative of Frederick Douglass* (Philadelphia: E. M. Davis, 1845) was distributed at no cost, and an edition was published at the *North Star* office in 1848.

With the aid of abolitionist friends, Douglass found sanctuary for almost two years in England, Ireland, Scotland, and Wales. Two editions of the *Narrative* were published in Ireland (Dublin: Webb and Chapman, 1845 and 1846). The first included a new preface in which Douglass states his threefold objective in visiting Great Britain. The second set forth in an appendix an attempted refutation of the *Narrative* by a former slaveholder, A. C. C. Thompson, together with the forceful reply made by Douglass, a self-liberated and self-educated slave. What has been listed as a third English edition was issued at Wortley, near Leeds, in 1846. A Dutch translation was published in 1846, and a French translation in 1848.

The New York *Tribune* was full of praise for this slave narrative, declaring, "We wish that every one may read his book, and see what a mind might have been stifled in bondage." The reviewer went on to observe, "Considered merely as a narrative, we have never read one more simple, true, coherent, and warm with genuine feeling. It is an excellent piece of writing, and on that score to be prized as a specimen of the powers of the black race, which prejudice persists in disputing" (New York *Tribune,* June 10, 1845; reprinted in *The Liberator,* June 20, 1845). Philip S. Foner shows that the *Narrative* became a fast seller: 30,000 copies were sold within five years and it had gone through nine editions in England by January 1848.

Perhaps because two subsequent autobiographies were published in 1855 and 1881, the *Narrative* appears not to have been issued again until the 1960 reprint, edited by Benjamin Quarles (Cambridge, Mass.: Belknap, 1960, 1967). Reprints were also issued in 1962 (Garden City, N.Y.: Doubleday) and 1968 (New York: New American Library). In a seventeen-page introduction to the Belknap edition, Benjamin Quarles gives a stirring, lucid, and scholarly appraisal of Douglass's career, and an objective appraisal of the *Narrative.* He concludes that the *Narrative* is "one of the most arresting autobiographical statements in the entire catalogue of American reform."

An expanded autobiography of Frederick Douglass published in 1855 was entitled *My Bondage and My Freedom* (New York: Miller, Orton & Mulligan), with an introduction by Dr. James McCune Smith, an Afro-American graduate of Glasgow University. "The style of Mr. Douglass in writing," wrote Dr. Smith, "is to me an intellectual puzzle. The strength, affluence and terseness may easily be accounted for, because the style of a man is the man; but how are we to account for that rare polish in his style of writing, which, most critically examined, seems the result of careful early culture among the best classics of our language." Of the three autobiographies, this version provides the most detailed and complete account of his years as a slave. It has several significant appendixes. Outstanding among these are the "Letter to his Old Master," the penetrating political analysis of "The Slavery Party," and the incisive philippic, "What to the Slave is the Fourth of July?" A second edition appeared in 1856 and a third in 1857. A German translation also was published, *Sclaverei und Freiheit, Autobiographie von Frederick Douglass* (Hamburg: Hoffman und Campe, 1860).

In recent years several reprints of *My Bondage and My Freedom* have been issued (New York: Arno Press, 1968; New York: Dover, 1969; and Chicago: Johnson, 1970). Lerone Bennett, Jr., in the foreword to the Johnson Ebony Classic, comments that this is "probably the best eyewitness account of American slavery." He further points out, "In addition to graphic descriptions of slavery and the anti-slavery movement, the volume offers theoretical insights of the first order on oppression, the impact of slavery on whites and blacks, the philosophy of reform, and relations between black and white leaders."

A revised and enlarged version of Douglass's autobiography was issued as *Life and Times of Frederick Douglass* (Hartford, Conn.: Park, 1881, 1882). This edition included an introduction by Judge George L. Ruffin along with two speeches by Douglass—"Abraham Lincoln" and "West India Emancipation." A further extended edition of the *Life and Times* with an account of his later life was published three times—in 1892, 1893, and after Douglass's death in 1895 (Boston: DeWolfe, Fiske). Foreign editions included an English publication with an introduction by John Bright (London: Christian Age Office, 1882); a French translation, *Mes Années d'Esclavage et de Liberté* (Paris: E. Plon, 1883, 1892), and a Swedish translation, *Lif och Samtid* (Stockholm: Schedins Fölag, 1895).

Almost half a century elapsed before a new edition appeared. Publication was revived by the issuance in 1941 of the Pathway Press edition, edited by Richard B. Moore, to mark the centenary of the emergence of Frederick Douglass on the public platform at Nantucket, Massachusetts. This edition featured an introduction by Alain Locke, dean of Afro-American literary scholars, a facsimile page of the author's handwriting, an index, a color portrait by Aaron Douglass, and illustrations by Carl G. Hill. In his foreword Locke declared that Douglass was the author of the classic of American Negro biography. He went on to observe that, "a chronicle of the initial struggles for freedom and social justice is . . . particularly pertinent again in our present decade of crisis and social reconstruction. . . . Obviously there is much in Douglass . . . which is vital and relevant to this present generation and to our world today."

Two decades later, the widespread demand for African and Afro-American Studies, especially among the youth, could no longer be ignored by academic institutions and publishers. Thus, several new editions came into print. The first of these was published by Collier-Macmillan in 1962, followed by one by Grosset & Dunlap in 1970. The Collier edition contained an introduction by Professor Rayford W. Logan of Howard University and an annotated bibliography. The opening statement of Logan's introduction declared, "The *Life and Times of Frederick Douglass* is a classic in American literature." He calls attention to the facsimile handwritten pages reproduced in the Pathway Press edition and emphasizes that, "unlike some slave narratives and, indeed, some messages of Presidents of the United States, Douglass's works were his own."

Although the importance of Douglass's autobiographical writings can hardly be overestimated, they may not have been as important during his lifetime as they were to become. His fame came primarily from his outstanding skill as an orator. It is ironic that the first American publication of a Douglass speech seems to have been in the proslavery pamphlet, *Abolition Fanaticism in New York: Speech by a Runaway Slave from Baltimore at an Abolition Meeting in New York, Held May 11, 1847* (Baltimore, 1847). This speech, "The Right to Criticize American Institutions," was also printed in the *National Anti-Slavery Standard* of May 20, 1847. Excerpts of a speech which he had delivered in December of 1841 had been printed in the *National Anti-Slavery Standard* on December 23, 1841. There had also been publication of several of his long speeches which had been delivered in England. Apparently none of these had appeared as publications in the United States.

Although many of Douglass's speeches were subsequently printed in whole or in part in the antislavery press as well as in pamphlets, no considerable collection of them appeared separately until fifty years after Douglass's death when Philip Foner edited the ninety-four-page pamphlet, *Selections From the Writings of Frederick Douglass* (New York: International Publishers, 1945). This was followed by his outstanding achievement, publication of the five-volume *The Life and Writings of Frederick Douglass* (New York: International Publishers, 1950–1975). Foner brought together all of Douglass's known speeches, writings, and letters. In reviews of the first two volumes (*Masses and Mainstream*, May 1950, and *Science and Society*, Fall 1951) W. E. B. Du Bois asserted that most American historians ignore Douglass but at last Foner has rescued from oblivion these important writings. Foner spent over eight years collecting and editing Douglass's writings which had been scattered in many libraries and historical societies. These five volumes are an indispensable storehouse of information on Douglass. Each is introduced by a biographical narrative covering the period of Douglass's life documented within that volume. The documents are presented in chronological order. In addition, there are valuable footnotes and an index in each volume. However, in the sections on Douglass's correspondence only letters from Douglass are included. The presentation would have been greatly enriched and enlivened if some of the correspondence to Douglass and writings about him had been included. An excellent research opportunity in this area remains.

Barbara Ritchie edited *The Mind and Heart of Frederick Douglass: Excerpts from Speeches of the Great Negro Orator* (New York: T. Y. Crowell, 1968), which contains excerpts from thirty-six of his speeches. This well-selected volume serves as a companion to her version of his *Life and Times*, adapted for a juvenile audience (New York: T. Y. Crowell, 1966).

Although, as was mentioned above, Douglass's fame derived largely from his skill as an orator, his principal work was as an editor. It is in the pages of his newspapers that valuable portions of his writings are available. They can be found in the printed as well as the microfilmed versions of the *North Star, Frederick Douglass' Paper, Douglass' Monthly, New Era,* and *New National Era.* Samplings from these publications have been included in the Foner volumes. Similar resources are contained in the pages of *The Liberator* and other contemporary newspapers and periodicals.

Practically all of Douglass's writings were nonfiction, with one exception. In March of 1853 he published in the pages of *Douglass' Paper* his one piece of fiction, a short story entitled "The Heroic Slave," which was also printed in *Autographs for Freedom* (Boston: Jewett, 1853), edited by Julia Griffiths. This was a fictionalized account of the mutiny on the brig *Creole* in 1841. It has seldom appeared in bibliographies of Douglass's writings and is now included in the fifth volume of Foner's work. Ronald Takaki included it in *Violence in the Black Imagination* (New York: Capricorn, 1972).

BIOGRAPHIES

The Douglass autobiographies were so thorough that most of the biographies have largely been drawn from them. The first, Frederick May Holland's *Frederick Douglass: The Colored Orator* (New York: Funk & Wagnalls, 1891, revised 1895) in the American Reformers Series, was comprehensive and outstanding for the period. Some of his new material came from interviews with Douglass and from unpublished lectures and letters loaned to him by Douglass. From the same period is James M. Gregory's *Frederick Douglass the Orator* (Springfield, Mass.: Willey & Co., 1893; rpt. New York: T. Y. Crowell, 1971). This account stressed Douglass's oratorical achievements and thus missed giving a full picture of the man and his work.

Charles W. Chesnutt contributed *Frederick Douglass* to the Beacon Biographies of Eminent Americans (Boston: Small, Maynard, 1899), an interpretive biography which some have found to be thoughtfully constructed and carefully written.

Booker T. Washington's *Frederick Douglass* (Philadelphia: Jacobs, 1907), in the American series of Crisis Biographies, expresses more of the accommodationist Washington than the militant Douglass. In the preface Washington characterizes the time of Douglass as "the period of revolution and liberation." He then hastened to assure the sons of the slave masters that "that period is now closed." Evidence now indicates that this biography, although expressing Washington's views, was largely or totally ghostwritten. Two other biographical sources are *In Memoriam: Frederick Douglass* (Philadelphia: J. C. Yorston, 1897) by the writer's widow, Helen Pitts Douglass, and John W. Thompson's *An Authentic History of the Douglass Monument* (Rochester, N.Y.: Rochester Herald Press, 1903; rpt. Plainview, N.Y.: Books for Libraries, 1971).

Altogether different in approach, tone, and scholarship is the modern biography, *Frederick Douglass* (Washington, D.C.: Associated Publishers, 1948; rpt. New York: Atheneum, 1968) by the very able Afro-American historian Benjamin Quarles. It is scholarly without being pedantic, and critical without carping. This is the best biographical study of Douglass to date.

Benjamin Quarles also edited, for the Great Lives Observed series, the volume *Frederick Douglass* (Englewood Cliffs, N.J.: Prentice-Hall, 1968), which gives selections from Douglass's work, offers favorable and critical assessments of Douglass by his contemporaries, and presents the appraisals of later historians. This unique tripartite approach, coupled with the high quality of the scholarship, makes this study noteworthy.

Equally scholarly and well researched, but reflecting a different perspective, is Philip S. Foner's *Frederick Douglass* (New York: Citadel, 1964), which brings together in one volume the introductory chapters of his earlier collection of Douglass's writings.

A recent full-length biography of Frederick Douglass is *Free at Last: The Life of Frederick Douglass,* by Arna Bontemps (New York: Dodd, Mead, 1971). This lively and readable account is firmly based on historical facts and presents information not generally known.

About 1940, Richard B. Moore proposed to the National Negro Congress that he would write a biography of Douglass if they would help publish it. However, whereas Moore envisioned a full-length book, the congress felt the biography should only be a pamphlet. Moore declined to write the pamphlet, so the congress had Steve Kingston write one which appeared as *Frederick Douglass: Abolitionist, Liberator, Statesman* (New York: National Negro Congress, 1945). The forty-five-page pamphlet demonstrates Kingston's unsuitability for the job and is hardly worth considering.

There have been a number of biographies of Douglass written for children, the earliest of these being *The Story of Frederick Douglass,* by Laura E. Wilkes (Washington, D.C.: R. L. Pendelton, 1899), reprinted in 1909 and 1918. Some librarians and bibliographers have classified Shirley Graham's *There Was Once a Slave: The Heroic Story of Frederick Douglass* (New York: Messner, 1947) as a children's book. It is well written in an engaging style and is enjoyable reading for young and old alike. It has been challenged as authentic biography, however, because of its inclusion of fictional material. It won the Julian Messner Award as one of the best books written to combat intolerance in America. Arna Bontemps and Jack Conroy combined their talents to produce the enjoyable and accurate *Frederick Douglass: Slave, Fighter, Freeman* (New York:

Knopf, 1959). One of the combined biographies for young people is *Four Took Freedom* (Garden City, N.Y.: Doubleday, 1967) by Philip Sterling and Rayford Logan. It contains short biographies of Harriet Tubman, Robert Smalls, and Blanche K. Bruce, in addition to Douglass.

Frederick Douglass is joined by Benjamin Banneker and Nat Turner in the portraits by Ruth Wilson in *Our Blood and Tears: Black Freedom Fighters* (New York: Putnam, 1972). She has a lively, provocative style combined with a militant tone. The title is taken from a line in Walker's *Appeal.* Wilson skillfully blends the words of historic documents in the narrative, giving the effect of dialogue. However, her enthusiasm for black militancy at times leads her to hyperbole.

Douglass was profiled in several nineteenth-century collected biographies by people who had personal contact with him. The earliest of these was Lydia Maria Childs's *The Freedmen's Book* (Boston: Ticknor & Fields, 1865; rpt. New York: Arno, 1968) which contains a chapter on Douglass. It was conceived as a textbook for newly freed slaves who were learning to read. Harriet Beecher Stowe, in *Men of Our Times, or Leading Patriots of the Day* (Hartford, Conn.: Hartford Publishers, 1868), gave a glowing tribute to Douglass, ranking him above all others in his achievements. Comparing him to Lincoln, she observed that "Frederick Douglass had as far to climb to get to the spot where the poorest free white boy is born, as that white boy has to climb to be president of the nation. . . . " William Wells Brown, an early Afro-American historian, shows strong favor for Douglass in *The Rising Son* (Boston: A. G. Brown, 1874; rpt. Coral Gables, Fla.: Mnemosyne, 1969). In addition to providing a biographical sketch, he places Douglass in his historical setting. It is interesting to note that W. E. B. Du Bois wrote the biographical sketch of Douglass for the *Dictionary of American Biography* (New York: Scribners, 1936).

An early attempt at interpretive biography is made by Howard Carroll in *Twelve Americans: Their Lives and Times* (New York: Harper, 1883). In addition to using the earlier autobiographies and other published materials by Douglass, the author informs us that much of his information was based upon conversations with Douglass. It is a well-structured short biography (forty-six pages) with carefully chosen selections from other documents.

Douglass is placed in perspective among other abolitionists by Benjamin Quarles in *Black Abolitionists* (New York: Oxford University Press, 1969). But Quarles had given him a much closer examination in his selection "Abolition's Different Drummer: Frederick Douglass" in *The Anti-Slavery Vanguard* (Princeton N.J.: Princeton University Press, 1965), edited by Martin B. Duberman. In that same volume, Leon F. Litwack discusses Douglass's break with the followers of abolitionist William Lloyd Garrison. Frank W. Hale takes a broader view in "Frederick Douglass: Antislavery Crusader and Lecturer" (*JHR*, 1st Quarter 1966), while J. W. Cooke looks at "Freedom in the Thoughts of Frederick Douglass" (*NHB*, February 1969). Consideration is given to the role of Douglass along with other famous runaways like Henry Bibb and William Wells Brown by Larry Gara in "The Professional Fugitive in the Abolition Movement" (*Wisconsin Magazine of History*, Spring 1965).

Periodical articles and parts of books dealing with Douglass have been numerous. Most of these have been concerned with his role as an abolitionist; however, many of them are, at the same time, largely biographical. The earliest of these was a chapter in David W. Bartlett's *Modern Agitators: or Pen Portraits of Living Reformers* (New York: Miller, Orton & Mulligan, 1855). He commented that "few living orators surpass Frederick Douglass in declamatory eloquence. . . . Mr. Douglass is a powerful writer, but we confess that we think he erred in attempting to maintain a weekly journal. . . . Nature intended Douglass for an orator." Henry Wilson devotes a chapter to Douglass in *History of the Rise and Fall of the Slave Power in America* (Boston: James R. Osgood, 1872). He saw Douglass as a champion in whom "not only did the colored race but manhood itself find a worthy representative and advocate." George Washington Williams, in his *History of the Negro Race in America* (New York: Putnam, 1883), gives attention to Douglass as an abolitionist and as an orator. Douglass's manly character is attributed to his mother's influence by William T. Alexander in *History of the Colored Race in America* (New York: Palmetto, 1888). He contended that "she was a woman of uncommon energy and strength of affection . . . [who] must have been one of that Mandigo tribe of Africans." In 1884 William C. Roberts included Douglass in *The Leading Orators of Twenty-Five Campaigns* (New York: L. K. Strouse, 1884).

Other late nineteenth- and early twentieth-century writers continued to provide interesting and helpful views of Douglass. Frederick May Holland, the biographer, gave a concise picture in his article, "Frederick Douglass" (*Open Court*, March 1895), whereas Kelly Miller did more of an interpretation of the significance of Douglass's career by setting forth six aspects of Douglass's greatness, which are "lessons to be derived from that life," in *The Voice of the Negro* (October 1904). He urged that Douglass be used to inspire the "aspiring colored youth of this land." The essay, "Frederick Douglass," is reprinted in Miller's book *Race Adjustment* (New York: Neale, 1908; rpt. New York: Arno, 1968), which also contains an excellent comparison of Douglass and Washington in the essay "Radicals and Conservatives."

DOUGLASS IN HISTORICAL PERSPECTIVE

In the first four decades of the twentieth century, writings about Douglass were scarce. His disappearance from historical writing was reversed by a pair of articles by Richard B. Moore in *The Crisis*. The first of these was the biographical sketch "Frederick Douglass" (February 1939), in which Moore observed that Douglass "challenged Negroes to press forward and achieve what at first seemed to be impossible. The principles for which he fought are the same as those for which you are struggling today." His second article, also titled "Frederick Douglass" (*The Crisis*, March 1941), marked the 100th anniversary of Douglass's first public appearance as a speaker on the abolitionist platform. He deplored the neglect by historians "who distort history." In the same issue of *The Crisis* there is an advertisement for the forthcoming Pathway Press edition of *Life and Times*, edited by Moore. During this period Benjamin Quarles gave an appraisal of "Frederick Douglass and the Woman's Rights Movement" (*JNH*, January 1940). Douglass had always been involved in the women's rights movement; the day of his death had been spent attending a women's rights meeting in Washington.

Angelo Herndon encouraged Afro-American participation in the war effort in "Frederick Douglass: Negro Leadership and War" (*The Negro Quarterly*, Winter–Spring 1943). He found that "clues to problems of our time are to be found by examining the role and leadership of Frederick Douglass." There is further discussion of Douglass's Civil War efforts in Arna Bontemps's essay "The Dilemmas of Frederick Douglass in the Civil War" (*Sepia*, August 1971), and in "Rose Out of Slavery to Lead His People" (in *New York State and the Civil War*, [Albany, N.Y.: New York Civil War Centennial Commission, January 1963]), by Rev. Richard K. McMaster. Other analytical and biographical articles about Douglass include: Herbert Aptheker's "Du Bois on Douglass" (*JNH*, October 1964), which contains the eulogy delivered by Du Bois at Wilberforce at the time of Douglass's death; Elliott M. Rudwick and August Meier's "Black Man in the 'White City': Negroes and the Columbian Exposition, 1893" (*Phylon*, Winter 1965); and Benjamin Quarles's "Frederick Douglass: Bridge-Builder in Human Relations" (*NHB*, First Quarter, 1966). August Meier's "Frederick Douglass' Vision for America" in *Freedom and Reform*, Harold R. Hyman and Leonard W. Levy, eds. (New York: Harper & Row, 1967; reprinted in *Blacks in White America*, edited by Robert V. Haynes [New York: David McKay, 1972]) attempts to give an analysis of Douglass's position on various issues of the day. Some emphasis is given to the similarity between the policies of Douglass and Washington. However, Meier stresses the differences between the two—"unlike Washington, Douglass was always clear and explicit about his desire for full equality." He never equivocated "his advocacy of agitation and political action." Additional perspectives are offered by William H. McClendon in "The Black Perspective of Frederick Douglass" (*BlackSch*, March–April 1972) and by Lerone Bennett, Jr., in "The Coming of Age of Frederick Douglass" (*Ebony*, April 1975).

One of the notable developments in Douglass's career was his change from a Garrisonian abolitionist (named for William Lloyd Garrison) to a more political and militant stance, which resulted in a break with Garrison. Their differences have been treated in several articles. Benjamin Quarles noted this parting of the ways in "The Breach Between Douglass and Garrison" (*JNH*, April 1938), in which he traces the change after Douglass's return from England. William and Jane Pease saw a different problem in "Boston Garrisonians and the Problem of Frederick Douglass" (*Canadian Journal of History*, September 1967). They felt the break was due to the subtle racial prejudice long evident among the white abolitionists. More of Douglass's role in political life is given by Charles H. Wesley in *Neglected History* (Wilberforce, Ohio: Central State College Press, 1965). His chapter, "The Participation of Negroes in Anti-Slavery Political Parties," gives particular attention to the changes in Douglass. Tyrone Tillery discusses the break in "The Inevitability of the Douglass–Garrison Conflict" (*Phylon*, Summer 1976). The change in Douglass was examined by Ronald Takaki in the essay "Not Afraid to Die: Frederick Douglass and Violence" in *Violence and the Black Imagination* (New York: Capricorn Books, 1972). This is a highly provocative article that traces Douglass's transition from the position of a Garrisonian "moral suasionist" (a pacifist who opposed slavery on moral rather than political grounds and refused to participate in political activism) to that of a political activist willing to accept "killing for freedom." Leslie F. Goldstein studies the same theme in "Violence as an Instrument for Social Change: The Views of Frederick Douglass, 1819–1895" (*JNH*, January 1976). He shows the influence of John Brown in Douglass's transition. Goldstein also has done admirable work in "Racial Loyalty in America: The Example of Frederick Douglass" (*Western Political Quarterly*, September 1975). He showed that while Douglass made no mystique of color, he always called upon his fellow Afro-Americans to "remember that we are one, that our cause is one, and that we must help each other."

The Douglass-Garrison dispute is reflected in the various National Conventions of Colored Citizens. These differences often resulted in heated and sometimes very personal cleavages among black leaders. Jane Pease and William Pease dealt with this in "Negro Conventions and the Problem of Black Leadership," (*Journal of Black Studies*, September 1971). Douglass seems very human in his petty bickering with Garnet and Remond. Howard H. Bell has performed a commendable service in editing *Minutes of the Proceedings of the National Conventions 1830–1864* (New York: Arno, 1964), thereby making it possible to trace Douglass's ascendency more easily. Further light is shed by Bell's essay, "The National Negro Convention 1848" (*Ohio History Quarterly*, October 1958) which describes Douglass's election as president and movement toward greater political involvement.

One of the clouded and controversial relationships in Douglass's career was with John Brown, the abolitionist. He discusses this at length in his *Life and Times* and in a lecture he gave at the fourteenth anniversary of Storer College at Harpers Ferry, West Virginia, May 30, 1881, which was printed as a pamphlet, *John Brown* (Dover, N.H.: Morning Star Job Printing House, 1881). This may be considered Douglass's definitive statement on Brown. It has been reprinted in *A John Brown Reader*, edited by Louis Ruchames (New York: Abelard-Schuman, 1959). There are also excerpts in Benjamin Quarles's *Blacks on Brown* (Urbana: University of Illinois Press, 1972). This lecture-essay was not included in Foner's collection. Barry Stavis did an excellent analysis and documentation of the relationship between Douglass and Brown in *John Brown: The Sword and the Word* (South Brunswick, N.J.: A. S. Barnes, 1970). Stavis also wrote *Harper's Ferry* (South Brunswick, N.J.: A. S. Barnes, 1967), a play which is a companion piece to the book. Another play dramatizing this relationship is *In Splendid Error* (1953) by William Branch. Originally titled *Frederick Douglass,* it was published in the collection *Black Theater,* edited by Lindsey Patterson (New York: Dodd, Mead, 1971). The play was reviewed by Herbert Aptheker as "The Drama of Frederick Douglass and John Brown" (*Masses and Mainstream*, November 1954), reprinted in Aptheker's *Toward Negro Freedom* (New York: New Century, 1956). In this volume Aptheker also included his article "Douglass and Lincoln," which originally appeared in *New Masses* (April 22 and 29, 1944). Another helpful article is Benjamin Quarles's "Frederick Douglass and John Brown" (*Rochester Historical Society Publications*, 17, 1939).

Most of Douglass's career was carried out from his home in Rochester, New York, where he lived for twenty-five years (1847–1872) and from which he published the *North Star, Frederick Douglass' Paper,* and *Douglass' Monthly.* This period is discussed in several articles. Shortly after Douglass's death, Janet Marsh Parker recalled these years in "Reminiscences of Frederick Douglass" (*Outlook,* April 6, 1895). It is an intimate and personal view of the Douglass family and the community by a sympathizer and neighbor. This was reprinted, without credit or citation, in Howard W. Coles's *The Cradle of Freedom: A History of the Negro in Rochester, Western New York and Canada* (Rochester, N.Y.: Oxford Press, 1941). Coles's book also has several biographical chapters on Douglass and other Afro-Americans.

Amy Hamner-Croughton sheds additional light on Douglass in "Anti-Slavery Days in Rochester" (*Rochester Historical Society Publications*, 15, 1936). Blake McKelvey, historian for the city of Rochester, gives a

straightforward account of the Rochester years without praise or prejudice in "Frederick Douglass Picks Rochester as Headquarters for His
Fight Against Slavery" (*New York State and the Civil War,* January 1963).
He discusses some of Douglass's political activities, including his running twice for the New York State Assembly and once for secretary of
state. One of Douglass's disappointments came in his fight against segregated schools in Rochester. Judith P. Ruchkin discusses this in "The
Abolition of 'Colored Schools' in Rochester, New York: 1832–1856"
(*New York History,* July 1970).

For an understanding of Douglass as an editor and writer, only lim-
ited materials are available. Some information on this subject is given in
Patsy B. Perry's "Before the *North Star:* Frederick Douglass' Early Jour-
nalistic Career" (*Phylon,* Spring 1974). There is also some reference in
I. Garland Penn's *The Afro-American Press and Its Editors* (Springfield,
Mass.: Willey, 1891; rpt. New York: Arno, 1969). The central issue of
Douglass's influence of as an editor has yet to be dealt with adequately.

Douglass was often criticized by his contemporaries for not being a
religious man. He was frequently critical of organized Christianity. His
views on religion are considered by William L. Van Deberg in "Frederick Douglass: Maryland Slave to Religious Liberal" (*Maryland Historical
Magazine,* September 1974). In a later article, "The Tragedy of Frederick Douglass" (*Christianity Today,* January 31, 1975), Van Deburg discussed the evangelical churches and their historic role. In the behavior
of church leaders, he finds an understanding of Douglass's response.
One white deacon had told Douglass, "We don't allow niggers in here."
Van Deburg seems to find that this is still the attitude of white churches
and asks, "Can we learn from past mistakes?"

After the disastrous fire which destroyed Douglass's Rochester home
and many of his records, including the only complete set of his newspapers, he moved to Washington, D. C., and ultimately purchased Cedar Hill at Anacostia. He resided there for the remainder of his life.
Some vignettes of Douglass's life at Cedar Hill and of the efforts to
have the residence declared a national shrine are contained in articles
by Archibald H. Grimke and Francis J. Grimke, both of whom were
close friends of the Douglass family. Archibald Grimke, in "Cedar Hill
or the Famous Home of Frederick Douglass" (*Voice of the Negro,* November 1905), gives an intimate view of family entertainment and of
the self-sacrificing efforts of Mrs. Helen Pitts Douglass to make the
home into a memorial. "She paid out of her small fortune to the heirs
of Mr. Douglass about fifteen thousand dollars in order to acquire
complete title to the property. She denied herself sufficient food and
proper clothing." However, this contention is challenged in a letter
from the younger son of the orator, Charles A. Douglass, who had
himself made no effort to save the home for posterity (*Voice of the*

Negro, December 1905). Francis J. Grimke, who performed the ceremony for Douglass's second marriage, took a different approach but reached the same conclusion as Archibald Grimke about the great sacrifices made by Mrs. Douglass. In "The Second Marriage of Frederick Douglass" (*JNH,* July 1934) he defended the marriage as "nobody else's business" despite his opinion that intermarriage "may not be a wise thing, in this country." He fills in some of the details concerning bequeathing the home as a memorial. More of Grimke's views on Douglass are contained in *The Works of Francis J. Grimke* (Washington, D.C.: Associated Publishers, 1942) edited by Carter G. Woodson. It includes three lectures on Douglass by Grimke and one on Helen Pitts Douglass. An editorial in *The Crisis* (May 1972) comments on the belated dedication of the Douglass home in Anacostia as a national shrine.

Douglass went abroad on four occasions. In his early years he fled twice to the British Isles, the first time after revealing his identity as a fugitive slave in the *Narrative,* and the second after a warrant for his arrest was issued for his participation in John Brown's raid. During these trips he visited Scotland, as was recorded in the article "Frederick Douglass and Scotland" (*JNH,* July 1953) by George Shepperson. The Scots gave him a very favorable reception as they did other Afro-American travelers and students. He was much impressed by the Scottish scholar George Combe. Gerald Fulkerson asserted that this was a crucial period in Douglass's life in "Exile as Emergence: Frederick Douglass in Great Britain, 1845–1847" (*QJS,* February 1974). According to Fulkerson, "Immediately upon his return [from England] to the United States . . . Douglass' colleagues acknowledged him as an emerging leader." One of Douglass's most important trips abroad was as foreign minister to Haiti. However, Douglass ran into difficulty because of his opposition to the United States taking over Haitian territory to set up a naval base. This unfortunate episode is examined in two articles: Louis M. Sears's "Frederick Douglass and the Mission to Haiti" (*Hispanic American Historical Review,* May 1941), which is less than complimentary; and Myra Himelhoch's "Frederick Douglass and Haiti's Mole St. Nicholas" (*JNH,* July 1971). This sympathetic view tries to explain Douglass's actions as a diplomat. A final piece by Theodore Stanton describes "Frederick Douglass in Paris" (*Open Court,* April 28, 1887).

Douglass's political and social views are examined by Herbert J. Storing in a chapter on Douglass in *American Political Thought,* edited by Morton J. Frisch and R. G. Stevens (New York: Scribners, 1971). He points out that "Douglass argued that the black's greatest struggle was the struggle to become a part of the American political community." This sense of the political urgency is further illuminated by an essay which Douglass had written for *Atlantic Monthly* (January 1867) with the title "An Appeal to Congress for Impartial Suffrage." This essay, which does not appear in Foner's *Life and Writings,* is made available by Herbert Aptheker in "Frederick Douglass Calls for Black Suffrage in 1866" (*BlackSch,* December 1973 and January 1974).

Douglass wrote many interesting and important letters, which are largely recorded in Foner's *Life and Writings.* But several additional pieces have been published which were not included in those memorable volumes. Joseph A. Borome has made letters available in the pages of the *Journal of Negro History* in his articles "Two Letters of Frederick Douglass" (October 1948) and "Some Additional Light on Frederick Douglass" (April 1953). Roland K. Huch examined one letter from Gerrit Smith to Douglass as a response to an earlier one from him in "Patriotism Versus Philanthropy" (*New York History,* July 1968).

The letters to Douglass are scattered in many large archival collections such as those of William Lloyd Garrison, Wendell Phillips, and Gerrit Smith. However, no one has studied and published these letters to and from Douglass in sequence. This could prove to be an interesting and enlightening analytical exercise and could shed more light on the characters of the persons involved as well as the nature of their relationships.

Booker T. Washington

The decline in the status of the Afro-American in the South during the last decade of Frederick Douglass's life was almost as rapid as the ascent during the early years of the Reconstruction period. Douglass used his considerable influence with the ruling Republican party in a futile effort to stem the tide of the decline. Militant demands for equality waned as Douglass aged, and all but ended with his death in 1895. Clearly there was the need to survey the field for potential successors to leadership. It would hardly have been likely to turn to Booker T. Washington, the largely unknown and decidedly unmilitant founder of the industrial school at Tuskegee, as the heir apparent.

Washington's Atlanta Address, which brought him to fame in 1895, gave unmistakable evidence of his acquiescence to what dominant America wanted. He expressed surprise at the reaction of many to his address. In *My Larger Education* (Garden City, N.Y.: Doubleday, 1911), he wrote:

> One of the most surprising results of my Atlanta speech was the number of letters, telegrams, and newspaper editorials that came pouring in upon me from all parts of the country, demanding that I take the place of "leader of the Negro People," left vacant by Frederick Douglass's death, or assuming that I had already taken this place.

He insisted that he had never given such a thought any consideration: "I did not know just what the functions and duties of a leader were, or what was expected of him."

For some time previously, however, Washington claimed to have been giving consideration to a need for change in the strategy of the Afro-American community. After extolling the achievements of Frederick Douglass, he demurred:

> But the long and bitter political struggle in which he had engaged against slavery had not prepared Mr. Douglass to take up the equally difficult task of fitting the Negro for the opportunities and responsibilities of freedom. The same was true to a large extent of other Negro leaders. At the time when I met these men and heard them speak I was invariably impressed . . . that there was something lacking in their public utterances. I felt that the millions of Negroes needed something more than to be reminded of their sufferings and of their political rights; that they needed to do something more than merely defend themselves.

The now-famous Atlanta address gave Washington the opportunity he needed to enunciate his new policy, which he said was "not of destruction but of construction; not of defense but of aggression; a policy not of hostility or surrender, but of friendship and advance."

AUTOBIOGRAPHIES

Booker T. Washington effectively tells the story of his life in a simple, folksy style in four full-length autobiographies and numerous articles and pamphlets. Five years after his Atlanta address he published his first autobiography, *The Story of My Life and Work* (Naperville, Ill.: J. L. Nichols, 1900), reprinted in 1969 by Negro Universities Press. A portrait of Frederick Douglass in the front of the book suggests a close association between Washington and Douglass. Notable also are the numerous portraits of white benefactors who helped to make Washington "the leader of the Negro people." A considerable portion of this book is devoted to detailing the history of Tuskegee Institute. Washington hastened to declare that all of his time, thought, and energy had been devoted to building the school and that "in any autobiography of mine, a history of Tuskegee is unavoidable and necessary." In 1915, Albon L. Holsey edited an updated version of this original autobiography as *Booker T. Washington's Own Story of His Life and Works* (Naperville, Ill.: J. L. Nichols, 1915).

Washington's second autobiography represented his major literary success. He tells us that *Up From Slavery* (New York: A. L. Burt, 1901) was "the outgrowth of articles, dealing with incidents in my life, which were published consecutively in *Outlook*. While they were appearing in that magazine I was constantly surprised at the number of requests which came to me from all parts of the country, asking that the articles be permanently preserved in book form." Evidence indicates, however, that he had intended to publish it as a book from the beginning. Emma

Thornbrough states that this autobiography became a world-wide best seller and was translated into Zulu as well as the chief European languages. There have been dozens of editions throughout the world which continue to be produced with amazing regularity in every decade since the original publication. Introductions have been written by such notables as Jonathan Daniels (London: Oxford University Press, 1945), William O. Douglas (Garden City, N.Y.: Doubleday, 1963), Louis Lomax (New York: Dell, 1965), and John Hope Franklin, in *Three Negro Classics* (New York: Avon, 1965). However, Louis Harlan suggests that *Up From Slavery* met a more modest response than the number of editions would indicate. "The response of the reading public to *Up From Slavery* was heartening and helpful to Washington's cause, but not overwhelming. Indeed, the evidence is that *The Story of My Life and Work* . . . actually outsold *Up From Slavery* in the American book market for several years."

Three years after the publication of *Up From Slavery*, Washington produced a third autobiographical volume, *Working With the Hands* (Garden City, N.Y.: Doubleday, Page, 1904). This contains a further development of his ideas about the necessity of industrial education for a people striving to raise themselves from the bottom of the social and economic order. It was reissued in 1969 by Arno Press and Negro Universities Press with an introduction by Thomas R. Cripps which views Washington as a "covert militant" and indicates recent sources which recognize this aspect. He "preferred to conceal his maneuvering behind the image created by his ghost writers."

Washington's fourth autobiography, *My Larger Education* (Garden City, N.Y.: Doubleday, Page, 1911), further spelled out his philosophy and attitudes, which were then under attack. He seems to have picked up a line suggested by Professor Barrett Wendell of Harvard, who, in a letter to Washington in 1901, wondered if Washington knew how lucky he was to have been driven by hardship to greater achievement. In his opening chapter, Washington finds advantage in every hardship and misfortune. He even seems to find it an advantage that he had never read many books and thus had to learn from his own experience and from the experiences of others. This book had appeared earlier in serialized form in *World's Work* during 1909 under the title "Chapters from My Experience."

OTHER WORKS BY WASHINGTON

In addition to the four autobiographies, Washington published at least nine other books between 1899 and 1913. In producing such an abundance of material he was assisted by some very capable writers and scholars, including Monroe N. Work and Emmett J. Scott (his personal secretary), whom he later commissioned to write an authorized biography. Other collaborators and ghostwriters included Max Webber, Max Bennett Thrasher, T. Thomas Fortune, S. Laing Williams, Alvis O. Stafford, and Robert E. Park. Emma L. Thornbrough declares that "in some cases these [books] were entirely ghost-written." There is no indication of coauthorship on the title page of any of these books, except in one case with Robert Park. Louis Harlan gives a good account of this matter in the introduction to *The Booker T. Washington Papers*, vol. 1 (Urbana: University of Illinois Press, 1972). This contains some of the autobiographical writings, including all of *The Story of My Life and Work* and *Up From Slavery*, and extracts from *My Larger Education, The Story of the Negro*, and "The Privilege of Service." Two other small pieces complete the collection. Harlan's introduction is probably the most interesting and valuable part of the book. Volumes two, three, and four of this projected fifteen-volume series contain the Washington correspondence and some other miscellaneous papers for the years 1860–1889, 1889–1895, and 1895–1898, respectively.

Washington's first book, *The Future of the American Negro* (Boston: Small, Maynard, 1899), was basically a collection of magazine articles and speeches. After its first publication, this book remained out of print until revived by the "black revolt" of the 1960s. It has recently been reprinted by Haskell House (1968), Negro Universities Press (1969), and Afro-American Press (1969). Charles W. Chesnutt, reviewing this book in *The Critic* (February 1900), rejected Washington's tacit acceptance of segregation with its implied if not declared inequality and inferiority. "To go slow," he wrote, "in seeking to enforce their civil and political rights . . . means silent submission to injustice. Southern white men may applaud this advice as wise, because it fits in with their purposes."

In 1900 Washington issued a forty-four-page monograph, *Education of the Negro* (Albany, N.Y.: J. B. Lyon), which was part of the education series edited by Nicholas M. Butler. He further expanded on his educational ideas and their implementation in *Tuskegee and Its People* (New York: Appleton, 1905), which he edited. It has recently been reprinted by Negro Universities Press (1969) and Books for Libraries (1971). The most valuable parts of this book are the seventeen chapters of autobiography by former Tuskegee students, which are primary sources for information on slavery and post-Reconstruction conditions. They show clearly the possibilities of successful achievement through industrial education.

Shortly after the appearance of *Souls of Black Folk* in 1903, Professor Ellis P. Oberholtzer, general editor of the American Crisis publications of George Jacobs & Co., asked W. E. B. Du Bois to write a biography of Frederick Douglass. Du Bois agreed to a contract, but Booker T. Washington expressed displeasure at the choice. He indicated his own desire to be the author of the biography of his great hero, Douglass. In spite of the contract already signed with Du Bois the company yielded, giving Du Bois the consolation of writing a biography of John Brown. With the help of S. Laing Williams and his wife, Fannie B. Williams, Washington issued the biography *Frederick Douglass* (Philadelphia: G. W. Jacobs, 1907; rpt. Westport, Conn.: Greenwood, 1969), which was simultaneously published in London by Hodder and Stoughton. Washington's first attempt at a historical work was made during the time that he was already at work on the Douglass biography. He turned the work of research and writing over to Robert E. Park (a white journalist and sociologist), Alvis Stafford (a black teacher), and Monroe N. Work (an Afro-American scholar). This team produced the two-volume *The Story of the Negro* (Garden City, N.Y.: Doubleday, Page, 1909). Another historical work, *The Story of Slavery* (Chicago: Hall & McCrea, 1913), was the last of his books.

Two other volumes credited to Washington are quite different in their content. *The Negro in Business* (Boston: Hertel, Jenkins, 1907), with reprints by Johnson Reprint (1970) and AMS Press (1971), extolled the achievements of successful Afro-American businessmen and the work of the National Negro Business League which Washington dominated. The principal function seemed to be to demonstrate how successful the new policy enunciated at Atlanta in 1895 was proving to be. The second work, *The Man Farthest Down,* written in collaboration with Robert E. Park (Garden City, N.Y.: Doubleday, Page, 1912), was an examination of the European peasants and urban poor. While Park is reported to have done the writing, it is in Washington's style and vernacular. They found the European peasants to be more degraded than poor blacks in the United States. Washington was impressed by the notion that "the position of the Negro in America, both in slavery and in freedom, has not been so exceptional as it has frequently seemed. . . . " There is no mention of "Jim Crow," discrimination, or lynching. The trip further persuaded the Tuskegee leader that there was little advantage in having political rights for the man farthest down, as was evidenced by the low state of workers in England. But in his usual optimistic style, he found progress everywhere.

Among the volumes of essays are some ascribed to Washington. *A New Negro for a New Century* (Chicago: American Publishing House, 1900) carries chapters attributed to him on the Spanish-American War and on education, as well as articles by N. B. Wood and a particularly interesting one on the role of women by Fannie B. Williams. This was reprinted in 1969 by Arno Press and Mnemosyne and is worthy of consultation as it contains valuable primary sources not readily available elsewhere. The style and tone of the first six chapters, which are attributed to Washington, offer an interesting study. They use the term "Afro-American," which is not used elsewhere in Washington's writings, and they contain a clear attack on Theodore Roosevelt for his slur on the courage of the "colored" soldiers at the Battle of San Juan. An interesting sidelight on Washington's attitude on the "question of the proper name for persons of African descent" is revealed in Gilbert T. Stephenson's *Race Distinctions in American Law* (London: D. Appleton, 1910), which contains part of a letter from Washington to Representative T. W. Sims of Tennessee in 1906 which declared: "It has been my custom to write and speak of the members of my race as Negroes. . . . To cast it off would be to separate us, to a certain extent, from our history. . . . " Light has been cast on these seeming inconsistencies by Louis Harlan in an interview with this writer. He indicated that Washington had written only the introduction to *A New Negro for a New Century* and had threatened to sue the publishers for showing him as the author. Further examination of the Washington papers may shed yet more light on this matter and on the whole question of ghostwriters.

The collection of essays titled *The Negro Problem* (New York: J. Pott, 1903) brought Washington and his chief adversary, W. E. B. Du Bois, together in the same book. Washington's contribution is a strong essay entitled "Industrial Education for the Negro." Du Bois counters with the essay "The Talented Tenth." There are several other important and historically significant essays by Charles W. Chesnutt, Paul Laurence Dunbar, and T. Thomas Fortune. Interesting also are articles by Wilford Smith and H. T. Kealling. Washington and Du Bois were reunited within the covers of another book—each of them contributed two lectures to *The Negro in the South*, which lists them as coauthors. (Philadelphia: G. W. Jacobs, 1907). This was reprinted in 1970 by Citadel Press with a helpful introduction by Herbert Aptheker, and in 1972 by Metro Books with a foreword by Blyden Jackson.

Because much of Washington's polemics and fame rested on his oratorical skills, it is not surprising to find that there have been numerous publications of his speeches. Among these, three are particularly noteworthy. The first was *Black-belt Diamonds: Gems from the Speeches, Addresses and Talks to Students of Booker T. Washington* (New York: Fortune and Scott, 1898). This selection carried an introduction by T. Thomas Fortune and has recently been republished by Mnemosyne and Negro Universities Press. A second, *Character Building* (Garden City, N.Y.: Doubleday, Page, 1902), contained many of Washington's Sunday evening talks to students at Tuskegee. These were largely centered on the Puritan ethic of hard work. The third was a more serious collection of his speeches edited by his son, E. Davidson Washington, *Selected Speeches of Booker T. Washington* (Montgomery, Ala.: Wilson, 1932). It includes speeches ranging from his first public address at the National Education Association convention at Madison, Wisconsin, in 1884, to his last before the American Missionary Association at New Haven, Connecticut, on October 25, 1915. One observes no sharp changes in direction, as was the case with Du Bois, but rather a gradual increase of criticism of the South. The last address includes significant statistics on Afro-American education and the discriminatory financing of segregated schools.

In *Eight Negro Bibliographies* (Millwood, N.Y.: Kraus Reprint, 1970), Daniel T. Williams lists over 200 articles by Washington which were published as pamphlets and in forty-nine different magazines. Most appeared in widely circulated periodicals such as *Outlook, Independent, World's Work, North American Review,* and the Hampton-based *Southern Workman.* The largest number was published, as one might expect, in *Tuskegee Student,* which had a relatively small circulation and may be difficult to find. The subjects covered range from a biographical sketch of Abraham Lincoln (*Tuskegee Student,* February 27, 1909) to "How Denmark Taught Itself Prosperity and Happiness" (*World's Work,* June 1911). Washington's constant purpose was the building of Tuskegee and the justification of his philosophy and plan for racial progress. Throughout, his penchant for optimism prevails. Much of his popularity seemed to rest, according to Miller and Harlan, on the practice of writing and saying what people wanted to hear.

In view of the fact that Washington was primarily an educator, it is only natural that most of his writings dealt with the subject of industrial education and its advantages. He was constantly advancing this idea and seeking to raise funds to support Tuskegee and its programs. The growth and financial success of the institute is evidence of the effectiveness of his speaking and writing. There was, however, little demand for his writing before 1900. During the first twenty years at Tuskegee, he published only nine articles, none of them before the Atlanta address of 1895. Notable among these early articles were "Awakening of the Negro" (*AtM,* September 1896), which tells of the advantages of industrial education over classical higher education, and "Industrial Education for Negroes" (*Our Day,* 1896).

With the fame that followed the Atlanta address, there came many opportunities to get into print. After the turn of the century, Washington wrote "Education Will Solve the Race Problem" (*NAR,* August 1900), which was a reply to an earlier *North American Review* article by John R. Straton of Mercer University. More typical of his style was "Chickens, Pigs and People" (*Outlook,* June 1, 1901), which stressed the importance of a practical education to the agricultural life of most black youth. He deplored the tendency of traditional education to draw young men from the farms to the city. Other illustrative writings on education include "Industrial Training for Southern Women" (*Tuskegee Student,* May 24, 1902), "Fruits of Industrial Training" (*AtM,* November 1903), "Education of the Southern Negro" (*NEA Proceedings,* 1904), "Farmers College on Wheels" (*World's Work,* December 1906), which describes one of Washington's pet projects for carrying training out to the farm, "Tuskegee" (*NAR,* April 1906), and "Industrial Education in Africa" (*Independent,* March 15, 1906), which tells of the work being done in Africa by Tuskegee graduates on a grant from the German government.

During his later years, Washington turned more of his attention to the ways in which graduates of Tuskegee were improving the schools and farms throughout rural Alabama. In "Educational Engineers" (*Outlook,* June 4, 1910), Washington presented his ideas of how a rural school should be developed and run. Relevance and self-help were the mainstays of his program. Similar were "Educate Six Million Negroes" (*World's Work,* June 1910), "A New Type of Rural School for Negroes" (*Survey,* March 15, 1913), and "Industrial Education, Public Schools and the Negro" (*Annals,* September 1913).

Acceptance and equality, which Du Bois thought would be won through higher education, Washington envisioned as coming through the Protestant ethic of hard work, clean living, and thrift. He emphasized this again and again, both in print and from the speaker's platform, with no appreciable change over the years. He related the work ethic to the needs of the black community in practically all of his social, political, and economic writings. Illustrative of his philosophy and policy was "Addresses to the Colored Farmers of Alabama" (*Annals,* March 1896), in which he stressed the importance of thrift, home ownership, and getting out of debt. In "The Case of the Negro" (*AtM,* November 1899), he informs the white South that the Negro is in the South to stay and that he will work hard and earn the respect of whites. More of the same can be found in "The Race Problem in the United States" (*Popular Science,* June 1899), "The American Negro and His Economic Value" (*International Monthly,* December 1900), "The Negro's Part in Southern Development" (*Annals,* January 1910), "Rural Negro Community" (*Annals,* March 1912), and "Solving the Negro Problem in Detail" (*Independent,* March 27, 1913), in which he mentions the need to go slowly and by individual advancement. He reveals his attitude toward Africa and slavery in "Religious Life of the Negro" (*NAR,* July 1905) by declaring it a great benefit for the "pagan" African to be brought here to gain "Christian civilization" through slavery.

Equally prevalent in his writings was his extolling of the virtues of building black businesses and communities. He tried to visit large centers of Afro-American population and all-black towns. He wrote of them in "Town Owned by Negroes: Mound Bayou, Mississippi"

(*World's Work,* June 1907), "Boley, A Negro Town in the West" (*Outlook,* January 4, 1908), and "Durham, North Carolina—City of Negro Enterprises" (*Independent,* March 30, 1911).

The business conducted in these towns was of high interest to Washington, who became the founder of the National Negro Business League at the same time that Du Bois was becoming interested in business. Washington frequently wrote about the advancement of black capitalism as the highest achievement of the race as exemplified in "National Negro Business League" (*World's Work,* October 1902), "Negro Enterprise" (*Outlook,* May 14, 1904), "Why Should Negro Business Go South?" (*Charities,* October 7, 1905), "Most Encouraging Convention" (*Independent,* September 20, 1906), which reported the first convention of black bankers, "Cheerful Journey Through Mississippi" (*World's Work,* February 1911), which was a survey of Negro enterprise in many communities, and "Opportunities for Negroes in Business" (*Commercial College Outlook,* January 1914).

Although none of his writing could properly be called protest, Washington was moving in that direction toward the end of his life. But even then the protest was carefully couched in questions or appeals. This changing mood could be seen in "Lynchings and International Peace" (*Outlook,* March 9, 1912) and "Is the Negro Having a Fair Chance?" (*Century,* November 1912). The latter was published as a thirty-four-page pamphlet by Tuskegee Press in the same year and given wide distribution. His final statement, "My View of Segregation Laws," written on September 13, 1915, was published posthumously (*New Republic,* December 4, 1915). In it he charged that "there has been no spontaneous demand for segregation ordinances." Such laws, he argued, were passed by politicians who appealed to "racial prejudices." He found that "attempts at legal segregation are unnecessary for the reason that . . . both colored and whites are likely to select a section of the city where they will be surrounded by congenial neighbors."

Washington released a number of biographical articles of questionable merit, which may have served to advance his policy of self-help and pride. Among these were: "Bert Williams" (*American Mercury,* September 1910), "Charles Banks" (*American Mercury,* April 1911), "Collis P. Huntington" (*Southern Workman,* June 1903), "Isaac Fisher" (*Everybody's Magazine,* April 1915), and "William Henry Lewis" (*American Mercury,* June 1913).

Washington did not concern himself with matters of foreign policy, but the foreign scene did give him material for several articles. They generally centered on the theme that the Negro in America is not the worst off of the peoples of the world. His "Impressions of Holland and France" (*Southern Workman,* November 1901) were observations from his first trip abroad. He pursued these further in "Women Who Work in Europe" (*Outlook,* June 10, 1911), and the previously cited "How Denmark Taught Itself Prosperity and Happiness," all of which were more fully developed in his book *The Man Farthest Down* (probably written, as discussed above, by Robert E. Park).

Other articles on the foreign scene brought Washington to the brink of overt protest. "Cruelty in the Congo Country" (*Outlook,* October 8, 1904) describes the barbaric cruelty and slavery of the Belgians, which Washington described as worse than anything experienced by blacks in the United States. In "Haiti and the United States" (*Outlook,* November 17, 1915), he decried the actions of the United States in that unfortunate island and pleaded for better treatment of black Haitians.

Several of the articles cited above are not listed in the bibliography by Daniel T. Williams (*Eight Negro Bibliographies*). Some other articles which are not listed include: "Extracts From Working With the Hands" (*Current Literature,* August 1904), "My Life Work at Tuskegee, Alabama" (*Teacher's Magazine,* June 1899), "Problems in Education" (*Cosmopolitan,* September 1902), "Influence of the Negro's Citizenship" (*NEA proceedings,* 1896), "Race Problem in the United States" (*Popular Science,* July 1899), "What the Negro is Doing for the Negro" (*Mississippi Review,* November 1904), "Negro's Life in Slavery" (*Outlook,* September 11, 1909), "Rise of R. S. Baker" (*American Mercury,* May 1908), "Story of the Negro" (*Outlook,* September 4, 1909), and "Observations and Comparisons Abroad" (*Independent,* November 19, 1903).

BIOGRAPHIES OF WASHINGTON

No significant biographies were written about Booker T. Washington until the year of his death, when a book-length biography appeared. This was basically a reworking of material gleaned from his autobiographies with some additions to cover the late years. The author of *Booker T. Washington, the Master Mind of a Child of Slavery* (Philadelphia: National Publishers, 1915; rpt. Westport, Conn.: Negro Universities Press, 1970), Frederick Drinker, was admittedly a great admirer of Washington and his book was intended to spread Washington's fame.

The next year saw two more biographies: Benjamin F. Riley's *The Life and Times of Booker T. Washington* (New York: Fleming H. Revell, 1916), and Emmett J. Scott and Lyman Beecher Stowe's *Booker T. Washington, Builder of a Civilization* (Garden City, N.Y.: Doubleday, Page, 1916). The latter was an authorized biography commissioned during Washington's life. Theodore Roosevelt wrote the preface, which praised Washington because "He was never led away, as the educated Negro so often is led away, into the pursuit of fantastic visions . . . he took precisely the right position as to the part the Black Man should try to take in politics." Twenty-three years elapsed before the next biography appeared, Theodore S. Boone's *The Philosophy of Booker T. Washington* (Ft. Worth, Tx.: n. p., 1939), a volume of unstinting praise.

Realizing that "no rounded, authoritative biography of Booker Washington, covering the whole of his life on a basis of firsthand research and interview, had so far been written," Basil Mathews undertook the task and produced *Booker T. Washington: Educator and Interracial Interpreter* (Cambridge, Mass.: Harvard University Press, 1948). It received favorable reviews as the most scholarly biography to that date, but it lacked adequate documentation. In making his apology for Washington's policies, Mathews frequently overstated or exaggerated the position of his critics.

What amounts to an abridged version of the Mathews biography was written by Samuel R. Spencer as *Booker T. Washington and the Negro's Place in American Life* (Boston: Little, Brown, 1955), which tells little that is new. Although it repeatedly uses slightly revised sections from the earlier biography without acknowledgement, and lacks footnotes, it received praise from Francis Broderick as "the best biography of Washington, fair to both Washington and Du Bois." It should be noted that Spencer had described Du Bois as a "self-appointed gadfly [who] had delusions of grandeur." Du Bois, in a review in *Science and Society* (Winter 1956), replied that Spencer "shows neither grasp nor understanding." He suggests that "Mr. Spencer, being a Southern white man, liked Booker Washington. . . . " He found the book to be a "fairy tale [which] may suit the present rulers of Mississippi and Georgia." Du Bois did not blame Washington alone for his shortcomings, for "this was the fault of the white South and the industrial North, which deliberately used Washington as a pawn to beat back ambitious Negroes." Richard Bardolph, in reviewing the book (*AHR,* October 1955), found Spencer "too insistently eulogistic." Ray Ginger was equally severe in his review (*The Nation,* November 5, 1955). He found that Spencer confused and concealed historical truth. Of Washington's faults he charged that Spencer "goes to hopeless lengths to interpret them away." He concludes that "the debate of a half-century ago between Washington and W. E. B. Du Bois about correct strategy for Negro progress is still a living and vital matter for us all. But Spencer, by neglecting the major issues and ranging the gamut of minor ones, has made the whole thing almost incomprehensible."

Two composite biographical works that followed a similar pattern were issued in the 1960s. The first, *Booker T. Washington and His Critics: The Problem of Negro Leadership* (Lexington, Mass.: Heath, 1962), edited by Hugh Hawkins, was one of the Amherst series called "Problems in American Civilization." It has a good introduction and helpful bibliographical notes, but lacks an index, and although each included excerpt is correctly cited, the footnotes from the originals are omitted. He offers writings by Washington, and favorable and unfavorable views of him by his contemporaries as well as by later historians (among them Rayford Logan, W. E. B. Du Bois, Francis Broderick, Kelly Miller, Emmett Scott, and Samuel Spencer).

The second of this pair is *Booker T. Washington* (Englewood Cliffs, N.J.: Prentice-Hall, 1969), ably edited by Emma Lou Thornbrough. Her twenty-five-page introduction, bibliographical notes, and index are especially noteworthy and helpful. The book contains defenses of Washington by such writers as T. Thomas Fortune and Ida Wells Barnett, and criticisms by Trotter, Chesnutt, and Du Bois.

Bernard A. Weisberger attempted to bring a better balance to the literature in *Booker T. Washington* (New York: New American Library, 1972). He clearly attempts to be fair to all sides but seems to assume "it was inevitable that he [Washington] would meet with resistance from his fellow blacks." However, he does go on to show that the opposition was based upon the shortcomings of the Washington program. It is unfortunate that Weisberger failed to include any footnotes, bibliography, or index.

Barry Mackintosh's well-written but brief biographical sketch, *Booker T. Washington: An Appreciation of His Times* (Washington, D.C.: National Park Service, U. S. Department of Interior, 1972), contains numerous well-chosen excerpts by and about Washington. They are well balanced in both praise and criticism. Nevertheless, although they are identified, full citations are not given.

Unquestionably the most outstanding and perhaps the only thoroughly scholarly biography of Washington is Louis R. Harlan's *Booker T. Washington: The Making of a Black Leader* (New York: Oxford University Press, 1972). This is the first volume of a projected two-volume work and covers the early years from 1856 to 1901. It is to be backed up by the projected fifteen volumes of Washington's letters and papers. John H. Bracey, Jr., reviewing this biography (*NYTBR,* March 4, 1973), found it "meticulous in reconstructing the life of Washington. The method and interpretation are in the best tradition of liberal scholarship." He also observed that "a lot of the 'old' Booker T. Washington remains . . . His shameless identification with and fawning on upper-class whites. . . . On the 'new' side are a number of facets of Washington that reveal more clearly the effectiveness of his power as a leader of black people." Willard B. Gatewood's review (*JNH,* April 1973) found this an "extraordinarily perceptive biographical assessment." An outstanding review article, "Of Mr. Booker T. Washington and Others" by J. R. Pole (*The Historical Journal,* December 1974), gives more than a review of the book. There is an illuminating and lengthy discussion of the similarities as well as the differences between Washington and Du Bois.

The most recent study of Washington is *Learn By Doing: A Projected Educational Philosophy in the Thought of Booker T. Washington* (New York: Vantage Press, 1974), by William H. DeLaney, in which DeLaney attempts an analysis of Washington's educational philosophy. He shows a close similarity between Washington's philosophy and that of John Dewey. DeLaney points out the emphasis which Washington placed on practical learning. His footnotes and bibliography are helpful.

There are several biographies of Washington geared to young people. The two best in this group were by outstanding Afro-American writers. Shirley Graham's *Booker T. Washington: Educator of Hand, Head, and Heart* (New York: Messner, 1955) is a vivid and inspiring story. Graham creates entirely plausible dialogue which seems quite in keeping with the situation. The brief but interesting 184-page narrative skims lightly over Washington's life and accomplishments without getting into any of the controversial aspects which created so much turmoil during and after his life. It is equally suitable for young readers and adults. *Young Booker: Booker T. Washington's Early Days* (New York: Dodd, Mead, 1972) by Arna Bontemps is effectively written. Bontemps does not embellish his writing with fictional conversation but rather adheres to firm historical principle. This book follows Washington's life up to the Atlanta Address of 1895. It, too, is equally suitable for young readers and adults.

Other juvenile books include *A Boy's Life of Booker T. Washington* (New York: Macmillan, 1922) by Walter C. Jackson, *Booker T. Washington: Leader of His People* (Champaign, Ill.: Garrard Press, 1962) by Lillie Patterson, and *Booker T. Washington* (New York: Putnam, 1968) by William Wise. A book for children notable for its negative qualities is Augusta Stevenson's *Booker T. Washington: Ambitious Boy* (Indianapolis: Bobbs-Merrill, 1950), one of the "Childhood of Famous Americans" series. This is more of a fairy tale of happy slaves who love their kind masters than a biography.

The number of books treating Washington's leadership continues to increase. The scene is effectively set in Hugh C. Bailey's *Liberalism in the New South: Social Reformers and the Progressive Movement* (Coral Gables, Fla.: University of Miami Press, 1969), which is outstanding. It goes far in explaining the seemingly inconsistent relations between the militant T. Thomas Fortune and the accommodationist Washington. C. Vann Woodward, a leading southern historian, has provided a very perceptive chapter in *Origins of the New South, 1877–1913* (Baton Rouge: Louisiana State University Press, 1951), which is the ninth volume of *A History of the South*, appropriately called "The Atlanta Compromise." He found race relations to be in a complete shambles at the end of the century, only forty years after emancipation had been hailed with such high hopes.

August Meier, in his *Negro Thought in America, 1880–1915* (Ann Arbor: University of Michigan Press, 1963), attempts to deal with intellectual development during the era of Booker Washington. He develops the thesis that "ambivalence has characterized the Negro's stance regarding integration into American life on the one hand and self-segregation on the other." Charles W. Thomas's review (*JNH*, October 1964) notes that Meier thought that self-help brought racial solidarity and self-segregation while ironically the opposite was the case. Meier found Du Bois's opposition to Washington "more from jealousy . . . than from conflicting educational philosophy." Melvin Drimmer (*Phylon*, Summer 1965) thought *Negro Thought in America* a well-documented study which saw Negro leadership in "bankruptcy."

Robert L. Factor's *Black Response to America: Men, Ideals, and Organization from Frederick Douglass to the NAACP* (Reading, Mass.: Addison-Wesley, 1970) gives a cold, selectively factual description of the economic and political views, alliances, and dilemmas of both Douglass and Washington. The major portion of the book is devoted to "The Reign of Booker Washington," making no excuse for Washington's gullibility as he is used by industrialists to serve their economic interests. There is considerable concern for the attitudes of both Douglass and Washington toward the growing labor unions.

WASHINGTON AS AN EDUCATOR

Booker T. Washington's work as an educator has received major attention, as most books on American education have a section devoted to him. The advancement of industrial education has been considered a boon not only to the least-advantaged Afro-American but also to the disadvantaged white. Merle Curti, in *The Social Ideas of American Educators* (New York: Scribners, 1935, with a more recent edition by Littlefield, Adams [Paterson, N.J., 1965]) devotes a chapter to "The Black Man's Place: Booker T. Washington." Curti maintains that the underlying purpose of Washington's educational philosophy was to show the South that industrial education "was in the true interest of the South—in the interest, in short, of the Southern white himself." Monroe N. Work (in *Southern Pioneers*, edited by Howard W. Odum [Chapel Hill: University of North Carolina Press, 1925]) has taken a similarly perceptive but uncritical view of Washington as an educator and a leader. There is also a very brief biographical sketch of Washington's career as a teacher in Mildred S. Fenner and Eleanor Fishburn's *Pioneer American Educators* (Washington, D. C.: NEA, 1944), reissued by Kennikat Press (Port Washington, N.Y., 1968). Their narrative reads like a Horatio Alger success story. It is notable, however, that Washington is the only Afro-American educator included in the book.

Works dealing specifically with Afro-American education have concentrated on the roles of Washington and Du Bois in shaping the course of late nineteenth- and early twentieth-century education. Horace Mann Bond's *The Education of the Negro in the American Social Order* (Englewood Cliffs, N.J.: Prentice-Hall, 1934; rpt. New York: Octagon, 1966) is the most comprehensive study of its type available. Bond followed it closely with the monograph *Negro Education in Alabama: A Study in Cotton and Steel* (Washington, D. C.: Associated Publishers, 1939; rpt. New York: Octagon, 1969), in which he assessed Washington's role in advancing Negro education in his chapter "The Influence of Personalities" and described Washington's struggle for public and private financial support for educational institutions. A more recent work, Henry A. Bullock's *A History of Negro Education in the South from 1619 to the Present* (Cambridge, Mass.: Harvard University Press, 1967), sheds interesting light on the differing approaches to educating the Afro-American in the South.

Roscoe Conkling Bruce has provided a biographical discourse on Washington and Tuskegee in *From Servitude to Service: Being the Old South Lectures on the History and Work of Southern Institutions for the Education of the Negro* (Boston: American Unitarian Association, 1905; rpt. Westport, Conn.: Negro Universities Press, 1969). In addition to a sensitive biographical sketch, Bruce provides a good description of Washington's achievements at Tuskegee. A strong defense of Washington was offered by M. B. Thrasher, one of his ghostwriters, in "Booker T. Washington's Personality" (*Outlook,* November 9, 1901) wherein he denies that Washington was politically active.

John Hope Franklin delivered the Founder's Day address at Tuskegee in 1959, which he titled "Booker T. Washington, the Man and the Educator." The text is printed in *Rhetoric of Racial Revolt* (Denver, Col.: Golden Bell Press, 1964) edited by Roy L. Hill. Franklin examined Washington and Tuskegee and the changes that had occurred in both in historical perspective. He saw Washington as "a realist of the first water" in whose "flexibility there was a consistency and a firmness." To him "Washington had many sides" and was infused with "a spirit of experimentation." Franklin's essay seemed strangely out of place in this book for it was neither "rhetoric" nor did it deal with "racial revolt."

WASHINGTON IN HISTORICAL PERSPECTIVE

Most writers recognized and tried to cope analytically with the many facets of Washington's career. Some, such as H. F. Kletzing in *Progress of a Race or the Remarkable Advancement of the Afro-American Negro* (Naperville, Ill.: J. L. Nichols, 1898), gave a glowing description of Washington and his work at Tuskegee. A very favorable account was given by another contemporary, Kelly Miller, in his *Race Adjustment* (New

York: Neale Publishers, 1908) in the chapter "Radicals and Conservatives." Doxey Wilkerson, in his foreword to the 1968 Arno Press edition, said that Miller's comparative assessment of Frederick Douglass and Booker T. Washington was "probably the most trenchant appraisal of these 'two superlative colored men' to be found in literature." Miller also has given a glowing, larger-than-life defense of Washington in "Booker T. Washington Five Years After" (in Miller's *The Everlasting Stain* [Washington, D. C.: Associated Publishers, 1924]). For him Washington "believed in attempting the thing possible and postponing the unattainable to the time of increased ability and power." The Arno reprint combines both Miller books in one volume.

Critical views of contemporary Afro-American leaders were given by William H. Ferris in *The African Abroad* (New Haven, Conn.: Tuttle, Morehouse & Taylor Press, 1913) and Francis J. Grimke in *The Works of Francis J. Grimke* (Washington, D. C.: Associated Publishers, 1942). Ferris, a leader of the anti-Washington group, catalogued the charges against Washington. He developed a lengthy philosophical justification for the struggle for full equality, giving numerous supportive public statements. There is an interesting description of his anti-Washington efforts at the Louisville meeting of the Afro-American Council. Grimke, in a sermon delivered in October, 1901, "The Roosevelt–Washington Episode, or Race Prejudice," was "glad of this episode because it will also have the effect of opening the eyes of Professor Washington himself. . . . Now the scales will fall from his eyes and he will see just what the Southern white men think of him."

Several books have sections that will be helpful to those who do not have access to original sources. Louis R. Harlan, the acknowledged authority on Washington, has provided an excellent study of the roles of Washington and Du Bois in the black business world. "Booker T. Washington, and the National Negro Business League" (in *Seven on Black* [Philadelphia: Lippincott, 1969], edited by William G. Shade and Roy C. Herrenkohl) reveals the congruence of the attitudes of Du Bois and Washington toward black businessmen: "The idea of the National Negro Business League was born in the brain of W. E. B. Du Bois, but it was Washington who took the idea and made it an institution." A broader view was undertaken by Herbert J. Storing in "The School of Slavery: A Reconsideration of Booker T. Washington" in *100 Years of Emancipation* (Chicago: Rand McNally, 1963), which is favorable to Washington and critical of the NAACP. More on Washington's relationship with the NAACP can be found in Charles F. Kellogg's *NAACP* (Baltimore: Johns Hopkins University Press, 1967). J. W. Schulte has given a clear and perceptive analysis of Washington in *The People That Walk in Darkness* (Netherlands: Van Longhum Slaterus, 1956; New York: Ballantine Books, 1960).

Key Issues in the Afro-American Experience (New York: Harcourt Brace Jovanovich, 1971), edited by Nathan I. Huggins, Martin Kilson, and Daniel M. Fox, contains two essays on Washington. The first, by Paul B. Wortham and James R. Green, "Black Workers in the New South, 1865–1915," focuses on Washington's appeal to southern employers and his antagonism to unions. The second essay, "The Gnawing Dilemma: Separatism and Integration 1865–1925," by Francis L. Broderick, examines the struggle for equal rights for blacks that continued throughout the careers of Douglass, Washington, and Du Bois.

A helpful view of Washington and his running battle with the "militants" is given by Steven R. Fox in *The Guardian of Boston* (Kingsport, Tenn.: Kingsport Press, 1970), a biography of the militant Monroe Trotter. Elliott M. Rudwick takes a close look at Trotter's role in "Race Leadership Struggle: Background of the Boston Riot of 1903" (*JNE,* Winter 1962).

The multitude of writings in periodicals and journals about Booker T. Washington is overwhelming. As in the case of the books, the articles can conveniently be divided into three major groupings: pro-Washington, anti-Washington, and those reflecting the ambivalence that many individuals had toward Washington. At best each group will represent only a sampling of the available materials, most of which are listed in Daniel T. William's *Eight Negro Bibliographies,* mentioned earlier. Unfortunately, William's work has numerous errors and omissions and is rapidly getting out of date.

The memorable address that Washington delivered at the Cotton States and International Exposition in Atlanta in 1895 catapulted him from near obscurity to national prominence almost overnight. A great deal of the literature on Washington includes some discussion of this address, which can be found in numerous publications. Roger M. Williams has attempted to discuss its significance in the popularly written and, at times, historically inaccurate "The Atlanta Compromise" (*American History Illustrated,* April 1968). It has been reprinted in *Annual Editions Readings in American History* (Guilford, Conn.: Dushkin, 1972). Williams defends Washington against his critics and finds that "his approach was right for his time." Practically all of the early articles supporting Washington's position were written by white writers. This may reflect their easier access to the media. In "Tuskegee Institute and its President" (*Popular Science,* September 1899), Max Bennett Thrasher gave a biographical sketch of the man along with a short history of the school, praising both. William Dean Howells wrote "An Exemplary Citizen," a long review article praising *Up From Slavery* (*NAR,* August 1901). H. C. Foxcroft offered praise tinged with racism in "Negro on Efficiency" (*Fortnightly Review,* September 1906). He considered it "remarkable" to find efficiency in "a man of color." Lavish praise was given by Walter Hines Page in "Booker T. Washington: The Characteristics of the Colored Leader Who Has Shown the Way to Solve the Hardest Problem of Our National Life," (*Everybody's Magazine*, April 1902), which was excerpted in Thornbrough's *Booker T. Washington*. Laudatory but obviously racist is F. E. Leupp's "Why Has He Succeeded" (*Outlook*, May 1902). Unusual praise is found in an editorial in *Education* (October 1900) which is so bigoted that it has to be read to be believed.

The most bitter racist attack to appear in a national periodical came from Thomas Dixon, Jr., in "Booker T. Washington and the Negro" (*SEP*, August 19, 1905). He was promptly and effectively answered by Joseph J. Brien's "Booker T. Washington and the Negro—A Reply to Thomas Dixon, Jr." (*Voice of the Negro*, October 1905).

More recent accolades include Charles H. Thomas's "Booker T. Washington Is Elected to the Hall of Fame" (*JNE*, Winter 1946), and Donald J. Calesta's "Booker T. Washington: Another Look" (*JNH*, October 1964). Calesta has used much of the same material published by August Meier seven years earlier to paint a picture of Washington as a civil rights militant who "surreptitiously worked toward undermining the American race system."

Articles by two outstanding Afro-American scholars fall largely within the group praising Washington. Carter G. Woodson, the dean of Afro-American historians, wrote "Honor to Booker T. Washington" (*NHB*, March 1947), which reprints the Atlanta address and makes a comparison with Douglass, whose "ideas as to educating the Negro were practically the same." The other eminent Afro-American was Kelly Miller, a contemporary of Washington. His essay "Washington's Policy" appeared in the Boston *Evening Transcript* (September 18 and 19, 1903). This is basically the same article previously mentioned as "Radicals and Conservatives."

On the other end of the spectrum there were, in the early years of Washington's career, a significant number of highly educated and talented Afro-Americans who were critical of both his philosophy and his plan. Alexander Crummell was sharply critical of Washington's views, although he did not mention Washington by name, in "The Attitude of the American Mind Toward Negro Intellect" in *Occasional Papers* #3 (Washington, D.C.: American Negro Academy, 1898). He complained that America "has refused to foster and to cultivate the Negro intellect." Horace Mann Bond, in his perceptive "Negro Leadership Since Washington" (*SAQ*, April 1925), makes it clear that the critics did not "develop a single and unchallenged leadership" until late in Washington's life. Their views were being expressed by men like Charles W. Chesnutt, the writer, whose review essay in *The Critic*, "A Plea for the American Negro," has previously been cited. In it he called for "rigorous condemnation" of racial discrimination and segregation. More critical was Professor W. S. Scarborough, vice-president of Wilberforce University, in "Booker T. Washington and His Work" (*Education,* January 1900). He found both the man and his work wanting. Tuskegee had "just enough book-learning work to make the industrial phase profitably intelligible." He found that friends of the race are "inimical when they become shortsighted and narrow . . . if they look upon a large part as the whole."

In spite of Washington's efforts, Afro-American publications continued to include criticism much as Monroe Trotter's editorials in the Boston *Guardian* and the editorial entitled "Tuskegee's Twenty-fifth Anniversary" in *Voice of the Negro* (May 1906). The Washington, D. C., *Bee* reported a speech by William H. Ferris, one of Washington's earlier critics, under the headline "Booker T. Washington, His False Theories Exposed by a Yale Graduate. The Position of the *Bee* Endorsed" (January 8, 1898). This has been republished in *Negro History Bulletin* (November 1970) as "William H. Ferris Criticizes Booker T. Washington."

One of the few white critics in the early period was J. S. Bassett, editor of *South Atlantic Quarterly,* who, in an article entitled "Two Negro Leaders" (July, 1903), observed that Booker T. Washington was "widely known because of his peculiar policy." Bassett showed a strong preference for Du Bois and his approach.

Recent writers and scholars who have examined the records have had a tendency either to be critical of Washington and his achievements or to take a more neutral position toward him. Jack Abramowitz, in three articles in *Social Education,* "Origins of the NAACP" (January 1951), "Crossroads of Negro Thought, 1890–1915" (March 1954), and "Emergence of Booker T. Washington as a National Negro Leader" (May 1968), observed that the death of Douglass left a void into which the white South thrust their candidate, Booker T. Washington, who until his Atlanta speech "was a minor figure in Negro life . . . a relative unknown." His statement that "it was mainly in the Southern press that he was accorded approval" largely concurs with the findings of Emma L. Thornbrough in "Booker T. Washington as Seen by His White Contemporaries" (*JNH,* April 1968; rpt. *Black Leaders of the Centuries,* edited by S. O. Mezu and R. Desai [Buffalo, N.Y.: Black Academy Press, 1970]). Her important article quotes many outstanding white political and industrial personalities who praised Washington because he permitted the blame to be placed on the Negro. But a New Orleans paper saw "the cunning of his race. . . . Booker, like other negroes, will not hesitate to create a fake impression if by doing so he can advance his own interest." Thornbrough's earlier article, "More Light on Booker T. Washington and the *New York Age*" (*JNH,* January 1958), had revealed some of Washington's devious relations with the black press and his false statements about it. These two articles should not be missed.

In spite of numerous requests from George W. Cable to Washington for information, Cable declined to respond favorably to Washington's requests for support. Philip Butcher, the noted Afro-American literary critic, examines all of the then-known correspondence between the two in "George W. Cable and Booker T. Washington" (*JNE,* Fall 1948). Cable apparently disliked industrial education and Washington's obsequious approach to the white South. Similar views were expressed by Oliver C. Cox in "The Leadership of Booker T. Washington" (*SF,* October 1951). He observed that Washington's leadership "must be thought of as spurious. . . . He never lost the attitude of the favorite slave."

Numerous scholars have attempted to unravel the apparent enigma of Washington's philosophy and career—was he a black separatist or an integrationist, a militant or an Uncle Tom? In so doing, scholars have evidenced a wide variety of attitudes. They have, however, remained neutral or have avoided making value judgments. Horace Mann Bond, the eminent Afro-American scholar whose career has largely been devoted to a study of Afro-American education in the South, wrote "The Influence of Personalities on the Public Education of Negroes in Alabama" (*JNE,* January 1937). Of Tuskegee he said, "Since the school was an instrument of social policy, it is difficult to tell where it is an educational institution, and where a social device." An interesting light is cast on the Atlanta address in the observation that before the Atlanta Exposition former Governor Bullock had announced, "The colored labor in our section is the best, safest, and most conservative in the world." This helps explain his delight when Washington confirmed his view in the address. Another Afro-American scholar, W. Edward Farrison, mixes praise and criticism in "Booker T. Washington: A Study in Educational Leadership" (*SAQ,* July 1942).

H. G. Wells appears objective but at times perplexed in "The Tragedy of Color" (*Harper's,* September 15, 1906). Another view is taken in "Negro Racial Movements and Leadership in the United States" (*AJS,* July 1937) by Guy B. Johnson, who, in spite of his southern experience, found the Afro-American so assimilated that "he is distinguishable from the white man only by his color."

One of the principal interpreters of Washington has been August Meier, who as long ago as 1957 viewed Washington as a secret militant because of his clandestine involvement in civil rights cases. In his essay "Toward a Reinterpretation of Booker T. Washington" (*JSH,* May 1957) he declared, "It is clear . . . Washington was surreptitiously engaged in undermining the American race system by a direct attack upon disfranchisement and segregation. . . . Washington's own correspondence is distinctly at variance with the ingratiating mask he presented to the world." This significant article is excerpted in Emma Thornbrough's book on Washington and reprinted in August Meier and Elliott M. Rudwick's *The Making of Black America* (New York: Atheneum, 1969). Meier went further in his study of Washington "to investigate the relationship between the popularity of this ideology and the changing Negro class structure" in his article "Negro Class Structure and Ideology in the Age of Booker T. Washington" (*Phylon*, Fall 1962).

The ever-burning "Uncle Tom" question surfaced in Jacqueline James's "Uncle Tom? No, Booker T." (*AH*, August 1968). She obviously used some of the Meier material, but only a small part of her article is devoted to this issue; most of it is concerned with Washington's early life and the real identity of his white father. John P. Flynn raised the question "Uncle Tom or Wooden Horse?" (*JNH*, July 1969), but shifted his discussion from civil rights strategy to the question of Protestant ethics versus Social Darwinism. An intriguing idea is offered by Irving Kristol in "A Few Kind Words for Uncle Tom" (*Harper's*, February 1965). Kristol sees a distortion of the significance of the original Uncle Tom, who was "regarded as a symbol of human nobility" with the "inner transcendent freedom which all noble souls possess." He sees similar qualities in Washington. "But there can be no doubt that much of our current disrespect for Booker T. Washington flows from the fact that he was not, by today's standards, a 'militant.' " Uncle Tom and Washington "were not equal to their white contemporaries only because they were superior to them."

Specific aspects of Washington's career are considered in several works. Jane Gottschalk analyzed "The Rhetorical Strategy of Booker T. Washington" (*Phylon*, Winter 1966); Willard B. Gatewood related the strange circumstances behind the serious beating given Washington in "Booker T. Washington and the Ulrich Affair" (*Phylon*, Fall 1969) and Elliott M. Rudwick examined "Booker T. Washington's Relations with the NAACP" (*JNE*, Spring 1960). Daniel Walden gave an inadequate account of "The Contemporary Opposition to the Political Ideas of Booker T. Washington" (*JNH*, April 1960). His coverage is narrow, focusing on the comments of Du Bois. Philip Foner promptly recognized this with his insertion of documents in response to Walden (*JNH*, October 1960). Lawrence J. Friedman pointed out many contradictory statements by Washington in "Life 'In the Lion's Mouth': Another Look at Booker T. Washington" (*JNH*, October 1974). Many details of the maneuvers necessary to get Washington to deliver his memorable address in Gainesville, Florida, are examined by Arthur O. White in "Booker T. Washington's Florida Incident, 1903–1904" (*Florida Historical Quarterly*, January 1973). White shows not only the virulence of the opposition to Washington, but also the harm it brought to his supporters.

A different approach to understanding Washington and Afro-American history is taken by Judith Stein in " 'Of Mr. Booker T. Washington and Others': The Political Economy of Racism in the United States" (*S&S*, Winter 1974/1975). She found "contradictions" in the analyses of other historians who saw racism as the root of the Afro-American's plight. She would substitute economic factors seemingly to the exclusion of racism. She comes to the strange conclusion that "Du Bois, like Washington, . . . saw no political role for black masses."

As might be expected, the best articles come from the current biographer and editor of the Washington papers, Louis R. Harlan. Writing in the *American Historical Review* (January 1966), he gave a twenty-six-page account of "Booker T. Washington and the White Man's Burden" in which he found that Washington "was substantially involved in African affairs . . . in Togo, Sudan, South Africa, Congo Free State, and Liberia." Washington recognized that the introduction and/or improvement of cotton growing would be important to Africa's economic development. Washington's interest in and influence on African industrial education was discussed in considerable detail in W. Manning Marble's "Booker T. Washington and African Nationalism" (*Phylon,* Winter 1974), which revealed the link between Washington and many of the important educational and political leaders of South Africa. Washington's concern for Africa led him to become vice-president of the Congo Reform Association and to condemn the brutal treatment of Africans in the Congo. Harlan joined forces with Pete Daniel to write "A Dark and Stormy Night in the Life of Booker T. Washington" (*NHB*, November 1970), in which they describe a mysterious incident when Washington was beaten up in a less-than-desirable neighborhood in New York City. Washington refused to explain why he was beaten or why he was in that neighborhood at that time. Hardly any other event more clearly demonstrates Washington's capacity for deviousness and the manner in which it might work to his discredit. Harlan let the chips fall where they may in "Booker T. Washington in Biographical Perspective" (*AHR*, October 1970), an important, concise biographical view.

W. E. B. Du Bois

Dr. W. E. B. Du Bois was known as a prolific writer during his long life. Herbert Aptheker, in his *Annotated Bibliography of the Published Works of W. E. B. Du Bois* (Millwood, N.Y.: Kraus-Thompson Organization, 1973), has provided basic identification of 1,975 items which he has been able to locate. These include twenty books covering the seventy-two-year period from Du Bois's first book, *The Suppression of the African*

Slave Trade to the United States of America, 1638–1870, Harvard Historical Series Number 1 (New York: Longmans, Green, 1896), to the posthumously published *Autobiography* in 1968. The variety of materials dealt with reflected the versatility of Du Bois's mind.

AUTOBIOGRAPHIES

Du Bois's autobiographical works are among his most noteworthy writings. Although he had written several short sketches of his life early in his career, the first full-length autobiography was *Dusk of Dawn, An Essay Toward an Autobiography of a Race Concept* (New York: Harcourt, Brace, 1940; rpt. New York: Schocken Books, 1968; Kraus, 1975), which he felt was "not so much my autobiography as the autobiography of a concept of race." Most readers welcomed this as an inner view of his endeavors; however, others saw in it evidence of egotism.

His second full-length autobiographical work, *In the Battle for Peace: The Story of My 83rd Birthday* (New York: Masses and Mainstream Publishers, 1952) is more than the story of a man; it is the story of a struggle in which the man, Du Bois, was the center of a storm. The book tells of his indictment, trial, and acquittal in 1951 and of the flurry of peace activities in which he was then involved. His emergence from the civil rights struggle into the world campaign for peace presaged by more than a decade the activities of Dr. Martin Luther King, Jr. The comments by Shirley Graham Du Bois appended to each chapter make this book a biography as well as an autobiography. The mixture of love and admiration in the comments make the story poignant and compelling.

His final work was the *Autobiography of W. E. B. Du Bois: A Soliloquy on Viewing My Life from the Last Decade of Its First Century* (New York: International Publishers, 1968). Julius Lester, in his very helpful bibliography in *The Seventh Son: The Thoughts and Writings of W. E. B. Du Bois* (New York: Random House, 1971), tells us that this book was first published in Russia in 1962. However, Aptheker contends that "shortened versions were published in their respective languages in 1964 and 1965 in the German Democratic Republic, the U.S.S.R., and the People's Republic of China."

SCHOLARLY BOOKS AND ARTICLES BY DU BOIS

During his early life, Du Bois prepared himself rigorously for work as a scholar in the social sciences. It is natural then that his historical and sociological works would be among his most important books. However, his experiences while he was becoming a scholar deeply impress upon him his identity as an Afro-American. He came to assert his African ancestry with fervor and pride. These experiences forced upon the young scholar the necessity for polemics, which are visible in all of his writings.

His first scholarly work was *The Suppression of the African Slave Trade,* which has been previously cited. This was his doctoral dissertation at Harvard and was published as the first of the Harvard Historical Series. There have been five printings of this work, the most recent by Russell and Russell in 1965. From this first historical undertaking, Du Bois turned his attention to sociological study in *The Philadephia Negro: A Social Study* (Philadelphia: Published for the University of Pennsylvania, 1899). Reissued by Schocken Books in 1967 with a long introduction by E. Digby Baltzell, this book has often been considered a model sociological study which others have followed.

Du Bois was able to continue his scientific research when he was offered a professorship at Atlanta University. Through a series of annual conferences, he planned "a careful search for truth conducted as thoroughly, broadly, and honestly as the material resources and mental equipment at command will allow." The first two Atlanta University publications (1896 and 1897) were issued before Du Bois's arrival on campus. The first issue edited by Dr. Du Bois was *Some Efforts of American Negroes For Their Own Social Betterment* (Atlanta University Press, 1898), followed by *The Negro in Business* (1899), *The College-Bred Negro* (1900), *The Negro Common School* (1901), *The Negro Artisan* (1902), *The Negro Church* (1903), *Some Notes on Negro Crime Particularly in Georgia* (1904), *A Select Bibliography of the Negro-American* (1905), *The Health and Physique of the Negro-American* (1906), *Economic Co-Operation Among Negro Americans* (1907), *The Negro-American Family* (1908), *Efforts For Social Betterment among Negro Americans* (1909), *The College-Bred Negro American* (1910), *The Common School and the Negro American* (1911), *The Negro-American Artisan* (1912), and *Morals and Manners Among Negro Americans* (1913). In the studies of 1910 through 1913 Du Bois was assisted by Augustus Dill as coeditor. Originally published by the Atlanta University Press, these studies have been reissued as the *Atlanta University Publications* (New York: Arno Press, 1968, 1969) in two volumes with an introduction by Ernest Kaiser.

One of Du Bois's grandiose ideas which failed to get off the ground was his plan for an encyclopedia utilizing "the best scholarship in the world" to present a description of "the past and present of the Negro race." After several years of work and the help of the Phelps-Stokes Fund he was able to issue only one volume with Guy B. Johnson as coeditor, *Encyclopedia of the Negro: Preparatory Volume with Reference Lists and Reports* (The Phelps-Stokes Fund, 1945). He later used this book as the framework for the *Encyclopedia Africana* after he went to Ghana. His death in 1963 prevented its completion.

Du Bois wrote only one full-length biography, *John Brown* (Philadelphia: George W. Jacobs, 1909), which he regarded as his favorite book. It was reissued by International Publishers (1962) and Metro Books (1972). He made no claim of presenting new information on Brown but rather sought "to lay new emphasis upon the material . . . and to treat these facts from a different point of view."

There were three general histories of the Afro-American experience, all of them tending to follow a set pattern: *The Negro* (New York: Henry Holt, 1915); *The Gift of Black Folk: Negroes in the Making of America* (Boston: Stratford, 1924), written at the request of the Knights of Columbus as one of their Racial Contributions Series; and *Black Folk Then and Now: An Essay in the History and Sociology of the Negro Race* (New York: Henry Holt, 1939). All were written as popular history without the evidence of scholarship displayed in earlier works. In 1935 Du Bois produced a solidly researched book which played an important part in redirecting the historiography of the period studied, *Black Reconstruction in America: An Essay toward a History of the Part Which Black Folk Played in the Attempt to Reconstruct Democracy in America, 1860–1880* (New York: Harcourt, Brace, 1935). This volume aroused more controversy than any of his other historical works, engendering strong support as well as severe criticism. Aside from offering a dubious Marxist interpretation of the period, it brought forward many important facts about the positive and creditable achievements of the Reconstruction governments and contradicted the racist views of most earlier histories. It has gone through a number of editions, including the more recent ones by World Publishing (Cleveland, 1964), Cass (London, 1966), Russell and Russell (1966), and the Atheneum paperback (1969). In his final chapter, "The Propaganda of History," Du Bois eloquently condemns the falsifications which have become part of our history textbooks and encyclopedias and thus explains why he had written this book.

It seems only natural that Du Bois's long and abiding interests in Africa would cause him to turn his literary talents in that direction. Most of *The Negro* is devoted to Africa and Africans. His next endeavors in this area were two small volumes for the Little Blue Book series, numbers 1505 and 1552. They were titled, respectively, *Africa, Its Geography, People and Products* (Girard, Kansas: Haldeman-Julius Publishers, 1930), and *Africa—Its Place in Modern History* (Girard, Kansas: Haldeman-Julius Publishers, 1930). In the latter stages of World War II, Du Bois wrote *Color and Democracy: Colonies and Peace* (New York: Harcourt, Brace, 1945), which gives an analysis of the role of the world's "colored" peoples, who constitute the majority of the population but are ironically held in a colonial status by European powers. He correctly anticipates the revolutionary activity which would soon occur among the colonized peoples. This book was soon followed by *The World and Africa* (New York: Viking, 1947), an enlarged edition of which was issued by International Publishers in 1965. In his *Annotated Bibliography*, Herbert Aptheker mentions another work on Africa which has not appeared on the American publishing scene—*Africa: An Essay Toward a History of the Continent of Africa*, which was published in Moscow in 1961; however, it is reported to have been written in 1959.

ESSAYS BY DU BOIS

As important as Du Bois's autobiographical and scholarly writings were, they were not his most widely read books, many commentators having indicated that he was not at his best in them. Perhaps his greatest genius was expressed in his essays, three books of which were published as collected writings. The first of these, and by far his most popular work, was *Souls of Black Folk: Essays and Sketches* (Chicago: A. C. McClurg, 1903), which has seen thirty editions. Du Bois commented in *Dusk of Dawn* that when McClurg asked for some essays they could put together in a book that he "demurred because books of essays almost always fall so flat." But he acquiesced, adding one new essay, "Of Mr. Booker T. Washington and Others," in which he "sought to make frank evaluation" of Washington. In 1953 he issued a new and slightly revised edition through Blue Heron Press. There have been other editions issued recently by Fawcett and Avon in *Three Negro Classics* (1965), but Aptheker cautions that they contain "errors, omissions and alterations." There have been foreign editions, including Constable (London, 1905), Présence Africaine (Paris, 1959), which was taken from the Blue Heron edition, and Longmans (London, 1965), which has an introduction by C. L. R. James.

A second book of writings was published as *Darkwater: Voices from Within the Veil* (New York: Harcourt, Brace, 1920; rpt. New York: AMS Press and Schocken Books, 1969). This volume included an autobiographical essay, "The Shadow of Years," describing his family background and his first fifty years, that had appeared in *The Crisis* in 1918 on the occasion of his fiftieth birthday. It was not until the year of his death that the third book of essays was published, *An ABC of Color* (Berlin: Seven Seas Publishers, 1963), which included selections from over half a century of his writings. Most of the items were taken from *The Crisis*.

In 1940 Du Bois submitted a manuscript of collected essays, "Seven Critiques of Negro Education, 1908–1938," to the University of North Carolina Press. It was returned to him in 1941 because they were "unable to publish at present for financial reasons." Herbert Aptheker came upon the manuscript thirty years later in 1971, added three more essays, and brought it out as *The Education of Black People: Ten Critiques 1906–1960* (Amherst: University of Massachusetts Press, 1973). Aptheker believes that this volume with the three essays which he added represents "the fullest expression of [Du Bois's] views as they developed in the last quarter-century of his life." The book contains helpful editorial notes by Aptheker, which give something of the historical setting, and a very valuable nine-page bibliography of Du Bois's published writings on education. These carry brief annotations.

OTHER WORKS BY DU BOIS

Du Bois's long and varied literary career found expression in a variety of forms. He made many forays into the realm of *belles lettres,* which included numerous pieces of poetry, but only one partial collection was published in *Selected Poems* (Accra: Ghana University Press, 1965). Many of his poems have been included in anthologies of Afro-American literature. Probably his most flamboyant effort was the pageant "The Star of Ethiopia" (New York: Horizon, 1913), which Du Bois produced first in New York and later in Washington, Philadelphia, and Los Angeles. Much more important were Du Bois's adventures into fiction. His first, *The Quest of the Silver Fleece* (Chicago: A. C. McClurg, 1911), was an attempt to encompass many facets of the "race problem" in a novel. Du Bois referred to it as "really an economic study of some merit." His second effort was *Dark Princess: A Romance* (New York: Harcourt, Brace, 1928), which he said was his favorite book. Late in life and shortly before leaving the United States, Du Bois wrote a trilogy, *The Black Flame* (New York: Mainstream Publishers). The first volume was *The Ordeal of Mansart* (1957); the second, *Mansart Builds a School* (1959), and the third, *Worlds of Color* (1961). This trilogy presents a fictionalized biographic history of the Afro-American from the post-Reconstruction period to the civil rights struggle of the 1950s. Some have thought that it was largely autobiographical.

As was the case with the other polemicists covered in this chapter, Du Bois has largely documented his own life. Francis L. Broderick has sarcastically suggested "characteristically for Du Bois, autobiography became an integral part of his sketches of the Negro's past." We have previously discussed his major autobiographical works, *Dusk of Dawn, In Battle for Peace,* and *The Autobiography of W. E. B. Du Bois.* In addition to these he wrote a number of shorter essays which have appeared in various publications. The first of these was "The Shadow of the Years" (*The Crisis,* February 1918), written for his fiftieth birthday celebration, and later included in *Darkwater.* In 1938, when Du Bois had returned to Atlanta University, he was asked to give a sketch of his life, which he did in "A Pageant of Seven Decades." This was published as a pamphlet by Atlanta University and reprinted in Foner's *W. E. B. Du Bois Speaks.* Other pieces include: "My Evolving Program for Negro Freedom" in Rayford W. Logan's *What the Negro Wants* (Chapel Hill: University of North Carolina Press, 1944); "Comments on My Life," written in 1942 but not published until 1965 in *Freedomways* (Winter 1965); "Editing *The Crisis*" (*The Crisis,* March 1951 and November 1970), which was reprinted in *Black Titan: W.E.B. Du Bois,* a compilation by the editors of *Freedomways* (Boston: Beacon, 1970); "A Negro Student at Harvard at the End of the Nineteenth Century" (*MR,* Spring 1960), which was reprinted in *Black and White in American Culture: An Anthology From the Massachusetts Review* (New York: Viking, 1971), edited by Jules Chametzky and Sidney Kaplan; and *W. E. B. Du Bois: A Recorded Autobiography,* in which Du Bois was interviewed by Moses Asch of Folkways Records in 1961.

Du Bois, one of the greatest essayists and journalists of the twentieth century, edited five different magazines. The first was the short-lived *The Moon Illustrated Weekly,* which began publication in 1906 as an anti-Washington publication in Memphis, Tennessee. It was succeeded by the founding of *Horizon* in Washington, D.C., in 1907, which continued publication until 1910, at which time Du Bois founded *The Crisis,* the organ of the newly formed NAACP. In 1920, during his tenure as editor of *The Crisis,* Du Bois, with Augustus Granville Dill, launched a children's monthly, *The Brownies' Book,* which was forced to fold after two years. Following his departure from the NAACP and the editorship of *The Crisis* in 1934, Du Bois returned to teaching at Atlanta University and conceived a new journal which would be "a university review of race and culture." Thus, *Phylon* began publication under his editorship in 1940.

These five periodicals became important outlets for his prolific pen, but they by no means consumed all of his time or writing. During that time he published in at least 211 magazines and newspapers. They ranged from the prestigious *Annals of American Academy of Political Science,* in which he had at least ten articles between 1898 and 1944, to numerous articles in Afro-American newspapers such as the *Amsterdam News,* for which he wrote a weekly column, "As The Crow Flies," from 1939 to 1944. He also wrote regular columns for the Pittsburgh *Courier,* "A Forum of Fact and Opinion," (1936–1938); the Chicago *Defender,* "The Winds of Time" (1945–1948); and Adam Clayton Powell's paper, *People's Voice* (1947–1948).

The availability of the white press to controversial Afro-American writers has always been sporadic and uncertain. The Afro-American press, however, from its founding in 1827 onward, provided a channel through which the four polemicists discussed in this chapter could reach and influence their primary audience. Du Bois's writings enjoyed great popularity in both white and black periodicals for many years. It is interesting to note, however, the sharp decline in the frequency of his articles in white periodicals after his departure from *The Crisis*. Thereafter he was increasingly confined to the Afro-American and leftist publications. Aptheker has annotated 739 newspaper columns written by Du Bois. There are also citations of 456 articles or speeches by Du Bois, most of which appear in the white press. It is not possible to make individual reference to these publications in this format, nor is it necessary, since they are readily available in Aptheker's *Annotated Bibliography*.

COLLECTIONS OF DU BOIS'S WORK

Some of the multitude of Du Bois's writings in the various media have been collected and published under the editorship of others, causing a flurry of publishing when they first appeared in 1970. Philip Foner brought together the two-volume collection, *W. E. B. Du Bois Speaks: Speeches and Addresses 1890–1963* (New York: Pathfinder Press, 1970). These speeches represent some of Du Bois's most revealing statements.They are not the highly rhetorical extemporaneous torrents which seem to characterize so many Afro-American orators; rather they were carefully prepared and structured papers more characteristic of Du Bois's scholarly training. Foner points out that, "As a speaker, Dr. Du Bois was no impassioned orator. His speeches, regardless of the type of audience he addressed, reflected the same clear, beautiful and dignified prose which his writings featured, and many of his speeches were published without the slightest change as articles." He cites the impartial observation in 1911 of the *Manchester Guardian:*

> Dr. W. E. B. Du Bois . . . spoke with astonishing mastery, lucidity and perfection of phrase. The manner was spontaneous, yet every sentence was in place. The address was so simple that an intelligent child could have followed the argument, yet it handled so closely the fundamental issue that no specialist who heard it would have refused his tribute of admiration.

Through these speeches we can observe and trace almost every issue with which Du Bois became involved and the shifting methods through which he would combat the problems confronting the Afro-American. One can also observe how similar as well as how different were his positions from those of the three other polemicists covered in this chapter. His close similarity to the attitude expressed by Douglass is evident in his statement that he would fight for every "right that belongs to a freeborn American . . . and until we get these rights we will never cease to protest and assail the ears of America." It is clear that he continued "to protest and assail" until his death in 1963. Foner has included a brief selected bibliography of books and articles about Du Bois along with an index.

A second important collection of Du Bois's prolific works was *The*

Selected Writings of W. E. B. Du Bois (New York: Mentor, 1970), edited by Walter Wilson and with an introduction by Stephen J. Wright. In the introduction, Wright envisioned Du Bois as "the bridge between the militant Frederick Douglass who died in 1895 and the current movement for racial justice and equality." He opined that although Du Bois was not a "great" novelist, poet, historian, or leader, he did write numerous other "superb" pieces for which he will be remembered. The selections in this anthology were mainly from those writings, the vast majority of which are excerpts from his books *The Philadelphia Negro, The Souls of Black Folk, Dusk of Dawn,* and the all-too-frequently neglected *John Brown, Darkwater,* and *Black Reconstruction.* Unique among these selections are those taken from *The Brownies' Book* which was written for "the Children of the Sun" designed especially "for Kiddies from Six to Sixteen." It includes a brief bibliography listing a few books about Du Bois and a helpful index.

Another book that reissued some of Du Bois's works was Meyer Weinberg's collection *W. E. B. Du Bois: A Reader* (New York: Harper & Row, 1970). Weinberg informs us that this book consists entirely of articles by Du Bois that were first published in various magazines and that the great majority have never before been collected. They represent the wide spectrum of Du Bois's thoughts and concerns and thus are valuable aids in an understanding of the man. The five-page introduction is one of the best analytical statements about Du Bois. The book contains a good bibliography, especially the section which lists chapters in books, which would be difficult to locate otherwise. There is also a good index.

The following year brought still more collections of Du Bois's work. Julius Lester edited the two-volume *The Seventh Son: The Thoughts and Writings of W. E. B. Du Bois* (New York: Random House, 1971), which has an excellent bibliography and index, and is the largest collection of Du Bois's writings. P. S. Prescott, in his review of this work in *Newsweek* (August 23, 1971), found it "more than serviceable" and that "Lester's introductory essay is a model of compression, expertly employing long extracts from Du Bois' own work." The introduction is a sympathetic but analytical 150-page biography. Selections in the book cover the span of Du Bois's writing career from his very first foray into writing as a lad of fifteen for a column in the *New York Freeman* to his last effort in his *Autobiography.* The first writing reveals a highly precocious teenager passing sage political advice to his elders. Lester's work is unquestionably a valuable resource in the quest for an understanding of Du Bois. Only publication of Du Bois's complete writings will fully replace it.

A collection along the lines of Lester's is that edited by Andrew G. Paschal, *A W. E. B. Du Bois Reader* (New York: Macmillan, 1971), with an introduction by Arna Bontemps. The similarity to the title of Weinberg's book should not mislead one to thinking that the books are similar. These selections from a full array of sources are highly race conscious and tend to accentuate and support Du Bois's nationalist or separatist views, as is evidenced in such selections as "Conservation of Races," "A Negro Nation Within a Nation," "On Blackness," and "Where Do We Go From Here?" In his preface, Paschal stresses the need to "understand" the life and philosophy of Du Bois; he further observes that "had white and black leaders not opposed and obstructed his program for economic cooperation," relations between blacks and whites would be much better today. He praised Du Bois's "relentless search for truth and the courage to express the truth when he found it." Arna Bontemps, in his introduction, gives a brief analysis of Du Bois and points out his "fondness for allegory" and his recognition of "the power of the symbol."

Henry Lee Moon, recently the editor of *The Crisis,* has given us a very creditable collection of Du Bois's editorials and articles from the pages of *The Crisis* in *The Emerging Thought of W. E. B. Du Bois* (New York: Simon & Schuster, 1972), which has a very good index. Some writers had held that Du Bois's twenty-four years with *The Crisis* were his finest and that its pages contained much of his greatest writing. Moon held that Du Bois, "more than any other single individual, developed the philosophy and set the goals of the twentieth-century Negro protest movement." Through these selections one can see that, confronted by the increasing presence of Jim Crow and the narrowing of opportunity in the North, Du Bois "began in the early thirties to embrace the doctrine of fighting 'segregation with segregation'." Moon observes that "he was ambivalent, paradoxical and self-contradictory," and that his purpose was to find some means "to end the senseless barriers between the races." This is an excellent mirror of the leading thought of the Afro-American community from 1910 to 1934.

The most recent collection of Du Bois's works is Herbert Aptheker's *The Education of Black People: Ten Critiques, 1906–1960* (Amherst: University of Massachusetts Press, 1973). There are also several anthologies which combine works by Du Bois with articles about him and therefore constitute a bridge to biographical writings. The first of these was the W. E. B. Du Bois memorial issue of *Freedomways* (Winter 1965), one-third of which is made up of Du Bois's writing, including such rarely published articles as "Africa and the French Revolution" (first published in *Freedomways,* Summer 1961) and "The African Roots of War." This volume was slightly enlarged and published in book form as *Black Titan: W. E. B. Du Bois,* cited earlier. Another of these combined anthologies, which appeared as a special issue in periodical literature, was *The Problem of Color in the Twentieth Century* (*JHR,* 1st Quarter, 1966), which carried the subtitle "A Memorial to W. E. B. Du Bois," edited by Daniel Walden. It is similar to the *Freedomways* prototype, which was considerably better. The final combined anthology was *W. E. B. Du Bois* (Englewood Cliffs, N.J.: Prentice-Hall, 1973), edited by William M. Tuttle, Jr., for the Great Lives Observed Series. More than half of this anthology is made up of well-chosen writings by Du Bois which mark the various stages of his development. They are topically grouped in a manner which is helpful to the reader. Unlike the previously cited combined anthologies, Tuttle's gives complete citations for all of the selections he used.

Two additions to the published works have been brought to attention recently by George Breathett (*JNH*, January 1975) and the editors of *Freedomways* (Fall 1975). The first, captioned "An Address to the Black Academic Community," was delivered to the Twenty-Fifth Annual Meeting of the Association of Social Science Teachers in 1960. Du Bois told his audience that if Afro-Americans adopt white values "we would cease to be Negroes." He regretted that "most schools and colleges are afraid to . . . tell how the larger part of the civilized world is adopting [socialism and communism]." The *Freedomways* document, "Behold the Land," is an address by Du Bois to the Southern Negro Youth Congress in 1946. He called upon the "young women and young men of devotion to lift again the banner of humanity and walk toward a civilization which will be free and intelligent." KTO Press of Millwood, New York, has reissued all of Du Bois's major works as well as *Book Reviews of W.E.B. Du Bois* (1977) as part of *The Collected Works of W. E. B. Du Bois*. They project future volumes of his poetry, essays that appeared in periodicals, newspaper columns, and government reports and studies along with testimony before government agencies.

BIOGRAPHIES OF DU BOIS

Biographical studies of W.E.B. Du Bois have been slow in appearing. Considering the multitude of activities in which he was involved, one might have expected more prompt attention to an analysis and interpretation of his life and achievement. It was not until the centennial of his birth that the first full biography was produced. Francis L. Broderick reworked his doctoral dissertation into *W. E. B. Du Bois: Negro Leader in a Time of Crisis* (Stanford, Calif.: Stanford University Press, 1959). Unfortunately, this first biography of Du Bois displayed a gross lack of understanding both of the man and his people. Andrew G. Paschal seems to have had Broderick in mind when he wrote of those "straining to locate faults in his scholarship and personality, seemingly so characteristic of some of the white writers who have undertaken to write of him."

A slightly more perceptive and equally well documented biography of Du Bois is Elliott M. Rudwick's *W. E. B. Du Bois: A Study in Minority Group Leadership* (Philadelphia: University of Pennsylvania Press, 1960), republished by Atheneum as *W. E. B. Du Bois: Propagandist of the Negro Protest* (1968) with a new preface by Louis R. Harlan and an added epilogue, "The Recent Years." Like Broderick's effort, this was a reworking of a dissertation and displays characteristics of a beginning scholar's attempt to interpret the heartbeat of the Afro-American community and the man who was "the most vital and compelling figure" during the first half of the twentieth century. The book should be read with caution for the numerous misinterpretations which result from exaggeration and a lack of intimate familiarity with Afro-American life. In the preface Harlan indicates part of the source of Rudwick's bias by stating, "It is clear that Professor Rudwick disapproves of the black nationalism which Du Bois always held under restraint and the radicalism to which he finally gave unrestrained vent. Rudwick deplores as an unrelieved personal disaster Du Bois's decision in 1961 to join the Communist party, whereas others might consider the decision a heroic protest against the official outlawing of this extreme form of dissent." However, Rudwick does not go as far in error as Broderick, who claimed that Du Bois wanted to be white.

A refreshing antidote to Broderick and Rudwick is found in Shirley Graham Du Bois's very personal biography, *His Day is Marching On: A Memoir of W. E. B. Du Bois* (Philadelphia: Lippincott, 1971). Her book could well be called an autobiographical biography, for it is a warm, intimate account which could only be given by one who lived with him during his later years, and is therefore as much an account of the author's life as it is of Du Bois. It speaks with the authority of first-hand experience without philosophical or rhetorical embellishments, and is a deeply moving story of a man always far ahead of his time. Above all it reveals the unknown and unseen side of a great and loving man. She has included almost verbatim many of the comments which she contributed to Du Bois's *In the Battle for Peace* (cited earlier).

The life and achievements of W. E. B. Du Bois were so monumental and inspiring that his story is well suited for children, and there are several biographies for young readers. One is by Leslie A. Lacy, who had met Dr. Du Bois in Ghana. This led him to write *Cheer the Lonesome Traveler* (New York: Dial Press, 1970). There is less of an orientation to "black power" in Emma G. Sterne's *His Was the Voice* (New York: Crowell-Collier, 1971). Its warm treatment reveals an acceptance of Du Bois's shifts toward socialism and communism. A third biography for young readers is Virginia Hamilton's *W. E. B. Du Bois* (New York: T. Y. Crowell, 1972). For the author, this work was the accomplishment of a lifelong dream. She concluded that "one cannot help wondering why he had waited so long to commit himself to communism." Another book for younger children which has more narrative and less interpretation is in the collected biography *Lift Every Voice* (Garden City, N.Y.: Doubleday, 1965) which was part of their Zenith Books series for junior high and elementary school students. This small volume by Dorothy Sterling and Benjamin Quarles also includes short biographies of Booker T. Washington, Mary Church Terrell, and James Weldon Johnson.

Other serious attempts to understand Du Bois appear in an anthology of previously published writings. This conglomeration of reactions, which includes both negative and positive views, is edited by Rayford W. Logan, who admired Du Bois but deplored his espousal of Marxism. The anthology, *W. E. B. Du Bois: A Profile* (New York: Hill & Wang, 1971), was compiled as part of the American Profiles series. The selections include pieces by the triumvirate of self-appointed interpreters of Afro-American history—Francis Broderick, August Meier, and Elliott Rudwick, who, along with Harold Isaacs in his article "Pan-Africanism as 'Romantic Racism,' " give a negative impression of Du Bois. Charles F. Kellogg portrays Du Bois as a contentious, disruptive element within the NAACP structure, one who continually created dissension and friction. Basil Mathews, in "The Continuing Debate: Washington vs. Du Bois," offers a more balanced account which manages to give a sympathetic view of both Du Bois and Washington without becoming the advocate of either. The chapters by William H. Ferris, Herbert Aptheker, and Vincent Harding are distinctly favorable to Du Bois. Ferris gives "A Contemporary View" in an excerpt from his *The African Abroad* (New Haven, Conn.: Tuttle, Morehouse & Taylor, 1913). Aptheker's contribution, "The Historian," was presented to the American Historical Association Annual Meeting in December 1968 at a panel which was devoted entirely to Du Bois's centennial. It also appears in his *Afro-American History: The Modern Era* (New York: Citadel, 1971) and the *Negro History Bulletin* (April 1969).

Among the anthologies of interpretive biographical essays about Du Bois, it is necessary to mention again the four publications which were cited under the collected anthologies of Du Bois's own writings. Each of them offer an important statement about his life and influence.

The *Freedomways* Memorial Issue (Winter 1965) is a collection of eulogies and essays about the contributions of Du Bois in many different areas. Aptheker contributed several of Du Bois's unpublished writings, including an autobiographical piece Du Bois had been asked to write on his seventy-fourth birthday. Among those offering praise were Kwame Nkrumah, Roy Wilkins, Langston Hughes, Horace Mann Bond, and Paul Robeson. A number of noteworthy articles were included, such as : "W. E. B. Du Bois as a Prophet" by Truman Nelson, "W. E. B. Du Bois, the Historian" by Charles H. Wesley, "W. E. B. Du

Bois' Influence on African History" by William Leo Hansberry, "Du Bois and Pan-Africa," by Richard B. Moore, and "A Selected Bibliography" by Ernest Kaiser of the Schomburg Collection, who is one of the best-informed librarians on Afro-American literature. The article by Moore on Pan-Africa is considered an excellent antidote to one done by Harold Isaacs in *W. E. B. Du Bois: A Profile.*

All of these articles were included in *Black Titan: W. E. B. Du Bois,* cited earlier with additional material by J. Saunders Redding, Vincent Harding, and Martin Luther King, Jr. Other additions include original review articles of *John Brown* by Ernest Kaiser and *The World and Africa* by Richard B. Moore. Although this book has the advantage of presenting a wide variety of views of Du Bois, it remains rather fragmented, as the essays are not woven together to present an integrated picture of Du Bois.

The special memorial issue (1st Quarter, 1966) of the *Journal of Human Relations* included many worthy articles on Du Bois, some of which had been previously published. Among the notable articles are: "W. E. B. Du Bois: Pan-Africanism's Intellectual Father" by Daniel Walden and Kenneth Wylie, "A Tribute to Du Bois" by Arna Bontemps, and "W. E. B. Du Bois" by Henry Miller. Unfortunately, this volume apparently has not been published independently for general circulation and is difficult to find.

The final anthology combining writings by Du Bois with writings about him was the perceptive volume *W. E. B. Du Bois* (Englewood Cliffs, N.J.: Prentice-Hall, 1973), edited by William M. Tuttle, Jr., for the Great Lives Observed series. This, like the previously cited biographies of Douglass and Washington, follows the format of viewing the character and achievement of a great world figure first through his own words, then through the opinions of his contemporaries, and finally through retrospective judgments. Not only did Tuttle present an outstanding selection of Du Bois's writings, as noted, but he also assembled a noteworthy collection of articles about him. For the contemporary views, selections by Kelly Miller (excerpts from "Radicals and Conservatives"), and by the southern white historian and editor John Spencer Bassett are marked by ambivalence toward Du Bois. Other contributors constitute a list of notables who opposed Du Bois, including Senator James F. Byrnes, Walter White, Marcus Garvey, A. Philip Randolph, Francis Broderick, and August Meier. There is also a brief defense of Du Bois by Truman Nelson in a selection from *Freedomways.* Tuttle provides a very good introduction in which he takes issue with Broderick's contention that Du Bois "abandoned race" in favor of the peace movement and the working class. He observes that Du Bois's "basic commitment remained constant: to equality of opportunity for attaining self-realization, human dignity, and a decent living without regard to race."

Three collected biographies contain short but well-written accounts of Du Bois's life. A close friend and long-standing associate in the NAACP, Mary White Ovington, wrote an early profile in *Portraits in Color* (New York: Viking, 1927), which gives a warm, knowledgeable account of his early career. Edwin R. Embree, in *13 Against the Odds* (New York: Viking, 1944), characterizes Du Bois as an elder statesman and recognizes that he was far ahead of current thinking. There is a twenty-page sketch of Du Bois's life in George R. Metcalf's *Black Profiles* (New York: McGraw-Hill, 1968), in which he, as others have done, erroneously asserts that Du Bois "abandoned the battle for Negro rights to devote all his energies to the quest for world peace."

Although there are numerous short biographical sketches of Du Bois in collected biographies of Afro-Americans, very few appear in magazines and periodicals. One of the earliest was "Rough Sketches—William Edward Burghardt Du Bois" (*Voice of the Negro,* March 1905) by John Henry Adams. Adams finds that Du Bois has "those manly attributes . . . which will ultimately bring to him lasting honor and fame." This illustrated article includes a photograph of Du Bois's high school graduating class. George Streator, formerly the managing editor of *The Crisis* and a close ally of Du Bois, wrote a strangely ambivalent biographical appraisal, "A Negro Scholar" (*Commonweal,* May 2, 1941), which evidenced strong anticommunist sentiment. It is careless both in interpretation and in fact.

A much better sketch is "Portrait . . . W. E. Burghardt Du Bois" (*ASch,* Winter 1948–49) by J. Saunders Redding. In contrast to the opinions of other writers who did not know Du Bois well, Redding asserts that Du Bois "did not seek the place of leader. His intellectual honesty, his far-length vision, and a fundamental integrity destined him to it."

William Allison Davis has given a unique and commendable account in *Du Bois and the Problems of the Black Masses* (Atlanta: W.E.B. Du Bois Institute for the Study of the American Black, n.d.). This analysis of three aspects of Du Bois's life—Du Bois's view of the problems of black Americans, his attempt to relate his proposed solutions to those problems to his own training and personality, and the fact that the validity of Du Bois's diagnosis of and prescription for the problems has been confirmed over the past twenty years—concludes that the grinding poverty of his early years and the prejudice he encountered produced Du Bois's rejection of whites. "The results in personality were his shyness and withdrawal. . . ." Furthermore, "his prime incentive was the middle-class reading and indoctrination he learned from his mother." Davis contends that the recent increase in job opportunities for blacks has been in the white-collar and professional fields and not in skilled labor as Booker T. Washington had expected.

DU BOIS IN HISTORICAL PERSPECTIVE

W. E. B. Du Bois was trained to be a scholar, and his career in several academic disciplines has been treated by numerous writers. Herbert Aptheker was eminently qualified to speak of "Du Bois as Historian," cited earlier. Charles H. Wesley contributed the excellent article "W. E. B. Du Bois: The Historian" to *The Journal of Negro History* (July 1965) and the *Freedomways* special edition. In it Du Bois characterized his own view of history by saying, "I realize that the truth of history lies not in the mouths of partisans but rather in the calm Science that sits between. Her cause I seek to serve, and wherever I fail, I am at least paying Truth the respect of earnest effort." In an earlier review of *Black Reconstruction*, "Propaganda and Historical Writing" (*Opportunity*, August 1935), Wesley commented that Du Bois wrote not "as a Negro historian but as an impartial historian . . . . He is the lyric historian, stringing his lyre. He is the literary knight with the plumed pen."

Earl E. Thorpe gave a critique of each of Du Bois's historical works in *Negro Historians in the United States* (published by the author, 1958) which was revised and enlarged as *Black Historians: A Critique* (New York: Morrow, 1971). Thorpe also devoted a chapter to Du Bois and his books in *The Central Theme of Black History* (Durham, N.C.: n.p., 1969), in which he provided an interpretive biography of Du Bois's intellectual and literary development. In addition, he gave a short commentary on many of Du Bois's books. Daniel Walden wrote a thoughtful and sympathetic article, "W. E. B. Du Bois: Pioneer Reconstruction Historian" (*NHB*, February 1963). Another view was given by Jessie P. Guzman in "W. E. B. Du Bois—the Historian" (*JNE*, Fall 1961), in which he observed that "as historian Du Bois is a crusader" who restored a balance to history.

Du Bois was equally important in the field of sociology, which he is credited with having helped establish as a scholarly scientific field. His development and influence in this discipline is given extensive attention in *Black Sociologists: Historical and Contemporary Perspectives* (Chicago: University of Chicago Press, 1974) edited by James E. Blackwell and Morris Janowitz. It contains three chapters devoted to Du Bois: "W. E. B.Du Bois: History of an Intellectual" by Francis L. Broderick, "W. E. B. Du Bois as Sociologist" by Elliott Rudwick, and "Black Sociologists and Social Protest" by Charles U. Smith and Lewis Killian. Rudwick's earlier article, "W. E. B. Du Bois and the Atlanta University Studies on the Negro" (*JNE*, Fall 1957), was a negative appraisal of Du Bois's attitudes as well as a critique of his work as a scientific sociologist. However, Rudwick came to Du Bois's defense in "Note on a Forgotten Black Sociologist: W. E. B. Du Bois and the Sociological Profession" (*American Sociologist*, November 1969). He argued that although Du

Bois's "training and research orientation toward both empiricism and reform was part of the mainstream of American Sociology," he was "ignored" because of "race prejudice." Broderick, in his article "German Influence on the Scholarship of W. E. B. Du Bois" (*Phylon*, Winter 1958), observed that "Du Bois went to Europe in 1892 an historian; he returned two years later a sociologist." This change Broderick attributed to the influence of Gustav von Schmoller. Further consideration of Du Bois's role as a scholar may be found in "Clues for the Future: Black Urban Anthropology Reconsidered" by Councill Taylor in *Race, Change and Urban Society*, edited by Peter A. Orleans and William R. Ellis, Jr., as volume 5 of the Urban Affairs Annual Reviews (Beverly Hills, Calif.: Sage, 1971). Taylor notes that "Du Bois initiated the field of black urban anthropology in 1896" with his *Philadelphia Negro.*

Du Bois probably gained his greatest prominence as an editor. Two of the periodicals which he launched—*The Crisis* and *Phylon*—continue to be published today and are tributes to his efforts. Du Bois dealt briefly with his role in an article in *The Crisis* (March 1951) which was reprinted along with several other important pieces in the sixtieth anniversary issue in November 1970. Elliott M. Rudwick examined his editorship in a pair of articles, "W. E. B. Du Bois in the Role of *Crisis* Editor" (*JNH*, July 1958) and "Du Bois's Last Year as *Crisis* Editor" (*JNE*, Fall 1958). In the latter, Rudwick cites comments of the Afro-American press concerning the fight with Walter White over the issue of segregation. He found that:

> Du Bois' failure [to sell segregation] in 1934 may be viewed in a sense as a measure of his success. For a whole generation as *Crisis* editor he had educated Negroes to demand social acceptance within the American milieu. It is an ironic fact . . . that he was drowned in the integrationist current he had done so much to generate and maintain.

In *The Crisis* (February 1968), Henry Lee Moon, its editor, wrote a favorable article, "The Leadership of W. E. B. Du Bois," which emphasized Du Bois's role as editor of *The Crisis*. He provided additional comment in "History of *The Crisis*" (*The Crisis*, November 1970). Moon also included a biographical chapter in his book, *The Emerging Thought of W. E. B. Du Bois* (New York: Simon & Schuster, 1972), which concerns itself primarily with Du Bois's role as editor. Comment on his early newspaper writing can be found in Paul G. Partington, "The Contributions of W. E. B. Du Bois to the New York 'Globe' and New York 'Freeman' 1883–1885" (*NHB*, February 1970).

One of Du Bois's earliest missions was the promotion of the idea of Pan-Africanism. Nkrumah referred to him as the "Father of Pan-Africa." One of the early articles was "Impressions of the Second Pan-African Congress" by Jessie Fauset (*The Crisis*, November 1921). She had been part of the American delegation which accompanied Du Bois on this mission and she provided an enlightening first-hand account of the proceedings. Clarence G. Contee devoted major attention to this aspect of Du Bois's career in several articles: "The Emergence of Du Bois as an African Nationalist" (*JNH,* January 1969), "A Crucial Friendship Begins: Du Bois and Nkrumah, 1935–1945" (*The Crisis,* August 1971), "Du Bois, The NAACP, and the Pan-African Congress of 1919" (*JNH,* January 1972), and "W. E. B. Du Bois and the Encyclopedia Africana" (*The Crisis,* November 1970). Edgar S. Efrat made an attempt to explore "Incipient Africanism: W. E. B. Du Bois and the Early Days" (*Australian Journal of Politics and History,* December 1967). Excellent articles on Du Bois and Pan-Africa can be found in *Freedomways* (Winter 1965), *Journal of Human Relations* (Spring 1966), and *Black Titan: W. E. B. Du Bois.*

Harold R. Isaacs devoted a chapter of his book *The New World of Negro Americans* (New York: John Day, 1963) to the relations between "Du Bois and Africa." This study of Du Bois's "racial fantasies" and "color astigmatism" is in part an anticommunist lament and in part a "psychoanalytic framework" for Du Bois's development. He found that "Du Bois' tie to Africa remains pure racial romance." This chapter is a slightly enlarged version of an earlier article by Isaacs, "Du Bois and Africa" (*Race,* November 1960). A recent book, *The Pan-African Movement* (London: Methuen, 1974) by Imanuel Geiss, is a translation by Ann Keep of *Panafrikanismus* (1968), which contains an important in-depth statement on the role of Du Bois in this movement. Discussion of Booker T. Washington's relation to Africa and the Washington–Du Bois controversy is also included.

One of the most balanced and informative articles relating Du Bois to Africa was Sterling Stuckey's "Du Bois, Woodson and the Spell of Africa" (*ND,* February 1967). Unlike many others, Stuckey does not argue the relative primacy of the attitudes of "Negritude" or of Pan-Africanism. Rather he sets out to study the views and roles of Du Bois and Woodson vis-à-vis Africa. He shows that these "leading advocates of African consciousness" were aware of "the harm being done to the American Negro's psyche by racist propaganda" about Africa.

The role of the polemicist and leader is one which inevitably lends itself to controversy and, in the case of Du Bois, seemingly to paradox more often than to understanding. Although his austere manner failed to generate many close friends, Du Bois had a large following of Afro-American intellectuals who, willingly or not, constituted the "Talented Tenth." However, it was a group whose members were often more limited in their thinking than was their mentor. Even Du Bois's supporters at times accused him of backsliding, apostasy, or worse. Thus in the articles written about Du Bois's ideas, plans, or programs, one needs to know something of the author and the time of writing in order to put the work in its proper context. Sadly, it seems to make considerable difference whether the writer is black or white (whites tend to be more critical), even though Du Bois had both friends and enemies in each group.

Efforts have been made to unravel the dilemmas caused by Du Bois's complex career. Worthy of consideration are commentaries by two of Du Bois's early contemporaries. Kelly Miller, in *Race Adjustment: Essays on the Negro in America* (New York: Neale Publishers, 1908), perceptively analyzes both Du Bois and Washington. A stronger proponent of Du Bois and sharper critic of Washington is William H. Ferris in *The African Abroad* (New Haven, Conn.: Tuttle, Morehouse & Taylor Press, 1913), although he maintained a reasonable balance with praise and criticism for each. Excerpts from his book also appear in Rayford W. Logan's *W. E. B. Du Bois: A Profile* (New York: Hill & Wang, 1971). Another contemporary and associate was the outstanding Afro-American educator Horace Mann Bond, who viewed the scene in his article, "Negro Leadership Since Washington" (*SAQ,* April 1925).

Du Bois's shift to racial economic separatism in the 1930s inspired numerous articles. "Negro Racial Movements and Leadership in the United States" (*American Journal of Sociology,* July 1937), by Guy B. Johnson, viewed the different types of leadership which developed in the first third of the century. Johnson disregarded Marcus Garvey and the nationalist movement, which, he felt, "had no sustained following, had almost no possibility of realization, and was significant chiefly as an example of fantasy and escape from reality." He did, however, examine the nature of the leadership offered by Washington and Du Bois along with the role of the NAACP. Benjamin Stolberg, in "Black Chauvinism" (*The Nation,* May 15, 1935), managed to misread history, find nothing worthy in black leadership, and give spurious advice to the Afro-American community. E. Franklin Frazier, in his article "The Du Bois Program in the Present Crisis" (*Race,* Vol. 1, 1935–36), provided an even more negative appraisal.

In contrast, William S. Braithwaite offered "A Tribute to W. E. Burghardt Du Bois" (*Phylon,* Winter 1949), and Truman Nelson envisaged "W. E. B. Du Bois: Prophet in Limbo" (*The Nation,* January 25, 1958). In this sympathetic, perceptive piece, Nelson analyzed the tragic aspect of Du Bois's career, in which the "final tragedy" was the silencing of the prophet who was "isolated by petty defamation, by suspicion, by officially contrived alienation." This article was reprinted in modified form in *Freedomways* and *Black Titan: W. E. B. Du Bois* without indication of the original source. Rayford W. Logan felt much the same way in an address given at Morgan State College, "Two Bronze Titans: Frederick Douglass and William Edward Burghardt Du Bois" (Washington, D.C.: Department of History, Howard University, 1972). He had known Du Bois for many years as a friend. He declared that he was "going to remain a disciple of the Du Bois of 1906 . . . " but that he regretted Du Bois's having joined the Communist party.

More recent efforts to comprehend Du Bois's career can be found in several books and articles. Raymond Wolters devotes two chapters to Du Bois in *Negroes and the Great Depression: The Problem of Economic Recovery* (Westport, Conn.: Greenwood Publishers, 1970), one of which concentrates on "Rift in the NAACP." Vivian Henderson observed that Du Bois "may have been the earliest person to bring into focus the impact of economic forces on workers and [Negro] people . . . " in "Race, Economics and Public Policy" (*The Crisis,* February 1975; and *Phylon,* Spring 1976). This address, delivered at Atlanta University, has been printed separately by the W. E. B. Du Bois Institute at Atlanta. S. P. Fullinwider, in *The Mind and Mood of Black America* (Homewood, Ill: Dorsey Press, 1969), devotes a chapter to "Du Bois and the Crisis in Intellectual Leadership," in which he seems to give excessive attention to the questionable "Christ-like myth" and "mission ideology." Nathan I. Huggins's *Harlem Renaissance* (New York: Oxford University Press, 1971) gives attention to Du Bois's role in the development of the Harlem Renaissance. The writings and policies of Du Bois during the 1930s were examined by James O. Young in *Black Writers of the Thirties* (Baton Rouge: Louisiana State University Press, 1973). The recent article by Joseph P. DeMarco, "The Rationale and Foundation of Du Bois's Theory of Economic Cooperation" (*Phylon,* Spring 1974), was yet another attempt to comprehend Du Bois's concept of segregation in the 1930s. Daniel Walden saw this transition in Du Bois from another aspect in "W. E. B. Du Bois: From Negro to Black" in *Forums in History* (St. Charles, Mo: Forum Press, 1974).

Du Bois was considered from a different perspective by William Toll in "W. E. B. Du Bois and Frederick Jackson Turner" (*Pacific Northwest Quarterly,* April 1974). Toll compared the thinking and attitudes of these two outstanding historians and found both similarities and differences. Notable among the differences, he found that "while Turner relegated formal leadership to a minor theme, Du Bois was to magnify its significance beyond its traditional role in historiography."

What was probably Du Bois's most bitter confrontation came with the highly volatile Marcus Garvey. Du Bois fought for equal rights for the Afro-American within an integrated society while Garvey advocated social and economic separatism for blacks. The contrast of the two men is well illustrated by the organizations they helped to found and lead: Du Bois in the integrated NAACP and Garvey in the all-black Universal Negro Improvement and Conservation Association, which advocated the "back to Africa" movement. Du Bois devoted several *Crisis* editorials to this, as did Garvey, whose editorials in *Negro World* were reprinted in *Philosophy and Opinions of Marcus Garvey* (New York: Atheneum, 1969) edited by Amy Jaques Garvey. The intemperateness of the arguments of Garvey and his proponents were further demonstrated in Sheppard Wheeler's vitriolic *Mistakes of Doctor W. E. B. Du Bois* (Pittsburgh: n.p., n.d.). Elliott Rudwick details the events of "Du Bois Versus Garvey: Race Propagandists at War" (*JNE*, Fall 1959), which he considered "abusive and acrimonious." He shows Du Bois as being more temperate, aloof, and intellectual than Garvey. Less heated and more illuminating discussions are offered by Ben F. Rogers in "William E. B. Du Bois, Marcus Garvey, and Pan-Africa" (*JNH*, April 1955) and by Richard B. Moore in "Critics and Opponents of Marcus Garvey" in *Marcus Garvey and the Vision of Africa* (New York: Random House, 1974), edited by John Henrick Clarke. *Life* contrasted these two leaders who "were as different as two men can be," in "Two Prophets of Race Pride" (December of 6, 1968). For more information on the Du Bois–Garvey relationship, one should also see Wilson J. Moses's "Marcus Garvey: A Reappraisal" in *Black Scholar* (November–December 1972). Theodore G. Vincent's *Voices of a Black Nation: Political Journalism in the Harlem Renaissance* (San Francisco: Ramparts Press, 1973) includes a chapter on this black nationalist conflict and views on Pan-Africa, segregation, and Marxism.

Criticism which is similar in tone to that of Garvey and his ilk is found in editorials by A. Philip Randolph in *The Messenger* in July, October, and December of 1919 in which he takes a strong quasi-Marxist thrust at Du Bois for being a "white folks' nigger" who is controlled by the "capitalist" board of the NAACP. These have been reprinted in part in Tuttle's *W. E. B. Du Bois,* and in *Negro Protest Thought in the 20th Century* (Indianapolis, Ind.: Bobbs-Merrill, 1965), edited by Francis L. Broderick and August Meier. Less polemical in tone and treatment were "Du Bois" in *Phylon* (Fall 1941) by Robert M. Lovett, and "William E. B. Du Bois' Concept of the Racial Problem in the United States" (*JNH,* July 1956) by Mary L. Chaffee.

In his later years, Du Bois found a different variety of critics emerging from the universities publishing "scholarly" articles. Francis L. Broderick projected "The Tragedy of W. E. B. Du Bois" (*The Progressive,* February 1958), and August Meier continued to chip away at the great image with his description of the fall from grace in his article "From 'Conservative' to 'Racial': The Ideological Development of W. E. B. Du Bois" (*The Crisis,* November 1959). Meanwhile Elliott Rudwick examined "W. E. B. Du Bois and the Universal Races Congress of 1911" (*Phylon,* Winter 1959) but found no worthwhile results. He was of the opinion that "the conclave was soon forgotten."

The death of Du Bois (1963) and the centenary of his birth (1968) seemed to signal new journalistic and scholarly forays and defenses. Du Bois had long since fallen under the Marxist cloud which largely excluded him, or any favorable writing about him, from the "capitalist" press. *The Journal of American History* could spare only one sentence to note his death in 1963. However, Werner J. Cahnman wrote a sympathetic article, "In Memoriam: William Edward Burghardt Du Bois," in the *American Sociological Review* (June, 1964). Unlike Broderick, Cahnman thought that Du Bois "never bartered the goal of liberty against the wages of expedience." From this point on, the Afro-American and progressive periodicals share the major part of the task of publishing articles about him.

The communist or Marxist point of view can be found in the prefatory dedication which Herbert Aptheker wrote in *Soul of the Republic: The Negro Today* (New York: Marzani & Munsell, 1964). It is perhaps more eulogistic than biographic. A more useful piece by the same author is an earlier article, "W. E. B. Du Bois: The First Eighty Years" (*Phylon*, Spring 1949). Aptheker salutes Du Bois on his ninety-fifth birthday in "To Dr. Du Bois—With Love" (*Political Affairs,* February 1963), in which he not only praises Du Bois's accomplishments but also extolls the validity of his Marxist or socialist positions fifty, sixty, and even seventy years earlier. Only a few months later he would write the obituary, "On the Passing of Du Bois" (*Political Affairs,* October 1963). In much the same vein is the essay by L. Hanga Golden and O. V. Melikian, "William E. B. Du Bois: Scientist and Public Figure" in *Black Leaders of the Centuries* (Buffalo, N.Y.: Black Academy Press, 1970), edited by S. Okechukwu Mezu and Ram Desai.

There is little doubt about the ambivalence of the American public toward Du Bois. He was only a memory following his flight to Ghana in 1961 to escape what he felt was continued persecution and possible imprisonment by the United States government. Shirley Graham (Du Bois) told how they were warned to leave the country before the anticipated Supreme Court decision of October, 1961, which would prohibit Du Bois from any further travel. Ghana proved to be a refuge for a weary warrior. This was hardly a voluntary exile, as many have claimed. However, Du Bois's influence remained and the Du Bois memory and image was preserved by Afro-American and progressive writers, including Marxists, who revered him for what he was and what he had been. The stunned silence and shock which fell like a shroud over the multitude gathered at the March on Washington in 1963 when Du Bois's death was announced stands as testimony to his memory and the fact that he was not only remembered but still honored. Another evidence of the reverence in which Du Bois was held by Afro-Americans was shown in the formation of the W. E. B. Du Bois Memorial Foundation and its efforts to establish a memorial to his memory at Great Barrington, Massachusetts. Dan S. Green tells of these efforts in "W.E.B. Du Bois Memorial Park" (*Freedomways,* 4th Quarter, 1975). It reveals clearly the continued hatred and disdain which many white Americans felt toward Du Bois. Green indicates the resurgence of interest in Du Bois in recent years in his article, "Resurrection of the Writings of an American Scholar" (*The Crisis,* November 1972). He notes that "during his career and until seven years following his death, only two volumes . . . had been published about Du Bois; from 1970 to 1972, sixteen volumes have appeared in print." Even this, he says, "is small tribute for his achievements, the legacy that he left, and the price that he paid struggling valiantly to better man's condition."

During the past decade Afro-American publications have continued to present frequent articles about Du Bois and his work. Lerone Bennett, Jr., one of the most articulate Afro-American journalist-historians, gave a memorable account, "W. E. B. Du Bois," in *Ebony* (May 1965). The article was made even more vivid by the high quality of the *Ebony* illustrations. William Brewer, editor of the *Journal of Negro History,* wrote the rousing "Some Memories of Dr. W. E. B. Du Bois" (*JNH,* October 1968), in which he pulled no punches in flailing Du Bois's foes. The *Negro Digest,* under its new name, *Black World,* published Earl Ofari's "W. E. B. Du Bois and Black Power" (August 1970). Lenneal J. Henderson offered the provocative "W. E. B. Du Bois: Black Scholar and Prophet" in *The Black Scholar* (January–February 1970). In this biographical study Henderson gave attention to Du Bois's development as a scholar and leader and deplored the fact that he was "perhaps the most discredited and maligned black scholar in the twentieth century." Andrew G. Paschal, also writing in *The Black Scholar,* offered a two-part biographical appraisal entitled "The Spirit of W. E. B. Du Bois" (October 1970 and February 1971) which was a full-blown defense of every position taken by Du Bois in the NAACP. Paschal describes Du Bois as "fighting alone on two fronts; the white enemy and their Negro cohorts, the Real Enemy!" The most recent analysis is of a very different nature. W. Maurice Shipley, in "Reaching Back to Glory: Comparative Sketches in the 'Dreams' of W. B. Yeats and W. E. B. Du Bois" (*The Crisis,* June–July 1976), noted the efforts of Du Bois and Yeats to "channel the creative arts . . . into a more meaningful" art.

The publication of Du Bois's *Autobiography* in 1968, the centenary of his birth, provided the opportunity for a salvo of review articles. However, a number of them were evaluations of Du Bois's life and career rather than analyses of the book. Irving Howe's "Remarkable Man, Ambiguous Legacy" (*Harper's,* March 1968) gave a perceptive analysis of the differing leadership styles of Du Bois and Washington in his review of the *Autobiography.* In addition to a portrait of Du Bois and a critical evaluation of the Washington–Du Bois conflicts, Howe spent considerable time deploring the fact that in the last decade Du Bois "had become a loyal and . . . courageous spokesman for Stalinism." However, considering the condition and treatment of the Afro-American, Howe concludes: "What is surprising is not that Du Bois turned toward a totalitarian outlook but that so few Negroes joined him." A similar though less analytical anticommunist point of view was expressed by Richard Kostelanetz in his review,"W. E. B. Du Bois" (*Commonweal*, November 1, 1968). An equally negative view of the *Autobiography* and the man was offered by Martin Duberman in "Du Bois as Prophet" (*NR*, March 23, 1968). Duberman found that the book "does nothing to change our view of Du Bois as a man of paradox" whose life was filled with "confusions" and "ideological twists and tactical turns." An opposing view was taken by Gilbert Osofsky in a refreshing and unusually penetrating review, "Master of the Grand Vision" (*SatR*, February 24, 1968). He states, "What chiefly impressed me about the last third of Du Bois's career was not its disjointedness but its continuity. So many of the themes he develops and the apparently new positions he takes on international issues are shadings of ideas he had expressed all his life." He makes the very discerning observation that "Du Bois was a seer who sensed the future before most of his contemporaries were aware of the present."

THE WASHINGTON–DU BOIS CONTROVERSY

Disagreement on the best way to achieve justice and status as a citizen in the United States has existed throughout the history of the struggle of the Afro-American for equality. David Walker was criticized by other black abolitionists for his audacious call for slave insurrections. Frederick Douglass was never the sole arbiter of the policy or tactics to be followed in the struggle against slavery or for full rights in the post-Civil War era. However, the sharpest clash among these great leaders was that between Washington and Du Bois. This has frequently been referred to as the Washington–Du Bois controversy and made to appear to be a clash of two men for leadership. Some writers have misconstrued these basic differences as a vacillating on the part of the Afro-American between integration and separatism. Others have found the variety and intermingling of themes as time has progressed bewildering. Irving Howe judged that "nothing in Du Bois's life, nothing in the history of the twentieth-century American Negroes, is more important than this clash." There is no doubt that this was one of the most significant struggles of ideological positions of the twentieth century. James A. Emanuel and Theodore L. Gross, who edited *Dark Symphony* (New York: Free Press, 1968), declared: "The ramifications of the Washington–Du Bois controversy invite a study of some length . . . The specifically literary repercussions of the controversy before 1920 can be glimpsed in works of several genres, among them the autobiography of James D. Corothers; the short stories of Chesnutt; the poetry of Leslie Pinckney Hill, Fenton Johnson and Du Bois himself; and the novels of at least eight Negro authors."

One of the most perceptive comments on this controversy was Dudley Randall's somewhat humorous and yet serious poem, "Booker T. and W. E. B.," in *Poem Counterpoem* by Margaret Danner and Dudley Randall (Detroit: Broadside Press, 1966).

The best sources for an understanding of the differences between Washington and Du Bois are to be found, of course, within the writings of the two men. Washington tended to adhere to the position expounded in 1895 in his Atlanta address, and this was spelled out more fully in his first book, *The Future of the American Negro* (Boston: Small, Maynard, 1899). The ambiguity of his language has been accepted as part of his strategy, allowing readers to interpret his meaning as they wished. Du Bois does not begin to voice significantly his disagreement with Washington's position until after 1900, when an early indication of his growing rejection of Washington's views could be seen in his review of *Up From Slavery* (*Dial*, July 1, 1901). His classic statement "Of Mr. Booker T. Washington and Others" in *Souls of Black Folk* (Chicago: A.C. McClurg, 1903) marked his full break with the Tuskegeean.

Washington and Du Bois had the opportunity to state their divergent views side by side in two early publications. In *The Negro Problem* (New York: James Pott, 1903; rpt. New York: Arno, 1969; Miami, Fla.: Mnemosyne, 1969), Washington gave his philosophy on "Industrial Education for the Negro" in which he criticized the fruits of higher education. He observed that "every slave plantation in the South was an industrial school." After emancipation

> those who had been trained as mechanics in slavery began to disappear by death, and gradually it began to be realized that there were few to take their places. There were young men trained in foreign tongues, but few in carpentry or in mechanical or architectural drawing. Many were trained in Latin, but few as engineers and blacksmiths. . . . We could find numbers who could teach astronomy, theology, Latin or grammar, but almost none who could instruct in the making of clothing.

Du Bois seemed to reply to this with his essay "The Talented Tenth" (in *The Negro Problem* [New York: J. Pott, 1903]), in which he stated, "The Negro race, like all races, is going to be saved by its exceptional men." Of these talented men, he said:

> Through political organization, historical and polemic writing and moral regeneration, these men strove to uplift their people. It is the fashion of today to sneer at them and to say that with freedom Negro leadership should have begun at the plow and not in the Senate—a foolish and mischievous lie.

The second joint appearance of Washington and Du Bois in print came with the publication in 1907 of their joint effort, *The Negro in the South* (Philadelphia: G. W. Jacobs; rpt. New York: Citadel, 1970; New York: Metro Books, 1972; New York: AMS Press, 1973). In his introduction to the Citadel edition, Herbert Aptheker indicated that "the contrast between Washington and Du Bois is especially sharp in this unique book where only the two appear, side by side." In one chapter, "The Economic Development of the Negro Race Since its Emancipation," Washington stressed the need to dignify labor and increase the "wants" of the Negroes so they would work harder and longer. To do this blacks would need the industrial education which Tuskegee had to offer. Du Bois in his chapter "The Economic Revolution in the South" leveled a powerful attack upon the systematic oppression of blacks in the South and the false promise of the Civil War. This was clearly a polemic to arouse protest and struggle.

In another early essay Du Bois restated his support for higher education. His article "Atlanta University" in Roscoe Conkling Bruce's *From Servitude to Service: Being the Old South Lectures on the History and Work of Southern Institutions for the Education of the Negro* (Boston: American Unitarian Association, 1905; rpt. Westport, Conn.: Negro Universities Press, 1969) related the building of one of the foremost Afro-American universities. This thought was further developed in the Atlanta University Publications paper on *The College-Bred Negro* (1900 and 1910). Many of his other writings make direct reference to Washington.

The establishment of the NAACP has been widely interpreted as an anti-Washington move on the part of those advocates, both black and white, of a more militant struggle for the rights of the Afro-American. The *Proceedings of the National Negro Conference 1909* (New York: Arno Press, 1969) records the initial step toward the founding of the NAACP, including two papers delivered by Du Bois. "Politics and Industry" has much of his argument against Washington's industrial education and noninvolvement in politics. Further light is shed on Du Bois's thought in "Evolution of the Race Problem." The other addresses and papers of the proceedings may be viewed as statements by members of both races of attitudes which were at variance with those of Washington.

Washington seldom made direct reference to Du Bois. He had a strategy of "benign neglect" by which he declined to advertise his adversaries. His feelings on Du Bois and others were at times expressed in his correspondence, in which he took them to task for their "misbehavior." No doubt more of this will be revealed as the letters and papers which are being edited by Louis Harlan become available. Similarly, the papers of Du Bois which are being edited by Aptheker will reveal more of his views of Washington.

There have been many discussions of the differences between the two men. A strong anti-Washington case was made by William H. Ferris in *The African Abroad* (New Haven, Conn.: Tuttle, Morehouse & Taylor, 1913), while Roscoe Conkling Bruce gave a pro-Washington view in his essay "Tuskegee Institute" in *From Servitude to Service.* Kelly Miller's pro-Washington blast, "Conservatives and Radicals" in *Race Adjustment* (New York: Neale, 1908), was primarily directed against Monroe Trotter as the malevolent schemer who used the "Boston Riot" as a device to gain Du Bois's open participation against Washington. Elliott Rudwick concerned himself with the same problem in "Race Leadership Struggle: Background of the Boston Riot of 1903" (*JNE*, Winter 1962). This well-documented article considerably extended the material in his biography of Du Bois and avoided favoring any of the participants. Horace Mann Bond offers an equally well-balanced perspective in "Negro Leadership Since Washington" (*SAQ*, April 1925). A favorable view of the Washington position was given by Charles S. Johnson in "The Social Philosophy of Booker T. Washington" (*Opportunity,* April 1928), in which he declared that "the ones who objected the most were the articulate Negroes who needed it least." Johnson went on to find that agitating for ballots was merely another of the "meaningless appurtenances"—such as higher education, language, music—to progress and improvement of the quality of life for Afro-Americans.

Numerous books concerning Afro-American leadership have sections dealing with these two differing philosophies. Earl E. Thorpe, in *The Mind of the Negro: An Intellectual History of the Afro-American* (Baton Rouge, La.: Ortlieb Press, 1961; rpt. Westport, Conn.: Negro Universities Press, 1970), devotes a well-balanced chapter to "The Washington–Du Bois Controversy." A briefer discussion is given by Thomas J. Ladenburg and William S. McFeely in *The Black Man in the Land of Equality* (New York: Hayden, 1969) in the chapter "The Great Debate." In *W. E. B. Du Bois: A Profile,* Rayford Logan devotes a generous part of his introduction to the Washington–Du Bois controversy. He also includes a selection by Basil Mathews, "The Continuing Debate." August Meier, in *Negro Thought in America, 1880–1915: Racial Ideologies in the Age of Booker T. Washington* (Ann Arbor: University of Michigan Press, 1963), devotes considerable attention to this conflict, as does Elliott Rudwick in *W. E. B. Du Bois: Propagandist of Negro Protest.* Henry Lee Moon adds his own comments on the dispute to the editorials quoted from *The Crisis* in *The Emerging Thought of W. E. B. Du Bois* (New York: Simon & Schuster, 1972). He acknowledges that "the issues were not clear-cut and unbridgeable." Tuttle has included two excerpts from Kelly Miller and John Spencer Bassett in *W. E. B. Du Bois* (Englewood Cliffs, N.J.: Prentice-Hall, 1973) which are directed at this controversy. Robert H. Brisbane has included a discussion of some aspects of the controversy in *The Black Vanguard* (Valley Forge, Pa.: Judson Press,

1970) with the chapter "The First Militants." He places much emphasis on the role of Trotter in launching the fight. Articles by Thornbrough, Meier, and Rudwick are included in *The Black Man in America Since Reconstruction,* edited by David Reimers (New York: T. Y. Crowell, 1970). Norman Coombs, in a somewhat superficial general history, *The Black Experience in America* (New York: Twayne, 1972), attempts a balanced analysis and points to the gradual change which was occurring in Washington's attitude toward the end of his life.

Herbert Aptheker examines one of the events in this running battle in an article, "The Washington and Du Bois conference of 1904" (*S&S,* Fall 1949), which was also reprinted in his books *Toward Negro Freedom* (New York: New Century Publishers, 1956) and *Afro-American History: The Modern Era* (New York: Citadel, 1971). The latter also contains a chapter called "The Niagara Movement." In the introduction to *The Seventh Son,* Julius Lester gives a strongly pro-Du Bois presentation in which he places the emphasis on their differing views of education. In addition to these illustrations, almost every general history and collection of writings on this period will contain some reference to the controversy.

The periodical literature similarly has abundant material on this topic, some of which has been reprinted in book collections. A markedly noncontroversial view was taken by Earl E. Thorpe in his article, "Frederick Douglass, W. E. B. Du Bois and Booker T. Washington" (*NHB,* November 1956). Although they are "thought of as greatly diverse personalities and types of leaders, the similarities among them are many." A similar view emphasizing similarities among the three was offered by Wesley C. Pugh in "The Inflated Controversy" (*The Crisis,* April 1974). However, Pugh's article was inconclusive and offered nothing new. Wilson Record, in "Negro Intellectuals and Negro Movements in Historical Perspective" (*AQ,* Spring 1956), took a middle-of-the-road position, finding both good and ill on each side. He also observed that there was more agreement between the disputants than they and some of their partisans recognized. A similar stance was taken by C. Spencer Poxpey in "The Washington–Du Bois Controversy and its Effect on the Negro Problem" (*History of Education Journal,* January 1957), but he emphasized the differences in personality and background. Daniel Walden examines Du Bois's position in a sympathetic manner in "The Contemporary Opposition to the Political and Educational Ideals of Booker T. Washington" (*JNH,* April 1960). An interesting sidelight on the dispute is given by Emma Lou Thornbrough in her study of "The National Afro-American League" (*JSH,* November 1961). Thornbrough concludes that the league was controlled by Washington operating behind the scenes with T. Thomas Fortune standing in the front for him. Its meetings became part of the battleground of the Du Bois–Washington conflict as partisans maneuvered. Little has been written from the perspective of the black nationalist or separatist contingents, but Nathan Hare infers in "The Battle for Black Studies" (*BlackSch,* May 1972) that both Washington and Du Bois were victims. "Burdened by the duality of racial oppression, black American education" reflected white America's educational dilemma. Probably the last word on this controversy was given by Du Bois in an interview granted to Ralph McGill in 1963 ("W. E. B. Du Bois," *AtM,* November 1965). Du Bois told McGill that "Washington bartered away much that was not his to barter." McGill reports, "There was no doubt in Du Bois's mind. He was sure, he said, that without Washington's position there would have been no Plessy-Ferguson decision in 1896." (This Supreme Court ruling upheld the constitutionality of segregation on Louisiana railroad lines and established the principle of "separate but equal" facilities.) Regarding the controversy with Washington itself, Du Bois characterized it as one that "developed more between our followers than between us."

Such controversies symbolize issues which continue to plague the American scene. Important studies on these conflicts are still waiting to be done, but a better understanding of the men and their ideas will have to come first. Any career as long, as productive, and as multifaceted as was that of Du Bois is bound to produce a large literary assemblage by and about the person. Add to this his importance to Afro-American development and the controversial nature of his varied policies and one introduces a multiplying factor. There seems literally to be no end to the materials about Du Bois in the libraries and archives of the nation. The complexity of his career is certain to produce yet more attempts to explain and analyze this "black titan." Unfortunately, this task will require a mind as eclectic, flexible, and broad in vision as that of Du Bois and possessing the literary articulateness and eloquence to reconcile scholar and polemicist, aristocratic Brahmin and proletarian advocate, black nationalist and integrationist, searcher for democratic truth and member of the Communist party. These and many more paradoxes must be reconciled but to date scholars have not accomplished this task.

Literary Criticism

PERSPECTIVES ON CRITICISM OF THE POLEMICISTS

The problem of presenting literary criticism of polemical writers is at best difficult. The old argument of art versus propaganda constantly plagues the critics. To apply criticism to Afro-American polemicists may be both risky and dubiously subjective. Critics, both black and white, appear to have had great difficulty in separating form from content. Sound criticism often floundered on the hidden rocks and reefs of subjective racial bias. Stephen Butterfield, in *Black Autobiography in America* (Amherst: University of Massachusetts Press, 1974), recognized this problem. "A critic has no choice," he wrote, "but to rely on his own biases, unless he wants to rely on the biases of others." He went on to spell out the special problem which confronts the Afro-American: "The main burden of the black writer, regardless of his class origins, has been to repair the damage inflicted on him by white racism, rend the veil of white definitions that misrepresent him to himself and the world, create a new identity. . . . It takes a certain kind of bias to appreciate such light."

Repeatedly, Afro-American writers and critics have voiced their awareness of a difference between the treatment of black writers and their white counterparts by an oppressing and belligerent white society. As early as 1913 Du Bois wrote an article on "The Negro in Literature and Art" (*Annals,* September 1913) confirming that "the Negro is primarily an artist." However, he went on to express regret that "the time has not yet come for the great development of American Negro literature. The economic stress is too great and the racial persecution too bitter to allow the leisure and the poise for which literature calls." He saw hope for the future (Du Bois was almost always an optimist): "Slowly but surely they are developing artists of technic. . . . The nation does not notice this for everything touching the Negro is banned by magazines and publishers unless it takes the form of caricature or bitter attack." Frederick Douglass similarly acknowleged that he was not pursuing writing as an art. In his *Life and Times,* he stated that writing did not come easily but was a struggle: "I write freely of myself, not from choice, but because I have, by my cause, been forced, morally forced, into thus writing."

J. Saunders Redding, in his volume of criticism, *To Make a Poet Black* (Chapel Hill: University of North Carolina Press, 1939; rpt. Washington, D.C.: McGrath Publ., 1968), acknowleged the special conditions imposed on the Afro-American writer by his social environment:

> Today no one who studies even superficially the history of the Negro in America can fail to see the uncommon relationship of his letters to that history; nor can one fail to remark that literary expression for the Negro has not been, and is not wholly now an art in the sense that the poetry and prose of another people, say the Irish, is art. Almost from the very beginning the literature of the Negro has been literature either of purpose or necessity.

This peculiar circumstance limited the materials which Benjamin Brawley felt he could use in *The Negro in Literature and Art* (New York: Duffield, 1918; rpt. New York: Dodd, Mead, 1929). He remarked that "we are here concerned with distinctly literary and artistic achievement, and not with work that belongs in the realm of religion, sociology, or politics."

A perspective similar to Brawley's was held by William Stanley Braithwaite, who expressed the view in "The Negro in Literature" (*The Crisis,* September 1924) that "the Negro as a creator in American literature is of comparatively recent importance. All that was accomplished between Phyllis Wheatley and Paul Laurence Dunbar, considered by critical standards, is negligible, and of historic interest only." He noted that "biography has given us a notable life story, told by himself, of Booker T. Washington. Frederick Douglass's story of his life is eloquent as a human document, but not in the graces of narration and psychologic portraiture which has definitely put this form of literature in the domain of the fine arts." These frequently quoted sentences are seldom balanced with other points made by Braithwaithe, who also declared: "The white writer [he might have added 'and critic'] seems to stand baffled before the enigma. . . . We shall have to look to the Negro himself to go all the way. It is quite likely that no white man can do it. It is reasonable to suppose that his white psychology will always be in his way." He implored the Afro-American writer to "reveal to us much more than what the Negro thinks" and feels. He must

> forget that there are white readers; he would have to lose self-consciousness and forget that his work would be placed before a white jury. He would have to be careless as to what the white critic might think of it; he would need the self-assurance to be his own critic. He would have to forget for the time being, at least, that any white man ever attempted to dissect the soul of a Negro.

Sterling Brown reaffirmed the defensive position of the Afro-American writer in "A Century of Negro Portraiture" (*MR,* Winter 1966), which also appeared in *Black and White in American Culture,* edited by Jules Chametzky and Sidney Kaplan (New York: Viking, 1971). Brown revealed that "an embattled people used literature as a weapon, as propaganda . . . as an exposé of injustice." He observed that Du Bois's *Souls of Black Folk* "was marked by impassioned polemics against compromise, incisive irony at hypocrisy."

This dilemma of the dual audience of the Afro-American writer and the problem it poses for the critic was echoed more recently by Addison Gayle, Jr., in the preface to an interesting anthology of "Essays by and about Black Americans in the Creative Arts" entitled *Black Expression* (New York: Weybright and Talley, 1969). While reminding us that "in much of Negro literature, the shout of racial protest is missing," he also predicts that "the Negro critic will still remain invisible. For his is the predominant voice in American criticism which calls upon the Negro writer to dedicate himself to the proposition that literature is a moral force for change as well as an aesthetic creation."

It is interesting to discover that despite the fact that Benjamin Brawley drew a distinction between works of "literary and artistic achievement" and those in the realm of politics, he included all four of the polemicists in *The Negro in Literature and Art* (New York: Duffield, 1918). This early critical work was reorganized and brought up to date as *The Negro Genius* (New York: Dodd, Mead, 1937; rpt. New York: Biblo & Tannen, 1966). It contains reviews of works by all four writers.

Vernon Loggins wrote an extensive critical work, *The Negro Author: His Development in America to 1900* (New York: Columbia University Press, 1931; rpt. Port Washington, N.Y.: Kennikat Press, 1964) which comments on all four of the polemicists. In this frequently cited source he indicates that his purpose is to make "a general survey of the field of American literature which our literary historians almost without exception have neglected." This doctoral study pays considerable attention to Douglass. However, Loggins found little of merit in Washington's writings or speeches, and only the two works by Du Bois which were written before 1900 were evaluated. It is unfortunate that Loggins did not include any works by Du Bois or any other Afro-American writer in *I Hear America* (New York: Biblo & Tannen, 1937), which studied the literature of the United States after 1900. Loggins thus gives credence to Gayle's argument that Afro-American literature "has never been considered an integral part of American literature."

It was not until 1974 that a comprehensive volume evaluating Afro-American writers from 1900 to 1960 was published. *From the Dark Tower* (Washington, D.C.: Howard University Press, 1974) was considered by its author, Arthur P. Davis, to be a sequel to Loggins's work. In his review in *Phylon* (Summer 1975), David Dorsey said that this work will "become a permanent and crucial reference point on the criticism of Afro-American literature." Davis contended that black nationalist writers tended to produce a new kind of literature and that the Afro-American critics have not yet succeeded in replacing the critical tenets of the Western literary tradition. Although a full chapter is devoted to a study of Du Bois's writing, only brief attention is given to each of his many books and journals. Unlike Robert Bone, who saw Du Bois as the "rear guard," Davis credits Du Bois with being one of "the scholars and creative artists who prepared the ground and planted the seeds of the New Negro Renaissance."

The works of Douglass and Du Bois are given ample attention in the previously mentioned *To Make a Poet Black* by J. Saunders Redding. This slim volume, one of the first works of criticism by an Afro-American, traces the work of selected Afro-American writers from the forerunners of the colonial period to the "New Negro." Douglass and Du Bois are treated as key figures illustrating the awakening of consciousness as the Negro's primary position in America progressed from abolitionist agitation to freedom and enfranchisement to social self-determination. Redding states that "no American biographies rank above Douglass' *My Bondage and My Freedom* and the first *Life and Times* in the literary qualities of simplicity, interest, and compression of style." The failure to recognize them "for what they are is attributable more to neglect than to the judgement of honest inquiry."

Two surveys done in the 1960s, David Littlejohn's *Black on White* (New York: Grossman, 1966) and Edward Margolies's *Native Sons* (Philadelphia: Lippincott, 1968), offer little of the polemicists. Margolies's comments on Du Bois are too brief and superficial to be considered as significant. Littlejohn does not believe that serious American Negro literature existed prior to 1940 and "would make no claim" for Douglass's *Life and Times* and Washington's *Up From Slavery*.

Quite different is the study of two forms of idealism in the chapter "Booker T. Washington and W. E. B. Du Bois" in *The Heroic Ideal in American Literature* (New York: Free Press, 1971) by Theodore Gross, who considers *Up From Slavery* and *The Souls of Black Folk* the "two books which inaugurate important Negro writing in America." Those two books are also the subject of chapters in other surveys of American literature. Robert B. Downs offers short summaries of them in *Famous American Books* (New York: McGraw-Hill, 1971), in which there is also biographical information on the authors but very little literary criticism. Kenneth Rexroth examined Douglass's writings in *The Elastic Retort* (New York: Seabury, 1973) and gave a short but engaging biographical sketch which argued that "Frederick Douglass was born free. His servile status was a juridical delusion of his owner." More extended discussions of the lives of Douglass and Du Bois are contained in *Landmarks of American Writing* (New York: Basic Books, 1969), edited by Hennig Cohen. "Narrative of the Life of Frederick Douglass" a chapter by Benjamin Quarles, is more properly a discussion of the book and its influence with some biographical insights. Everett S. Lee's chapter on "W. E. B. Du Bois: *The Souls of Black Folk*" is mainly biographical. He admits, "It is hard to be fair to W. E. B. Du Bois." He found little to praise but much to criticize in his heavily negative writing. Additional commentary can be found in: Arna Bontemps's "The Negro Contribution to American Letters" in *The American Negro Reference Book* (Englewood Cliffs, N.J.: Prentice-Hall, 1966), edited by John P. Davis; Sterling Brown's "A Century of Negro Portraiture" and J. Saunders Redding's "The Problems of the Negro Writer," both in *Black and White in American Culture* (New York: Viking, 1971), edited by Jules Chametzky and Sidney Kaplan; E. Wright's "*Souls of Black Folk* and My Larger Education" (*JNE*, Fall 1961); and Jerold J. Savory's "The Rending of the Veil in W. E. B. Du Bois's *The Souls of Black Folk*" (*CLAJ*, March 1972). The introductions to the various editions of the autobiographies and *Souls of Black Folk* also contain commentary which should be consulted.

Brief discussion can be found in various anthologies of Afro-American literature. One of the earliest was *The Negro Caravan* (New York:

Dryden Press, 1941; rpt. New York: Arno Press, 1969) edited by Sterling A. Brown, Arthur P. Davis, and Ulysses Lee. It is one of the few which gives a selection from "The Heroic Slave," a fictional work by Frederick Douglass. It also gives some attention to the speeches and other minor writings of the polemicists. Additional selections and commentary are given in Benjamin Brawley's *Early Negro American Writers* (Chapel Hill: University of North Carolina Press, 1935); *Dark Symphony* (New York: The Free Press, 1968), edited by James A. Emanuel and Theodore Gross; *Black Writers of America* (New York: Macmillan, 1972), edited by Richard Barksdale and Keneth Kinnamon; *Afro-American Writing*, edited by Richard A. Long and Eugenia W. Collier (New York: New York University Press, 1972); and *Black Literature in America* (New York: McGraw-Hill, 1971), edited by Houston A. Baker, Jr.

The most significant work of literary criticism on Afro-American writing uses the works and lives of Walker, Douglass, Washington, and Du Bois as the basis for understanding the whole field of Afro-American literature. Houston A. Baker, Jr., contends in *Long Black Song* (Charlottesville: University Press of Virginia, 1972) that "Black America . . . possesses a true culture—a whole way of life that includes its own standards of moral and aesthetic achievement." In order to understand the culture and the aesthetic works it produces, one must understand the history which is identified by Baker as "the primary factor." We will find then "that both Frederick Douglass and David Walker produced works which expressed the spirit of their age [and] which transcend the limitations and hazards of time." He offers one of the most penetrating analyses of Walker's *Appeal.* Entire chapters are devoted to Walker, Douglass, Washington, and Du Bois to illustrate the common black experience which undergirds all Afro-American writing. He stresses the oral, collectivistic, and repudiative features of the literature and further contends that combining recognition of these distinctive characteristics with an understanding of "the prime motivating forces" in the lives of men like Walker, Douglass, Washington, and Du Bois will be "more rewarding than a struggle to force both the literature and the culture into preexisting molds that were not designed to contain them."

CRITICISM OF ORATIONS AND RHETORIC

Criticism of oratorical achievements of the polemicists is scant and varied. Most of the available material concentrates more on the philosophical and political content than on the oratorical style, structure, and form. In addition, much of the criticism is limited to commentary accompanying collections of orations. Such anthologies, with speeches by Douglass, Washington, or Du Bois, range from one of the earliest collections, edited by Alice Moore Dunbar, *Masterpieces of Negro Eloquence,* (New York: Bookery Publishers, 1914; rpt. New York: Johnson

Reprint, 1970), which has no commentary, to Arthur L. Smith's *The Rhetoric of Black Revolution* (Boston: Allyn & Bacon, 1969), which includes several chapters discussing revolutionary rhetoric along with one chapter of speeches.

Carter G. Woodson's volume, *Negro Orators and Their Orations* (Washington, D. C.: Associated Publishers, 1925), is still one of the basic references and includes several orations by Douglass and Washington with appropriate commentary on each. Woodson discusses the nature of oratory and its importance in the history of the Afro-American. He considers oratory a special art form and quite different from written literature. "Few speeches," he says, "can bear the colorless photography of a printed record." He finds that the orator "is essentially a partisan. His aims are conviction and persuasion." Roy L. Hill, in *The Rhetoric of Racial Revolt* (Denver, Colo.: Golden Bell Press, 1964), includes some discussion of the oratory of Douglass and Washington. However, despite the impression given by the title, his work is mainly a collection of speeches. Ernest G. Bormann's *Forerunners of Black Power* (Englewood Cliffs, N.J.: Prentice-Hall, 1971) is also basically an anthology with brief comment on Douglass.

Several writers have not attempted to separate the discussion of oratory from other literary achievements of Afro-American writers. At the same time they have not confined themselves to offering an anthology of speeches and writings; rather, they have given extended discussions of the nature of those works. Notable among these is Arthur L. Smith's *The Rhetoric of Black Revolution,* cited previously, which is primarily an analysis of "the origins, context, strategies, topics, and audience of the rhetoric of black revolution." Smith contends that "the authentic rhetoric of black America has always been militant and revolutionary." For him David Walker was the true revolutionary, while Douglass "believed strongly in reform." Du Bois became "the most productive source for the secular themes in the rhetoric of black revolution."

A similar structure and approach has been used by James L. Golden and Richard D. Rieke in *The Rhetoric of Black Americans* (Columbus, Ohio: Merrill, 1971). They have devoted an extended introductory chapter to analysis and criticism of black rhetoric in which they, too, recognize the burden that circumstances have placed on Afro-American writers, noting that " . . . black Americans from the colonial period to the present have been confronted with a rhetorical situation that demanded a meaningful response." They have also provided significant analytical commentary as an introduction to each group of documents and have concluded that "the rhetoric of black Americans cannot be viewed as simply a part of American oratory."

It should be noted that Benjamin Brawley devoted a chapter to the oratory of Douglass and Washington in *The Negro in Literature and Art*

(New York: Duffield, 1929). He observes that "the Negro is peculiarly gifted as an orator. To magnificent gifts of voice he adds a fervor of sentiment." Even more outstanding "is the romantic quality that finds an outlet in vast reaches of imagery and a singularly figurative power of expression." Brawley draws a sharp distinction between Douglass the "subjective" orator, and Washington, the "objective," polished public speaker.

One of the most penetrating studies of oratory is the chapter entitled "Booker T. Washington" by Karl R. Wallace in *A History and Criticism of American Public Address,* Vol. 1 (New York: McGraw-Hill, 1943; rpt. New York: Russell and Russell, 1960), edited by William N. Brigance. He attributes Washington's great success to his skill as an orator, calling him a consummately persuasive speaker. Wallace notes Washington's "sincerity" and "simplicity" of both statement and style and his endeavor to please his audience by systematically finding out "what a particular audience wanted to know."

By far the most comprehensive study of oratory is Marcus H. Bouleware's *The Oratory of Negro Leaders 1900–1968* (Westport, Conn.: Negro Universities Press, 1969). This work is especially helpful as it brings together commentary from many secondary sources. Bouleware devotes considerable attention to Washington's skill as a public speaker who "studied every detail and weighed every word" in order to make the impression he desired. The description of Du Bois contrasts greatly with the homey style and appearance of Washington. "The tone of the voice of Du Bois was that of an articulate scholar. . . . His platform posture was dignified, his diction perfect and clear, but he lacked the forceful emotional delivery demanded of an orator." Although Bouleware's book is seriously marred by the absence of citations for some of his sources and ideas, he has given a commendable history of Afro-American oratory in the twentieth century. He acknowledges in his preface that his is not a strict rhetorical criticism of Negro public speaking.

CRITICISM OF AUTOBIOGRAPHIES

Autobiography is one of the most important means of establishing the place in history of three of the four polemicists. It is, therefore, to their autobiographical works that most students turn for an understanding of these men's writings.

In *Witness for Freedom* (New York: Harper & Bros., 1948), Rebecca Chalmers Barton makes a unique study of twenty-three autobiographies, including *Life and Times of Frederick Douglass, Up From Slavery,* and *Dusk of Dawn.* She examines not only the role of Afro-American writers but their personalities as well. Alain Locke contends in the foreword that she presents a "composite and accordingly more balanced and representative picture of Negro life experience." He states that she demolishes the commonplace stereotypes of Afro-American writers. Although the author's purpose was not primarily criticism, the study does provide insight into the techniques and effectiveness of the autobiographies.

The most extensive exploration of the autobiographical form as expressed by the polemicists is offered by Stephen Butterfield in *Black Autobiography in America* (Amherst, Mass.: University of Massachusetts Press, 1974). He views autobiography as a problem of identity. "This identity crisis occurs most acutely in W. E. B. Du Bois. . . . It was W. E. B. Du Bois who gave the most conscious, explicit statement, in autobiographical form, of the struggle to unite and harmonize the pieces of the divided self." He devotes a full chapter to Douglass and states that "it was Frederick Douglass, among all the slave narrators, who made the best use of his materials, who mastered and assimilated the rhetoric of the literary mainstream, stamped it with his personality and experience, and most ably turned it to whatever purpose he chose." There is considerable literary discussion of Washington and Du Bois throughout this excellent book.

There are a number of articles concerning autobiography in which critics have explored the work of individual polemecists; this offers an opportunity for greater study of each of the works. Nancy Clasby's "Frederick Douglass's *Narrative:* A Content Analysis" (*CLAJ*, March 1971) is as much concerned with psychological as literary and structural analysis. She found the book "unexcelled in clarity and controlled intensity of passion." Another interesting study is William W. Nichols's "Individualism and Autobiographical Art: Frederick Douglass and Henry Thoreau" (*CLAJ*, December 1972). Nichols went beyond an analysis of *Walden* and *My Bondage* to face the compelling question of why his training in American literature during the 1960s assumed the importance of *Walden* and ignored the existence of *My Bondage*.

CRITICISM OF DU BOIS'S WORKS OF FICTION

Du Bois was the only one of the polemicists to write any fiction. One of the earliest critics to study his work in this genre exclusively was Hugh M. Gloster, who provided insight into black writers in *Negro Voices in American Fiction* (Chapel Hill, N.C.: University of North Carolina Press, 1948; rpt. New York: Russell and Russell, 1965). He recognized that "Negro fictionists . . . undertook to provide literary defense for their people." They "were the public prosecutors of racism." He discussed at some length Du Bois's *The Quest of the Silver Fleece* and *Dark Princess*.

Ten years later Robert Bone published *The Negro Novel in America* (New Haven: Yale University Press, 1958). In an almost entirely negative view of Du Bois and other most highly respected Afro-American writers and leaders, he notes that " unfortunately, his [Du Bois's] social and economic insights far surpassed his artistic powers." Like Francis L. Broderick he asks, "What sort of empathy could this young intellectual feel for the black masses . . . ?" It is fitting then that Bone should see Du Bois as the "conservative faction" during the period in the 1920s known as the Harlem Renaissance. According to Bone, Du Bois was of the rear guard, one of those who lagged behind.

Two articles that deal effectively with Du Bois's fictional writings are Richard Kostalanetz's "Fictions for a Negro Politics: The Neglected Novels of W. E. B. Du Bois" (*XUS*, vol. 7, no. 2, 1968), and Arlene A. Elder's "Swamp Versus Plantation: Symbolic Structure in W. E. B. Du Bois' *The Quest of the Silver Fleece*" (*Phylon*, Winter 1973). Kostelanetz observed that "as a writer, Du Bois has mastered the gamut of expository forms from academic essay to polemic to poetic prose-pieces." He gives extensive consideration to all of Du Bois's fictional writings and finds that *Black Flame* is, in some ways, superior to its predecessors— " . . . the trilogy achieves a polemical effectiveness absent from Du Bois' earlier fiction." The symbolism in Du Bois's first novel is given lengthy analysis by Elder. She finds that Du Bois "achieves unity of plot and statement through a carefully constructed framework of contrasting symbols" and that the "symbolic structure is his attempt at an artistically effective framework for presenting his convictions about social, political, and economic tensions, North and South, black and white."

As in the case of fiction, Du Bois produced the only poetry to become the subject of literary criticism. Jean-Paul Sartre, in his essay "Black Orpheus" in *The Black American Writer, Volume II: Poetry and Drama* (Deland, Fla.: Everett/Edwards, 1969), edited by C. W. E. Bigsby, spotlights the role of poetry for the Afro-American. He states, "It is necessarily through a poetic experience that the black man, in his present condition, must first become conscious of himself." It seems appropriate then, that critical emphasis concentrates on Du Bois's *Darkwater*, which included his most frequently reprinted work, "A Litany at Atlanta," along with five other poems. Jean Wagner, in *Black Poets of the United States* (Urbana: University of Illinois Press, 1973), originally published as *Les Poèts Nègres des Etats Unis* (Paris: Libraire Istra, 1963), noted that "the new Negro poetry was first manifested by W. E. B. Du Bois . . . in 'A Litany at Atlanta.' " He further observed that "externally, his poems are sometimes reminiscent of the poetic prose of the biblical line, but his too-numerous alliterations and his addiction to grandiloquence often lead him far from the sober style of the Holy Writ." Sterling Brown, in *Negro Poetry and Drama* (Washington, D. C.: Associates in Negro Folk Education, 1937; rpt. as *Negro Poetry and Drama and The Negro in American Fiction* [New York: Atheneum, 1969]), had previously struck the same chord, commenting that Du Bois "often affects alliteration to the extreme . . . and generally uses a rhapsodic free verse, more akin to the Bible than to Whitman." All of these comments predate the publication of Du Bois's *Selected Poems* and therefore fail to comment upon his range of theme and style. Interestingly, Kwame Nkrumah, in the foreword to *Selected Poems*, refers to Du Bois as a "sensitive fighter-poet." Shirley Graham (Du Bois), in the exposition, reminds us that "his poems . . . were not written as lyrical entities but . . . as passionate outcries, . . ." and thus his poetry was another form of expression for a fervent polemicist.

CRITICISM OF JOURNALISM AND ESSAYS

The press has long been one of the most effective media for the dissemination of the rhetoric of polemicists. It was probably more far-reaching than their oratory and books combined. As has been noted, Douglass published his own newspapers for many years and his speeches and statements appeared widely in papers and periodicals throughout the years. Du Bois edited his own journals, which were the main vehicle for his views. Washington had either part ownership or great influence in many newspapers which regularly published his "news" releases. In spite of this volume of published materials, there is practically no mention of any of it in the critical literature. There remains the need for a careful and scholarly study of the polemical press, its quality and its influence.

The essays of Douglass, Washington, and Du Bois have been published in national periodical and scholarly journals as well as in pamphlet form. In spite of their abundance and significance, no critic has undertaken a study of them as a genre. These two needs remain, in addition to the need for an in-depth study of these writers who were also preeminent leaders in the Afro-American community.

CONCLUSION

The field of criticism is at best subjective. The difficulty of value-laden judgment when literary criticism crosses cultural and racial lines has been stressed by many critics. The malevolent effect has been particularly noted by Afro-American writers and critics. Du Bois delivered an address at the NAACP annual convention in Chicago on "Criteria of Negro Art" which was later published in *The Crisis* (October 1926). After describing the conditions which confronted the Afro-American and the state of his art, he declared:

> Thus all Art is propaganda and ever must be, despite the wailing of the purists. I stand in utter shamelessness and say that whatever art I have for writing has been used always for propaganda and gaining the right of black

folk to love and enjoy. I do not care a damn for any art that is not used for propaganda.

It would seem that such a dedication would require different criteria from those that were developed for and suited to the needs of Euro-centric writers. There is a need for criteria suited to the requirements of oppressed minorities wherever their literature may be found.

I wish to acknowledge the assistance and encouragement that my wife, Joyce Turner, has given toward the completion of this essay.

MODERN BEGINNINGS:
William Wells Brown, Charles Waddell Chesnutt, Martin R. Delany, Paul Laurence Dunbar, Sutton E. Griggs, Frances Ellen Watkins Harper, and Frank J. Webb

RUTH MILLER
PETER J. KATOPES

Early American authors generally limited themselves to writing with a rhetorical purpose—promotion tracts, community histories, sermons, biographies and autobiographies, or didactic poems. Black writers were well acquainted with these forms, and when they combined this awareness with their familiarity with the slave narrative and the Afro-American oral tradition, they created a medium out of which a distinctively black fiction easily emerged.

The transition made by black authors from nonfiction to fiction is easy to explore—the slave narrative was transformed into fiction in the work of William Wells Brown. His slave narrative was published in 1847 under the title *Narrative of William Wells Brown*. Encouraged by its success, he expanded it in 1848 and again in 1849. Then he simply borrowed freely from himself, bringing into existence *Clotel,* the first work of black American fiction.

Brown, however, did not invent a new form: rather, he provided the model for the transition from the slave narrative to early black fiction. Black American novelists developed a tradition of constructing suspenseful plots with didactic themes, creating stereotyped characters, and furnishing realistic descriptions. They were also known for their use of anecdotes, dialogue, personal experience, a variety of emotions, and mingled writing styles, all of which had been experimented with in the slave narratives and were now crystallized in fiction. Novels written by black writers in the nineteenth century came out of this tradition, and continuing practice and further experimentation in the mode culminated in the Harlem Renaissance of the 1920s.

Bibliographies

There are several general and individual bibliographies that concentrate on this phase of black American literature.

GENERAL BIBLIOGRAPHIES

Monroe N. Work's massive compilation, *A Bibliography of the Negro in Africa and America* (New York: Wilson, 1928; rpt. New York: Octagon, 1965, 1970), contains references to almost every aspect of Negro life from ancient times to about 1928. Work's listings include several early black novelists; however, there are at least two glaring omissions: Martin R. Delany's *Blake, or the Huts of America* (*Anglo-African Magazine*, 1 [1859]; rpt. Boston: Beacon, 1970) and Frank Webb's *The Garies and Their Friends* (London: Routledge, 1857). Work's practice of identifying the race of a particular author is especially useful.

Maxwell Whiteman's valuable *A Century of Fiction by American Negroes; 1853–1952: A Descriptive Bibliography* (Philadelphia: Albert Saifer, 1955; rpt. 1969) lists all books and complete stories that appeared in anthologies or in pamphlet form, or in magazine issues if they contained a complete novel. Reprint information is not included except where textual differences have been noted, titles changed, or introductions added. However, significant variant texts are mentioned. Entries are chronological and the original publisher is noted, indicating whether the firm was an established one, or whether the volume was the result of a private printing. Appended to this is the racial identification of the publishing house. Helpful also are Whiteman's brief synopses of the works of fiction, and his mention of significant historical and critical studies. This compilation includes entries on Brown, Chesnutt, Dunbar, Delany, Griggs, Harper, Webb, and others.

Also useful, although its emphasis is on the twentieth century, is Darwin T. Turner's *Afro-American Writers* (New York: Appleton, 1970). Turner's entries are based on each author's current critical reputation or popular status, or on the historical or stylistic significance of a particular work. The bibliography offers a representative listing of several early black American writers, but there is no mention of Martin R. Delany. Also excluded are anthologies and scholarly works that Turner feels are not particularly significant because they lack what he considers an appropriately black cultural perspective. However, his compilation covers drama, fiction, and poetry, and includes guides to related topics such as history, sociology, art, music, journalism, and folklore. Helpful are his "aids to research," which note significant bibliographies, collections, and periodicals. Of particular value is Turner's listing of articles in popular magazines and in encyclopedias, two important but overlooked sources of information about black Americans and their works.

Another significant compilation is Robert A. Corrigan's "Afro-American Fiction: A Checklist, 1853–1970" (*MASJ*, Fall 1970). Corrigan attempts to identify all works of fiction by Afro-Americans published in book form. Each entry includes author, title, original publisher, place and date of publication, pagination, and reprint information about both soft- and hard-cover editions. This checklist supercedes Corrigan's "A Bibliography of Afro-American Fiction, 1853–1970" (*SBL*, Summer 1970), and is itself augmented by his "Afro-American Fiction: Errata and Additions" (*AmerS*, Spring 1971).

Somewhat helpful, although marred by several errors, is *Black American Writers Past and Present: A Biographical and Bibliographical Dictionary* (Metuchen, N.J.: Scarecrow, 1975), compiled by Theressa Gunnels Rush, Carol Fairbanks Myers, and Esther Spring Arata. It offers unannotated listings of an author's works, as well as short biographical notes. Most of the articles cited have appeared in magazines devoted to black authors. Because these journals are not usually indexed in conventional bibliographies, such as the *MLA International Bibliography,* this feature is extremely valuable. The compilers also have noted the specific page in a work on which an author is mentioned, greatly aiding students who seek material on lesser-known authors.

Black American Writers, 1773–1949: A Bibliography and Union List (Boston: G. K. Hall, 1975), compiled by Geraldine O. Matthews and the African-American Material Project Staff, offers a representative listing of works by early black American writers, but it does not deal comprehensively with any one author. When possible, library locations of works have been noted.

Useful also is *The Negro Almanac* (New York: The Bellwether Co., 1971), edited and compiled by Harry A. Ploski and Ernest Kaiser, which offers short biographies and bibliographies of writers who spearheaded the modern movement in black American letters.

Robert Bone's *The Negro Novel in America* (New Haven, Conn.: Yale University Press, 1965) contains an unannotated bibliography of works by American Negroes. In order to sidestep possible semantic controversy, Bone defines a "Negro novel" as one written by a Negro, "regardless of subject matter." The entries are chronological by date of publication and include works by most early black American authors.

Vernon Loggins's bibliography in *The Negro Author: His Development in America* (New York: Columbia University Press, 1931; rpt. Port Washington, N.Y.: Kennikat Press, 1969) lists works according to both genre and period. Included are the works of Brown, Chesnutt, Delany, Dunbar, Harper, and Webb, in the categories of fiction, poetry, and nonfiction. The main problem with Loggins's compilation, despite its comprehensiveness, is that its organization may cause inexperienced researchers some difficulty unless they know in what category to search for a particular work. For example, the novelist Frank Webb is listed under "Miscellaneous" for the period 1840–1865.

BIBLIOGRAPHIES OF INDIVIDUAL AUTHORS

William Wells Brown   The most comprehensive bibliography on William Wells Brown is in W. Edward Farrison's *William Wells Brown, Author and Reformer* (Chicago: University of Chicago Press, 1969). Farrison offers a complete listing of Brown's published works, including dates of subsequent editions and locations of rare items. He also cites several secondary works relating to slavery, a number of articles on Brown, and the names of newspapers that Farrison found useful for his own research. His brief listing of manuscripts and miscellaneous collections offers the student further resources for study.

Charles Waddell Chesnutt   The most complete listing of Charles Waddell Chesnutt's published work is "The Works of Charles W. Chesnutt: A Checklist" (*BB*, January 1976) by William L. Andrews. Particularly useful also is Andrews's "Charles Waddell Chesnutt: An Essay in Bibliography" (*RALS*, Spring 1976). *A List of Manuscripts, Published Works and Related Items in the Charles Waddell Chesnutt Collection of the Erastus Milo Cravath Memorial Library, Fisk University* (Nashville, Tenn.: Fisk University, 1954) by Mildred Freeny and Mary T. Henry is of some value despite its incompleteness and often incorrect publication data.

Another useful listing is Joan Cunningham's "Secondary Studies on the Fiction of Charles W. Chesnutt" (*BB*, January 1976) which supercedes Dean Keller's bibliographical essay on Chesnutt (*ALR*, Summer 1968). Less comprehensive is "Black Fiction at the Turn of the Century: Charles Waddell Chesnutt and Paul Laurence Dunbar," a brief bibliographical essay which appears in *Blacks in America: Bibliographical Essays* (Garden City, N.Y.: Doubleday, 1971) by James M. McPherson et. al.

Good bibliographical introductions to the basic materials for the study of Chesnutt are the checklist by Julian D. Mason, Jr., in Louis D. Rubin's *Bibliographical Guide to the Study of Southern Literature* (Baton Rouge: Louisiana State University Press, 1969), the listing in *Black Writers of America: A Comprehensive Anthology* (New York: Macmillan, 1972) by Richard Barksdale and Keneth Kinnamon, and *Charles W. Chesnutt: A Reference*

Guide (Boston: G. K. Hall, 1977), edited by Curtis W. Ellison and E. W. Metcalf, Jr. Darwin T. Turner's listing on Chesnutt in his *Afro-American Writers* (New York: Appleton, 1970), besides being a good introductory bibliography, also lists articles on Chesnutt in popular magazines not usually included in major academic listings. A good critical assessment of the six dissertations written on Chesnutt has been done by Elisabeth Muhlenfeld and is included in Noel Polk's "Guide to Dissertations on American Literary Figures, 1870–1910: Part One" (*ALR,* Summer 1975).

Paul Laurence Dunbar Because of his prolific output of both poetry and prose, Paul Laurence Dunbar has been the subject of several bibliographies. Jacob Blanck's *Bibliography of American Literature* (New Haven, Conn.: Yale University Press, 1957) includes a complete listing of Dunbar's published works, as well as several significant secondary items. A very useful bibliography is in Virginia Cunningham's biography, *Paul Laurence Dunbar and His Song* (New York: Dodd, Mead, 1947; rpt. New York: Biblo & Tannen, 1969). Cunningham lists Dunbar's books of poetry and prose in order of appearance and includes references to reprints. Cited also are his nonfiction works, fiction published in other than book form, dramatic sketches and musical shows to which he contributed, and song lyrics by him that did not appear in the musical shows. Added to this is a listing of secondary sources, as well as references to newspaper and magazine articles and reviews of Dunbar's works.

A more recent contribution is *Paul Laurence Dunbar: A Bibliography* (Metuchen, N.J.: Scarecrow, 1975), by E. W. Metcalf, Jr. Metcalf divided the material into three sections: works by Dunbar, works about him, and microfilm collections of material by him. Unfortunately, this compilation is not as good as it might have been had a bit more care been taken with it. The listing is enumerative rather than annotative, and it is weakened by a severely inadequate index, which includes only proper names and the titles of Dunbar's books. Missing are references to publishers, and titles of short stories, individual poems and songs, and newspapers and magazines.

Also of use are the listings appended to *The Paul Laurence Dunbar Reader: A Selection of the Best of Paul Laurence Dunbar's Poetry and Prose, Including Writings Never Before Available in Book Form* (New York: Dodd, Mead, 1975), edited by Jay Martin and Gossie H. Hudson. The editors include a checklist of books by Dunbar from 1893 to 1906, citing subsequent editions during that period, and a short but helpful selected bibliography with brief annotations. Useful also, although by no means comprehensive, is "Black Fiction at the Turn of the Century: Charles Waddell Chesnutt and Paul Laurence Dunbar," mentioned earlier, in *Blacks in America: Bibliographical Essays* by McPherson et al.

Jean Wagner's *Black Poets of the United States: From Paul Laurence Dunbar to Langston Hughes,* translated by Kenneth Douglas (Urbana: University of Illinois Press, 1973) includes a bibliography that lists several secondary works relating to Dunbar and his contemporaries, gives a brief checklist of his books of poems, and includes a bibliographical supplement by Keneth Kinnamon.

Editions

The recent renewal of interest in black literature has encouraged a number of reprint editions, both soft- and hard-cover, of the works of many early black authors.

WILLIAM WELLS BROWN

William Wells Brown's *The Black Man: His Antecedents, His Genius, and His Achievements* (1863) was reprinted in 1969 by Arno Press and the Johnson Reprint Company, both of New York.

An excellent edition of *Clotel; or the President's Daughter: A Narrative of Slave Life in the United States* (1853), is that introduced and edited by William Edward Farrison (New York: Citadel, 1969). This edition reprints the original London version of Brown's seminal black American novel, and includes *The Narrative of the Life and Escape of William Wells Brown.* A good paperback edition is *Clotel; or, the President's Daughter: A Narrative of Slave Life in the United States,* with an introduction by Arthur P. Davis (New York: Collier Books, 1970). J. Noel Heermance's *William Wells Brown and Clotelle: A Portrait of the Artist in the First Negro Novel* (Hamden, Conn.: Archon, 1969) contains a facsimile reprint of the 1864 edition of *Clotelle: A Tale of the Southern States,* published in Boston by James Redpath. Heermance's long critical introduction (almost two hundred pages) gives some biographical data, offers an excellent discussion of the slave narrative as a genre, and analyzes *Clotelle* and Brown's *Narrative,* although the text of *Narrative* is not included. Of interest here is Farrison's searing review of the Heermance edition, entitled "One Ephemera After Another" (*CLAJ,* December 1969).

CHARLES WADDELL CHESNUTT

Chesnutt's five books of fiction have been made available by Gregg Press of Boston. *The Wife of His Youth"* (1899) was reprinted in 1968; *The Conjure Woman* (1899) and *The Marrow of Tradition* (1901) were reprinted in 1969. The University of Michigan Press has published paperback editions, with short introductions, of the following: in 1969, *The Conjure Woman* and *The Marrow of Tradition;* in 1968, *The Wife of His Youth.* Darwin T. Turner introduces Collier-Macmillan's 1969 reprint of *The House Behind the Cedars* (1900). In 1969 Mnemosyne (Coral

Gables, Florida) produced a facsimile edition of *The Colonel's Dream* (1905). The Johnson Reprint Company reprinted Chesnutt's *Frederick Douglass* (1899) in 1970. Chesnutt's conjure stories have been edited by Ray A. Shepard and published in standard English for younger readers in his *Conjure Tales of Charles W. Chesnutt* (New York: Dutton, 1973).

Sylvia Lyons Render's *The Short Fiction of Charles W. Chesnutt* (Washington, D.C.: Howard University Press, 1974) collects Chesnutt's magazine fiction and other individual stories. A significant review of this edition, noting bibliographical and editorial problems, is by William L. Andrews (*MissQ*, Fall 1975). "Baxter's Procrustes," a short story by Chesnutt, was reprinted in 1966 by the Rowfant Club of Cleveland, Ohio, and contains a biographical introduction by John B. Nicholson, Jr.

MARTIN R. DELANY

In 1970 *Blake, or the Huts of America* by Martin R. Delany (1859) was reprinted, with an introduction by Floyd J. Miller, by Beacon Press of Boston. There is a review by Julianne Malveau of this edition in *Black Scholar* (July–August 1973). In 1969 Arno Press reprinted Delany's *The Conditions, Elevation, Emigration, and Destiny of the Colored People of the United States, Politically Considered* (1852).

PAUL LAURENCE DUNBAR

Because of their enduring popularity, the works of Paul Laurence Dunbar have merited several reprint editions. *Candle-Lightin' Time* (1901) was reprinted in 1969 by Mnemosyne, and in 1972 by AMS Press of New York. *The Complete Poems of Paul Laurence Dunbar* was published by Dodd, Mead in 1913 and includes the introduction to *Lyrics of Lowly Life* by William Dean Howells, as does the "Complete Poetry" section of Lida Keck Wiggins's *The Life and Works of Paul Laurence Dunbar* (Naperville, Ill: J. L. Nichols, 1970). *The Fanatics* (1901) was reprinted by Negro Universities Press of Westport, Connecticut, and Mnemosyne, both in 1969. *Folks From Dixie* (1898) was reprinted in 1968 by Gregg Press and in 1969 by Books for Libraries of Plainview, New York, Negro Universities Press, and Mnemosyne. *The Heart of Happy Hollow* (1904) was reprinted in 1969 by Mnemosyne and Negro Universities Press and in 1970 by Books for Libraries. *Howdy, Honey, Howdy* (1905) was reprinted in 1969 by Mnemosyne and in 1972 by AMS Press. In 1969 Negro Universities Press reprinted *In Old Plantation Days* (1903), Mnemosyne reprinted *Joggin' Erlong* (1906), and Mnemosyne and Negro Universities Press reprinted *The Love of Landry* (1900). *Lyrics of Lowly Life* (1896) was issued in 1968 by Gregg Press, in 1969 by Mnemosyne, and in 1972 by AMS Press. (The 1899 edition of *Lyrics of Lowly Life* was reprinted in 1969 by Arno Press.) *Lyrics of the Hearthside* (1899) and *Lyrics of Sunshine and Shadow* (1905) were both issued in 1969 by Mnemosyne and in 1972 by AMS Press. *Majors and Minors: Poems* (1895) was reprinted in 1969 by Mnemosyne. In 1969 and 1972 AMS Press reprinted *Poems of Cabin and Field* (1899), and in 1975 it reprinted *Speakin' O' Christmas and Other Christmas and Special Poems* (1914). *The Sport of the Gods* (1902) was offered in 1969 by both Mnemosyne and Arno Press, and in 1970 by Collier-Macmillan. In 1969 both Arno Press and Mnemosyne reprinted *The Strength of Gideon and Other Stories* (1900). *The Uncalled* (1898) was issued in 1969 by Mnemosyne and Negro Universities Press and in 1972 by AMS Press. *When Malindy Sings* (1903) was reprinted in 1969 by Mnemosyne and in 1972 by AMS Press.

Of particular value is *The Paul Laurence Dunbar Reader,* edited by Jay Martin and Gossie H. Hudson, mentioned earlier. This anthology includes over one hundred sixty separate essays, short stories, and poems, as well as a substantial selection from *The Sport of the Gods.* More than one-third of these pieces have been taken directly from Dunbar's manuscripts and appear here for the first time. Included are eighteen poems which appeared in Dunbar's early volumes, but were not included in the *Complete Poems.* There is a general introduction by the editors which offers biographical data on Dunbar, as well as a chronology of important dates. The material within each section—both published and unpublished works—is arranged in a single chronological format and preceding each section there is a short introductory note.

OTHER WRITERS

The works of Sutton E. Griggs have also enjoyed a reprint revival. *The Hindered Hand* (1905) was reprinted in 1969 by AMS Press and Mnemosyne. *Imperium in Imperio* (1899) was reprinted in 1969 by Arno Press and Mnemosyne and in 1975 by AMS Press. *Pointing The Way* (1908) and *Unfettered* (1902) were reprinted in 1974 and 1971, respectively, by AMS Press. *Wisdom's Call* (1909) was issued in 1969 by Mnemosyne.

Frances Ellen Watkins Harper is represented by reprints of *Atlanta Offerings: Poems* (1895) by Mnemosyne (1969); *Idylls of the Bible* by AMS Press (1975); *Iola Leroy; or, Shadows Uplifted* (1893) by AMS Press (1971); *Poems* (1871) by AMS Press (1975). *The Poems of Frances E. W. Harper* was published by Books For Libraries in 1970.

Frank J. Webb's novel *The Garies and Their Friends* (1857) has been reprinted by Arno Press, and includes the original introduction by Harriet Beecher Stowe.

Manuscripts and Letters

Original manuscripts of nineteenth-century black American authors— with the notable exceptions of Chesnutt and Dunbar—are difficult to find; however, original published editions are generally accessible. The following dictionary catalogues of major collections of Negro literature, all published by G. K. Hall of Boston, should be consulted to determine holdings: *The Dictionary Catalog of the Schomburg Collection of Negro Literature and History, the New York Public Library* (1962), with two supplements (1967 and 1972); *The Dictionary Catalog of the Jesse E. Moorland Collection of Negro Life and History, Howard University Libraries, Washington, D.C.* (1970); *The Dictionary Catalog of the Arthur B. Spingarn Collection of Negro Authors, Howard University Library, Washington, D.C.* (1970); and *The Dictionary Catalog of the Negro Collection of the Fisk University Library, Nashville, Tennessee* (1973). Particularly useful in locating the letters of these authors is Walter Schatz's *Directory of Afro-American Resources* (New York: Bowker, 1970). The student should be cautioned, however, that although this directory is generally reliable, it does contain several inaccurate and misleading entries.

CHARLES WADDELL CHESNUTT

The Charles Waddell Chesnutt Collection of the Fisk University Library (Nashville, Tennessee) is the single most important repository of Chesnutt's manuscripts and letters. *A List of Manuscripts* by Freeny and Henry, mentioned earlier, provides titles, dates, and occasional descriptive comments about the holdings. Freeny and Henry also identify the letters in the collection. Helen M. Chesnutt's biography of her father, *Charles Waddell Chesnutt, Pioneer of the Color Line* (Chapel Hill: University of North Carolina Press, 1952) includes edited versions of several letters held by Fisk, as well as numerous letters which are not part of the Fisk collection. An important critical study of the editing of Chesnutt's private papers in this biography is William L. Andrews's "A Reconsideration of *Charles Waddell Chesnutt, Pioneer of the Color Line*" (*CLAJ*, December 1975).

In addition to the holdings at Fisk, Chesnutt's papers may be found at the Western Reserve Historical Society Library in Cleveland, Ohio. The letters at this library cover primarily the final fifteen years of Chesnutt's life, and the manuscripts here are mainly fragmentary versions of those in the Fisk collection. Chesnutt material is located also at Harvard University's Houghton Library, the Library of Congress, the Beinecke Rare Book and Manuscript Library at Yale University, the Tennessee State Library and Archives, the Chatauqua County Historical Society (Chatauqua, N.Y.), the Atlanta University Archives, the Rutherford B. Hayes Library (Fremont, Ohio), the Moorland-Spingarn Research Center at Howard University (Washington, D.C.), and the Schomburg Collection of the New York Public Library.

PAUL LAURENCE DUNBAR

The largest repository of the papers of Paul Laurence Dunbar is the Ohio Historical Society in Columbus. The collection includes a number of Dunbar's prose and poetry manuscripts, as well as several manuscripts of his song lyrics. The collection has been microfilmed and is available for purchase or loan from the Society, as is an inventory of the collection.

The Schomburg Collection of the New York Public Library possesses approximately one hundred letters from Dunbar and his wife to their literary agent, Paul R. Reynolds. Other Dunbar letters are also scattered among various collections kept at the Houghton Library at Harvard.

Biography

WILLIAM WELLS BROWN

The definitive biography of William Wells Brown is W. Edward Farrison's *William Wells Brown: Author and Reformer* (Chicago: University of Chicago Press, 1969). Farrison focuses on Brown's activities as a social reformer, although he by no means shortchanges Brown's career as an author. Indeed, if this biography has a major flaw, it is perhaps that Farrison tells us too much about Brown and in so doing, as Robert Cruden has pointed out in his review (*AHR*, February 1970), tends to obscure the context of Brown's times so that the "nonspecialist reader may miss the full significance of some of Brown's changes in outlook." There are also two minor but irksome flaws in this work. The first is a number of annoying typographical errors, and the second is the surprisingly abbreviated index. However, the appended bibliography is excellent and the biography is interesting, readable, and indispensible to scholarship on William Wells Brown. Material from several articles by Farrison—"A Flight Across Ohio: The Escape of William Wells Brown From Slavery" (*Ohio State Archeological and Historical Quarterly*, July 1952), "William Wells Brown in Buffalo" (*JNH*, October 1954), and "A Theologian's Missouri Compromise" (*JNH*, January 1963)— has been incorporated into this biography. Farrison's "*Phylon* Profile, XVI: William Wells Brown" (*Phylon*, Spring 1948) offers some biographical information as well as a brief analysis of Brown's drama, *The Escape; or, A Leap for Freedom* (1858).

William Wells Brown and Clotelle: A Portrait of the Artist in the First Negro Novel (Hamden, Conn.: Archon, 1969) by J. Noel Heermance, although primarily an introduction to a reprint of the 1864 edition of *Clotelle* published in Boston by James Redpath, also contains biographical data on Brown. However, Heermance's study lacks an index and the bibliography is mediocre.

Significant biographical information is also found, of course, in Brown's own *Narrative of William W. Brown* (Boston: Anti-Slavery Office, 1847) and its subsequent editions. Also useful, although it repeats much of the material in Brown's *Narrative,* is the *Biography of an American Bondman, By His Daughter,* written by Josephine Brown and published in Boston by R. F. Wallcut in 1856.

Jean Fagan Yellin's *The Intricate Knot: Black Figures in American Literature, 1776–1863* (New York: New York University Press, 1972) offers useful biographical data on Brown intertwined with an intelligent analysis of his *Narrative* and of the different versions of *Clotel.* Of some interest, too, is a short, eulogistic sketch by Pauline E. Hopkins, entitled "William Wells Brown," which appeared in *Colored American Magazine* (January 1901), if only because it reflects Brown's status as a symbol of achievement for the turn-of-the-century black American community.

CHARLES WADDELL CHESNUTT

Despite its adulatory approach, Helen M. Chesnutt's biography of her father, *Charles Waddell Chesnutt, Pioneer of the Color Line* (Chapel Hill: University of North Carolina Press, 1952), remains the most comprehensive study of his life. John W. Parker's "Chesnutt as a Southern Town Remembers Him" (*Crisis,* July 1949) tells of Chesnutt's boyhood in Fayetteville, North Carolina. Hiram Haydn's "Charles W. Chesnutt" (*ASch,* Winter 1972–1973) describes the local reaction to the Chesnutt family's arrival in a primarily white Cleveland, Ohio, community.

The North Carolina *State Normal Magazine* for October, 1900, describes Chesnutt's career as a court reporter in "The History of Shorthand Writing in North Carolina" by C. H. Mebane. Chesnutt's relationship with George Washington Cable through the Open Letter Club is recounted in Philip Butcher's *George W. Cable: The Northampton Years* (New York: Columbia University Press, 1959). The biographical backgrounds to "Baxter's Procrustes" are described by John B. Nicholson's introduction to the 1966 Rowfant reprint edition of this work mentioned earlier.

In Chesnutt's own "Post-Bellum-Pre-Harlem" (*Colophon,* February 1931) he discusses his breaking into print in the *Atlantic Monthly* and offers both his personal estimate of the significance of his writings and the turn-of-the-century critical estimate of them.

MARTIN R. DELANY

The most comprehensive portrait of Martin R. Delany is Victor Ullman's *Martin R. Delany, The Beginnings of Black Nationalism* (Boston: Beacon, 1971). George E. Kent, in his review of this work in *Phylon* (Winter 1974), lauds it as an important study of "a leader who understood the meaning of power." Biographical material also appears in Yellin's *The Intricate Knot,* mentioned earlier, as well as Loggins's *The Negro Author* and Bone's *The Negro Novel in America.* For information on Delany's medical career, see Kelley Miller's "The Historic Background of the Negro Physician" (*JNH,* April 1916). A. H. M. Kirk-Greene's "America in the Niger Valley: A Colonization Centenary" (*Phylon,* Fall 1962) is an interesting account of Delany's Niger Valley exploring party, which aimed to recolonize West Africa with American Negroes.

PAUL LAURENCE DUNBAR

The earliest significant biography of Paul Laurence Dunbar is Lida Keck Wiggins's *The Life and Works of Paul Laurence Dunbar* (Naperville, Ill.: J. L. Nichols, 1907). Wiggins's study is divided into two parts: part one, which is slightly more than one hundred pages long, consists of biography; part two, almost three hundred pages long, consists of Dunbar's *Complete Poems* (with Howells's introduction to *Lyrics of Lowly Life*), and a selection of his "best short stories." Wiggins's gives a rather simplistic account of Dunbar's life, portraying the poet as a gentle, childlike soul. Unfortunately, this kind of portrait reveals little of Dunbar the man. Wiggins gives us few private glimpses of Dunbar, casually skimming past the less pleasant episodes of his life, such as his marital difficulties and his reliance on alcohol to ease the discomfort caused by his tuberculosis. The text is patronizing in its effort to demonstrate how a black man, if he were possessed of enough talent and determination, and had a mild temperament, could succeed in America. Much of Wiggins's material was collected firsthand through interviews with Dunbar and his associates, yet she failed to make any of the people in this biography come alive. Her characterizations are too shallow, the dialogue too formal, and Dunbar's reaction to adversity too sedate to be satisfying to the reader. Further, the work is not indexed, although it does contain an adequate selection of Dunbar's poetry and prose. Benjamin Brawley's *Paul Laurence Dunbar: Poet of His People* (Chapel Hill: University of North Carolina Press, 1936; rpt. New York: Kennikat Press, 1967) is another eulogy masquerading as biography. Brawley's work improves on Wiggins's only because it includes a bibliography and an index.

Paul Laurence Dunbar and His Song (New York: Dodd, Mead, 1947; rpt. New York: Biblo & Tannen, 1969), by Virginia Cunningham, attempts to portray Dunbar the man, rather than Dunbar the symbol, and herein lies its strength. Cunningham's research was based on interviews with people who knew Dunbar, as well as on a study of his letters and manuscripts. She treats with more depth than either of her two predecessors Dunbar's marital difficulties and other unpleasant episodes in his life. Also significant is her unwillingness to parade indiscriminately before the reader those important personages who contributed so much to Dunbar's success. Although this biography lacks an index, it does include an excellent bibliography, as noted earlier.

The most recent biography of Dunbar is *Oak and Ivy: A Biography of Paul Laurence Dunbar* by Addison Gayle, Jr., (Garden City, N.Y.: Doubleday, 1971). Gayle's failure to utilize the wealth of Dunbar manuscripts and letters available to the researcher is what keeps this study from being the definitive Dunbar biography. As Gossie H. Hudson suggested in his review (*JNH*, January 1973), this biography is likely to be more popular with the nonspecialist than with the scholar.

An interesting remembrance of Dunbar by a man who knew him is Edward F. Arnold's "Some Personal Reminiscences of Paul Laurence Dunbar" (*JNH*, October 1932). In "Paul Laurence Dunbar and William Dean Howells" (*Oregon Historical Quarterly*, April 1958), James B. Stronks uses the letters between Dunbar and Howells as documentation for an analysis of their relationship. Another brief study of a literary relationship is Philip Butcher's "Mutual Appreciation: Dunbar and Cable" (*CLAJ*, March 1958).

OTHER WRITERS

Biographical data on Sutton E. Griggs and Frances Ellen Watkins Harper can be found in Robert Bone's *The Negro Novel in America* and in Hugh Gloster's *Negro Voices in American Fiction*. Additional information on Griggs is available in *The Way of the New World: The Black Novel in America* by Addison Gayle, Jr., (Garden City, N.Y.: Doubleday, 1975). Vernon Loggins offers some additional data on Harper in *The Negro Author*.

The only significant biographical data about Frank J. Webb is in Harriet Beecher Stowe's introduction to Webb's *The Garies and Their Friends* (London: Routledge, 1857; rpt. New York: Arno, 1969), in which she describes Webb as "a young colored man, born and reared in Philadelphia . . . of the better class of colored citizens." This is virtually the extent of our knowledge about him.

Criticism

Critics of early black American literature generally have placed themselves in one of two camps. The first, consisting primarily of white critics, has measured this early literature by traditional literary standards, and by so doing attempted to place these authors within the mainstream of American literature. The second camp, made up mainly of black critics, has formulated a "black aesthetic," and insisted that black American literature be judged according to it. They see the necessity for this separate-but-equal aesthetic rising out of the black's unique cultural and historical position in America. This disparity between the two positions has made for a continuing and lively critical debate.

Robert Bone, in *The Negro Novel in America,* suggests that the early black novelist exploited the romantic tradition because melodrama's "moral extremes make it a natural vehicle for racial protest." He shows how these early novelists employed "counter-stereotypes" rather than literary realism to respond to those stereotypes of the Negro prevalent in plantation literature. In a more recent study, *Down Home: A History of Afro-American Short Fiction From Its Beginnings to the End of the Harlem Renaissance* (New York: Putnam, 1975), Bone argues that Afro-American short fiction emerged from the struggle between the pastoralists (those who write about rural life and themes) and the antipastoralists, and that these black writers were indebted to, and even dependent upon, white authors. Bone's analysis contains several flaws, which Darwin T. Turner has identified and examined in his review of this work (*AL,* November 1976). Bernard W. Bell, in "Literary Sources of the Early Afro-American Novel" (*CLAJ,* September 1974), seems to agree substantially with Bone's thesis, stating that the black novelist's "philosophical and aesthetic needs were served by melodrama." However, Bell contends that the tradition of the black novel reaches back beyond the conventions of abolitionist literature, as exploited by Brown, Delany, Harper, and others, to a Christian tradition which embodied the principles of faith, hope, and charity. He concludes that the major trends in the black literary tradition are romantic, protestant, and messianic.

Tilman C. Cothran's "White Stereotypes in Fiction by Negroes" (*Phylon,* Fall 1950) surveys several early and more recent black novels and lists the traits ascribed to whites in these novels. He argues that a "significant bias toward the sordid and unlovely side of white characters" pervades a great deal of black fiction. A similar analysis is James W. Byrd's "Stereotypes of White Characters in Early Negro Novels" (*CLAJ,* September 1957). Byrd suggests that there are six major stereotypes to be found in early black fiction: the benevolent white father of mulattoes, the kind aristocrat, the poor-white villain, the mean planter, the brutal overseer, and the Northern champion of the Negro. He points out that these stereotypes were a natural reaction to plantation literature, and that they are prevalent in the fiction of Chesnutt, Griggs, and others. Byrd believes the use of these stereotypes, which offer views of white characters that are just as distorted as the views of black characters in the literature of the plantation tradition, constitutes a major flaw in the early black novel.

Toni Trent's "Stratification Among Blacks by Black Authors" (*NHB,*

December 1971) examines the portrayal of mulattoes in the fiction of Brown, Chesnutt, and others. Priscilla Ramsey's "A Study of Black Identity in 'Passing' Novels of the Nineteenth and Early Twentieth Centuries" (*SBL,* Spring 1976) analyzes the "passing" theme in the works of Brown, Chesnutt, and Webb. Robert E. Fleming's "Humor in the Early Black Novel" (*CLAJ,* December 1973) discusses the use of humor "as an avenue to mass appeal." He points out that humor provided relief from some of the sordid episodes in these novels, as well as helping "to render the blatant propaganda more palatable to white readers." Fleming's study concentrates on the fiction of Brown, Chesnutt, Delany, Griggs, and Webb.

The significant recent study by Addison Gayle, Jr., *The Way of the New World: The Black Novel in America* (Garden City, N.Y.: Doubleday, 1975), is an extended argument in favor of the "black aesthetic." Gayle maintains that the black novelist traditionally has been engaged in a "war for control of images, a battle to recreate legends of the past, create symbols, images, and metaphors, in order that the Black man might be redeemed in myth if not in actuality." The black novel, Gayle suggests, is a social vehicle rather than a cultural artifact, and therefore must be judged, not in terms of form, structure, dialogue, or characterization, but rather in terms of content. Gayle's discussions of individual authors will appear later.

WILLIAM WELLS BROWN

The foremost authority on William Wells Brown is W. Edward Farrison, who has published several articles on Brown, as well as *William Wells Brown: Author and Reformer.* This definitive biography, mentioned earlier, includes analyses of Brown's writings.

In "William Wells Brown, Social Reformer" (*JNE,* Winter 1949) Farrison describes how Brown's zeal as a reformer is reflected not only in his *Narrative* and *Clotel,* but also in his historical works, *The Black Man, His Antecedents, His Genius, and His Achievements* (1863) and *The Rising Son; or, The Antecedents and Advancement of the Colored Race* (1874; reprinted by Johnson Reprint in 1970). Farrison excuses certain inaccuracies in these works, and their gross lack of documentation, by citing Brown's educational deficiencies. He concludes that Brown employed literature and history to the same end, to promote his ideas on reform.

A companion article to this one by Farrison is Edward M. Coleman's "William Wells Brown as an Historian" (*JNH,* January 1946). Coleman attempts to discover to what extent Brown employed contemporary historical methodology in his studies of the Negro race, both fictional and nonfictional. Like Farrison, Coleman concludes that Brown's historical method often was inadequate. However, again like Farrison, he suggests that Brown's educational deficiencies tend to mitigate any harsh judgments of his historiography.

In "Clotel, Thomas Jefferson, and Sally Hemings" (*CLAJ*, December 1973) Farrison provides an "essay in research" exploring both fact and rumor about Jefferson's alleged liaison with Sally Hemings, which Brown purported to be the source for *Clotel*. Farrison's earlier study in *Phylon* (Winter 1954), "The Origin of Brown's *Clotel*," offers additional information about this relationship.

Farrison explores a lesser-known side of Brown's literary career, his experience as a dramatist, in two significant articles. "Brown's First Drama" (*CLAJ*, December 1958) is a short history of the development of Brown's unpublished play, *Experience, Or How To Give a Northern Man a Backbone* (1856). "*The Kidnapped Clergyman* and Brown's *Experience*" (*CLAJ*, June 1975) explores the similarities between Brown's drama and the earlier anonymous one (1839).

Vernon Loggins is somewhat unsympathetic toward Brown as a writer of fiction. In *The Negro Author* Loggins faults Brown for "cramming enough material for a dozen novels" into *Clotel*. He further suggests that Brown's eagerness to score rhetorical points with his audience caused him to under-utilize the dramatic aspects of his plot. Unsympathetic for different reasons is Addison Gayle, Jr., in *The Way of the New World*. Gayle criticizes Brown for exploiting in *Clotel* certain aspirations of the black middle class—for example, assimilation into white society. He suggests that Brown's portrayal of the "tragic mulatto" demonstrates the assimilationist philosophy of his fiction. Gayle further notes that it was the adherence to this philosophy that prevented Brown and other early novelists from moving the black novel in "the right direction."

Another helpful study is Jean Fagan Yellin's *The Intricate Knot*, mentioned earlier, which offers intelligent analyses of several of Brown's works.

CHARLES WADDELL CHESNUTT

There have been a number of studies of the varied aspects of the works of Charles Waddell Chesnutt. Julian D. Mason, Jr., in "Chesnutt as Southern Author" (*MissQ*, Spring 1967), suggests that the key to an understanding of Chesnutt's fiction lies in viewing him as a southern author. In "The Image of the Negro in Popular Magazines, 1875–1900" (*JNH*, April 1972), George R. Lamplugh examines Chesnutt's atypical view of the antebellum South and the southern black in his conjure stories, which appeared in the *Atlantic Monthly*. A more detailed discussion of black characters in Chesnutt's work is found in *Black Portraiture in American Fiction* (New York: Basic Books, 1971) by Catherine Juanita

Starke. In *The Folk of Southern Fiction* (Athens: University of Georgia Press, 1972), Merrill Maguire Skaggs analyzes Chesnutt's handling of the South's "plain folk." Sylvia Lyons Render's "Tar Heelia in Chesnutt" (*CLAJ*, September 1965) examines the incidence and influence of North Carolina in Chesnutt's fiction. Chesnutt's use of dialect is discussed in Render's "North Carolina Dialect: Chesnutt Style" (*North Carolina Folklore*, November 1967). William L. Andrews's "Chesnutt's Patesville: The Presence and Influence of the Past in *The House Behind the Cedars*" (*CLAJ*, March 1972), examines Chesnutt's use of Fayetteville, North Carolina, as the locale for his first novel. Chesnutt's use of folk materials is analyzed in Donald M. Winkelman's "Three American Authors as Semi-Folk Artists" (*JAF*, April–June 1965), and the magical elements of Chesnutt's conjure tales are examined by Robert A. Smith's "A Note on the Folk Tales of Charles Chesnutt" (*CLAJ*, March 1962). Houston A. Baker compares the influence of the folk and literary traditions on Chesnutt and Dunbar in "Balancing the Perspective: A Look at Early Black American Literary Artistry" (*NALF*, Fall 1972).

June Socken has used several of Chesnutt's essays, speeches, and book reviews as documentation in "Charles Waddell Chesnutt and the Solution to the Race Problem" (*NALF*, Summer 1969) in an attempt to demonstrate that large-scale miscegenation was Chesnutt's solution to America's racial difficulties.

Chesnutt's fiction is placed within the muckraking tradition of Frank Norris, Jack London, and Upton Sinclair by Russell Ames in "Social Realism in Charles W. Chesnutt" (*Phylon*, Spring 1953), and Wendell Jackson argues in "Charles W. Chesnutt's Outrageous Fortune" (*CLAJ*, December 1976) that Chesnutt's "propaganda motive," as well as his premature efforts as a novelist, stimulated public hostility toward his novels. Continuing to discuss the social significance of Chesnutt's fiction is Robert M. Farnsworth's "Charles Chesnutt and the Color Line" in *Minor American Novelists* (Carbondale: Southern Illinois University Press, 1970), edited by Charles Alva Hoyt, which examines social themes of and contemporary reactions to *The Wife of His Youth, The House Behind the Cedars,* and *The Marrow of Tradition.* Noel Schraufnagel argues that Chesnutt's use of counter-stereotypes and his propagandistic techniques severely weakened his literary efforts in *From Apology to Protest: The Black American Novel* (Deland, Fla.: Everett/Edwards, 1973). Approaching this question from a slightly different angle is Walter Daykin in "Attitudes in Negro Novels" (*Sociology and Social Research*, November–December 1935), although he places Chesnutt with Du Bois as among the most outspoken and "rebellious" black novelists.

Chesnutt's *The Conjure Woman* (1899) has received perhaps the most critical attention of any of his books. Early reviews by James MacArthur (*Outlook*, July 1, 1899), Florence Morgan (*Bookman*, June 1899), and others praised Chesnutt's portrayal of the antebellum South, as well the character of Uncle Julius (cited by many reviewers as the best feature of the collection).

Recent criticism has for the most part conformed to this early assessment. In his introduction to the 1969 reprint of *The Conjure Woman* by the University of Michigan Press, Robert M. Farnsworth describes how Chesnutt was able to comment on social and racial issues without offending his mainly white audience. David D. Britt's "Chesnutt's Conjure Tales: What You See is What You Get" (*CLAJ*, March 1972), and Melvin Dixon's "The Teller as Folk Trickster in Chesnutt's *The Conjure Woman*" (*CLAJ*, December 1974) examine Chesnutt's method of "masking" his protest behind the seemingly noncommittal tone of his stories. Similarly, James R. Giles's "Chesnutt's Primus and Annie: A Contemporary View of *The Conjure Woman*"(*MarkhamR*, May 1972) analyzes the tension between the book's "honest protest and its racial condescension." In "Gothic Sociology: Charles Chesnutt and the Gothic Mode" (*Studies in the Literary Imagination*, Spring 1974), Robert Hemenway traces Chesnutt's debt in *The Conjure Woman* to both the American and English Gothic traditions. The literary method of *The Conjure Woman* is explored by Richard E. Baldwin in "The Art of *The Conjure Woman*" (*AL*, November 1971). The social implications of the conjure tales have been examined by Theodore R. Hovet in "Chesnutt's 'The Goophered Grapevine' as Social Comment" (*NALF*, Fall 1973). William L. Andrews's "The Significance of Charles W. Chesnutt's Conjure Stories" (*SLJ*, Fall 1974), is a discussion of the place of these tales in American and Afro-American literary history.

Critical response to *The Wife of His Youth* has been more mixed than it was for Chesnutt's first book. Early reviews like Carolyn Shipman's "The Author of 'The Conjure Woman', Charles W. Chesnutt" (*Critic*, July 1899) and Nancy Huston Banks in her review, "The Wife of His Youth," (*Bookman*, February 1900) each generously praised the title story of the collection. However, Banks was less kind concerning what she considered to be a lack of good taste in Chesnutt's depiction of miscegenation in some of the other stories. Benjamin W. Wells's significant assessment in "Southern Literature of the Year" (*Forum*, June 1900), notes Chesnutt's use of tragedy, irony, and pathos in *The Wife of His Youth*, and is echoed over two decades later by Carl Van Vechten in "Uncle Tom's Mansion" (*NYHTBW*, December 20, 1925).

The best short analysis of Chesnutt as a writer of short fiction was stimulated by the success of his first two books. William Dean Howells's "Mr. Charles W. Chesnutt's Stories" (*AtM*, May 1900) praises Chesnutt as a realist, favorably comparing his work to that of James, Jewett, and Maupassant. Also significant here is Howells's suggestion that Chesnutt's stories should be judged according to their aesthetic appeal rather than merely by their presentation of the black consciousness. William L. Andrews has further explored the Howells–Chesnutt relationship in his important study, "William Dean Howells and Charles W. Chesnutt: Criticism and Race Fiction in the Age of Booker T. Washington" (*AL*, November 1976). Andrews concludes that Howells's tendency "to psychologize the black writer, particularly in the area of his social views and emotional allegiances" seriously impaired his ability to evaluate Chesnutt's art. Another important early assessment stimulated by the publication of Chesnutt's two books is Hamilton W. Mabie's "Two New Novelists" (*Outlook*, February 1900), in which he suggests that Chesnutt is less a humorist than a tragic artist.

More recently, Julian D. Mason, Jr., has provided a careful and thorough examination of *The Wife of His Youth* in "The Stories of Charles W. Chesnutt" (*SLJ*, Autumn 1968). A somewhat helpful assessment of *The Wife of His Youth*, although burdened by factual errors and a tendency towards critical ambiguity, is "A Pioneer Black Writer and the Problems of Discrimination and Miscegenation" (*Costerus*, No. 3, 1973) by Robert A. Smith. Eugene Arden's "The Early Harlem Novel" (*Phylon*, Spring 1971) suggests that *The Wife of His Youth* was a forerunner of those Harlem Renaissance works which were concerned with intraracial color stratification.

Two articles that examine "The Sheriff's Children" as a parable of social and historical developments in the South are Gerald W. Haslam's " 'The Sheriff's Children': Chesnutt's Tragic Racial Parable" (*NALF*, Summer 1968) and Ronald Walcott's "Chesnutt's 'The Sheriff's Children' as Parable" (*NALF*, Fall 1973). Haslam suggests that the story dramatizes "the moral dilemma inherent in chattel slavery in the American South," and Walcott views the moral significance of the story in terms of its relationship to the tale of Cain and Abel.

Sylvia Lyons Render's valuable introduction to *The Short Fiction of Charles W. Chesnutt*, mentioned earlier, examines the elements of local color in the stories, critical and popular reaction to them, and their various stylistic and thematic aspects. Considerably less valuable, because of its brevity and the substitution of plot summary for analysis, is Joan Cunningham's "The Uncollected Short Stories of Charles Waddell Chesnutt" (*NALF*, Summer 1975). An excellent evaluation of "Baxter's Procrustes" is Robert Hemenway's study in *CLAJ* (December 1974), " 'Baxter's Procrustes': Irony and Protest."

The Life of Frederick Douglass (1899), Chesnutt's first full-length narrative, has been all but ignored by modern critics. Some contemporary reviews praising the work are in *The New York Times Saturday Review* (January 13, 1900), and William Dean Howells's assessment (*NAR*, August 1901).

Chesnutt's first novel, *The House Behind the Cedars* (1900), was generally maligned by early critics as unoriginal in concept and weakened by Chesnutt's clumsy handling of his characters. The only extensive modern study of this novel is Robert P. Sedlack's "The Evolution of Charles Chesnutt's *The House Behind the Cedars*" (*CLAJ*, December 1975). Sedlack uses the five manuscripts of the work to document its thematic development, as well as Chesnutt's increasing literary sophistication, both of which occurred during the ten-year lapse between Chesnutt's original conception of the work and its eventual publication. In Darwin T. Turner's introduction to the Collier-Macmillan paperback reprint of *The House Behind the Cedars* (1969), he discusses the historical importance and the aesthetic shortcomings of this novel.

Publication of *The Marrow of Tradition* (1901) revealed Chesnutt's rather militant position on race problems in the South, accounting, perhaps, for some of the adverse reaction to the novel. A reviewer for the *Bookman* (January 1902) chastised Chesnutt for his unattractive characterization of whites, as did John H. Nelson over twenty years later in "The Negro Character in American Literature" (*Bulletin of the University of Kansas Humanistic Studies*, No. 1, 1926). Even Howells commented on the bitterness in *The Marrow of Tradition* in "A Psychological Counter-Current in Recent Fiction" (*NAR*, December 1901), and evaluated the effects of the novel's rhetorical content on its stylistic aspects.

An excellent modern analysis of *The Marrow of Tradition* is Robert M. Farnsworth's introduction to the 1969 reprint by the University of Michigan Press of the novel. A provocative examination of the unresolved thematic conflict between the work's condemnation of contemporary social conditions and Chesnutt's own assimilationist tendencies is John M. Reilly's "The Dilemma in Chesnutt's *The Marrow of Tradition*" (*Phylon*, Spring 1971). Significant also is John Wideman's "Charles W. Chesnutt: *The Marrow of Tradition*" (*ASch*, Winter 1972–1973). An interesting Marxist interpretation of *The Marrow of Tradition* is Samuel Sillen's "Charles W. Chesnutt: A Pioneer Negro Novelist" (*Masses and Mainstream*, February 1953), in which Sillen praises Chesnutt's use of the character of Josh Green to articulate a militant ideology.

The most neglected of Chesnutt's novels is unquestionably *The Colonel's Dream* (1905). Contemporary critics responded to the novel halfheartedly, if at all. More recently, Vernon Loggins, in *The Negro Author*, called *The Colonel's Dream* "the most poignantly tragic and yet perhaps the most realistic" of Chesnutt's novels. Echoing Loggins is Cary D. Wintz in "Race and Realism in the Fiction of Charles W. Chesnutt" (*Ohio History*, Spring 1972). Wintz considers the pessimistic elements in Chesnutt's writings, particularly those in *The Colonel's Dream*, to be realistic assessments of the turn-of-the-century black American social condition. In *Negro Voices in American Fiction* (Chapel Hill: University of North Carolina Press, 1948; rpt. New York: Russell & Russell, 1965),

* Hugh Gloster briefly discusses the conflict between long-standing racial prejudice and idealistic Reconstructionist reform which is illustrated in *The Colonel's Dream.*

A number of comparisons have been made between Chesnutt and his contemporary, Paul Laurence Dunbar. One of the earliest is Elizabeth L. Cary's "A New Element in Fiction" (*Book Buyer,* August 1901), which suggests that the "imagination and profound sentiment" of Dunbar's plantation fiction was inferior to that found in Chesnutt's tales. Loggins praises Dunbar as a better recorder of black dialect, but argues that the artistic achievement of a work like Chesnutt's *The Conjure Woman* far surpasses any of Dunbar's efforts. In "Testing the Color-Line—Dunbar and Chesnutt" in *The Black American Writer* (Deland, Fla.: Everett/Edwards, 1969), edited by C. W. E. Bigsby, Robert M. Farnsworth suggests that Chesnutt was intellectually and artistically superior to Dunbar. Kenny J. Williams, in *They Also Spoke: An Essay on Negro Literature in America, 1783–1930* (Nashville, Tenn.: Townsend, 1970), praises Chesnutt's use of psychological realism over the mere "local color or surface realism of Dunbar."

The degree to which the plantation school of literature has influenced Chesnutt remains a controversial subject. Loggins accuses Chesnutt of blatantly imitating Joel Chandler Harris and Thomas Nelson Page, while Gloster, among several others, responds that Chesnutt was by no means a "slavish imitator," although there is evidence of the plantation school's influence in his fiction.

Some recent general studies of Chesnutt's literary career are Carol B. Gartner's "Charles W. Chesnutt: Novelist of a Cause" (*MarkhamR,* Fall 1968), a somewhat disorganized introduction to the study of Chesnutt; Walter Teller's unsatisfying summary (*ASch,* Winter 1972–1973), "Charles W. Chesnutt's Conjuring and Color-Line Stories"; and A. Robert Lee's excellent " 'The Desired State of Feeling': Charles Waddell Chesnutt and Afro-American Literary Tradition" (*Durham University Journal,* March 1974). Of particular value is William L. Andrews's lecture on Chesnutt, available on cassette tape from Everett/Edwards, Inc., which surveys Chesnutt's total literary achievement and suggests reasons for the author's success.

An important full-length study of Chesnutt is J. Noel Heermance's *Charles W. Chesnutt: America's First Great Black Novelist* (Hamden, Conn.: Shoestring Press, 1974), which represents a culmination of Chesnutt scholarship to date. This work is not definitive, however, as Heermance's approach to the fiction is sometimes unsystematic and inconsistent. Heermance has succeeded nonetheless in diligently exploring the available Chesnutt journals for indications of the author's personal ideals and literary motives.

Chesnutt's place in American literary history is as yet unclear. The

critical tendency has been to lump him among the southern regionalists•
and leave it at that. J. Saunders Redding, however, in "The Problems
of the Negro Writer" (*MR*, Autumn–Winter, 1964–1965), has argued
that Chesnutt's skill as a novelist far exceeds that of William Dean
Howells. Robert Bone, in *The Negro Novel in America*, commends Chesnutt's shorter works, but suggests that the author was too concerned
with producing black propaganda to master the intricacies of the novel.
Generally agreeing with Bone are Redding and Sterling Brown. In *The
Negro in American Fiction* (Washington, D.C.: Associates in Negro Folk
Education, 1937), Brown insists that many of the aesthetic flaws in
Chesnutt's novels result directly from his attempts to "answer propaganda with propaganda." In *To Make A Poet Black* (Chapel Hill: University of North Carolina Press, 1939), Redding suggests that Chesnutt's
contributions to black American literature are best illustrated in his two
collections of short stories.

MARTIN R. DELANY

Critical work on Martin R. Delany's one novel, *Blake; or, The Huts of
America: A Tale of the Mississippi Valley, the Southern United States, and
Cuba* (1859) is sparse, although modern critics have begun to rediscover
the work in the context of an increasingly militant black community in
America.

Robert Bone, in *The Negro Novel*, suggests that "*Blake* is a remarkable
novel, closer in spirit to Karl Marx than to the New England abolitionists." In *The Way of the New World*, Addison Gayle, Jr., also praises
Blake's departure from precedents established by Brown and Webb,
citing its strength in its espousal of "racial unity instead of racial division, rebellion instead of passive resistance, and nationalism instead of
assimilation." Gayle further notes the inability of subsequent black novelists to exploit Delany's breakthrough and suggests that this meant
that "no viable literary tradition was possible until after *Native Son*."
Julianne Malveau also comments on Delany's breakthrough in "Revolutionary Themes in Martin Delany's *Blake*" (*BlackSch*, July–August
1973). Malveau calls Delany the literary father of black nationalism,
and sees the significance of *Blake* in its expression of a radical and
nationalist philosophy.

John Zeugner compares *Blake* to the works of some modern black
militants, like Eldridge Cleaver, in "A Note on Martin Delany's *Blake*
and Black Militancy" (*Phylon*, Spring 1971). He suggests that *Blake's*
"one strident message . . . violent purification through insurrection,"
earns it a place in black literary history as the seminal work of militant
fiction. Also noting the rhetorical aspects of *Blake* is Roger W. Hite in
his " 'Stand Still and See the Salvation': The Rhetorical Design of Martin Delany's *Blake*" (*JBLS*, December 1974).

Pointing out that Delany, unlike his contemporaries Brown and Webb, did not believe in the mulatto's inherent superiority to the darker members of the race, is Robert E. Fleming in "Black, White, and Mulatto in Martin R. Delany's *Blake*" (*NHB*, February 1973). Instead, Delany's hero is a man of pure African blood, demonstrating the author's belief in the need for black unity, and his dissatisfaction with the tendency among blacks to segregate themselves on the basis of skin tone.

PAUL LAURENCE DUNBAR

The central critical issue in regard to Dunbar's work is the degree to which his racial awareness (or lack of it) is reflected in his fiction and his poetry. The earliest significant critical assessment of Dunbar's poetry, and the one which simultaneously established his reputation and directed the course that Dunbar criticism was to follow well into the twentieth century, is William Dean Howells's famous "Review of Dunbar's *Majors and Minors*" (*Harper's Weekly*, June 27, 1896). Howells's suggestion that Dunbar's genius lay in his dialect verse rather than in his literary verse had a profound effect on at least two subsequent generations of critics.

Charles Eaton Burch's article in *Southern Workman* (May 1921), "The Plantation Negro in Dunbar's Poetry," reflects Howells's influence in Burch's suggestion that Dunbar has given a true and honest interpretation of the southern black, "who toiled and sang during the busy hours of the day and grew not tired of song" in the evening. He further states that Dunbar's poetry surpasses all other literary efforts in its portrayal of the "kindlier side" of the relationship between master and slave. Also reflecting contemporary critical attitudes is Burch's "Dunbar's Poetry in Literary English" (*Southern Workman*, October 1921), in which he argues that Dunbar did not produce any great works in this mode, although he did manage to contribute "a few charming poems to the native literature."

Reflecting a modern shift toward Dunbar's nondialect verse is Allan B. Fox's "Behind the Mask: Paul Laurence Dunbar's Poetry in Literary English" (*TQ*, Summer 1971). Fox argues that a careful examination of Dunbar's literary verse reveals a subtle irony toward those literary conventions of the 1890s which made him a popular poet. Fox points out that it is in this innovative and generally overlooked aspect of his poetry in literary English, rather than in the shallow humor and sentimentality of his dialect poems, that Dunbar makes a significant contribution to American poetry.

"Paul Laurence Dunbar: *Dialect et la Négritude*" (*Phylon*, Fall 1973) by Gossie H. Hudson further develops Fox's thesis. Hudson argues that

Dunbar's awareness of negritude caused him to reveal his racial pride in his poetry. Dunbar's dialect poetry was not meant to be derogatory, Hudson suggests, but rather it was meant to be "used as a living language to depict the life of rural Blacks." The fault in this, however, was that Dunbar tended to describe blacks in terms of a single being—the rural southern black. But when he wished to make a serious statement about being black in America, he "discarded dialect and child-like simplicity" and wrote in literary English. An earlier note which briefly hints at Hudson's thesis is Theodora W. Daniel's "Paul Laurence Dunbar and the Democratic Ideal" (*NHB,* June 1943). Hudson examines Dunbar's role as a "local color" poet in "Paul Laurence Dunbar: The Regional Heritage of Dayton's First Black Poet" (*AR,* Summer 1976).

An excellent analysis of Dunbar's poetic technique, as well as of his relationship to his contemporaries, appears in Wagner's *Black Poets in America,* mentioned earlier. Wagner explores the influence of the plantation tradition on Dunbar's poetry, the charge of pessimism which was often leveled against him, and the poet's own racial consciousness. Also of interest is Wagner's brief biographical introduction to the section on Dunbar.

An interesting psychological study is Walker M. Allen's "Paul Laurence Dunbar, A Study in Genius" (*Psychoanalytic Review,* January 1938), in which Allen uses several of Dunbar's poems to document an analysis of the psychoanalytic results of the poet's conflicts with his father, his turning to his mother for comfort, his marital problems, his racial awareness, and his tuberculosis.

Eugene Arden's "The Early Harlem Novel" (*Phylon,* Spring 1959) suggests that Dunbar's last novel, *The Sport of the Gods,* was the forerunner of the Harlem school of fiction because of its treatment of Negro life in New York. Arden also calls it a naturalistic novel, noting how the "forces of the city . . . quickly demoralize the protagonists." In "The Novels of Paul Laurence Dunbar" (*Phylon,* Fall 1968) Charles R. Larsen suggests that this movement toward literary naturalism, as well as an increased racial awareness on Dunbar's part, are clearly evident in *The Sport of the Gods.* Significant here also is Larsen's mention of Dunbar's novel in the context of two pioneer naturalistic works, Frank Norris's *McTeague* and Theodore Dreiser's *Sister Carrie.* Larsen suggests that many incidents in these novels are similar to events occurring in *The Sport of the Gods;* however, he is unclear as to whether Dunbar had read either of the earlier works.

Vernon Loggins, in *The Negro Author,* has little good to say about Dunbar's novels, calling *The Sport of the Gods* the "most interesting and the most imperfect" of the four. About Dunbar's poetry, however, he is kinder, calling the publication of *Lyrics of Lowly Life* in 1896 "the greatest single event in the history of American Negro literature."

Victor Lawson's *Dunbar Critically Examined* (Washington, D.C.: Associated Publishers, 1941), examines Dunbar's dialect and nondialect poetry, as well as his short stories and novels. He argues that Dunbar's nondialect poems were mere "romantic echoes," and his dialect poetry a reflection of his "conscious or unconscious" stance as apologist for the plantation tradition. Lawson's assessment of Dunbar's prose is "that it was very important in helping him to make a living."

In *The Negro Novel in America,* Robert Bone accuses Dunbar of "trying to amuse rather than arouse his white audiences," and by so doing considerably weakened the impact of each of his novels. Bone praises *The Uncalled* (1898) as a "spiritual autobiography," and comments on Dunbar's exploration of the conflict between the natural and the artificial. Bone considers *The Love of Landry* (1900) to be Dunbar's worst novel because of its reliance upon romantic conventions. *The Fanatics* (1901) is a "well-disguised attempt at racial protest, so carefully veiled that only the subtlest reader will grasp it." Bone accuses Dunbar of resorting to caricature in this novel in order to pander to the bigotry of his white audience. Finally, *The Sport of the Gods* is to Bone a mere reiteration of the plantation-school contention that "the rural Negro becomes demoralized in the urban North." Bone further suggests that Dunbar's "mid-western agrarian values" often paralleled the anti-industrial bias prevalent in plantation fiction, thus making escape from industrial civilization the dominant motif in his writings. Defending Dunbar from Bone's allegations is Darwin T. Turner in "Paul Laurence Dunbar: The Rejected Symbol" (*JNH,* January 1967). Turner suggests that perhaps readers and critics have traditionally expected more from Dunbar as a writer than he was prepared or equipped to offer. Turner describes him as a "talented, creative, high-school graduate, whose views reflect the limited knowledge of many historians, economists, and social philosophers of his day." Gregory L. Candela also disagrees with Bone's assessment in "We Wear the Mask: Irony in Dunbar's *The Sport of the Gods*" (*AL,* March 1976). Candela argues effectively that Dunbar's strength as an artist was in his ability "to mix the seemingly inflexible elements of melodrama with the consciousness of an ironic mask that the black people in America know so well."

Hugh Gloster's analysis of Dunbar's novels in *Negro Voices in American Fiction* is similar to Bone's, although Gloster goes a step further by acknowledging the naturalistic elements in *The Sport of the Gods.* More significant, however, is Gloster's careful analysis of Dunbar's short stories, which he insists are generally restricted by the limitations of the plantation tradition.

A valuable collection of essays is Jay Martin's *A Singer in The Dawn: Reinterpretations of Paul Laurence Dunbar* (New York: Dodd, Mead,

1975). These essays were originally presented as lectures at the Dunbar Centenary Conference conducted at the University of California at Irvine in 1972. The section on Dunbar's poetry begins with Darwin T. Turner's important article, "Paul Laurence Dunbar: The Poet and the Myths," which also appears in *College Language Association Journal* (December 1974). Turner argues that Dunbar's achievements as a poet have been obscured by reliance upon myths about him, rather than on a critical examination of his work. He goes on to explode six of these myths, those dealing with versification, tone, subject, diction, attitudes toward black characters, and Dunbar's talent in general.

"Racial Fire in the Poetry of Paul Laurence Dunbar," by James A. Emanuel, examines twenty-five poems which contain "substantially whatever racial fire Dunbar could express in verse." Emanuel suggests that Dunbar's lack of inherent inferiority to others accounts for the fact that the fire of racial pride "glows only in one poem out of every twenty that he wrote." This ratio, however, does not lessen his stature either as a man or as a poet, according to Emanuel.

Dickson D. Bruce, Jr., argues in "On Dunbar's 'Jingles in A Broken Tongue': Dunbar's Dialect Poetry and the Afro-American Folk Tradition," that Dunbar, rather than being a mere teller of tales, was actually an interpreter of a way of perceiving the universe that was prevalent in folk tradition—that is, that man was a being in a world governed by forces greater than himself. Bruce uses "An Ante-Bellum Sermon" and "Accountability" to illustrate his point.

In "Dunbar and Dialect Poetry," Myron Simon uses a linguistic approach to suggest that the literary and oral traditions of black poetry begin to come together in Dunbar's work.

Addison Gayle, Jr., opens the section dealing with Dunbar's fiction with "Literature as Catharsis: The Novels of Paul Laurence Dunbar." Gayle suggests that Dunbar's failure to see the novel as a means by which to create new and positive images of the black man led to a "schizophrenia," which caused him to remain unsure of his identity— was he a conventional American or was he a black after the fashion of the plantation school. The black side of Dunbar is represented by his short stories, his dialect poetry, and two of his novels, *The Fanatics* and *The Sport of the Gods;* but, says Gayle, the man he wished himself to be, the free, white, and independent American, is revealed in the poems written in literary English and in his other two novels, *The Uncalled* and *The Love of Landry.* This view is further explored by Gayle in *The Way of the New World*, in which he accuses Dunbar of being unable to "regard Blacks as other than the stereotypes and images created in the minds of Euro-Americans." Kenny J. Williams, on the other hand, argues in "The Masking of the Novelist" that Dunbar had to veil his protest in order to succeed as a black writer in a predominantly white society. Williams examines Dunbar's novels as "exercises in masking his views."

In "The Lyrical Short Fiction of Dunbar and Chesnutt," Bert Bender insists that each author in his own way attempted to create a new aesthetic—Dunbar through lyricism and Chesnutt through irony—and in so doing helped to create a new direction for the short story. (Other comparative studies of these two authors have been noted earlier.)

SUTTON E. GRIGGS

The predominant critical debate concerning the writings of Sutton E. Griggs has focused on the degree of militancy evident in his fiction. Hugh Gloster, in "Sutton E. Griggs, Novelist of the New Negro" (*Phylon,* Winter 1943), hails Griggs as the chronicler of the demise of the servile black and the arrival of the new Negro. Gloster discusses Griggs's five race-motivated novels from this perspective, and praises *Imperium in Imperio* (1899) as the first black American novel with a strict political emphasis. Gloster concludes with a brief comparison between Griggs and Chesnutt, in which he suggests that Chesnutt was the better artist, but that, unlike Griggs, Chesnutt failed either to glorify negritude or to offer the black community a political solution to their problem. Much of the material in this study is incorporated into Gloster's section on Griggs in *Negro Voices in American Fiction.* Taking issue with this analysis is Robert Bone. In *The Negro Novel in America,* Bone insists that Griggs is merely "an old-fashioned Southerner who relies on 'quality white folks' to provide a solution to the race problem." Because of this, he contends, Griggs must be willing to compromise, and Bone argues that compromise is not the way of the new Negro.

Attempting to reconcile these opposing views is Robert E. Fleming in "Sutton E. Griggs: Militant Black Novelist" (*Phylon,* Spring 1973). Fleming suggests that a careful examination of Griggs's novels "as he wrote them" makes more logical the development of accommodationist philosophy from *Imperium in Imperio* to the later novels.

Taking Bone to task for his assessment of Griggs is Addison Gayle, Jr., in *The Way of the New World.* Gayle contends that Griggs's strength lies in his being a novelist of ideas rather than a stylist, and that Griggs was the first novelist since Delany to engage in "the war for control of the images." Griggs, Gayle assures us, is indeed "the prophet of the new Negro." Also helpful for a study of Griggs is Campbell Tatham's "Reflections: Sutton Griggs' *Imperium in Imperio*" (*SBL,* Spring 1974).

FRANCES ELLEN WATKINS HARPER

Most of the criticism of Frances Ellen Watkins Harper's work appears in general surveys of black American literature. Loggins discusses both her poetry and her novel, *Iola Leroy; or, Shadows Uplifted* (1892), in *The Negro Author,* and concludes that she was "an author of poor stories and fair verse." Bone calls *Iola Leroy* a transitional novel which combines abolitionist elements with "incipient attacks on caste." He identifies it as a protest novel, although he concedes that it lacks the urgency of others written in the same mode. Gloster, too, calls *Iola Leroy* a transitional novel, suggesting that it bridges the ante- and postbellum periods by helping to develop certain middle-class black characters in order to counteract the stereotypes of the plantation school. He also suggests that Harper drew heavily from Brown's *Clotel* for material for her own novel. Gayle generally agrees with these assessments, although he accuses Harper of extolling the accommodationist ideas of Webb and Brown, while ignoring the strides made by Delany.

FRANK J. WEBB

Loggins calls Frank J. Webb's only novel, *The Garies and Their Friends* (1857), an important work because of the power of its emotional content, which enables Webb to convey effectively the pathos of his characters. Bone has suggested that *The Garies* has much in common with the protest novels of the 1890s because of Webb's concern, not with slavery, but rather with the artificial barriers to success which confront the free Negro. Arthur P. Davis, in *"The Garies and Their Friends:* A Neglected Pioneer Novel" (*CLAJ,* September 1969), argues that *The Garies* is better written than *Clotel* and in a way more significant because it contains a number of "firsts": it was the first novel to deal with the problems of free blacks, to treat intermarriage "with any appreciable depth," to portray a lynch mob in a free state, to treat with irony the vagaries of the "color line," and to focus on the middle class, an aspect of the black novel that continued until the appearance of *Native Son.* James H. DeVries attributes the current unpopularity of *The Garies* more to its indictment of northern racism than to its reliance on the conventions of the sentimental novels. His "The Tradition of the Sentimental Novel in *The Garies and Their Friends"* (*CLAJ,* September 1972) suggests that other novels employing sentimental conventions, especially *Clotel,* have enjoyed popularity in spite of them. R. F. Bogardus's "Frank J. Webb's *The Garies and Their Friends:* An Early Black Novelist's Venture Into Realism" (*SBL,* Summer 1974), suggests that Webb's work was a transitional novel which sought to break out of an effete romantic tradition and move closer to literary realism.

The authors wish to acknowledge their indebtedness to William L. Andrews's "Charles Waddell Chesnutt: An Essay in Bibliography" (*RALS,* Spring 1976) for their discussion of Chesnutt scholarship.

THE HARLEM RENAISSANCE:
Arna W. Bontemps, Countee Cullen, James Weldon Johnson, Claude McKay, and Jean Toomer

RUTH MILLER
PETER J. KATOPES

Charles Hamlin Good's article "The First American Negro Literary Movement" (*Opportunity*, March 1932) tells of the literary activities of the *cordons bleus*, a community of wealthy mulattoes in New Orleans during the nineteenth century. Led by Arthur Lanusse, this group began publishing a magazine in 1843 that featured the works of the city's Negro literati. The publication, which was written entirely in French and called *L'Album Litteraire, Journal des Jeunes Gens, Amateurs de Litterature*, included poems, short stories, and essays. The editors also offered advice to the magazine's young readers, encouraging them to assert their rights as individuals, as well as the rights of their race in general. Encouraged by a favorable response to this effort, Lanusse later collected eighty-seven poems in French by seventeen different "men of color," all natives of New Orleans. The anthology was called *Les Cenelles* (the holly berries) and appeared in 1845.

Eighty years after this pioneer effort there appeared a collection of writing by another group of Negroes who were geographically as well as culturally distinct from their predecessors. This collection appeared in an issue of *The Survey Graphic* dedicated to Harlem (March 1925), and contained a selection of works by Harlem writers, as well as the now famous and influential essay by Alain Locke, "The New Negro." The success of the issue was immediate, and Locke quickly enlarged the collection to include materials of national and even international scope. Calling the volume *The New Negro: An Interpretation* (New York: Albert & Charles Boni, 1925), Locke struck the keynote of the intellectual and literary highlight of the phenomenon which became known as the "Harlem Renaissance," a rich fulfillment of Lanusse's prophetic effort of the 1840s.

The new Negro, according to Locke, will no longer accept being treated as one apart from the mainstream of American life. He is the common man who has been transformed from a dependent ward into a self-reliant, self-respecting citizen of the democracy. The new Negro is intellectually dynamic and, quite literally, on the move, migrating not to escape the South, but rather to embrace the new freedom that awaits him in the North. The new Negro is emblematic of an awakened racial pride, a pride fostered not only by his American heritage, but also by his African roots in a race of warriors and kings. Locke's prediction that out of this new consciousness would come a blossoming of the arts, with the emphasis on craftsmanship, and new forms of expression, was fulfilled during the 1920s, the decade of the Harlem Renaissance.

Bibliographies

GENERAL BIBLIOGRAPHIES

There are several general as well as individual bibliographies available to the student of the Harlem Renaissance. Robert Bone's unannotated bibliography in *The Negro Novel in America* (New Haven, Conn.: Yale University Press, 1965) lists Negro novels from 1853 to 1952 chronologically by date of publication. Robert A. Corrigan's "Afro-American Fiction: A Checklist, 1853–1970" (*MASJ*, Fall 1970) attempts to identify all works of fiction by Afro-American writers published in book form. Each entry includes author, title, original place and date of publication, publisher, pagination, and—of particular value—information about both hard- and soft-cover reprints. This checklist updates Corrigan's earlier compilation, "A Bibliography of Afro-American Fiction, 1853–1970" (*SBL*, Summer 1970), and is itself augmented by "Afro-American Fiction: Errata and Additions" (*AmerS*, Spring 1971).

Another useful bibliography is appended to *Dark Symphony: Negro Literature in America* (New York: The Free Press, 1968), edited by James A. Emanuel and Theodore L. Gross. This listing cites several major repositories for manuscript materials, a number of black periodicals, and primary and significant secondary sources for the major Harlem writers. Hugh M. Gloster's bibliography in *Negro Voices in American Fiction* (Chapel Hill: University of North Carolina Press, 1948; rpt. New York: Russell & Russell, 1968) is an alphabetical listing of fiction by Negro authors of both the early modern period and the Harlem Renaissance. Also included are references to works of literary history and criticism, magazine and newspaper articles, and book reviews. The bibliography, which appears in *Images of the Negro in American Literature* (Chicago: University of Chicago Press, 1966), edited by Seymour Gross and John Hardy, includes a helpful listing of significant books and articles on Cullen, Johnson, McKay, and Toomer. Another useful general bibliography is Helen R. Houston's "Contributions of the American Negro to American Culture—A Selected Checklist" (*BB*, July–September 1969), which notes several significant critical works dealing with the Harlem Renaissance.

"The American Negro and American Literature: A Checklist of Significant Commentaries" (*BB*, January–April 1947), by John S. Lash, lists almost six hundred anthologies, literary histories, periodical references, and study guides and outlines relating to Negro expression. There are brief descriptions of some articles and books, and this list is especially helpful regarding the poetry of the Harlem Renaissance. Useful also is Lash's "The American Negro in American Literature: A Selected Bibliography of Critical Materials" (*JNE,* Fall 1946).

Blacks in America: Bibliographical Essays (Garden City, N.Y.: Doubleday, 1971), compiled by James M. McPherson et al., includes a short general bibliography of the Harlem Renaissance, and brief individual listings for Cullen, Hughes, Johnson, McKay, and Toomer. *Black American Writers, 1773–1949: A Bibliography and Union List* (Boston: G. K. Hall, 1975), compiled by Geraldine O. Matthews and the African-American Materials Project Staff, offers a representative listing of works, citing library locations of copies, when known. Elizabeth W. Miller's *The Negro in America: A Bibliography* (Cambridge, Mass.: Harvard University Press, 1966) contains a short section on literature, with brief annotations. The selections are primarily limited to modern works and appropriate secondary resources.

Black American Writers Past and Present: A Biographical and Bibliographical Dictionary (Metuchen, N.J.: Scarecrow, 1975), compiled by Theressa Gunnels Rush et al., is an unannotated listing of works by black authors. Most periodical references are to black magazines, many of which are not usually noted in established academic bibliographies. Particularly useful in this listing, despite several inaccuracies, is the citing of specific page numbers on which an author is mentioned in a particular book or article. Dorothy B. Porter's two compilations, *A Working Bibliography on the Negro in the United States* (New York: Xerox Corporation, 1969), and *The Negro in the United States: A Selected Bibliography* (Washington, D.C.: Library of Congress, 1970), are helpful resources. Darwin T. Turner's *Afro-American Writers* (New York: Appleton, 1970) focuses on twentieth-century drama, fiction, and poetry, and offers guides to related topics such as history, sociology, art, music, journalism, and folklore. Of particular value is Turner's listing of articles appearing in popular magazines and encyclopedias which, although they are often important sources of information for the study of Afro-American literature, are rarely included in major academic listings. *The Negro in the United States: A Research Guide* (Bloomington: Indiana University Press, 1965), by Erwin K. Welsch, is also useful. Maxwell Whiteman's *A Century of Fiction by American Negroes, 1853–1952: A Descriptive Bibliography* (Philadelphia: Albert Saifer, 1968) attempts to list all books published by Negroes during this period. Included in this listing are the major Harlem writers, as well as a representative group of some lesser-known authors of the Harlem Renaissance.

Jean Wagner's *Black Poets of the United States: From Paul Laurence Dunbar to Langston Hughes* (Urbana: University of Illinois Press, 1973), translated from the original French by Kenneth Douglas, provides an extensive bibliography and supplement (by Keneth Kinnamon) dealing with the Harlem Renaissance authors, as well as a list of general works of sociology, psychology, history, and criticism. Another useful listing devoted primarily to the Harlem movement is Roger Whitlow's "The Harlem Renaissance and After: A Checklist of Black Literature of the Twenties and Thirties" (*NALF*, December 1973), which includes primary and significant secondary works relating to this period.

ARNA BONTEMPS

Despite his prolific career, the works of Arna Bontemps have not had any exhaustive bibliographic study, perhaps because critics have placed him on the periphery rather than at the center of the Harlem movement. A comprehensive listing for Bontemps appears in Arthur P. Davis's *From The Dark Tower: Afro-American Writers, 1900–1960* (Washington, D.C.: Howard University Press, 1974), which also includes a bibliography of anthologies, collections, and critical studies, as well as listings for the other Harlem Renaissance authors. Useful also is "Arna Bontemps: Dedication and Bibliography," (*BlackW*, September 1971). Included here are Bontemps's collaborations with Langston Hughes, Jack Conroy, and W. C. Handy, as well as references to chapters by Bontemps appearing in recent books.

COUNTEE CULLEN

A good list of works about Countee Cullen appears in *Modern Black Poets, A Collection of Critical Essays* (Englewood Cliffs, N.J.: Prentice-Hall, 1973), edited by Donald B. Gibson. Margaret Perry's *A Bio-Bibliography of Countee Cullen* (Westport, Conn.: Greenwood, 1971), offers a complete list of Cullen's works, including his books and reviews of them, individual poems, plays, short stories, recorded works, articles by Cullen, and his unpublished works. Another section of the bibliography is devoted to writings about Cullen (over two hundred entries) and lists material in newspapers and magazines, and in parts of books, as well as obituary notices and tributes. Perry also notes some twenty-three untitled newspaper references to Cullen and about seventy anthologies in which his poems appear.

JAMES WELDON JOHNSON

The definitive bibliography of the works of James Weldon Johnson appears in Eugene Levy's excellent biography, *James Weldon Johnson: Black Leader, Black Voice* (Chicago: University of Chicago Press, 1973). The listing is preceded by an essay discussing various resources for studying Johnson, including some which appeared too late for Levy to use. The bibliography itself is divided into ten sections, listing Johnson's published writings in chronological order, several manuscript collections and their locations, published correspondence, government and institutional reports related to his career, a number of newspapers Levy used in his research, over one hundred seventy books and articles offering information about Johnson and his times, dissertations, and two interviews in which Johnson participated. Another useful compilation is J. Saunders Redding's list of works about Johnson which appears in Louis D. Rubin's *A Bibliographical Guide to the Study of Southern Literature* (Baton Rouge: Louisiana State University Press, 1969).

CLAUDE McKAY

Manuel D. Lopez's "Claude McKay" (*BB*, October–December 1972), is a comprehensive listing of McKay's published works and also notes relevant secondary sources. Another excellent bibliography appears in *The Passion of Claude McKay: Selected Poetry and Prose, 1912–1948* (New York: Schocken, 1973), edited by Wayne Cooper. Cooper lists McKay's published books, with references to editions, book reviews, articles about McKay, and publication data on his individual poems and short stories. A list of works about McKay is found in Gibson's *Modern Black Poets*, mentioned earlier.

JEAN TOOMER

Bibliographical material on Jean Toomer is generally restricted to lists of works about him. The most comprehensive listing is John M. Reilly's "Jean Toomer: An Annotated Checklist of Criticism" (*RALS*, Spring 1974). Reilly lists in chronological order all items offering commentary on Toomer which were published between 1923 and 1973. Included also are a number of complete but unpublished dissertations. Darwin T. Turner's list of secondary works in Rubin's *A Bibliographical Guide to the Study of Southern Literature,* and Gibson's list in *Modern Black Poets* are useful.

Editions

The revival of interest in black American literature has prompted a number of reprints of the works of many authors of the Harlem Renaissance as well as the compilation of several anthologies.

An excellent recent collection is Nathan Irvin Huggins's *Voices From the Harlem Renaissance* (New York: Oxford University Press, 1976), which includes selections from minor as well as major figures of the movement. *Black Writers of America: A Comprehensive Anthology* (New York: Macmillan, 1972), edited by Richard Barksdale and Keneth Kinnamon, includes a particularly useful selection of Harlem Renaissance writers. Offering a helpful Harlem Renaissance selection is Ruth Miller's *Blackamerican Literature, 1760–Present* (Beverly Hills, Calif.: Glencoe Press, 1971), featuring poems by Fenton Johnson and an excerpt from *'Cruiter,* a play by John Matheus. Of interest also are *Dark Symphony: Negro Literature in America* (New York: The Free Press, 1968), edited by James A. Emanuel and Theodore Gross; Abraham Chapman's *Black Voices; An Anthology of Afro-American Literature* (New York: New American Library, 1968); *Kaleidoscope: Poems by American Negro Poets* (New York: Harcourt, Brace & World, 1967), edited and introduced by Robert Hayden; Langston Hughes's *The Best Short Stories by Negro Writers: An Anthology From 1899 to the Present* (Boston: Little, Brown, 1967); *The Poetry of the Negro, 1746–1949* (Garden City, N.Y.: Doubleday, 1949), edited by Hughes and Arna Bontemps; Bontemps's *American Negro Poetry* (New York: Hill & Wang, 1963; revised 1974); *The Negro Caravan* (New York: Dryden, 1941), edited by Sterling A. Brown, Arthur Davis, and Ulysses Lee; Countee Cullen's *Caroling Dusk: An Anthology of Verse by Negro Poets* (New York: Harper & Bros., 1927; rpt. Harper & Row, 1974); *Four Negro Poets* (New York: Simon & Schuster, 1927), edited by Alain Locke and including poems by Cullen, Hughes, McKay, and Toomer; Locke's *The New Negro: An Interpretation* (New York: Albert & Charles Boni, 1925); *Plays of Negro Life: A Source-Book of Native American Drama* (New York: Harper & Bros., 1927), edited by Locke and Montgomery Gregory; and James Weldon Johnson's *The Book of American Negro Poetry* (New York: Harcourt, Brace & World, 1922; second ed., 1931).

Arna Bontemps's two most popular novels, *God Sends Sunday* (1931) and *Black Thunder* (1936), have each been reprinted, the former in 1972 by AMS Press of New York, and the latter by Beacon Press of Boston in 1968. *Personals* (1963), a collection of Bontemps's poems, was reprinted by the Broadside Press of Detroit in 1974.

In 1970 Arno Press of New York reprinted Countee Cullen's *Color* (1925). His novel *One Way to Heaven* (1932) was reprinted by AMS Press in 1975.

James Weldon Johnson's autobiography, *Along This Way* (1933), was reprinted in 1973 by Da Capo Press and in 1968 by Viking (both publishers are located in New York). Johnson's *The Autobiography of an Ex-Coloured Man* (1912) was reprinted in 1960 by Hill & Wang (New York) and includes an introduction by Arna Bontemps. The autobiography also appears in John Hope Franklin's *Three Negro Classics* (New York: Avon, 1965), along with Du Bois's *The Souls of Black Folk* (1903) and Booker T. Washington's *Up From Slavery* (1901). *Black Manhattan* (1930) was reprinted in 1968 both by Arno and by Atheneum (New York). *Fifty Years and Other Poems* (1917) was reprinted in 1975 by AMS Press; *Negro Americans, What Now?* (1934) was reprinted in 1973 by Da Capo; and *The Book of American Negro Poetry* (1922, 1931), in 1969 by Harcourt Brace Jovanovich of New York.

A Long Way From Home (1937), Claude McKay's autobiography, was reprinted in 1970 both by Arno Press and by Harcourt Brace Jovanovich; the latter also reprinted *Banana Bottom* (1933) in 1974, as did the Chatham Bookseller (Chatham, New Jersey) in 1971, and *Banjo* (1929) in 1970. Harcourt Brace Jovanovich reprinted *Harlem: Negro Metropolis* (1940) in 1972, and *Selected Poems* in 1969. *The Dialect Poetry of Claude McKay, Two Volumes in One* (1912), a facsimile reprint of his *Constab Ballads* and *Songs of Jamaica*, is a product of Books For Libraries (Plainview, New York) as is a facsimile of *Gingertown* (1932). *Home to Harlem* (1928) was reprinted in 1973 by the Chatham Bookseller; Twayne (Boston) published the *Selected Poems of Claude McKay* in 1971; and Howard University Press (Washington, D.C.) published *My Green Hills of Jamaica* in 1975.

The Selected Poems of Claude McKay: With an Introduction by John Dewey and a Biographical Note by Max Eastman (New York: Bookman Associates, 1953) includes approximately eighty-five poems. The material is divided into five parts. The first includes some of McKay's West Indian verse; the second selects poems representative of McKay's developing racial awareness; the third includes poems about city life; part four presents verse about McKay's travels to Europe and Russia; and the final section offers poems exploring sexual themes.

Perhaps the best edition of McKay's work is Wayne Cooper's *The Passion of Claude McKay: Selected Poetry and Prose, 1912–1948* (New York: Schocken, 1973). The selections attempt to trace the external development of McKay's life, as well as the progress of his racial awareness. Cooper has included an excellent critical commentary, a good set of notes, a fine bibliography, a helpful index, and a number of unpublished letters and other writings which appear here for the first time.

The material is divided into seven parts: "Early Articles, 1918–1922"; "The Russian Experience, 1922–1923"; "Selected Poems, 1912–1925"; "An Article and Letters"; "Experiments in Fiction"; "Letters and Essays, 1934–1948"; and "The Move to Catholicism, 1944–1948."

Jean Toomer's *Cane* (1923) was reissued in 1971 and 1975 by Liveright, in 1967 by University Place Press, and in 1969 by Harper & Row. This last edition includes an introduction by Arna Bontemps (all publishers are located in New York).

Manuscripts and Letters

Fortunately, the manuscripts and letters of several Harlem Renaissance writers are available in large and small collections throughout the country.

The James Weldon Johnson Memorial Collection at the Beinecke Rare Book and Manuscript Library at Yale University contains a great deal of relevant material. Although the items in this collection have not been catalogued, and therefore are not easily accessible to researchers, the holdings are extensive and in excellent condition. Several manuscripts by Arna Bontemps, both hand- and typewritten, are included in this collection, as are almost two hundred letters. Countee Cullen is represented by a number of items, including the complete series of *The Lost Zoo* manuscripts, with Cullen's notes. Also of particular interest is a typescript carbon of Cullen's play *Medea,* which includes both a prologue and an epilogue excised from the published version, and a handwritten manuscript of this same prologue and epilogue, with Cullen's revisions. Available also are the manuscripts of *The Black Christ, One Way to Heaven* (both the novel and the play), Cullen's French notebook, and over one hundred letters. The holdings include handwritten drafts of James Weldon Johnson's autobiography, *Along This Way;* typescripts and working drafts of *Black Manhattan, The Autobiography of an Ex-Coloured Man,* and *God's Trombones;* a rare book copy of Claude McKay's *Constab Ballads;* as well as other manuscript items by McKay. In addition, several other figures prominent in the Harlem Renaissance, non-writers as well as writers, are represented.

The Arna Bontemps Collection at the George Arents Research Library at Syracuse University consists of over fifty boxes of manuscripts and letters by Bontemps and others. There are drafts of several of Bontemps's books, such as *The Black Napoleon,* and *Chariot in the Sky;* fragments and completed drafts of a number of others (notably the first draft of *Black Thunder*); a draft of an unpublished novel, *The Chariot in the Cloud;* as well as letters, memorabilia, legal papers, and a miscellany of writings by other authors.

The Amistad Research Center at Dillard University in New Orleans holds approximately ninety letters from Bontemps to Countee Cullen in a collection called "Papers of Countee Cullen." Also included are approximately twelve hundred of Cullen's letters, several manuscripts, and his 1928 diary. These papers are available on microfilm from Dillard.

The Countee Cullen Memorial Collection of Atlanta University's Trevor Arnett Library contains some five thousand items and continues to grow. Included are proof sheets of Cullen's *The Brown Girl, The Lost Zoo,* and *On These I Stand,* as well as manuscripts of several of his individual poems. Represented in this collection are Hughes, Johnson, McKay, Carl Van Vechten, and several others connected with the Harlem Renaissance.

The Department of Special Collections of the University of California in Los Angeles holds ten letters from Cullen to Edouard Roditi, and the Joseph Regenstein Library of the University of Chicago holds several letters that Cullen wrote to Harriet Monroe while she was editor of *Poetry Magazine.* Fisk University has approximately one hundred items relating to Cullen, and the Schomburg Collection of the New York Public Library also contains several items.

The Library of Congress, The Hampton Institute in Virginia, and the Schomburg Collection hold several items of Johnson's, and Fisk owns several manuscripts of his songs and poems.

Additional material on Claude McKay can be found at Harvard University's Houghton Library, where there are ten of his letters (eight to W. S. Braithewaite and two to Lewis Stiles Gannet). The Schomburg Collection also holds some miscellaneous items relating to McKay.

The papers of Jean Toomer are at the Fisk University Library. Included among the various manuscripts and letters are manuscripts of Toomer's "Eight-Day World" and "From Exile and Being."

Biography

Biographical material on most of the Harlem writers is included in the numerous general studies of Black American literature, such as Robert Bone's *The Negro Novel in America* (New Haven: Yale University Press, 1965), Hugh Gloster's *Negro Voices in American Fiction* (Chapel Hill: University of North Carolina Press, 1948; rpt. New York: Russell & Russell, 1965), and Arthur P. Davis's *From The Dark Tower: Afro-American Writers, 1900–1960* (Washington, D.C.: Howard University Press, 1974). *The Negro Almanac* (New York: Bellwether, 1971), compiled by Harry A. Ploski and Ernest Kaiser, *Black American Writers Past and Present: A Biographical and Bibliographical Dictionary* (Metuchen, N.J.: Scarecrow, 1975), compiled by Theressa Gunnels Rush et al., and several other similar works are useful.

There is as yet no full-length biography of Arna Bontemps. However, two short articles in *Black World* (September 1973) commemorating his death offer some useful biographical data. "Arna Bontemps: A Memoir," by Houston A. Baker, Jr., is an account of Baker's relationship with Bontemps when the latter taught at Yale. Sterling A. Brown's "Arna Bontemps: Co-Worker, Comrade," offers insight into why Bontemps was not really a member of the Harlem Renaissance coterie.

The only full-length biography of Countee Cullen is Blanche E. Ferguson's *Countee Cullen and the Negro Renaissance* (New York: Dodd, Mead, 1966). Unfortunately, this work glosses over his life rather superficially and reads very much like a biography aimed at children. Ferguson offers no documentation and appends a rather mediocre bibliography. Despite the implications of the title, she explores none of the psychological, social, or literary ramifications of the Harlem Renaissance. Margaret Perry's *A Bio-Bibliography of Countee Cullen* (Westport, Conn.: Greenwood, 1971) offers a sixteen-page sketch of the poet's life, as well as a complete and perceptive analysis of his poetry. "Countee Cullen: The Lost Ariel," in Darwin T. Turner's *In A Minor Chord: Three Afro-American Writers and Their Search for Identity* (Carbondale: Southern Illinois University Press, 1971), describes Cullen as a prodigy who, because of "conflicting emotions, diverse friends, exotic settings, and indolence," never realized his early promise. Helpful biographic information about Cullen is found in Stephen H. Bronz's *Roots of Negro Racial Consciousness, The 1920's: Three Harlem Renaissance Authors* (New York: Libra, 1964), and Jean Wagner's *Black Poets of the United States: From Paul Laurence Dunbar to Langston Hughes* (Chicago: University of Illinois Press, 1973), translated from the French by Kenneth Douglas.

The definitive biography of James Weldon Johnson is Eugene Levy's excellent *James Weldon Johnson; Black Leader, Black Voice* (Chicago: University of Chicago Press, 1973). Levy intertwines the varied aspects of Johnson's life to give us not only a solid portrait of the man, but also an interesting account of the times. The biography is well written and researched and Levy appends an extensive bibliography. Two significant reviews of this study are by Walter B. Weare (*JAH,* September 1975) and by William M. Tuttle, Jr., (*AHR,* April 1975). Lynn Adelman's "A Study of James Weldon Johnson" (*JNH,* April 1967) is a brief survey of Johnson's adult life from the 1890s until his death in 1938. Noted in the article is Johnson's role in founding *The Daily American,* a Negro newspaper in Jacksonville, Florida, as well as his theatrical ventures, his brief law practice, and his stint as a United States consul to Venezuela. "James Weldon Johnson and Atlanta University" (*Phylon,* Winter 1971) by Clarence A. Bacote, is an account of Johnson's six years as a student at the famous Southern school. Additional biographical information can also be found in Bronz's *Roots of Negro Racial Consciousness* and Wagner's *Black Poets of the United States.*

There is no full-length biography of Claude McKay; however, valuable information about McKay's life is found in James R. Giles's *Claude McKay* (Boston: Twayne, 1976), Wagner's biographical introduction to the section on McKay in *Black Poets of the United States*, Addison Gayle, Jr.'s brief study, *Claude McKay: The Black Poet at War* (Detroit: Broadside, 1972), Kenneth Ramchand's *The West Indian Novel and Its Background* (New York: Barnes & Noble, 1970), Matthew Anthony Hoehn's *Catholic Authors: Contemporary Biographical Sketches 1930–1947* (Newark, N.J.: St. Mary's Abbey, 1948), and in Stephen H. Bronz's study. Phyllis Martin Lang's article "Claude McKay: Evidence of a Magical Pilgrimage" (*CLAJ*, June 1973), uses material from the Soviet newspapers *Pravda* and *Izvestia* to supplement McKay's own comments about his trip to Russia during from 1922 to 1923.

There also is no full-length biography of Jean Toomer, although Mabel Mayle Dillard's dissertation, "Jean Toomer: Herald of the Negro Renaissance" (Ohio University, 1967), offers some biographical data, as does Fritz Gysin's *The Grotesque in American Negro Fiction: Jean Toomer, Richard Wright, and Ralph Ellison* (Bern, Switzerland: Francke Verlag, 1975). Particularly helpful is "Jean Toomer: Exile" in Darwin Turner's *In A Minor Chord*, mentioned earlier, in which Turner explores certain aspects of Toomer's childhood in order to suggest the reasons for the author's isolationist tendencies. Wagner's short analysis of Toomer's poetry in *Black Poets of the United States* also includes some biographical information. Information on Toomer's interracial marriage is available in Daniel P. McCarthy's "Just Americans: A Note on Jean Toomer's Marriage to Margery Latimer" (*CLAJ*, June 1974), and Merle Richmond's response to McCarthy in (*CLAJ*, December 1974), "Jean Toomer and Margery Latimer." Charles Scruggs, in "Jean Toomer: Fugitive" (*AL*, March 1975), analyzes Toomer's denial of his Negro identity and cites two events, Toomer's reading of Romain Rolland's *Jean-Christophe*, and his acquaintance with Waldo Frank, as being critical in the development of this attitude. Cynthia E. Kerman examines Toomer's inability to be accommodated by any group to which he belonged in "Jean Toomer—Enigma?" (*Indian Journal of American Studies*, January 1977).

Criticism

BOOKS AND PARTS OF BOOKS DEALING WITH HARLEM RENAISSANCE WRITERS

An excellent discussion of the artistic, cultural, and intellectual difficulties encountered by the twentieth-century black American writer is *The American Negro Writer and His Roots: Selected Papers From the First Conference of Negro Writers, March, 1959* (New York: American Society of African Culture, 1960). Essays included are by a number of well-known black writers and critics, among them Bontemps, Davis, Saunders Redding, Hughes, and John Henrik Clarke.

A significant book-length study of the Harlem movement is Nathan Irvin Huggins's *Harlem Renaissance* (New York: Oxford University Press, 1971). Huggins approaches the Harlem of the 1920s not as the focus, "but as the lens through which one might see a new view; white and black men unknowingly dependent in their work to shape American character and culture." Huggins assesses the rather important role Carl Van Vechten played in the Harlem Renaissance, as well as the general relationship between white patron and black artist, in an attempt to demonstrate that the movement was more a white creation than a black one. As Huggins is primarily a historian, it is not surprising that his literary analysis is somewhat weak. Perhaps recognizing his limitations, he has not offered an in-depth study of any individual writer, choosing rather to survey the movement in terms of its cultural significance. The work is well indexed, but no bibliography is provided. However, the weaknesses do not seriously detract from the overall importance of the study. Three significant reviews are George Kent's (*Phylon,* Winter 1972), August Meier's (*AHR,* October 1972), and Charles T. Davis's (*AL,* March 1973).

Absolutely essential to a study of the Harlem Renaissance, and black American literature in general, is *The Way of the New World: The Black Novel in America* (Garden City, N.Y.: Doubleday, 1975) by Addison Gayle, Jr. Gayle argues that the Harlem Renaissance failed because black writers were forced to depend too much upon white benefactors (such as Carl Van Vechten), and because division within their own ranks "limited a full-scale assault on the image created to define Blacks." He suggests that the Harlem writers were divided into two groups. The first, represented by Jessie Fauset, James Weldon Johnson, and George S. Schuyler, supported a conservative approach, advocating a subordination of the black cultural experience to the overall American experience. The other, more radical, group, led by Langston Hughes and Claude McKay, believed in fidelity to the black experience, and saw the function of the black writer as being "the caretaker of the cultural heritage." Besides these major literary figures, Gayle's discussion of the movement also includes a number of nonliterary figures, notably Marcus Garvey.

A valuable collection of essays is *The Harlem Renaissance Remembered* (New York: Dodd, Mead, 1972), edited by Arna Bontemps. The book includes a memoir which offers an interesting insider's view of the Harlem milieu of the 1920s. George E. Kent's "Patterns of the Harlem Renaissance" describes how the Harlem writers sought "to assert, with varying degrees of radicality, a dissociation of sensibility from that enforced by American culture and its institutions." Hiroko Sato's "Under the Harlem Shadow: A Study of Jessie Fauset and Nella Larsen" is a study of two of the best-known women writers of the Harlem Renaissance. Patricia E. Taylor's "Langston Hughes and the Harlem Renaissance, 1921–1931: Major Events and Publications" is an overview of the achievements during this decade of perhaps the best-known of the Harlem writers. "Portrait of Wallace Thurman" by Mae Gwendolyn Henderson offers information on another important Harlem Renaissance figure, as does Robert Hemenway's "Zora Neale Hurston and the Eatonville Anthropology." Theodore Kornweibel, Jr., analyzes the drama criticism of Theophilus Lewis in "Theophilus Lewis and the Theatre of the Harlem Renaissance." Of particular value is Ronald Primeau's "Frank Horne and the Second Echelon Poets of the Harlem Renaissance," which discusses, in addition to Horne, the contribution of Anee Spencer, Donald Jeffrey Hayes, Gwendolyn Bennet, Waring Cuney, Helene Johnson, Arna Bontemps, and Georgia Douglas Johnson. Also of interest are Patrick J. Gilpin's "Charles S. Johnson: Entrepeneur of the Harlem Renaissance," and Warrington Hudlin's "The Renaissance Re-Examined."

In *The Negro Novel in America,* Robert Bone suggests that the Harlem Renaissance had a sociological rather than a literary motivation. He notes that this becomes evident when one examines how this "period of self-discovery . . . reversed the assimilationist trend of the pre-war period."

A useful short study is Stephen H. Bronz's *Roots of Negro Racial Consciousness, The 1920's: Three Harlem Renaissance Authors,* mentioned earlier. Bronz analyzes the writings of Cullen, Johnson, and McKay in an attempt to understand their relationship to Harlem and to Negro history. He examines Johnson's belief in the necessity of "respectable white recognition" of the Negro, and how he often resorted to irony in his poetry in order to vent his protest. He suggests that Cullen's shunning of the "confrontation with the realities that his times and his race imposed upon him" were emblematic of the shortcomings of the entire Harlem movement, which depended for its sustenance upon the approval of wealthy white and middle-class black audiences. McKay was the most effective protest poet of the Renaissance, according to Bronz. He also says that although McKay's novels are "weak as literature," they have sociological value because of their consistent and sometimes fierce reaction to racial prejudice. In this study, Bronz somewhat successfully bridged the gap between "the fawning, dissembling Uncle Tom of the Reconstruction Era and the determined, outspoken Negro of today." Amritjit Singh's recent study, *The Novels of the Harlem Renaissance: Twelve Black Writers, 1923–1933* (University Park: Pennsylvania State University Press, 1976), which examines the works of Bontemps, Cullen, Du Bois, Fauset, Fisher, Hughes, Larsen, McKay, Schuyler, Thurman, Toomer, and White, is also helpful. However, *Silence to the Drums: A Survey of the Literature of the Harlem Renaissance* (Westport, Conn.: Greenwood, 1976) by Margaret Perry is a disappointing summary which offers no new insights.

Sterling Brown's *The Negro in American Fiction* (Washington, D.C.: Associates in Negro Folk Education, 1937; rpt. Port Washington, N.Y.: Kennikat Press, 1968) offers an interesting perspective, suggesting that the Harlem Renaissance writers committed the same errors as did earlier white writers who explored the plantation tradition. Brown observes that just as the plantation writers deliberately underplayed or ignored the daily horrors of slave life—the lashings, the auction block, the separation of families—so the Harlem Renaissance writers deliberately ignore the daily horrors of life in Harlem—the unemployment lines, the grossly overcrowded schools, prevalent street crime, and the "surly resentment" of the average man—in favor of the cabaret and the glamour of night life. In *Native Sons: A Critical Study of Twentieth-Century Negro American Authors* (Philadelphia: Lippincott, 1968), Edward Margolies echoes Brown when he describes the Harlem Renaissance as a "swing to Romanticism, sometimes dangerously racist, sometimes curiously exotic, but always self-congratulatory. The trouble is . . . Harlem is not—and never was—a happy jungle, and to describe it as such only perpetuates the minstrel stereotype in another form."

David Littlejohn's shrill outburst, *Black on White: A Critical Survey of Writing by American Negroes* (New York: Grossman, 1966), defines the Harlem Renaissance as "one more fad of the faddish 20's—something modish and insubstantial, and perhaps even a little corrupt." He attributes the "built-in obsolescence" of many Harlem novels to an "excessive concern for a colorful surface and a fixation with the social mores of the Negro middle class." He is somewhat more favorably disposed toward the Harlem poets, however, who he says "took themselves and their art far more seriously" than did the novelists. Unfortunately, Littlejohn's study, which could very well have been an important contribution to black American literary scholarship, is less literary analysis than pure vitriol.

Arthur P. Davis's *From The Dark Tower: Afro-American Writers, 1900–1960* (Washington, D.C.: Howard University Press, 1974) is a useful study geared to the student rather than to the specialist. Davis offers a brief overview of the backgrounds of the Harlem Renaissance, and his volume is a helpful quick-reference guide to the major and minor writers of the movement.

Hugh Gloster's *Negro Voices in American Fiction* (Chapel Hill: University of North Carolina Press, 1948; rpt. New York: Russell & Russell, 1968), includes a valuable analysis of lesser-known writers of the Harlem Renaissance. He discusses the early postwar fiction of Herman Dreer, Fenton Johnson, William Pickens, and Joshua Henry Jones, as well as the work of Fauset, Walter White, Larsen, Schuyler, Thurman, Fisher, and Eric Walrond. Also valuable is James O. Young's *Black Writers of the Thirties* (Baton Rouge: Louisiana State University Press, 1973), which, although it focuses upon the economic and political writing of the day, nevertheless offers a chapter on each of the black poets and fictionists of the period.

An outstanding study of the poetry of the Harlem Renaissance is Jean Wagner's *Black Poets of the United States: From Paul Laurence Dunbar to Langston Hughes* (Chicago: University of Illinois Press, 1973), translated from the French by Kenneth Douglas. Wagner offers an excellent analysis of the social, political, and psychological backgrounds of the Harlem Renaissance, as well as an examination of the "interrelationship of racial and religious feeling in the poets." Included are individual sections on Cullen, McKay, and Toomer (whom Wagner calls the "great lyric poets" of the movement), suggesting that each used some form of religion as a means of transgressing the dilemma of the black poet in America. Opposed to this group are Johnson, Hughes, and Sterling Brown, who reject any type of religion, and want rather to "rehabilitate, praise, and defend" the black race as a group.

ARTICLES ABOUT HARLEM RENAISSANCE WRITERS

A contemporary condemnation of the Harlem Renaissance was Benjamin Brawley's "The Negro Literary Renaissance" (*Southern Workman*, April 1927). Brawley is outraged at the Harlem writers' "preference for sordid, unpleasant, or forbidden themes," and accuses them of being "loafers" masquerading as artists. He calls *Cane* "artificial," Cullen an artistic novice, and Hughes "the sad case of a young man of ability who has gone off on the wrong track altogether." On the positive side, Brawley praises Eric Walrond's collection of stories, *Tropic Death* (1926), as the "most important contribution made by a Negro since the appearance of Dunbar's *Lyrics of Lowly Life*," and observes that McKay's poetry "shows due regard for the technique of versification."

Walter Daykin's early article in *Sociological and Social Research* (January–February 1935), "Social Thought in Negro Novels," examines the implied or expressed social criticism in the Negro novel. Daykin divides the Harlem writers into two groups. The first, represented by Du Bois, White, Fauset, and Larsen, reacts negatively to anything degrading to the race, whether or not it is true, and by so doing attempts to elevate the status of the Negro by positive fictional representation. This is one reason, Daykin suggests, that these novelists frequently use the "refined and educated mulatto" as their main character. The second group, represented by Rudolph Fisher and McKay, protests against the social order by stressing the vulgar aspects of Negro life and employing proletarian characters to fill their novels.

The aims of the Harlem Renaissance writers are also explored in Charles Glicksberg's "The Negro Cult of the Primitive" (*AR*, Spring 1944). Glicksberg suggests that these writers, by a return to their primitive origins in Africa, attempted to form cultural and political alliances with other black people throughout the world. He further suggests that this was an impossible task exactly because of the vast cultural differences from their African counterparts. Glicksberg concludes that the Negro artist cannot achieve self-definition as long as he is "enslaved by his racial complex." In "Primitives and Saviors: Cultural Images of Blacks in the 1920's" (*Minority Voices*, Spring 1977), James F. Smith, Jr., examines how blacks are portrayed by the Harlem Renaissance writers, as well as by such white writers as John Dos Passos.

Abraham Chapman's important article, "The Harlem Renaissance in Literary History" (*CLAJ*, September 1967), offers a lengthy discussion of the literary and psychological aspects of the Harlem Renaissance, and rightly criticizes the general lack of reference to the movement in several well-known literary histories. In " 'All Dressed Up But No Place to Go': The Black Writer and His Audience During The Harlem Renaissance" (*AL*, January 1977), Charles Scruggs examines the "problem of a suitable audience for black writers [which] preoccupied the best minds" of the Harlem Renaissance. "The Harlem Renaissance: Toward a Black Aesthetic" (*MASJ*, Fall 1970), by Addison Gayle, Jr., discusses the Harlem writers' attempt to create new values and images for the Negro through their literature. This article previews much of the material in Gayle's *The Way of the New World*, mentioned above.

An interesting study is Robert C. Hart's "Black–White Literary Relations in the Harlem Renaissance" (*AL*, January 1973), which explores, "from the Black side," the implications of these relationships. Hart points out that it was rather significant that the important figures of the "white renaissance" of the 1920s—Fitzgerald, Faulkner, and Hemingway, to name a few—had no association with the Harlem writers. Instead, black writers formed friendships with second-rank white artists, and these associations ultimately developed into patron-writer relationships. An informative, if sometimes testy, memoir of the Harlem Renaissance is John O. Killens's "Another Time When Black Was Beautiful" (*BlackW*, November 1970). In the same issue, "The Harlem Renaissance: Its Artists, Its Impact, Its Meaning," by John A. Williams, suggests that the movement developed primarily because "Black artists were exotica for whites."

"The Expatriate Consciousness in Black American Literature" (*SBL*, Summer 1972) by Lloyd W. Brown examines the movement from the perspective that the Harlem writers were "transplanted Africans" searching for their cultural roots in a primitive past, while simultaneously trying to redefine or rediscover their more immediate ties in America. Priscilla Ramsey examines the use of the "passing" theme by several Harlem Renaissance writers in "A Study of Black Identity in 'Passing' novels of the Nineteenth and Early Twentieth Centuries" (*SBL*, Spring 1976).

Charles R. Larson's "Three Novels of the Jazz Age" (*Crit*, No. 3, 1969), suggests that Cullen's *One Way to Heaven* (1932), McKay's *Home to Harlem* (1928), and Van Vechten's *Nigger Heaven* (1926), combine to constitute the "cultural birth" of the new Negro. Larson sees the strength of McKay's novel in its ability to catch "the pulsation of Negro life, the beat of Harlem." Van Vechten's work is also strong on atmosphere and local color, but weak on plot. Cullen's effort, however, does not capture the "throb of Harlem life," concentrating rather on the full development of the story.

In "Fantasies of Affirmation: The 1920's Novel of Negro Life" (*CLAJ*, December 1972), Michael L. Lomax accuses the "novelists of Negro life"—Fauset, Larsen, Fisher, Cullen, and White—of showing contempt for that life by portraying black middle-class existence merely as a "darker version" of the white standard.

Waters E. Turpin's "Four Short Fiction Writers of the Harlem Renaissance—Their Legacy of Achievement" (*CLAJ*, September 1967), is a study of Toomer's "Blood-Burning Moon," Fisher's "Miss Cynthie," Hughes's "Slave on the Block," and McKay's "Truant."

Eugenia Collier's "Heritage From Harlem" (*BlackW*, November 1970) considers the way in which the Harlem poets rejected the false images of the Dunbar tradition and the detachment of the Negro romantics, and turned instead to folk culture by substituting the language of "real" blacks for the dialect of Dunbar, by exploiting themes not previously stressed in Negro poetry, and by a celebration of negritude.

Collier's "I Do Not Marvel, Countee Cullen" (*CLAJ*, September 1967; reprinted in *Modern Black Poets, A Collection of Critical Essays,* edited by Donald B. Gibson [Englewood Cliffs, N.J.: Prentice-Hall, 1973]), suggests that Negro poets, by protesting hatred and injustice, by demonstrating their pride in themselves and their race, and by seeking economic and social equality, are indeed "voicing the American Dream." She considers three poems from this perspective—Cullen's "From the Dark Tower," Brown's "The Odyssey of Big Boy," and McKay's "The Harlem Dancer." Collier also touches on poems by Bontemps, Fenton Johnson, Hughes, James Weldon Johnson, Helene Johnson, and Waring Cuney.

Two general essays regarding Harlem Renaissance poetry are Michael Furay's "Africa in Negro American Poetry to 1929" (*African*

Literature Today, January 1969), which explores the poets' use of African imagery and symbols, and Gerald Moore's "Poetry in the Harlem Renaissance" in *The Black American Writer: Poetry and Drama,* edited by C. W. E. Bigsby (Deland, Fla.: Everett/Edwards, 1969), which suggests that within the poetry of the Harlem movement is found a "world of real anguish and real desire struggling to find expression."

INDIVIDUAL AUTHORS

Arna Bontemps Critical material on Arna Bontemps is sparse. Although his work is usually touched upon in general critical works dealing with black American literature, there are few long studies devoted to him. Robert Bone, in *The Negro Novel in America,* calls Bontemps a transitional figure "bearing the mark both of the Renaissance and the Depression," and in so doing perhaps pinpoints why critics deal rather casually with this writer. Bone discusses *Black Thunder* (1936), commending Bontemps for a well-rounded characterization and a "narrative technique reminiscent of Dos Passos." Gloster, in *Negro Voices in American Fiction,* calls *Black Thunder* and *Drums at Dusk* (1939) important experiments in historical fiction, and praises *God Sends Sunday* (1931) for its lack of race consciousness. Even Littlejohn, in *Black on White,* favorably comments on Bontemps's work, especially his poetry. An important article is Dorothy Weil's analysis of the importance of the "folk credo" in *Black Thunder,* "Folklore Motifs in Arna Bontemps' *Black Thunder*" (*SFQ,* March 1971).

Countee Cullen A useful introduction to Countee Cullen's poetry is *A Many-Colored Coat of Dreams: The Poetry of Countee Cullen* by Houston A. Baker, Jr., (Detroit: Broadside Press, 1974). Bone calls Cullen the most talented poet of the movement, citing his use of humor and satire, and has high praise for his novel *One Way to Heaven* (1932). Gloster suggests that this novel helps to offset the more lurid emphasis of the Van Vechten mode by its focus on respectability and its satiric thrusts at Harlem socialites. Littlejohn calls Cullen "a fairly good nineteenth-century poet . . . a queer twentieth-century example of an English traditionalist, loving the measured line and skillful rhyme."

"Major Themes in the Poetry of Countee Cullen," by Nicholas Canaday, Jr. (in *The Harlem Renaissance Remembered,* edited by Arna Bontemps [New York: Dodd, Mead, 1972]) examines the various themes in Cullen's poetry, particularly race, death, Christianity, and heritage. Arthur P. Davis's "The Alien-and-Exile Theme in Countee Cullen's Racial Poems" (*Phylon,* Winter 1953) studies Cullen's concept of the American Negro as a perpetual alien, a spiritual and geographical exile, and discusses how this forms the thematic focus of several of his poems. Highlighting Cullen's use of traditional poetic techniques is "Countee

Cullen's Use of Greek Mythology" by David F. Dorsey, Jr. (*CLAJ*, September 1969). Michael L. Lomax suggests in "Countee Cullen: A Key to the Puzzle" (*Studies in the Literary Imagination*, Fall 1974) that Cullen's juxtaposition of racial and nonracial poems in *Color* (1925) is the clue to the "central contradiction in Cullen's appraisal of his own racial identity." Another examination of this tension in Cullen's verse is Beulah Reimherr's "Race Consciousness in Countee Cullen's Poetry" (*Susquehanna University Studies*, June 1963).

Robert A. Smith's "The Poetry of Countee Cullen" (*Phylon*, Fall 1950), suggests that Cullen's acute sensitivity to discrimination prevented him from achieving any kind of world view in his poems. Harvey Curtis Webster argues, in "A Difficult Career" (*Poetry*, July 1947), that this shortcoming accounts in great part for Cullen's "mediocrity" as a poet. Bertram L. Woodruff, in "The Poetic Philosophy of Countee Cullen" (*Phylon*, Fall 1940), suggests that Cullen's poetry "reveals his sincere attempt to discern what ever spiritual adjustment there may be for suffering, passionate, and weak souls in a hostile world."

Cullen's poetic technique is further explored in Catherine H. Copeland's "The Unifying Effect of Coupling in Countee Cullen's 'Yet Do I Marvel' " (*CLAJ*, December 1974), and Richard Lederer's "The Didactic and the Literary in Four Harlem Renaissance Sonnets" (*EJ*, February 1973). For an insight into Cullen's critical perspective, Walter C. Daniel's "Countee Cullen as Literary Critic" (*CLAJ*, March 1971) is useful.

James Weldon Johnson Robert Bone considers James Weldon Johnson to be "the only true artist among early Negro novelists" because Johnson favors artistic considerations over racial ones. Gloster agrees, citing Johnson's dispassionate characterizations in *The Autobiography of an Ex-Coloured Man*. David Littlejohn, on the other hand, describes the *Autobiography* as an "utterly artless, unstructured, unselective sequence of Negro-life episodes, written in a style as flat and directionless as the floor of an enormous room." Another negative opinion, albeit for some different reasons, comes from Clarence A. Amann, whose review of John Hope Franklin's *Three Negro Classics* (New York: Avon, 1965), "*Three Negro Classics*—An Estimate" (*NALF*, December 1970), is a comparative evaluation of Washington's *Up From Slavery*, Du Bois's *The Souls of Black Folk*, and Johnson's *Autobiography*, in which the last "emerges as the paranoid wailing of a bohemian wastrel."

Robert E. Fleming's significant "Irony as a Key to Johnson's *The Autobiography of an Ex-Coloured Man*" (*AL*, March 1973) examines the "sustained and many-faceted irony" which is the chief artistic merit of the book. Fleming goes on to explore Johnson's use of an unreliable narrator, allowing the author to "convey his vision of Black life in America through irony rather than by means of the heavy-handed propagandistic techniques of his predecessors." Marvin P. Garret's

"Early Recollections and Structural Irony in *The Autobiography of an Ex-Coloured Man*" (*Crit,* No. 2, 1971) suggests that the key to the novel lies in the narrator's recollections, which continually reveal his fallibility. Stephen M. Ross, in "Audience and Irony in Johnson's *The Autobiography of an Ex-Coloured Man*" (*CLAJ,* December 1974), argues that instead of directing his irony at the ex-colored man, Johnson is in fact attacking a hypothetical white audience. The narrator is unreliable, therefore, less because of his own hypocrisy, than because the author wishes us to see him as a man betrayed by and enmeshed in a white system of values.

"Contemporary Themes in Johnson's *The Autobiography of an Ex-Coloured Man*" (*NALF,* December 1970) by Robert E. Fleming suggests that the autobiography introduces for the first time many themes found in later black fiction. These themes—namelessness, racial self-hatred, the black mother's ambiguous role, and the characterization of the white liberal—all appear in the writings of Richard Wright, James Baldwin, Ralph Ellison, William Demby, Ann Petry, and John A. Williams. The influence of Johnson's novel on subsequent black fiction is noted by Houston A. Baker, Jr., in "A Forgotten Prototype: *The Autobiography of an Ex-Coloured Man* and *Invisible Man*" (*VQR,* Summer 1973). Baker argues convincingly that the "cultural situation that produced the *Autobiography,* the manner in which the story is set forth, and the antecedent works which influenced its author, lead one easily to the informing sensibility and significant patterns of action in [Ralph Ellison's] *Invisible Man.*" Eugenia Collier's "The Endless Journey of an Ex-Coloured Man" (*Phylon,* Winter 1971), suggests that Johnson's autobiography is constructed upon a framework of two journeys—one physical and one psychological—and that the narrator's perspective is that of an outsider looking in.

Johnson's poetry has also elicited critical response. In "A Weapon of My Song: The Poetry of James Weldon Johnson" (*Phylon,* Winter 1971), Richard A. Long divides Johnson's poetry into four groups—lyrics in standard English, dialect poems, folk-inspired free verse, and the long satirical "Saint Peter Relates an Incident of the Resurrection Day"—and suggests that Johnson was concerned mainly with influencing opinion in his early poetry (as in the first two groups), but eventually forged his verse into a "weapon" of protest. Eugenia W. Collier suggests in "James Weldon Johnson: Mirror of Change" (*Phylon,* Winter 1960), that the general changes in the black poet's handling of folk material, from the traditional dialect to an "imitation of the idiom," is evident in Johnson's work more than in that of other poets of his generation.

"Black Racial Spirit: An Analysis of James Weldon Johnson's Critical Perspective" (*Phylon,* Winter 1971), by Richard A. Carroll, summarizes

Johnson's poetic philosophy and suggests that it has as much relevance for the present time as it had for Johnson's own era. "James Weldon Johnson's Theories and Performance Practices of Afro-American Folksong," by Wendell Phillips Whalum, in this same issue of *Phylon*, is a useful article dealing with yet another side of this versatile artist, his considerations of Afro-American music.

Claude McKay In *Negro Voices in American Fiction*, Hugh Gloster discusses Claude McKay's *Home to Harlem* (1928), *Banjo* (1929), and *Gingertown* (1932—a collection of stories), and comments that for the most part McKay capitalizes on the "selling points of the Van Vechten vogue"—sex, the cabaret, atavism. Robert Bone sees the failure of *Home to Harlem* as McKay's inability to develop Jake's negative relationships with Ray and with contemporary society. True to form is Littlejohn's assessment of McKay as a "doctrinaire eroticist whose plotless works were made up of pure voluptuous jazzing." Littlejohn also sees little to recommend in McKay's poetry, attributing its weaknesses to the poet's "small-mindedness and poetic inability."

A significant article is Michael B. Stoff's "Claude McKay and the Cult of Primitivism" (in *The Harlem Renaissance Remembered*, edited by Arna Bontemps, mentioned earlier). Stoff examines both McKay's life and his art, and concludes that the writer's quest for a lost innocence doomed him to "an existence directly opposed to the life he apotheosizes in his art."

An excellent study of McKay's novels appears in Kenneth Ramchand's *The West Indian Novel and Its Background* (New York: Barnes & Noble, 1970), in which Ramchand calls *Banana Bottom* (1933) the "first classic of West Indian prose," because in this work McKay has created a world "to which it is possible to belong." Another important article is Richard Priebe's "The Search For Community in the Novels of Claude McKay" (*SBL*, Summer 1972). Priebe, like Ramchand, sees as the controlling theme in McKay's novels the search for community, for the imaginative structuring of a society in which the blacks could forego the cultural dualism now necessary to their survival in America.

In his "Symbolism and Irony in McKay's *Home to Harlem*" (*CLAJ*, March 1972), Richard K. Barksdale takes that novel beyond its traditional assessment as a naturalistic exposé, and suggests that it is a symbolic conflict on two levels: order versus disorder, and the rational versus the animalistic.

The vagabond elements in McKay's picaresque novels, in his sexual ideas, and in his religious and psychological uncertainty, and how these relate to his art, are explored in Sister Mary Conroy's "The Vagabond Motif in the Writings of Claude McKay" (*NALF*, March 1971). Conroy suggests that this motif is actually a psychological gesture by McKay as he attempts to escape the harshness of life.

George E. Kent challenges the traditional assessment that the identity problems raised in McKay's earlier novels are resolved satisfactorily in *Banana Bottom* in his article, "Claude McKay's *Banana Bottom* Reappraised" (*CLAJ,* December 1974). Helpful also is Jacqueline Kaye's study of "Claude McKay's *Banjo*" (*Présence Africaine,* No. 73, 1970), in which she suggests that *Banjo* is an attempt to return to whatever racial roots are still available to the decultured Afro-American. Addison Gayle, Jr., in *Claude McKay: The Black Poet at War* (Detroit: Broadside, 1972), suggests that McKay, through his protest poetry, fulfilled the role of "warrior-poet of his people," in the battle to change the traditional images of the black man. Arthur D. Drayton, on the other hand, argues in an article in *Black Orpheus,* "McKay's Human Pity: A Note on His Protest Poetry" (June 1965), that McKay's sense of humanity often caused his protest poetry to transcend racial bitterness, and utter instead "a cry for the race of mankind."

Eugenia W. Collier explores "The Four-Way Dilemma of Claude McKay" (*CLAJ,* March 1972), which she finds reflected in his poetry. Collier suggests that McKay is confronted with a geographical dilemma, a dilemma of heritage, a dilemma of "double consciousness," and a dilemma rising out of the paradox of the black man's place in a democracy. Wayne Cooper's "Claude McKay and the New Negro of the 1920's" (*Phylon,* Fall 1964; reprinted in *The Black American Writer, Volume II: Poetry and Drama* [Deland, Fla.: Everett/Edwards, 1966], edited by C. W. E. Bigsby), surveys McKay's works and concludes that he was one of the first writers of the Harlem Renaissance to express the spirit of the new Negro. Helen Pyne-Timothy examines the role of the "multi-faceted" black woman in "Perceptions of the Black Woman in the Work of Claude McKay (*CLAJ,* December 1975). McKay's concern with the interrelationship of art and politics is explored by Mark Helbling's "Claude McKay: Art and Politics" (*NALF,* June 1973). Similarly, Robert A. Smith's "Claude McKay: An Essay in Criticism" (*Phylon,* Fall 1948) discusses McKay's hatred of racial discrimination and explains his writing as a means of attacking the status quo. An intelligent analysis of McKay's most famous poem is Robert A. Lee's study (*CLAJ,* December 1974), "On Claude McKay's 'If We Must Die.' " Richard Lederer's "The Didactic and the Literary in Four Harlem Renaissance Sonnets" (*EJ,* February 1973) discusses McKay's poetic technqiue.

Jean Toomer Although his reputation rests for the most part upon the success of one book, *Cane* (1923), there has been perhaps more written on Jean Toomer than on any other Harlem Renaissance writer except Langston Hughes.

Robert Bone recognized the critical problems that such a complex work as *Cane* would present when he observed that analysis of *Cane* is "frustrating." He also recognized, however, that in *Cane* Toomer had broken new ground in the use of the myth and symbol. Gloster also recognized the experimental nature of *Cane,* and attributed its "occasional incoherence" to this quality. Arna Bontemps's "The Negro Renaissance: Jean Toomer and the Harlem Writers of the 1920's" (in *Anger and Beyond: The Negro Writer in the United States,* edited by Herbert Hill [New York: Harper & Row, 1966]) credits Toomer with providing the "cue" for the writers of the Harlem Renaissance, imploring them to see life "with the Negro, through him."

A longer study of Toomer is Mabel Mayle Dillard's dissertation "Jean Toomer: Herald of the Negro Renaissance" (Ohio University, 1967). Dillard offers little more than a survey of Toomer's life and work, although her study is valuable as an introduction. Of particular help is a chronology of Toomer's life which Dillard has included as a reference guide. Another useful study, although sometimes heavy-handed, is Fritz Gysin's *The Grotesque in American Negro Fiction: Jean Toomer, Richard Wright, and Ralph Ellison* (Bern, Switzerland: Franke Verlag, 1975). *The Merrill Studies in Cane* (Columbus, Ohio: Merrill, 1971), compiled by Frank Durham, is a helpful collection of several critical essays on Toomer's work from 1923 to 1969. Included are Waldo Frank's foreword to the 1923 Liveright edition of *Cane,* as well as Bontemps's introduction to the more recent Harper & Row reprint (1969), and essays by W. E. B. Du Bois, Robert Kerlin, Gorham Munson, Montgomery Gregory, Robert Bone, and others. Of particular interest in this collection is Eugene Holmes's "Jean Toomer—Apostle of Beauty" (*Opportunity,* August 1932). Holmes insists that Toomer will remain one of the more important black poets because his "message is beauty and the mystery of life," and that his poetry will endure "because it is the stuff of pure poetry." There are a number of problems with Durham's edition, one of which is that he incorrectly identifies the race of some of the critics he has included. For more information about this, see W. Edward Farrison's "Jean Toomer's *Cane* Again" (*CLAJ,* March 1972), which analyzes *Cane,* recaps critical attitudes toward the work, and reviews *The Merrill Studies in Cane.*

An early study of *Cane* appears in Paul Rosenfeld's *Men Seen: Twenty-Four Modern Authors, 1925* (New York: Dial, 1925; rpt. New York: Books For Libraries, 1967), in which Rosenfeld favorably compares Toomer's novel to Joyce's *The Portrait of the Artist as a Young Man.* Rosenfeld's article is reprinted in *The Merrill Studies in Cane,* as is S. P. Fullenwider's important study of Toomer's identity crisis, "Jean Toomer: Lost Generation or Negro Renaissance?" (*Phylon,* December 1966). Darwin T. Turner explores the contrast in *Cane* between the natural and the artificial in "Jean Toomer's *Cane*" (*ND,* January 1969), and finds weakness in Toomer's inability to interpret satisfactorily the southern Negro, his continually changing point of view, and his "substitution of satire for sympathy" in the later sections of *Cane*. An important study is Todd Lieber's "Design and Movement in *Cane*" (*CLAJ*, September 1969), which goes beyond a study of "thematic" unity to an analysis of the "comprehensive design that transcends and encompasses its separate bits and a progressive movement that is sustained from beginning to end," designed to operate both on an objective and a subjective level.

Donald G. Ackley's "Theme and Vision in Jean Toomer's *Cane*" (*SBL*, Spring 1970) is a discussion of recurrent images, themes, and symbols, as well as an analysis of the special critical problems *Cane* presents because of its unorthodox structure. James Kraft suggests, in "Jean Toomer's *Cane*" (*MarkhamR*, October 1970), that the tension in *Cane* rises out of the "reconciliation of the warring elements that exist in the American experience."

Arguing that despite its lack of external exuberance there exists in *Cane* an underlying spirit of celebration is Sister Mary Kathryn Grant in "Images of Celebration in *Cane*" (*NALF*, March 1971). In "Is There a Unifying Theme in *Cane?*" (*CLAJ*, March 1972) Patricia Watkins suggests that if there is, it is the theme of man's inability to interact with his fellow human beings, the inability, ultimately, to love.

"Jean Toomer: As Modern Man," by Larry E. Thompson (in *The Harlem Renaissance Remembered*, edited by Arna Bontemps) explores Toomer's quest for singularity through an analysis of *Cane* and of Toomer's plays. Another important study of Toomer's plays is Darwin T. Turner's "The Failure of a Playwright" (*CLAJ*, June 1967). Turner argues that Toomer did not deliberately rebel against the dramatic conventions of his era; rather, he imitated the German Expressionistic playwrights, "who posited each character for a human type," and therefore was forced to resort to experimental forms in order to express his concepts. John M. Reilly's "The Search For Black Redemption: Jean Toomer's *Cane*" (*SNNTS*, Fall 1970), proposes that *Cane* is a symbolic record of the sensitive author's attempt to relate to his past. He also suggests that this symbolic return, as well as Toomer's poetic "linking" techniques, were anticipated by Du Bois's *The Souls of Black Folk*.

Benjamin F. McKeever's "*Cane* as Blues" (*NALF*, July 1970) suggests that the dark vision of life generated in *Cane* is an effect similar to the blues, "a mood ebony for a condition which can only be described as chaos." Picking up on this musical idea is Bowie Duncan in "Jean Toomer's *Cane:* A Modern Black Oracle" (*CLAJ*, March 1972). Duncan describes *Cane* as an "elaborate Jazz composition," in which Toomer is continually developing variations on a theme, causing the reader to seek out the relationships between these variations.

Charles W. Scruggs's important study, "The Mark of Cain and the Redemption of Art: A Study in Theme and Structure of Jean Toomer's

Cane" (*AL,* May 1972), is based upon Scruggs's examination of the unpublished Toomer papers at Fisk University. He analyzes the interrelationships within each of the sections of the novel, and suggests that they point to Toomer's deliberate attempt at a mythic representation of the black experience in America. Another important structural analysis of *Cane* is Bernard W. Bell's "Portrait of the Artist as the High Priest of Soul: Jean Toomer's *Cane*" (*BlackW,* September 1974). Bell proposes that *Cane*'s division into three major sections can be compared to such concepts as Freud's theory of a three-fold personality, a Hegelian dialectic, the Gurdjieffian triad, or all three.

Roberta Riley sees *Cane* as a record of Toomer's "Search for Identity and Artistry" (*CLAJ,* June 1974). Mabel Dillard's "Jean Toomer—The Veil Replaced," in the same issue, discusses how Toomer's theories on the formation of a new race were incorporated into two of his poems, "Brown River, Smile" (1932), and "Blue Meridian" (1936).

An analysis of Toomer's exploitation in *Cane* of his blackness and his knowledge of the South, as well as of how these two factors influenced his imaginative consciousness, is found in Charles T. Davis's "Jean Toomer and the South: Region and Race as Elements Within a Literary Imagination" (*Studies in the Literary Imagination,* Fall 1972). In "Toomer's *Cane:* The Artist and His World" (*CLAJ,* June 1974), George C. Matthews uses an unpublished letter (written by Toomer to Waldo Frank in 1922) that explains the three critical angles from which Toomer thought *Cane* should be analyzed.

Using the "new criticism" of P. D. Ouspensky's *Tertium Organum,* which Toomer had studied, Catherine L. Innes examines "The Unity of Jean Toomer's *Cane*" (*CLAJ,* March 1972). A more detailed analysis of Ouspensky's influence upon Toomer is Alice Poindexter Fisher's "The Influence of Ouspensky's *Tertium Organum* Upon Jean Toomer's *Cane*" (*CLAJ* (June 1974).

Bernard Bell attempts to explicate and examine the interrelationship of the poems in *Cane* in "A Key to the Poems in *Cane*" (*CLAJ,* March 1971), and Udo Jung discusses two poems from *Cane,* "Cotton Song" and "Prayer," in "Spirit-Torsos of Exquisite Strength" (*CLAJ,* December 1975). Louise Blackwell considers Toomer's use of Biblical myth to express the experience of his people in "Jean Toomer's *Cane* and Biblical Myth" (*CLAJ,* June 1974). Susan L. Blake's "The Spectatorial Artist and the Structure of *Cane,*" in the same issue, analyzes Toomer's use of a "creative persona" through which he attempts to give form to experience in *Cane.*

Rafael A. Cancel argues that Toomer's female characters, unlike the males, are "rich with sensibility, beauty, and fertility, and that the effect of modern civilization is the atrophy of that sensibility" in "Male and Female Interrelationship in Toomer's *Cane*" (*NALF,* March 1971). Patricia Chase's "The Women in *Cane*" (*CLAJ* March 1971) suggests that the women characters serve to weave *Cane* together, and that Toomer's vision of his aggregate woman culminates in the character of Carrie K. "The Aggregate Man in Jean Toomer's *Cane*" by William G. Fischer (*SNNTS*, Summer 1971) proposes that Toomer has delineated a "representative Afro-American protagonist, an aggregate man whose identity is confirmed by the collective experience of all the male characters in *Cane.*"

William J. Goede, in his study in *Phylon* (March 1969), "Jean Toomer's Ralph Kabnis: Portrait of the Negro Artist as a Young Man," argues that the sketch "Kabnis" illustrates the problems Toomer faced as a Negro writer, as well as being the first portrait of a Negro writer in American literature. A brief but significant study is Michael J. Krasny's "Design in Jean Toomer's 'Balo'" (*NALF*, June 1973), which suggests that in this sketch Toomer wanted to reveal the "social forces which have separated Black people from their emotions." Hargis Westerfield's "Jean Toomer's 'Fern': A Mythical Dimension" (*CLAJ*, March 1971) argues that Toomer's use of the surname Rosen points to his deliberate exploitation of Jewish and Christian myth in the story. Also concentrating on the same section is Marian L. Stein, who in "The Poet-Observer and Fern in Jean Toomer's *Cane*" (*MarkhamR*, October 1970), suggests that "Fern" is the "intense pivot of the whole novel." Edward Walrond's "The Search For Identity in Jean Toomer's 'Esther'" (*CLAJ*, March 1971) proposes that Toomer has injected an allegorical element into this section, so that "beneath the individual seeking consciousness of Esther lies a racial search." George Kopf, in "Tensions in Jean Toomer's 'Theatre'" (*CLAJ*, June 1974), suggests that this short story, which appears in *Cane,* is the "product of its author's perceptions of tensions and countertensions in the reality of the black experience in the U.S."

Two articles that explore the relationship between Toomer and Sherwood Anderson are Mary Jane Dickerson's "Sherwood Anderson and Jean Toomer: A Literary Relationship" (*Studies in American Fiction*, Autumn 1973), and Darwin T. Turner's analysis of letters between the two, "An Intersection of Paths: Correspondence Between Jean Toomer and Sherwood Anderson" (*CLAJ*, June 1974). Suggesting a possible influence for *Cane* in Hart Crane's "Black Tambourine" (1921) is Victor A. Kramer's "The 'Mid-Kingdom' of Crane's 'Black Tambourine' and Toomer's *Cane*" (*CLAJ*, June 1974).

LANGSTON HUGHES

Blyden Jackson

Langston Hughes is not the easiest subject for a bibliographer to survey for he is not typical, bibliographically, of the Negro writer, even of the present post-Wright era in literature, when Negro writers as a group certainly write more than they have ever written at any time before. Langston Hughes wrote prolifically and in many genres, including works for radio, phonograph records, and television.

He may be said to have begun to publish when he finished grammar school. Members of his eighth-grade class in the little town of Lincoln, Illinois, elected him poet for their graduation exercises in 1916. Before the audience of proud parents, he read a sixteen-stanza poem that launched his half-century of productivity. Five years afterward, when he was twenty years old, a poem of his was published in *The Brownies' Book,* a children's magazine under the aegis of *The Crisis,* whose famous editor, W. E. B. Du Bois, had printed Hughes's verses in its monthly issues. Hughes thus embarked on a writing career that continued until his death in 1967. He tried his hand at virtually every form of expression open to a writer. His name is attached, singly or as a collaborator, to more than forty books. He wrote two novels and sixty-six short stories; the sketches or stories about Jesse B. Semple, out of which he gathered five collections; poetry that appeared in many magazines, as well as in more than ten books of poetry; long and short plays; critical essays and other articles; musicals, librettos, and song lyrics; and at least one apprentice's experiment that can be termed an opera. In conjunction with the Negro film star Clarence Muse he created the scenario for a movie. He also developed a strange hybrid of theater and opera or musical comedy which he called a *drame.* He also wrote two accounts of his own life, books for children, popularizations of subjects like Negro history and jazz, newspaper columns, scripts for radio and television, and recording scripts. In addition to all of the foregoing, he edited, he anthologized, and he translated.

Bibliography

By far the most extensive bibliography of Hughes's work is Donald C. Dickinson's *A Bio-bibliography of Langston Hughes, 1902–1967* (2nd rev.

ed.; Hamden, Conn.: Archon Books, 1972). Dickinson, a university librarian, divides his bibliography into eight parts: books by Hughes; books edited by Hughes; book-length translations by Hughes; works by Hughes which were published in foreign languages but for which there are no editions in English; Hughes's appearances in collections not his own; prose and drama by Hughes; poems by Hughes; and works about Hughes, including "selected reviews" of Hughes' "major" works. He indicates, in an explanation at the beginning of his bibliography, that he does not list Hughes's publications in newspapers, or lyrics for published songs, or readings on phonograph recordings.

In listing books by Hughes, Dickinson proceeds chronologically from the first edition of *The Weary Blues* in 1926 to the posthumously published *Don't You Turn Back* in 1969, two years beyond the terminal date in Dickinson's title. Dickinson also gives, for each book, all of its editions, domestic and foreign. For example, Hughes's novel *Not Without Laughter,* we learn from Dickinson, followed its original edition in 1930 with thirteen other editions: two English; one Argentinian; two Dutch; one French; one Italian; two Japanese; one Russian; and three Swedish. Accordingly, editions of Hughes's work in eighteen languages and nineteen nations appear in Dickinson.

For those of Hughes's books that are collections of previously published material, Dickinson lists the individual pieces in each book. Like most authors who lead busy publishing lives, Hughes was not above occasionally doubling back on his own tracks. For example, the short story "Little Dog" appeared in his first collection of short stories, *The Ways of White Folks,* in 1934. The same story is in Hughes's *Something in Common and Other Stories,* a collection published in 1963, twenty-nine years later. There were other stories and poems that appear in more than one of Hughes's books. Dickinson, by his reduction of Hughes's "collections" into their constituent components, renders the identification of such duplications a relatively easy matter. Moreover, in two sections of the bibliography, "Prose and Drama by Langston Hughes" and "Poems by Langston Hughes," Dickinson lists alphabetically by title every play, poem, and piece of prose to which he has made a reference. Beneath each title are all the places where the piece may be found, whether in a book by Hughes or as a contribution to a collection, such as an anthology. One may determine from Dickinson when and where Hughes's minor poems appeared. Dickinson also recognizes Hughes's several collaborators, not all of whom were writers. Some were musicians and at least two were excellent photographers. Dickinson reproduces Hughes's dedications to his work, and names Hughes's illustrators. (Jacob Lawrence, the painter, illustrated *One Way Ticket.*)

Although Dickinson's bibliography is, on the whole, a valuable resource, it is possible to find some fault with it. The middle name of Paul Laurence Dunbar, for example, is consistently misspelled. The last section of the bibliography lists reviews—as the bibliography stipulates, "selected" reviews—of Hughes's "major" works. All of the reviews so listed—far from all of the reviews of Hughes's work—are from American journals only. However, Dickinson does include items from foreign commentators among the books and articles listed in the last section of his bibliography. *Good Morning Revolution* (New York and Westport, Conn.: Lawrence Hill, 1973), edited by Faith Berry and appropriately subtitled, with reference to Hughes, as his "Uncollected Writings of Social Protest," should be added to Dickinson's list of books by Hughes (it was not available when Dickinson compiled his bibliography). The notable omissions which can be discovered in Dickinson relate to Hughes's activities as a writer of radio and television scripts, and of lyrics for popular songs.

Therman B. O'Daniel's "Langston Hughes: A Selected Classified Bibliography" is available in a volume edited by Therman O'Daniel, *Langston Hughes, Black Genius: A Critical Evaluation* (New York: Morrow, 1971). A precursor to this bibliography had been published earlier in a memorial issue for Hughes of *College Language Association Journal* which appeared in June of 1968. Moreover, O'Daniel's 1968 bibliography was a successor to a bibliography of Hughes's works which O'Daniel had published earlier in the same publication's precursor, *College Language Association Bulletin* (Spring 1957).

O'Daniel's bibliographies of Hughes have evolved over the years. His second was an expansion of the first. His third, and fullest, builds upon his second. This latest bibliography is organized into twenty-eight sections, among them "Lyrics for Dramatic Musicals," "Opera Librettos," "Screenplays," "Radio Scripts," "Radio Scripts in Collaboration," "Television Scripts," "Lyrics for Songs," and "Recordings." The sections just named offer information which Dickinson elected to exclude. O'Daniel does not offer discussion of individual poems and short stories, which is, as previously noted, provided by Dickinson, so Dickinson's work is much longer than O'Daniel's. Yet O'Daniel's is a substantial work, based, like Dickinson's, on a careful and exhaustive presentation of the central corpus of Hughes' canon—the many books, in poetry, prose, and drama, of which Hughes was either the sole or a collaborating author.

O'Daniel covers such categories as poetry, novels, children's stories, short stories, autobiographies, biographies and histories for young people, histories, translations, photo essays, edited anthologies, full-length plays, one-act plays, gospel song-plays, and a Christmas cantata. In the main, these categories tend to reflect judgments quite comfortably assimilable to familiar conventions. In his section on novels, however, O'Daniel includes four of the five books into which Hughes eventually gathered the sketches about Simple (full name: Jesse B. Semple), a Virginia-born black migrant to Harlem, a man of the people and an unsung colloquial philosopher. Simple was probably Hughes's finest portrait of the so-called ordinary Negro. Simple made his world debut through the columns of the Chicago *Defender,* the weekly newspaper that was once a sort of bible for Negro America. (Simple, incidentally, had a rather eminent identity for years not only through the columns of the *Defender,* but also in other publications, including the *New York Post.*) Whether any of the Simple books constitutes a novel is debatable, despite the narrative continuities which link various sequences of the Simple sketches.

O'Daniel's bibliography includes a section listing books and articles about Hughes. This list is selective but fairly comprehensive. It represents all of the critical approaches to Hughes and is knowledgeably assembled and highly useful. The reviews cover only books by or about Hughes which appeared prior to publication of the bibliography in the *College Language Association Journal.*

Of the less comprehensive bibliographies of Hughes, three are especially reliable and useful: James A. Emanuel's in *Langston Hughes* (New York: Twayne Publishers, 1967), a volume in the Twayne United States Authors Series; Ernest Kaiser's "Selected Bibliography of the Published Writings of Langston Hughes" (*Freedomways,* Spring, 1968); and Milton Meltzer's in *Langston Hughes: A Biography* (New York: T. Y. Crowell, 1968).

Emanuel's bibliography lists—in one chronological, undifferentiated grouping—book-length publications with which Hughes was connected as an author (singly or in collaboration), an editor, or a translator. The pamphlet-like publications *The Negro Mother, Scottsboro Limited, A New Song,* and *Freedom's Plow* do not appear on this list, nor, of course, does any publication after 1967 (the year of Hughes's death). Emanuel also lists books to which Hughes contributed introductions or chapters, a limited number of articles by Hughes, seven interviews in which Hughes participated, and, under the heading "Secondary Sources," a brief, selective list of books and articles about Hughes's work.

Kaiser's bibliography is in an issue of *Freedomways* that focused on Hughes and appeared shortly after his death. It is explicitly "based largely" on Dickinson and Emanuel. It also is restricted to books and pamphlets with which Hughes was connected as author, editor, or translator, introductions and chapters in books written by Hughes, and selected magazine articles both by and about him.

Meltzer's bibliography lists Hughes's books, but does not list *The Negro Mother, Scottsboro Limited, A New Song,* or *Freedom's Plow.* It does, however, list recordings by Hughes of some of his poems, and four books about Hughes.

A bibliography about Hughes appears in Darwin Turner's *Afro-American Writers* (New York: Appleton, 1970). However, it is not as full as it might be, as it lists only Hughes's books for adult readers, in poetry or prose fiction. However, it does include *Five Plays by Langston Hughes*, edited by Webster Smalley (Bloomington: Indiana University Press, 1963). It lists also the previously cited works by Dickinson, Kaiser, and O'Daniel in a section called "Autobiography, Biography, and Criticism." Although not exhaustive, Turner is judicious. His list of autobiographies, biographies, and criticism, moreover, reflects the several kinds of criticism of Hughes. It omits little of genuine importance. The preface makes clear that throughout *Afro-American Writers* Turner has excluded from the bibliographies "short articles on minor points" and book reviews.

The short bibliographical essay on Hughes in *Blacks in America: Bibliographical Essays* by James M. McPherson et al., (Garden City, N.Y.: Doubleday, 1971) is placed within the context of the history of Negro poetry in America. Thus the essay, understandably, emphasizes Hughes's poetry and the printed reactions to it. The essay engages, perhaps a little too confidently, in evaluations in addition to listings.

Interest in Hughes may well increase rather than diminish. It seems significant, then, that there is a paucity of information in existing bibliographies about reviews of Hughes's publications, for Hughes was not a writer whom reviewers ignored. Indeed, Emanuel, in his *Langston Hughes*, refers to ninety-one reviews of *The Ways of White Folks* (1934) alone. Yet *The Ways of White Folks* was hardly Hughes's most talked-of book. Lewis Leary's *Articles on American Literature* (Durham, N.C.: Duke University Press, 1954, 1970) surveys journals both in America and abroad. The first and subsequent volumes of *Articles* are of interest to those who seek essays about Hughes that appeared in foreign periodicals.

Editions

POETRY

"I think it was de Maupassant," Hughes observed in *The Big Sea* (1946), "who made me really want to be a writer." Hughes's first book was a volume of poetry, *The Weary Blues*, which was published in 1926 by Knopf in a first edition of 1,500 copies. The poems were praised for their realism and spontaneity. An inexpensive edition of *The Weary Blues* was printed in 1931; a Danish edition appeared in 1945; and a Japanese edition, in 1958. In 1927, only one year after the first edition of *The Weary Blues*, Knopf published *Fine Clothes to the Jew*, including within it "A Note on the Blues." Hughes was to enjoy a long association with Knopf, which published most of the volumes of Hughes's poetry.

Among the friends Hughes made as he expanded his circle were Joel Spingarn, the distinquished critic and active supporter of the NAACP, and his wife, Amy, from whom Hughes had received a scholarship to Lincoln University. On the Spingarns' estate at Amenia, not far from

New York City, a conference of consequence to students of Negro history had been held in 1916. The Spingarns operated a small publishing enterprise on their estate, the Troutbeck Press. In 1931 they produced a private printing of 100 copies of *Dear Lovely Death,* a slender sample of Hughes's poetry on twenty unnumbered pages, largely for circulation among Hughes's friends. In the fall of 1931, Hughes began a nine-month tour, going from coast to coast along a southern route and reading his poetry wherever he could do so for a fee. On this tour he sold *The Negro Mother,* a twenty-page booklet printed by the Golden Stairs Press specifically for sale to his tour audiences. In 1932 the Golden Stairs Press issued another booklet by Hughes, *Scottsboro Limited,* eighteen unnumbered pages containing four poems and a play, and intended by Hughes as a fund raiser for the defense of the Scottsboro Boys. There was a Russian edition of it in 1932, the year of its first edition. In 1938, after Hughes returned from Spain, the International Workers Order, as part of a literary series it had started, published his thirty-one-page *A New Song,* with an introduction by Michael Gold, the proletarian radical. *Freedom's Plow,* more patriotic than radical in many ways, was read over a national radio network by Paul Muni, the noted actor, on Monday, March 15, 1943, and was published in the same year by the Musette Publishing Company. Also in 1943 the thirty-page *Jim Crow's Last Stand* was published in Atlanta by the Negro Publication Society of America. In 1951 the seventy-five-page *Montage of a Dream Deferred,* containing the now rather popular "Theme for English B" and the poem from which Lorraine Hansberry was to take the title of her play, *A Raisin in the Sun,* was published by Henry Holt. There are, then, seven books of poetry by Hughes which were not published by Knopf.

In the 1930s Knopf published only one volume of Hughes's poetry, *The Dream Keeper and Other Poems.* This volume, which appeared in 1932, was aimed at young readers, and included sixty poems, twenty of which had already been printed in *The Weary Blues,* seven from *Fine Clothes to the Jew,* and one from *Dear Lovely Death.* In 1942 Knopf published *Shakespeare in Harlem, Fields of Wonder* in 1947, and, in 1949, *One-Way Ticket,* whose title alludes to Negro migration from the South. In 1959, Knopf published, in an unusually large first edition, *Selected Poems of Langston Hughes,* and in 1961, *Ask Your Mama.* In 1967 *The Panther and the Lash* appeared and, in 1969, *Don't You Turn Back.* Most of these are still in print.

NOVELS

Knopf published Hughes's first novel, *Not Without Laughter,* which has remained in print since 1930. Several of the thirteen foreign editions have titles which do not translate into anything having to do with laughter. *Tambourines to Glory,* of which there have been three foreign editions, was published by John Day in 1958.

OTHER PROSE FICTION

Hughes became seriously interested in the short story while in Russia, although it was D. H. Lawrence's work which ignited his interest in the form. After Hughes's return from Russia, Knopf published, in a first edition of 2,500 copies, and containing fourteen stories (five of them written in Moscow), Hughes' *The Ways of White Folks.* There would be five foreign editions of this volume. Hughes's second book of short stories was brought out in 1952 by Henry Holt. In 1963, Hill & Wang published a third book of short stories, *Something in Common and Other Stories.* Simon & Schuster brought out the first two Simple books, *Simple Speaks His Mind* (1950) and *Simple Takes a Wife* (1953). Hughes shifted to Rinehart for the third Simple book, *Simple Stakes a Claim* (1957). For the last two Simple books, *The Best of Simple* (1961) and *Simple's Uncle Sam* (1965), he committed himself to Hill & Wang, and thus was already involved with them in 1963, when *Something in Common* was ready to be submitted to a publisher.

Popo and Fifina, a children's story illustrated by the well-known E. Simms Campbell, which Hughes wrote in collaboration with Arna Bontemps, was published in 1932 by Macmillan in a first edition of 4,000 copies.

AUTOBIOGRAPHY AND HISTORY

An account of Hughes's early life appeared in the autobiographical *The Big Sea* (1940). Hughes continued this personal account sixteen years later in *I Wonder as I Wander.* There have already been nine editions of *The Big Sea,* the first of which was published by Knopf. Seven of the succeeding editions were published abroad. *I Wonder as I Wander,* originally a Rinehart publication, has had three editions, one of them abroad.

To some extent, Hughes's ventures into history reflect his repeated and highly sincere efforts to render himself agreeable as well as communicative to less-sophisticated readers. Characters like Simple commanded Hughes's genuine respect. Hughes thought it was not admirable for a writer to spurn the Simples of this world because of their intellectual shortcomings. Moreover, as Hughes thought of Simple, in a like manner he thought of children. In the 1950s Dodd, Mead published a series of biographies by Hughes aimed at young people: *Famous American Negroes, Famous Negro Music Makers,* and *Famous Negro Heroes of America.* Almost simultaneously Hughes produced for Franklin Watts, also for young people, the "first book" series, which contained *The First Book of Negroes, The First Book of Rhythyms, The First Book of Jazz, The First Book of the West Indies,* and *The First Book of Africa.* In 1962 he told the story of the NAACP, hoping to reach a wide audience, in *Fight for Freedom: The Story of the NAACP,* published by Norton. Earlier he had joined with Milton Meltzer to write *A Pictorial History of the Negro in America,* published by Crown. In the year of Hughes's death (1967), Prentice-Hall issued *Black Magic: A Pictorial History of the Negro in Entertainment,* which Hughes wrote with Milton Meltzer.

DRAMA

James A. Emanuel has been instrumental in calling attention to Hughes's activity as a playwright. The theater had always been an important part of Hughes's existence. While still in high school Hughes worked in amateur theater at Karamu House in Cleveland. Later he started three community theaters: one in Harlem, one in Los Angeles, and one in Chicago. He composed, or participated in the composition of, long and short plays, operas, musical comedies, and a curio of his own invention, the gospel song-play. No manuscripts of Hughes's work in drama have yet been published. Only *Five Plays by Langston Hughes,* which Webster Smalley edited and the Indiana University Press published in 1963, is available in book form. Included in *Five Plays* are "Mulatto," "Soul Gone Home," "Little Ham," "Simply Heavenly," and "Tambourines to Glory." "Simply Heavenly" is a musical based on the Simple stories, and "Tambourines to Glory" is a play with music based on Hughes's novel *Tambourines to Glory.*

OTHER WORKS

Hughes anthologized himself, both as a poet and a writer of prose, in *The Langston Hughes Reader* (New York: Braziller, 1958). He served as sole or joint editor of some nine anthologies. Two of these anthologies, *Four Lincoln University Poets* (Lincoln University, Pa.: Lincoln University, 1930) and *Lincoln University Poets* (New York: Fine Editions, 1954), obviously connect him with his undergraduate alma mater. Two others, *An African Treasury: Essays, Stories, Poems By Black Africans* (New York: Crown, 1960) and *Poems From Black Africa* (Bloomington: Indiana University Press, 1963) show his interest in African writers. In *The Poetry of the Negro, 1746–1949* (Garden City, N.Y.: Doubleday, 1949) Hughes and Bontemps, as editors, pioneered in the recognition of Lucy Terry, thus playing key roles in the correction of the long-unchallenged assumption that Jupiter Hammon was America's first Negro poet. *The Book of Negro Folklore* (New York: Dodd, Mead, 1959), also edited by Hughes and Bontemps, is notable for its excellent introduction and for the range of material covered. *The Book of Negro Humor* (New York:

Dodd, Mead, 1966) and *The Best Stories by Negro Writers: An Anthology from 1899 to the Present* (Boston: Little, Brown, 1967), as well as the Negro Poets Issue in the winter of 1950 edition of *Voices: A Quarterly of Poetry,* all represent editing tasks which Hughes performed unaided. Hughes's *Best Short Stories by Negro Writers* contains stories which well justify the designation accorded them and which certainly exhibit Hughes as an excellent judge of literary merit.

Hughes translated, from the French, in collaboration with Mercer Cook, the novel *Gouverneurs de la Rosée* by the Haitian novelist Jacques Roumain. The translation is entitled *Masters of the Dew* and was published by Reynal and Hitchcock in 1947. In 1948, *Cuba Libre,* poems by Nicolás Guillén, translated from the Spanish by Hughes and Ben Frederic Carruthers, was published by Anderson and Ritchie in Los Angeles. Hughes spent several months in Loyalist Spain. To him the Spanish poet Garcia Lorca was a martyr for the cause of right and freedom. Hughes translated Lorca's *Romancero Gitano.* As *Gypsy Ballads* his translation appeared as the first *Beloit Poetry Chapbook* in 1951. Indiana University Press issued Hughes's translation of *Selected Poems of Gabriela Mistral* in 1957.

Two of the books with which Hughes was associated have been called "photo essays" by Therman O'Daniel. One of these, *The Sweet Flypaper of Life,* united the writing of Hughes with the sensitive photography of Roy Decarava. Published in 1955 by Simon & Schuster, *The Sweet Flypaper of Life* also presented a protagonist, Mary Bradley, who has been viewed as a forerunner to the main character of Ernest Gaines's novel, *The Autobiography of Miss Jane Pittman.* The photo essay *Black Misery* was published by Paul S. Ericksson in 1969.

Hughes made a number of records on which he not only read his own poetry but also spoke at length about jazz. On another record he told for children the story of Negro history. Most of these were released by Folkway Records. He also made records for MGM, United Artists, Vanguard, Columbia, and Caedmon.

Available paperback editions of Hughes's work include: from Hill & Wang, *The Big Sea, I Wonder as I Wander, Tambourines to Glory, Simple's Uncle Sam, The Best of Simple,* and *Something in Common and Other Stories;* from Apollo, *Five Plays by Langston Hughes;* from Lawrence Hill, *Good Morning Revolution: The Uncollected Social Protest Writings of Langston Hughes;* from Macmillan, *Not Without Laughter;* from Knopf, *The Panther and the Lash;* and from Random House, *The Ways of White Folks.*

Manuscripts and Letters

A comprehensive survey of Hughes's manuscripts and letters has not yet been undertaken. It has been reported that most of Hughes's unpublished letters and papers are to be found in the James Weldon Johnson Memorial Collection at the Yale University Library. The Johnson Collection contains, as noted by James A. Emanuel in *Langston Hughes,* "letters to hundreds of correspondents; autographed revised drafts and typescripts of published and unpublished work; lecture notes; 'Simple' columns; magazine and newspaper clippings; pamphlets and handbills; etc." Among its hundreds of letters are 110 pieces of correspondence between Hughes and the Knopf publishing firm spanning the years from 1925 to 1958, and 170 letters exchanged between Hughes and his literary agent, Maxim Lieber, from 1937 to 1955.

There are additional materials in the Schomburg Collection of the New York Public Library, at the library of Lincoln University in Pennsylvania, and in Fisk University's Negro Collection. Donald Dickinson has a collection of fifty letters and postcards sent to him by Hughes from 1956 to 1965. A considerable collection of material is now in the custody of George Houston Bass of Brown University, executor of the Langston Hughes estate.

Biography

There is no official biography of Hughes and virtually all of the biographical works about him are based on one or both of his autobiographies, *The Big Sea* and *I Wonder as I Wander.*

Hughes begins *The Big Sea* as he is leaving the port of New York at the age of twenty-one on a freighter bound for Africa. The reader then goes back with Hughes through the years that preceded the sailing from New York. Thus Hughes shapes the first part of *The Big Sea,* which he calls "Twenty-One." The second part, "Big Sea," follows him to Africa and through his subsequent experiences in Western Europe. The third part, "Black Renaissance," carries through the last five years of the 1920s into 1930—through the years when Hughes, somewhat belatedly, attended college, and the Negro was, as Hughes put it, "in vogue."

I Wonder as I Wander begins where *The Big Sea* leaves off, in the beginning of the 1930s. It covers not quite a whole decade. Hughes is in Paris on New Year's Eve, hearing the bells ring in the new year of 1938, when the book ends. Combined, then, *The Big Sea* and *I Wonder as I Wander* account for thirty-five years (from 1902 through 1937) of Hughes's sixty-five. Almost half of his total existence, and more than two-thirds of his adult career, is thus left untouched by these two works. Moreover, Hughes obviously tells only what he chooses to of his first thirty-five years.

The closest approach to a lengthy biography of Hughes, Milton Meltzer's *Langston Hughes: A Biography* (New York: T. Y. Crowell, 1968), obviously was written for as wide an audience as Meltzer could command

and was aimed, therefore, as much at children as at scholars. Meltzer enjoyed an acquaintance with Hughes, he and Hughes having collaborated on two books. Some of Meltzer's biography capitalizes on this acquaintance. Clearly, Meltzer interviewed Hughes more than once, apparently with the preparation of a biography in mind. Even so, the book depends heavily on Hughes's autobiographies. Over half of Meltzer's work, indeed, is closely identifiable with *The Big Sea*. Much of the remainder quite unmistakably derives from *I Wonder as I Wander*. Meltzer imparts to his biography his own highly favorable reactions to Hughes's personal qualities. But he adds little to the knowledge of his friend and collaborator already supplied by Hughes in Hughes's own works.

Black Troubadour: Langston Hughes (Chicago: Rand McNally, 1970) is a biography of Hughes written by librarian Charlemae H. Rollins primarily for older children. *Black Troubadour* appeared five years after Mrs. Rollins's *Famous American Negro Poets* (New York: Dodd, Mead, 1965), a volume in the Famous Biographies for Young People series. In *Famous American Negro Poets*, Mrs. Rollins presents a five-page biographical sketch of Hughes. As with Meltzer's book, this sketch and *Black Troubadour* rely heavily on Hughes's autobiographical statements.

Perhaps the most critically inclined biographical treatments of Hughes are in works about Hughes which are not solely, or even mainly, biographical. The concentrated attention to Hughes's life in James A. Emanuel's *Langston Hughes* is a prelude to a searching analysis of Hughes's performance as a writer. The biography in Donald A. Dickinson's *A Bio-bibliography of Langston Hughes* serves to introduce the bibliography. Therman B. O'Daniel sets the stage for the critical essays in *Langston Hughes, Black Genius: A Critical Evaluation* (New York: Morrow, 1971) with a brief biography. Emanuel, Dickinson, and O'Daniel depend heavily on *The Big Sea* and *I Wonder as I Wander*, although they all touch upon Hughes's life after the Spanish Civil War, as do Meltzer and Rollins.

François Dodat's *Langston Hughes* (Paris: P. Seghers, 1964), which is written in French and is largely a miscellany of Hughes's poetry, contains a biography of Hughes similar to those already described. A particularly laudatory presentation of Hughes may be found, under the title "Shakespeare in Harlem," in *13 Against the Odds* (New York: Viking, 1945), biographies of thirteen distinguished American Negroes written by Edwin R. Embree. It is clear from "Shakespeare in Harlem" that Embree knew Hughes and that he makes good use of this knowledge in his portrait. Even so, and with due allowance for Embree's encomia, Embree's Hughes is fundamentally the Hughes of *The Big Sea*, from which Embree requisitions the general shape of the life he constructs, a store of anecdotes, and many direct quotes.

A very early account of Hughes is in Mary White Ovington's *Portraits in Color* (New York: Viking, 1927). Of course, it deals only with Hughes's youth and first years as a writer. There are numerous brief portraits of Hughes in anthologies. At least two of these are notable for their excellence, although neither breaks new ground and both are adjusted to the requirements and limitations of an anthology. They are in *Dark Symphony: Negro Literature in America* (New York: Free Press, 1968), edited by James A. Emanuel and Theodore L. Gross, and volume two of *American Literature: The Makers and the Making* (New York: St. Martin's Press, 1973), edited by Cleanth Brooks, R. W. B. Lewis, and Robert Penn Warren. Emanuel has had a long, continuing interest in Hughes. Presumably he wrote the biography of Hughes in *Dark Symphony*. Although literary criticism dominates the book, it is a masterful summation of the important phases of Hughes's life. Moreover, it is one treatment of Hughes's life which conveys, in something like a due proportion, an impression of Hughes's activity as a major dramatist. The biographical sketch in *American Literature: The Makers and the Making* summarizes the important phases of Hughes's career.

In the issue of the periodical *Freedomways* devoted entirely to Hughes (Spring 1968), Arna Bontemps's "Langston Hughes—He Spoke of Rivers" tells of his first meeting with Hughes in about 1924; Louise Thompson Patterson, in "With Langston Hughes in the USSR," shares her experience as one of the twenty-two Negroes, including Hughes, who went to Russia in 1932 to make the film (never actually produced), "Black and White"; and Lindsay Patterson, an aspiring writer who received aid and encouragement from Hughes, wrote "Langston Hughes—An Inspirer of Young Writers."

A sense of coterie flourished among the writers of the Harlem Renaissance. They produced some satire, not a little of which was directed at themselves. It is not unusual, therefore, to find manifestations of the *roman à clef* in the fiction of these writers. Four novels of the Harlem Renaissance, insofar as they are *romans à clef,* seem to contribute, however slightly, to a biography of Hughes. They are Rudolph Fisher's *The Walls of Jericho* (New York: Knopf, 1928), Wallace Thurman's *The Blacker the Berry* (New York: Macaulay, 1929) and *Infants of the Spring* (New York: Macaulay, 1932), and Countee Cullen's *One Way to Heaven* (New York: Harper, 1932). In *The Walls of Jericho* the character Langdon appears to be Fischer's characterization of Hughes as an innocent-looking "rascal." Thurman places a character named Tony Crews, a "curly-headed poet," in *The Blacker the Berry.* This same Tony Crews appears at a salon of Harlem Renaissance writers in *Infants of the Spring.* Both Tonys seem to be very thin disguises for Hughes. The character of Lawrence Harper, a poet, although seen very little in *One Way to Heaven,* has the same initials as Hughes and seems to be a satirical picture of Hughes by Cullen.

Criticism

Therman B. O'Daniel's *Langston Hughes, Black Genius: A Critical Evaluation* not only contains, as elsewhere discussed, a biography of Hughes and a bibliography of works by and about him, but it also collects twelve critical essays which deal with Hughes as a literary artist. Six of these essays were written expressly for this volume. All twelve of the articles, moreover, relate to one another, and together make this volume a comprehensive general study of Hughes's literary art. A group of essays—one each by Arthur P. Davis, Nancy Bullock McGhee, and Donald B. Gibson—examines Hughes as a poet. One essay, by Darwin T. Turner, studies Hughes as a playwright. Another, by William Edward Farrison, concentrates on Hughes's novel, *Not Without Laughter*. Three essays—by Eugenia W. Collier, Harry L. Jones, and Blyden Jackson—are concerned with the Simple stories. James A. Emanuel, in one essay, treats Hughes's short fiction and, in another, Hughes's literary experiments. John F. Mathews discusses Hughes as a translator, and George E. Kent, in "Langston Hughes and Afro-American Folk and Cultural Tradition," relates Hughes's work to important folk elements of Afro-American life. The volume originated as a token of respect for Hughes's memory. All of the contributors were friends of Hughes. All are black members of the College Language Association and represent the attitude of Negro critics toward Negro literature. Even so, these essays constitute an excellent introduction to the aesthetic and cultural properties of genuine significance which can be found in Hughes's work. They tend to be summaries, although they are not wanting in explicit analysis. A great virtue of *Langston Hughes, Black Genius* is that it expresses what can reliably be considered a consensus among the scholars who, rightly or wrongly, feel that they are closest to the sources of Hughes's creative life.

There are no other collections of essays about Hughes in book form. However, five articles (Margaret Burroughs's "Langston Hughes Lives," Mari Evans's "I Remember Langston," Julia Fields's "The Green of Langston's Ivy," Addison Gayle, Jr.'s "Langston Hughes, a Simple Commentary," and Julian Mayfield's "Langston"), all in the *Negro Digest* of September 1967, and all by black writers and critics, constitute a collection about Hughes within an issue of a periodical. Additionally, seven articles in *Freedomways* for Spring 1968, including a bibliography by Ernest Kaiser and biographical contributions by Arna Bontemps, Louise Thompson Patterson, and Lindsay Patterson, all mentioned previously in this essay, constitute a second collection of essays about Hughes within one issue of a periodical. Four of the articles in *Freedomways* may be classified as criticism. In "Langston Hughes, Philosopher-Poet," Eugene C. Holmes argues that Hughes was a philosopher, "in the accepted sense," because he had "developed a *Weltanschauung*, a cultural pluralism and commonality which endure because of his spokesman's role as a freedom fighter in the long and checkered history of the struggle for human freedom." In "Robert Burns and Langston Hughes," Aaron Kramer likens Hughes to Burns. And in what may well be one of the most important articles about Hughes's short stories, "The Short Fiction of Langston Hughes," James A. Emanuel speaks of where Hughes's short fiction has been published and of its themes, images, symbols, plotting, and characters.

There is one critical study of Hughes of considerable length, James A. Emanuel's *Langston Hughes,* which has, like *Langston Hughes, Black Genius: A Critical Evaluation,* already been cited in this essay for the biography and the bibliography it contains. However, in *Langston Hughes* Emanuel's view of Hughes is restricted, in the main, to Hughes's poetry and short prose fiction, with little attention given to his novels or plays. Emanuel organizes his study primarily as an identification and anatomizing of the themes which recur with notable frequency and with telling effect in Hughes's poetry and fiction. In successive chapters Emanuel finds Hughes markedly interested in "The Cult of the Negro"; racial discrimination; religion (and Negro interactions with it); "Love, Life, and Negro Soul"; and Harlem, the black metropolis. Emanuel's study is more descriptive than evaluative. Although it is far from devoid of the expression of philosophic judgments, it is notable primarily as a highly objective résumé of the *content* of much of Hughes's imaginative output. Emanuel does not close his eyes to the fact that Hughes was an artist much involved with race. He merely avoids political huckstering in his confrontation with that fact.

Benjamin Brawley, the dean of Negro critics some two generations ago, speaks of Hughes more in sorrow than in anger, and certainly than in praise, in *The Negro Genius* (New York: Dodd, Mead, 1937). In this book Brawley expresses some of his misgivings about Hughes after Hughes had published such works as poems connecting himself with the Harlem Renaissance; the novel *Not Without Laughter;* the short-story collection *The Ways of White Folks;* the volumes of verse *Dear Lovely Death, Scottsboro Limited,* and *The Dream Keeper and Other Poems;* the children's books *Popo and Fifina;* (with Arna Bontemps) *Children of Haiti;* and the play *Mulatto* (for which the Broadway production constituted its publication). To Brawley, the good life was the life of genteel tradition. He subtitled *The Negro Genius* "A New Appraisal of the Achievement of the American Negro in Literature and the Fine Arts." But his less than five pages of appraisal of Hughes reflect sensibilities that were easily distressed. The "abandon and vulgarity" (Brawley's words) of the poetry written by Hughes during the Harlem Renaissance would be upsetting to anyone with Brawley's strong sense of "propriety" in art. Brawley was prepared to concede some credit to Hughes as a realist, largely, it seems, on the basis of Hughes's performance as a novelist in *Not Without Laughter*. But he was incapable of traveling a meaningful distance toward actual *rapprochement* with Hughes, for Brawley lacked either the latitude of appreciative taste or the experience of life which would have permitted him to sympathize with jazz and the *habitués* of cabarets. Hughes for him, then, was an *enfant terrible*. Indeed, he found in Hughes's poetry for the young (*The Dream Keeper and Other Poems*), rather than in Hughes's more serious attempts at interpreting the human comedy, the "best things" that Hughes had done.

Two other works of a survey nature in which important commentators on Negro life and literature refer in general terms to Hughes are J. Saunders Redding's *To Make a Poet Black* (Chapel Hill: University of North Carolina Press, 1939) and Margaret Just Butcher's *The Negro in American Culture* (New York: Knopf, 1956). Of a later breed of critic than Brawley, and not constrained by Brawley's super-conservative attitudes toward conduct indecorous and "crude," both Redding and Butcher understand, and esteem, Hughes's ability to articulate the psyche of the "ordinary" Negro. Writing, like Brawley, at a time when much of Hughes's career was still in the future, Redding saw Hughes compassionately as a new Negro, yet as a new Negro possessed by desperation rather than emancipated by the "joy" of the new Negro's new world. Redding contrasts Hughes with Countee Cullen. If Cullen can be said to think racially, Hughes has been "swept," in Redding's judgment, with a great tide of racial feeling. In other words, "professors, ministers, physicians" may cerebrate with Cullen. But "domestics, porters, dock hands, factory girls, streetwalkers," all of these belong emotionally to Hughes. In his concern for form, and thus in his incorporation into his verse of such folk-born phenomena as blues and shouts, Hughes is not the creature of intellectuals. Of Hughes's prose fiction, incidentally, Redding says nothing at odds with his observations about Hughes's verse. Butcher, writing later than Redding and even more summarily, connects Hughes likewise with Cullen, but also with Sterling Brown, for Butcher feels that both Hughes and Brown have learned well from, and speak well of, the Negro folk. There are passing references in Butcher to Hughes as a novelist and dramatist. References to Hughes are scattered, but consistently more positive than negative, in David Littlejohn's *Black on White: A Critical Survey of Writings by American Negroes* (New York: Grossman, 1966). Indeed, Littlejohn calls Hughes the "surest Negro classic." In *Native Sons: A Critical Study of Twentieth-Century Negro Authors* (Philadelphia: Lippincott, 1968), by Edward Margolies, the succinct treatment of Hughes is able and judicious, without being pretentious.

Two criticisms of Hughes's work represent blatantly political approaches to literature. A Russian writer, Lydia Filatova, in "Langston Hughes: American Writer" (*International Literature,* No. 1, 1933), argues that Hughes was at first under the spell of decadent fantasies which fatuously projected the integration of the Negro into a "capitalist paradise," and was deceived and captivated by "bourgeois estheticism," but grew in grace as he became increasingly aware of the true nature of the class struggle and the urgent necessity for revolution in thought and action. Filatova follows predictable paths and uses predictable clichés in her doctrinaire criticism of Hughes. Equally as doctrinaire, as predictable, and as addicted to clichés, albeit exactly opposite in ideology, is Elizabeth Staples in "Langston Hughes: Malevolent Force" (*American Mercury,* January 1959). To Staples it is clear that Hughes should not be tolerated by decent, loyal Americans—he is an insufferable renegade, who, although he has the effrontery to deny it, is a Communist. Faith Berry, in her introduction to *Good Morning Revolution* (Westbury, Conn.: Lawrence Hill, 1973), accepts Hughes's denial that he ever was a Communist even while she maintains that Hughes's consistent leftism in much that he wrote has failed to receive the attention it deserves. Hughes, Berry avers, is fashionably construed as little other than a folk poet, when, as a matter of fact, he frequently champions the cause of radical, and often left-wing, social change.

James Presley's "The American Dream of Langston Hughes" (*SWR,* Autumn 1963) depends for the development of its argument upon the postulate that Hughes did espouse the so-called American dream. Presley implies for Hughes's American dream terms of the purest and loftiest political and social idealism. Presley has attached himself to an issue of importance in the criticism of Hughes by relating Hughes to dreams, particularly utopian dreams, and consequently to Hughes's version of the American dream. For the word "dream" occurs in the titles of two of Hughes's books of verse, and the presence of leading characters who are dreamers establishes much of the tone of the Simple stories and of *Not Without Laughter.* As Presley observes, it is through exposures of discrepancies between the American dream and actual practices that Hughes's protest in both his poetry and his prose is expressed.

One special note of protest in Hughes that can be differentiated from others has been studied by Arthur P. Davis with rather spectacular results. As early as 1925 Hughes had given some attention, in a twelve-line poem entitled "Cross," to the theme of the tragic mulatto, a major theme for students of the Negro novel, if not also for students of Negro poetry. Davis uses "Cross" and five other works by Hughes in "The Tragic Mulatto Theme in Six Works of Langston Hughes" (*Phylon,* Summer 1955) to follow Hughes's handling of this theme over more than a quarter of a century and through the forms of poetry, short story, drama, and opera. Hughes's mulattoes have white fathers and black mothers. They are especially bitter toward their white fathers, by whom they are never acknowledged in a satisfactory way. Davis concludes that, for Hughes, the tragic-mulatto theme really reduces to a drama of rejection. It is always the story of a disowned son. Davis, furthermore, suggests a connection between Hughes's use of the theme and his experiences with his own (mulatto) father.

Hughes's poetry has been widely anthologized. Hence, brief critiques of it are fairly numerous. A goodly proportion of these anthology notices, moreover, tend to be excellent résumés and reliable evaluations of Hughes's poetry. Surely the longest and fullest critique is in the ninety-page section devoted to Hughes in the study of major Negro American poets by French scholar Jean Wagner, *Black Poets of the United States: From Paul Laurence Dunbar to Langston Hughes* (Urbana: University of Illinois Press, 1973).

Wagner's work on Hughes is commendable in many ways. First, Wagner respects his subject. No note of condescension, no hint of a superior white man patronizing creatures of a lower order, creeps into what he says. Second, Wagner has not only read Hughes's poetry, but he has also made good use of pertinent authorities and commentators. Third, Wagner benefits from an adequate and active sense of context. He has acquired, for example, a knowledge of the world in which Hughes existed. Finally, Wagner possesses critical acumen. He rates Hughes highly as a poet for sound reasons.

Wagner begins with an account of Hughes's life as a boy and a young man which he modulates by easy stages into an account of Hughes's career as a poet. Wagner presents a record, both chronological and interpretive, of Hughes's activity as a poet—a record which, however, he permits to end (probably because of publication dates) without reference to *The Panther and The Lash* (New York: Knopf, 1967), Hughes's final volume of verse. Human beings tend, as they age, to change, to pass through different stages. Hughes changed as he passed from youth to maturity, even as in certain ways he remained very much the same. Wagner catches the essence of Hughes's basic self as well as the Hughes who progressed from racial romanticism to decidedly more valid conceptions of his own racial past (and present). Wagner identifies the folk Negro solely with the agrarian South. Hence, for Wagner, Hughes tends to be the poet of a citified Negro common man, not a folk poet in a proper sense. Wagner's interpretation of Hughes's poetry reaches its high point in an extended explication of the text of *Ask Your Mama,* which Wagner regards as a synthesis of the content and form of Hughes's poetry.

Hughes's poetry is examined at length in *Black Poetry in America* (Baton Rouge: Louisiana State University Press, 1974) by Blyden Jackson and Louis D. Rubin, Jr. The intended emphasis here is upon historical interpretation. In *Black Writers of the Thirties* (Baton Rouge: Louisiana State University Press, 1973), James O. Young examines Hughes's poetry of that decade. (Young makes only brief allusions to Hughes' fiction.) It is true that Hughes's ties with communism were close and highly visible in the 1930s. Young speaks of these ties briefly, yet accurately. He does not feel that the expression of protest improved Hughes's poetic art.

Robert Kerlin's "A Pair of Youthful Poets" (*Southern Workman*, April 1924), amiable though it is, is nothing more than a rapid salute to Countee Cullen and Hughes. Norman Macleod's more substantial "The Poetry and Argument of Langston Hughes" (*The Crisis*, November 1938) concentrates on a single mission. Macleod detects in Hughes one personality which feels and another personality which thinks; Macleod contends that the Hughes who feels is a poet, but that the Hughes who thinks is not. Y. Carmen's "Langston Hughes, Poet of the People" (*International Literature*, No. 1, 1939) defines poets and people in an obvious manner. John W. Parker, in " 'Tomorrow' in the Writings of Langston Hughes" (*CE*, May 1949) introduces a distinction which probably should not be lost in a review of critical expression about Hughes. Although Hughes's tomorrow, as Parker analyzes it, has its dark side, there is hope in it and the promise of possible good.

It may well be that no more perceptive article has been written about Hughes as a poet than Arthur Davis's "The Harlem of Langston Hughes' Poetry" (*Phylon*, Winter 1952). In emphasizing that the first Harlem in Hughes poetry is, in Hughes' own term, "Jazzonia," the "sundown" city of Harlem's night life, Davis is not announcing a discovery that he alone has made. He may well be in step with Parker. Even so, his use of his special and superior knowledge in his analysis of "Jazzonia" and of the gradual process by which, in Hughes's poetry, "Jazzonia" is replaced by another, less simplistic Harlem, is exceptional enough to merit citation. A similar special and superior knowledge of jazz and blues and of the culture from which they came contributes to the value of Nat Hentoff's "Langston Hughes, He Found Poetry in the Blues" (*Mayfair*, August 1958). The references to Hughes's poetry in Harold Isaacs's "Five Writers and Their African Ancestors" (*Phylon*, Fall 1960) occur only in relation to Isaacs's discussion of the appearance of Africa in the work of some Negro writers other than Hughes, above all, in Lorraine Hansberry's *A Raisin in the Sun*. Theodore R. Hudson's "Langston Hughes' Last Volume of Verse" (*CLAJ*, June 1968) confines itself largely to a cursory description of *The Panther and the Lash*. Hudson, however, is one of the better critics and his brief description says much in a few words. Phyllis Klotman makes perceptive observations about Hughes as an artist and about the character Jesse B. Semple, better known as Simple, in "Jesse B. Semple and the Narrative Art of Langston Hughes" (*JNT*, January 1973). It is Klotman's thesis that, in the Simple stories, Hughes borrows quite profitably from vaudeville the technique of the skit played by two stand-up comics. James Presley, in "The Birth of Jesse B. Semple" (*SWR*, Summer 1973) relates how Simple evolved in Hughes's mind and first appeared in print. Gary F. Scharnhost's "Hughes' 'Theme for English B'" (*Expl*, December 1973) affirms, through its reference to the juxtaposition within the poem of black and white cultures, the essential unity of all races, an assertion which may not represent adequately the attack in the poem upon white insulation from black experience. Martha K. Cobb's "Concepts of Blackness in the Poetry of Nicolás Guillén, Jacques Roumain and Langston Hughes" (*CLAJ*, December 1974) links Hughes as a poet to Guillén and Roumain, especially through the themes of confrontation, dualism, identity, and liberation. Rita B. Dandridge's "The Black Woman as a Freedom Fighter in Langston Hughes' *Simple's Uncle Sam*" (*CLAJ*, December 1974) emphasizes aspects of Hughes's characterizations of the black women found in the Simple stories.

Surprisingly, virtually no criticism other than the notices of the reviewers exists for Hughes's second, and last, novel, *Tambourines to Glory*. Hugh Gloster's indispensable pioneering study, *Negro Voices in American Fiction* (Chapel Hill: University of North Carolina Press, 1948), contains a treatment of *Not Without Laughter* which is basically a plot synopsis. Gloster, however, esteems the novel, especially as a sensitive transcript of Negro life. In what is easily one of the best-known comments about Hughes, Robert Bone, in both editions of his *Negro Novel in America* (New Haven, Conn.: Yale University Press, 1958 and 1965), attributes "ideological ambivalence" to *Not Without Laughter* and calls the whole work mediocre. Carl Milton Hughes, in *The Negro Novelist* (New York: Citadel, 1953), allots only three lines to *Not Without Laughter*.

Arthur P. Davis, a student of many aspects of Hughes's career, has presented a study of the character of Simple that synthesizes superb literary criticism, relevant sociological observation, and a sense of Negro history in "Jesse B. Semple: Negro American" (*Phylon*, Spring 1954). In *Witnesses for Freedom* (New York: Harper & Bros., 1948), Rebecca Barton devotes a chapter to a critical résumé of *The Big Sea*.

The Big Sea was reviewed by, among others, Edwin Embree, Oswald Garrison Villard, and Richard Wright. It can be said of Hughes not only that he was widely reviewed, but also that he was reviewed by interesting and illustrious people. The reviewers of his poetry include Countee Cullen, Jessie Fauset, Alain Locke, DuBose Heyward, Babette Deutsch, Kenneth Fearing, Abbe Niles, William Rose Benét, Mary Colum, Alfred Kreymborg, David Daiches, Dudley Fitts, Owen Dodson, Rolfe Humphries, J. Saunders Redding, Arna Bontemps,, and James

Baldwin; of his prose, John Chamberlain, V. F. Calverton, Sterling Brown, Sherwood Anderson, Lewis Gannett, Martha Gruening, Vernon Loggins, Carl Van Vechten, Bucklin Moon, August Meier, Herbert Aptheker, Roi Ottley, Nick Aaron Ford, James Ivy, Arna Bontemps and J. Saunders Redding. There is at least one "critical war" reflected in his reviews. White reviewers—as, for example, Babette Deutsch in *Bookman* (April 1927) and Julia Peterkin in *Poetry* (October 1927)—tended to laud *Fine Clothes to the Jew*. Black reviewers writing in black journals—as in black newspapers such as New York's *The Amsterdam News*, Chicago's *The Whip*, the Philadelphia *Tribune*, and the Pittsburgh *Courier*, as well as in the Negro magazine *The Crisis*—tended to attack *Fine Clothes to the Jew* on the grounds that it gave an unnecessarily scurrilous picture of Negro life which was, moreover, badly timed. The reviewer in the *Amsterdam News* called Hughes a "sewer dweller." The reviewer in *The Whip* named Hughes the "poet lowrate of Harlem."

Critics have not written voluminously of Hughes's connections with the theater. Webster Smalley's introduction to the previously cited volume of plays by Hughes which he edited is almost the only critical essay on the five plays within the volume. Oriented largely toward a personal history of Hughes, as well as a history of the circumstances accounting for the plays, it gives favorable assessments of Hughes as a playwright. A judgment of Hughes as a dramatist based extensively upon the plays in Smalley, but with some reference to Hughes's play *Mule Bone*, and attributing to Hughes a style in the sense of a "controlling manner of thought," constitutes the substance of T. J. Spencer and Clarence J. Rivers's "Langston Hughes: His Style and Optimism" (*Drama Critique*, Spring 1964). Darwin Turner, however, in "Langston Hughes as a Playwright" (*CLAJ*, June 1968), a rather conventional scrutiny of Hughes's skill in the craftsmanship of drama, tends to be considerably less pleased with Hughes than either Smalley or the critical team of Spencer and Rivers.

The author gratefully acknowledges the substantial assistance of Joan Barrax, Rose Hart, and Thomas Scheft on this essay.

NAME INDEX

OPEN MIC NIGHT IN MOSCOW

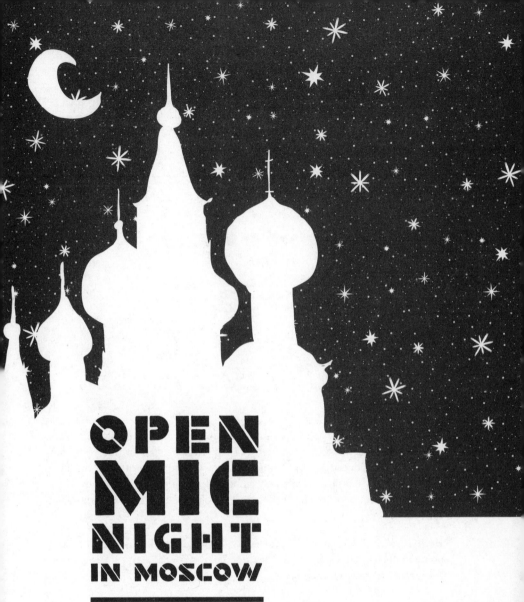

OPEN MIC NIGHT IN MOSCOW

And Other Stories from My Search for Black Markets,
Soviet Architecture, and Emotionally Unavailable Russian Men

AUDREY MURRAY

WILLIAM MORROW
An Imprint of HarperCollins Publishers

HarperCollins books may be purchased for educational, business, or sales promotional use. For information, please e-mail the Special Markets Department at SPsales@harpercollins.com.

FIRST EDITION

Designed by Leah Carlson-Stanisic

Star illustration by Yana Alisovna/Shutterstock, Inc.

Map of Soviet Union by Serban Bogdan/Shutterstock, Inc.

Library of Congress Cataloging-in-Publication Data has been applied for.

ISBN 978-0-06-282329-8

18 19 20 21 22   LSC   10 9 8 7 6 5 4 3 2 1

For Mom, Dad, Angela, and Andrew

CONTENTS

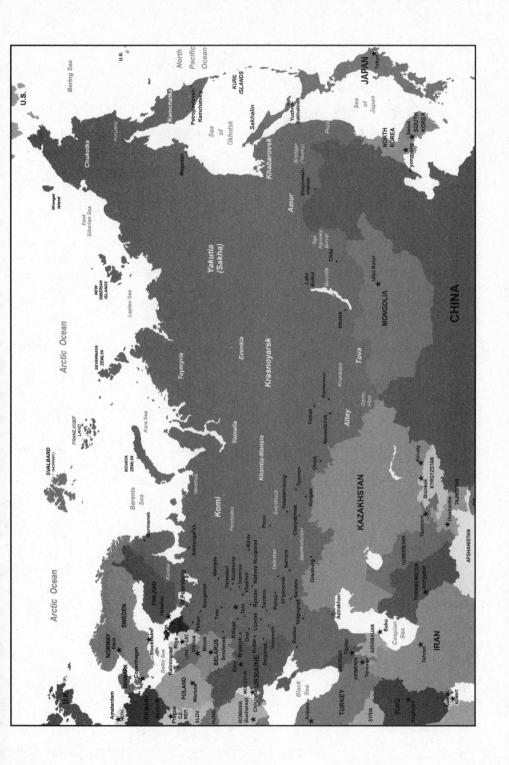

"(C) Lonely Planet 2014. No part of this publication may be copied, stored in a retrieval system, or transmitted in any form by any means . . . without the permission of the publisher."

—*Lonely Planet Central Asia*

"Ничего особенного. Так, поставить галочку. Все очень помпезно, неуютно, официально. Угрюмое местечко."

—*TripAdvisor User Lihman, on Red Square*

"I want to thank my accountants . . . They are both geniuses."

—Why Men Love Bitches *(acknowledgments section)*

INTRODUCTION

Hello, I'm Audrey. Welcome to my book.

I've never written a book before, but in researching this one, I opened dozens of them, and I noticed that many start off with the same mistake. The first page contains a few quotations that obviously mean something to the author but are presented without context or explanation. As a result, they fall flat, sound pretentious, or make you wonder, "Why is a cookbook leading with an excerpt from Machiavelli?"

To avoid falling into this trap, I'm going to explain the significance of the quotes from my epigraph.

The first comes from the 2014 Lonely Planet guide to Central Asia, which I obtained by illegally downloading it from a Russian website and used it extensively while planning portions of my trip, and later while crafting the copyright page of this book. I found the copyright page to be one of the most daunting to write. How do you strike the right balance between keeping it light but also sounding legally threatening? What makes a good ISBN? Is it gauche to list your parents' home address? The Lonely Planet guide to Central Asia helped me navigate not only the Pamir Mountains and a fire crater in the desert of Turkmenistan, but also the supple ins and outs of a well-honed Library of Congress catalog entry.[*]

The second quotation is more meaningful to me. It comes from a TripAdvisor user's review of Red Square in Moscow, and because

------

[*] Update: it turns out you don't get to write your own copyright page. Your publisher does that for you, and it can—and will—ignore multiple e-mails with reasonable demands that the page include more of your lucky numbers.

it's in Russian, I don't understand what it means. But it speaks to me just the same, in the way that poetic truths transcend language, time, and copyright laws. (Update: I just ran the quote through Google Translate, and it turns out that it means, "Nothing special. So, tick the box. Everything is very pompous, uncomfortable, formal. A gloomy place." So yeah, confirmed—immortal words.)

The final quote comes from my roadmap to life and favorite book of all time, *Why Men Love Bitches*. If you've never read it, go return my book and use the store credit to buy a copy. *Why Men Love Bitches* lays out a life philosophy that its predecessors (the Torah, Bible, and Koran) were grasping for, but never managed to reach. That philosophy is basically: do what makes you happy, don't worry about what other people think, and when it comes to dating, play a little hard to get. I'm including an excerpt from the acknowledgments section as a reminder that I need to file my taxes.

Now that the quotes are out of the way, here's a quick overview of the book so you know what to expect, and also have something to say if you find yourself in a situation where you need to pretend to have read it (e.g., core curriculum of the near future, a literary salon). Truly, I understand: if I could have, I would have pretended to have written it. My plan had been to just pull an all-nighter and bang it all out the day before publication, but it turns out that publishing a book is a little different from writing a high school essay.

Basically, it's about this twenty-eight-year-old woman (aka me) who decides to spend a year traveling through the former Soviet Union (aka the best place ever) because she's insanely obsessed with the Russian language and culture (aka all of her boyfriends were Russian), and along the way she learns a lot and and meets a bunch of people and winds up in situations that are awkward and funny and occasionally poignant (aka give her the Pulitzer Prize?).

It's hard to say how my fascination with all things Russian began. Was it my first Russian boyfriend (Oleg)? My second Russian boyfriend (Anton)? My third Russian boyfriend (back to Oleg again)?

It happened in bits and pieces, without my particularly noticing, but by the time I turned twenty-eight, I'd become so obsessed with the countries that gave us beets, Dostoevsky, and websites for streaming pirated movies that it seemed perfectly logical to spend a year traveling through the former Soviet Union and trying to learn Russian.

This was not something I'd seen coming.

Before I turned twenty, I'd been outside of the United States exactly once, when I was six months old and my parents took me to England. I have no memory of this trip, but it did leave me with an infant passport that I used for years as a backup form of identification. Bouncers everywhere were mystified.

In college I spent a semester in Paris and came back feeling very worldly. I started eating dinner at eight p.m. and annoying every French person I encountered by responding in my high-school-level French to their perfect, unaccented English. Then I met Oleg, and through him, Russian.

After I graduated from college, I took a real job, then quit and moved to China. In Shanghai, I did comedy, wrote plays, paid my rent and funded my habit of getting my bicycle stolen by SAT tutoring, and had the honor of being a free hotline's most frequent caller of the year. I met Anton, and through him came more Russian.

But unless she's lucky or raised in a matriarchal society, there comes a time in every young woman's life when she faces increasing pressure to cool it and settle down. While the world has gotten better at allowing young women to explore their passions, there is still an unspoken (and sometimes spoken, repeated, and followed up in e-mails) expectation that she will put them aside in order to find love. Back in America, my friends were starting to get engaged and my parents wanted me to move home and do the same more than I wanted anything in particular for myself. And so after almost four years in China, I moved back to the U.S. and set out to settle down.

The only obstacles to my plan were the fact that I wasn't really sure what settling down entailed, that I was unsure how you were supposed to do it, and that I knew that I definitely didn't want to.

But I was certain I could make it work. If I could make a life for myself on another continent and be a distinguished guest at a free hotline's annual gala, where if I'm being honest things got a little awkward when the operators came out and performed skits making fun of the people who called in but we got over that, I could work out how to become the type of person who drove a minivan.

In the dreamy and aspirational sense, I wanted to travel through the former Soviet Union. But it was a pipe dream. Not something I ever expected to achieve in this lifetime. Or at least, not something I thought would be financially feasible before the age of 70, unless my Beanie Baby collection shot up in value.

What I hadn't realized was that sometimes an incredible stroke of luck takes a form other than a stuffed animal with a tag protector.

A few months after I'd arrived in New York, a former boss in Shanghai asked if I'd like to come back and SAT tutor for the busy seasons. I'd return to Shanghai for one- or two-month stretches, work truly horrendous hours but make bank, and then go back to New York for a few months.

Or, I thought, instead of going back to New York, I could go to Russia.

This was my version of winning the *Hamilton* lottery, or maybe even the actual lottery.

But as soon as the thought popped into my head, I banished it. I still didn't know what settling down looked like. But I was pretty sure it did not involve yurts.

I had come back to the U.S. for one purpose (to put an end to my anxieties about dying alone by marrying the first person who shared my belief that the maximum amount of time you should spend at a sporting event is thirty minutes), and I felt that I had to put everything else on hold until that happened.

But when I dreamed, it was never of the job, boyfriend, wedding, or babies I was willing myself to long for. (Though it was sometimes of steamy hookups with really hot guys who seemed emotionally unavailable.) It always was of this one adventure that kept coming back to me. Only now, it wasn't a pipe dream.

I tried to tell myself that was the kind of thing you did after you settled down and built some semblance of a normal life. I'd been trying to do that in New York. I had signed a lease on an apartment and stopped flying to countries with lax pharmaceutical regulations to stock up on over-the-counter Xanax. Those seemed firmly planted in the adulthood column! But I was also starting to get the sinking feeling that my ambitions didn't square with the traditional path I saw around me.

Not that that mattered! Most people, I reminded myself, hadn't spent their childhoods dreaming of going into corporate litigation. But they did it anyway, because it was the responsible choice. If everyone else could find a way to make it all work and still be happy, couldn't I?

The truth was that the answer was no, and I knew that for a long time before I admitted it to myself, and even longer before I did anything about it.

When a passing fancy metastasizes into an all-consuming passion, there can be an urge to ascribe it to fate or higher meaning. There has to be a *reason* you sleep in yurts in Mongolia and Tajikistan; that way, destiny can be held responsible for any havoc it wreaks. Deciding to devote your life to the study of prehistoric ferns or to marry Brad the Lawyer is dangerous, because if things don't work out, you'll have no one but yourself to blame.

When future scholars look back at the written record left by twenty-first-century Americans, they'll find a history in "moments in which we knew." We write college essays about the instant we realized our passion for biomedical engineering. We bond with strangers by trading revelations: our moment of deciding to quit our jobs, for their moments of realizing their bodies were sensitive to gluten.

I never have these moments. Sometimes I think I do (e.g., while waiting in line at a coffee shop: *I should open a coffee shop!*; while waiting in line for a bathroom: *I should write a poem about craft beer in Brooklyn!*; after drinking too much craft beer in Brooklyn: *I should call my ex-boyfriend!*), but when I reexamine them later, I recognize them for what they were: terrible ideas masquerading as insight.

The things I have figured out have dawned on me so gradually that it's hard to draw the line between when I knew and when I didn't.

Each time I buy a $90 West Elm dinner plate off a wedding registry, I wonder whether, on the night Hannah opened her door and found Brad holding her favorite smoothie, she *really* gazed lovingly into his eyes and thought, *One day, we're going to make all of our friends stay in a block of rooms at a Hampton Inn.* Because I think it's far more likely she went, *That thing BETTER not have any fucking banana in it.*

So, there was no good reason why I loved Russian and wanted to spend a year traveling through the former Soviet Union, but there were plenty of good reasons not to do it. Such as: I was twenty-eight, single, seasonally employed, still using my parents' residence as my home address, and convinced that the best way to iron something was to hang it up in the bathroom while I showered. I was, as they say, "still figuring things out," unless *they* are my dad, in which case it's "putting in your 10,000 hours of partying."

For the entire time it was around, the Soviet Union was the largest country on Earth. If you're interested in a brief history, I highly recommend Wikipedia, but the condensed version is basically: communism, Stalin, is Anastasia still alive but living in New Jersey?

In the early 1990s, the fifteen republics that had made up the Soviet Union decided to go their separate ways and became the independent nations of Russia, Latvia, Lithuania, Estonia, Belarus, Ukraine, Moldova, Georgia, Armenia, Azerbaijan, Turkmenistan, Uzbekistan, Tajikistan, Kazakhstan, and Kyrgyzstan. I originally planned to visit all of them, but because of time constraints and the fact that I haven't yet figured out how to get people to keep depositing money into my bank account when I'm not working for them, I will only make it to eleven. I purposefully decided to save for another trip to the Caucasus (which, in this part of the world, means Georgia, Azerbaijan, and Armenia, not a bizarre Midwestern voting ritual where everyone gets locked in a barn and has to stay until the whole room is standing under the name of one candidate), legitimately forgot about Moldova (honest mistake!), and showed up in Mongolia thinking it had been part of the former Soviet Union and then quickly learned it had not (honest but expensive mistake!).

I remember the moment I decided to buy a one-way ticket to the former Soviet Union in rich, vivid detail. The rain-slicked streets of Brooklyn glittered in the early twilight, like the cover of an acoustic album inspired by a breakup. I'd been feeling pretty miserable, because I missed living abroad, because I was still hung up on Anton, and also maybe because I had stopped taking my antidepressants without consulting a medical professional. I looked up to the heavens, where the stars winked back at me, and then down at my hands, which I was shocked to see were holding *my own destiny*.

In that moment, I realized that the answer to my problems lay not in deliberate introspection or mindful goal-setting or finding a full-time job, but rather in traveling for a year through the former Soviet Union, and I also knew that I would study biomedical engineering and quit my job and marry Brad.

That's obviously not how it happened.

In truth, the decision to go was, like all of my major life choices, random and incremental and maybe a little impulsive.

But I'm glad I did it, because it worked out. And if it hadn't, it would have been a huge waste of time and money, and maybe the biggest mistake of my life.

ONE THE SILK ROAD

OPENING FOR A MEDITATIVE DRUM CIRCLE IN ALMATY (KAZAKHSTAN)

The first rule of comedy is probably "Never say no to a gig." The second rule is likely an addendum to the first, and it's "even if it's opening for a meditative drum circle in Kazakhstan."*

Which is why I'm standing in front of a group of confused Kazakhstanis, trying to explain what stand-up is. In case you're wondering, this is not the ideal way to start a show. There's a reason Beyoncé doesn't open her concerts with "Please raise your hand if you're familiar with music."

"Who here has seen stand-up comedy before?" I ask.

Two hands go up.

"Maybe I should back up—how many of you understand English?"

This time, half of the room raises its hands, which is better, though it does occur to me that some of them might not understand English and could just be raising their hands because they see the people around them doing it. In fact, most of the time I raise my hand, it's for exactly this reason. But I'm going to think positively. The glass is half-full, and the audience is half-fluent. Not a dream setup for an art form that's basically just talking, but my third rule of comedy is "A language barrier is no excuse for a comedy failure."

---

* I assume this is true, though I've never read any rules for stand-up out of a general distrust for rules, with the exception of my aforementioned favorite book and intermittent personal Bible, *Why Men Love Bitches*.

I turn to the bongo player.

"Do you know those drum stings they play after jokes on TV?"

I'm thinking there's maybe a 50 percent chance he can even understand me, and a one-in-five shot he knows what I'm talking about. I'm reminded that I never took statistics as he surprises me by doing a pretty good *ba-dum-tss* on the bongos.

Okay. A room full of people who mostly don't speak the only language I can perform in, and an accompanying late-night band that's just one guy on bongos. To say that I can work with this would be to vastly overestimate my abilities. To accurately read my capacity for obstinacy is to know I'll try.

"So I'm going to tell some stories," I continue. "If you want to laugh, great, and if you don't know when to laugh . . ." I gesture to the bongo player, who's right there with me. *Ba-dum-tss.* Nervous laughter. (If there's a fourth rule of comedy, it should be "Tip your bongo players.")

I look out at the young Kazakhstanis sitting cross-legged on the common room floor of the Loco Hostel. I look down at my socks, which I'm performing in for the first time, because not even the stage gets a break on the no-shoes-inside policy. This is the kind of moment where you'd expect me to pause and go, *Wow, I never thought I'd be doing stand-up in Kazakhstan.* But instead, all I can think is, *Should I talk about dating or ask them what's up with those buses that don't come to a complete stop?*

Twenty-four hours earlier

I didn't plan on showing up in Kazakhstan severely underprepared for a yearlong journey through the former Soviet Union. But on the flight to Almaty, I discover that this is what happened.

Sure, I'd illegally downloaded a guidebook with every intention of reading it, but then life, and more precisely the Internet, got in the way. I have kind of, sort of, looked into which countries require me to arrange visas in advance, concluded that the answer is most of them, and then mentally filed that information away under Problems for Future Audrey. I'd made one hostel reservation—for one night in Kazakhstan—and I'd booked that the day before I left.

The one thing I did do was study Russian for approximately one hour a day for a solid six weeks. I feel extremely confident in my budding abilities right up until the flight attendant asks me what I want to drink.

"Oh, um, *nyet* Russian," I stammer, realizing, for the first time, that I have not learned how to say, "I can't speak Russian." Come to think of it, there are a lot of seemingly useful phrases I have not learned, including: "How much does this cost?" "Take me to the hospital," and "Where are you going with my valuables?"

Well, I guess I'll just have to work with what I've got. The flight attendant is still standing beside my armrest expectantly.

"Um . . ." I try to imagine what the word *water* might sound like in Russian. "Vater?" I guess.

This is not correct. After attempting to pantomime the not-so-charades-friendly phrase *bottled water*, I reflect on some of the phrases Rosetta Stone did opt to teach me before tackling the non-essentials like "water" and "help." I would never find myself in an emergency in which I was unable to tell a Russian speaker, "They are riding horses," "Women swim," or, "That is a man."

In other words, my Russian would be fine for the purposes of eyewitnessing a not-terribly-elaborate murder at a Russian country club, but definitely more wanting in all other scenarios.

This is when I start to panic.

I look around the plane. Most seats sit empty on the late-night flight from China's capital Beijing to Kazakhstan's former capital Almaty, which had its status stripped and transferred to a mostly empty plot of land in the middle of the desert. (The president, worried Almaty's population of ethnic Russians could thwart his authoritarian ambitions, announced in 1997 that he was moving the capital from Almaty to a new city called Astana, which he intended to build from scratch. He did, and the results were . . . kind of like when you're going for flashy but end up with a mall shaped like a tent.) The few dozen other passengers are mostly businessmen and the Chinese Olympic water polo team, whose presence somewhat calms me, because they are all extremely hot. I'm the only woman traveling alone, and I'm certainly the only twenty-eight-year-old following her heart and harboring vague aspirations of "finding herself."

I'm all for taking the road less traveled. But when you find yourself on a thoroughfare mostly used by people negotiating contracts or playing competitive water sports, it can make you wonder if you're on a life path where you might get lost and starve to death only twenty feet from the trail.

The TVs hanging over the line at passport control do little to quell my sense of impending doom. As we wait to have our passports stamped, they launch into what's either a news segment or a commercial for some kind of baby swimming class. It's hard to tell, because whoever was behind the camera went in for a few perfunctory, almost begrudging, shots of the babies and then spent the rest of his time time panning up and down the bikini-clad bodies of the women holding them. This segues into something about tractors. Finally, a brief clip of rapidly scrolling text explains Kazakhstan's visa-free entry program.

At some point, I read or heard that Americans don't need visas for Kazakhstan, and I'd accepted that as truth that didn't require further fact-checking.

This video says that Americans don't need visas for a trial period from July 2014 to August 2015. Which is troubling, because it is two days into September of 2015.

The lusty swimming babies video starts up again. *Wait,* I telepathically implore the television, *can we go back to that visa thing?*

Where had I even heard this visa rumor? Would "I'm pretty sure it said so on Wikipedia" hold up in immigration court?

The man in the passport control booth is wearing what looks like full combat gear, but might appear to a less terrified person as more of a standard border-patrol uniform. He slowly thumbs through my passport as I try to maintain eye contact that's aggressive, but not in an *I'm trying to illegally enter your country but not on purpose* way. He removes a few staples left over from visas that had been ripped out upon exit from other countries; I can't tell if he's trying to intimidate me or procrastinating work by cleaning. I have visions of being deported, although the question of where they would send me is intriguing enough that I almost want to see how it plays out. Will they put me on a plane to America, the country on my passport, or back to China, the country I've flown in from? Are there even any flights from Almaty to America? Would it be nice to just get a free trip home at this point and call the whole thing a wash?

Before I can get an answer to this question, the guard is pounding my passport with one of those perplexingly hefty visa stamps that looks like it could also, in a pinch, make fresh-squeezed orange juice.

The arrivals hall in Almaty is equipped with everything you'd need to walk straight through it and on to your final destination. There are a few small shops, a row of five adjacent ATMs, and something called "Caviar Palace." The only thing that's missing are the people from my hostel, who are supposed to be picking me up.

It's almost midnight, and I'm reminded that I'm alone in a country I've barely heard of, where, if my attempts to order water on the plane are any indication, my language skills are more likely to get me into trouble than out of it. I'm finally on the verge of tears when a loud group bursts into the arrivals hall. A man and a woman dressed in full-body animal costumes carry balloons and a giant sign, while a dreadlocked photographer follows.

I smile. I may be all alone but at least I'm not walking into an embarrassing airport greeting.

And then I squint at the sign they're holding, because my name appears to be written on it.

Newlyweds Almas and Kassya, freshly derobed from furry costumes, just opened Loco Hostel a few weeks ago. I'm the first guest they picked up from the airport, so they wanted to surprise me with the costumes and balloons.

"Were you surprised?" Almas asks. "You seemed surprised."

I assure him that I was.

We're having drinks at a bar we stopped at on our way to the hostel. When we park outside, I ask if it's safe to leave my suitcase in the car. Almas, Kassya and Darya, the photographer, look at me like I've asked if the vehicle works underwater. "I would die if I lost my beauty products," I want to whisper, but don't.

Inside, it's karaoke night, an event no customers seem to have attended on purpose. The manager has forced an extremely attractive bartender to perform a 20-minute set, which, to his credit, he's nailing.

"He's so handsome," I blurt out.

"Yes," Almas says. "I think he's Korean."

I'm surprised. "Like, he's from Korea?" I ask.

Almas shakes his head. "Probably his grandparents were."

The nineteenth and twentieth centuries brought waves of Korean immigrants to the Russian Empire and the Soviet Union, and ethnic Koreans still make up a small percentage of the population in many post-Soviet states.

Our table is another reflection of the post-Soviet melting pot. Almas and Kassya are ethnic Kazakhs, and Darya is ethnically Russian. What are national borders today were more like state lines in the Soviet Union, and Darya's family has been living in Almaty since before she was born.

Kazakhstani and Russian both became official languages when Kazakhstan declared independence, and so I ask Darya if she speaks Kazakhstani. Judging from the reaction this gets, I might as well have said, "Let's go around at the table and talk about which members of our families were murdered by Stalin." My three companions shift uncomfortably.

"Maybe I would like to one day . . ." Darya replies.

Almas quickly changes the subject.

"So you do comedy?" he says. "I have a joke: yellow blue bus."

Kassya and Darya giggle, so I do too, because I don't need to look stupid. But then curiosity gets the better of me.

"I don't get it," I admit.

"In Russian, it sounds like 'I love you,'" Darya explains. "*Ya lyublyu vas.*"

"What's your comedy about?" Almas asks.

"Strangers I meet at karaoke nights," I say.

This turns out to be a terrible choice of retort.

"Do it now!" they implore. "With the karaoke microphone!"

I ungracefully refuse, but Almas is insistent.

"Could you make a show at our hostel?" he asks.

"Do you have a microphone?" I reply, because the answer to that question is usually no.

He nods. "We're having, like, a meditative drum circle tomorrow night. So . . . maybe you can do your comedy before?"

Oh boy. You don't really see stand-ups, or, come to think of it, anyone, hustling for that sweet spot right between after people show up for a meditative drum circle and before the meditative drum circle goes on. And I say that as someone who ran a comedy show in the basement of a bookstore.

But the show must go on! Or maybe that's not the right saying, because it sounds like the show will go on, it's just a question of whether I'll be in it. But when in Kazakhstan . . . !

"Sure," I reply. And then, because this strikes me as something I should have checked before saying yes, I ask, "Will people speak English?"

Almas laughs. "We'll see."

Kazakhstan is the largest of the five Central Asian republics that became countries after the USSR collapsed. It combines with the other four—Kyrgyzstan, Tajikistan, Uzbekistan, and Turkmenistan—to form a region often referred to as Central Asia or, "the 'stans."

Stan can sound scary to an American ear or to anyone who's heard Eminem collaborate with Dido, but it's actually just Persian for *land of.* Central Asia has five major ethnic groups, which can be crudely divided into the traditionally nomadic herders (the Kazakh and Kyrgyz), the traditionally settled traders (the Tajiks and Uzbek), and the traditionally terrifying warriors (the Turkmen). The majority of Central Asians are Muslim, though they practice a form of Islam that incorporates indigenous animist and shamanistic traditions.

Central Asia is marked by harsh terrain, expansive deserts, and precipitous mountains that can make simply moving around a challenge. Ironically, the region served for centuries as the overland trade link between Asia and Europe that most of us know as the Silk Road. When sea routes rendered the caravan obsolete, some parts of the region fell into decline, and much of the territory was gobbled up by the Russian Empire in the nineteenth century.

Kazakhstan declared independence in 1991, and one of its first official acts as a sovereign nation was to launch a cosmonaut into space. It did this before the country settled on a name. This was obviously a piece of political theater designed to demonstrate the new government's power and legitimacy and it was thanks to a random coincidence. The Soviet Union's version of Cape Canaveral was located in Kazakhstan, and when the USSR dissolved, newly independent Kazakhstan found that it owned a space center.

But it was also a sign that, though the Soviet Union had ended, some things would be slow to change.

Kazakhstan was luckier than some former Soviet Republics. Its land was rich in natural resources, which fueled steady economic growth that began in the early 2000s. Oil revenues brought foreign investors and Western brands and built some (legitimately) flashy skyscrapers in the new capital, Astana.

But in other ways, Kazakhstan fared no better than other post-Soviet states. Many hoped that the collapse of the Soviet Union would bring freedom and democracy to the newly independent nations, but most countries simply swapped a Soviet dictatorship for a homegrown version. Kazakhstan has had the same president since the country declared independence twenty-four years ago. Kazakhstanis have neither freedom of speech nor freedom of religion, dissenters are often jailed, and the government shuts down organizations it deems threatening.

For a while, it seemed like Kazakhstan's leadership had convinced its citizens that they'd made the tacit tradeoff of political freedoms for economic growth that was trending in authoritarian circles in the 1990s and 2000s. People saw their standard of living rise and, the theory went, were willing to accept a more restrictive government in exchange for continued prosperity. But a worldwide decline in oil prices has hit Kazakhstan's economy, along with that of its biggest trading partner, Russia. The pace of economic growth has slowed, and it's unclear if the terms of this agreement will need to be renegotiated.

The shopkeepers of Almaty do not enjoy making change.

"No, no, no, no!" the woman at the grocery shouts while pushing me out of her store after I try to buy a 5-tenge loaf of bread with a 5,000-tenge note.

If a sandwich costs 350 tenge, a 500-tenge note is unacceptable. Change is sometimes so hard to come by that it's given in the form of similar-value goods. I buy a 150-tenge bottle of water and get packs of gum back as change. My purse slowly fills with Orbits where there'd normally be loose coins.

The Kazakhstani tenge took a precipitous nosedive two weeks before I arrived. Kazakhstan's central bank had announced that it would no longer set the currency's exchange rate, and in one day, the tenge dropped 26 percent. On August 18, 2015, 1 U.S. dollar got you 188 tenge. By August 21, it got you 252 tenge.

When I arrive in Almaty on September 2 of that year, people are still figuring out how to adjust.

For the most part, life seems to be more or less carrying on as usual. Stores stay open. Smiling grandparents push baby strollers through parks. A woman sitting next to me in a Georgian restaurant uses a special stylus to send text messages, because her fingernails are too long for her to touch the screen.

The only hint of economic uncertainty comes in the beauty aisle.

Almaty has no shortage of cosmetic stores; in the city center, there seems to be one on every block. I feel underdressed in my tinted ChapStick.

I spend an afternoon wandering the city, and behind each floor-to-ceiling beauty-store window, I see saleswomen hunched over merchandise with cotton balls and bottles of rubbing alcohol, scrubbing furiously. Sometimes the male security guards have been pressed into service too, and they perform their duties with significantly more resentment.

I finally walk inside one to figure out what's going on. The cotton balls and rubbing alcohol are being used to remove the price tags. All of the merchandise is being marked up.

Almaty glows with the luster of something long coveted. I ogle each tree and trash can with the awe of a parent entranced by a newborn's toes. This apple is from Almaty! This window was made in the Soviet Union!

Almaty sits at the base of snowcapped mountains that hover over the wide, leafy avenues and enormous Soviet buildings. Much of what the Soviets built remains, a preservation perhaps aided by the fact that the city is no longer the capital.

Almaty therefore retains buildings from each Soviet period. There are the regal neoclassical buildings painted bright colors and trimmed with casings that look like piped frosting, known, ironically enough, for Joseph Stalin, the man who popularized them. Stalin, I'm left to conclude, was a ruthless dictator in the boardroom, gingerbread-house man in the drafting room. Beside these sit otherwise ordinary structures with strange abstract flourishes from the Constructivist period, which sought to infuse public and industrial buildings with the avant-garde aesthetics of Russian Futurist art. Concrete lattices drape over facades; supports and engineering fixtures protrude as if to highlight the buildings' guts.

The dominant architectural feature is the Soviet tendency to go big or go home, with buildings constructed on such a grand scale, I sometimes wonder if the builders accidentally doubled the proportions: the Hotel Kazakhstan, a twenty-six-story tower that looks like it's wearing a crown; Ascension Cathedral, a colorful onion-domed church made entirely of wood and hidden in the middle of a public park; the Central State Museum, which has a look I can only describe as "Greek Pantheon meets the Space Age, also big enough to accommodate the entire population of Kazakhstan if everyone decides to visit on the same day."

Cyclists will tell you the best way to see a city is on a bike; subway enthusiasts espouse the virtues of experiencing a place as its commuters do. A couple once swore to me that you can only get to know a country by hitchhiking. After a series of mishaps, I'm exploring Almaty by hopping on and off of its public buses while they're still moving.

A visa errand has left me stranded on the edge of town, which is a convenient place to discover that I don't know how to say Loco Hostel in Russian. I have also, in what I now realize was an unwise move, ventured out without a copy of the address. The facts of the situation are this: I'm standing on the side of a highway with no plan and a vague sense of the direction my hostel lies in. A taxi is linguistically out of the question, and my phone doesn't have data. There are, however, a fairly steady stream of city buses rolling up to a station beside me to discharge and pick up passengers.

It's becoming clear that I'm going to have to jump on a bus headed in an unknown direction and try to get off somewhere that looks familiar. And I mean "jump on" quite literally, because the buses never come to a complete stop. Instead, they slow as they approach the station, and when the doors open, people jump out of and into buses that are very much still moving.

My plan, as I leap through the open doors of a still-rolling bus, is to jump off the bus when it veers off course, find one headed in a more promising direction, and repeat this process, edging closer to the hostel each time. If all else fails, I will call Kazakhstan's version of 911. Although, come to think of it, I'm not sure what that number is. But I do know I need to head roughly straight-leftish.

The bus follows the highway back into the city center, passing an American-style strip mall and an American-style mega mall. The side of the road is edged with rosebushes, still in bloom. I jump out at the city's main east-west artery and jump onto another bus headed toward my hostel. When this turns up a street I'm not expecting it to, I jump off again, walk back to the main road, and try again. Somehow, I make my way back.

I enter the hostel common room, stunned that my plan has worked, and with renewed faith in my abilities to navigate a trip I could have just better planned for. Well, who cares? I wasn't a Boy Scout, but I'm pretty sure that their motto is "The first step to preparedness is to start out completely unprepared."

Travel can turn the smallest errands into triumphs that feel like major accomplishments. Grocery shopping, riding public transit, and making it through immigration all fill you with a sense of achievement that's sometimes even more sweet because you were forced to do something you never thought you could.

Almas is still sitting at a table in the common room and looks up as I come in. "So, the show starts at seven," he reminds me.

I smile and lie. "I can't wait."

Halfway through my set, the bongo player jumps in to provide an unsolicited beat. But the audience is engaged and fairly responsive, except for one woman, who gets a call in the middle of a joke and ANSWERS it.

"Sorry," she tells me after, through a friend who translates. "I didn't understand it anyway."

People who don't do comedy (aka "noncomics" or "people who

have never tried to do their own dry cleaning with a blow-dryer and a gut feeling") often ask if I get nervous before I go onstage, and I always say, "I do sometimes, but it doesn't bother me." People imagine that you stop feeling nervous, but for me anyway, it's more that you get used to it. The first time you have an *awful* set—the kind of truly horrendous bombing that makes you want to go hang out with organized criminals, in the hopes that you'll witness a crime and be placed in the witness protection program—you realize that bombing doesn't kill you. I get nervous before some shows, but I get nervous every time it looks like the person in front of me is ordering the last everything bagel. Of the two worst-case scenarios, the bagel is more devastating. And all of this is the truth, but only half of it.

The half I'm leaving out is that the nerves are the whole point. They're what stop most people from ever trying comedy. They're what give you that rush when you step off the stage—the risk was huge, and everyone watching you knew it.

After the show, I sit outside in the kind of cold that stings your nose while the drum circle's flutist smokes cigarettes. He's a handsome, charismatic guy who has the irresistible aura of someone who is both sincere and stripped of self-consciousness.

"Do you like Sartre?" he asks.

"Um . . ." I do not casually read things like Sartre, but the fact that he clearly has is only adding to his sexy vibe, and I have enough sense to know I'll be shooting myself in the foot if I tell him I've recently been on a thrillers-about-women-who-go-missing kick.

"I love *No Exit*," I say, which is true in the sense that I saw it once and kind of understood it.

"What do you think is the message of it?" he asks.

I shrug. "Hell is other people. Fucking up is inevitable." He shakes his head. "To me it is about freedom." To him, he shares, freedom is when you know yourself, and when you're at peace with yourself, there's a light inside you, and when you look at someone else, you're offering him that light. When your mind and heart are sufficiently open, you can experience things without naming or judging them, and this is true freedom.

"Anyway," he says. "Sorry, my English isn't very good."

This entire conversation has gone down in English with no linguistic problems on his end. This has not stopped him from apologizing for his English, profusely. I don't have the heart to tell him that earlier this evening, I tried to convey that I wanted to order takeout by saying, "Hello, I would like to eat . . . and stand."

I ask him what other languages he speaks.

"Russian," he begins, ticking off on his fingers. "Kazakh. Urdu. Uyghur."

His grandparents, he explains, spoke these languages. One was Kazakh, another Pakistani, another Uyghur, an ethnic group found in Western China, and the final something he calls "Mountain Jew."

"A what?" I ask.

"You don't know what a Mountain Jew is?" he asks.

I shake my head.

"Well, I am one."

A perfectly thin blonde woman standing beside him nods. Though she speaks no English, I decide she must be kind, because any time anyone stubs out a cigarette on the porch railing, she picks up the pack and proffers another. There's a warmth in this gesture that transcends language and makes up for the fact that she was the one who answered her cell phone during my set.

The blonde woman says something to the flutist, and he turns to me. "My girlfriend wants to know why you wanted to come to Kazakhstan."

This catches me off guard, because, by this point, I had assumed that the flutist and I were halfway through the process of falling in love, and that I had found my life partner forty-eight hours into my trip.

I'm also fumbling because by now I should be used to this question, but I still haven't come up with a good answer.

I have variously described my trip as "like *Eat, Pray, Love*, but with yak-herding," or "like *Wild*, but in Turkmenistan."

I say these things, because mediocre jokes are always a great way to get out of giving an honest response to a question that's complicated and difficult to answer.

So I go with what I've learned is the most satisfying explanation for strangers. It's the truth, but far from the whole story.

"I've had a lot of Russian boyfriends," I reply.

CROSSING A LAND BORDER FROM
KAZAKHSTAN TO KYRGYZSTAN

If you want to seem suspicious to a seasoned traveler, all you have to do is offer to help her.

"Do you speak English?" a young Kyrgyz woman asks me.

I'm sitting on a bus in Kazakhstan that will depart any minute for Bishkek, Kyrgyzstan, and as it happens I do speak English. But why does she? It seems most likely that she mastered this second, or perhaps seventh, language to rob, cheat, and/or identity thieve me.

"Yes," I reply cautiously.

She says that the driver is trying to tell me that a ticket to Bishkek costs 1,500 tenge, which is even more suspicious, because that's how much it's supposed to cost. So what's her scam? I thank her and pay the driver. I'll keep an eye on her.

I've been dreading this bus trip, because I'm extraordinarily prone to motion sickness. To me, the two most terrifying words in the English language are "whale watch." Before leaving, I stop at a pharmacy to pick up some necessary supplies.

A thick layer of protective Plexiglas separates me from the pharmacist.

"Hello," I say in Russian, "I am inside a car, I am vomiting." Actually, I don't say *vomiting*, so much as pantomime it with sound effects.

He nods and pushes a tiny glass bottle that looks like it came from an old-timey apothecary through a sliding drawer.

"Will this medicine make sleep?" I ask, because I'm also prone to drowsiness.

"No," the pharmacist replies. "You want sleeping pills?"

"No, I *don't* want to sleep."

"Okay, no problem. These aren't sleeping pills."

"And they won't make me sleep?"

"No."

"You're sure?"

"Yes," he assures me.

"Great," I say. Then, casually, "By the way, do you sell Xanax?"

Sitting on the bus behind the "helpful" Kyrgyz woman who is almost definitely casing me, if a person can be cased in the same way as a house, I take out the glass bottle of allegedly nondrowsy motion-sickness pills I purchased earlier.

I pass out about three minutes after taking one.

I wake up at a rest stop, which, in my drug-induced haze, I mistake for the border. I cause a lot of confusion when I hand my passport to the babushka manning the women's bathroom.

I remain semi-awake as the bus makes its way through parched, stunning valleys to the actual border. The land stretching out before us is a dusty reddish brown that takes on different hues as it rises to form mountains of green and blue and purple. But all of the formations and colors are made of soil. The same brown dust that clings to the sides of my jeans no matter how violently I scrub them.

On maps, borders appear as neat lines that partition the world into shapes so familiar they seem almost inevitable. It can be strange to look out from an airplane window and remember that the land doesn't conform to the order we impose upon it, that the people who spray paint lines on soccer fields haven't been hired to mark the boundary between China and Nepal.

That was how I'd crossed most borders in my life: at an altitude of twenty thousand feet. At that distance, you don't notice the transition from one country to another. Even getting your passport stamped feels like part of the airport, not a migration between geo-political entities.

A land border is much more deliberate. You feel each step that takes you out of one nation and into another. It's a transatlantic flight, with more mindfulness, and ten times the chaos.

Oh, is there chaos! First our bus pulls up to Kazakhstan's exit door, which is actually a series of buildings connected by narrow gravel paths lined with chain-link fences. We have to collect all of our luggage and drag it through the gravel, because gravel is kryptonite to a suitcase's ability to roll. Then we huddle in front of a line of booths where officers will stamp us out of Kazakhstan. The other travelers yell and smoke and carry bulky bags of cement mix. Next, we drag our suitcases through more gravel to customs, which is located in another building. There's no one directing us through all this; we just follow whoever looks confident.

A Kazakh woman takes pity on me, probably because I look extremely distressed. She is small but fierce, and she pushes our way to the front of the not-line.

"This is just the checkpoint to exit Kazakhstan," she assures me. "Kyrgyzstan will be much more organized."

This turns out not to be true. After I'm given official permission to exit Kazakhstan, I once again have to drag my suitcase through a confusing maze of snaking, unpaved walkways to reach the Kyrgyz entry point. By now, I'm so disoriented that I attempt to enter Kyrgyzstan as a vehicle.

I find my way back to where I'm supposed to cross my first border as a pedestrian. As we're waiting to get stamped into Kyrgyzstan, my new Kazakh friend asks me if I want to skip the bus and split a taxi to Bishkek.

"Can't we just wait for the bus to pass through customs?" I ask.

She tells me it takes a long time for the bus to get through, and that, anyway, the bus drops you off on the outskirts of town, so you have to take another taxi to get into the city.

This sounds like either a plausible explanation, or a practiced opening to a well-rehearsed scam.

"I don't have any Kyrgyz money," I say, which is both true and, I figure, a noncommittal response.

"Okay," she replies, "I'll pay for you."

Now I'm both more wary and slightly horrified. If this is a scam, it's getting more elaborate, and if it isn't, I'm not letting this kind woman pay for my taxi.

The Kazakh flutist's girlfriend raised a good point last night: What am I doing here, crossing the desert from Kazakhstan into Kyrgyzstan, and more broadly, on this meandering and poorly planned journey through the former Soviet Union?

The summer before my senior year of college, my best friend set me up on a blind date with her friend Oleg. He took me out for sushi and told me he was Russian. Though I smiled, I was terrified. Not because he was Russian, but because, like any good American, I had only vaguely heard of most foreign countries, and I wanted to avoid being asked follow-up questions like, "Have you been to Russia before?" or "Do you know the name of the current president?"

I fell in love with Oleg for all the reasons people fall in love, and then I fell in love with Russian because I thought Oleg was Russian. Unfortunately, he wasn't. Oleg was born in the Soviet Union and lived in Ukraine until the age of eight, when his family immigrated to upstate New York.

But his family spoke Russian and felt culturally Slavic, and it would take me years to learn the many nuances of the word Russian. In the meantime, I was fascinated by Oleg's stories of the Soviet factory his grandfather ran, his memories of ration cards, the snippets of Russian I would hear when his parents called. I sent Oleg home with a long list of questions to ask his grandparents, whose answers he begrudgingly recorded, translated, and relayed back to me.

The more I learned about the Soviet Union, the more it fascinated me. It sounded kind of like the U.S., but with table caviar. Like America, the Soviet Union was a huge country that saw itself as the predominate geopolitical power. Its territory spanned regions with distinct languages and cultures, which it too (eventually) attempted to unite with the aspirational melting pot. As in America, the diverse cultures "melted" so that everyone spoke, dressed, and behaved like the majority culture. Also like in America, the Russian ethnic majority tended to be monolingual and figured the rest of the world should just learn to speak its language.

People who harbor intense fascinations with and affinity for Russian culture often find themselves struggling to explain why they find this part of the world so captivating. Sometimes I'll go off on a rambling explanation of how hard the language is, how the challenge of learning it carries the irresistible allure of other things people do precisely because they're hard, like climbing mountains and dating people who take a week to respond to a text message. Other times I'll point to the surprisingly similar ideologies that shaped the childhoods of my parents and those of their Soviet counterparts. How my dad, who was raised to speak one language, geek out over space, and fear that any day now, the Soviet Union was going to destroy his country, would have had been told similar things in Moscow, except swap out the Soviet Union for the U.S. At some point, my listeners' eyes glaze over, and so I reveal the boyfriend thing. "Oh," they brighten. "Next time, just say that."

But if Oleg had been Danish, I suspect I might have written a (much shorter) book about traveling through Scandinavia. Or if I'd met him a week after discovering an intense passion for beekeeping, I might have loved him but never learned to stop calling it "the Ukraine."

So this whole trip had been a dream for a while, but a distant one. The kind you dip into during a boring meeting but know will never happen.

Unless you find a second Russian boyfriend.

When the Kyrgyz border guard sees my identification, he calls for backup and then disappears with my passport.

When your passport vanishes into a back room at a border crossing, the appropriate response is panic, but I'm too caught up in my neurosis re: Is this woman conning me? If not, what should I do? Where will I find an ATM? Will we become lifelong friends, or is she about to bring up her friend's "art gallery?" I look up and find that while agonizing, I have paced my way into the guards' private living quarters, which seems like a terrible place to be caught at a border without your passport.

I return to the guard, who gives me back my passport, and find my new Kazakh friend, who, in turn, has found the Kyrgyz woman who helped me buy my bus ticket and who now also wants to get in on this shared taxi action.

Okay, I think. *This is probably not a scam.*

But as we drag our suitcases down the final unpaved no-man's-land that leads to the taxis, they start speaking to each other in Kazakh and Kyrgyz, which makes sense, because why wouldn't they communicate in their native languages? But could it also be a sign that they know each other and have been planning some elaborate ruse from the start?

We reach a parking lot, and the women head off to negotiate a taxi while I duck into a small wooden shed to change money.

The Kazakh woman is waiting for me outside. "Is 450 som okay for you?" she asks.

I try to make it seem like I'm thinking while I discreetly type the number into a currency converter on my phone. The dollar equivalent pops up: $70 U.S.

"Whoa," I yelp. "That's really expensive."

If her reaction includes a facial expression, I can't read it.

"Maybe I should just take the bus?" I venture.

She points to a bus that is, as in a movie, pulling out of the parking lot. "It just left," she says.

"I thought you said it took a while for the bus to get through the border?!" This woman is now, without a doubt, tricking me.

She shrugs. "I guess it went through quickly. Anyway, you don't want to go to the bus station; it's very far away from the city."

"450 is expensive . . ." My voice trails off, because what choice do I have?

"Maybe you should talk to the driver," she suggests.

Now I'm furious, in part because I'm going to have to part with 70 bucks, but perhaps even more so because no one wants to be seen as an easy mark. *These girls and the driver are old friends,* I fume. *They saw me the second I got on that bus, and they sent each other a secret signal that means, "Let's pretend not to know each other for the duration of this six-hour bus ride so we can extort $70 from that drowsy American."*

The driver is a young guy with great English, which makes him seem even more suspect. *Who speaks English,* I wonder again, *except people trying to cheat tourists?*

I get him down to 250 som, which is still a whopping $46 U.S. dollars. I want to pay 200 som, or $36.80 US, which is still outrageous, but, I have decided, the price point at which I can retain some semblance of dignity.

"200," I say again.

"Come on, 250 is a fair price," he says for the tenth time.

I glance over at my Kazakh and Kyrgyz friends and notice that their eyes appear to be popping out of their heads. Now I can read both facial expressions, and they are ones of horror.

"You're arguing about 50 som," the driver continues, sounding exasperated. "That's 50 cents in U.S. dollars."

That's when I look down at my converter app, and realize I've been converting into *Tajikistani* som. In Kyrgyzstani som, the original 450 he'd asked me for is $6.50 U.S. The 250 I've bargained him down to is $3.63.

Well, now I know why the women look horrified.

But I can't bring myself to admit my mistake. "Fine," I say coolly. "Your price is acceptable."

Out of the three people in the car, the driver speaks the best English. He also seems to have forgiven me for the bargaining fiasco, because he's explaining how Kazakhs and Kyrgyz communicate.

"They speak to us in Kazakh," he says, "and we respond in Kyrgyz."

"And everyone can understand each other?" I ask.

"It's almost the same language. Like American English and British English."

I'm impressed, not only because his linguistic abilities far exceed my own, but also because he's culturally savvy enough to know that if you want Americans to understand something about another part of the world, you need to give it to us in an analogy that we star in. I wonder what that says about Kyrgyzstan's economy, that someone fluent in at least five languages is driving a taxi.

The Kyrgyz girl introduces herself as Nazima and asks me how old I am.

"I'm twenty-eight," I say.

"And you're traveling alone?"

I tell her I am.

Her eyebrows raise. "I'm very afraid for you," she says. "I'm worried that Bishkek is maybe very dangerous. Please, take my phone number, and call me if you have *any* problems."

Now I'm back to being terrified. Is Kyrgyzstan dangerous?

When we arrive in Bishkek, I pay the driver the amount he originally asked for and then find myself facing a new conundrum. I don't have an address for the Airbnb that I booked, and I also booked the wrong nights. I call my host Dmitri, whose Airbnb reviews have all indicated that he's very nice and is still learning English.

"Hello, this is Audrey," I say gravely, hoping my tone will tell the rest of the story.

"Who?" Dmitri asks.

"Audrey, from Airbnb."

This elicits no response.

"I'm supposed to stay in your apartment," I try again.

There's a long pause in which Dmitri attempts to grasp the gravity of the situation and/or figure out who I am. "I have many, many apartments," he replies, finally. "Please, which apartment?"

Through the magic of Google Translate and an English-speaking bartender, I convey my problem to Dmitri.

I expect Dmitri to tell me that I'm out of luck, but he doesn't. Instead, he tells me it's no problem, and that he'll put me up in another apartment.

This is really above and beyond the call of duty, so while I'm waiting for him to come pick me up in his car (!!), I decide to take another look through his Airbnb profile.

I notice one curious detail: Dmitri has put several people up in apartments that differed from the ones guests had selected on Airbnb. "The apartment was nice," they all say, "but not the one we booked."

Aha! I have found his scam.

Let's pause for a moment, and consider all of the people I have suspected of cheating me today:

-the Kyrgyz girl who helped me buy a ticket to Bishkek

-the Kazakh woman who helped me enter Kyrgyzstan as a pedestrian, and not as a vehicle

-the Kyrgyz taxi driver who wanted me to pay $6 for a forty-five-minute taxi ride

Now let's tally the people who actually took advantage of me:

Does that stop me from adding Dmitri to the list of Highly Suspicious Persons Who Are Most Likely Trying to Cheat Me?

Not at all. Not even when Dmitri calls to tell me that he's coming to pick me up in his own car to drive me to the other apartment. Not even when he shows up at the bar with his wife. Not even when I notice they are both dressed up in a way that makes me hope that I have not interrupted a date/an important event/their wedding.

Listen, you don't understand. Dmitri and his wife are only doing their best to make polite conversation and going out of their way to help me to reel me in for the big con!

"This apartment is much bigger than the one you booked," Dmitri says, smiling, as he carries my suitcase into a concrete high-rise apartment building. Dmitri, like most of the men I've encountered here, refuses to roll my suitcase. Even after I tell him it rolls, show him how to make it roll, and try to pry it from his hands so I can roll it myself. Instead he prefers to hand-carry my four-foot-long, fifty-pound bag. The effort does make him at least 60 percent more attractive.

He smiles again as we stuff ourselves into the tiny, decrepit elevator whose shaky ascent makes me wonder if it's operated by an old man with a rope and pulley.

"So, this is my brother's apartment," Dmitri says as he opens the door to what I can only describe as a Kyrgz gangster palace.

I booked a tiny studio apartment. The apartment I'm standing in is a freshly renovated, three-bedroom penthouse with a Jacuzzi.

After Dmitri leaves, I walk around the apartment turning on all the lights. It's creepy to be in such a big, opulent apartment all by myself.

And then I stop and have a Moment of Realization. I've caught Dmitri at his game! He has tricked me by giving me an apartment that's too big and too nice.

Thus satisfied that I've discovered the way in which I've been cheated, I crawl into bed and sleep more soundly than I have in days.

The strangest thing about Kyrgyzstan is its 3-dollar coin. (Technically its 3-som coin.) Three feels like such a clunky, uneven denomination that I keep expecting shopkeepers to be unable to make correct change. Other foreigners I meet are equally baffled.

"I calculated all the different ways that you could make change, and it's the same as having a 2-euro coin," a Dutch traveler tells me. "But still! 3! How strange!"

Kyrgyzstan is less developed than Kazakhstan. Sidewalks crumble underfoot and street fronts are crammed with general stores selling plastic mop buckets next to fans and digital alarm clocks. At night, pedestrians navigate the mostly unlit streets with flashlights. Almaty's modern bus network, in Bishkek, becomes crowded minibuses I am too intimidated to flag down.

Cars drive on the right side of the road and have steering wheels on either the right or the left side; the orientation appears to be a matter of personal preference rather than something regulated by law.

Culturally, Kyrgyzstan feels similar to Kazakhstan. Like the Kazakhs, the Kyrgyz are descended from nomadic herders. Plenty of semi-nomads still pitch yurts in summer pastures and return to houses and apartments for the colder months. Outside of the cities, people use horses as a form of transportation. Women cover their hair and make bright, geometric felt ornamentations for the yurts. The men wear tall, embroidered white hats.

Over the next few days, multiple Kyrgyz women, upon learning that I'm traveling alone, give me their phone numbers and insist that I call if I have problems, just like Nazima did. This leads me to conclude that Bishkek is potentially at war with something and barricade myself in the gangster palace each night.

The most memorable number comes one morning when I'm trying to hail a taxi. A car pulls over and I open the door and get in, only to discover that the back seat is already occupied by a very pregnant woman.

"I'm sorry!" I yelp, moving to close the door, but the driver and the pregnant woman insist that I stay. The driver says he'll drop her off first and then take me where I need to go. I agree to this arrangement reluctantly, because my fellow passenger is probably the most pregnant woman I've seen who is not actively giving birth.

The pregnant woman also speaks perfect English. "Here's my phone number!" she exclaims, after I tell her I'm by myself in Bishkek. "If you have problems, call me *anytime*."

"Thank you," I say, knowing full well that, even if I'm in the process of being murdered, I will not place a two a.m. phone call to a woman who is possibly ten months pregnant.

But I'm so touched by her gesture that after she gets out, I try to express my gratitude to the driver. Unfortunately, my terrible Russian makes it difficult to get my point across.

"Woman good!!!" I tell him. "Inside woman, baby."

RIDING A HORSE IN THE MOUNTAINS OF KYRGYZSTAN

Bishkek and Almaty have been great, but to really kick-start my Russian and dive into the "real" Central Asia, I decide I need to get out of the city, ride a horse to a lake in the mountains, and sleep in a yurt.

Guidebooks have a way of tricking me into thinking I enjoy nature. Maybe that's because the wilderness descriptions are the one section where writers really get to run wild, which seems to lead some to forget that they're writing a Lonely Planet and not *Leaves of Grass* fan fiction.

"Distantly ringed by a saw-toothed horizon of peaks, the wide-open landscapes of Song-Köl create a giant stage for constant performances of symphonic cloudscapes," reads the Lonely Planet introduction to a Kyrgyz alpine lake. *Wow*, I think, *I belong outdoors.*

You only have to meet me once to realize that the only times I belong outdoors are during a fire drill and while dining al fresco. I sunburn easily and was once terrorized by a goldfish. But I don't have anyone around to remind me of that, so I head to Song-Köl.

"Getting to Song-Köl is a large part of the experience," Lonely Planet says of the two-day trek to Song-Köl lake from the nearest village, Kochkor, and, indeed, the trip's highlight is the stunning scenery afforded by the journey through mountains and valleys.

But for me, the adventure begins when I take a six-hour shared taxi to Kochkor, with a driver who enjoys driving on both sides of the road.

The journey of a thousand miles begins with a single step, or, in Kyrgyzstan, a single shared taxi.

Shared taxis are private cars that charge passengers by the seat and travel pretty much everywhere. They're generally the most convenient way to get around in Central Asia. Given the region's communist history, it's an ironic example of the free market stepping in to satisfy demand that government and official businesses can't meet.

Long-distance shared taxis usually congregate outside the long-distance bus stations. While official buses travel the same routes, shared taxis are faster, make fewer stops, and depart more frequently.

The only downside is, if you're the first passenger to sign up, as I am now, your fate and departure time are determined by how quickly your driver can sell the other seats in his car.

My driver is a large man with a boxy sedan whose windshield is spiderwebbed with cracks. I'm watching from inside as he slouches around the parking lot muttering the name of our destination: "Kochkor, Kochkor, Kochkor." When he gets discouraged, which is often, he stops for a cigarette.

It's not a persuasive sales pitch. I want to get out and give him a few tips I've picked up from corralling people into stand-up comedy shows. Things like smiling, approaching someone with a clear, confident sales message—"You two look like you could use an adventure! How about Kochkor?"—and fewer smoke breaks.

A young man slides into the back seat, and our driver's face appears by my window. "Three children," the driver says in solemn English. It takes me a moment to realize he's confusing the words *children* and *people*. Meaning he has three seats left to sell.

I'm reminded of one of my first students in Shanghai, a nineteen-year-old boy who had given himself the English name Kingsley. Kingsley's father was a wealthy businessman who wanted his son to follow in his footsteps; at nineteen, Kingsley was content to enjoy the life of leisure fate had afforded him. I liked Kingsley, but he was a terrible student. In the six months we worked together, I think he did his homework twice. His English may have even gotten worse. After misunderstanding a story he told me and supplying the wrong vocabulary word, I accidentally taught him to go around telling people that ghosts kept stealing his cell phone. (I've lost touch with Kingsley, but I do hope he's since learned that the word he was looking for was *thief*.)

I met Kingsley just after I'd quit my job and moved to Shanghai on a dare. Before that, I'd been working as a consultant in Washington, DC at my first real postcollege job. I hated it, partly because my duties involved periodically flying to rural Michigan to count light bulbs in strangers' homes, and partly because I felt destined for something greater, the way all twenty-three-year-olds with few tangible skills do.

Test-prep tutoring in China offered the creative's dream: a solid paycheck, flexible hours, and ample free time you could theoretically devote to your own projects. (Although in practice, it was sometimes ample free time you could devote to procrastinating and then furiously working once someone held a deadline to your head.)

I had always wanted to be a writer, but I found I didn't mind test-prep tutoring. The majority of my students were bright, motivated, thoughtful teenagers, and because we worked one-on-one for months at a time, I got to know them. They taught me about their lives, about China, and about the strange world of Korean boy bands, which all have to disband for a few years while their members complete compulsory military service. Just as I had once memorized the color of Justin Timberlake's eyes and the details of his childhood, my students rattled off their idols' favorite foods and the dates they would report for army basic training.

My students and I also had a common enemy. The more I grew to know and love my tutees, the more I despised the standardized tests they had to take to apply to American schools. Most had worked hard for the chance to be educated abroad, but their acceptance prospects often hinged on how well they scored on poorly designed, outdated exams. My middle-school students, for example, had to memorize all the English words for groups of animals (a gaggle of geese, a coven of crows), along with the words for male and female animals (stallion and mare, boar and sow), and their offspring (calf, kid, joey) to make it through an analogy section that included questions like BEVY: SWAN:: _____: TIGER. Why did boarding schools care about such obscure, arcane terminology? Did they want to make sure students could file an accurate campus security report if they were chased across the lush, sprawling campus by two or more chickens?

I liked the mechanics of test-prep. I loved breaking down the tests into question types and coming up with tricks to help students boost their scores. I also loved that no boss will hold you to lower professional standards than a fifteen-year-old boy.

When I moved back to the U.S., I figured that was that. But I left at a time when the Chinese education market was insane. Companies had gotten into the habit of flying "experts" from other countries in for short but intense teaching sprints. Some contracts were rumored to be so lucrative that people were making a living flying back to China a few times a year.

When an old boss reached out to ask me if I'd like to try, I was initially skeptical. I still wasn't sure what this whole "settling down" thing was about, but I was pretty sure it did not involve switching continents every two months.

But I'm also not one to turn out all the lights and pretend I'm not home when opportunity knocks. I pitched it to myself as a way to save cash for Operation Conform to Adulthood in New York, which I was definitely not abandoning! Slowly, I started to wonder if I could take this trip instead.

The door of the sedan opens and a grandfather gets in followed by his granddaughter. "One children," the driver says.

Then there are no children, and we are off to Kochkor.

As soon as we leave the city, I begin to understand why there are so many cracks in the windshield.

The steering wheel is on the car's right-hand side, and perhaps for this reason, the driver feels more comfortable driving in the left-hand lane. The problem is that this lane is reserved for oncoming traffic. Each time we barrel toward a head-on collision, the driver swerves into the correct lane at the last minute, lays on his horn, and lights up a cigarette. I momentarily forget to breathe, and then glance back at the other passengers, who all appear unfazed.

The driver's preferred cruising speed is 140 kilometers per hour, which I decide not to convert into miles per hour. The car shakes and rattles loudly as we whip around switchbacks and fly over crests of hills, sometimes literally. I try to meditate.

We reach Kochkor, a small, dusty town hunkered down behind some mountains, in late afternoon. There are no Airbnbs or hotels in Kockhor, and so I've arranged to stay in a guest house.

If you've never seen a yurt, picture a tent, but round. The outside is usually a simple pale-colored felt covering, but inside, yurts are intricately decorated. Brightly colored carpets and ornamental hangings customarily cover the walls and floors. An opening in the ceiling lets light in during the day and ventilates smoke from the stove used for cooking and heating at night. Each item serves a purpose and has been designed for maximum portability, from the wall hangings that double as silverware drawers to the frame held together without nails. Yurts traditionally served as the portable homes of Central Asian nomadic herders, who move seasonally between pastures. "Our ancestors had thousands of years to perfect the yurt," many will tell me in the next few days.

This yurt is in the driveway of my Kochkor guesthouse. Like bed-and-breakfasts, guesthouses are typically family homes that have been expanded and outfitted so that rooms can be rented out to travelers. This guesthouse belongs to the family of a young Kyrgyz man named Azamat, who has arranged a horse trek to Song-Köl—I will be joining.

Azamat's family was one of the first in his hometown of Kochkor to participate in a movement called community-based tourism, or CBT, which seeks to help people in rural areas develop sustainable tourism businesses. CBT came to Kyrgyzstan in the early 2000s. At the time, the idea must have seemed strange. Historically, Kochkor had been farmland surrounded by grazing pastures, and the economy revolved around agriculture and herding. A pivot to tourism would have felt like telling South Dakotan farmers to start taking strangers camping at Mt. Rushmore.

But Kochkor was surrounded by stunning natural scenery, particularly in the mountains circling the glass-surfaced Song-Köl lake, which made it appealing as a base for nearby tourist excursions.

A decade and a half after Azamat's parents opened the guesthouse, the family is doing well. Their compound has been expanded into generous quarters that now offer Wi-Fi. Azamat and his wife have lived all over the world, most recently in Australia, where they met and befriended a young Spanish man whose sister, Mireia, is to be my companion on this trip to Song-Köl.

Mireia and I have a long trek ahead of us. The ride to tonight's campsite will be at least six hours, maybe more, depending on how bad we are at riding horses. It's now past lunchtime, but no one seems to be in a particular rush to finish tea.

In Kyrgyzstan, tea is served alongside endless plates heaped with bread, cookies, candies, and fruit, while flies circle glass bowls of syrupy homemade jam. I keep throwing back scalding cups of tea in the hopes that someone will see that I'm done and suggest that we leave, but each time my cup approaches empty, Azamat's mother, an older woman with a soft face perennially lifted in a smile, pours more. This will turn out to be a terrible decision, bladder-wise, in a few hours.

While we wait to head out, I learn Mireia is a proud Catalonian who works for a notary in Barcelona. She studied film in school and dreams of teaching, but the economic climate in Spain has forced many with artistic aspirations to pursue more practical methods of earning a living.

"Mireia is like family," Azamat informs me. "So while she is here, nothing bad will happen to her." I pause and wait for him to say nothing bad will happen to me, either. He doesn't.

At the departure camp, Mireia and I are given a two-minute lesson on how to ride a horse. Unfortunately, it's in Kyrgyz, a language neither Mireia nor I speak. My only real takeaway is that *choo* means "giddy-up" in Kyrgyz; it's up to me, I guess, to figure out how to make the horse stop and how not to fall off. But at last, it seems, we're off!

Kind of. My horse refuses to move. I kick his flanks and say, "Choo," but he just stands there, unfazed. He continues to feign indifference as everyone from the yurt camp comes over and starts shouting "Choo!" at him, and finally the guide just shrugs and switches horses with me.

"The horses know who should ride them," Mireia tells me. If memory serves, she's backed up by the movie *Wild Horses Can't Be Broken.*

This isn't Mireia's first horse trek, and it shows. She wears hiking pants and a sturdy fleece jacket, while my attire consists of makeshift outdoor gear and things I don't mind being ruined: a raincoat over an old college sweatshirt, and a pair of awkwardly baggy designer jeans I bought on a website that didn't allow returns.

The horses plod us through pristine landscapes. Sheep graze on sloped pastures rolling off of treeless hills whose naked faces reveal each mound and scratch. Wild horses raise their heads as we pass. A stream wraps around a grassy knoll; the first cold snap has left a few leaves blushing. There are no people.

Here's the thing the guidebooks don't tell you about horse trekking: it's really boring.

The writers, too busy scribbling lyrical poetry about a guest yurt's variety of breakfast foods, neglect to mention the most important detail, which is that the novelty of riding a horse wears off after about thirty minutes, and after that, you're stuck on top of a smelly animal whose maximum speed rivals that of a moving sidewalk. With nothing to do but think, for two whole days.

We're forty-five minutes into our trek, but it feels like it's been forty-five hours. Two days is going to be a lifetime. The time stretches out before me like an abyss into which my mind gleefully dumps all the things I don't want to think about: fears, insecurities, the probable caloric value of my breakfast, various bodily irregularities that could be the first signs of a fatal illness, various bodily irregularities that are definitely benign but somehow more distressing (am I getting wrinkles?), conjectures about which ex-boyfriends I could get back together with if I had to, the likelihood that my enemies are suffering more than I am, musings on why I have enemies, realization that my number of enemies has decreased with age, brief burst of pride, fear of aging, fear of death.

Our guide has been singing to himself since we left. At first, I worried this was a sign of insanity, but I now understand this is something he does to keep from going insane.

The first time I meet Anton, he tells me how much he hates when people ask him where Belarus is.

"It's like, come on, I shouldn't have to tell you," he says.

"Yeah, totally," I reply. "Who doesn't know Belarus?"

"Lots of people don't even know it's in Europe," he tells me, which is how I learn Belarus is in Europe. "They don't know anything about it."

"So crazy," I say, making a mental note to Google, *What is Belarus?*

Anton and I fall for each other quickly and intensely. We both love short stories and witty turns of phrase. He has a disarming smile and unwavering faith in his own convictions. When he kisses me I melt.

How do you describe what you love about someone? Maybe that sounds like a cop-out, but it's also a legitimate question I've been wondering. I could say that his face was so smooth and chiseled that I sometimes wished I could carry it around with me and run my fingers over it when I was feeling sad and that spending time with him was like being on the kind of fun drugs they give you for dental surgery. I could say that it instantly felt like I'd known him forever, that we seemed to understand each other so completely that we would sometimes stop and marvel at the fact that we'd come from such different places. But every description falls short of the things we hold most precious.

One summer Sunday early on, I take him to a party at a pool in Shanghai with a swim-up bar and an afternoon DJ. It's a hot, slow, blue-sky summer day, too perfect to do anything but waste. We sip beers with my friends in the pool bar and talk about nothing and everything. At one point we drift away from the crowd toward the deep end—we say we want to swim, but really it's just an excuse to be alone together, to hold each other without anyone watching, because it feels so unnatural for our bodies to not be entwined.

"Are you sick of me yet?" he asks. He came over on Friday to help me move and hasn't left my side since.

I shake my head. "Are you sick of *me?*"

He shakes his head.

It's settled.

A few days later, he texts me: *I fucking miss you, man.*

I write back: *I don't blame you, because I'm a man.*

Him: *extra words to conceal the emotion*

Me: *which words are extra?*

Him: *fucking, man.*

We go to see a friend's play—*No Exit*, as it happens—in an old wharf on the river. I borrow a friend's bike for Anton and we ride there. It's night, but above us the sky glows from the neon lights of skyscrapers and billboards and dumpling restaurants. I think there's a cut-through in the old city, and we duck into a maze of dark alleys and low gable-roofed houses that have been there for a century. We get so lost we miss the first scene. Stages always seem to suck me in physically; I come to when the lights go up and find myself perched on the lip of my chair, my chin hovering over the shoulder of the stranger in front of me. Afterward, the director teases us. "You were watching the play," he tells me, "but your boyfriend was watching you." He's not my boyfriend yet, but we don't correct him.

Outside, we discover that someone has stolen my bike while we were watching the play. We're miles from my house and we need to get my friend's bike home.

"I don't know how to ride on the back of a bike," I tell Anton.

He doesn't know how to ride with someone on the back. But we eliminate all other options.

"I'm really ticklish," he warns. Which means I can't hold his sides to stay on.

We take a different route back, this one beside a highway. We shriek and laugh and almost die a million times because when I slip and grab his waist to catch my balance, he loses his. We keep stopping; I don't think either of us thinks we'll make it, but we don't say that. When we pull up outside the apartment building, it feels like, if we could make it through that—two people who don't belong on one bicycle—together we can do anything.

Anton wants us both to be great, but first we have to be better. From the start, we see in each other the things we could be. We've both been waiting our whole lives to fall in love with someone else who dreams of writing a passable short story and understands they still have a long way to go. We set deadlines and send each other pieces for feedback. We both have day jobs we fantasize of one day putting behind us, and we make each other believe that our passions are possible. We push each other to take them more seriously.

In a lot of ways, it's a typical start to a brand of passionate relationship between a twenty-five-year-old and a twenty-seven-year-old, but in one very notable way it's not, which is that Anton is married.

Well, kind of. It's complicated: he and his wife, Elena, are no longer in a romantic relationship, but they're still married, for visa reasons, and living together, out of financial considerations and also because it's the easiest way to coparent their five-year-old son, Vadik. Anton tells me all of this the first time I meet him.

I meet Elena and Vadik a few weeks after I meet Anton. They live in a city twenty-five minutes outside of Shanghai. I go out there on weekends and stay with them. I sleep in Elena's bed, she sleeps with Vadik, and Anton takes the couch. I know, by the reaction I get when I explain this, that it should feel so strange and awkward, and sometimes it does, but mostly it doesn't. Elena tells Anton that I seem frightened by her, which is kind of true. But I like her, and I fall in love with Vadik almost as quickly as I do with Anton. We cook dinners and go grocery shopping and take Vadik to karate. I'm trying on a domestic routine and responsibilities that are still years away for me. I'm twenty-five.

The whole time, Belarus floats in the ether. It's where Elena goes to visit her fiancé when the school where she teaches piano has holidays. It's a place Vadik knows, but not as home, and the homeland Anton is always trying to put behind him. Sometimes Elena cooks blinis and they tell me stories. For Anton, Belarus is poverty, despair, loneliness; for Elena, it's snow, forests, family.

Sometimes I stay with Vadik while Elena is out of town and Anton is at work. We color, read, and use Chinese when there's a word one of us doesn't know in the other's language. I wonder what it would be like to do this, not in China, but in Minsk.

"You have to see it," Anton tells me. We'll go.

"How old are you?" the guide asks me suddenly in Russian, interrupting my daydreams.

I've gotten this question a lot so far in Central Asia; I'm starting to sense it's the local small talk.

"I'm twenty-eight," I tell him. "How old are you?"

He tells me he's thirty-two and then gestures to Mireia. "How old is she?" he asks.

I stammer. "Um, Mireia, the guide wants to know . . . how old you are."

She looks taken aback. "Thirty-four," she says, after a brief pause.

"I'm twenty-eight and he's thirty-two!" I blurt out before translating her answer back to the guide. He nods, and doesn't speak to us again for hours.

Anton and I break up, partially because it gets tiring to commute between cities to see each other, and partially for the reason everyone said we would, which I hate. I hated the way people would say, "Oh, he's married?" and assume they knew everything. Elena and Vadik are supposed to move back to Belarus a year after Anton and I meet, after which Anton would come to Shanghai, but then Elena gets cold feet and I can't fathom another year of us catching trains on Fridays and Sundays.

The breakup floors me like nothing has before. This surprises me, because I never pictured things with Anton lasting forever. But it feels like they ended too soon.

I miss him in a way that's terrifyingly novel and all-encompassing. I move through the world and see only reminders of someone I desperately want to talk to, but can't. The fact that I've never felt this before makes me fear that I'll never not miss him. People say it takes time, but when the emptiness doesn't fade, after the first weeks, then months, your fate starts to seem sealed.

I mean, in some ways, it does get better. Everyone says that, too, and while it's true, that's not the point. Sure, I stop crying and I no longer have to fight the urge to call him when I see something and go, "Dude, do you remember . . ." But I still think about him constantly, and there remains a dullness to everything, a lingering longing even in moments where my thoughts do manage to turn to something else. The fact that this counts as progress isn't comforting.

Anton and I used to make crazy pacts: write five new minutes of material each week, work on a play, write a song. It worked because we spent so much time apart; when we were together, the hours disappeared.

Now I feel like I don't know how to move onto the next step without him pushing me there.

Months after we break up, I e-mail Anton, and he comes to Shanghai to meet me for dinner. He asks me if I still think of him, and I say no, because in tough times, I always find comfort in the wisdom of *Why Men Love Bitches*. Then I ask him if he still thinks of me and he says all the time. "Sometimes I think, *What was I doing a year ago today?* And the answer is always: I was with you."

Here I should mention that I have problems with altitude. I was given doctor's orders to stop climbing mountains after I had an episode of high-altitude cerebral edema and tried to take a nap on a glacier at nineteen thousand feet. I pretended to find this diagnosis disappointing, but in truth, I was relieved. Clearly, many people enjoy ascending a mountain by climbing it, but if it's an option, I'd just as gladly drive.

I was told never to go above an altitude of fifteen thousand feet: any higher than that and, I assume, I'm supposed to stop, drop, and roll my way down to safety.

Song-Köl is at an elevation of ten thousand feet, which I decide will be fine. I really want to see Song-Köl. I may not enjoy outdoor activities like hiking, waterskiing, and doing trust falls with co-workers, but I do like nature. Or I want to like it.

As the afternoon fades into evening, I start to feel woozy and spacey. I know this is a bad sign, but I glimpse a circle of yurts in the distance. It's just over this combination hill/field, which I'm sure has some beautiful poetic or geographical term, but I can't think of it because I'm too busy not vomiting. I fix my eyes on the yurts and will myself to stay upright by envisioning all of the wonderfully satisfying ways in which I can murder my horse.

Why is riding a horse so exhausting? The only thing I have to do is not fall off a slightly larger animal tasked with carrying me and all my luggage over countless mountains, while refraining from eating his favorite food, which literally grows at his feet, and I'm somehow the more fatigued. The valley that stands between us is probably turning pink and purple as the light fades, but all I can focus on is the fact that these goddamned yurts have grown only slightly larger, because, again, we're inching along at the pace of an energy-efficient escalator. Although I have a few survival instincts, including an impeccable sense of direction, one that I don't have is the will to persevere in the face of physical discomfort. I start feeling worse. The world spins; I don't; a nap would be nice; I would like to vomit.

I yell something like "Time-out!" as I gracelessly tumble off the horse. The guide and Mireia rush over.

I don't want to get back on the horse. The ground feels safe and familiar, like a couch that got you through a dark period. "I'll just walk," I say weakly, first in English, and then kind of in Russian. "I'll meet you guys there."

The look on their faces says this is not an option. Which, fair enough, I was just going to try to roll the rest of the way.

Mireia smiles and gets down from her horse. "How about we walk together for a while, and if you feel better, you can get back on the horse?" she offers.

"I'm never getting back on," I whisper hoarsely.

She nods. "Okay."

We walk through the meadow holding our horses' bridles; Mireia tries to distract me by asking about my life, my trip, my family. I shake my head. "Tell me everything about Franco's Spain," I croak. I know that there is a thing called Franco's Spain, and I have a general sense that it was bad and that's about it. Now seems as good a time as any to get informed.

Soon I'm so busy asking questions I can only get away with because I'm ill ("How were the Catalonians repressed?") that I don't even notice that I'm swinging my leg back over the horse. Well, technically, I'm not really doing the swinging: the guide is holding my torso up with one hand and swinging my leg over with the other. But the point is, I'm back on the horse.

I think about how, of all the jobs I'd be bad at, horse guide probably tops the list. How does our guide stare at mountains all day without going mad? What does he know that I don't?

The sun finally slips behind the mountains, rimming the horizon in a soft pink glow. We pull into a small yurt encampment on a gentle slope. Next to a hitching post, two horses nuzzle each other. It's quiet and still, and I finally feel something approaching contentment. Still, I'd be lying if I said I didn't check my cell phone to see if the yurt camp had service. (It doesn't.)

We're shown into the guest yurt, a dark, warm room filled with rugs, blankets, and pillows. The family sleeps in the yurt next door. I'm surprised to see a solar panel, which powers the single light bulb dangling from the yurt's ceiling, and a simple sink in which water collected in a small cistern flows into a basin via a foot pump.

The matriarch, a sturdy woman of sixty, serves us tea while her small grandchildren filter in and out. The guide tells her about my collapse, and she returns a few minutes later with a stethoscope and blood pressure cuff. She smiles sweetly, takes my blood pressure, then lets her granddaughter take my blood pressure, take my blood pressure again, and does not seem to reach a diagnosis. "Do you want medicine?" she asks.

After dinner, the grandmother pushes the table we ate on into a corner of the room and removes a decorative cover to reveal a giant pile of bedding. She stacks blankets and pillows into three piles that form remarkably warm, comfortable beds. We crawl into them and turn off the light, and I sit in bed with my lighted Kindle, surprised at how cozy the yurt is. *See?* I think. *This is how people used to live. What a beautiful, simpler time, when we lived off the land, and went to bed when the sun went down, and didn't have to–*

Out of nowhere, a bug lands on my head. I slap my face out of reflex. It's gone; I shiver in disgust and go back to reading.

Then I feel something in my hair.

I sit up and hit the top of my head, but I don't feel anything but hair. Maybe I just imagined it? But then a moth lands on my Kindle, right next to my light. I kill it with my blanket, which only seems kind of gross after I've done it. I try to flick the moth carcass away, but it gets stuck on my finger, which is even more disgusting, and I start shaking my hands and slapping myself until I realize that there are other people in the room, calmly compose myself, and hide under the covers.

I burrow into an airtight cocoon of blankets, but after a few minutes, I hear what sounds like an incoming kamikaze, and then feel one moth hit my blanket. And then another. The moths are dive-bombing me.

I throw back the covers and start killing all the moths I can see with my Kindle cover. The guide gets up and does the same, except he kills the moths by squeezing them between his fingers. We find them crawling on the floor and landing on our blankets. We continue killing until all that's left are dead moths, which the guide oddly arranges in a pile on a small table between our beds.

I go back to reading, above the covers. And then I feel something in my hair.

I shine my light up to the ceiling, where I see hundreds of moths fluttering beneath the yurt opening.

The guide laughs. I see no humor in this situation. I click off my Kindle light and crawl back into my blanket cocoon. This will quickly become too hot, and I'll continue being dive-bombed for the rest of the night. My sleep will be fitful and punctuated by dreams of moths crawling up my leg, which will cause me to wake up, convinced that I am, in fact, being molested by a moth.

But for now, I allow myself a small moment of triumph, because I realize that I conducted a semi-medical semi-emergency entirely in Russian.

"Were you viciously attacked by moths last night?" I ask.

Mireia laughs. I assume it's a nervous laugh, fueled by fear that the moths are lurking in some corner of the yurt, waiting for the first sign of weakness to resume their assault.

But her smile is easy. "I just had to turn off my light and go to sleep," she says.

HAD to go to sleep? I think. I spent the night cowering under the covers, flinching every time a moth's aerial attack gently pinged my blanket. Sleep hadn't been an option, much less a solution.

We're sitting at the table, which has been dragged back to the center of the room and covered in breakfast foods while our beds have turned back into a single, tidy stack of blankets. There is, I realize, an intense efficiency to this whole yurt setup. It's only one room, but, with a little rearranging of the furniture, that room transforms from a kitchen to a bedroom to a living room to a dining room, kind of like a Barbie Dreamhouse.

I take another sip of scalding tea, which I'm starting to suspect contains no caffeine. I'm no less groggy than I was three cups ago, and I'm now missing most of my taste buds, along with a significant portion of the roof of my mouth.

"I'm kinda going crazy on that horse," I confess to Mireia. "Like, I don't know what to think about? And then my mind just sort of . . ."

She nods. "You know, I do yoga now, and I just think of it as a practice for that."

Wow, I think, *this really is just like* Eat, Pray, Love, *but with pack animals.*

We spend the morning climbing hills whose surfaces resemble the texture of crumpled paper. The day is bright and cool. Locals call this the golden season, because the grass that covers everything has started to die, and the brittle, yellowed stalks glow in the sunlight.

I'm pretty sure my horse has scurvy. Sure, all I know about scurvy is that it's something that happens to sailors who don't eat enough oranges, and sure, all I know about horses comes from a weird movie about a girl who rides horses off of a diving board that my sister and I for some reason watched over and over as children, but I feel confident in my diagnosis.

First, there's the fact he's walking so slowly, I'm pretty sure I would beat him in a potato sack race in which only I had to wear a potato sack. We often fall thirty minutes behind Mireia and the guide, and every so often, the guide gets fed up, rides back, and ties us to his belt.

My horse has also started stumbling. So has Mireia's. It's terrifying: I'm riding along and suddenly, I'm pitched forward toward the ground. Each time the horse gets back up I'm shaken, but what can I do?

"My friend hired horses in Cuba," Mireia whispers. "And they were really skinny and sickly. Our horses look okay, but I think maybe they're the same."

Mireia's yoga suggestion isn't really working for me. While we crest the top of a mountain range, I wonder how much money is left in my checking account. As we descend a gentle path beside a pair of wild horses, I try to calculate how many calories we've burned since yesterday.

Man, do I think about a lot of stupid, useless shit! Even in the face of raw, unspoiled nature. *Especially* in the face of raw, unspoiled nature.

My favorite yoga teacher once said that Tibetan Buddhists believe that at any one time, each person is dealing with seven problems. I've avoided fact-checking this, because I like how it sounds, and the person who said it is an American yoga teacher, which experience has shown to be the demographic least informed about Eastern religions.

Sometimes it feels like all I do is run through my seven problems, most of which aren't really problems. Did I choose the wrong line at the grocery store? How many calories was my dinner? How will I ever go on if someone I love one day dies? Will I ever find someone I love as much as I loved Anton?

We reach the lake at lunchtime. The water is a smooth pane of glass that reflects the puffs of clouds on a blue sky. Close to shore, we can see the pebbles that form the lake bed through the bathwater-clear waves gently lapping at the beach. Sheep graze on the golden field beside us; mountains rise on the far side of the lake. I decide to pardon my horse from his murder sentence.

We eat lunch in a yurt with a bespectacled, dour German man who has just finished a PhD program and is traveling through Central Asia, supposedly to celebrate. But he doesn't seem like the kind of guy well suited to celebrating.

"Are you happy to be done?" I ask.

"I guess." He sniffs. "But now the German government will no longer pay me."

"They were paying you, like paying your tuition?"

"No, I got a salary also."

I'm impressed.

"And a lot of vacation."

"Paid vacation?"

"Of course. Several months each year."

He'd used that time to travel extensively through Central Asia, the Caucasus, and Eastern Europe. He seems disdainful of all of them.

The German has hiked in, which, he's quick to tell us, is probably faster than horseback riding. His guide, who speaks English, reaffirms this, first to us, in English, and then to our guide, in Kyrgyz.

"And you know," the German continues, "that in Uzbekistan, you should buy money on the black market?"

I don't want to admit that I don't know this, so I make a noncommittal grunt, and then urge him to keep going. Uzbekistan is a stop on my trip, so this could be useful information.

"In Uzbekistan, the government sets the value of the currency, and they set it much too high," he explains. "It's totally ridiculous. In a free-market economy, the value would be much lower, so people just buy and sell currency on the black market. But everyone does it," he explains. "It's totally open: you go to your hotel, and they tell you, 'Okay, here is where you should buy money on the black market, and here's how much it should be.'"

"That seems . . . crazy," I say.

He shrugs. "And another thing: the money is worthless. The biggest note they have is maybe 50 euro cents. So they give you these giant plastic bags full of, well, paper that's worth nothing."

"Wow." I shake my head.

But he's not done. "Actually, I heard from a friend who is a tour guide, that one time he was on a bus, and a guy on his tour, he ate something bad, and he had to shit a lot. But they were in the middle of the desert, no bathrooms, so they pulled over, and he started to shit in the desert. And after a while, he ran out of toilet paper, so they decided to use the currency. Because it's worth nothing." He becomes serious for this final pronouncement.

We finish lunch and stand outside in the warm sun as our guides prepare for the final leg of our journey, to the yurts we'll sleep in at the other end of the lake. We talk about our travel plans: Mireia's meeting up with her family, the German is, apparently, on a tour of places that fail to impress him, and I'm telling him about my plans for the former Soviet Union.

"If you like the Soviet Union, you'll love Belarus," the German says. He doesn't know it, but he's pouring salt on a wound. Whenever anyone hears about my bizarre fascination with the USSR, they all tell me to head straight to Belarus. "It's the closest you can get to seeing what life was like behind the iron curtain," they say.

"Oh!" they exclaim when they find out I'm American. "Never mind. You'll never get the visa."

This, of course, only makes me want it more. But from everything I've read online, it's a nightmare for Americans to get visas to both Belarus and Russia, which Future Audrey will need to figure out at some point, because my flight back to Shanghai leaves from St. Petersburg.

As we split up to head for the lake—we're riding, the German's walking—the German's guide hoists his own pack onto our guide's horse, but not the German's. *That poor guide,* I realize. *He hates the German just as much as I do.*

That night, Mireia and I have dinner with a literal Czechoslovakian couple. He's from the Czech Republic; she's from Slovakia. He has long blonde hair and works for an antivirus company; she has short blonde hair and works for a university. He speaks to her in Czech, and she responds in Slovak. The two languages are close enough to be mutually intelligible, but I still imagine it would be strange to be married to someone and never have a conversation in the same language.

"When we were born, it was all one country," he reminds us.

They're traveling through Kyrgyzstan with a tall, stoic Kyrgyz driver. When Mireia tells him she's from Barcelona, he says, "Oh, Catalonia."

"Wow," she replies. "I'm impressed that you know that."

He stares at her. "I read the news," he says.

Mireia thoughtfully doesn't mention that until recently, so I wasn't sure if Franco was the bad guy or the good guy.

The Czechoslovakians are excited about everything. First and foremost, my English.

"You speak English so well!" they exclaim after I introduce myself.

For a moment, I'm flattered. This is the first sincere compliment I've received on my ability to speak a language. Then I remember that I'm a native speaker. Crestfallen, I admit that I'm American.

"Ah, that explains it," the Czech man says.

Then they're excited about Turkmenistan—this visit is turning out to be a veritable preview of my itinerary. "In our last yurt, we were watching Turkmenistan TV," the Slovak woman continues.

"Wait, your yurt had a *TV*?" Mireia and I ask.

"Oh, yes!" she tells us. "These yurts had showers, and real Western toilets, and electricity!"

Mireia and I haven't seen a toilet that's not a hole in the ground in days.

"So!" she continues. "Turkmenistan TV: it's the strangest thing I've ever seen!"

"You cannot imagine," her husband muses, shaking his head.

"The Turkmen president had just come back from a visit, and they were having a parade to welcome him back."

"But it's a GIANT parade. Like, an entire city."

"And people are going crazy!"

"Like, they're standing on the side of the street, waving flags, screaming!"

"And then, at one point, he gets out of his car, and he starts riding on a bicycle!"

"And everyone loses it! They're cheering, and . . . Wow!"

"I'm trying to go to Turkmenistan," I tell them. "But my visa keeps getting rejected."

Turkmenistan is supposed to be the North Korea of the former Soviet Union. It's an insular dictatorship whose leader fosters a cult of personality. I'm trying to get a transit visa, but the embassies in Almaty and Bishkek have raised the very legitimate point that it's not imperative that I travel through Turkmenistan to transit between the two countries listed on my application—Uzbekistan and Kazakhstan—because Uzbekistan is next to Kazakhstan.

We somehow start talking about Christmas. In Spain, we learn, presents are exchanged at Epiphany, and it's the Three Wise Men who bring children presents. In America, I tell them, Santa delivers kids presents on Christmas Eve.

"Who brings your Christmas presents?" I ask the Czechoslovakians.

"The baby Jesus," she says, without blinking.

That night in my yurt, I think about how the Czechoslovakians might be the happiest people I've ever met, and how I want to be that happy. Do they not have the same fears and worries that I do? Have they just found a better way to deal with them? Or maybe, have the happy people just realized that we have so little control over some of the things that scare us most, and that there's a certain freedom that comes with accepting that? Like how I always feel weirdly less afraid on an airplane than I do driving a car, because if the plane crashes, at least it wouldn't be my fault?

I can't decide if the point of this excursion was the lake itself, or the journey to the lake, or maybe to learn how to see life as being about the journey and not the destination, or maybe the universe reminding me why it's good I didn't go into entomology?

Maybe it's a reminder that we're less alone than we think we are, even when all we think we want is a little peace and quiet to wallow in our own self-inflicted misery.

THE MOST TERRIFYING FLIGHT ON EARTH (TAJIKISTAN)

The thing to do in Tajikistan is to take a road trip along the border with Afghanistan, and the way to do it is to organize everything a year in advance. Because, in characteristic fashion, I'm winging everything at the last minute, I'm waiting to board what's known in travelers' circles as the most terrifying flight on Earth.

The flight goes from Dushanbe, the capital of Tajikistan, to Khorog, a small city high in the Pamir Mountains on the Afghan border. To get there, a rickety prop plane from the Soviet days has to clear cloud-scraping peaks that threaten the plane's maximum altitude. It flies once a day, weather permitting, which it's usually not. The route cuts through dramatic mountain passes that are at times so close you feel like could stick your hand out the window and touch the peaks, which you could theoretically do, because the cabin isn't pressurized. The runway in Khorog dead-ends into a mountain, leaving no room for error. Also, the flight path passes through Afghan airspace, which apparently isn't actually dangerous, but still sounds bad.

So far, the boarding process has consisted of hanging around on the tarmac while Tajik Air crew members circle the plane with clipboards and conduct a visual inspection. This feels like a little too much behind-the-scenes secrets when we would have been fine believing in the magic. Up close, the plane seems too small to stay up in the air. Which makes no sense when I think about it, but there we have it. Aerodynamics has never really been my strong suit.

Eventually, a flight attendant places a small step stool on the ground and opens the plane's trunk. Apparently, this is not actually called a trunk, but it should be. I've never boarded an airplane before by climbing in under the tail. As I do, I notice that our luggage is bungee-corded to the walls.

It's a full flight: a small boy naps on his father's lap; a puppy is stowed in a box in the center of the aisle; there's no seat for the flight attendant, who squats on stairs in front of the open cockpit.

The pilot turns on one propeller, then the other, and the plane fills with the smell of diesel, which strikes me as bad but doesn't seem to worry anyone else. A frail elderly woman stares out at the crowd of well-wishers, who are, yes, standing on an active runway, waving us off. The plane shakes violently as we accelerate down the airstrip, then lifts a little, falls a little, and works its way off the tarmac. Through the space where there should be a door to the cockpit, I see that the pilot's headphones are wrapped in hospital-issue booties.

We slowly rise above the city. No one has asked us to turn off our cell phones; the flight attendant is using his to play Candy Crush. Also, what is the point of the flight attendant? It's not like there's going to be a beverage service.

I keep expecting the pilot to get on the intercom and announce that we've reached our cruising altitude of eight feet, but that would, of course, be ridiculous: this plane doesn't have an intercom. Beside him, the copilot openly naps.

The city's features begin to blur. I put on music and wait for that surge of airplane emotion that usually compels me to weep during the safety demonstration.

Urban sprawl slowly gives way to harsh, unbridled nature. I can almost see the paths ancient glaciers ripped through the jagged, rocky peaks below, as they get closer and closer.

Because the cabin isn't pressurized, our cruising altitude is capped at 13,700 feet. The distant peaks are suddenly significantly less distant, and then they're beside us, six inches from my window.

It's strange, and terrifying, to look out of an airplane and see mountains *above* you.

On second thought, should I be concerned?

Three days before all this, I get my first taste of scary flights by flying to Dushanbe on an airline that's been banned from entering EU airspace.

At arrivals in Dushanbe, I'm the only unaccompanied woman.

A tall, gangly young man with rosy cheeks approaches me. "Audrey?" he asks softly.

I nod.

He grabs my suitcase. "Okay, let's go."

I put my hand out to stop him. "Wait, who are you?" I ask.

He stares at me.

I'm renting an Airbnb apartment from a man named Jafar, who has generously offered to meet me at the airport, take me to buy a SIM card, and to "make sure [I] have a great stay in Dushanbe!" He signs each message, "With optimism, Jafar."

For this kindness, I repay him with the utmost cultural insensitivity: each time I read his name, I picture the Disney villain.

Does Aladdin *take place in Tajikistan?*

Well, no. Aladdin takes place in a fictitious, geographically and ethnically ambiguous city called Agrabah. The characters and setting in the Disney film have a Persian feel, but the story actually comes from a French author who heard the tale from a Syrian guy and included it in his French translation of *Arabian Nights*.

Aladdin is, however, a good reference point for understanding the biggest way in which Tajikistan differs from Kazakhstan and Kyrgyzstan. While the Kyrgyz and Kazakh speak mutually intelligible Turkic languages, Tajiks speak Persian dialects and share cultural similarities with Iranians, from whom they are descended. The Soviets more or less invented the Tajik ethnicity in a campaign overseen by Stalin, a high-school dropout who somehow managed to become the Soviet Union's ranking expert on the subject of nationality. In perhaps a display of the extent of his cultural awareness, Stalin took the word *Tajik*, which meant "Persian speaker," and decided it made an empowering identity for a wide range of people who had anywhere from little to nothing in common.

Unlike their nomadic neighbors, Tajiks have a long history of being settled. They also have a rich literary tradition and strong cultural influence over some of Uzbekistan's best-known cities.

"Jafar?" I ask the guy holding my luggage.

"Jafar," he says.

"Wait, you're Jafar?"

He smiles shyly and tells me his English is very bad.

I figure I'm in one of two scenarios: either this is a random con man who walks up to every Western woman exiting the terminal and tries to guess her name, or this is Jafar. The former would make more sense if he were throwing out characters from popular '90s sitcoms ("Rachel? Elaine? Sabrina the Teenage Witch?"), and also if there were more Western women exiting the terminal. I decide this must be Jafar.

"Should we get a SIM card?" I ask, gesturing to a nearby counter.

He shakes his head. "Airport, no."

It's a long, awkward drive to the apartment. Each time I try to speak to Jafar in Russian, he responds in mangled English, and each time he speaks to me in English, I'm confused. Eventually, we give up and stare out the window. Although it's mid-September, the air is hot and dry, and a bright sun wanders across a cloudless sky. The men on the streets wear polo shirts, jeans, and flip-flops. The women dress more modestly, in bright, patterned tunics and scarves that cover their hair.

We pull into a compound of new, hastily constructed high-rises. Jafar parks next to a staircase, which seems to have been mistakenly connected to the second floor. To enter the ground-floor lobby, we have to walk through a tunnel under the staircase.

Beside the front door, a welder puts finishing touches on a vaulted archway directly above a jungle gym. Children scramble up plastic ladders and catapult down slides, oblivious to the sparks raining down on them.

Jafar and I get into the elevator, and as soon as the doors close, the power cuts out. Jafar chooses this moment to ask me if I'm single.

"I'm engaged," I snap. "And my fiancé is coming to Dushanbe tomorrow."

This has been my go-to defense against unwanted advances in many shared taxis, restaurants, and, in one case, a print shop where I went to get my passport Xeroxed.

"So beautiful, and not married?" asked the man making the copies.

"I'm engaged," I replied hastily.

"When is your wedding?" he asked.

I hadn't anticipated this question, so I blurted out the first date I could think of. "April 27."

He looked down at my passport, where my date of birth is listed as April 27.

"We're doing it on my birthday," I stammered, "so that we only have to do one party."

"Congratulations," he replied without smiling.

Sometimes, I feel guilty about lying. Most people who ask if I'm married aren't planning to get down on one knee to ask me to make them the happiest men in Tajikistan. In cultures that place such strong emphasis on family, it's a natural topic of conversation. I show strangers pictures of my parents, they tell me about their wives, and boom, we're friends! But I'm always wary of seeming flirtatious—sometimes for good reason. A taxi driver taking me from a monument to a restaurant recently repeatedly asked me for the name of my hotel, which seemed irrelevant until he revealed that he would be glad to meet me there later.

This time, I've prepared a less incriminating, but equally readily recalled wedding date—July 4—but Jafar doesn't ask me that. He simply moves on to the next subject.

"How old are you?"

In Central Asia, guests are treated with such magnanimity that guidebooks warn travelers about inadvertently burdening people who might be graciously offering more than they can spare. Friends at restaurants fight over who gets to pay the bill. Taxi drivers and fruit vendors sometimes refuse my money after learning that I've come from so far away.

This level of hospitality is so startling at first that, as in Kyrgyzstan, I mistake people trying to help me for people trying to scam me.

Dushanbe reminds me of China, because that's where everything but the buildings appears to come from. The manhole covers, traffic cones, and recycling bins were all made in China, and I know this because all the writing is in Chinese.

The Chinese goods both make sense and don't. Tajikistan is one of the poorest Central Asian republics: it has the second-lowest GDP per capita, and almost half of its GDP comes from migrant workers sending money back home. The landscape can be unforgiving. Over 90 percent of the country is mountainous, and droughts and famines still affect some of the more remote regions. China, with its heaps of cheap consumer goods, is just across the Pamir Mountains, and a Chinese trucking route runs straight through Tajikistan. But some products seem out of place, like the manhole covers that only say "power line" in Chinese.

I'm getting a tour of all the Chinese products, because Jafar and I are trudging all over the city, trying to find a place that will sell me a SIM card, which I need to buy every time I get to a new place to have basic phone service and navigation.

Everything Jafar does increasingly irks me, which then makes me annoyed with myself because he's being so nice. When we get to his brand-new, meticulously wallpapered apartment, I ask him for the Wi-Fi password. He looks confused. "No Wi-Fi," he tells me.

What kind of Airbnb doesn't have Wi-Fi? I fume to myself. My face must betray this aggravation, because Jafar immediately offers to go get a USB stick with Internet and bring it back. When he returns, forty-five minutes later, it doesn't work. He offers to take me to get a SIM card instead.

Why didn't we just get one at the airport? I want to politely scream. But instead, I follow him back outside, assuming there's a store around the corner.

It turns out to be around more like fifteen corners, necessitating a twenty-minute walk in awkward silence. When we get to the store, Jafar strides in and shakes hands with the guy behind the counter. The handshake is a gesture I recognize—it's how men greet one another, even strangers, in Central Asia—but the cell phone guy gives Jafar a weird look. Then he says that he can't sell a SIM card to a foreigner. Chastised, Jafar scurries out of the store. *Why don't you just buy the SIM card for me and say it's for you?!* I seethe.

We go back to the apartment, where I'm horrified to find that Jafar's mother has been waiting this whole time in an un-air-conditioned car. "I'm so sorry," I try to say, but his mother has stepped out of the car and is enveloping me in a warm hug. I feel even worse. Jafar wants to drive me to a cell phone company's headquarters, where it's not clear if SIM cards are even sold or if it's open on Sunday, and at this point I would rather permanently sever any potential connection to the Internet than spend any more time with Jafar, who has no business running an Airbnb business, which I would tell him if I could figure out how to pantomime it. I somehow convince Jafar and his mother to leave, but not before they call his sister Nilofar to translate the message that Jafar will return with an Internet-enabled laptop tomorrow morning.

I finally wander out onto the main street in the last rays of sunlight. It's a long avenue that traverses the entire city, with block after block of beautiful, perfectly preserved Soviet neoclassical buildings. It's odd: the countries I'm visiting have retained progressively less of their ethnic Russian populations, and progressively more of their buildings. Kazakhstan had tons of Russians and few Soviet relics mixed in with contemporary high-rises, Kyrgyzstan had a well-preserved downtown and a handful of Russians, and

now Dushanbe is a veritable time capsule left behind by a population that is no longer there.

I eat dinner at a Ukrainian restaurant that has Wi-Fi. When I get
online, I see that Jafar has sent me a bunch of messages.

"My younger brother Sayed will pick you up at the airport," the
first reads. "Looking forward to hosting you! With optimism, Jafar."

Oh no. The guy who has been helping me all day isn't some bum-
bling, incompetent technophobe trying to start an Airbnb business.
He's a kid helping his older brother.

I put down my fork. I feel so terrible. How had I missed that?

It would be easy to blame the language barrier. Sayed and I
couldn't communicate, and so he couldn't tell me that he was Jafar's
younger brother, and I couldn't pick up on verbal cues that might
have outed him as the twenty-year-old I will later learn he is. But I
don't think that's it. If I'd spent just two minutes trying to understand, or even just paying attention, I would have seen a teenager
still adjusting to the new feel of certain adult rituals. There was the
awkward, timid way he drove the car. Whatever faux pas he made
with the handshake. The look that he wore all day: a deer-in-the-
headlights-fear of being exposed as a teenager. I was annoyed when
he didn't pretend to buy the SIM for himself and then give it to me,
but maybe he hasn't yet mastered the essential adult skill of lying.

I realize, with great shame, that what made me miss all these
clues is the fact that, because money is exchanging hands, I had
seen our relationship as a commercial transaction.

Airbnb is somewhere hazy between putting a stranger up on your
couch and opening a hotel. You're inviting a random person to sleep
in your house, but he's paying a modest rate to be there.

In Central Asia, it gets even hazier, because guests are so venerated.

Because I'm paying Jafar to stay at his apartment, I had seen myself as the customer, and Sayed as the person whose job it was to
make sure I got what I paid for. And because, in my mind, every
Airbnb should have Internet, I expected Sayed to do anything up

to and including personally laying transpacific fiber-optic cables to make that happen.

While I'm sure Jafar, Nilofar, and Sayed set up the apartment to bring in a little extra money, that didn't stop them from still seeing me as their houseguest. All of Jafar's e-mails have indicated as much. "I hope you like the apartment." "Good night Audrey :)"

A quick Google search reveals that most homes in Tajikistan don't have Internet because monthly subscription costs exceed average wages. Oh great: I am a spoiled Westerner, even more so because that thought had never crossed my mind. And if Internet in the apartment isn't a given, Sayed going back and forth to the apartment with potential SIM cards and tomorrow's computer went above and beyond the call of duty adhered to by typical Airbnb hosts, who like to provide their guests with a "chill" vibe by responding to questions like, "How do I get to your house?" days after your scheduled visit. ("Oh, sorry! Looks like you found it after placing frantic, expensive international calls to Airbnb customer support! It was great meeting you!")

What makes the whole thing even worse, I realize, is that I was so quick to forgive my own mistakes, and so unforgiving when someone didn't provide me with a service I felt I'd paid for.

I walk into the first cellphone store I see the next day and buy a SIM card with no problems.

In the course of this transaction, I learn that text messaging is currently down in Tajikistan.

"Oh, no, I want a SIM card that can send and receive SMS," I tell the saleswoman, assuming I misunderstood.

"No, no," she replies. "For one week, all of Tajikistan, no SMS."

My mission in Dushanbe is to book a flight to Khorog, a city in Tajikistan's southeastern tip that's within walking distance of Afghanistan. From there, I want to travel along the border through the fertile Wakhan valley and then up into the moonscaped Pamir Mountains. The problem is, I need to find someone to do it with.

If I link up with other travelers, we can all split the cost of hiring a guide with a Jeep for the entire ten-day journey. If I can't, I'll have to hitchhike along the Afghan border, which does not seem like the best mode of transport for a woman traveling alone with an eighty-pound suitcase.

It does concern me that e-mailing strangers on message boards is my "safer" alternative, but I've only been able to find one person whose dates come anywhere close to matching my own. An enigmatic user named V has posted on multiple forums looking for someone to join a trip that leaves the exact day I want to. I've been e-mailing him daily, but so far he hasn't responded to any of my messages.

The more he ignores me, the more I become convinced that his trip is *perfect*, and the more desperate I am to join him. He's starting in Dushanbe and ending in Kyrgyzstan, taking the exact route I'd picked out in between. His dates coincide with mine so perfectly that I've made sure to stay in Dushanbe until the day he leaves, on the off chance that he gets back to me. But that's now only two days away, and the chances of hearing from V seem slim.

Tajikistan is a small country shaped like a cowboy riding a bucking bull while waving a ten-gallon hat. The Wakhan valley is a lush, green strip along the bull's hind hoof. It straddles the Panj River and butts up against the Hindu Kush mountains in Afghanistan and the Pamir Mountains in Tajikistan.

If V doesn't get back to me, my last chance to avoid hitchhiking is to fly from Dushanbe to Khorog, the biggest city in the Wakhan, and try to arrange something from there.

The flight is rumored to be harrowing. It's supposedly the only commercial flight for which Soviet pilots received hazard pay.

Demand for a seat, however, is through the roof. To get a ticket, you have to go to the airport two days in advance and put your name on a list. If you're one of the first fourteen names on the list, you go back the next day and get in the ticketing line, which is subject to the whims of the airline staff. If either of the two previous days' flights were grounded, those passengers get the next day's seats, and you have to come back and try again the day after.

It's an awfully long shot, I think, for a journey that could leave me stranded sans travel companions in a remote corner of Tajikistan.

The Tajik Air ticketing office has set up shop in the back of an apartment complex. To get there, I take something called a "3 taxi." Named for the 3-somoni fixed price of each ride and identifiable by the 3 affixed to their windshields, 3 taxis are unlicensed cabs that run along fixed routes like public buses. They're privately owned vehicles that travel up and down the main boulevards, picking up passengers who flag them down and dropping them off at predetermined points along the way.

"When they see the police, they hide the sign and pretend not to be a taxi," Nilofar tells me. "But you don't worry!"

When I arrive in midafternoon, the Tajik Air office is still closed for lunch. A foreign couple is waiting in a rare patch of shade, and we eye each other suspiciously. She has blonde hair and colorful patchwork sneakers; he has dark curly hair, light eyes, and a sturdy-looking backpack.

A young Tajik Air employee in a bright patterned dress eventually shuffles up to the door with keys. We pour in behind her: me, the foreign couple, and a crowd of Tajik men. We rush for the counter. There's fifteen minutes of yelling and fist-banging, after which the Tajik Air woman apparently decides she's had enough. She announces she's closing up shop for an hour. The foreign couple and I wearily make for a set of couches, which are, at least, out of the heat. But no, no, she wants to literally lock up, and until she gets back, we have to wait outside.

This is how I formally meet the couple, Joanne and Maarten.

Joanne and Maarten are from Holland. They live in a small city where she coordinates volunteer opportunities for the municipal government, and he does odd jobs. They're on a three-week Central Asian jaunt: they've just come from Uzbekistan, where, they warn me, border security is so strict that they open your laptop and go through all your pictures.

They're friendly and easy to talk to, and they're also, it turns out, picking up a guide with a Jeep in Khorog. He'll take them through the Pamirs on the exact route I'm looking to follow. Our dates line up perfectly. I start laying on the charm.

An hour later, we all have our names on the list to get plane tickets tomorrow, and they've given me their driver's e-mail address, although not, unfortunately, an invitation to join their trip. We shake hands in the parking lot, and laugh about how strange this whole ticketing process has been.

As soon as they're gone, I'm alone again. I'm suddenly aware of how few opportunities I've had lately to talk to people in the only language I've mastered (English), and how wonderful human interaction can be. I kick myself for not inviting them to dinner. If I prowl the most popular foreign restaurants in the city, will I casually bump into them?

I send an e-mail to their driver and wander off toward the world's tallest flagpole, which is one of Dushanbe's tourist attractions listed in my guidebook.

Joanne and Maarten's guide e-mails me back almost immediately. He tells me I can join a trip starting in two days with a French guy who "loves photography," for the reasonable price of $1,000 U.S. I'm hesitant about dropping so much money to go on a ten-day road trip with a man I've never met. What if we hate each other? Also why the mention that the Frenchman "loves" photography? I tell the guide I'll think about it.

I stroll through gardens with rosebushes in full bloom. I stare enviously at couples walking hand in hand and groups of friends laughing on benches. I miss my friends in Shanghai, my friends in New York, my parents, my brother and sister. I think about the sun setting where they are.

I check my phone and find four new e-mails from the guide. The first assures me that the Frenchman is a "kind" person. The next successively lowers the price, and implores me to leave Dushanbe in a shared taxi first thing in the morning. My response is noncommittal: I'm not eager to take a bumpy twenty-four-hour taxi ride, and plus we might get tickets for the flight.

I finally find the tallest flagpole in the world. It's not hard: it towers over everything around it. It's easily the tallest flagpole I've ever seen, though it does occur to me that a country doesn't build the world's tallest flagpole by accident. Dictators love world records, and I imagine Tajikistan's search for a practical, economical feat.

"Biggest mall!" "Too expensive." "Longest roller coaster!" "Too logistically challenging." "Tallest flagpole?" "We could probably swing that!"

My phone buzzes. I have two new e-mails, each insisting that this is the "final price." The second is almost half of the original offer. I sigh. What's the right price for a ten-day vacation with a stranger?

At the Tajik Air office the next day, Joanne, Maarten, and I are third, fourth, and fifth on the list to buy tickets. We learn, miraculously, that tomorrow's flight is tentatively good to go. But as we cluster around the ticket counter, I begin to fear that the list won't be the final say.

Each time the ticketing agent calls out the next name on the list, twenty people shove passports and cash under her nose. A phone beside her rings incessantly, and when she can ignore it no longer, she halts the whole ticketing process to answer it.

I try to join the other customers in annoyingly foisting my passport and money on the overwhelmed ticketing agent, but Joanne and Maarten wait calmly off to the side. They appear resigned to our fate: either we'll get the tickets, or we won't, and they seem convinced that pushing and shoving won't affect the outcome.

A young man in a Tajik Air uniform appears behind the counter and starts talking to us in English.

"You want to fly to Khorog?" he asks.

We tell him we do.

"Don't do it," he advises.

"What?!" we exclaim.

"I did that once." He shakes his head. "Scariest flight of my life. You fly so close to the mountains, and the plane—have you seen it?" We've seen photos. "It's so small, and so old, you wonder how it can even fly. I'll never do it again."

Not a great sign when the airline's own employees are too afraid to take the flight.

"There's a Dutch woman with a travel TV show," Joanne says, "and she also took this flight. And she has done so many crazy, scary things—climbing mountains, and jumping off of high places—and she also says this is the worst thing she's ever done."

Much of my conversation with Joanne and Maarten has been devoted to how much I'm dreading this flight. I've seen photos of a tiny prop plane that looks less like a photograph of aviation achievement and more like the backdrop for an inspirational quote about persevering against all odds. I've read accounts by people who swear the plane was about to crash. Now that I've spent twenty-four hours trying to get this ticket, I'm wondering if I even want it.

"You can drive," the guy offers. He frowns. "But actually, the roads are so bad. Cars crash all the time. You heard there was a huge mudslide recently?" I haven't, but I nod knowingly. "I think driving might actually be more dangerous than flying."

Well, at least there's that.

But then he brightens. "Actually, there is one safe way to get to Khorog: ride a horse."

Miraculously, the ticket woman calls us over. She shoos away the other customers, who beseech her to skip us. Suddenly, we're filling out endless forms, handing over cash, holding tickets in our hands.

Outside, we exchange giddy high fives and congratulate ourselves on our good fortune. But then I look down at my ticket and see a problem.

"My name is spelled wrong on the ticket," I say.

Maarten checks his. "So is mine."

"Me too," Joanne chimes in.

We debate: Do we go back inside? Will we risk losing our tickets? Maybe they'll let us on the flight with minor misspellings?

But I once booked flights for a vacation with Anton and forgot that on his passport, his name is written with Belarusian spelling instead of the Russian spelling he usually uses. When we got to the airport, the airline wouldn't give him a boarding pass.

Joanne, Maarten, and I go back inside and push our way back to the counter. The woman asks us how many mistakes we have on our tickets.

How many mistakes? "I guess . . . two letters are wrong?" I say.

The woman takes our tickets, stamps each twice, and then hands the tickets back, mistakes intact. She goes back to the swarm of would-be ticket buyers.

"Wait!" Maarten exclaims. "Our names are still spelled wrong!"

A guy standing next to us intervenes. "Each stamp means one mistake is okay," he explains. "So, two stamps: two mistakes."

"But I also have two stamps," Joanne adds, perplexed. "And I only have one mistake."

"Well," he says, "you have an extra, just in case."

The next morning, Sayed knocks on my door at five forty-five. He hands me a pile of clothes that his mother hand-washed and line dried, and then drives me to the airport as the first streaks of pink spill over the horizon.

Later, I will re-read my e-mails with Jafar and cringe when I see that my revelation in the Ukrainian restaurant didn't result in immediate behavior modification on my part. Instead, I will re-watch myself happily taking Jafar up on each generous offer of hospitality—that would be great if your mom could hand-wash my clothes! well, if Sayed happens to be up at 5 a.m. and doesn't mind swinging by the apartment!—when I should have politely declined.

As I walk into the Dushanbe airport, a stray dog gallops past me, chased by two members of the Tajik army.

The flight to Khorog leaves from a tiny terminal directly adjacent to a pancake stand, where I find Joanne and Maarten waiting, along with a large, graying Frenchman and his Tajik fixer—a local foreigner can hire to translate and help navigate foreign environments.

The Frenchman wears a heavy-duty vest and serious sunglasses. He tells us he works for an NGO and that he's taken this flight many times before.

"Is it terrifying?" I ask.

He shrugs with breezy indifference. "It's worse on the way back," he says, "because right after you take off, you have to make it over a very tall mountain. Sometimes, the pilot only clears it by a few centimeters."

We hear a loud bang. "Ah, well, they shot the dog," he says.

Joanne, Maarten, and I are horrified.

"You saw the stray dog running around?" the fixer asks. We nod. "So, they killed him."

"But why?!" I ask.

"It's a big issue in Dushanbe right now," the fixer explains, "what to do about stray dogs. Because we can bring them to shelters, but there are too many of them, and in Tajikistan, people don't adopt animals. So they're going to get killed anyway. Why not now?"

I nudge the conversation toward another pressing concern: the renegade general.

About a week ago, a high-level general learned he was about to be fired, so he rounded up some supporters, grabbed a bunch of weapons, and fled, supposedly to the Pamir Mountains, where we're heading. On his way out of town, the general and his cohorts shot up an ATM in Dushanbe. Travel blogs have been warning tourists to stay out of the Pamirs, where he's rumored to be hiding out. Should we be worried?

"Yes," the French guy says dryly. "Like you, this general is very lazy. So he's also probably traveling through in the back of some guy's Jeep."

It takes me a moment to realize he's joking.

We're still not sure if the plane will fly—a slight change in the weather in Khorog could ground us at any moment—but a calm, clear sky hangs over Dushanbe, portending good fortune.

The check-in process is slightly frazzling, and then my suitcase exceeds the weight allotment, which isn't surprising, given that all it would take for my weight to drop below that of my suitcase would be a minor case of food poisoning, but then I have to pay a luggage fee to one specific guy, in U.S. dollars, which I don't have, so I have to track down an ATM dispensing U.S. dollars in Tajikistan. I find one in another part of the airport and make my withdrawal quickly: the story of the general is still fresh in my mind.

Joanne and Maarten's guide, Januzak, texts me to say he'll meet us at the airport in Khorog. I allow myself one last wistful moment of mourning for my would-be travel partner V, and then the Tajik Air staff announces that we can begin boarding.

The French NGO guy raises his eyebrows. "Now," he says, "the real adventure begins."

A TEN-DAY ROAD TRIP THROUGH TAJIKISTAN

My first glimpse of Januzak, the guide who will take me on a ten-day road trip through Tajikistan, is of a yellow Ukraine baseball cap bobbing up and down behind the concrete barrier surrounding the tiny airport in Khorog, Tajikistan.

On particularly energetic bobs, the hat is accompanied by a man grinning and feverishly waving, seemingly at us.

"I guess that's Januzak," Maarten says.

This is where I'll part ways with this lovely Dutch couple—in the two days since we met in a parking lot, they have come to feel like close friends. Joanne and Maarten will travel with one of Januzak's employees and take a slightly different route through the Pamir Mountains; I'm going in Januzak's Jeep with the Frenchman Januzak has described repeatedly and possibly two times too many as "kind." Januzak is also bringing his assistant guide, a woman named Norgul, so I can "have a friend."

To be fair, my French travel companion does seem pretty kind. His name is Vianney, he sells champagne, and he insists that I sit in the front seat.

"I was in the front all of yesterday, and the day before," he says. "You should sit up front, to see the views."

"No, no!" I exclaim. I point out that he's over six feet tall, while I, at five two, can barely see over the top of my rolling suitcase. I'm used to being tucked into small spaces; the long-limbed, on the other hand, are constantly being boxed in by vehicles and society.

"Really," he insists. "I'm almost tired of the view!"

We agree to a compromise: Vianney will sit up front for now, but we'll switch places this afternoon.

I look up and see Januzak has been watching this whole exchange with a look of bewilderment. I sense that he shares the prevailing view toward seating arrangements in Central Asia: men in the front, women in the back.

As we start driving, it becomes clear that Vianney is extremely prepared for this trip.

"Is that Mount Something Something?" he asks Januzak, pointing to a peak in the distance. "No," Januzak tells him, it's "Mount Whatsitmacalled." "Ahhh," Vianney replies, "Mount Whatsitmacalled—the place where the animal thingamajigger comes from!" "Yes," Januzak confirms.

"Wow," I venture. "You know a lot about this area."

Vianney demurs. "Oh, it's just years of reading about it in books."

This area is called the Wakhan valley, and I have not spent years reading about it in books. I thought I would be okay with this, but Vianney's almost childlike sense of wonder and unbridled enthusiasm for the landscape outside our windows kind of shames me, and again reminds me that you're supposed to read the guidebook *before* you show up somewhere. I feel like the *Idiot Abroad* to Vianney's Kofi Annan.

What I do know is what I can see, which is that the landscape really is spectacularly beautiful. The Panj River beside us is a vibrant turquoise trickling between red rocky banks.

A few trees and bushes form a thin strip of green that lines each side of the river. Beyond that, the desert swallows up the landscape, which rises into mountains on the far side of the water.

We pass a group of tiny children dressed up like adults for school. They can't be older than five, and they're trying to hitchhike. (When we ask Januzak about this later, he seems confused by our question. "Is it safe for kids that young to take rides from strangers?" we ask. "Of course!" Januzak declares.) The girls wear white button-down blouses tucked into black skirts; the boys, doll-sized suits. They almost look like they're headed to a baby networking event.

"*Salam alaikum*," Vianney calls through the open window. The kids shriek with laughter.

"Is that correct?" Vianney asks, turning to Januzak. "*Salam alaikum* is how to say 'hello'?"

Januzak shrugs. "For a man, *salam alaikum* is nice, but if it's just a woman, *salam* is okay." Vianney and I flinch at "just a woman," and the car fills with awkward silence.

"I'm glad you'll be spending the week with me and Audrey," Vianney finally says smoothly. "By the end, hopefully, you will realize that men and women are equal."

Our journey begins in the Wakhan valley, a verdant oasis sprouting from the banks of the Panj River, and then we'll climb up into the Pamir mountain range, and finally end in Kyrgyzstan at the foot of Peak Lenin, the highest point in the former Soviet Union.

Each geographical feature serves as a kind of border. The Panj divides Tajikistan from a tiny strip of Afghanistan that juts in between Tajikistan and Pakistan. This nonsensical cartographical move comes from nineteenth-century tensions between the British and Russian empires, who had decided that they were best equipped to exploit the resources of Central and East Asia and were busy colonizing all the territory they could conquer. As each expanded toward the other's holdings, an increasing number of public beheadings and military skirmishes threatened to lead to all-out war, so they carved out Afghanistan's Wakhan Corridor in the name of peace. It served as a barrier between Russian Central Asia and British India. In typical colonialist fashion, they expended exactly zero energy worrying about the implications for people living there.

The mountains surrounding the Wakhan valley are best known for killing the people who tried to cross them. On the Afghan side, there's the Hindu Kush, whose name supposedly means "killer of

Hindus." The British hoped the Pamirs, on the Tajik side, would serve a similar purpose if the Russians tried to invade India.

Januzak is small in stature, but outsized in personality and stores of energy, which he replenishes with disconcertingly frequent naps. We return from a mini-excursion or bathroom break to find Januzak in the throes of REM sleep. When we knock on the window, he leaps out of his seat. "Okay!" he exclaims. "Let's go!"

Norgul is much calmer and quieter. She's the Melania to his Donald, silently absorbing the occasional bursts of casual misogyny from the back seat. She has long hair and a pretty smile, and, at least in English, she's fairly shy, I suspect because she doesn't feel as comfortable in it as she does in the four other languages she speaks (Tajik, Farsi, Kyrgyz, and Russian). Januzak is training Norgul to be a guide for his company, which I hope means that one day she'll be driving and relegating men to the back seat.

We make an odd foursome, the two guides, plus the ever-cheerful, seemingly unflappable Vianney, and then me, conversationally engaged but frequently carsick.

Januzak and Norgul both come from Murghab, one of the poorest cities in Tajikistan, surrounded by one of the poorest provinces in Central Asia. The areas that we're traveling through are unfortunately just as remarkable for their striking natural beauty as they are for their poverty. Eastern Tajikistan is isolated and remote, cut off from the rest of the country by mountains that can only be crossed by the terrifying flight or the only slightly less harrowing roads. It's also been hard-hit by war: first the Soviet campaign in Afghanistan, and then a five-year civil war that ravaged Tajikistan after independence.

As in Kyrgyzstan, NGOs tried to combat poverty by introducing tourism. The NGOs arrived in the early 2000s, bringing training and resources, and tourists soon followed. Adventurers were drawn by the soaring, snowcapped peaks and moonscapes in between.

Januzak's first clients were a group of Swiss tourists with whom he could not communicate. He drove them through the mountains in a borrowed car, and by the end of the trip, he decided he'd found opportunity. He taught himself English however he could: impromptu lessons with his clients on long drives, the odd book, but, he's quick to stress, no formal English-language schooling. He packs his English with jokes and expressive outbursts. He substitutes sound effects for words he doesn't know and is eager to expand his vocabulary. "How do you say, when they take a man's *whooooop* and cut off the *chiup?*" he asks us. We teach him the word *circumcision.* "Yes," he says, shaking his head. "Very painful."

Januzak worked his way up at another tour company and then was selected to travel abroad for further NGO-sponsored training. When he returned, he was elected president of the regional tourism association. Last year, he started his own company.

The turquoise waters of the Panj slice through dusty mountains, brush clinging to the rocky banks. We turn down a road that runs directly beside the river, so close that it feels like the water could splash our tires.

"It's so strange, to be so close to Afghanistan," Vianney is saying.

I nod, but I actually don't find it that strange. "Afghanistan is right behind those mountains?" I ask, pointing to the peaks across the river. To me, the country is some far-off, hypothetical place that exists on the news but, for the purposes of my life, might not even be real. But Vianney shakes his head and instead points to banks on the other side of the narrow, low river, not ten feet away, and says, "No, *that's* Afghanistan."

That changes things.

I had no idea what it would feel like to stand ten feet from Afghanistan. In truth, I didn't think it would feel like anything. I imagined staring at trees and mountains and experiencing the letdown that comes from straddling an imaginary line that divides two countries, or two continents, and willing yourself to think, *Holy shit, I'm in two places at once!*

It's not like that at all. I gape, openmouthed, at trees and mountains and think, *Holy shit! That's Afghanistan.*

I'm looking at a country my country's been at war with for most of the time I can remember. The trees are rooted in a place where men hiding in caves evaded what I'd been raised to believe was the most powerful military in the world.

I'm entranced. So is Vianney. We're at a loss to describe why just looking at Afghanistan is making us so awestruck.

"You have to understand," Vianney tells Januzak when we stop to examine an abandoned Soviet tank left over from the Afghan war. "For my whole life, Afghanistan was a place that fought the most powerful nations on Earth. And won."

The Panj River marks the border between Afghanistan and Tajikistan but does little to stop people from crossing it. While the river is supposedly more menacing when it swells with mountain runoff in springtime, in the fall, when we visit, the river is low and you don't have to travel far to find a spot that looks easy to ford.

The Tajik government worries about crime and religious extremism flowing over the border, which happens occasionally, but the most regular traffic comes from something far less abstract but apparently less worrisome: drugs.

Opium poppies from Afghanistan are thought to be the source of 90 percent of the world's heroin, and Badakhshan Province, just across the river, is a major hub for smuggling it out of the country.

An Afghan looking across the Panj River into Tajikistan sees paved roads, modern homes, and a relatively regular flow of traffic.

Where he stands, twenty yards away, roads are dirt, houses mudbrick, cars rare.

On the Tajik side, long-haul truckers in jeans and flip-flops ferry cheap Chinese goods across the country. In Afghanistan, women in chadors carry cumbersome baskets up and down the main road.

Tajikistan's Wakhan valley is poor, but it's much better off than Afghanistan's Badakhshan Province across the river.

The river that divides the two countries is slow and shallow, at times more exposed land than water. Smuggling drugs at this time of year seems like only slightly more work than being an Instagram influencer, and yet, on the Tajik side, it doesn't feel like a major drug artery. Families sell fruit on the side of the road. Five-year-olds hitchhike to and from school, an act that would seem wildly dangerous in the safest American suburb, but apparently isn't a stone's throw from one of the world's most porous opium borders.

The only evidence of the drug trade is the massive, incongruous satellite dishes sitting outside some homes on both sides of the border. The satellites, Januzak tells us, are purchased with drug money.

"But now that the Taliban outlawed drugs, the violence is much less," a Swedish volunteer at our guesthouse for the night tells us. "Well, okay, a few tourists were beheaded the other year," he concedes. "But I would still really like to go."

The road the next morning alternates between densely shaded settlements and vast, open expanses. The snowcapped mountains across the river seem to rise out of nowhere and soar into the clouds. We pull off at particularly picturesque points and take pictures of the turquoise river or beams of light piercing gray clouds. I keep marveling at the fact that I'm photographing Afghanistan.

We pass a large utilitarian building that looks like a development project. Vianney asks what it is, and Januzak tells him it's a school "that our president built for our children."

Vianney and I exchange looks. Januzak has had plenty of positive things to say about "our" president of Tajikistan, a man regularly condemned for human rights violations and who, shortly after we leave, will take the title "Founder of Peace and National Unity, Leader of the Nation, President of the Republic of Tajikistan, His Excellency Emomali Rahmon."

The majority of post-Soviet republics have had the same president since shortly after the fall of the USSR. I always assumed, naively, that dictatorships would be difficult to sustain. I imagined that most people would resist giving one man all the power (for equality's sake, I would support a *brief* reign of the world's first female dictator). But the period that followed the Soviet Union was characterized by chaos and turmoil, and the post-Soviet autocrats seized and held onto power by promising to restore order—a pledge they often made good on with crackdowns and restrictions on rights and freedoms. For many, the memories of the 1990s loom large, and at least their current corrupt leaders are known entities.

Still, it seems strange that Januzak, who has traveled abroad and works extensively with foreigners, would be so earnest in his admiration for the president. I assumed that people exposed to the outside world would have access to news that contradicts the state-run media, and that the truth would put an end to the kind of unabashed support Januzak is espousing.

But I'm starting to see that as a flawed, simplistic way of thinking. To be fair, Januzak's positive comments have mostly been limited to much-needed development projects, likely associated with the president to combat the region's general aversion to being governed by him (eastern Tajikistan declared independence after the collapse of the Soviet Union and has clashed with the central government ever since). But there could be a billion other explanations for Januzak's comments: lack of interest in politics, lack of exposure to critical commentary (after all, it's not like I get to another country and immediately Google "What is the U.S. government lying to me about?"), perceived lack of alternatives.

Or maybe he knows, but doesn't feel like getting into it. If a solution to the country's political ills even exists, it's unlikely to be figured out by the four of us in this car. Especially given the geography and the fact that I can't tell the difference between a hill and a mountain. What can Vianney and I do except shake our heads and say, "That's terrible"? We could return to our home countries and bemoan the oppression in Tajikistan. And our friends and family would likely reply, "What's Tajikistan?"

Each time we stop—for gas, for dinner, for a mandatory military checkpoint—Januzak tries to buy someone's car. These vehicles are rarely for sale. Often, they're currently being driven by the confused owners he's propositioning.

Toward evening on the second day, we stop at the birthplace of a Sufi mystic. It's been transformed into a museum dedicated to both the mystic, Mubarak Kadam Wakhani, and the traditional Pamiri home, a unique construction that reflects the rhythms and rituals of life in rural Tajikistan. That's about all I can tell you, because that's about all Norgul can translate.

Januzak, as usual, wants to nap in the car, so he sends Norgul to help us communicate. At first, it's fine: in a cool antechamber with pottery and metalwork displayed on carved wooden shelving, Norgul tells us that our guide—the kindly older Pamiri gentleman who created the museum—collected a lot of artifacts. When we ask where he got them from, there's some awkward silence and confusion, so we pose holding guns from the nineteenth century, and then the guide pulls out an old-timey wooden pointer to deliver a passionate lecture on the life of the mystic, who turns out to have been his great-, or maybe great-great-grandfather. We pick up on the odd detail: He was an astronomer, who translated the Koran into Pamiri, or maybe Tajik? Or maybe Persian?

Next, he takes us to the main room of a traditional Pamiri house. The Pamiri home's design dates back 2,500 years. The main room consists of a sunken dining and common area surrounded by a raised platform on which the entire extended family sleeps: men on one side, women on the other. Each house has five pillars, symbolizing the five members of the prophet Muhammad's son-in-law's family, which feels kind of random until you learn that the five pillars originally represented five Zoroastrian gods. When Islam arrived in Central Asia, Muslim proselytizers scrambled to make their faith fit into the grooves Zoroastrianism had carved into Pamiri life and society. It's harder to sell people on your new religion if you tell them they need to rebuild their houses. Better to just repurpose their symbolism. If Scientology ever makes it to Eastern Tajikistan, the pillars will probably stand for the five tentacles of a thetan.

Four layers of recessed squares frame a skylight in the center of the ceiling, each representing one of the four Zoroastrian elements. "Earth, water, air, and"—Norgul pauses before translating the final element—"fish," she finally offers hesitantly.

"Do you mean fire?" we ask.

No, no, she assures us. The fourth element is fish.

Our final stop on the second day is in a tiny village where Januzak deposits us with two boys who can't be more than twelve but tell us that they're sixteen. When we ask ten minutes later, they tell us they're seven. It's unclear whether they don't understand our question, or don't know their own ages.

Januzak has told them to take us up the side of a hill to see a Buddhist stupa.

I regret not waiting in the car about two minutes into the fairly arduous climb. I don't even know what a Buddhist stupa is.

The boys tell us to peek inside a small cave dug into the side of the hill. I'm expecting this Buddhist stupa thing, but instead I find myself face-to-face with a *human skeleton*. I jump.

"Who is that?!" we ask.

The boys shrug: no one knows. It's been there for a long time, they assure us, but I'm not convinced.

As we get higher up, the boys point to clouds of dust billowing up behind a tiny matchbox car on the Afghan side of the valley. "That's an American army base," they announce.

Vianney and I lunge for his binoculars. "How do you know?" we ask.

"Everyone knows," they tell us.

Indeed, all the attempts at inconspicuousness are what outs it as such. A cluster of low, nondescript buildings bunkered together in the middle of nothing. Telecom equipment trying to pass as low-key.

We see a tiny speck meandering around an imaginary perimeter: someone on patrol.

Staring at an American army base in Afghanistan turns out to be even stranger than being an American staring at Afghanistan. It feels like a celebrity sighting. How much of my childhood was shaped by the fact that all the dyed-in-the-wool liberals who raised me were morally, vehemently opposed to the very thing I'm now staring at?

We reach the Buddhist stupa. It's a pile of rocks that can no way compete with the binocular view of an AMERICAN ARMY BASE IN AFGHANISTAN. I stand on the stupa to get a better view of the base. The boys point to their school, a low, blue building, and then try to convince us to stay at their family's guesthouse. When we tell them we can't, they pull a bunch of sparkly red stones from their pockets, declare them to be rubies, and try to sell them to us.

The evening's guesthouse is quiet. We are, in fact, the only people there. We eat dinner with the proprietor, a friendly man who serves us dinner and sits down to chat. He's a retired teacher; he and his wife grow all of the food in their garden. They are very proud of this fact.

He kindly offers us fresh yogurt, which Vianney and I happily accept. It is only after the first bite that I realize "fresh" means "unpasteurized." The taste is difficult to describe: it's sour and heavy and tastes, to a child of the 1990s American suburbs, like poison.

But I don't want to hurt our host's feelings, or offend his wife, so I breathe through my mouth and force it down as Vianney asks the owner about his ancestry. He tells us about his grandparents, who came from Iran.

As a kid, I assumed the obsession with tracing your family back to earlier places of inhabitation was uniquely American. I attributed it to guilt over a mostly ignored displacement of indigenous populations or an attempt to distance oneself from the unsavory parts of American history that predate ancestors' arrivals.

The Soviets drew borders in a way that left people separate from the country to which their ethnic group was native. Januzak and Norgul are ethnically Kyrgyz, but hold Tajik passports.

But even Vianney traces his ancestry to other parts of Europe.

It's strange how we cling to these roots as part of our identity. How American teenagers in baseball hats show up in Milan and expect to find an affinity with men in pointy shoes and neatly styled hair just because they both have the last name Cogiliano. How disappointing it is when we don't.

Maybe we all want to believe we come from someplace else. Somewhere better, cooler, more exotic. We want to wake up one morning and discover that we belong to different people.

The next morning is our last in the Wakhan valley. Before we turn off onto the road that will take us up into the mountains, Januzak pulls over at one final lookout. It doesn't seem particularly picturesque: a few camels grazing on the far bank in Afghanistan, the same turquoise water creating a divide that transformed lives on either side of it.

Januzak motions to a small cairn on our side of the river. "You know," he says, "that's the border with Afghanistan."

"So if we walked past the rocks, we'd be in . . . Afghanistan?"

Januzak nods.

It's unguarded, and we're the only people for miles, so alone it's hard to imagine that ideas like borders and countries could matter so much. For a moment, it seems no more serious than the lines marked for tourists to stand in two places at once.

Does it feel different, sneaking past the rocks and planting my feet on the ground in Afghanistan?

Perhaps, in that I feel absolutely terrified. I take one shaky selfie in which I grin maniacally, look around, try to create some meaningful memory, and then sprint back into the relative safety of Tajikistan.

The biggest difference is that when I left the no-man's-land of half Canada, half New York, I felt silly. When I stepped from Afghanistan back into Tajikistan, I felt like I'd been somewhere.

In the afternoon, we climb into the Pamir Mountains on a narrow, switchbacked dirt road. Our progress keeps being impeded by herds of livestock. The winding road, shouldered by a hundred-foot drop, is periodically blocked by shoulder-to-shoulder sheep.

"Tajikistan traffic jam," Januzak grumbles.

Each time, he lays on the horn as shepherds try to beat a Jeep-sized path through the crush. The shepherds' faces are obscured by bandannas and ski masks they wear to protect against high-altitude sun and wind, but also kind of make them look like they rob banks.

Up in the mountains, the landscape changes. The verdant valley becomes a craggy moonscape, more barren than anything I've seen. Everything is brown and dusty. Iron oxide deposits lend some hills a reddish hue; others somehow shimmer like fish scales in the bright sunlight.

Januzak pulls off the main highway, an unpaved road, and onto something even more rudimentary: a pair of parallel tire ruts that cut through the jagged landscape.

It's strange to get downgraded from an unpaved road. Before, the ride was bumpy. Now it's like we're driving through an earthquake.

A more practical argument for a seat belt presents itself: Norgul and I are tossed around the back of the car like dice in a Yahtzee shaker. We get in a lot of core work attempting to anchor ourselves to the headrests in front of us and the overhead hand strap, whose purpose I once believed to be limited to hanging dry cleaning.

Januzak and Norgul confer in hurried, urgent Kyrgyz.

"I'm trying to find the right way," Januzak explains.

There are dozens of ruts of varying ages and permanence. It's hard to tell which were made by what, and where they lead. Every so often, Januzak mutters something under his breath, throws the car in reverse, and tries another. It feels like we're following a dashed line to the cartoon X on a pirate treasure map.

Suddenly, the landscape is dotted with alpine lakes, the water so deep and clear it's almost black. Everything else is the same brown, barren earth, some heaps piled together to form peaks, the rest flattened out in between.

We pull up to a lookout so stunning I gasp. It's incredible: a black lake wrapped around undulating peaks colored deep blues and purples. Vianney and I are reduced to monosyllables—wow, wow, wow—and Januzak grins.

"We never tell clients we are going here," he says finally, "because, sometimes, we can't find it."

"Have you noticed," Vianney asks, "that, if you go anywhere else in the world, and you tell someone where you're from, they'll know one famous person from your country? Like when you say you're American, people say, 'Obama!' Or for me, they'll name some famous soccer player. But here, people just say, 'Oh. America.'"

The one person everyone in the Pamir mountains does know is the Aga Khan, a wealthy celebrity who breeds horses and attends star-studded galas and still finds time to lead a spiritual movement.

The Aga Khan's development foundation was one of the first NGOs to come into eastern Tajikistan and provide aid, and it continues to implement relief projects today. Pamiris, in turn, feel understandable gratitude toward the Aga Khan, who, in all fairness, seems like he does a lot of good work, even though he marries models and hangs out on yachts.

Many Pamiri families hang a photo of the Aga Khan in a location that suggests he's a member of the family, which is incredibly confusing, because he's visibly not Pamiri. For the first few days, I'm baffled—do all these families have a middle-aged European son?—and then Vianney explains who he is.

It's well past lunchtime, and my rumbling stomach is starting to sour my mood. Januzak's keeping an eye out for a yurt in which we can stop and grab a bite, and he seems anxious, like he's picked up on my hunger-fueled aggravation.

"Dear guests, are you okay?" he asks. "I notice, you are not talking."

"Oh, I'm more than okay," Vianney assures him. "I've just been read-ing and dreaming about this place for twenty years. It's so amazing to be here." He turns to me. "Audrey, I'm sure for you it's the same."

Now doesn't seem like the time for honesty, so I lie. "Oh, yes." I smile. "Me too."

For a rugged stretch of land cut off from the rest of the country, the Wakhan valley seemed, at least to me, to offer inhabitants a modest but adequate standard of living. The Panj River provides arable land and flat terrain on which roads are easier to maintain. We stayed in homes that had electricity and bought fruit from families selling produce on the side of the road.

All of these comforts disappear the moment we ascend into the Pamir Mountains. Now we're on a rocky, high-altitude plateau where little seems to grow and the elements make quick work of eroding infrastructure. Electricity is rare and mostly produced by oil-powered generators; roads are unpaved and cut through vast ex-panses of open space connecting the small towns that dot this re-mote district. Nomadic herders have long used parts of the region for summer pasture—Januzak's grandparents among them. He's prone to nostalgia when he looks out over the landscape. "It reminds me of the land of my childhood," he says, shaking his head. "Happy times."

Januzak likes to be off the road well before sunset. The roads, difficult enough to find in the day, disappear in the dark. At night, the only light comes from the stars and our headlights.

The mountains, brush, and dust around us have turned purple in the fading twilight and threaten to fade to black at any moment. Januzak's following a set of tire tracks that winds into the horizon, and I can almost feel him sweating.

He's looking for a yurt camp near a summer pasture, where he knows a group of yak herders who can put us up. But he's not sure if he'll be able to find them because, depending on whom you ask, the pasture season is either almost over, or definitely over, meaning they would have packed up for the winter.

We pull into a few encampments, but they're all dark, with no trace of the life they must, at some point, hold. In Kyrgyzstan, the yurt dwellers dismantled their homes and hauled them away in the back of pickup trucks, but Tajik herders must leave their summer abodes behind in these remote fields each winter when they depart.

Januzak's anxiety has now spread to the rest of the car. We ride in silence while Januzak mutters about driving to the nearest city, if we have to, and spending the night in a hotel. We haven't seen a city in days, but now doesn't seem like the best time to point this out.

The darkness engulfs and ensconces us, and in my mind I can almost zoom out until I see us, from hundreds of feet above, two tiny specks of light in a vast, empty landscape of desert and mountains.

Just when all seems lost, we pull up to a row of yurts, and a woman pokes her head through the door. Relief floods the car.

Minutes later, we're drinking hot tea and spreading jam on bread while Januzak chats with our host. When she leaves, he turns to me.

"Did you see the woman's sons, the shepherds?" he asks. "They were going crazy when you arrived. I think . . . they will love you."

Do yaks eat humans? These ones look like they'd at least like to try. They have long brown fur and menacing horns, and they're definitely shooting me death stares. I stand beside the relative safety of the outhouse in the early-morning light, marshal my courage, and then sprint past them and back into the main yurt.

Vianney is chatting amiably with everyone, even though he only shares a common language with Januzak and Norgul. This doesn't surprise me. Over the past few days, I've noticed that Vianney has a way of connecting with people that I can't quite put my finger on. He's curious about everyone we meet. While he's sensitive to the ways in which his life and mine have differed vastly from those of the people we interact with, he talks to the yak herders the same way he speaks to Januzak, which is the same way he talks to me and spoke with the

French-speaking Belgian couple we overlapped with at a guesthouse. He asks about their jobs, lives, families, cities. He has inside jokes with Januzak and Norgul from before I met up with them. Why does his way of being in the world stand out to me? It feels almost reductive to say that he's treating everyone equally, because, duh, that's what everyone says they do, or at least aspire to do. I sit at the breakfast table and try to name what it is that I'm observing. He's . . . genuine? Gracious? Generous? I feel like I'm stuck on the gs.

Everyone's talking about the altitude. The plateau that we're sitting on ranges in elevation from eleven thousand to thirteen thousand feet above sea level; the mountains add another few thousand feet. I learned my lesson in Kyrgyzstan and am planning to limit physical exertion to dipping my bread in jam and raising it to my mouth. Still, we're all going to feel headachy and cranky until we acclimatize.

As we get up to leave, Vianney asks the family if they have ibuprofen and acetaminophen in their first-aid kit. The mother checks; she does not.

"Here," Vianney says, opening his backpack and taking out his pain relievers. "Tell her to take these." When Januzak hesitates, Vianney reasons with him. "It's probably difficult for her to find places to buy this." He shrugs. "I'll get more in France."

Shaimak is near the spot where Tajikistan, Afghanistan, China, and Pakistan all come crashing together to form what must be one of the world's most volatile borders.

If you Google "Shaimak," you're inundated with search results for an Indian choreographer named Shiamak, whom Google is so confident that you're actually looking for that it automatically corrects your spelling. This, I think, says a lot about Shaimak.

We've come to Shaimak for its two hot springs, which seem to constitute about three-quarters of the village's permanent structures. I skip them because I'm not feeling well; while Vianney takes a dip, heavy snowflakes begin to fall from the sky. They float down slowly, almost hanging in the air before disappearing the moment they touch the earth.

The day's drive is mercifully short but painfully monotonous, punctuated only by a break to take blurry pictures of a distant peak in the Hindu Kush about which Vianney is extremely excited and of which I pretend to have heard.

As the morning wears on, the temperature drops. The hills are suddenly dusted with snow, and patches of frost linger on the ground.

At midday, we reach Alichur. It's a step up from Shaimak, although the step is modest. There is one store. It does not sell toilet paper.

Vianney and I are given spacious, comfortable rooms in the home of a kind family in the midst of extensive renovations. This presents some awkward challenges: the workers on the roof are afforded a sweeping view of the uncovered outhouse, which has, disconcertingly, two adjacent holes and not the slightest attempt at a privacy barrier in between.

There's not much to do in Alichur. Our house doesn't have electricity, though there is a gasoline-powered generator that the family turns on at night.

We're looking forward to this, because we haven't had power in two days. While I hadn't noticed the absence of electricity as much in the yurt, it's jarring to walk around a village with a shop and normal-looking houses and realize that everyone has learned to live without electricity during the daytime. And I mean learned, because most villages had electricity in Soviet days.

One of the few upsides to being forced to joyfully join the Soviet Union was that Tajikistan benefited from Soviet development projects and social programs. At the outset of the USSR, Tajikistan was considered the least developed and least socially progressive republic. Its topography made it difficult to grow food, build infrastructure, and produce goods.

The Soviets set about building roads and growing cotton, and they brought in goods that were more easily produced in other regions.

Many of these gains in Tajikistan disappeared after the collapse of the Union. Products that had been readily available in Soviet days were now expensive and in short supply. Schools closed; damaged power lines were never repaired. In the deserts, people sometimes drive on the sand beside the old Soviet highways, which still mark the way, but are too marred by cracks and potholes to traverse.

This has made some people—particularly older generations—nostalgic for the Soviet Union. It's easy to understand why, especially in places like Tajikistan, where standards of living have fallen. But it's hard to know what to make of this.

This, again, is why I'm lucky to be traveling with Vianney.

Vianney is perhaps one of the world's best travelers. He is, above all else, understanding and easygoing.

Each time we meet travelers struggling to find a ride to the next town, Vianney offers to squeeze them into our Jeep. There are unnecessary detours in which Januzak tries to chase down someone who owes him a car part, and there are days when we eat lunch at four p.m. These minor inconveniences often leave me seething; Vianney's mood never sours. He finds small opportunities to be generous. He covers the nominal cost of Januzak and Norgul's admission to tourist attractions. He gives away things that other people need more that I would have nevertheless held on to on the off chance that I'd want to use them. At the end of the trip, he gives Januzak his Tajik SIM card, prompting me to do the same. (I part with mine begrudgingly, out of an irrational fear that I might need it.) He never makes me feel bad for ranging from underinformed to straight-up clueless.

I could learn a lot from Vianney.

In the afternoon, Vianney and I decide to go for a hike. There's a river meandering through a few hills that look like they'd afford a nice view. Walking toward this, we attract the attention of some kids playing outside of a house, which, in turn, draws a few adults, who insist that we come in for what we assume will be tea.

We quickly realize that what we've been invited to is much more than tea. We're led into a room full with Kyrgyz men, which I mistake for a bachelor party until Vianney points out that the women are likely in a separate room. Our hosts graciously offer to let me sit with the men, but, no, no, I'm going to culturally assimilate!

I proceed to be the world's most disappointing guest.

Imagine, if you will, that you're a Kyrgyz woman from a small, isolated village that probably doesn't get many strangers coming to town. One day, a Frenchman and an American woman show up and you kindly invite them to some as-yet-unidentified party at your house.

In the men's room next door, you can hear the Frenchman speaking basic but intelligible Russian with the assembled guests, who laugh and shout and pass around his iPhone. You smile and shake your head. *How fun it would be to have our own guest from a strange, far-off place*, you think, because you've completely forgotten there's an American woman sitting right beside you.

I couldn't be a less interesting guest if I tried to explain office politics. Without Januzak, Vianney, and Norgul around to translate, I freeze. I neither employ the little small talk I can make in Russian nor attempt to pull up a few photos of my family before my phone dies. Without the security blanket of my companions, I'm suddenly reminded of how far my Russian still has to go and this humbles me to the point where I can't recover. Part of me wonders if being reduced to a toddler's level of communication has made me feel like I'm confirming the notion of women so many of the men here cherish— helpless, meek, not worthy of attention. Or maybe that's a cop-out.

The entire room quickly forgets about me. While Vianney's stealing the show next door, I'm getting tripped over because I'm blending so seamlessly into the wall. I sit silently, trying to solve the mystery of what celebration Audrey and Vianney are attending.

Here are the clues:

About thirty women and children circle around a blanket that's been spread over the floor and covered with nuts, breads, candies, jam, and dried fruit. The mood seems happy and festive. Maybe it's a wedding?

Someone passes me a bowl of light broth that turns out to have a surprisingly powerful, gamey flavor. I immediately set about trying to pantomime that I'm very, very full.

Thirty excruciating minutes pass. Then a woman arrives with the kind of plastic bag full of plastic bags that can probably be found under any kitchen sink in the world. The bags are distributed to the guests, and then another woman brings in a large plate of freshly cooked meat that I think, judging from the face, is goat.

I assume this signals the start of the feast, but it seems to do the opposite. Everyone starts packing up. They fill the plastic bags with every food item still left on the table, and when the meat gets passed around, people take almost ceremonial bites of their servings before tossing that in the bag, too.

The woman next to me helps me fill my bag, though I feel kind of awful taking one. To not take one, I realize, would be even worse.

Another woman arrives with a bag full of dresses and headscarves, which she presents to each attendee in a very specific order, starting with the eldest women seated in the place of honor. She says a kind of blessing as she places a scarf on each woman's head. I get one, too, and the women next to me immediately help me tie it on. It's not a good look for me: my head makes it look like a pair of underwear.

I'm getting the sense that whoever threw this party had to buy a new wardrobe and a week's worth of groceries for each attendee. This is really making me curious about what would merit this kind of celebration, and then, as if on cue, a baby is carried into the room with pomp and circumstance reminiscent of *The Lion King*.

The party turns out to be a celebration for his first birthday, and we all crowd around him for a group photo. I've made so little of an impression that I'm relegated to the far edges, very likely outside of the frame.

When the men pose for the same photograph with Vianney, they have him stand in the middle and hold the baby.

That night, alone with only my thoughts and the gentle hum of a generator that's about to cut out, I think about the baby. I wonder if, when he grows up, his parents will show him the photo and tell him, "When you were one, we threw you a birthday party with an American girl who didn't know how to talk."

The next morning, we drive to Murghab. It's the region's capital and the largest settlement for thousands of miles, and in my imagination, it has risen to mythical, Oz-like status. I haven't showered since Dushanbe. The sheen of grease that covers my hair has me alternating between wearing my new head scarf, out of consideration for others, or avoiding the few mirrors we encounter, out of consideration for myself.

Januzak keeps telling us we can bathe in Murghab, that we'll be able to shop at a market and plug in our phones. I expect it to rise out of the desert like an emerald city with Wi-Fi and charging stations.

None of us slept well last night because of the altitude. I'm practically chewing Tylenol, but the altitude still gives me a headache that presses on the back of my eyes and makes it painful to look anywhere but straight ahead. Perhaps we pass more stunning scenery on our way to Murghab? I only take in the headrest in front of me.

Halfway there, our tire starts leaking. Januzak notices at the lip of a crater he's taken us to see. This is problematic, because he lent his spare to another driver, who hasn't yet returned it.

I'm not sure what to think when Januzak unveils his plan. "We will drive to Murghab," he declares gravely, "but we will drive very fast."

The ride to Murghab is quiet in the way that a full flight turns silent in turbulence.

Each time we slow down, I think of the air slowly escaping from the rubber tube beneath us, and I think of how desperately I don't want to be stranded on the side of the road when we're *so close* to the bustling metropolis of Murghab.

The tire makes it to Murghab, which does, as promised, have a market with SIM cards, toiletries, and the highest concentration of Chinese electronics I've seen outside of China, along with giant

sacks of rice and the few root vegetables that can grow at high alti-
tudes. The stores have been fashioned out of old shipping containers.
Outside of electronics, shampoo, and starchy vegetables, selection is
limited.

Though Murghab is technically a capital city, it feels more like
a capital town. Its population hovers around four thousand and
doesn't seem to have a lot of hometown pride. "Murghab is certainly
not a beautiful town," the website of the Murghab Ecotourism Association reads, "however there is no denying the attractiveness of the
surrounding region."

The shower is a welcome bucket of warm water administered by
ladle, and as I wash off four days' worth of dust, I find myself thinking again about Soviet nostalgia.

The closer I get to Moscow, the less Soviet nostalgia I find. I can
almost feel the flow of funds that left the industrialized Western
USSR and poured into the impoverished republics in the East. In
Central Asia, the Soviets brought political oppression and plenty of
imperialism, but they also brought inoculations and ended the practice of child brides.

Another stark contrast between the past and the present comes
in education. The Soviet campaign to "liquidate illiteracy" proved
remarkably effective—by the 1950s, almost every citizen of the
USSR could read and write. Schooling was compulsory for all Soviet citizens, which brought education to women in places where
girls hadn't traditionally been sent to school. In some places, and
especially in the poorer rural parts of Central Asia, these education gains have been lost. Women don't always finish school if they
marry before graduation, which means young brides may receive
less of an education than their grandmothers did. The older generation often speaks more Russian than the younger.

This creates an odd dynamic for travelers. Anywhere else in the
world, if you want to find someone who speaks the lingua franca,
you approach young people. In the former Soviet Union, you start
with the oldest people you can find.

I'd always assumed that Soviet citizens saw the collapse of the USSR as a welcome harbinger of freedom and independence. Many did, particularly at the time, but few were prepared for the period of political and economic chaos that followed. A majority of the fifteen post-Soviet states traded one dictatorship for another, and for many of their citizens, it's hard to see what was gained.

It reminds me of a conversation I had with Anton years ago that I'd never been able to wrap my head around until now.

We were discussing Mikhail Gorbachev, the final leader of the Soviet Union. When I'd learned about him in school, he'd always been painted in a positive light, and I was surprised to hear that the opposite had been true for Anton.

"Some people see him as a coward," he said, "because he let the Union fall apart."

"Yeah, and that liberated, like, millions of people—including you," I said.

"Audrey, you don't understand. One night you go to bed, and you're part of the Soviet Union, the largest and most powerful country on Earth. And the next morning, you wake up, and you're Belarus."

Mountains speckled with what I've come to call Central Asian graffiti—white rocks arranged to spell out words on the sides of impossibly steep cliffs—guide us out of the settlements toward the Ak-Baital Pass, the highest point on the Pamir Highway. As we ascend, the landscape becomes increasingly barren, until it's just different variations of rock. There's solid rock that engineers had to blast through to lay the highway, smaller stones that catch underfoot as I scramble to find a suitably private spot to relieve myself on the side of the road, and the fine dust of former rocks that cakes my clothes in a soft layer of powder.

The mountains turn more colorful: greenish browns and vivid reds swirled together like marbles. There are moments when I look out my window and see the mesas and badlands of the American southwest; others when all I glimpse are snow-covered peaks and open sky. I snap a panorama while squatting on the side of the road.

Early British explorers nicknamed the Pamirs "the Roof of the World," which doesn't make much sense to me. A roof descends from above, while mountains rise from below. I would have called them something simpler, like "Severely Conducive to the Aging Process."

We drive by a lone cyclist bundled up in a red Windbreaker struggling up toward the pass, and he raises one arm in salute. "You'd have to be crazy," we all mutter, although I wonder if I might secretly have it in me to finish my trip on a bicycle.

We pull up to the sign that marks the highest point on the pass. I'm dizzy from the altitude. We snap a picture. I've made it, I guess, to the Roof of the World.

The penultimate stop on our journey is Karakul Lake, a stretch of clear, turquoise water ringed by snow-covered mountains that's pooled in the gash left by meteorite impact.

I've already been to Karakul Lake, although not *this* Karakul Lake. Across the border in China, there's another body of water with the same name. The two do look remarkably similar. For a moment, I wonder if they share a name because someone mistook one for the other, but then I learn Karakul just means *black*, and this kind of makes sense, but also doesn't, because what strikes me most about both of these lakes is the vivid blue of their waters.

We're staying in a tiny town that's more like a cluster of houses huddled together against the high-altitude elements. I get lost wandering the unnamed streets as the wind and sun burn my skin.

Januzak points out the tip of Peak Lenin across the waters. "It's the highest point in the former Soviet Union," he tells us.

Highest seems to be the superlative most frequently bestowed upon this part of the world. We've visited the highest town and the highest pass, while traveling along the second-highest highway in the world. Karakul Lake seems eager to snatch the title "highest navigable lake" from the hands of Lake Titicaca: in 2014, it hosted the Roof of the World Regatta, which was, as I might have guessed, the highest sailing regatta in the world. Outdated calendars in our guesthouse still boast about this distinction, with pictures of sailboats tacking on the lake's still waters.

After lunch, I sneak down to the lake for a moment of solitude. The water sits, still as glass, in the crater basin. It's so quiet I can hear the silence. The sun glitters off the lake.

Back at the guesthouse, I find a rugged American couple who've recently dismounted from bicycles. They're young, outgoing, and funny; and, most notably, they're the first native English speakers I've encountered on my trip.

People say you have different personalities in different languages, which for me has been true because I've never mastered a second language. Linguistic deficiencies have forced me to be less expressive and talkative—a more muted version of who I am when I don't have to think about vocabulary.

Even with Vianney, who spent part of his childhood in Australia and speaks perfect English, there are still cultural references I can't make and small details you never think of as being specific to your language or country. It's like an American and an Australian doing improv: one says, "Let's get in the car," they sit down on two chairs beside each other, and they both think they're driving. The Americans and I joke and speak quickly and watch the sun set over the lake. I feel myself relaxing, letting my guard down, and slipping into a version of myself that feels more natural.

It doesn't hit me until after dinner, when we're lounging on pillows, watching a Tajik news program we can't understand. I realize that what I'm doing with these Americans, Vianney does with everyone. I'm unconsciously putting everyone I meet into one of two boxes—other and not other—and changing how I relate accordingly. In the name of being sensitive, I'm also being more guarded, acutely aware of my identity and how it colors interactions.

Vianney maintains this sensitivity while also just operating under the assumption that some common, uniting humanity supersedes cultural and situational differences. He finds common ground— work, family, food—and then has a normal conversation. Most strikingly, he doesn't turn into the worst version of himself when he's in an unfamiliar environment. It's so easy to do that when you're traveling. You're in a new place and don't know the language, rules, and best snack foods. It's easy to go on the defensive: to look out for danger and swindlers instead of keeping an open mind. It's harder to be a Vianney. But it seems like it might be a challenge worth undertaking.

The last mountains we see look like frosted red velvet cupcakes. They're rich with iron and topped with snow. They sit behind the Chinese border, a line clearly marked with posts that once had barbed wire connecting them. Some still do. The only people who'd be thwarted by that border fence would be people carrying wide loads who didn't think to turn sideways.

Vianney and I begin speaking about the trip as though it's already ended.

"It's lucky we found you," he's saying, "because I was posting on these websites, looking for someone to join us, and no one was responding."

I tell him that I was the lucky one, because I was messaging the V guy with the perfect dates, the perfect itinerary, which, now that I think about it, is actually pretty similar to our own, so maybe it all worked out in the end—

And then it clicks. That the V guy I kept trying to reach on those message boards. The *V* stood for Vianney.

TOURING THE BLACK MARKETS OF UZBEKISTAN

A friend recently asked how I knew where to find the black markets in Uzbekistan.

I blinked. "You just ask people."

At restaurants, you flag down the nearest waiter. "Could I get the check?" you ask. "And by the way, where's the nearest black market?" You point to a pyramid of apples at a fruit stand and ask the woman peddling them how much they cost. "Also, is this the black market?" When you ask a cop for directions, you don't ask about the black market, but you get the sense that you probably could.

It turns out that the snooty German I met back in Kyrgyzstan was right—in Uzbekistan the black market is *the* place to exchange currency.

Like many post-Soviet states, Uzbekistan spent the early 1990s putting out the fire that was its economy. When the USSR disbanded, what had once been a unified, centrally planned economy was broken up and divided among the fifteen newly independent nations. Adding further strain, almost all of these countries planned to transition to free-market economies. "Transition" here was a loose term: many governments were so excited about this that they decided to abandon gradual change for instant capitalism (technically called "shock therapy"). Prices immediately skyrocketed, ushering in an era of shortages and rampant inflation. The Uzbek government attempted to combat this by setting an "official" exchange rate that's about as in touch with reality as the weight I self-report on health forms. The official rate, which is used by banks and mandated by law in Uzbekistan, makes the Uzbekistani som more valuable than it would be if the government didn't intervene. Uzbekistani citizens and business would rather hold their wealth in U.S. dollars, because the som is so unstable. But because the banks and government lose money each time they sell dollars at the official rate, the pool of hard U.S. currency available through legal channels is limited. The black markets step in to fill the gap, and everyone loses, except the people coming into Uzbekistan with U.S. dollars. When I was there, the official rate was around 2,500 som to the dollar. The black market rate was close to 5,000. Each time I changed $100, I was getting $200 worth of Uzbekistani currency.

The Uzbek border is a dusty, desolate expanse of desert barricaded behind miles of fence and barbed wire. I'm nervous; although I've added a few more land-border notches to my crossing-between-territories-belt, I've heard that the Uzbek border is the most restrictive in Central Asia. Guards apparently inspect each item in your suitcase to check for drugs and sensitive materials, a broad and subjective category that includes pornography, documents promoting religious extremism, and photographs of borders. I've been warned to discard any medication that could possibly be construed as a narcotic and go through my computer to ensure I don't have any pictures of borders or men with beards. I'm particularly worried about the border photos. I spent last night going through years of pictures and deleting anything that kind of even looked like an international divide.

Inside a crowded customs hut, a soldier in an olive-green uniform instructs me to fill out an exhaustive form declaring the value of everything I'll bring into Uzbekistan. The example provided is: "Sellphone (1). Used."

I hesitate, wondering whether to correct the error. Would that be pretentious? Is this a test to weed out the obnoxious know-it-alls? "Sellphone," I finally write. "(1). Used."

I struggle to hoist my suitcase onto the row of folding tables where soldiers inspect the contents of travelers' suitcases. A female guard begins unzipping my pouches of night creams and antacids.

"Do you have any drugs?" she asks.

I'm about to say no when I remember that I do—that is, if you count Xanax as a drug, which, if memory serves, most law enforcement does.

I'd been so focused on scrubbing my computer of potentially incriminating fences that I'd completely forgotten about the Xanax. I'm now remembering that Uzbekistan has a zero-tolerance drug policy and that an online forum warned about a British couple who were thrown in jail for having cough syrup that's sold over the counter in the UK. A group of cyclists had told me they'd had to account for each pill in their first-aid kit.

"I'd toss anything that's not, like, Tylenol or Tums," one cautioned. "Just to be safe."

"No," I say as the customs agent opens the backpack containing my drugs. "No drugs."

She pulls out the plastic sandwich bag of medications. From it, she removes the blister pack of Xanax, the back of which is clearly labeled, in capital letters, *XANAX*.

"What's this?" she asks.

"Medicine," I whisper.

"What for?"

"For . . . headaches."

She frowns and picks up an old prescription bottle whose label wore off long ago. This is where I carry the rest of my pills—ibuprofen, Ambien, fish-oil pills, and antimalarial medication all jumbled together. The flaws in this system have been revealed many times, as when I went for a dose of what I thought was ibuprofen and ended taking six times the recommended daily dosage of antimalarial medicine.

"What are these?" she asks, shaking the bottle.

If she opens it, the forty mismatched pills might not do me any favors. "Also . . . for . . . headaches," I whisper.

She shrugs and puts the bottle back in my bag.

I realize, as I drag my suitcase to the next station, that though she's been trained to scour suitcases for Xanax, she's likely never been taught what the word looks like in English.

Tashkent is a mix of crumbling Soviet infrastructure and beautiful Islamic architecture. Blocks of concrete apartment buildings adorned with vaguely Middle Eastern designs abut tiled mosques and madrases. In the right parts of town, fountains splash over verdant grass, and in the wrong parts, people pour water on the sidewalks to keep the dust down. When you walk down those streets, you learn to watch for the women flinging bucketfuls of water.

Uzbeks are the largest ethnic group in Central Asia, and Tashkent, Uzbekistan's capital, was always the de facto capital of Russian- and Soviet-controlled Central Asia. The fertile farmland in Uzbek territories was well-suited for growing cotton, which is why the tsar decided he needed it. His decision to invade and conquer the various Uzbek khanates was also easy to justify, because the Uzbeks had a habit of kidnapping Russian citizens and keeping them as slaves.

Today agriculture remains an important sector of Uzbekistan's economy, but domestic demand has shifted to something the country doesn't produce. "Right now, people are going crazy for dollars," the manager of my guesthouse is telling me, shaking his head. He's checking me in, a process made tedious by government regulations requiring foreigners to obtain registration slips accounting for each night of their stay. Some managers have printed forms; others scribble the details onto the backs of Post-it notes. I have to carry these slips around with me and hand them over on my way out of the country in order to be allowed to leave—a reminder that Big Brother is watching, but can't track me via computer.

"You should change money at the black market," the manager continues. "It's completely illegal, but perfectly safe."

This is music to my ears. I love any chance to feel like I'm living dangerously without risking arrest, bodily harm, or mild embarrassment.

I'm also excited to see a black market in person. In China, I used illegal money changers and bought knockoff Louis Vuitton purses from a crawl space hidden under a dental surgery clinic, but I've never been to a shopping center that calls itself the Black Market (although I have admittedly shopped at White House Black Market).

"And where is the nearest black market?" I ask.

At the fruit market, he tells me. All the good black markets, it turns out, are in fruit markets.

But I have a more pressing concern: my Russian visa.

Half of the countries I want to visit require Americans to obtain visas in advance. Because I'm not traveling on a tour, I have to arrange my own visas, a task I've made more difficult for myself by applying outside of my home country. On the plus side, I'm learning more than I ever thought there was to know about various foreign bureaucracies. For example, did you know most embassies get mildly offended when you show up to apply for a visa and say, "Sorry, can you remind me of the name of your capital?"

Some of the embassies are so small that the ambassador personally processes visa applications. Each time I submit my documents to an ambassador, it feels like an exchange for which he is vastly overqualified. On two occasions, I have to haggle over the visa price using a calculator as an interpreter between myself and his excellency.

I'm at the Russian embassy in Tashkent, which looks like something built by the Cold War. By that, I don't mean that its structure seems ideologically fueled by the paranoia and posturing of U.S.-Soviet relations in the 1960s. I mean that it looks like it was designed, planned, and constructed by a nuclear missile.

The building is surrounded by gates, fences, and razor wire. The entrance is a steel door guarded by men with machine guns and further cordoned off by a series of gates.

I'm standing in a crowd of people so tightly packed together that we'd be fully prepared if the ambassador stepped outside and announced that he wanted to stage dive. But this mosh pit is for Uzbekistani citizens, who have a special visa agreement with Russia.

When a guard sees my American passport, I'm whisked to the front of the line, where I deposit my bag in a locker, then proceed through a six-inch-thick steel door into the vestibule, where a guard protected by bulletproof glass asks to check my documents. I realize that I left those in the locker, and he rolls his eyes because I am clearly *amateur hour* when it comes to heavily fortified, steadfastly bureaucratic embassies, so I have to go back and sheepishly retrieve my documents from the locker, which makes the armed guards roll their eyes, too, because *how did I mess up the first and easiest part of this whole thing?* I show my documents and then pass through a metal detector and a second steel door into the custody of another guard who escorts me to the visa window, which is located deep inside the bowels of a labyrinthine collection of fluorescent-lit corridors that have the interior design sensibility of a public swimming pool.

Things are not going well for the European tourists in front of me at the visa window.

"It's Airbnb," they're trying to explain to the woman sitting behind yet another panel of bulletproof glass.

The visa woman is shaking her head.

Russia requires that citizens from countries whose leaders don't capitulate to Vladimir Putin obtain letters of invitation to apply for tourist visas. In theory, a letter of invitation is supposed to come from someone inviting you to Russia for a semi-legitimate reason, but in practice, I've learned, it's something you buy from a sketchy company on the Internet.

An Airbnb host has to apply in person for the tedious paperwork required for private citizens to invite their friends to Russia; a shady tourist agency can issue a falsified document in minutes.

I lean toward the woman. "You can just buy a fake one online," I whisper.

She eyes me suspiciously. "But we really *are* staying with this woman on Airbnb," she explains.

"It's really cheap," I assure her. "And way faster."

I share what I've learned in my weeks of compulsive Googling, and within minutes, I've convinced her that it's completely illegal, but perfectly safe.

Buoyed by pride in my own detective skills and general ingenuity, I step up to the visa window full of confidence.

The woman behind the window wears her hair in a soft perm and her lips in a straight line that passes for a neutral expression in Russia, and would be considered a frown anywhere else.

She does not speak English. Our conversation quickly surpasses the bounds of my Russian. We struggle for a few minutes, and then she sighs. "*Habla español?*" she asks.

Somehow using a combination of phrases gleaned from Taco Bell commercials and French pronounced in a bad Spanish accent, we reach an understanding: I printed out the wrong letter of invitation, and I need to go get another copy.

I head back outside to try to find someone with a printer. I'm not sure where to begin: most of the businesses around the embassy are small shops, and, as is true anywhere in the former Soviet Union, one out of every four businesses is a notary.

It's impossible to imagine a story that begins, "So I was in a former Soviet republic, and I could not, for the life of me, find a notary!"

I'm not kidding: the storefronts that you pass on any former Soviet street go something like this: notary, grocery store, notary, convenience store, notary, notary, notary, monument to hero of the people.

Not far from the embassy gates, I find an overworked notary on the verge of a nervous breakdown. A dozen clients with stacks of papers in plastic sheaths hover around her desk or wait patiently in a row of chairs as the notary buries her face in her hands and emits loud, dramatic sounds of distress.

I decide this will be a good place to print my letter.

I get to cut the line because I'm the only one who doesn't need anything notarized, and also, I think, because as soon as they realize I'm a foreigner, they want to get rid of me. I ask the notary if I can get on the Wi-Fi and e-mail the letter to her. She stares at me. There is no Wi-Fi.

Our conversation is labored and heavily impeded by the language barrier. Finally, the notary shouts something into a back room, and Camilla appears.

For the first time in my life, I understand the urge that some men have to save certain women, because this is how I instantly feel about Camilla. She's tiny and pretty and exudes a certain air of helplessness, although she will end up solving every problem I stumble across in the next forty-eight hours. I want to pick her up, pack her in my suitcase, and ferry her off to a better life in Turkmenistan.

Camilla sits me down at her computer and has me pull up the invitation letter. "So," I begin, "I kind of need this signature to look . . . like it didn't come from a printer."

She nods. We get to chatting. Camilla is ethnically Russian and speaks decent English. When I ask her how, she tells me she studied to be an interpreter—her dream job. I tell her she seems qualified to work as a translator, and then her responses become more vague. At some points, she intimates that she might not have finished school; at others, she seems to indicate that a woman, or a Russian, can't run a company, although I want to point out that her boss is at least one of those things. Camilla strikes me as smart and capable, and, above all else, very young.

As she finishes printing, I realize I need to exchange my currency in order to pay her.

"Thanks," I tell her, when she hands me my new letter of invitation. "By the way, where's the nearest black market?"

She stares at me like I'm crazy. "In the fruit market, of course."

It's one thing to know that the black market is inside the fruit market; it's another to locate the black market *aisle*.

I assume I'll know it when I see it. I picture shady characters lurking on the edges with big black bags, scanning the room for eye contact.

Instead, I find a pretty normal-looking outdoor fruit market, with the slow trickle of shoppers you'd expect at eleven a.m. on a Wednesday.

So I ask people. I wander up and down the rows of tables murmuring, "U.S. dollars?" like someone peddling drugs outside of a nightclub. I stop to ask a kid selling apples and a group of women hawking SIM cards.

I'm surprised when they all point me not to a thuggish man scowling beside a pole, but to a small, unassuming woman selling Korean salads. When I approach her, only the top of her head peeks out from a pile of shredded carrots.

"I'm looking for . . ." I begin timidly.

Before I can finish my sentence, she whips out a calculator and types in the exchange rate. Her offer is great—higher than anything I've heard—but I counter out of habit. She shakes her head and retypes the original number. I slide over a hundred-dollar bill, and she hands me a black garbage bag stuffed with thick wads of cash rubber-banded together. She seems surprised when I dump it all out and begin counting right in front of her.

I guess I wasn't expecting a black market transaction to be as straightforward as buying a sweater at the Gap.

Back at the embassy, the woman at the visa window checks over all of my documents, nods at everything, and then disappears into a back room. A solid thirty minutes pass. I entertain myself by studying the bulletins on the wall, which show the right and wrong ways to take a passport photo. A picture of a woman smiling is covered in a giant red X; the corrected photo beside it shows her frowning. Another *NO* photo features a man wearing a rainbow clown wig; the *YES* picture is the same man, sans wig. I wonder if Russia has had an influx of Clowns Without Borders.

The visa woman reappears with an even more serious man. "Everything is okay with your documents," he declares in English. "Except that your visa application must be filled out in the Russian language."

I stare, incredulous. For a brief, poorly considered moment, I try to reason with him. Why didn't they tell me that before? Why is the visa application form on their website in English?

"If a Russian wants to go to America, so, he must submit a visa application in English," he explains. "American citizens must do the same in Russia."

I can't find fault in his logic. But I also can't translate my application into Russian. I try one last Hail Mary.

"The visa office closes in thirty minutes," I say. "And tomorrow is Teacher's Day."

The guesthouse manager warned me about that this morning. "Tomorrow is Teacher's Day," he told me, grimly.

At the time, this didn't strike me as particularly earth-shattering information. In America, Teacher's Day is more or less on the same level as Arbor Day: the type of holiday that shows up on a calendar and then disappoints you by not bringing presents or a reprieve from homework. Suddenly, though, it feels like a potential ace up my sleeve.

"Yes," the man at the visa office says.

"And I plan on celebrating," I lie, "because I am a teacher."

He stares at me, unmoved.

"Also," I continue, "won't you be closed for Teacher's Day?"

"Of course not," he replies.

The instructions on the Russian visa application clearly state that the application can only be prepared by the person obtaining the visa or a licensed tour operator. But by this point in the day, I'm too deep into a life of crime to stop. Out on the street, I contemplate how I can hire someone to illegally translate my application. Camilla's face pops into my head.

Back at the notary office, the notary–cum–Virginia Woolf character agrees to translate my documents, but rather than handing them off to Camilla, she sends me to a skinny kid in an office across the street who's blasting Akon, chain-smoking cigarettes, and not at all conversant in English.

I fume. I wonder where Camilla is, and why she isn't the one doing this. I'm also curious about why this guy was banished to an empty office across the street, and why, given that the embassy closes in twenty minutes, he's putting together a DJ set instead of translating my documents.

"The office closes at noon," I say. "You need to start now! Fast, fast!"

My boy DJ Tashkent is pretty stumped from the get-go. He has to look up words like *America* and *name*. Eventually, he just gives up and calls Camilla, who, I want to point out, should have been doing this all along! (If only so we can spend more quality time together, and I can encourage her to start an organization to empower young women.) She joins us in the smoky office, but steps outside to draw on her own slim cigarettes and exhale long, thin trails of smoke.

Even from outside, he calls to her.

"University?" he asks.

"*Universitet*," she calls back.

He flies through my work history and family tree, and it's starting to look like I might *just* make it back in time to drop off my documents before noon, but then we reach the worst part of the application.

This section requires me to list the dates of travel for every country I've visited in the past *ten years*. I'd been surprised, when filling it out this morning, to discover that the past decade had brought me to dozens of countries. *If I'd have known all that travel would turn out to be such a liability*, I think bitterly, *I would have stayed home*.

Translating the country names and filling in the travel dates is so tedious and time-consuming that they eventually decide to start skipping most of them.

"They will not check every country," Camilla declares confidently. She delivers this, as she does every line, with a seriousness usually reserved for handing down death sentences.

"They won't?" I ask, surprised.

"Most probably, no," she says. "But maybe yes."

Noon comes and goes, with DJ Tashkent wanting to know how to say *China*, and Akon wanting to make love right now (na na), and me now forced to spend another day in Tashkent.

"You should be running this place, Camilla," I snap.

She's been nervously eyeing my purse, which I've dropped unceremoniously onto the floor beside me. "You shouldn't put your bag on the ground," she says finally. "It's bad luck."

While Camilla and DJ Tashkent finish illegally translating my Russian visa application, I grapple with an even more overwhelming conundrum: Should I offer to buy Camilla lunch?

The thing is, I know my relationship with Camilla is strictly professional, but a part of me senses the tingle of a blossoming friendship. Is it crazy that I'm picturing us giggling over beers at an exclusive, locals-only party later that evening? Or meeting up in New York years later, laughing as we recognize the familiar faces hiding beneath sleeker haircuts and more sophisticated makeup?

"And, sign here," she tells me, pointing to a line beside a statement swearing that no one helped me prepare my visa application, which, if I'm being honest, I can't even read.

Plus, I tell myself, *Camilla really did all the work here, and I bet DJ Tashkent is going to get* all the credit. *That's what it's like to be a* WOMAN *in* UZBEKISTAN!

They hand me back my application, and I try to say, "Can I buy you some fried dumplings?" It comes out, "I'm going to run to the embassy to see if I can still turn this in!"

How did that happen? I wonder, as I make my way back down the hot, dusty street to the embassy gates. Men with creased faces stand smoking cigarettes in the paltry shade cast by a thin line of trees.

Maybe it's all for the best, I think. *Maybe she would have been weirded out by the whole—* Hang on! I interrupt myself. *You're telling me, in a part of the world where people invite strangers to babies' birthday parties, it would have seemed weird to buy someone lunch to say thanks for helping?*

Well, when you put it that way . . . I concede.

The embassy is, of course, closed, because if there's one thing bureaucrats do efficiently, it's break for lunch. As I head back to the main street, and my unexpected extra day in Tashkent, I resolve to invite Camilla for lunch.

But then I chicken out and scurry past her office.

Come on, Audrey! I scold myself as I reach the main street. *You're submitting semiforged documents to a government that still poisons dissidents, and you're scared of a little social rejection?*

Good point! I agree.

I march back toward Camilla, first full of confidence, and then pretending that I'm just looking for something I dropped.

As I reach the embassy crossroads at the end of the street, I suddenly feel very silly. This whole lunch no longer feels worth the internal turmoil. I turn around and resolve to head back to the guesthouse, and as I walk past Camilla's office for the final time, she steps outside.

I smile and wave. "I was going to ask you if you've eaten," I say.

She gives me a strange look and tells me she hasn't.

"I'd be happy to buy you lunch," I continue, "to thank you for everything."

She shakes her head. "We have lunch at the office. So we don't take a break."

I toe the dirt with my sneaker, unsure if she's telling the truth or letting me down gently. "Wow," I finally reply. "That's tough work."

"Oh, yes," she says. "Every day."

There's an awkward silence, so I ask her what her hours are like.

"We begin at nine," she says, shrugging, "and then, at night, sometimes we work until seven, sometimes nine, sometimes ten."

She says this without histrionics or a bid for sympathy, but as I walk back to the main street, I can't help but feel sorry for her. Her boss, in my head, has transformed from a Virginia Woolf character on the verge of a nervous breakdown to a callous Dickensian guardian, forcing her to scrub the floors while translating legal contracts into English, and it isn't until I reach the main street that I realize, *Wait, when I'm tutoring and performing, I basically work the same hours.*

I wonder why I was so awkward about all this as I reached out my hand to flag a taxi. Maybe spending so much time alone makes each potential friendship seem like a once-in-a-lifetime opportunity. If you blow it, you'll never have a companion for lunch again.

The knowledge that you're carrying around hundreds of dollars in garbage bags changes your personality. You become more paranoid. You find yourself possessive of meaningless belongings. You begin locking your toiletries.

In your eyes, every person is a potential thief. You eye the toddler crawling around at your feet with suspicion. *Maybe*, you think, *he's one of those babies who's been trained to steal fistfuls of cash from strangers' garbage bags.* You can't remember if that's something you made up, or a tip you read in one of those chain e-mails forwarded by elderly relatives with a subject like "RE:FWD:FWD:FWD:RE:FWD: KNOWING THESE CRIMINALS' SECRET TRICKS COULD SAVE YOUR LIFE." You begin to understand why drug dealers say they don't know who their real friends are.

Before I leave my guesthouse in the morning, I gather up all the bills floating in my purse. I pull bills from the loose change that accumulates at the bottom. I shake my guidebook, and a few thousand som tumble out.

It briefly occurs to me that if someone wanted to rob me, he'd first have to organize my bag.

The next morning, I head back to the Russian embassy to turn in the application that DJ Tashkent took too long to translate.

In the early-morning light, Tashkent, like all Soviet cities, seems at once hopeful and hopeless. The concrete apartment buildings that will look gray and worn by noon glow in the hazy, golden light. We pass a stocky, inelegant building with no windows called Next Mall of Tashkent. Billboards on its walls advertise an ice-skating rink and a restaurant called American Pizza.

I walk past Camilla's office and briefly wonder if I should buy her a present in Samarkand. Would that be weird? Will she think I'm hitting on her? Does she *already* think I'm hitting on her? *Am* I hitting on her?

Things go a little more smoothly at the embassy this morning. The woman at the visa window looks over my application, now written in perfect Russian, nods, and disappears again. When she returns, she tells me, in her signature blend of Spanish and Russian, that everything looks good, and then asks if I want to pick the visa up in ten working days, or spring for the express service and get it in five.

My mouth goes dry. "I want to pick it up *tomorrow*."

Picture Uzbekistan as a shadow cutout of Walt Whitman's beard. Tashkent is located at the tip of the beard, just before it starts to curl up, and I want to make it to the chin. In ten days.

Plus, I want to get out of Tashkent, an interesting but Soviet city, and on to the rest of Uzbekistan, where ancient mosques covered in turquoise mosaics rise from expansive deserts. I planned to visit Samarkand, home to epic madrassas and six-hundred-year-old ruins; Bukhara, a fortress with Zoroastrian temples; and Khiva, an ancient walled city.

I beg and plead and get transferred to the scowling man from yesterday. Is there any way I can pick up my visa tomorrow?

"It's impossible," he says with a sigh that makes me believe it's out of his hands. "It takes five days just to get permission from Moscow," he says.

Moscow. Just the sound of the name sends shivers down my spine. Part of me still can't believe I'll get to see it. Another part of me still can't believe that *Moscow* is the thing that makes me all weak-kneed and dizzy. Not a handsome stranger or the promise of professional success. Not even a city it might make sense to have strong feelings about, like Paris or Cory Booker–era Newark.

I sigh. "How much will the express visa cost?"

"450 U.S. dollars," he replies.

My eyes pop. "450 *U.S. dollars?!*"

"Yes."

"But, but . . ." My head spins. 450 *DOLLARS?!* I try to remember the last thing I spent that much money on. "Can I think about it?" I croak.

I return to my corner with my friends from passport phototutorial. Do I hang out in Tashkent and scrap my plans to wander through ruins in Samarkand? Do I go and then come back to Tashkent? How do I get back and forth? Uzbekistan has a rail system left over from the Soviets' zeal for infrastructure, and though I can take day trains from Tashkent to Samarkand, Samarkand to Bukhara, and Bukhara to Khiva, I'd almost certainly have to take an overnight train to come back to Tashkent and get my visa. An overnight train in western China that my sister and I shared with a flock of chickens made me swear I'd never sleep on the rails again, and to get from Tashkent to Khiva . . . I don't know what I'd do. Fly, I guess? If buying a plane ticket between two relatively unknown cities a week out isn't prohibitively expensive?

Suddenly, I have an idea. I rush back to the visa window.

"Can I pay the visa fee in local currency?" I ask, breathless.

"Of course," the man says. "You have to."

"And you calculate that . . . at the official rate?"

He nods.

"I need to run to the black market," I say. The government official is unfazed. "Also, do you know where I could buy a plane ticket around here?"

Before I leave the embassy, I go on a fact-finding mission. The guard who's escorted me to and from the bathroom tells me how I can take trains to Samarkand and Bukhara, and the guard who sits behind the bulletproof glass at the door recommends I fly to Khiva and draws directions to the train station on the back of a Post-it note. The guard outside with the machine gun explains how and where to purchase an airline ticket.

Here's what I've realized: most guesthouses and tourism busi-nesses in Uzbekistan that quote prices in U.S. dollars calculate the exchange using the going rate at the black market, not the official government rate. The embassy, however, does not.

Take my guesthouse in Tashkent. On its website, it says a room costs $20 U.S. a night. Right now, the government rate says that 2,500 som equals $1 U.S., but at the black market, I can get 5,000 som for each dollar. At the official rate, $20 U.S. would be 50,000 som, but if I want to pay in local currency at my guesthouse, they'll use the black market rate and charge me 100,000 som, which is more fair.

Embassies being an extension of the government, paying for a visa will be done at the official government exchange rate, using currency I obtained for half the price, so my $450 visa fee will be cut in half. In fact, any visa I arrange in Uzbekistan will be half the price it would be anywhere else. I want to get as many visas as I can. When you see a list of visa fees on an embassy wall, America is always the only country followed by three digits. "Canada: $10, UK: $25, France: $25, America: $148." I mentally scroll through the list of any visa-restricted countries I *might* visit in the next ten years. I briefly contemplate renewing my passport.

And I immediately call the Belarusian embassy.

I'd almost given up on the idea of visiting Belarus.

Out of all the former Soviet Republics, it's Belarus that I most want to see. Really, out of all the countries on Earth, Belarus has been the place I've most longed for, for years, because of Anton. But even he sometimes has misgivings about my going.

"What will you do when we go to Belarus?" he asks one day.

I shrug. "Hang out with you."

"But what if I have to work one day, or go with Elena to get di-vorced?"

He looks panicked; I can't understand why. "I dunno," I say. "What do most people do?"

"My hometown is . . . you know, it's kinda small." He's sitting on my bed, cross-legged, his voice dropped down a register and usual playfulness gone, like this is a gravely important conversation.

I pull up his hometown on Wikipedia. "I mean, I wouldn't be going because I want to see monuments or museums," I say. "I want to see where you're from." I hand him the phone with the Wikipedia page.

"Oh yeah, the fort!" He jumps up, his voice flooding with relief. "I forgot about that."

"Okay . . ." I fiddle with the corner of my fitted sheet that is always coming untucked.

"It's pretty cool actually," he goes on. "Lots of people come to my hometown just to see it."

"Sure," I say. "But I'm not worried about sightseeing. It'll be interesting just because, you know, it's where you grew up."

He starts kissing me, and in between his smile is back. "So, okay, everything's fine now," he assures me. "You'll go to the fort."

Like Russia, Belarus requires would-be tourists to obtain a letter of invitation. Unlike for Russia, I can't just buy one on the Internet.

Everything I read says I need to book a tour through an official Belarusian agency authorized to hand out invitation letters. These agencies are, unsurprisingly, not cheap.

"For us to provide a letter, you need to book all of your hotels through us, plus one excursion," one travel agent writes me. "Might I suggest the excursion of taxi pickup from Minsk train station ($50 U.S.)?" I look up the distance from the train station to the hotel on a map: it is a twenty-minute walk. Fifty dollars for the taxi excursion seems excessive, and also way out of my accidentally-haggling-over-fifty-cents budget.

To make matters worse, tourists need special health insurance, which I don't have and assume is expensive. I've spent weeks researching everything before reluctantly conceding defeat. Barring an urgent telegram revealing that I'm secretly Habsburg, or a prompt marriage to a Minskovite, visiting Belarus appears to be off the table. I'm crushed and heartbroken all over again.

But now I'm emboldened by my coup-de-grace at the Russian embassy.

Maria, the woman who answers the phone at the Belarusian embassy, is far more helpful than her Russian counterparts.

After I explain my problem with the invitation letter, she has an idea. "Maybe your hotel could invite you?" she suggests.

I jump online and stumble on a post from a backpacker who visited Belarus. He mentions, offhand, that he got the invitation letter from his hostel.

I immediately call every hostel I can find in Minsk, and they are all like, "Yeah, if you book a dorm bed for one night, we'll give you a letter."

"But a hostel bed is, like, eight bucks!" I exclaim.

"Yeah," they reply, not seeing what the big deal is.

So why wouldn't everyone just book a hostel bed and not stay there? I wonder but do not say out loud. Instead, I ask, "How soon can you send me the letter?"

I call Maria back to make sure an invitation from a hostel will pass muster. "Don't worry," she says, "I'll call the hostel and tell them exactly what to write." I should introduce her to Camilla.

She goes over a few more details—I have to get my entire passport translated, but luckily, I know a girl—and then she brings up the health insurance.

"I have my card right here," I say, just to add perjury to my criminal-conduct punch card.

"And does it say, somewhere on the card, that this insurance will cover the Republic of Belarus?" she asks.

"It covers Belarus," I assure her.

"And does it say so?" she asks.

My heart sinks. "No," I admit.

Well, I think, *this is it*. I came so close, but maybe Anton and his family and the gods of Belarus were right: I'm not meant to stand in the famous fort or visit the homeland of . . . someone? There has to be one famous Belarusian? Marc Chagall? It was fun, I suppose, while it lasted, and maybe the lesson, if there's one to be had, is that sometimes you need to know when to let go.

"Audrey, just one second," she says. "Maybe my friend can help you."

Because I wasn't expecting to drop 1.3 million som on my Russian visa, I run back to my guesthouse to grab more cash.

The manager directs me to the black market aisle of the nearest bazaar, where I find a group of twenty-something guys in flashy T-shirts who won't give me the same rate I got from the woman selling Korean salads. We go back and forth, and I make a show of storming away, but I quickly realize they're the only black market around. I return, somewhat sheepishly, and change $200, which turns out to be *thousands* of Uzbek bills.

"Make sure to count out money from black market changers," all the guidebooks warn. "Remember, they're not regulated, and totally illegal."

But I struggle with the stacks of bills. I'm standing in the middle of a crowded bazaar, trying to count thousands of bills while juggling my purse and guidebooks and official documents.

"It's okay," the guys tell me. "You don't need to count it." One of them calls his number from my phone so that I have it, and tells me to call him if any money's missing. I can't tell if this should reassure me, or put me even more on guard, because it messes up my counting, and I have to start all over again.

I'm so flustered that I call the guesthouse manager.

He listens to my story, and then agrees that I don't need to count it. "These guys, they will not cheat you."

I look at the kids, standing next to me with their starched dress shirts and simple cell phones, and I realize I don't think they're trying to cheat me, either. They could have taken off as soon as they had my money, but instead, they're sticking around, trying to end my performance of *Distressed White Woman in a Foreign Country*.

How odd, I think, *to be in a country where the black market is more honest than some of its ambassadors.*

The black market is right next to the metro, and so I decide to take the underground back to the Russian embassy.

Tashkent metro stations only have one entrance. You access them through the entrance doors, if you know what you're doing, or the exit doors, if you don't.

It's not like New York, where one subway stop might branch off into thirty-two different exits, some of which dump you out blocks away from where you want to be, others that empty out in Staten Island.

If you want to get on the Tashkent metro, you just walk through the door. You pass through a metal detector so old it might be steam-powered. The three guards chatting beside it pointedly ignore the beeping sounds it emits. At an old-fashioned ticket window with blinds and bars, you struggle to understand the woman's words that burst forth from a square, staticky speaker.

You slide your money through an opening in the glass, and in return the woman gives you something so amazing you blink in disbelief.

It's an antique plastic token, blue and chipped and translucent, stamped with an *M*. It's the type of collector's item you'd expect to see on eBay or in a severely underfunded museum. *This actually gets you on the metro?!* you think.

It does, because the Tashkent metro seems to operate on the honor system. You drop your novelty-style token into a novelty-style turnstile, and you walk through an empty space that probably once had fare gates. You get the sense that you could just as easily not drop your novelty token in the novelty turnstile and still walk through.

The sight of the escalator leading down to the tracks surprises me. It looks like it was lifted from a department store fifty years ago. Retro steps with thick teeth descend wood-paneled balustrades punctuated by lamps.

The weirdest part is, it all seems familiar. The lightning speed with which the steps fly away from the platform, the small leap of faith it takes to get on, the thick, rubber handrails you grip so that you don't topple forward.

I remember these, I think, as I run my hands along the wooden siding and feel the jolt of the motor under my feet, but of course I don't. This type of escalator would have been out of use long before I was born. When I get to the bottom, there's an attendant booth *right where I'm expecting it,* but how did I know this?

When I reach the platform, I freeze. An elegant marble floor stretches out beneath a vaulted ceiling, and beside the track, I see an old, boxy train car, painted summer-sky blue. It looks like an old model train come to life.

It's as if time stopped in 1979 in this station. Everything, from the font used to label the map of stops on the wall, to the train's cushioned, leather seats, belongs to another era, and it delivers the emotional gut punch that comes from catching the whiff of the renovation fumes that lingered in your first apartment, or rummaging through a junk drawer and knocking against a forgotten childhood toy.

But, of course, these artifacts don't belong to my lifetime. They're memories inherited from my parents and grandparents. It looks familiar because I've seen it in movies, old photographs, heard about it in my parents' stories.

Why do I feel paralyzed by a powerful swell of nostalgia? Am I longing for the '70s? For bell-bottoms and recessions and some of the worst music ever created? Even my dad, who puts on rose-colored glasses any time he looks back in time, never misses a chance to yell, "The seventies sucked!"

The past is something I'm used to experiencing at a distance, reconstructed in museums, where it's cordoned off and viewed from behind glass cases and velour ropes. To be able to walk through and interact with it, and to be the only one to whom this isn't completely normal, provides a brief, tantalizing illusion that we can go back in time.

If an old escalator can dump me out in 1977, maybe the next one will ferry me back five years, or two, or three months, and I can go back and undo all my mistakes. Maybe I can tell Anton I'm sorry.

I stare at the train.

Here's the other weird thing: there's something about all this that feels so American. I can't quite put my finger on it. It's not the New York subway system, and it's not Boston's, although it's maybe vaguely reminiscent of DC's, which makes sense, because Tashkent and Washington opened their metros within a year of each other.

It's less the design elements and more the feel. Some sense that it was inspired by a mix of grandiosity and worship of human progress. The insistence on wide, clean open spaces. The feeling of looking toward the future my parents were promised, the one in which technology would ferry us into a new era of flying cars and anthropomorphic robots.

Which is not to say that there aren't differences. Each Tashkent metro station is a work of art: some simple, others dripping with ornate chandeliers and detailed murals. One station feels like a church, with painted cupolas and marble columns, another a memorial to the cosmonauts, with bronze reliefs of Yuri Gagarin.

I'm struck more by what feels familiar. It's not the last time that I'll notice that, as the U.S. and Soviet Union were facing off in a nuclear war that could destroy the world as they knew it, they were also designing buildings and erecting infrastructure that carried eerie echoes of those built by their sworn enemies.

I show up at the Russian embassy thirty minutes before it closes with a few million som in garbage bags. The guard grins as he checks me in. I've finally worn him down.

"Did you buy your ticket?" he asks.

"I bought four!" I tell him proudly.

I'm escorted to the payment window upstairs, which is staffed by the same woman from the visa window, only this time, she's hidden behind tinted glass. I dump mountains of cash from the garbage bags into the sliding drawer, assuming that the woman on the other side will have some sort of electronic bill counter.

But when I squint through the window, I see that she's counting it out by hand, and she's called another colleague over to help. I try to do the same on my side, but I keep getting confused and having to start over. Every so often, the women yell for more money, and I dump more from the garbage bags into the sliding tray. There are times in life when you just have to trust people counting your money behind tinted windows.

Eventually, they indicate that I've paid enough, and even pass me back some change, along with a receipt and a notarized copy of my passport photo page.

I leave the embassy, with the promise of a visa obtained for almost half the price, four transportation tickets, and an overwhelming sense of accomplishment. Also camaraderie. I've spent two days with the embassy staff, complaining and queuing and waiting, and in that time, they've somehow come to feel like old friends.

On the way out, I have an urge to high-five the guard at the door. I remember just in time that we're separated by three inches of bulletproof glass.

Maria from the Belarusian embassy puts me in touch with her friend Alonya, who sells health insurance plans that cover Belarus. I take the subway to Alonya's office more or less on a whim; from what little I know about health insurance, there's no way I'll be able to afford it.

Alonya is an ethnically Russian Uzbekistani woman in her midtwenties with shiny blonde hair and long painted fingernails. She speaks good English and has a decent job working for an insurance company in Tashkent. In the handful of years since she finished school, she became a young bride and a slightly less young divorcée.

Alonya loves Nicholas Sparks and Ivanka Trump. Both were

sources of comfort and support instrumental in getting her through her divorce. It's October 2015, and I've barely heard of Ivanka Trump. I tell Alonya this, and she gasps.

"You don't know her website, Women Who Work?" she asks.

"She works?" I reply.

Alonya nods admiringly. "She believes women can have a career *and* a family."

"I believe that, too," I concede.

People tend to marry younger across the former Soviet Union. Anton and his wife wed when he was twenty-one and she was twenty; they were parents a year later. In Central Asia especially, women who marry while still in school are less likely to finish their education.

Alonya has been galvanized by her divorce. She started taking English lessons and learning about America.

"How is Newark?" she asks me. "I've always wanted to go to Newark."

"You mean New York?" I ask.

"No," she corrects me. "Newark." New York is too big and flashy, but Newark seems smaller and more manageable. Then she has another question. "Can Democrats and Republicans get married?"

Of course, I tell her. Her post-divorce English classes were taught by an American man who somehow left the class with the impression that in his country, people on opposite ends of the political spectrum couldn't marry.

"It's probably hard," I acknowledge. "But it's definitely allowed."

Alonya shakes her head. "In our country," she explains, "nationality is a barrier, but not politics." Her most recent boyfriend was Uzbek. I realize this must have been how that ended, and I feel for her.

Alonya is keeping up this conversation while filling out paperwork for my Belarusian health insurance, which I haven't had the heart to tell her I'm worried I won't be able to afford. She continues to insist that I check out Ivanka Trump's website.

"Before I found it, I had never heard these ideas!" she exclaims. "That it's also good for women to have jobs—that way we can be strong and independent." She sighs. "Ivanka Trump is my hero."

I have probably never felt so conflicted. On the one hand, I want to tell her that Ivanka Trump is a largely irrelevant socialite (oh, would that that were still true!). But maybe it's best not to shoot Alonya's messenger if the right message is getting through. (Though perhaps Camilla can start a website for the next Alonya?)

"Sign this," Alonya declares, pushing paperwork across the table.

I gulp. "How much is health insurance for a week in Belarus?"

Alonya frowns. "Let me check." She looks up something on her ancient desktop computer and types numbers into a calculator. My heart sinks because I'm sure I already know the answer. It's going to be $100, $200—some number too large for me to justify going to Belarus.

Alonya turns the calculator screen toward me. "In American money, it will be 5 dollars."

I blink. "5 . . . U.S. dollars?"

"Yes."

I'm so giddy I could kiss Alonya. "I'll take it!" I exclaim. I'm going to Belarus! This must be what it feels like to find out you're inheriting a small fortune or that you finally mastered contouring. I think of the time I spent with Anton imagining this very moment— having a Belarusian visa on lock—and how much further away it seemed in the years since we split up.

Alonya walks me outside. "I'm so happy you came," she tells me. "My ex-boyfriend and I used to speak in English, and now . . ."

"I'm happy we met, too," I tell her. And it's true: Uzbekistan, I'm realizing, is where dreams come true.

Before I leave, Alonya has one last question. "Your comedy," she asks, "is it cruel?"

7

TRAINS, TOMBS, AND OVARIES
(UZBEKISTAN)

As a tourist in Uzbekistan, you are culturally, aesthetically, and morally obligated to see Samarkand. When you imagine a dreamy Central Asian city rising like an oasis from the desert, you're picturing Samarkand. It's filled with blue-tiled domes and jaw-dropping madrasas that you hear look the same today as they did six hundred years ago.

In the 1300s, Samarkand became the capital of an empire founded by a brutal warlord named Timur. He was known for his love of the arts, and his love of ruthlessly murdering his enemies. His citadel, Samarkand, reflects both interests.

The problem, if indeed it is one, is that the oldest parts of the city have been heavily restored.

If you're in Central Asia, this is all you hear about Samarkand. "It's beautiful," people will tell you after stepping off a whirlwind bus tour. "But, you know, it's basically been rebuilt." They say this as though the decision to not leave ancient structures lying in ruins is an unequivocal moral failing. The most vitriolic offer the most damning condemnation. They lean in and whisper, shuddering, "It's like *Disneyland*."

Samarkand fell into decline along with the empire that built it. Its once mythic buildings crumbled as the landlocked empire was cut out of trade profits as sea routes supplanted the overland Silk Road. The region's predisposition to earthquakes wasn't doing architectural preservation any favors. By the twentieth century, the historic quarters were turning to rubble. The Soviets started restoring Samarkand's historic sites in the 1960s, and conservation work continues today.

Because I want to see this all for myself, I'm taking a train to Samarkand. I'm somewhat dreading this journey because I'm not too crazy about trains. Yes, the views are nice, but trains are slow and we don't want to know how the bathroom works.

I've never understood people who buy Eurail passes or dream of taking the Trans-Siberian Railway. I won't even watch the thriller *Transsiberian*, because I'm worried I'd scream at the wrong parts, like when the camera pans to the tiny sleeping berths.

Although as soon as I see my train, I soften slightly. It's a stately green-and-white-striped Soviet model, with curtained windows and a hammer and sickle on the outside of each carriage.

Like with the subway in Tashkent, stepping onto this train feels like stepping back in time. An attendant in a pillbox hat checks my ticket against my passport before ushering me into a carpeted hallway lined with old-fashioned compartments.

My compartment-mates are four older men in embroidered four-sided hats and a quiet, cherubic six-year-old girl. She wears a pressed checkered dress and spotless white tights; her hair is curled and carefully pinned back. Strangest of all, her grandfather has brought *nothing* with which to entertain her: no toys or books or paper to draw on. She sits quietly and stares straight ahead.

As the train pulls out of the station, the men pull back the curtains and chat amiably, after a while with me.

"New York!" one exclaims after hearing where I'm from. "There are *many* Uzbeks living in New York."

"Really?" I say.

They're surprised that I didn't know this. "In Brooklyn," one adds.

"I lived in Brooklyn!" I exclaim.

"They live near the *velodrome*," one says.

Though it's an English word, I've never heard it before, and it takes me a minute to figure out it's some kind of arena for bicycles. I can think of few things that sound more Soviet. "Oh no, we don't have that in Brooklyn," I assure them.

Guess who turns out to know more about what is and is not in Brooklyn? (Hint: it's the Uzbek grandpas who have never been there.) Although why are all the Uzbeks congregating around the velodrome?

The men start spreading newspapers over the table in our compartment and laying out bread and jam and meats. They insist that I have some. Before we eat, they offer a blessing over the food, and I know how to do the part at the end, where we all run our hands over our faces.

Anton and I take a lot of trains. We live in cities separated by a thirty-minute trip on a high-speed rail, and it feels like one of us is forever on a train, the other waiting for it to arrive.

They are sleek, bullet-nosed engines that tear between cities at speeds displayed in real time on monitors inside the carriage. I watch the number climb beside the familiar blur of scenery: 100 kilometers per hour, city high-rises; 150 kph, factory sprawl; 180, field of power lines; 200, farmland. It always maxes out in the mid-220s, but I stare at the number anyway, willing it to go higher.

Anton saves all of our tickets, sky-blue cards the size of a driver's license.

After we break up, I throw away all the tickets I hadn't yet given him, and gradually, everything else that reminds me of him. My pride is wounded and I need to destroy the evidence. Each day I carry a few more things out to the garbage bins behind my apartment. One day the notes, the next the cheap sunglasses he bought glue to fix while I was sleeping. In the end there are, inevitably, the few things I can't bring myself to discard with kitchen trash: his clothes, Vadik's drawings, an oversized sweater he'd given me for Christmas. These are stuffed in a bag and shoved into the back of a closet and I tell myself at least I'll never have to walk around my apartment and see things that make me think of him. It doesn't help; even without visual reminders, he's all I can think about.

A few months later I'm moving to New York and Anton comes to Shanghai to say goodbye. I take out the bag and hand it to him. He starts pulling things out, happy at first ("my sweatshirt!"), but when he gets to the sweater, he looks surprised. It's navy blue with red and orange Charlie Brown stripes. There was a time when I wore it constantly.

"It was a gift," he says. "You don't have to give it back."

"I know," I reply, "but I wouldn't want to wear it with the next person . . ."

I'd wanted to say that but pretend it slipped out when his face stiffens and he closes the bag and stuffs it in his backpack. "I'm sorry," I lie.

"No, you're right," he replies, all fake cheerful.

It's the reaction I wanted, but not the outcome. He goes into the kitchen and starts putting on his shoes.

All day we've been waiting for the other to read our mind. I'd headlined my last show in Shanghai the night before, and though we only had plans to meet today, Anton came to Shanghai a night early and slept in a hostel.

"You should have known to call me and tell me to come to your show," he said earlier. "Then we would have had this whole romantic night together—that was how it was supposed to happen."

You should have known just to come, I thought.

Back in my kitchen, Anton is texting someone—from his smile, it feels like a woman, but I don't ask—and anxious to leave. He looks up and glances around the kitchen. "I can't believe this is the last time I'll be in this apartment," he says.

I start crying. "Sorry," I say. "You remember—I cry really easily, and it looked like you were going to cry."

"I wasn't going to cry," he says, shaking his head. He stands up. "I have to go."

Is dyslexia with directions a thing? If it is, Anton has this. I have to walk him to the metro station he's been to a thousand times before, because he never learned the way. I take the least direct route possible. Even he notices.

"Did you take us a really long way on purpose?" he asks. "Because you don't want me to go?"

"Yes," I admit.

Later that night he texts me. "There's a woman on the train wearing the sweater you gave back to me. It's a sign."

I write back, "Haha, sign of what?"

He never responds.

In the years that follow, Anton's picture sometimes pops up on my feed, and I quickly scroll past, because whatever it is, it's easier not to know.

But a few times something catches my eye and I can't help myself. I go back and look at the picture more closely. He's wearing my sweater.

Los Angeles is a city built on the entertainment industry. Washington, DC, exudes power and influence. Modern Samarkand's vibe is "Welcome, tourists!"

It's a city ruled by coach buses full of retirees. I actually kind of have to give them credit for coming to Uzbekistan. They are, presumably, aware of Florida.

Still, it's an unsettling change of pace from the rest of Central Asia, where friendly strangers invite you to their babies' birthday parties. In Samarkand, the friendly strangers are most likely soliciting bribes to take you up a minaret.

I meet Farhod in the parking lot of the Samarkand train station, where he's idling his car and blasting his air-conditioning. When I tell him, in terrible Russian, where I want to go, he shoots me a look of disgust.

"Do you speak English?" he asks. "Speak to me in English, okay."

Like everyone else in Samarkand, Farhod is trying to sell me something, but unlike everyone else, he makes no attempts to be polite, friendly, or likable.

This initially seems like a good thing. While everyone else is asking me where I'm from or trying to lure me into small talk in order to blindside me with a sales pitch, Farhod prefers to insult me.

As soon as I've hired him to drive me around Samarkand for the day, he begins offering unsolicited feedback.

First, there's my choice of guesthouse.

"That place is terrible," he tells me. He says that a guidebook rebranded an old, dusty accommodation as "cozy" and "charming," and that he knows a much better place.

I assume that he "knows" the much better place because they "give him a cut of the deal," but I let him take me to both—first the place I booked, which seems quaint but is, as promised, a little worn and loved, and then Farhod's place, which is newer and cheaper and more centrally located. I decide that even if Farhod is getting a kickback, I'd rather stay here.

"I'll take it," I tell Farhod.

Then, in a move I did not see coming, he turns to the manager and throws a fit.

The room they've offered me is on the ground floor, and for this, Farhod wants a steep discount. I wonder if this is part of the charade, but then the shouting continues and he bargains them down so low that he would presumably eat up much of any potential kickback.

He finally nods and tells me I can move my stuff in. The manager glares at Farhod until he understands that he should wait outside.

I'm beginning to see why Farhod has to find clients outside of the train station.

Next we go to lunch. "Putin's birthday was yesterday," Farhod tells me, in an attempt at small talk.

"Oh," I say.

"When's Obama's birthday?" he asks.

I tell him I have no idea.

"You don't know your own president's birthday?" He shakes his head.

I want to point out that Putin isn't his president, either, but instead I ask about the history of Uzbekistan. It turns out he's much more interested in telling me about prison tattoos and pointing out how great it is that you can buy guns in America.

"So who built Samarkand?" I ask.

"One of our great heroes, Timur," he says. Then he glances furtively around the restaurant. "I was just looking for prison tattoos," he confides.

Prison tattoos became prevalent in the Stalinist era and served as a way of distinguishing political criminals from "common law" convicts. I ask Farhod how he knows this, hoping there's some interesting story behind his fascination. "Wikipedia," he tells me.

As Farhod and I work our way through *plov*, a tasty, oily staple of Central Asian cuisine made from rice, meat, and spices, I glean a few details about Farhod's life.

Like many people from Samarkand, Farhod's ancestors are a mix of Afghan, Uzbek, and Tajik. Ancient cities famed for being centers of trade and learning remain, unsurprisingly, culturally diverse today.

Samarkand is part of modern-day Uzbekistan, but its citizens are predominantly ethnic Tajiks. They carry Uzbekistani passports but tend to identify, culturally, as Tajik, and they speak Tajik, not Uzbek, at home.

Samarkand has a long history of being ethnically Tajik and administratively something else, having been ruled by, among others, Alexander the Great, the Turks, Genghis Khan, the Timurids, some emirs, the Russians, the Soviets, and now the Uzbeks. Some Tajik nationalists call for Samarkand and the nearby predominantly Tajik city of Bukhara to be "reunited" with Tajikistan, but it's complicated, and perhaps a little like Xi Jinping trying to reincorporate Chinatown into regular China.

Farhod spent a few years in Korea in his early twenties. When I ask him what he did there, he tells me he built a house for Jackie

Chan. Farhod says it was fun and free, and then gazes wistfully at the artwork above my head, which happens to depict two mermaids in the throes of copulation. I decide to ask no further questions about that.

Farhod moved back to Uzbekistan to settle down and start a family. His wife just had their fourth child. He tells me it's important to have a family, especially for women. I want to say that it sounds a lot like he would rather be back in Korea.

"I hope you don't like girls," he says. "My last client was a Finnish novelist, and she was also a lesbian."

At this point, Farhod is driving. He takes out his phone, without pulling over, and starts scrolling through pictures to show me what she looked like.

"I don't mind!" he insists, showing me pictures of the Finnish woman, smiling, in a gun range in the desert. "I was just shocked!"

I'm starting to realize I mind Farhod.

Farhod claims to be the only guide in Samarkand with a Wi-Fi hot spot in his car. He does not see why people visiting a five-hundred-year-old city might not care about Wi-Fi. Farhod wears a Bluetooth headset and is messaging someone on WhatsApp, the free intentional communication app, whenever he's not talking and occasionally while he's driving.

He takes me to the Ulugh Beg Observatory, which was built atop a giant, curved ramp that looks like the kind of thing you'd roll a metal ball down in a science museum. Farhod delivers a lively, engaging lecture on the history of Samarkand, its most famous ruler, Timur, and his grandson Ulugh Beg, a terrible ruler but decent astronomer whose greatest achievements include allowing his empire to crumble and building this ramp and an adjacent observatory in the 1420s. The observatory was promptly destroyed by religious fanatics, and the ramp, which is all that has survived, was rediscovered by a Russian archaeologist in 1908.

"They could look at the ramp," Farhod explains, "and know exactly what time it was." He walks up to the observation platform and yells at a group of middle-aged tourists until they move away. "See?"

"Ohhh," I say, trying to sound like I do.

"Ulugh Beg also found mistakes in other maps of the stars," he says, "and Samarkand was too far away to know that!"

"Wow," I say, nodding knowingly but thinking that doesn't quite make sense.

"I think you don't understand," Farhod snaps. But he doesn't explain anything further.

In an adjacent history museum, Farhod walks me through a brief overview of the Timurid Empire, under which the aforementioned Timur united much of Central Asia and the predecessor of modern Uzbekistan. The Uzbeks claim Timur because he came from Samarkand and because he makes a good hero, as long as you end the story after he handily captures most of the Middle East and before he heads off to China to die of a cold.

Farhod leaves me to wander around the compound. Wedding parties line up to take photos outside of the museum. In Central Asia, people take wedding portraits in front of local tourist attractions. On the day of the wedding, the couple rents a limo and heads out with the wedding party and a photographer, and stops at each famous site. Many brides have taken to wearing white wedding dresses, often with what looks like forty pounds of tulle and sequins, instead of the colorful traditional Uzbek gowns. Outside of the observatory, I find a solitary acrylic fingernail on the ground. I think of the bride, wandering around Samarkand on the most important day of her life, trying to conceal one finger in her wedding photographs. Or maybe her friend brought spares? Or maybe the fingernail belonged to her friend? Or maybe losing a fingernail is good luck at an Uzbek wedding?

Farhod and I visit tombs and madrases and the Registan, an iconic plaza of buildings dating back hundreds of years and Samarkand's main tourist attraction today. Farhod delivers more rousing lectures on Uzbek culture and history and then, with almost psychopathic abruptness, goes back to messaging someone on his phone with his screen tilted away from me.

The buildings are stunning. They're elongated two- and three-story structures of sand brick with arched windows and ornate entrances made to seem larger with a series of inlaid arches. Turquoise cupolas and columns extend from the façade, which is the real draw. The façades are covered in tiles every shade of blue and turquoise imaginable, which come together to form intricate patterns and designs that punctuate the architectural undulating shapes.

Farhod soon abandons any pretext of likability. He begins quizzing me on names he mentioned earlier and, when I can't remember them, declares that he won't read my book. If I appear anything less than blown away by each detail he tells me, he overexplains it until I feign shock and awe.

"The pomegranate symbolizes fertility," he says, gesturing to a piece of embroidery.

"Oh," I say.

He stares. "You knew that already?"

I tell him I didn't.

"A pomegranate has many seeds," he continues. "So it's like fertility."

"Ohhhhh," I reply, mimicking the way my Chinese teacher taught me to vocalize the hardest rising and falling third tone. "Pretend that someone has just explained something to you that you never understood," she would say.

"See?" Farhod asks.

"Yeah. Wow!"

"You didn't understand at first."

Farhod asks me if I'm married, and I decide to tell him the truth. I'm not exactly sure why. I guess I'm getting tired of lying about having a fiancé, though part of me is sad to see him go. I've built up quite a backstory about my fiancé, Alex, or sometimes Mikhail, whom I met in college, or followed to Tajikistan, or caught in a candid moment while he was crossing the street in Almaty. Before the copy shop incident, we always plan to marry on my birthday, and he's from Ukraine, or sometimes Belarus. Often he's just Anton or Oleg with a few details changed, or not.

Unless there's a visa on the line, I don't really enjoy or excel at lying. My fiancé only opens the door for more lies, when people follow with polite questions like what's his name, how old is he, can I see a picture? This last one has left me scrambling to pull out my phone and pull up the first picture of a male I stumble on, which is often Vianney or Januzak, and sometimes a stranger in the background of a picture I was taking. "Yes," I say, "we like doing this thing where he walks by a Lenin statue while I stand across the street taking a picture of the statue and trying not to catch him in the frame."

"No," I tell Farhod. "I'm not married."

"Boyfriend?" he asks.

Again, I opt for honesty. "Nope."

"And you're twenty-eight?" Farhod exhales sharply and shakes his head. "You need to get married soon."

I shrug. "Maybe."

"You need to start having children soon," he implores.

Sometimes I wonder if firefighters evacuating a woman from a burning building in Central Asia would run into a room and yell, "THE BUILDING IS ON FIRE! By the way, do you have a husband?"

Most of the time, people here ask if I'm married in the same way people back home ask what I do for a living. They're just trying to find something to talk about. I wonder if they ask if I'm married because they assume I don't have a career, and if men get asked about their job.

I'm more uncomfortable when a man asks me about my marital status. I sometimes worry he's doing preliminary research before proposing. Or worse.

But I've started to doubt a made-up fiancé would save me from serious harm. If someone wants to harass or hurt me, would he stop if he believed I was betrothed? People who engage in predatory behavior aren't known for making sure potential victims are single. I've never heard a catcaller yell, "BEFORE I TELL YOU HOW GOOD YOUR ASS LOOKS IN THOSE SWEATPANTS, LET ME CHECK TO MAKE SURE YOU'RE EMOTIONALLY AVAILABLE."

I reason I can just as easily ward off unwanted advances by standing up for myself. But Farhod's unwanted advances aren't romantic overtures, they're pep talks from the 1950s.

"Why aren't you married?" he asks.

"Because I haven't met anyone I wanted to marry," I say honestly.

"Do you want children?"

"Maybe someday."

This line of questioning continues throughout the tour of Samarkand's extraordinary turquoise-tiled tombs and its ancient Jewish cemetery.

"If you don't have children, who will take care of you when you're old?" he asks as he leads me through the graveyards.

Who will take care of you if all of your children die? I want to ask. At first, these inane inquiries roll off my back, because I could not care less what Farhod thinks of my future plans, but over the course of the day, his questions close in on the nerve he's trying to hit.

It's not that Farhod is the first to suggest there's a bomb strapped to my chest, counting down to the moment I hit menopause. There's nothing he can say that I haven't freaked out about a thousand times. In leaving for this trip, I felt I had made as much peace with these questions as two decades of internalized patriarchal notions would allow.

But there's something about being alone and having to explain deeply personal things to strangers that's making me question everything again. I understand that in Uzbekistan, these questions don't sound like an interrogation, and they're not intended to function as the relationship equivalent of graphic health warnings on cigarette packs. But from an American perspective, they make me feel deeply flawed and irredeemably unlovable.

I try to steer the conversation toward Samarkand, Uzbek history, or anything else, but I sense resistance.

"Look!" Farhod finally explodes. "You're twenty-eight. If you wanna have kids, you have ten, maybe eleven good years left!"

This unsolicited advice is probably not medically sound and also one of the meanest things anyone has ever said to me.

In the movie version I've played out in my head countless times since this day, this is the moment when I demand that Farhod pull the car over, get out without paying him, and walk off while describing, in very vivid languages, the numerous and varied ways in which he can go fuck himself. I'm vulgar and defiant in every way that he thinks a woman should never be.

In reality, I force myself to sound cheerful. "If it happens," I tell him, or I don't know, maybe myself, "it'll happen."

The train to Samarkand had opened me to the possibility of falling in love with the iron horse; on the overnight train back to Tashkent, this romance comes to a screeching halt.

The first train charmed me with its old-fashioned comforts: the compartments and carpets and tablecloths. I expected the overnight train to resemble a miniature apartment on rails, like the flights to Dubai with personal showers.

Instead, I find four bunk beds crammed into a tiny compartment filled with three large men. This is not the gender ratio of the slumber party I'd envisioned.

The first thing that becomes clear is that there's no space for my suitcase, which is as bulky and easy to maneuver as a rolling fourth grader. But the men gamely lift it over their heads and attempt to shove it into some unseen bulkhead, while I fret that they'll drop it on their heads and get concussions and/or ruin their hats.

They try to tell me something in Russian, which is probably, *You have eighty pounds of crap in a suitcase with the buoyancy of a stack of folding chairs*, but I don't understand. I look around helplessly. I realize that I had been right about trains: they're horrible, inefficient modes of transportation that trap you inside scary compartments with too many men and not enough room for your beauty products. I wonder if it's too late to hitchhike back to Tashkent.

A young boy pokes his head into the hallway. "Do you speak English?" he asks.

"Yes!" I cry. He has kind eyes and a soccer jersey, and he is here to save me.

The boy's name is Husein, and he's traveling to Tashkent to take the IELTS exam with his identical twin, Hasan. To me, they look nothing alike.

"You're twins?!" I ask.

They look surprised. "You didn't notice?" Hasan asks.

The boys have arranged for me to swap spots with a random man in their cabin, so now, instead of spending the night with three Uzbek men, I'm spending it with two Uzbek teenagers, and their managed chaperone.

Husein jumps down from the top bunk and stands next to Hasan so that I can verify their twinness. Husein is more solidly built than his brother, who still has a child's long, bony limbs and soft torso.

"You're not . . . fraternal?" I ask delicately. "*Fraternal* means . . ." I try to look up the word in my dictionary, but Hasan cuts me off.

"I know," he says. I nod. This bodes well for his IELTS.

IELTS stands for International English Language Testing System and is pronounced, nonintuitively, *i-elts*. Knowing this is often an indication of direct personal experience with the exam, which is administered to some 2.5 million test takers each year.

IELTS is supposed to measure a nonnative speaker's English language proficiency, and foreign students applying to most schools in the UK, Canada, and Australia are required to submit an IELTS score. In theory, it should be the kind of exam you can't study for, but in practice, a sufficiently motivated student will study for a Rorschach test.

Husein and Hasan are taking the IELTS because they want to apply to a British university that recently opened a satellite campus in Tashkent.

They're in luck, because the one skill people regularly pay me for is teaching kids how to take standardized tests.

I spent most of my twenties eking a living out of teaching, a job that I often performed begrudgingly and for an entire month each spring, under the influence of allergy medication that was not non-drowsy.

A friend originally told me to move to China because he said I'd be able to make a living teaching English part-time, leaving me plenty of time to write.

"But I don't know how to teach English," I said.

He rolled his eyes. "It's the easiest job in the world. You just talk to people."

Ten minutes into my first lesson, I realize he has been very mistaken.

Talking to someone for two hours is the easiest job in the world if that someone is a friend, a lover, or famed linguist named John McWhorter. When the someone is an eight-year-old girl, keeping up a conversation for two straight hours becomes a Herculean task.

"But wait!" you say. "My niece is in second grade, and when I hang out with her, the whole day flies by."

To that I say, yes, but her mother isn't hovering in the next room with the expectation that your conversation will be vaguely academic. You can't color. You can't pull up a YouTube video. You can't gossip about your brother or furtively pump her for family secrets. If you tried to make one hundred and twenty minutes of uninterrupted small talk, unaided by a parent or a snack or even a comfortable pause in the conversation, you, too, would begin SAT tutoring.

Like most IELTS takers, the twins are nervous about the speaking section. In it, they'll have to sit across from an IELTS examiner and speak for a full minute in response to such inspired questions as "What is your favorite animal?" and "Can you describe one of your neighbors?"

I offer to help them practice, and Hasan eagerly accepts, handing me a book of questions. Husein, I sense, would be just as happy if the helpless American girl he rescued from a compartment of strange men didn't return the favor by giving him homework.

Through their practice responses, I learn that both twins dream of celebrating New Year's under the Eiffel Tower in Paris. I learn that Husein's hero is Cristiano Ronaldo, and Hasan's is his father, because he worked hard and gave has family a good life. Hasan asks me if I've tried *plov*, and I tell him I have, and he asks me if I ate it with my hands, which I didn't.

"You should eat it with your hands," he tells me. "Because it's a different taste than eating it with a spoon, and it makes you full faster."

Hasan and Husein have been sent to Tashkent with their father's friend, a quiet man in his twenties who's brought along two liters of beer to entertain himself and an equal amount of Pepsi for the boys. He speaks a little English but is shy to use it.

When we take a break from studying, the chaperone asks me, through the boys, if I'd like a drink. I gratefully accept, assuming he'll pour some beer into a plastic cup. Instead, he reaches for the Pepsi.

It's a weird moment, and it shouldn't be a big deal, but for some reason it feels like I've been, perhaps not slapped in the face, but pinched lightly by a cooped-up sibling. I realize that it would never occur to him to offer me beer, because I'm a woman.

I'd seen our carriage as divided into two worlds: the adults (the chaperone and me) and the kids (Hasan and Husein). But I realize that, while the other three see a divide, they'd lumped me in with the children. I'd seen the chaperone as my equal; he probably hadn't seen me as his. I look at his freshly pocked face and naked wedding finger and realize I might be older.

And I know, I know, I know, that he didn't mean any harm, and that it's a cultural difference, but for a brief moment, I'm so, so glad that I get to walk out of this world at the end.

The twins are quadrilingual: they speak Tajik, which they use at home; Uzbek, which they learned when they got to school; Russian, which they studied later; and English, which came most recently.

Their school offered two tracks: one in Russian, the other in Uzbek. Both boys started out in Uzbek, but Hasan switched to the Russian program in middle school.

"And you could understand everything, right from the start?" I ask.

He shakes his head. Both boys strike me as fairly serious, but Hasan more so. Each word he uses feels so measured and carefully chosen that I feel like I'm talking to a forty-five-year-old who has aspirations of one day running for public office, and not an Uzbek teenager.

"At first, it was very hard," he tells me.

"So how did you take your classes?"

"Many of the students speak Uzbek, so they helped me," he says. "But it was very hard."

I take a sip of my Pepsi.

They ask me what I'm doing in Uzbekistan, and I tell them that I'm traveling through the former Soviet Union, studying Russian, writing about it, the whole spiel, minus the Russian boyfriends.

Hasan stares at me thoughtfully. "What are your interesting stories?" he asks.

Wow. That's a damn good question, and I do not have a good answer.

"Umm . . ." I try to think. "I did a comedy show in Kazakhstan? Opening for a meditative drum circle?"

Blank stares. "A meditative drum circle is like . . ." I think. "Do you want to see pictures?"

I fumble for my computer and feel deeply disturbed by the fact that the whole point of this trip is to generate and tell interesting stories, and I've utterly disappointed my first audience.

"Whoops, my computer's dead."

Hasan looks taken aback. "In English, if something has no electricity, you say, it is dead?" he asks.

I think back to my days as an English teacher, when students would ask me questions about aspects of grammar no native speaker ever considers, like the difference between the simple present and the present continuous. I'd run through examples in my head, trying to tease out a pattern, or say something like, "That's a good question. Class, can anyone give her an answer?"

I test a few sentences to see if they sound okay: *the calculator is dead, the phone is dead.* "I guess so," I say finally. *The fan is dead. No,* I think, *that doesn't sound right.* "Well, if, it's, like, something that holds a charge . . ."

Hasan's face is blank.

"Like, something you can plug in?" I try again, but no, a fan also plugs in. "Yeah, I guess, sure," I conclude, giving up.

Hasan considers. "In Uzbek language, you can also say a computer is dead," he concedes. "But in Russian, it would be very rude."

I make a note to remember this.

The chaperone has almost finished getting slowly, quietly drunk in the corner, and before we go to bed, I run through a few more questions with Hasan.

"What are the benefits of marriage?" I read off the page of his book.

He considers for a moment. "I don't know," he admits. "When people get married, they start to have problems."

8

AN INVITATION TO A STRANGER'S WEDDING (UZBEKISTAN)

I'm flying to Urgench, Uzbekistan, a city of little note except that it happens to have an airport. From Urgench, I will take a taxi to Khiva, another ancient city half-buried in the desert, allegedly given a fresh coat of paint to attract French pensioners.

While I'm waiting in line at the airport, probably wearing my face in its perpetual mask of *Am I lost?*, a guy my age in a sharp suit asks me, in English, if I'm flying to Urgench.

He has a sweet smile, and I tell him I am.

"You're in the right line," he assures me.

I thank him and turn back around, because I'm old enough to know the dangers of mixing small talk with air travel. Also, my experience with Farhod the tour guide/aspiring guerrilla fertility specialist has made me wary of interacting with the opposite sex.

This guy doesn't get the hint.

"What are you doing in Urgench?" he asks.

"I'm going to Khiva," I say, pressing my lips into a tight smile.

"What are you doing there?" he continues.

His name is Aziz, and he works as some kind of economic advisor for the government of Uzbekistan. The fact that he works for the state raises flags, because the Uzbekistani government is one step away from having to put up those posters that say, "It's been __ days since the international community condemned us for something that we think is totally okay and normal!" He lives in Tashkent, but he grew up in Urgench, and he's flying home to be the best man in his best friend's wedding.

"Are you traveling alone?" he asks, inevitably.

I nod and brace myself for one of three responses: *Are you afraid? You must be frightened!* And, as of earlier this morning, *That must be boring!*

But instead, he smiles and says, "That's cool."

He's cute, seems nice, and doesn't appear to be working up the courage to propose to and/or murder me, but I'm still wary. We chat more, and I learn he went to graduate school in Korea and travels all over the world for work. But this, too, seems suspect. What kind of economic advisor travels abroad for his job? Is this just a cover for more sinister work, like, perhaps *tracking down Uzbekistani dissidents abroad and bringing them to injustice?* Oh, except it's more like meeting with people about investment opportunities and joint ventures. Sometimes he goes to Shanghai. He describes a bar he went to on his most recent visit, and I recognize it from details he recounts.

This last reveal makes my heart soar with how small and knowable the world can be, how much more interconnected we all are than we think! I'm so high on this that I'm not prepared for the question he asks me as the bus drops us off at the stair car next to our airplane.

"Maybe we can ask someone to switch seats, so that we can sit together?"

I'm horrified.

Like anyone who constantly feels busy while juggling little to no actual responsibilities, I believe that a flight is *my time.* Airplanes are sacred for me because they are blissfully free of distraction. No one can call or text or send you a link to a Twitter-feed black hole that will swallow the rest of your workday. The hours that I spend with my devices in airplane mode are my most productive. My ritual for the fourteen-hour flight home from China includes pulling up my notes and interviews for a business report I've been avoiding, banging out the article, catching up on some reading, watching a movie, washing an Ambien down with a glass of wine, and then, depending on whether or not I've eaten dinner, potentially spilling my guts to the non-English-speaking grandmother beside me.

But I can't think of a good excuse fast enough, and so I say sure and pray that our seatmates will be unaccommodating.

Aziz exchanges a few words with a man in the aisle, and then turns to me and grins. "He says it's no problem."

Great, I think.

Aziz, like the little girl on the train, has brought NOTHING with which to distract himself on the flight. As we take off, Aziz and I continue to chat about our lives and our work and our travels, and when the conversation peters out, he stares serenely at the seat ahead of him, hands folded in his lap.

I wait for these pauses to grow long enough that I can politely switch on my Kindle, but each time we approach that critical moment, Aziz turns to me with another question.

I hear more about his work for the government, his trips to China. We chat about the differences between Central Asian cultures, and I ask him why the country shut down for a day in honor of a national teachers' holiday. "Teachers are very important to us," he says solemnly.

Aziz keeps bringing up Urgench, casually, almost shyly, suggesting I should visit, hinting that he'll show me around, and I feign a blissful obliviousness to protect myself from being murdered in a city whose Wikitravel page has a long, robust "Getting In" section, and nothing under "See," "Do," "Buy," "Eat," or "Drink."

Aziz tells me about Uzbekistan and I tell him about my trip, and at some point a flight attendant comes by with sandwiches that have the wrong bread-to-mayo ratio, which if you're even measuring in rations, you have a problem. I pick at mine politely while Aziz inhales his. After the food has been cleared, I'm staring at the clouds through the window, trying to finagle a way to turn on my Kindle, when Aziz turns to me.

"What are you doing tomorrow?" he asks.

I know where this is going and try desperately to deflect. "You know, like, looking around Khiva, and, um . . ." I trail off, defeated.

"You should come to the wedding with me."

Should I?

Arguments in favor: When the flight attendant announces we're about to land, I'm surprised. It feels like we just took off. Somehow, my conversation with Aziz made the flight zip by. I suddenly realize how handsome he is.

Arguments against: At baggage claim, Aziz turns into a different person. In the air, he'd been zen and demure, hands folded like a Buddhist monk, but on the ground, he's glued to his cell phone. He's distracted. He keeps cutting me off.

This frazzled, phone-addled Aziz is kind of making me hope that he's forgotten about this whole wedding invitation thing, but no, no, he wants me to come back to Urgench tomorrow so that he can show me around and then take me to his friend's wedding.

Outside the train station, there's a driver waiting with my name on a sign. I'm embarrassed by how ostentatious this seems, and also because the sign says "Mr. Audrey Murray."

"Your surname is *Murray?*" Aziz laughs. I tell him it is. I don't ask why it's funny. I promise to see him tomorrow, though I'm kind of hoping I won't. Although, crap, now he knows my full name.

By the next morning, I'm full of indecision over whether I want to go to the wedding. On the one hand, weddings are fun, and I'm eager to disprove the taxi driver from the airport who insinuated that I have no friends, and therefore no life. On the other hand, I can't shake the feeling that inviting a stranger on an airplane to a wedding feels like something only a murderer would do. A polite murderer. But still.

I decide to check out Khiva in case I have to meet Aziz for a tour of this stupid city Urgench, whose main tourist attraction Aziz has described as a statue of a book.

The guidebook swears that Khiva is best viewed at dawn from a high vantage. It suggests that I watch the sunrise from atop the Islom Hoja Minaret, letting the majestic splendor of the ancient mudstone buildings wash over me and inspire me to paint or write poetry or leap to my death. Instead, I climb to the roof of my guest-house, where I catch the last pink twinges of sunrise hovering over the patchwork of flat roofs, punctuated by turquoise cupolas. I am awash in feelings of coldness, and also hunger.

After breakfast, I call Aziz to see where he wants to meet and what he meant by "afternoon." He doesn't answer.

Unfazed, I head out to explore Khiva.

I wander into an old temple with matchstick pillars burrowed un-der the street. Inside, it's cold and dark, save from light streaming in through a skylight, and empty, except for a woman selling knitted shoes.

Climbing the dark, winding stairs of the adjacent tower, I pass a young Uzbek couple passionately making out, oblivious to the American tourist awkwardly trying to step around them while sud-denly realizing why Uzbekistan might have so many towers.

From the top, the city is a swath of buildings as brown as the sand that birthed them. At the bottom, I call Aziz again. No answer. I send him a text message. My screen darkens with the heaviness of an unanswered question.

I begin to wonder if I've been uninvited from the wedding.

"So, I can wear anything to a wedding?" It's still unconfirmed whether I'll be going, but I'm soliciting wardrobe advice from my guesthouse manager, Jaloladdin, who, if I'm being honest, is start-ing to freak me out a little. His tendency to speak without facial expression is coupled with a habit of appearing in rooms suddenly, without noise or warning. He's already made me yelp twice, and not in the *I have very strong opinions about this bakery* sense.

"Yes." He nods. He looks at my jeans and turquoise Windbreaker. "This is fine to wear to the wedding."

I'm horrified. "No, no," I say. I hold the black dress I've brought down from my room to show him. "I have this dress," I explain. "But I'm not sure if it's bad to wear black to a wedding in Uzbekistan?"

"It's not a problem," he insists.

I'm suspicious of any sartorial tips from someone who suggested I wear outdoor gear to a wedding, so I ask Jaloladdin to check with his non-English-speaking sisters in the back room. Jaloladdin emerges from a "discussion" thirty seconds later and assures me that they agree.

At the very least, I suspect it would be inappropriate for me to expose my bare legs, so I head to a market just inside the gates of the old town. It's the type of Central Asian one-stop shop where you can buy everything from knockoff DVDs to a freshly slaughtered goat. The one thing that turns out to be difficult to find is tights.

I wander the aisles of fruit and Chinese electronics and underwear, casually striking up conversations with vendors who might be able to give me fashion tips.

"My friend is getting married," I say. "In Uzbekistan, wedding, black?"

The more I fear my invitation has been rescinded, the greater my need to run the potential story by strangers, gauge their reactions, and see what I might be missing. I check my phone: still no response from Aziz.

I finally find a woman selling tights. The only pair for sale is loose-fitting and slouchy, with a control top that offers no control and is covered in butterflies.

"I'm going to my friend's wedding," I say.

She smiles and nods.

I stare at my phone, as though I can will the black screen to light up with an incoming message.

I visit an ancient palace filled with elegantly tiled courtyards and a pop-up store that sells PVC piping.

"Women in Khorezm are famous for special dancing," Aziz told me on the plane, which makes me even sadder for what could have been, dance floor–wise. I've mastered the sacred wedding party rituals that are the Macarena and the Cotton-Eyed Joe, and I can usually even fake my way through the Electric Slide.

Finally, at the hostel, I call one last time, reasoning that, if I keep this up, Aziz will have just cause for filing a restraining order. This time, someone picks up, and after a long breath, I hear, "Hello?"

Now that the wedding attending is back on, so are my concerns that I might be out of place, or severely underdressed, or at risk of being murdered.

But while there are plenty of people I can pester about wearing black, I don't have anyone to whom I can say, *Is this weird?* I can't ask Jaloladdin, because I've insinuated, via repeated insistence, that the person getting married is a friend, and it seems a little late to clarify that when I said *friend*, I meant *stranger*.

I put on my dress and my butterfly control-top tights and stare at myself in the mirror. I decide that I will be brave. And if that doesn't work, I'll do what people do when they're uncomfortable at weddings the world over: get drunk.

The driver chauffeuring me to Urgench flashes a thumbs-up to each car we pass. At first, I assume he's having an unusually great day, or that he finds the sight of the purple twilight creeping up over the fallow cotton fields as moving as I do, but just to check I ask him.

"It means there are no police," he tells me.

Oh, great. So he's scouting for murder locations, too.

The driver drops me off outside of a hair salon where Aziz is getting a trim. Aziz rushes out with a towel still draped around his shoulders. There's an awkward second where we're unsure how to greet each other, but then he reaches out and shakes my hand, and, in this moment, I know I'll be okay. I know Aziz won't try to murder or sacrifice or embarrass me. He apologizes for not being ready, then shows me to his car and rushes inside to finish his haircut.

As we drive to the groom's house for some kind of prewedding festivity, I find out why Aziz wasn't answering my calls this morning.

"There was a lot of vodka last night," he admits.

So he wasn't debating rescinding my invitation; he was hungover.

"Do you know about these houses?" Aziz asks, gesturing to a row of identical one-story yellow houses that keep reappearing between fallow fields. He tells me they're part of a rural housing initiative. In Uzbekistan, poverty is concentrated in the countryside, where, according to government statistics, 70 percent of the country's poor reside. An underdeveloped mortgage market makes it difficult for people to buy real estate with anything but cash; the housing initiative built homes and provided would-be home buyers with access to loans to buy them.

We pull into one of these developments, where the groom's parents live. Aziz leaves the car running as we head inside.

The house is small, but a fairly open-plan interior creates a sense of spaciousness. The floors are carpeted, and flies buzz lazily above the copious spread of fruits and candies, perhaps because the open windows have no screens.

The groom and his father wear identical tracksuits and seem unhurried in their preparations for the impending wedding.

Aziz says something to the groom, who turns to me and says hello in Chinese.

I blink. "Why do you speak Chinese?" I blurt out.

"I studied in China," he tells me. "And I go back every year for work."

Chinese feels stiff and ungainly in my mouth as I work to untangle it from the Russian I've spent a month leaning on for survival. The human brain has an annoying tendency not to distinguish between foreign languages, and mine has shelved French, Chinese, and Russian together on a rack labeled, "Languages you should not try to use in a medical emergency." I can say much more in Chinese than I can in Russian, but I find Russian words slipping into my Chinese. It's annoyingly simple words, too—things I've known how to say in Chinese for years. *Perhaps you were looking for the Russian word for work?* my brain offers. *Even though that constitutes a solid 10 percent of your total Russian vocabulary?*

The groom's mother fusses over us, making comments I don't understand.

"She's curious if you drink Coke," Aziz translates.

"Coke is American!" I exclaim, before realizing this answer makes no sense. "I am American," I add meekly.

Aziz announces it's time to go, and outside, I realize that his car has been idling for the past thirty minutes.

The wedding takes place in a cavernous reception hall the size of a small cruise ship. The ceilings are thirty feet high and dripping with chandeliers. The other guests are dressed in a wide array of attire. Most men wear suits, but some wear jeans, as do a few of the women. Most of the older women wear traditional tunics; the younger, modest dresses. It turns out Jaloladdin wasn't steering me wrong: I probably could have worn my Windbreaker.

Aziz drops me off at an empty table and, with an apologetic smile, abandons me to perform his best-manly duties. A bowl of fruit, loaves of bread, and two liters of vodka with mixers are spread out on the table.

I feel awkward sitting by myself, a sensation I remedy by taking four unnecessary trips to the bathroom.

I come back from one to find my table filled with fifteen guys who went to school with the groom and Aziz. They wear Western suits, sans ties, and the youthful grins of a reunion.

"We call him Titanic," one says, gesturing to a handsome man blushing on the other side of the table.

"Huh?"

"He looks like Leonardo DiCaprio, no?"

I consider. I suppose Titanic does resemble Leonardo DiCaprio, in that both men are incredibly good-looking and otherwise look nothing alike. "Oh, yeah," I say.

Everyone at the table speaks English because the boys attended a rigorous boarding school that they tested into but paid no money to attend. I feel a growing sense of commonality with my tablemates, who, like me, are twenty-eight, and speak English, and have traveled abroad.

And then there are ways in which we differ.

"How do you motivate your students?" Ruslan asks.

I'm sitting between Ruslan, an affable guy whose shirt stretches tight to reach across his belly, and his business partner Tim, who has a thin build and even thinner smile. Tim recently left his job at Coca-Cola to start a TOEFL training center with Ruslan because he wanted to be his own boss, which I guess means millennials also exist in Uzbekistan.

I try to give a brief overview of the specific strategies I've come up with for each section of the test, and then I ask them the same question in return.

"Corporal punishment!" they exclaim.

They are adamant that I try this approach.

"You know, some mothers, they come to me, and they say, 'How can I help my son do well on his test?' and I say, 'Let me hit him.'"

"Oh, wow!" I say. "That's probably—"

"You should visit our school tomorrow!" Ruslan adds, brightening.

My powers of observation evidently dulled by those trips to the bathroom, I'm slow to notice that men and women are sitting on opposite sides of the room.

When I do, I realize, to my horror, that I'm sitting on the men's side.

A dance floor divides the room in half: men on the left, women on the right, Audrey unwittingly shattering the glass ceiling in the middle. I'm not sure what to do. Should I feign ignorance? Use another gratuitous bathroom visit to join up with my sisters in arms? Run away?

Before I have time to answer this question, the wedding begins with a crescendo of thumping club music.

The groom has changed from his tracksuit into a regular suit, and we clap as he makes his way up the aisle, followed by his grooms-men. It's like an American wedding procession, only with Pitbull in place of Pachelbel's Canon.

The bride is the last to enter. She looks beautiful and *very* young. I spend the rest of the evening trying to discern her age: everyone pegs her for early twenties, a few years younger than her husband, but not scandalously so. I can't ask this, and no one offers confirmation, but to me, she seems far more attractive than the guy she's marrying, though my eye has yet to align with local beauty standards, like how unibrows are in.

Brides younger and more beautiful than their husbands are maybe the only thing more universal than feeling too big for the life you were born into or the polarizing effect of cilantro. But there's something unsettling about the couple standing alone on a stage that also awkwardly resembles a canopy bed.

I'm momentarily distracted, because the guys have cracked open the handle of vodka and are pouring shots into glasses that would pass for small wine goblets in America. They don't even bother offering me one, and, as I raise my glass of Coke to join their toast, I know that they skipped my glass for the same reason the identical twins' guardian poured me soda without thinking. They assume that, as a woman, I don't drink.

When they go to pour the next round of shots, I hold my glass out. Tim raises his eyebrows.

"You want?" he asks.

I remind myself of Ivanka Trump's words, delivered by Alonya: women can have a family and a career and a vodka.

"I want," I say.

The biggest difference between American and Uzbek weddings is that, at an Uzbek wedding, it's not all about the bride. It's not *her* day. In fact, for a solid chunk of the wedding, we seem to forget about the newlyweds, who are seated side by side on the stage, silently eating eat their dinners.

Meanwhile, I'm taking vodka shots, arm in arm, with the guys at my table. This is attracting a lot of attention. Two videographers have been hired to film the wedding, and for a while, they're giving me full coverage. I'm wondering if we really need two cameras on Audrey as she tosses back yet another vodka shot. Maybe they'd like to focus on the other wedding guests, and/or the bride and groom?

Attention is momentarily diverted from me as the emcee begins making a series of long announcements in Uzbek.

I look around the room. It's packed.

"There must be four hundred people here!" I whisper to Ruslan.

He shakes his head. "Probably eight hundred."

"Eight hundred people?!"

He shrugs. It's normal.

"Do the bride and groom know all of them?"

He considers. "Probably some, yes. Maybe others, they've never met. By the way, they just made a small hint about you."

"Really?" I ask.

"He said, 'We are proud to have many guests here from all over the world, even one from America!' Everyone will know it is you."

A man approaches our table, and Uzbek Leonardo DiCaprio leaps up, grinning. Uzbek Leo and this new man lean in toward each other, as if they're going to kiss, but at the last minute, they bump their temples together, first on one side, then on the other. I've seen men do this all week: it's an odd combination of head-butting and the French double-cheek kiss. I ask Ruslan about it.

"It's the cool way for young guys to greet each other," he tells me. "But the old people, they say it is not respectful."

The older generation wants men to bow slightly while placing their hands over their hearts. I watch the man head-butt *bisous* his way around the table, and I find myself oddly touched by the affection and physical contact the young men are exchanging in this hypermasculine culture.

I get weepy at weddings. This isn't surprising, given that I also cry at graduations, holiday celebrations, YouTube videos, and the occasional inspired boarding announcement. But the head-butting isn't what does me in.

My tear ducts start tingling a few minutes later, when the boys all jump up and line up in front of the stage. All the men's tables are getting up, one at a time, to congratulate the bride and groom and present their wedding gifts (cash, only cash). Uzbek Leo discreetly pats his pocket for the wad of cash, and in that moment, I see his mother kneeling beside ten-year-old Uzbek Leo, helping him maneuver his arms into a suit jacket, explaining the rules for weddings. Only sit with members of your own gender; hand over some cash when you get onstage; if you don't have a suit, just wear your hiking gear.

There's something touching about watching everyone follow unwritten rules dictated by culture. I'm reminded of the time my friend Allison brought her non-Catholic boyfriend Matt and friend Laura to a Catholic wedding. When it was time to exchange the sign of the peace, Allison turned to Matt and kissed him. Matt and Laura, assuming this was the standard peace offering, turned to the strangers around them and began kissing them.

The part that makes me cry comes later, when a group of older men and women walk into the room. The boys are immediately on their feet, grinning and slightly starstruck.

"They are our teachers," Ruslan whispers to me.

Having your teacher come to your wedding is a huge honor, the boys tell me. I think about the national holiday for teachers and the high esteem in which Uzbekistan seems to hold all educators, and I see the men swarm their teachers like they're the sample bar at Trader Joe's.

Maybe it's culturally proscribed and maybe it's regimented respect, but it's still enough to ruin my mascara.

After dinner, professional dancers with long, braided wigs perform an elaborate dance, and then I get pulled up to dance in front of all eight hundred guests. One of the groom's female relatives is a specially trained dancer, and I try to follow her moves, until Aziz leans over to me and whispers, "Just freestyle is okay."

The bride and groom are supposed to have their first dance, but halfway through, she flees the dance floor, and I get yanked up to perform again.

"She's very shy," the boys explain.

I'm kind of horrified. I think about how I haven't seen her smile all night. For most of the evening, she's been stuck up on the canopy-bed stage, eating with a blank expression. I start to worry that she's been coerced into the wedding, and that my dancing is enabling this coercion, but eventually, I continue dancing, and she comes back down and makes it through the first dance.

Then the women all come up and give her money, just like the men did for her new husband, only she has to stand there and bow to each of them. Tim explains that an Uzbek bride is supposed to be modest and demure on her wedding day, deflecting attention and acting like she doesn't want to be there. And certainly a lot of people get nervous on their wedding days, even Brooklyn couples who've been living together for over a decade and already have three children.

Still, it's hard to tell whether she's being pushed into a wedding she doesn't want, or she's a naturally talented actor.

Not long after, the couple decide they're done, and they get up to leave. We all follow them out, pausing at the door to run our hands over our faces in prayer.

I creep back into the guesthouse, feeling slightly badass for having stayed out past eleven. Jaloladdin nods at me.

"How was the wedding?" he asks me.

I beam. "It was wonderful."

He nods. "That's what you wore?"

I look down at my tight black dress and the butterfly control top that's slowly slipping down my thighs. "Yep," I say.

"That's perfect."

A VISIT TO A SECRET MUSEUM (UZBEKISTAN)

The world's second-largest collection of Russian avant-garde paintings sits in a relatively unknown museum in the middle of the desert in Uzbekistan. According to some, this is no coincidence. The museum's origin story, as presented by a smattering of Western media outlets and travel books, goes something like this: a brazen collector amassed the collection as an act of dissidence and then hid it in a remote museum where no one would think to look.

Something about this story gives me pause. So in Khiva, I search for a taxi to take me three hours into the desert.

In 1966, Igor Savitsky opened the Nukus Museum of Art in a remote city in the Uzbek desert. Nukus was small, obscure, and hard to reach, making it an ideal location for a nuclear testing facility or a secret underground lab, and a less logical place to put an art museum.

Unless the point was to keep certain people from visiting.

The Soviet government didn't take kindly to abstract art or the people who made it. During Stalin's purges, almost anything could be used as an excuse for arrest, including and often especially writing, thinking, and painting things not sanctioned by the Communist Party.

But this party, along with the government it ran, was headquartered in Moscow. To the Soviet leaders, Nukus was far away and not particularly important, and no one in the Kremlin was paying close attention to the city or a tiny museum inside it.

And so the museum became a refuge for art persecuted by the Soviet regime. Savitsky salvaged thousands of works hiding in basements and attics, waiting to be destroyed or forgotten, and gave them a home in his museum. In the end, art triumphed over tyranny. It's a great story. Maybe too great.

The museum's origin story bothers me because it's too simple, too clear-cut. It's missing the messiness and moral ambiguity of real life. I worry that it's a convenient backstory for a museum in an inconvenient location.

I want to believe in abject heroism in the face of tyranny, but valiant deeds seem more often stumbled into than carefully premeditated. You don't start out planning to save one thousand people from Auschwitz. You begin as a Nazi industrialist with a factory.

Did Savitsky go to Uzbekistan with the intention of risking his life to save art? Or is his legacy something that happened along the way?

I find a driver who will take me from Khiva to the museum. He's a reticent man who stops before we leave town to stock up on a frozen snack called "ice milk." I hope, for his sake, that's a mistranslation.

Outside the city, the land empties into open vistas of sky and sand. The same unchanging reel of brown desert and scruffy shrubs cycles past our windows. Clouds hang low in the sky and swirl above our heads.

I wonder whether I'm going to a place Savitsky went in order to save a bunch of paintings, or a place where he happened to be living when he had the idea to open a museum.

It quickly becomes a long ride.

Igor Savitsky was born in Kiev in 1915 and grew up in Moscow in the years following the Russian Revolution. As a child, he dreamed of becoming an artist. He took painting lessons while he was young and enrolled in art school as an adult, though perhaps as a backup plan, he trained as an electrician.

In the Second World War, the art institute at which Savitsky was studying was evacuated to Samarkand. He spent the war in Uzbekistan, and returned after completing his studies to work on a major archaeological excavation in the desert region of Khorezm. There, he studied artifacts and folk art created by the Karakalpak people. In his free time, he painted landscapes of the sandscapes that surrounded him. He still clung to his dreams of making great art.

A few years later, Savitsky returned to Moscow with his paintings of Uzbekistan. He showed them to Robert Falk, a prominent Russian painter whom Savitsky greatly admired. Falk declared them to be terrible.

This was a huge blow to Savitsky. Devastated, he cut up his canvases. He decided that he was finished with the Moscow art world, and he returned to Uzbekistan. He settled in the small city of Nukus, where he continued his work in archaeology and ethnography.

There, Savitsky began collecting art and artifacts of the native Karakalpaks. He amassed jewelry, headdresses, pottery.

At some point, he decided he wanted to open a museum with his Karakalpak collection. But the Soviets tended to be skittish on cultural heritage, seeing it as a dangerous weapon groups could rally around to question the authority of the Union.

It's said that Savitsky browbeat local authorities into giving him his museum. Or maybe Moscow was far away and didn't feel particularly threatened by an exquisite collection of earrings.

Either way, Savitsky opened his museum in 1966.

And then he began collecting paintings.

Anton's mother was an artist. She died when Anton was eight. On the wall in Vadik's bedroom hangs one of her pieces: a weaving of a woman wearing an enigmatic expression.

"Do you think it's your mom?" I ask Anton.

"No," he says. "I think it's just a random woman."

I can't see the woman in the weaving as anyone other than Anton's mother. I can't not feel like she's watching while Vadik and I color on the floor of his bedroom, while Anton and I sleep there on summer nights when Elena and Vadik are back in Belarus. When I read to Vadik or sit in his bed making up fairy tales that he forbids from including names from his own life, I try to decipher the woman's expression. It always eludes interpretation.

What would Anton's mother think of all this, of the grandson she never met, of this bizarre setup we all accept so casually? Whenever I tell anyone about Anton, I can sense in their reaction that they feel it is doomed. I know what it looks like, but I hate how no one believes in us.

Would she? I'm haunted, less by her approval, but more by the omniscience it's easy to project onto the dead. In my mind, she knows how the story ends. But she won't tell me.

Anton is haunted in a different way. "What if her art . . . wasn't good?"

The Nukus Museum is a blocky space-agey building that looks like the losing entry in a 1969 design competition for a public library. This could, I suppose, be intentional.

When the Bolsheviks came to power, they brought with them ideas of what art should be. It should be easy to understand and relevant to people's lives. It should glorify the worker and support the state.

By 1934, the Soviet government had issued a list of standards to which it declared all art should aspire. It had to be proletarian and realistic, it had to represent scenes of everyday life, and it had to support the aims of the state and the party. Art that met this criteria was "approved"; everything else was not. An exemplary piece might depict young, rosy-cheeked communists smelting iron with joy. Abstract painting, a category into which almost all of the avant-garde fell, was now condemned as bourgeois and decadent.

Artists who failed to conform to official tastes were removed from their jobs and barred from exhibiting, or arrested, or worse. Some left. Chagall and Kandinsky took refuge in Europe. Malevich stayed behind and had his paintings confiscated. There are doubtless other names we'll never know, either because they chose to live by painting smiling iron smelters, or because they didn't.

Within the Soviet Union, the avant-garde movement withered and died.

Except, the Nukus Museum of Art asks, what if it didn't? What if some artists kept painting subversive work in secret? What if they hid the results in places where they'd never be found? What if the events that seem most improbable unfold in ways that make it look easy?

At the ticket counter, I notice a sign offering a private English tour of the collection. I do the math and realize it costs $5 U.S.

A few other foreigners mill around in the lobby holding tickets or reading guidebooks. Why, I wonder, is no one else booking the private tour? Maybe it's terrible. Maybe all of their guidebooks say, "Whatever you do, don't take the $5 private tour!" Maybe there's no such thing as a free lunch, and also no such thing as a good $5 private tour.

I'd kind of like to explore the museum myself, but to not ask about the $5 private tour feels like declining the gift horse without even looking it in the mouth.

I ask the woman behind the desk if there are any English private tours today. I'm kind of hoping she'll say no and let me off the hook. That way, I'll be able to say I at least *asked* about the $5 private tour, and I'll console myself by reasoning that if you book a private tour that costs less than the average sandwich, you probably get what you pay for.

To my dismay, she says there is.

"Is it starting soon?" I ask nervously.

She frowns and tells me to wait. She disappears behind a door and then returns, nodding.

"She can do it now," she says.

Some of the first paintings Savitsky purchased were by a Russian artist living in Uzbekistan named Alexander Volkov. Once a distinguished painter awarded the title People's Artist of Uzbekistan, Volkov had fallen from grace after Stalin ramped up the campaign to replace abstraction with Socialist Realism. Volkov's paintings were labeled "counter-revolutionary" and removed from museums. He was fired from his teaching post. He spent the remainder of his life in isolation, prevented by the local artists' union from having any contact with the art world.

Savitsky bought his first Volkov paintings a decade after the artist died. This acquisition inspired Savitsky to travel around Uzbekistan looking for "art that the history of our times condemned to obscurity."

But art isn't always condemned to obscurity because it's subversive. Sometimes, it fades into obscurity because it's not that great.

I knew things wouldn't last forever with Anton long before we start handing back copies of each other's keys and making threats we don't quite have the courage to follow through on.

I've gotten good at explaining him to people. "Tell me about your boyfriend," they say, and I reply, "Well, he's from Belarus," and they quickly mask the look of concern that flickers across their faces. "But he went to high school and college in the U.S.," I continue, and then they relax, because this proves to them that he has another way to live in the U.S. legally and that he isn't scheming to use me for a green card. They ask me what he does and I just cut to the juicy stuff, which is Elena and Vadik, because it's better to just get that out of the way. I explain that Anton and Elena are getting divorced, and they give me a look, like they've heard that before. And I know what they mean, but I also know that Anton and Elena really will get divorced. The only thing I don't know is that it will happen a few months after Anton and I break up.

It's a lot of explaining for something that never seems that complicated in the moment. The commute is annoying and their shower is broken. I keep a baby pair of slippers in my apartment for Vadik. But mostly, I'm happy.

My guide's name is Gulmara. She's quiet and thoughtful, and she knows the history of the museum and its paintings with an obsessive attention I've never achieved outside of the biographical details of members of '90s boy bands.

Before we enter the collection, she makes me leave all of my belongings in a locker.

"Can I bring this?" I ask, holding up my phone.

She shakes her head.

"This?" I hold out a notebook and pen.

She considers, then decides it's allowed.

The museum's director recently resigned in the midst of a murky controversy. The government alleged that she'd been forging paintings from the archives and selling the originals to wealthy collectors. Her supporters allege that the government fabricated this story in order to push her out, so that it could quietly implement this exact scheme.

Gulmara does not tell me any of this, but she does, in one rare, unguarded moment, declare how much she admires the former director, her former boss, and she says this with such fierce intensity that I would want to believe her even if evidence pointed to the contrary.

Paintings cover the walls from floor to ceiling. No inch of wall space is wasted. In some rooms, the art feels less on display and more just really jammed in there. There's a sense of urgency, a need to exhibit as much of the collection as humanly possible.

After his Volkov purchases, Savitsky spent the next 20 years traveling around Uzbekistan in search of paintings that had been hidden in attics or stashed in the back of closets for fear of getting their creators labeled counterrevolutionaries. Sometimes, the paintings' "subversive" qualities were limited to abstract forms. Other works were more explicit in their critique of communism, the Soviet government, and the way of life in the USSR.

Savitsky undoubtedly saved some work that would otherwise have been destroyed, but he might have just set out to collect paintings, not preserve a piece of a modernist movement. Unapproved work that couldn't be shown in official galleries might have been easy to acquire. So could paintings that no one else wanted.

When people say he hid the paintings in the desert, they usually don't mention that the desert was also where he lived. Perhaps he brought the art to Nukus to keep it safe, or perhaps he brought them there because it was the most obvious choice.

But now I'm starting to question how much his motives matter.

Oleg's parents once told me a story about reading Aleksandr Solzhenitsyn, the famed Soviet writer who lived in exile and published works criticizing the Soviet regime. One of his most famous, *The Gulag Archipelago*, told the story of the brutal gulags where prisoners, intellectuals, and innocent civilians were sent to toil in work camps that claimed over one million lives.

Oleg's family, like most in the USSR, was aware of Stalinist repressions because of a personal connection. An uncle who had risen through the ranks in local government had been executed in a political purge. In the relative thaw that followed the Stalinist period, Soviet officials acknowledged that Stalin had gone too far, but few ordinary citizens knew the extent or specifics of the gulag system.

The Gulag Archipelago detailed the horrors of the prison labor camps and quickly became a sensation when it was published abroad in 1973. The book was of course banned in the Soviet Union, but Oleg's father had a friend with a father high up in the Communist Party, and she was able to get them a copy of the book. The only catch was, they could only keep it for one night.

"We sat down with my parents at the kitchen table," Oleg's mother told me, "and we stayed up all night reading it." They divided the book up into four parts and took turns reading each section. "We would read each piece as fast as we could and then pass it to the next person," she remembered. "It was all so shocking."

Later I mentioned that I couldn't imagine a book so important to Americans of my generation that we'd stay up all night reading it.

"For us, it was not even a question," she said. "We were happy to stay up all night and read, because we wanted to know."

Here is an expressive, chaotic canvas in which forms bleed into the shape beside them.

"It's a caravan," Gulmara tells me.

Here are landscapes, deconstructed; faces, chopped up and re-assembled; portraits barely recognizable as such; here are vibrant bursts of color, scenes of daily life; here is a woman, here is a man, here is a mood, idea, intimation. Here is a collection of art that overwhelms the space it's in; here are portraits, stacked five on top of one another, covering the walls, leaving barely any white space in between, hinting at the hundreds or thousands of more unseen in basement storage.

Here is the collection's pièce de résistance. It was painted by a man named Vladimir, or maybe Evgenney, Lysenko, an artist about whom little is known, except that he was arrested and probably died in a mental institution, possibly not because he suffered from mental illness, but because the authorities wanted to keep him from painting.

The painting is titled *The Bull*. A secondary title is, apparently, *Fascism Is Approaching*. It's hard to find much information on the painting. Some sources use the second title; others only the first. It's unclear if the artist gave the work its politically charged name, or if that was added later. It's unclear when it was made. Most of all, it's unclear why, without the second title, it would be considered so slanderous to the Soviet Union.

Especially given how openly the other paintings brazenly mock and disparage the powers that were.

Here is a painting called *Drink to the Dregs*. Do I see the influence of German expressionism? Look at the caviar label pasted onto the canvas. This was a luxury brand favored by the political elite, who lived private lives of lavish comfort while publicly condemning decadence. Do I see the political critique?

Here is another canvas, called *Capital*. A grotesque couple smile in front of a backdrop of floundering workers, the couple's material comfort apparently built on the backs of others' labor. Gulmara tells me that the work is only the top half of a larger painting. The bottom is missing.

Gulmara says that many of the works were painted on top of existing pieces, because, at that time, it was cheaper to buy an old painting than a blank canvas. To get a sense of what was underneath, the museum staff X-rayed the pieces at a hospital in Nukus.

Some of the paintings compel me to keep standing in front of them after Gulmara finishes her explanation. Others don't, but sometimes I pretend to be absorbed and enthralled, because I want Gulmara to feel like I love each painting as deeply as she seems to, that I, too, am reveling in the precise, meticulous details she shares with me.

I'm trying to discern if these paintings were on the verge of being forgotten because they were forbidden, or because they weren't particularly memorable. I feel guilty wondering about this, because being here has made me realize how terrifying and difficult and hopeless it must have felt to live through the Stalinist purges.

Is there such as thing as objective aesthetic value for art made under duress? Does it get graded on a curve? Do the paintings left behind preserve the story of the risk and sacrifice required to make them, and hint at the works that weren't painted? Would that story have been conveyed if I'd just wandered through the galleries, staring at the paintings unguided?

Anton occasionally sends me stories after we split. I try not to respond to the e-mails, but I always devour the words. They invariably read like lightly fictionalized accounts of his relationships—some from his past that I recognize, others set in a post-Audrey world that I don't. The women range in importance from Elena to one-time flings. There's not even one tiny detail I recognize myself in.

How am I so absent in his stories? Did I leave so little of an impression on someone who had such an outsized impact on me? Of course, there is a more logical explanation. Why would he send me a story about me? We can be unreliable narrators when we try to tell the stories of things that matter most to us.

"I would never write about you," he tells me another time. "I have too much respect for what we had." I don't believe him; I assume he's trying to dissuade me from ever turning him into a character. But also, if you respect something, how can you not try to immortalize it?

Here is one way to understand the story of Savitksy and the Nukus Museum: a failed artist built a collection of works by artists who similarly failed to gain recognition. Here is another way: a man had a vision to preserve endangered art in the middle of the desert.

The result is the same. Savitksy put together the world's second-largest collection of Russian avant-garde work. The only other is the Russian Museum in St. Petersburg, a massive collection in a city known for its mind-numbingly massive collections. This makes Savitsky's accomplishment impressive regardless of how or why it happened. How many private collectors assemble a catalog that rivals that of a state museum of the largest country on Earth? How many fewer did so without access to wealth, by simply persuading artists and their families to give him work that they didn't want?

This is where the collection is most vulnerable to criticism. Some argue that Savitsky's collection dates from a period when the avant-garde was in decline, and that it lacks works from the movement's most well-known artists. Art critics have said that the pieces in the Nukus Museum are, for the most part, unremarkable.

But it must have been hard to become remarkable when you couldn't study abstract techniques in schools or look at the movement's masters in exhibitions.

One of the last paintings Gulmara shows me is a bright, happy scene of a family at a picnic. A blanket spreads over the ground, and Gulmara points to the baby in the center of it. She smiles. "That's me."

At first, I'm confused. She feels like a picnic?

No, no. "My father was one of the artists in the museum," she tells me.

The pieces click together.

"Do you tell everyone on the tour?" I ask her.

Her smile becomes more mysterious. "Only some."

In the end, I'm left with a sense that the museum might mean more to someone who has stayed up all night passing pieces of a book around a table than it would to someone who hasn't. That Anton's mother's work is good in a way that has nothing to do with composition or technical mastery, because it's something of hers that he has. That hanging a painting on a wall doesn't erase the pain of losing a parent or knowing a relative was shot for no reason or being told that your work isn't good enough or having to paint in secret because the government dictates what you can and cannot make. That I don't know if the majority of these artists set out to make dissident works. That paintings probably don't change the world or erase the past or save us from being condemned to repeat it. That the $5 tour is always worth it. That sometimes it's worth taking a taxi to the middle of the desert and coming away without any concrete answers but an interest in trying to understand.

CAMPING BESIDE THE DOOR TO HELL (TURKMENISTAN)

My first glimpse of Turkmenistan is from the Turkmen embassy on the outskirts of Bishkek, where a silent man in a plaid shirt and reflective sunglasses escorts me through a walled-off compound that houses embassy staff and operations. In the middle of the courtyard sits an empty, uncovered swimming pool.

My second glimpse of Turkmenistan is from the Turkmen embassy in Dushanbe, where I have to go because my visa application was rejected in Bishkek. A young official with expertly applied eyeliner at the embassy in Dushanbe asks me about my passport as soon as her boss leaves the room. "I've heard Americans can travel to many countries," she says. "Where can you go?"

The collapse of the Soviet Union brought greater freedoms to most of the nations that emerged from it. Turkmenistan is one of the exceptions. Today, it's a closed, isolated country, with a government that controls all access to information and fosters a cult of personality.

I want to visit Turkmenistan because I imagine seeing it with my own eyes will yield even some small understanding of what life is like under these political conditions. I also want to see a crater that's on fire.

In 1971, Soviet engineers were surveying for oil in the Karakum desert of Turkmenistan. It wasn't easy work. Temperatures could fluctuate wildly, soaring above ninety degrees Fahrenheit at midday and then dropping below freezing at night. With the exception of a small nearby village, the surrounding area was empty, with nothing but sand stretching out in every direction.

The desert had once been home to bands of nomadic Turkmen tribes renowned and feared for their ferocity in battle. Hardened by desert living and centuries of conflict with neighboring empires, the Turkmens were widely regarded as the wildest Central Asians, among the last to be subdued by the Russian Empire.

Now, the tsar's socialist successors believed they'd found oil in the desert they'd once conquered. A rig and base camp had been installed to investigate the sand that earlier surveys suggested was covering a massive oil field.

The engineers soon realized that the site contained natural gas, not oil, and that they'd set up shop on top of a gas pocket. Not long after, the earth under the rig suddenly collapsed, the desert opening its mouth to swallow the equipment and work site. Miraculously, no one was hurt. But the newly formed crater was now leaking gas, and fumes were spreading across the surrounding terrain.

Fearing that the leak could pollute a nearby settlement, the engineers decided to light a fire to burn it off, which sounds dangerous but I guess is standard practice on gas fields. They figured all the gas would burn off within a few days, a few weeks, at most.

What they started wasn't so much a fire as a conflagration. Flames shot up into the air, ten, twenty, maybe thirty feet above the crater. You couldn't go anywhere near it. It burned for weeks, and then months.

It's still going today, more than forty years later.

These days, it's known as the Darvaza Crater, or, if you're feeling dramatic, the Door to Hell. People come from all over the world to see it: from Japan, from America, from Japan, from Russia, from Japan, from Germany, from Japan. They say the best way to see the crater is to spend the night camping beside it. I want to go. But there's no way, I tell myself, that I am camping.

I, of course, end up camping beside the crater.

There are two ways to get to Turkmenistan. You can book a tour with a state-licensed operator, which comes with a state-licensed guide-slash-chaperone, or you can apply for a five-day transit visa. I opt for the latter for many reasons, the most important being that I want to see the "real" Turkmenistan. I don't want a guide following me around, spouting government rhetoric and making sure I don't see anything I'm not supposed to. I want to have real conversations with real people unafraid to tell me what they really think.

But not booking a guide means I'm on my own for getting to the fiery crater in the middle of the desert, and finding a ride is turning out to be harder than I expected.

I spent the past week e-mailing dozens of Turkmen tourist agencies, but it's the end of the tourism season, and everyone is either shuttered for the winter or exorbitantly expensive.

A mile-wide strip of no-man's-land runs along the Uzbek-Turkmen border, and a guy with a minivan is driving me and a few men to the Turkmen side. When he hears I don't have a way to get to the crater, he brightens and tells me he knows someone. He pulls out his phone and starts texting while driving, which I normally condemn but can't bring myself to speak up about, given that the only other living creatures around are cacti, and none of them are driving.

The first thing I see in Turkmenistan is a border outpost whose façade is adorned with a giant portrait of the president. He flashes us a welcoming, benevolent smile.

When you hear that a country hangs pictures of the president from the top of its buildings, you don't quite get a sense of how sinister this will seem in real life. After all, celebrities wink at us from the top of Times Square, imploring us to buy watches and carbonated beverages. We resent this blatant commercialization, but let me tell you: it's much creepier when it's a politician. You feel like he's watching you, keeping tabs on what you're up to. More than anything, you realize that someone who can put his face on the side of a government building probably has few things he can't do.

In 1991, the Soviet Union dissolved, granting Turkmenistan independence. As in other post-Soviet states, a former high-ranking party official was elected president of the new country of Turkmenistan. His name was Saparmurat Niyazov, and he quickly realized he had few rivals.

Within a decade, Niyazov had amended the constitution to declare himself president for life. He started going by *Turkmenbashi*, which translates to something like "father of all Turkmen people." Children studied his bizarre book of autobiography-cum-philosophical-musings in school. His portrait hung on the insides and outsides of buildings, and he erected gold statues of himself all over the country. Foreign journalists enumerated his eccentricities: he renamed months and days of the weeks for members of his own family; he made newscasters swear an oath of loyalty before "reporting" the government-scripted evening news.

This news, of course, spoke little of the outside world, and when it did, it was all in service of legitimizing Niyazov's regime. Niyazov turned his borders into an airtight seal, cutting his country off from the rest of the world.

One big difference between Niyazov's Turkmenistan and the Kims' North Korea or the Castros' Cuba is that Turkmenistan has huge amounts of natural resources. It has the world's sixth largest reserves of natural gas, but only 5.6 million people. Though profits mostly stay concentrated in the hands of a small political elite, fossil-fuel revenues mean that famine and extreme poverty didn't plague Niyazov's rule, nor have they that of his successor, Gurbanguly Berdimuhamedow, a slightly more progressive dictator.

Berdimuhamedow, who began his career as a dentist, got rid of some of Niyazov's more extreme measures, like the oath of loyalty and the Niyazov-family-themed calendar names. But Berdimuhamedow still hangs his portrait in airports and bus stations, and his administration continues to purge political opponents and top the lists of worst human rights records. In the most recent election, some of Berdimuhamedow's most enthusiastic supporters were the seven men running against him.

I want to know if people see through the propaganda. I want to understand how it feels to be monitored by an autocrat whose face is everywhere. I want this, not because I crave a taste of totalitarianism before skipping back into the free world, but because I think it will help me understand something that seems inconceivable.

Inside, the Turkmen border outpost I pull up my visa, which is actually just an e-mail from the Turkmen ambassador's personal account.

"Did you print it?" the guards ask. "You were supposed to print it."

My face falls. "Errr . . ." I stare at the three young men in uniform. They could easily refuse to let me into the country, which would not be ideal, because I don't have a visa to go back into Uzbekistan either. I'll be like Tom Hanks in *Terminal*, except, rather than being stuck in a fancy airport, I'll be stranded in a sandy and possibly land mine–ridden no-man's-land, and I'll have to befriend that guy in the minivan and see if he'd be cool with me squatting in the trunk.

"No problem." The guards shrug. "We can print it."

This helpfulness so catches me off guard that it emboldens me, and I ask them if I can call Ulugbek, the minivan driver's friend, to negotiate a ride to the crater. Sure, they say, no problem, don't let him charge you more than X. Turkmenistan was supposed to be one of the least free places on Earth. But these border guards almost feel like they're here to guard me from myself.

Until one hears me tell Ulugbek the name of an ancient town that's not on my handwritten itinerary.

"You can't go there," he cuts in sharply.

After the visa is in my passport, another guard hand-searches my luggage.

"Do you have carpets?" he asks.

I shake my head. "No."

He frowns and carefully opens every pocket and pouch, as though I might be hiding a carpet in my makeup case. When he finds none, he asks me again. "No carpets?"

I'm confused. "No carpets," I repeat.

"In Uzbekistan, you buy carpets?"

"I have no carpets," I insist. Although I'm starting to wonder: do I have carpets? Did I buy them in Uzbekistan and forget? I'm kind of afraid he'll continue interrogating me until I admit that I'm carrying a carpet factory, but he shrugs and lets me go. I gather my belongings, and I walk out the door to Turkmenistan.

In pictures, the crater looks like a portal to a terrifying dimension, or an artist's rendering of the Rapture, or an underfunded metal band's album cover. It's strange to see the earth burning without any visible fuel source. It's like the moral to an environmental disaster movie, the earth exacting revenge for all those times we left the AC on when we ran to the grocery store.

I have no reason to camp beside it. As my recent experiences with horse treks and yurt stays have reminded me, I'm better off being one with the indoors.

Still, for some reason I find myself telling Ulugbek that I want to rent a tent and sleeping bag, and spend the night snoring beside a potentially haunted crater.

Ulugbek is tall and friendly, and though the man in the minivan bragged that Ulugbek speaks excellent English, it quickly becomes clear that he does not.

"You? Smoking?" he asks, pantomiming taking a drag of a cigarette.

I shake my head. "Good," he says. "In city, smoke, NO!" (The president, in an effort to kick his own cigarette habit once and for all, has outlawed smoking in all urban areas.)

This becomes a common sentence pattern.

"Here, kielbasa, okay. There, kielbasa, NO!" "Here, president, [indecipherable hand gestures]." "Turkmenistan, gas, goooood!"

I respond to all of these statements with a knowing, "Ohhhh!" Ulugbek pulls over to get gas.

"America, gas, free?" he asks.

"Free?" I repeat.

Gas used to be free in Turkmenistan, he tells me. Under the new president, it now costs $0.30 Turkmen manat a liter, which works out to about $0.32 U.S. per gallon.

Turkmenistan's natural resources provided the country with better economic prospects than other post-Soviet states. But many argue that central planning and bizarre subsidies, like free gasoline, have prevented Turkmenistan from reaching its full economic potential. The average monthly salary in 2012, the most recent year for which data is available, was around $330 U.S.

"How do you know the man who gave me your number?" I ask Ulugbek as he fills his tank.

He grins. "He is my brother."

Ulugbek is bringing his girlfriend with us to the crater so that I'll feel more comfortable.

"Two girls, okay!" he proclaims.

His girlfriend is a young, pretty blonde named Jirnelle. We pick her up at her mother's house, where she lives with her two young children. At twenty-five, she's fourteen years younger than Ulugbek. Her face is scrubbed clean, and she wears a T-shirt and tracksuit.

She joins Ulugbek in the front, and they begin talking and laughing in a mix of Uzbek and Russian. Glad as I am to have her here, I quickly start to feel like a third wheel.

I try to suss out Ulugbek and Jirnelle, to see how much they know about the outside world, but also to figure out how they *really* feel about their country and the government that isolates it. I imagine that, when I'm not around, it's all they talk about.

They offer more promise of worldliness than most. Ulugbek was born in the Soviet Union, not Turkmenistan, and, as an ethnic Uzbek, he's a minority in Turkmenistan. Plus, the fact that he works as a guide puts him in regular contact with foreigners. Jirnelle is half-Uzbek, half-Turkmen. She studied in Moscow for five years, a biographical detail that I can't square with the fact of her school-aged children, who are not Ulugbek's. She must have had children very young and then left them with her mother while she finished her education.

"In America, do you have the sandwich shop Subway?" she asks dreamily. When I tell her we do, she replies, modestly, that she used to work at Subway in Moscow, a chain I will soon learn is an almost replica of the American version, but with draft beer.

When we stop for lunch at a roadside cafe, I watch for my chance to steer the discussion toward politics.

Over dumplings and soup, Jirnelle asks me if I've noticed the power outages in Turkmenistan. I've only been in the country a few hours, so I haven't, but she assures me they're a regular occurrence.

"Do you know why?" Ulugbek asks.

I'm guessing inadequate infrastructure or political issues, but I don't know how to say either of those things in Russian, so I just shake my head.

Ulugbek leans in and confides that Uzbekistan is stealing Turk-menistan's electricity.

"And also petrol," Jirnelle adds.

I'm trying to imagine what this would look like—soldiers creep-ing over the border at night and making off with oil drums? Secret wires running under the no-man's-land that funnel Turkmenistan's hard-earned electricity into Khiva?

Ulugbek is referring to Uzbekistan's 2009 exit from the power grid that once fed all five Central Asian Soviet republics, a move said to have caused shortages in the other four nations, particularly Tajikistan. How Uzbekistan is stealing oil is less clear. The source of this intel, as it would be for all information outside the realm of their personal lives, is the state-run media.

Any first impressions I had about Ulugbek and Jirnelle's famil-iarity with the outside world fall away as lunch progresses. Ulugbek doesn't understand why it's hard for French, German, and Japanese tourists to speak English, because English is widely spoken in their home countries, no?

"I don't think so," I say.

But their languages are similar to English, right?

No, I say. Very no for Japan.

He shakes his head. "Japan tourists, speak English: NO!"

Jirnelle's English is a tiny bit better than Ulugbek's, and she asks me about my trip. I list the places I've been, but I get blank stares in return.

"Bishkek?" I say with disbelief. "It's in Kyrgyzstan?"

She blushes. "Sorry," she says. "I don't know."

I try to play this down like it's no big deal, but it's stunning. Bishkek is the capital of Kyrgyzstan, a nation only two countries over from Turkmenistan. When Jirnelle's parents were born, Kyrgyzstan and Turkmenistan were part of the same country. Her not knowing Bishkek would be like a Bostonian never having heard of Philadelphia.

Ulugbek's favorite phrase is "No problem." He uses it to punctuate each sentence.

After I finish my meal: "Finished? No problem?"

When the check comes: "Ten manat. No problem!"

When it's time to leave: "We go, no problem."

It's not hard to believe Turkmenistan is 80 percent desert. Outside of the cities, that's all there is.

We speed toward the ancient ruins the border guard told me I wasn't allowed to visit. I've decided not to share this information with Ulugbek.

If I had to describe Ulugbek's driving style in a word, it would be: reckless. He tails ambulances and then cuts in front of them. He puts on his seat belt as we approach checkpoints and takes it off once we're past. He avoids traffic by getting off the road and driving around it.

Just before sunset, we arrive at Konye-Urgench, the site of Turkmenistan's most spectacular Silk Road ruins. Compared to Uzbekistan's, they feel almost untouched. It's not that they haven't been restored—although a gaping hole in one roof suggests that the work has been more modest—it's that there's practically no one else there. Other than a group of women praying for fertility at one mosque, we have the whole place to ourselves.

Or, I should say, I have the place to myself. When we pull up to each ruin, Ulugbek walks me to the entrance, attempts to impart some basic facts, and then gets back in the car with Jirnelle. As I duck inside a mausoleum that I'm not sure I'm supposed to enter, I worry that I'm holding Ulugbek and Jirnelle up. And then I remember that they're here for me . . . some combination of their outnumbering me and my being, for all intents and purposes, mute, has made me feel like an awkward guest on their couples' getaway they're hoping will disappear.

Our last stop is a spindly sand-colored minaret that rises 200 feet up to the sky like a teetering pencil. It's the only structure that remains from a fourteenth-century mosque.

Ulugbek tells me that Turkmenistan has the second-tallest minaret in the world after India. "Bukhara, Khiva, no!" he shouts.

"Huh," I reply.

"Okay, I wait you!" Ulugbek calls, already bounding back to the car.

We head out into the desert to find the crater, and I'm still wondering how much I can ask Ulugbek and Jirnelle about politics. Have they spent enough time outside of Turkmenistan to be skeptical of what's reported on state-run media? Are they critical of Berdimuhamedow? Are they waiting for me to bring it up? Worried I might be a spy?

And if they are opposed to the president and his oppressive regime, how are they just . . . sitting there? Why do they go about their lives like normal people, instead of rioting in the streets?

We pass a herd of unaccompanied camels, nonchalantly ambling down the road, as though being a herd of unaccompanied camels roaming freely through the desert is a totally normal thing.

One of the camels has a leash and a bell tied around its neck. "Does anyone own them?" I ask, confused, because there's no one around.

Ulugbek and Jirnelle are adamant: no one owns them.

I try to picture how a herd of camels could have come to escort itself down a highway. I decide that the animals are owned by a camel herder who sent them on a journey after selecting the one with the leash as lead camel. "You're in charge now," he whispered before releasing them.

We cross a rickety, Soviet-era bridge spanning a roaring river. Ulugbek wants me to check out either the bridge or the river, so he stops the car and we get out. He points to a new bridge being built a little further down. "This bridge is being built by Turkey," he tells me. When the Soviet Union ended, Turkey saw an opportunity to strengthen relationships with the Turkic-speaking Kazakhs, Kyrgyz, Uzbeks, and Turkmen. Ankara offered aid and sought closer ties with leaders of all four nations. These efforts have been most successful in Turkmenistan, perhaps because the country's two languages are closest and mutually intelligible.

"Did you know that, every Sunday, the president rides a horse around the hippodrome?" Ulugbek asks me.

My ears perk up. "Wow," I reply cautiously. "How . . . funny."

He either ignores my bait, or I used the wrong word. "This Sunday, he did not," he continues. "He was busy."

I had worried that a guide on an official tour would try to censor what I saw in Turkmenistan. Now I'm not sure that's true, because Ulugbek tells me he also works as a guide on official tours. He may not be particularly fluent in English or interested in the details of history, but he's also not trying to keep me from seeing anything. When we pass billboard-sized portraits of the president hanging on the walls of public buildings, he slows down so I can photograph them, even though it's illegal to do so.

We're driving along a desert highway, surrounded by darkness. It's the kind of empty black that reminds you that there's nothing and no one else out here. A red glow appears in the distance, the crater announcing itself from miles away.

The glow grows as we approach, a red orb of light trapped in the thick air hanging above the fire. It's unexpectedly creepy, menacing even, kind of in the way I expected the whole country to feel.

Up close, it's even stranger than in pictures. Flames jump and skitter across the crater's rocky bowl. It doesn't seem real, this fire raging but burning nothing. My eyes scan the edges, looking for the trick. It's hard to wrap my head around it. I think: rocks cannot catch fire. But that's exactly what I'm seeing.

As far as tourist pull-offs go, it's not bad. It's borderline incredible. I'm momentarily overwhelmed with gratitude that I found Ulugbek, that he brought me here, that I got to see this.

And then the novelty wears off. A burning crater is spectacular for approximately fifteen minutes, after which you realize there's not much more to see or do or think about. I don't need to see it at sunrise. I'm very much wishing I'd arranged to have Ulugbek drive me to the closest town after a quick crater visit and then found my own way to Ashgabat in the morning. But he's already dragged Jirnelle all the way out here, and it feels a little late to back out of sleeping in this tent.

I did not know that as soon as the sun goes down, a desert becomes extremely cold. I have always pictured deserts as places where people died of heatstroke, not places where you can potentially contract frostbite, which is what I fear has sucked all the feeling out of my toes.

I'm curled up in a ball and burrowed deep inside my sleeping bag. I'm wearing two layers of long underwear, wool socks, a down jacket, and a hat. I've never been so cold in my life. Ulugbek has given me a tent and a sleeping bag, but no sleeping pad to stop the cold from seeping up through the bottom of the tent. I shift my weight, stamp my feet, and try to wiggle my toes. Nothing.

My heart sinks with the realization that I have, in fact, contracted frostbite. I curse myself for falling for the camp-beside-the-crater trap. Tomorrow morning, Ulugbek will drive me to a hospital in Ashgabat, where they'll amputate my toes, or maybe, if I'm really unlucky, my whole foot. I start to cry.

Ulugbek and Jirnelle are not as cold as I am, because they're sleeping in the car beside me. With the engine running. Ruefully, I imagine them snuggled into blankets, lost in tranquil dreams while several of my appendages wither and die.

Eventually, I fall asleep, but I toss and turn all night, the cold waking me on the hour. Finally, just after sunrise, I give up. I get out of my tent and go sit beside the crater, which has the benefit of giving off heat, because it's on fire.

In the early-morning light, the flames look far less dramatic. They seem smaller, less menacing. I can see the rusting carcass of the rig that fell into the crater. The heat shimmers above its twisted limbs. Also, bonus revelation: I did not contract frostbite last night.

It dawns on me that I could have gotten up and slept in the car with Ulugbek and Jirnelle, and I wonder why I didn't. My head throbs with lack of sleep.

The only other people at the crater are a group of Japanese tourists with tripods and long lenses. When I pass them, they nod.

"Welcome to Japan," one says, in English.

I suspect that this is not what he meant to say, so I smile back at him. "Welcome to Japan," I reply.

When I come back to camp, Ulugbek and Jirnelle have set up for breakfast. Instead of spreading a blanket over the sand, they've rolled out an oriental rug.

"It was cold last night," Ulugbek announces.

I glare at him. "I know."

Ulugbek slices a sausage on top of an unfolded newspaper. When I look closer, I see that the front page has a very obviously Photoshopped picture of the president planting a Christmas tree. His shovel looks like it's made of marble. Ulugbek laughs when he sees me studying it.

"Can I take a picture?" I ask.

He nods, but tells me not to get his hand in the photo, which is strange, because how would anyone know that it was his hand? Does Turkmenistan keep a database of everyone's finger shapes? On second thought, he might not be thinking about repercussions at all—he might just worry that my picture will look worse if his hand is blocking it.

Ulugbek wants to wash his car before we leave, so I wander back toward the crater. A camel lingers wearily behind a sand dune, and I step toward it for a picture. The camel stares at me, then suddenly turns and gallops off. I didn't know camels could gallop. I turn and see Ulugbek, who watched the whole encounter, buckling with laughter.

It feels like the first exchange we've had where we both understood everything. This, or maybe all the time to myself beside an only slightly-more-exciting-than-usual crater makes me realize that Ulugbek and Jirnelle's reluctance to talk politics may have nothing to do with what they know of the world outside their borders, but rather, an intense familiarity with the one inside them. Maybe it's not that they don't want to discuss these things with me, but that they've gotten out of the habit of discussing them with anyone. I now highly doubt this is all they talk about when I'm not around.

When I get back to the car, Ulugbek is wiping the hood down with a rag and bottled water. His phone is tucked between one ear and shoulder.

"My brother." He grins, gesturing to the phone. "He, you: 'hello.'"

I wanted to go to Turkmenistan because I hoped it would be unlike anything I'd ever seen before. It is, but not in a good way.

Ashgabat is the capital of Turkmenistan and the country's second-biggest tourist attraction, after the burning crater. I thought I'd find this all strange and interesting, because I didn't understand how years of authoritarian rule can wipe away any potential for charm. Copenhagen is quirky. Ashgabat is gloomy.

Saparmurat Niyazov's stylish, week-renaming eccentricities are all over Ashgabat, which had once been a typical Soviet city, and is now a combination marble preserve and shrine to Niyazov and Gurbangaly Berdimuhamedow. These are not elegant marble buildings. They are marble buildings for the sake of being marble buildings, with design plans that look like they were lifted from a geometry textbook. In between the buildings are gold statues of the country's two presidents, or gold statues of Niyazov's self-published memoir (which he forced everyone to read), or indiscernible gold statues that might as well be of the president.

Something about Ashgabat immediately gives me the creeps. Maybe it's the citywide ban on photography, which only makes me want to photograph everything. Perhaps it's the ubiquitous portrait of president Berdimuhamedow, who smiles back at me from the walls in every building.

The people I meet in Ashgabat are kind and generous, but most seem to have limited information about the outside world. When a taxi driver learns I'm twenty-eight and childless, he tries to explain how sex works.

What gnaws at me most is the sense that the whole country runs on a set of unwritten rules obvious to everyone else, but incomprehensible to me. Which perhaps is how I end up spending my whole trip to Ashgabat staying in a hotel run by the secret police.

I did not make reservations for the secret police hotel. I end up there because it is the only place that admits to having vacancies, and also because I am not an artist.

First, I get dropped off at a place listed in my guidebook: the Hotel Syyahat. In an unexpectedly chaotic lobby, I'm asking a receptionist for a room.

She stares at me. "Are you an artist?" she asks.

I tell her I'm not.

She shakes her head. "If you're not an artist, you can't stay here."

Perplexed, I head to the next-best hotel in the Lonely Planet. This time, I'm prepared.

"Hello," I say. "I'd like a room, and I'm an artist."

But this hotel is full, as is the next one, and the one after that, which has a travel agency inside the lobby.

"Do you know why all of the hotels are full?" I ask the woman working there.

She looks confused. "They're full?" She offers to go check something. She's gone for a long time. When she comes back, she seems surprised to still find me waiting. "I don't know why the hotels are full," she tells me.

I start to panic. What if I can't find a hotel? I'd like to think of myself as the kind of person who could, in an emergency, hole up in a bus station for the evening, but that seems like a risky move in an authoritarian state, and also that would mean skipping my night-cream routine.

Two university students I stop on the street for directions seem to pick up on my distress. They also speak English. When I tell them my story, they insist on accompanying me to the next hotel, and also, because this is Central Asia, on carrying my suitcase.

"It rolls," I protest, and while they do acquiesce to rolling it, they insist on being the ones to do the rolling.

Like all male students in Turkmenistan, the boys are dressed in plain black suits affixed with pins of the flag of Turkmenistan. Their female counterparts wear floor-length dresses of vibrant green, traditional hats, and two long braids. It's strange to see a city full of young people all wearing the same outfits.

I ask the boys why their English is so good.

"The Russians are stealing all of our jobs," one says, shaking his head. "For the future, we must speak English."

This job-stealing claim seems curious, given that I've seen exactly zero ethnic Russians in the prosperous capital, and that all of the government ministers pictured on various walls and buildings appear to be Turkmen men. But I remember that I am helpless and homeless, so I say nothing.

The next hotel is full, too. So is the one after that, and, at this point, I beg the boys to go back to whatever they were doing before I inadvertently suckered them into escorting an ill-prepared foreigner to various disinterested hotels, but they refuse.

"You don't understand," one says. "I think most people here . . . they won't even know how to talk with foreigners."

What he's trying to say, I think, is that these hotels aren't quite sure how to deal with me. The government has enacted byzantine requirements for foreigners staying in local hotels to ensure that money is changed at the official rate, and not on the black market. For me to stay at a hotel, I learn, the hotel has to give me paperwork, which I need to bring to one specific branch of one specific bank, where I need to change the total charge for my stay into local currency, which the bank needs to confirm via endless stamps on said paperwork, which I can then bring back to the hotel to begin the process of checking in. While doing this, I will discover that none of my credit or debit cards work in Turkmenistan. Some of the places I first visited might have pretended to be full to avoid the headache, or perhaps feared the repercussions of making a mistake along the way.

The one place that admits to having vacancies is the MKD hotel. If I knew my Soviet history, I would have known in advance that the MKD was a Soviet-era secret police force. But because I don't, I'm merely confused when I notice that everyone who passes through the lobby is wearing a full police uniform.

I will later speculate that the hotel is operated by the MKD to raise funds, the way some police forces hold bake sales. But for now, I simply find it strange when I open the door to my room and find a police officer scrubbing the toilet.

He finishes and leaves, allowing me to look around the space, which is billed as a deluxe suite. It comes with a living room, bedroom, and bathroom, which is helpful, because I'm sharing my room with an entire colony of cockroaches.

Not eager to spend much time getting to know my new roommates, I head out to explore Ashgabat.

In order to respect the ban on public photography, when I see something I want to take a picture of, I discreetly open my iPhone camera and place the phone to my ear like I'm taking a call. I attempt to hold the phone perpendicular to the ground and press a volume button on the side, which snaps the shutter. This is my small act of rebellion, and I perform it with as much stealth as a person slinking into a department store to use the bathroom. Most of my photos come out severely tilted, or obscured by strands of my hair.

The city feels like it was designed and built for a population that never materialized. The wide sidewalks and marble underground passageways are mostly empty. The marble high-rises appear minimally inhabited. The only people reliably found on the street are police officers, who are everywhere, guarding what often seems like nothing. There's a pair posted up at the entrance to a square not far from my hotel, and they tell me I can't walk through. It's closed, they say, for rehearsals for an upcoming military parade.

I smile. "That's interesting," I say. "Can I see it?"

We chat for a few minutes, and then they concede that I can walk through if I do it "quickly," and I'm congratulating myself on once again skirting the rules when one of the officers tells me he wants to take me on a date tonight and asks for my phone number.

I'm instantly terrified. I don't dare give him a fake number, because, in a police state, it seems like a bad idea to romantically reject the police. I scribble my real number on a piece of paper and scurry away, resolving not to answer my phone for the duration of my stay, but it turns out there's no need—he never calls.

Oddities abound. I find a park being built, not by construction workers, but by students. This happens in communist countries too—students and teachers are sometimes given "holidays" that they're required to spend helping with a harvest or contributing manual labor to a government project. For this, they're paid only in the "honor" of serving the country.

I pass countless statues of angry-looking warriors holding swords, which I keep jumpily mistaking for actual people. I pass another square closed for a changing of the guards, but when I ask a guard if I can walk through anyway, he grumbles and then also says yes. As I'm walking, one of the less-disciplined guards breaks from his goose-stepping to stop and stare at me.

The rules seem most heavily enforced by the people who stand to lose the most if they're caught breaking them. I came to Turkmenistan wary of the police, but it's never someone in uniform who glares at me when I'm illegally taking a picture. It's an ordinary citizen, who, I suspect, knows the limits of his own ability to protect himself against the state.

One night, I end up in a lively restaurant filled with Turkish expats, who apparently make up a good portion of the labor force in Turkmenistan. I'm the only woman in the room, with the exception of the waitresses, who are all wearing fully transparent shirts. A bookish young guy in glasses at the table next to me strikes up a conversation in English, and I ask him, delicately, about the nature of the relationship between the clientele and the women working here.

He picks up on my meaning and laughs. "No, no," he protests. "Turkish men, we can't talk to women here. It's forbidden to . . . go on a date. Unless you're married."

This turns out to be true, an arrangement that, unsurprisingly, creates more problems for the Turkmen women than it does for their foreign suitors. If the couple is caught, it's the local woman whom the government can punish.

At ten forty-five p.m., the Turkish man turns to me again. I've finished my dinner, but have stayed at my table, reading a book in a room full of drunk people, because this seems preferable to reading my book in a hotel room full of cockroaches.

"Are you driving home?" he asks me.

I shake my head.

"You should go now, then," he says. "The curfew starts at eleven."

"What?!" I say.

Yes, he explains, people aren't allowed out on the streets after eleven.

"How can you live here?" I ask.

He shrugs. "It's not so bad. The work is pretty good."

Turkmenistan is not hooked up to the World Wide Web.

Internet access is all but impossible to come by. There's no Wi-Fi in hotels, restaurants, or coffee shops. Few people have Internet service at home, and most of the country rarely goes online.

By the end of my second day, I feel completely isolated. In most places I visit, I can get intermittent texts and e-mails, which act as a virtual security blanket—here my solitude grows apparent with each passing minute.

I decide to get a drink at the old Sofitel, which is now no longer a Sofitel, but that's what most people still call it. It's the same upscale hotel, except now with local management and a Turkmen name. Most important, it's the only place I've seen in the entire country with Wi-Fi. After a confusing dinner at a Turkish pizza parlor, I head out into the street to find a taxi that will take me there.

In Central Asia, any car is a potential taxi. When you want a ride, you wave your arm until a driver pulls over and asks where you're going. If he's heading in your direction, he tells you to get in. If he's not, he drives away without saying another word.

It's dark, and the streets are empty, so I'm relieved when a car makes a U-turn to pick me up.

But this does strike me as odd. Drivers don't usually change direction to pick people up, because they don't normally take passengers who aren't heading where they're already going.

The man driving this car looks like he's in his early twenties, and his friend sits in the passenger seat. This, too, isn't unusual—drivers in Central Asia often bring friends along if they're taking passengers at night.

I tell them I'm heading to the Sofitel. We go back and forth negotiating a price, and then I get in.

Then another strange thing happens: as soon as we start driving, we stop being able to communicate.

In Russian, they ask me where I'm from and I tell them. But what they say next is impossible for me to understand. In Russian, I ask them to repeat it, and when they do, I still can't make out a single word. They're speaking something that *sounds* Russian but isn't. My ear grasps at each sound, trying to latch on to a word I recognize.

This, too, is troubling. Taxi small talk tends to follow a fairly standard script—where are you from, what are you doing here, are you married, do you have children, you better get pregnant soon!—and I've been running these lines daily for a month now. To understand *nothing* is so strange and frustrating I refuse to accept it.

For a few minutes, I struggle to communicate. "What?" I keep saying, "I don't understand. Repeat, please?" Each time, they say something that sounds like I should be able to follow, but I can't even find simple subjects—me, I, you, us. Eventually, I give up and sit back, exasperated.

By itself, this wouldn't be cause for alarm, either. Anti-Russian sentiment in Turkmenistan has grown since the fall of the Soviet

Union, and the younger generation doesn't always speak the language of its former colonizers. Perhaps they are speaking Turkmen or heavily accented Russian. *But why does it sound Russian?* I wonder. *Why could we understand each other before I got in the car?*

I stare out the window. Ashgabat is far from picturesque during the day, but at night, darkness softens the jarring marble buildings, which shine gently under spotlights. I'm thinking about how it almost looks pretty when the driver cruises past the street for the Sofitel.

Okay, I think. *That was strange.* But the streets in this neighborhood have been closed for rehearsals for the upcoming military parade. I remind myself that most of the taxis I've taken in Ashgabat have driven unbelievably circuitous routes, often, it seemed, out of a genuine enthusiasm for driving. I could ask why he skipped the turn, but I'm not anxious to revisit the linguistic barrier.

We keep driving. Ten minutes pass, and then fifteen, and something begins to feel very wrong. The glitzy downtown buildings start to give way to a crumbling old city I haven't seen before. *How, I wonder, will this get us to the Sofitel?*

Then the driver turns north.

This is bad. The Sofitel had been *south* of where he'd picked me up. We're now much farther west than we need to be, and there's no plausible explanation for why we're now heading north, and out of the city.

"Do you know where the Sofitel is?" I ask.

"Yes," the driver says, suddenly able to understand me again and respond in Russian.

"It's not north," I reply.

He's silent.

"Not north," I try again.

"It's there." He gestures.

I repeat the name in Turkmen, and ask, again, if he's *sure* he knows where it is.

"Yes, yes," he keeps saying, and I believe him, because no one in

Ashgabat doesn't know the Sofitel. It's easily the city's most famous hotel and a well-known landmark in its own right. To be unfamiliar would be like a New Yorker going, *What did you say it's called? Time's squared?*

As the buildings become increasingly spaced out, my nervousness skyrockets.

I try to think very carefully. It is, I suppose, theoretically possible that my normally very acute sense of direction is off, and that we are not, as I suspect, far northwest of where we need to be. I don't have Internet, so I can't check a map on my phone. But this should have been a ten-minute ride, and we've been driving for what feels like three times that.

"This isn't right!" I try again.

Suddenly, they're back to speaking incomprehensibly, and I'm starting to panic.

"No!" I say firmly. "The Sofitel, behind!"

I start yelling; they remain unflinchingly calm.

"It's okay," they keep saying in such soft and unworried tones that I start to doubt myself. Maybe I'm overreacting? Maybe they do know where we're going?

I start running through my options, in case my gut feeling is right. I don't know Turkmenistan's emergency number, but I can probably look it up in the Lonely Planet on my phone. Should I call and try to explain what's happening? See if they can translate? Look up the number for the U.S. embassy?

And then, to my horror, I see that we're approaching a highway leading out of the city. I know, instantly, that I'm in a very bad situation.

"Stop," I scream, in Russian and English. "Stop. STOP. STOP!"

They stay calm. The car slows but doesn't stop. "It's over there," the driver repeats, gesturing.

"STOP!" I yell again and open the door for emphasis.

I've imagined this moment in countless daydreams. What would I do if someone tried to kidnap me? I've pictured myself jumping out of a moving car, and in these fantasies, I land, scraped and shaken, but otherwise unharmed.

We can't be going more than twenty miles an hour, but as soon as I see the asphalt rushing past in a blur beneath the door, I know I won't jump.

"It's there," the driver repeats.

I close the door, because staying in the car seems less terrifying than jumping out of it, and because I'm still clinging to the last threads of hope that he's telling the truth.

And there's still the fact that they're so calm! Aren't criminals angry and jumpy and jittery? Don't they scream at their captives and accidentally fire their guns when a clanking radiator startles them? I'm hysterical, and these guys seem unperturbed. Maybe the hotel is just up ahead?

Then we pull onto the highway.

Scenes of the endless desert I drove through to get here play through my mind. Once you leave Ashgabat, it's all desolate, uninhabited stretches of sand.

Suddenly, I'm not wondering whether I should call the U.S. embassy or look up Turkmenistan's emergency number. I know I need to get out of this car immediately.

"STOP," I yell, and again I open my door. We're now driving highway speeds, and I know there's no way I'm jumping out of the car, but I also know that my last hope involves not closing this door.

The last exit before the city ends is for the airport, and though we've passed the off-ramp, there's an on-ramp up ahead for cars leaving the airport to get on the highway.

"STOP," I scream. "STOP NOW."

The cars around us start honking in response, I assume, to a sedan casually driving down the highway with one door wide open.

"I can't stop," the driver says. "There's a car."

And he's right—a car merging from the airport on-ramp is blocking the path to the shoulder, but this car lays on its horn so furiously that the ones behind follow suit. Up ahead in the distance, I see a vast, deserted *nothingness*.

I keep my door open, and I keep yelling, and the cars around us keep honking, and then he's slowing down, he's pulling over, he's stopping.

I jump out of the car and run in the opposite direction.

The initial burst of adrenaline carries me 100 feet before I turn back around. The car hasn't moved. I continue to back away, pulse electric as if I'm staring down a predator. The car stays where it is for a few moments. Are they waiting for me to get back in? The brake lights go off—they're going to drive away. The car rolls only a few feet and then stops again, as if the two men in the car are debating something. I watch, heart pounding, ready to start sprinting again if they get out. But they don't, and a few moments later, they drive off and disappear down the highway.

I want to cry more badly than I ever have in my life. I want to sit on the side of the highway and sob until my eyes are puffy and my eyeliner runs down my cheeks.

But I'm stranded on the side of the highway on the outskirts of Ashgabat with no clue where I am, and a good cry is a luxury I can't afford.

A steady stream of traffic passes by on the highway, which is well lit for the next few hundred yards. There's a pedestrian overpass in front of me. But there are no other pedestrians.

The neon outlines of Ashgabat's skyscrapers glimmering far off in the distance confirm my suspicions: I'm far outside the city center, and we were heading farther out. I look around. I'm not even in a suburb. There's nothing out here but the highway, a set of railroad tracks, a train guardhouse, and empty land.

Through the open guardhouse door, I see a disheveled-looking older man in a rumpled uniform.

I call the U.S. embassy to say that I'm ready for my Navy SEAL rescue.

Unfortunately, I reach the U.S. embassy's voice mail.

It lists an after-hours emergency number, which I dial, assuming it will be manned/womanned by a Navy SEAL dispatcher.

The man that I reach does not seem to have access to the Navy SEALs.

"Yeah . . ." he says, after I finish my story. "What I'd recommend is, walk back in the direction you came from."

"But I'm really far outside the city!" I protest. "I'm at least a twenty-minute drive!"

"Oh." He pauses. "Well, in that case, you're probably better off taking a taxi."

My jaw drops. "I'm on the side of a highway! I don't see any taxis, and anyway, I wouldn't really feel comfortable getting in one again, because of, you know, what just happened . . ."

"I'm not really sure what to tell you . . ." He trails off.

"Can you speak Russian?" I ask. "There's this guy guarding a train crossing—"

He tells me he doesn't. He also doesn't speak Turkmen. I want to ask how he got an embassy job in a country where he doesn't speak any of the local languages, but instead I say, "Are you . . . in Ashgabat?"

"I am," he answers, "but I'm new here, and I'm not too familiar with the city."

"So there's nothing you can do to help me?" I ask.

He confirms.

I am never paying my taxes again, I think as I hang up the phone.

My next recourse is the train guard.

He does not seem particularly fazed by the appearance of a distraught American woman at his guardhouse in the middle of nowhere. His eyes stare off in two different directions.

"Where am I?" I ask.

He names the locality we're in.

"Are we in Ashgabat?" I ask.

He seems confused and points to the distant skyline.

My already imperfect Russian, perhaps downgraded by my acute hysteria, prevents our conversation from progressing, so I call Oleg to translate. Through Oleg, I learn that I am, as I thought, far north of the city, and that the only way back to the glittering skyscrapers downtown is to cross the highway and flag down a car.

The hardest part of being potentially kidnapped and stranded on the side of a highway on the outskirts of Ashgabat is working up the courage to trust someone enough to get back to safety.

I'm determined to get in a car with at least one other woman in it. The first driver who stops is a single man, and I wave him on. But he waits, and I notice his car is a BMW, which, for some reason, reassures me. Criminals never have nice cars, right? At least, not the kidnapping kind.

His name is Azat, and he speaks good English. When I tell him what happened to me, he bangs on the steering wheel. "Those fucking bastards!" Then he brightens. "Don't worry! God sent me to save you."

Azat speaks five languages and, until recently, had been working in logistics, although he's vague about the sequence of events that culminated in his driving a taxi. So far, he's been unsuccessful in his attempts to find a new job because of "the fucking people in this country!"

Part of me wants to suggest that his anger issues could be part of the problem, but then the other part of me remembers where I am.

Azat does his best to cheer me up. He is very certain that God played a hand in everything from my abduction to his having found me. "When bad things happen, it's always for a reason, and good things, too," he says in a way that makes me think he is perhaps talking more about his own life than mine.

Azat drops me off at the Sofitel with a copy of his résumé, in case I know someone in the oil processing industry looking for a polyglot with a specialization in logistics.

"Finally, I want to tell you about something, Audrey," he says, and from the way that he says it, I have a hunch that "something" is going to be "God." Sure enough, he opens with a declaration that "Whether you're Christian, Muslim, whatever, God is God," and then rambles his way to something about, "If you go somewhere and you die, it's okay, because God says it's time for you to die. And if you don't die, you don't worry, because—"

"Okay, bye!" I say, jumping out of the cab in the middle of his sermon. It's as if God has inspired me to take flight.

It's hard to know what to think about what has happened. The waiter at the Sofitel bar first says that he thinks the guys were up to no good, but then changes his mind, and says it's more likely that the boys hadn't understood me. He suggests that they might not have spoken Russian, or that they were from out of town, and he, too, notes taxi drivers' tendencies toward roundabout routes. He tells me that Ashgabat's suburbs are slowly filling with luxury ho- tels (which I'm never able to find any evidence of), and that they may have heard the name "Sofitel" and assumed it was out of town, although when he draws me a map that includes the Sofitel, the location of the new hotels, and the place where I'd jumped out of the cab, this theory starts to fall apart. The new developments are con- centrated on the east side of town, while we had been far to the west.

He tells me that laws in Turkmenistan are so strict and the pun- ishment so severe that people don't commit crimes on impulse. He underscores the one thing that was most confusing to me, which was that they did eventually stop the car and allow me to go. But he also concedes that the Sofitel is the city's most famous hotel, and that "everyone" should know where it is.

My hotel calls an English-speaking tour operator, who tells me that he's never heard of anything like this happening to tourists, which, to me, doesn't seem to prove anything. "Anyway, you're safe," he says, "because your hotel is run by the police."

"Huh?" I say.

"You didn't notice that it's all police working there?"

The Lord's sentinel Azat is adamant that the highway we were driving on in the sedan led only out of Ashgabat, and although he clearly has misplaced rage issues, maps that I later study seem to confirm this.

Whether the men stopped the car because they were worried that an open car door on a major car highway would attract too much attention or because they genuinely weren't trying to hurt me, I'll probably never know. My gut feeling is that it was bad. I've taken plenty of taxis in countries where I don't speak the language, and usually, when you start shouting, the driver pulls over and shouts back. These guys never lost their cool.

The more I talk to people, and the more I learn about Turkmenistan, the more I suspect the worst. A few months later, a Russian friend tells me about a Turkmen gang that was busted for kidnapping women and trafficking them into the sex trade.

"Someone committing a crime for the first time would have freaked out when you started freaking out," one of my students says. "Only people who've done this many, many times before would have been calm."

The first full Russian phrase I learned was for a joke I had written about my upcoming trip. "I'm learning Russian because I'm traveling through Central Asia for a few months," it went, "and so far, the only thing I've learned how to say is как интересно. я хочу уехать из туркменистана прямо сейчас. Which means, *Oh, how interesting! I would like to leave Turkmenistan now.*" It looks like the joke was on me.

12
HOW TO GET OUT OF TURKMENISTAN WHEN YOU'RE OUT OF CASH

If you should ever find yourself, as I will shortly, in Turkmenistan, out of cash, on the run from a restaurant in which you dined and dashed, and in desperate need of a $60 ride to the border on the day your visa expires, do not despair. Your situation is not good, but it's not hopeless. You can make it to Kazakhstan, but you must maintain faith, commit to courage, and above all, not tell anyone.

The morning after the taxi ride, I fly to Turkmenbashi, a city near the border with Kazakhstan. I would have just flown to Kazakhstan, but my visa will only allow me to exit the country via one land border on the Caspian Sea. The border is a four-hour drive from Turkmenbashi, and by the time I arrive, it's too late in the day to make the trip. Though I'm anxious to leave Turkmenistan, I'll have to spend the night here.

I'm running low on cash because I hadn't realized my debit and credit cards wouldn't work in Turkmenistan. This could have presented an even bigger problem, but luckily, I'd withdrawn a good amount before leaving Uzbekistan. It probably would have been enough to get me through if I hadn't panic-purchased the plane ticket to the border.

I won't be able to withdraw money until I leave the country. I should be sweating, but I feel oddly calm. After the ill-fated cab, marble-clad Ashgabat seemed even more menacing. By contrast, the normal-looking streets and buildings of Turkmenbashi put me at ease.

My guidebook only lists one hotel for the city, so I head there to get the day over with. The receptionist hears one syllable of my Russian and informs me that I can't have a room.

But I'm not taking no for an answer. "Here's my passport," I say, in English that she doesn't speak.

"Not possible," she replies, in Russian.

We go back and forth like this: her pointing at my passport and insisting I can't stay, me trying to climb over the desk and grab one of the keys. Finally, she calls out to an unseen backroom, and a young blonde woman appears.

Her name is Vera, and she now has the unfortunate task of translating a battle of the wills.

"Americans . . . can't . . . live here," she labors to communicate in rusty English.

"I don't mind," I reply cheerfully. "I'll stay here anyway."

The receptionist's stance is unwavering; I try begging and threatening and finally explaining myself. "Yesterday, I was . . . do you know this word . . . kidnapped," I begin. It's the first time I've used that word—all day, I've been telling myself it must have been a misunderstanding—and as soon as I finish saying it, I burst into tears.

Maybe Vera understands, or reads the look on my face, or maybe crying is all it takes. Either way, I can suddenly stay. Vera is going to accompany me to one specific branch of one specific bank, where, just as for the secret police hotel, I'll exchange the amount of currency for my bill and get notarized proof.

On the walk to the bank, I ask Vera how she learned English, and she tells me she'd been taking lessons, but had to stop when her level surpassed that of the teachers. "It's hard to get good English teachers to come here," she sighs.

"Why don't you take online classes?" I ask.

"Online?" she replies, confused.

I explain how online classes work, and she shakes her head. To get online, she has to go to an Internet cafe, where the connection is too slow and expensive for video classes.

Vera dreams of being a translator. But she needs more English to get there, and until a better teacher shows up in Turkmenbashi, there's nothing she can do to further her ambitions. She's stuck at the hotel, waiting.

On our walk back, we pause to take a selfie in front of a monument.

"What's your e-mail address?" I ask. "So I can send you the picture."

She shakes her head. "I don't have one."

After paying for the hotel, I'm down to my last twenty dollars. This is a problem, because I've negotiated a ride to the border for the next morning for $60 U.S. But it's been a long two days: I decide to let Future Audrey handle this.

I still have half a day to kill, which Vera suggests I do at a beach on the Caspian Sea. A ride there is less than three dollars, which I calculate that I've earned.

The beach is beside a new development full of ritzy hotels, and I share my taxi there with a Turkish engineer heading over to check out a work site.

"It looks like Abu Dhabi," I observe as we draw near.

"You have a good eye," he replies. "We copied most of the designs from buildings there."

The swanky development is, unsurprisingly, empty. The hotels haven't had a lot of success convincing tourists to take a beach vacation in Turkmenistan. Not that it matters: the development is just an ego project for the president.

I get out beside one of the hotels and make my way down to a thin sliver of public beach separated from the pristinely manicured resort beaches by a rocky jetty. I look up and down the beach: I see no one else.

Entirely alone, I can finally let my guard down. For the first time since it happened, I think about last night in Ashgabat. I return to that moment on the side of the highway.

A cold wind whips in off the waves that a halfhearted afternoon sun has rendered a dull gray. I tuck my hands into my coat pockets and look down at the sand, where I notice a few seashells. I lean down and pick one up.

Suddenly, I'm crying, sobbing actually, because I'm overwhelmed by a powerful but unfamiliar feeling. I can't even name it: it's something like gratitude, or maybe love in its purest form. Everything else melts away and life suddenly seems so simple. No matter what I call to mind, I can feel only love. Grudges and resentments seem ridiculous in the face of this all-encompassing sense of good. I'm incapable of feeling anger, even at my most reliable targets. Terrorism. Republicans. Anton. I forgive everyone. I forgive myself.

It's like a switch has been flipped and I suddenly understand some powerful, larger truth. Not that life is good or that there is some good in everything, but that there is some privilege in this: in simply being here, in simply being alive.

I stay on the beach for as long as I can, because I want to hold on to this feeling. I somehow know that I'll lose it as soon as I step off the sand, and I'm desperate to trap it inside of me. I don't want to go back to that other way of being, of getting annoyed at a long wait for a train or condemning people for the wrongs they do me.

Why can't I carry this truth with me? Is it because it's an illusion, or because I still have a lot of growing up to do?

I wish I could say that after that moment I never again poison a relationship or summon the conductor when someone takes a call on the quiet car. But this feeling is fleeting, its truth unsubstantiated, and by the time I am home, the effects of this day will have dwindled to an occasional, passing thought when I catch myself being petty. *I'd be a way better person*, I think, *if I could get kidnapped every once in a while*.

It never occurs to me to abandon the trip after the kidnapping scare.

It's not that I have never felt unsafe traveling alone as a woman.

There have been moments that gave me pause and dark streets I hurried along. I try not to stay out late or draw attention to myself. As much as I can, I stay alert to my surroundings, and I listen to my gut.

In spite of that, the ride to the Sofitel could have easily ended differently. I'll take credit for the quick thinking that led to creating a diversion and drawing attention to our car, but if any number of tiny details had been different—if there hadn't been anyone around to honk, if one of the men had pulled out a weapon—the outcome might have been something that no amount of quick thinking could have prevented.

But in this moment, the overwhelming sense I have is that something bad happened and I got myself out of it.

Later, a well-meaning relative tries to insinuate that an angel saved me.

"No," I snap. "I saved myself."

I go to a nearby restaurant and order a dinner that I think costs $10, but when the bill comes, it's for $40.

"I'm so sorry," I tell the waitress, "but I don't have enough cash."

She's confused.

I open my wallet to show her and then offer her all three of my credit cards. As I suspected, none work.

She can see I'm getting upset. "Don't worry!" she says. "Can you come back tomorrow and pay?"

I know that I can't.

I've never stolen anything in my life, and I feel awful as I lie to the waitress and tell her I'll return in the morning with the money to cover my bill. I feel even worse that she seems to trust me completely as she carefully writes the address and a reminder of how much money to bring on a card that she gives me.

"See you tomorrow." She smiles.

The next morning, I show up for my ride to the border. I haven't mentioned that I have no way of paying for it. My plan is to remain very silent on the subject.

Our driver is a young Turkmen man with a wife and small children at home; my companions, three older, weathered Kazakh men. It's very unclear why anyone besides me is making this trip. There's vague mention of family: one of the Kazakh men seems to be the Turkmen driver's uncle, and it seems families are scattered on both sides of a border that was once more like a state line.

Two of the Kazakh men are short, round, and difficult to tell apart, but the third is easily distinguishable. He's tall and thin and has dressed in a worn pin-striped suit and battered cowboy hat for the ride. There's something regal about the way he holds himself, though his nose looks like it's been broken, and a cigarette burn mars his right sleeve. On one hand is a small homemade tattoo.

His two stout friends smile convivially; the Kazakh cowboy shoots me a pointed question. "Do you have a husband and children?" he asks.

I tell him I don't.

"I am *not* married," he declares. His tone is less flirtatious, more wedding guest about to request "Single Ladies."

I smile and say nothing, reminding myself that I have no way of paying for this ride, and therefore no right to complain.

On our ride to the border, we pass burning smokestacks, empty oil containers sitting in front yards, mountains, and heavy machinery.

Turkmenistan's northwest border is dominated by heavy industry. Specifically, oil. It scars and chews up the landscape, which is really saying something, because the landscape is mostly barren desert.

The ride is so bumpy that we put on our seat belts. Tires have cut paths in the sand beside what appears to have once been a functioning highway; several times, eighteen-wheelers barrel down it toward us.

The men chat in local languages—a mix of Kazakh and Turkmen and Russian—and I stare out the window, wondering how I will pay the driver and contemplating my other options. Now that

I've skipped out on one check, I am an accomplished, if guilt-ridden criminal. I suppose I was in Uzbekistan too, but those were laws everyone else was breaking too, and doing so didn't violate my principles. This time, it feels like I stole from a person. Perhaps I am now really living a life of crime. Maybe from this day forward, I won't be able to resist the urge to hop turnstiles, commit fraud, and jaywalk.

The problem is that rides to the border normally end at the border. The driver drops you off at an ominous-looking gate, and then you walk through the space in which one country ends and another begins. At the end, you reach another gate, and negotiate another ride onward to your final destination. I know I can get money out of an ATM in Kazakhstan, but our driver will be long gone.

It's safe to assume that no one will be happy when I announce that I am out of cash. It's equally safe to assume that the driver does not accept Venmo. I'm considering asking one of the Kazakh non-cowboys to spot me until we hit the first ATM in Kazakhstan. I've been furtively looking up Russian words I haven't needed yet in my dictionary: *borrow, pay back, also ran out on a check in Turkmenbashi and don't really need you to do anything about that, just wanted to get it off my chest.*

Just before the border, we pull off at a cairn, where my companions step out to pray. I realize this must be a holy site.

Many rides I've taken in Central Asia have included a stop off at a holy site whose historical origins seem murky. Everyone, it seems, has a spot where the prophet Mohammed's daughter or son-in-law visited or was buried or was once buried before his grave was moved. But the ritual is always the same: the devout run their hands over their faces as reflexively as Americans offer benedictions after sneezes.

I came to Central Asia a month ago knowing little about the place, except that it had once been part of the Soviet Union. Since then, I've wandered through countries I'd previously barely heard of, trying to both mask my ignorance and rid myself of it.

Travel is often espoused as a way of understanding the world and the people in it, but the things I now know about Central Asia are still vastly outnumbered by the things I don't: which parts of this ritual belong to what religion, many of the words these men speak to me, the landscape, the desert, the Kazakh cowboy. Maybe I'm supposed to understand that these are people, just like you and me!, though if I didn't know that before, how will a four-hour drive through the desert change that? But maybe for the rest of my life, when I hear the word Turkmenistan, I will remember this moment and the name will mean something to me that the names of places I haven't been do not, or maybe my face will flush with anger when I remember the men whose car I jumped out of on the side of a highway, or maybe I'll feel a pang of guilt about running away from an unpaid check, or maybe all of these things will happen at once in a flash, and then I'll be back to worrying about money and what there is to eat in the house and whether I should go out and get snacks.

There's a long line of trucks waiting to cross the border, and our Jeep slips in behind them. We turn off the engine. This is nice, because I now have extra time to fret about our impending farewell from the driver, who will likely ask me for the money for this trip, which I do not have.

One of the non-Kazakh cowboys is nudging me, pointing to the truck beside me. "It's from Belarus!" he marvels.

I look at the license plates, and he's right. For a moment, I assume he is marveling for the same reason I am: because Belarus is Europe's last dictatorship, because what a strange place it must be, because what must it be like to be from a place with so little freedom and such systemic corruption and ineptitude weighing down on you? And then I realize that Turkmenistan is no different, and that he's marveling because Belarus is so far from where we are now.

We crawl toward a border outpost more desolate than any other I've seen, which is saying something, because I crossed from Tajikistan into Kyrgyzstan in mountains surrounded by no-man's-land. But the isolation here is even more apparent, because the land is flat, and you can see for miles in every direction and all you can see is sand and a sad-looking outhouse.

While I'm patronizing the outhouse, it briefly occurs to me that I could avoid this whole no-cash-to-pay-for-the-ride mess by just not returning from the outhouse, waiting until the Kazakh cowboy has crossed and the Jeep has headed back to Turkmenbashi, but then I remember that they have my luggage, and besides, I don't think I want to be the type of person who travels the world regularly leaving debts unpaid.

I return to the Jeep as the traffic lets up, and suddenly we are all getting out of the car with our luggage to walk through the border checkpoint while our driver stays with the car.

The Kazakh cowboy insists on carrying my suitcase into the border outpost.

"He's going to Kazakhstan?" I ask nervously, re: the driver.

The Kazakh cowboy says yes.

Well, maybe things are looking up.

Inside, things are casual. There's no line demarcating where Turkmenistan ends and Kazakhstan begins, but there is a queue (which is largely ignored) and an X-ray machine (which seems equally optional). The men pass through with no problem, but the border guard, who is wearing a novelty FBI hat, takes one look at my U.S. passport and refuses to touch it. I try to pass it to him, and he puts up his hands like my passport is a gun and this is a stickup.

He calls over a more senior guard, who frowns and tells me I need a visa to go to Kazakhstan.

I stare in disbelief. "Americans don't need visas," I assure him.

He looks at me for a long time, trying to decide whether to believe me. This seems crazy: Can't he look it up? It occurs to me that this border might be so remote that they don't have telecommunications, but shouldn't they have some kind of documentation, or even a handy cheat sheet of nationalities that are and are not allowed in? "Are you sure?" he asks finally.

"Yes!" I exclaim. I open my passport to show him the stamps from when I entered and exited Kazakhstan a month ago.

With nothing, I guess, to dispute my claim, he begrudgingly stamps me in.

We walk out of the border outpost and into Kazakhstan. I could fall to my knees and kiss the ground, which is strange, because I did not previously know myself to be the type of person to do that, but I have the sensation of having survived some kind of ordeal, and of having put it behind me by leaving Turkmenistan. I feel light, almost giddy. Even more so when I see our driver getting back into the Jeep, which I think means that he will drive us to our final destination, and that I can pay him there, that I can be a woman of my word, or something like that.

As we get back in the car, the Kazakh cowboy asks me what I'm writing about, and I try to explain.

"My son wrote a book," he says.

This comment gets lost as we pack ourselves back into the car, so he says it again.

"My son wrote a book," the Kazakh cowboy repeats. "It was about how I drank too much. And I hurt my family." He shakes his head. "I cried and cried as I read it."

I am unsure if I misunderstood him, because the last thing I'm expecting this weathered Kazakh cowboy to tell me is that his son wrote a book and he cried and cried, but his friend jumps in and confirms.

"He hasn't had a drink since then," the friend says.

The Kazakh cowboy nods. "Seven years."

The mood on the other side is lighter, celebratory even. It's like Turkmenistan was weighing on all of us, and now we are free. We stop at a convenience store made of wooden planks and buy celebratory rounds of energy drinks that taste like some combination of sugar, medicine, and poison.

We haven't gone far into Kazakhstan when we pass a car broken down on the side of the road.

Our driver pulls over without any discussion, and the men hop out to help the stranded vehicle. Well, maybe *help* is a stretch, because our driver appears to be the only one who knows anything about cars, but what the Kazakh cowboy and his friends lack in mechanical know-how, they make up for in shared snacks and camaraderie. They all shake the car from side to side and then stand around, laughing and chatting.

To make strangers seem familiar, all you have to do is add other strangers. Next to even less recognizable faces, the Kazakh cowboy's looks like one I've known all my life.

I realize now why he was so quick to declare his singlehood when we got in the car. He destroyed his family and then tried to right his wrongs, but it was too late.

Maybe the one thing that most unites all of us is not love of family or fear of death or inability to stick to diets, but the fact we're constantly messing up and trying to make amends. No matter how hard we strive to be good and virtuous, we all end up reading the book that shows us our sins. Our lives are all shaped by past mistakes. And in the moments when the mistakes seem most grave, our greatest ambition isn't love or money or recognition, but rather, the fortitude to get up and put on a suit and cowboy hat and drive across the desert to a place where one thing ends and another begins.

So, in conclusion, if you should ever find yourself in Turkmenistan, out of cash, and on the run, there's no need to panic. The driver will be very understanding when he returns from fixing the stranger's car and you tell him you don't have any money. When your offer to stop at the first ATM and pay him in Kazakh currency comes off as terrified and pleading, he will laugh and tell you not to worry. And you shouldn't. It all more or less sorts itself out in the end.

13

CLUBBING WITH STRANGERS
FROM A CONVENIENCE STORE IN
KAZAKHSTAN

The first thing you need to know about Aktau is that the city was built long after the rest of the world had adopted the street name + number convention of assigning addresses. The White House had been at 1600 Pennsylvania Avenue for a century and a half; government leaders had been moving in and out of 10 Downing Street for hundreds of years; even Sherlock Holmes had long ago established residency at 221B Baker Street. The point is that people were using this system, and it seemed to be working.

For reasons that are not immediately obvious to visitors, Aktau's city planners decided to try something new. Whether because they were tired of coming up with street names or because Russian doesn't have a saying that means, "If it ain't broke, don't fix it," we'll never know. In any case, the addresses in Aktau are a string of three numbers, separated by dashes, seemingly indecipherable to visitors, residents, and Google Maps alike, making the most reliable method of navigation not directions, but luck.

Instead of 34 West Third Street, an address in Aktau will be given as something like 12–19–04. You could be forgiven for thinking that the person sending you this accidentally messaged you her date of birth.

It turns out that the first number denotes the microdistrict, a Soviet administrative division somewhat analogous to a neighborhood. In Aktau, the microdistricts are numbered, from one to twenty-nine, not in order. Microdistrict three sits between microdistrict six and microdistrict one, which is not adjacent to microdistrict two. The coastline goes: microdistrict four, microdistrict five, microdistrict seven, microdistrict nine, microdistrict fourteen, microdistrict fifteen. Microdistrict twenty-four is also microdistrict twenty-five; microdistricts sixteen through twenty-one are missing.

The second number is the building number, which again seems to follow no discernible pattern. While looking for building thirteen, you might pass building eight, then building eleven, then building fourteen. You would perhaps check across the street, assuming that, as in most places, even- and odd-numbered buildings are on opposite sides of the street, that building eleven is sandwiched between buildings eight and fourteen because someone made a mistake, which you can forgive, because we're all human, aren't we? But why does the other side of the street go building five, building six, building fifteen? What kind of anarchy is this? What sins of my forefathers am I atoning for? How badly do I need to eat dinner in this Indian restaurant?

The final number is the room number. For all I know, these numbers might follow an entirely intuitive system of logic. I can't say because, in my three days in Aktau, I was never able to successfully locate a restaurant or establishment using its 11–19–03 locker combination.

To be fair, if you're looking at Aktau on a map, the address system kind of makes sense. Patterns that don't make sense on the ground become logical from a bird's-eye view. The only problem is, I'm not a bird.

I came to Aktau to fly out of Kazakhstan, which means I have low expectations. When you visit a place specifically for its transportation offerings, you're not expecting a city that inspired a *Paris, je t'aime* spin-off. There's a *New York, I Love You*. There's no *Newark, I Appreciate Your Airport*.

I arrive in Aktau in a shared taxi with two men and a stylish forty-something woman. She wears large sunglasses and carries her belongings in a chic leather purse.

The Central Asian equivalent of A/S/L is A/H/C (Age? Husband? Children?), and so we all go around and share. I brace myself for the usual reaction of horror to "twenty-eight/no/not that I know of," but it turns out the other woman is also unmarried.

"In America, that's very normal," I declare, although that is not technically true.

"Maybe," she says, "but here you are . . . *bodak*."

"Well," I say proudly, "then I am *bodak*."

This lands better than any joke I've told onstage. The car is in stitches. "You shouldn't say that!" the men exclaim, almost in tears. I suspect I've confidently declared, "I am an old maid."

Aktau is a city that combines laid-back beach vibes with aggressive exploitation of fossil fuels. It does so in a manner that I can't, in good conscience, call "seamless." On my way into town, I pass menacing machines with spidery appendages sucking the earth dry, and then a billboard with a smiling family splashing in the waves.

The receptionist at my hostel is a scowling woman with hair that has been bleached and cropped with commitment. When I arrive, she's in a heated argument on her cell phone (perhaps with the person who gave her the aforementioned hairstyle?). I take a seat beside a black-lit fish tank and stare at a colorful grouper whose only options for friendship are a few tiny minnows and an uninspiring rock. I wonder what happened to his former fish companions. Did they die? Or maybe he ate them? Is excessive concern about aquatic social life a sign that I need more human interaction?

The receptionist has stepped outside to shout and gesticulate more freely, so I tap my fingernail gently on the glass. I know from my visits to aquaria that this is not something you're supposed to do, because tapping on the glass somehow traumatizes marine life in a way that capturing them from the ocean and sentencing them to life in a doctor's waiting room does not. But this, too, fails to elicit any response, and I sigh and stare out at the empty boardwalk.

When the receptionist needs a breather from her fight, she leads me through the kitchen and down a dark staircase into a basement hallway flanked with dorm rooms. She opens the door to a small room with a jail-cell window and two dusty twin beds.

"This is a single room?" I ask.

She nods. "Yes."

"So this room is just for me?"

"Yes."

"Not shared?"

Another nod.

"Okay."

Back upstairs, I pay for three nights, and after we both sign the receipts, she casually adds, "So, maybe another person will join you in your room tonight?"

"What?!" I exclaim.

"Just maybe," she clarifies. "But probably."

The main activity in Aktau seems to be getting lost, which is kind of fine, because Aktau is in peak off-season. The city has the eerie feel of an empty elementary school at night. It feels wrong to be here now, with the sleeping storefronts along the boardwalk, the fading billboards advertising summer fun. Down the street from my hotel, I find an amusement park that seems like it would amuse most people for a maximum of ten minutes. It, too, is closed, except for the central bar, which is open, sound blaring from TVs that play four different channels at once. Outside, a smiling dragon whose brightly colored torso has been chopped up into roller coaster cars sits frozen on a track.

The whole town feels empty. The one restaurant reliably open is a hamburger joint that serves something that manages to taste not entirely like a hamburger. It has notes of off-brand ketchup and the wrong kind of pickles.

"You!" the waiter asks in shaky English. "How many . . . 'Happy birthday!'?"

By two p.m., I have exhausted (or failed to locate) everything there is to do in Aktau. This includes "walking around in boredom" and "staring out at the ocean in boredom," both of which I make a mental note to add to the Aktau TripAdvisor page. I guess I'll have to kill the next three days at the eternal flame.

Almost every Soviet city has an eternal flame that's part of a war memorial commemorating the estimated twenty million Soviets killed in the Second World War.

Before I came to the former Soviet Union, I didn't have much experience with eternal flames. The only one I'd ever seen had been on an eighth-grade field trip to Arlington National Cemetery. At the time, I was less focused on figuring out how the flame worked than on the fact that my parents were hundreds of miles away, and so eternal flames came to be one of those things I just accepted but couldn't explain, like physics or the popularity of musicals. If you'd asked me how they worked, I would have said that the fire was feeding on some kind of material that burned forever. Whatever they used in the original Hanukkah. I assumed if one went out, it would be an international scandal.

Eternal flames are still big in the former Soviet Union, despite the fact that they have all outlived the country that lit them. There are still some four thousand in Russia alone. But many of these eternal flames have been downgraded to occasional flames.

A fuel source, it turns out, is the key to the "eternal" part, and the flames require a constant supply of propane or natural gas. Anyone who has ever contemplated the purchase of a grill understands that this is expensive. The eternal flames are therefore sometimes turned off to save money, or otherwise burn out due to neglect.

A village in Russia made headlines when it replaced its eternal flame with a cardboard cutout of a fire, reportedly due to fuel shortages. In response, Putin set aside funding to ensure that all eternal flames were burning for the upcoming Victory Day celebrations. A BBC report on the story gleefully noted that, "Even though Russia has the world's largest reserves of natural gas, a third of the country's households are not connected to gas pipelines."

The eternal flame in Aktau is surrounded by a circle of towering pillars that evoke the image of a yurt from the outside and a huddle of grieving mothers inside.

As an American, I look at the flame and see irony and hubris, but maybe the Kazakhstanis see something else. Perhaps to them, it's a reminder of their country's rich reserves of natural resources, or the horrors of war, or maybe they just see a petite American woman standing by herself.

Not all who wander are lost, but most people in Aktau are.

One night, I try to find an Indian restaurant listed in all the guidebooks and end up in an apartment courtyard. I spot two women around my age dressed up for a night out and make a desperate dash toward them.

"Do you know where this is?" I ask, thrusting an address in their faces. I'm suddenly conscious of the fact that I've been wearing the same sweatshirt for three days, after the hostile hostel lady tried to charge me $2 per *piece* of laundry.

They seem equally baffled, but they offer to help me find the place. Normally, I'd insist that they continue on to the glamorous plans that clearly await them, but three of my most recent meals have been eaten directly outside grocery stores.

We wander up and down a busy street, the girls scanning for building numbers and pausing to check their phones. Everything about them seems perfect: their hair brushed and wrapped into neat buns, their eyebrows plucked and penciled into dramatic arches, their eyeshadow applied with something other than fingers. I wonder how I must look to them in my sneakers and skinny jeans that lack of laundry has relaxed into a "boyfriend" fit.

"Where are you from?" they ask.

"America," I say.

They nod politely, but I can see them trying to work out what I'm doing here at all, and also in October.

Because I'm obsessed with your language and country, I want to say, but this seems like it will only make me sound weirder, plus I don't know how to say *obsessed* in Russian.

We cross the street back and forth three times. Finally, they take me up an unlit stairwell, and on the second floor of a deserted strip mall, we find the Indian restaurant!

"Wow!" I exclaim.

It's closed. Whether for the season or permanently, it's hard to say. I sigh and ask them if they know *any* restaurant.

Twenty minutes later, they're in a cab headed somewhere exciting, and I'm in a hookah bar that also serves food. But hey: people who've been eating sour cream straight out of the tub because they thought it was yogurt can't be choosy.

I've felt very lonely in Aktau, which is maybe unsurprising, given that every shop, restaurant, and stadium is as close as a place can get to, without technically being, empty. Though I know it's the city shaping my mood, it feels like the opposite. *I've ended up in a deserted beach town*, I think, *because it's where I* belong.

And to be fair, it's hard to feel like you're living your best life when you're eating dinner alone at a hookah bar.

Being asked if I'm married by so many strangers has made me think about the fact that I'm not, and it has made me wonder, if only because traveling alone inevitably brings moments of loneliness. Though I've been quick to assure everyone who seems surprised that I'm 28 and unmarried, that this is normal for women where I'm from—and it is undoubtedly much more acceptable in the U.S. than it is in the former USSR—I don't mention that a class of self-supporting, unwed women is not exactly what my culture aspires to. I did, after all, return home because I felt pressure to marry.

Why did I feel that pressure? I'm surprised to find that I've never asked myself this before.

I assume a creeping fear of never finding lasting love afflicts many people in their late 20s. Particularly women, who are told that we'll age out of our desirability. I do also miss being in love, and sometimes I'm terrified that I'll never again feel the way that I did with Anton.

Those feelings had once seemed so important that I would have done anything to find them. Even hiking. Marriage came to look like an attractive insurance policy against future heartbreak. It's embarrassing to admit all this, both because it's mortifying to want something so nakedly, and also because it didn't work. Plus, I almost didn't go on this trip for the same reasons, and I'm still not sure I made the right move.

But still, why did I feel like the world was pushing me to settle? It's a complicated question. Certainly my childhood home was not exactly an incubator of progressivism. My parents loved us and did their best, but they explained adulthood in terms they couldn't have imagined being interpreted as betraying a value judgment. We would grow up, we would go to college, and we would marry someone who could beat my dad at chess. (It's lucky that I developed a thing for Russians.) But I had easily shaken so many of their old-fashioned ideas—why had this one stuck?

I wonder if the progress my home culture had made had blinded me to its shortcomings. The first of my female friends had started to put their careers on hold for a year while they planned elaborate weddings. My disapproval of that is my own value judgment—and one that is popular, but perhaps not taken further. People roll their eyes at this behavior, but they don't think about the implications. And then I, along with I'm sure millions of others, internalize the tacit message.

There's no greater motivator than panic. Many college applications and tax returns owe their completion to threat of a looming deadline. And perhaps turning 30 was starting to feel like April 15.

I want to find love, yes, but what am I willing to sacrifice in service of just *trying* to find it? Why did I think I had to return home to get married? And do I even want that?

This trip has been about five million steps backward in terms of my one-time goal to settle down. And yet, in almost every moment, it has felt more right than anything I was doing in New York.

But what does feeling "right" even mean? The only arbiter of intuition is time.

More than anything, I wish I didn't worry about all this. The Audrey on the beach on the Caspian Sea would have seen beyond these things. The Audrey eating tandoori chicken in a room full of sweet-smelling shisha can't turn away from them.

The only other guest staying at my hostel is either a German man or a German ghost. A gauze bandage wrapped several times around his head suggests a troubling wound underneath, though the mummy-like wrapping is unsettling. No wound explains the need to circumnavigate his head, unless someone sawed off the top and he's trying to reattach it.

The first few times I happen upon him, he's on his cell phone, speaking animated German. The cell phone feels like less of a ghost move, which is nice, because it suggests that, though I'm staying in a deserted beach town, I'm not sleeping in a haunted hostel.

Maybe he did the bandaging himself? But why wouldn't he just fold the gauze into a square and tape that over the wound?

But slowly, I start to worry for him. I try to avoid eye contact while studying his cranium each time I see him. But he's always in the lobby, and I'm picking up on more of his story, and also getting a sense of where his head injury might have come from. He spends hours talking to the receptionist, soliciting a good deal of legal advice from a woman who charges for laundry by the sock. He has asked her, several times, if she thinks he should go down to the police station to answer some questions. The gauze wrapped around his head, I'm beginning to surmise, is somehow related to a sex worker he refers to in euphemistic language. I can understand, but I'm concerned that the receptionist, who seemed to have learned English as a Scowling Language, might not know what to do with

". . . and she is, how do you call, a lady, just a friend, but not just a friend."

He so obviously needs to call his embassy and/or hop on the next Jeep headed out of the country, but I can't bring myself to offer him unsolicited advice. After all, it's his life. He might know something that I don't about how he wants to live it.

On my last day, I stop in at a convenience store to buy a bottle of water and strike up a conversation with the woman working there. It's a garbled exchange that relies heavily on body language and is sustained only by my desperation for human contact. Her name is Alira. She's a petite Kazakh woman in her forties with bright red fingernails and plans to go dancing with her girls tonight. She asks me if I want to join.

Do I ever. I would go dancing with anyone at this point—my college enemy, a blood relative, the stars.

We exchange numbers and make plans to meet later.

Socializing with strangers turns out to be slightly more trying when there's a sizable language barrier. Nadia and Olga have blonde and red hair, respectively, and no English. I want to tell them that, with Alira, their range of hair colors makes them look like Charlie's Angels, but I don't know how to say *angels*, or Charlie's, and I'm also not sure that movie made it to Kazakhstan.

So instead, I break the ice by telling them my story about getting kidnapped in Turkmenistan.

When I'm done, I'm so proud of myself for getting through the whole thing in Russian that it takes me a moment to register their horrified expressions. They shake their heads. This story was maybe a little too heavy to lead with.

Olga is wearing a formfitting dress made of leather and chiffon, Nadia's donned a tight red dress and leather boots that reach up to her thighs, and Alira's dressed in boot-cut jeans and a comfortable sweater. She's still wearing her scarf. For the first and only time on this trip, I'm wearing a pair of heels and a skirt that I packed. For the second time, I'm wearing the butterfly control-top tights I bought for the wedding in Uzbekistan.

The women have ordered a liter of vodka, which they're sipping alongside cranberry juice, and the look on their faces when I ask the waiter for a beer tells me I've ordered the wrong thing.

Somehow I had imagined that tonight's dancing would take place in a more nightclub-like venue, but this feels more like a casual Italian restaurant that's been rented out for a bat mitzvah. We're sitting at a table with a tablecloth made from the same fabric as the chair coverings. A dance floor has been cleared in the center of the room, a stage for the live band erected in front of it. Colored spotlights flash from the ceiling as people get up to dance or sit down to eat dinner. Maybe it actually feels more like a wedding: guests ranging in age from young children who seem like they're in an inappropriate environment to grandparents who mostly watch from the sidelines.

I ask Olga if she, Nadia, and Alira come here often, and she says yes, of course. Maybe nightlife in Aktau has more of a function-hall feel in the off-season. The mural facing us is painted to look like a brick wall with a couple salsa dancing through it. A few actual pieces of brick have been glued on to amplify this effect.

We get up and dance for a while, which removes the burden of talking. The dance floor is surrounded by strategically placed mirrors that allow us all to watch ourselves dance, which is exactly what we do. There's something that feels nakedly honest about a social activity in which everyone just stares at their own reflections. Then we sit down and drink. The women toast to me, and then I toast to them. The band takes a break and is relieved by a DJ accompanied by a bongo player. We return to the dance floor, then to our table when a slow song comes on. It feels like I'm back at a middle school dance: a few couples slow dance, while the single people sit and stare daggers. A more upbeat song brings us out of our chairs, and then I get danced into a corner by a kid in a tracksuit with his back to me. I'm getting tired and sit down with Olga and Nadia.

Alira has befriended a group of men who look closer to my age, and we watch her dance and flirt and laugh with them, and I marvel at the fact that it's Alira, in her straight-from-work jeans and sweater, who's the star of the show.

When Alira returns, I tell the women I have to go because I have an early flight in the morning, which is true, but we've also exhausted the limits of small talk that can be made through gesticulation alone.

Alira walks me outside and we hug goodbye, and as I start back to my hotel, I think about the different paths our lives will take, and how strange it is to spend each day interacting with people you assume you'll never see again, but most of all, I think about how kind it was for Alira to invite me dancing. It might not have gotten me out of my head, and in fact, has made me slightly worried that I will be spending my evenings at places like that when I'm in my forties—but then I think about how happy Alira looked the whole night, and I think maybe it wouldn't be that bad.

So where do Aktau's addresses come from?

Some suggest that they're deliberately abstruse. Aktau was once a closed city (meaning permits were required to enter) while uranium mining was carried out in the surrounding hills. Perhaps the Soviets wanted to make it difficult for outsiders to navigate a city that contained sensitive information linked to the country's nuclear program?

I was never able to find a good answer. But I do know that Aktau is a good place to be lonely. The confusing streets force you to interact when you otherwise wouldn't, which might lead you to befriend a stranger you meet in a convenience store, or to groove out beside a couple salsa dancing through a wall. Worst-case scenario: you end up a German ghost.

TWO EASTERN EUROPE

14

AN AFTERNOON IN CHERNOBYL
(UKRAINE)

"So how many people died here?" Janice asks. This is her favorite question; she has asked it, in various forms, at the power plant, at a school, in a swimming pool, and now most sensitively, at a memorial to the victims.

"No, no one died here," our guide, Misha, explains. "This is just, like, maybe art project to remember people who is died."

"It's a memorial," Daniel, a thin, serious British student, adds quietly.

"Oh," Janice replies, sounding disappointed.

Janice is an older Canadian schoolteacher on her way back from somewhere that doesn't seem like the type of place Janice should go—I think Kazakhstan, or maybe Mongolia, possibly Thailand. Janice seems like the type of person who should stick to Canada, maybe occasionally venture down to the United States, and even then, not do much talking around people who may have experienced any kind of hardship.

As we've learned, Janice's flight back to Canada includes a twenty-four-hour layover in Kiev, and there is only one thing she wants to see in all of Ukraine: the site of the Chernobyl nuclear disaster. She has gotten off the plane and boarded a bus she prebooked with a tour group to take her straight to the reactor. She keeps telling us how grateful she is to be here.

Janice probably came to Chernobyl for the same reasons we all travel to unfamiliar places: to see something unlike anything we've seen before. The novelty of new locales can be exciting, eye-opening, sometimes frightening. Perhaps Janice thought, as I did, that in coming here she would learn something new and gain a greater understanding of the infamous disaster. But as I've learned time and time again on this trip, direct observation doesn't always yield insight.

People often point to the Chernobyl disaster as the beginning of the end of the Soviet Union. They say that the accident became a flashpoint for people's unaired grievances against the government that set the wheels of regime change in motion, and that those wheels would later drive Boris Yeltsin into Moscow on a tank to declare the end of the communist party.

The more I learned about the Chernobyl accident, the more I became interested in the causes instead of the effects. The explosion at reactor four in the Chernobyl Nuclear Power Plant came to look like the perfect embodiment of all that was wrong with the Soviet system, each event leading up to its destruction representing a different ill that was undermining the foundations holding the country in place.

If you're anything like Janice, or me before I visited Chernobyl, most of what you know about the accident might be a little bit off.

You probably assume, as I did, that it happened in a place called Chernobyl, which it didn't, and that the surrounding area was immediately abandoned, which it wasn't. How many people died in the initial explosion? If you'd asked me before I went to Ukraine, I would have guessed somewhere between a few hundred and a few thousand. The actual number is two.

This isn't to say that the Chernobyl accident wasn't bad, because it was, or that its victims weren't numerous, because they were.

But in visiting I feel, above all, I'd spent my whole life being told the wrong story.

Just before one thirty a.m. on April 26, 1986, two explosions destroyed a reactor at the Chernobyl Nuclear Power Plant. In the days that followed, the reactor released large quantities of radioactive material into the atmosphere.

As a result, radioactive particles covered the surrounding areas and were carried by winds as far as Western Europe. The majority of the waste fell in Belarus, which received 70 percent of all radioactive material released in the accident.

It can be difficult to quantify Chernobyl's human toll. Death estimates are hard to come by and subject to heated debate, because the diseases caused by radiation can take a long time to appear.

The problem in Chernobyl was less initial exposure, which caused thirty-one deaths in the days and weeks immediately after the accident, but rather, the long-term effects of contamination. In Belarus, and also, to lesser degrees, in Ukraine and Russia, land, water, agriculture, livestock, and wildlife all absorbed radiation to which humans would eventually be exposed when they ate, drank, bathed in, or otherwise came in contact with these contaminated entities.

Many people did so unknowingly, because the Soviet government's overwhelming response to the Chernobyl accident was to try to cover it up.

I haven't come to Ukraine intending to visit Chernobyl. Before I arrive, I'm not even sure it's possible. Chernobyl is, after all, the site of the world's worst nuclear disaster, and I figure the area would be off-limits to everyone except scientists, well-connected journalists, and maybe the occasional boy band trying to launch a comeback.

I'm therefore surprised to learn, at an insane-asylum-themed bar in Kiev, that Chernobyl is a quick, easy day trip from Kiev. A tour company will arrange all the permits, pick me up in Kiev, and return me at the end of the day, taking care of all food, transportation, and guiding in between.

I don't know much about Chernobyl. I know it was an accident at a nuclear power plant, and that the radiation it released caused health problems for thousands of Soviet children. Children were the face of Chernobyl in 1990s America. A family in my neighborhood hosted Chernobyl children each summer—just being in the U.S., we were told, added years to their lives. As a result, the image I have of Chernobyl is of a place still teeming with fallout.

Presumably because I'm not the only one with this picture, the agencies that run trips to Chernobyl produce videos and detailed reports explaining how safe it is to take a day trip to the Exclusion Zone, a one-thousand-square-mile territory that was evacuated after the accident. Though I get the sense that no scientists have been consulted in the making of these materials, I also get the sense that enough people go that it can't be that bad. The agencies pitch Chernobyl not as a nuclear fallout zone, but rather as a unique example of a once-thriving city that has now been abandoned, like a modern-day Pompeii.

I e-mail one of these tour companies because I'm curious. I feel guilty about doing this; it seems like gawking at tragedy. But despite my efforts to divert my attention to more wholesome sightseeing, like . . . churches?, I keep wondering what it would be like, a place so haunted by its past, a town that has been so quickly and irrevocably abandoned. I tell myself I won't hurt anyone by going. All the bad stuff has already happened. Besides, I'm so close. What harm is there in getting closer? Well, you know, besides radioactivity.

Maybe as a way of easing my conscience, the day before I leave for Chernobyl I go to a cave monastery.

I've never been to a cave monastery before, but it's pretty much exactly what it sounds like: an underground network of churches, living spaces, and tombs that monks started digging in the eleventh century.

I've learned that the Russian Orthodox churches across the former Soviet Union are usually worth ducking inside. The interiors are festooned in spectacular paintings, the altars covered by gold-leaf grates. The most striking difference between these and Catholic churches is that here you aren't allowed to sit down. There aren't any pews, because worshipers remain standing throughout services. If you do find a bench and sit down for a moment of reflection, you'll be shooed away by an angry babushka.

I've also developed an irrational fear of Orthodox holy men, who roam church grounds in floor-length black robes, long beards, and sometimes black veils. They exude a heavy masculine vibe and remind me of the time one publicly chastised me for wearing shorts.

Unbeknownst to me, I'm standing in line to descend directly into the tomb portion of the cave monastery, where the remains of Orthodox monks are displayed in glass cases.

I've covered my head, using the scarf bestowed upon me at the Tajik stranger's baby's birthday party, but apparently this is not a sufficient display of modesty, because a monk is now pulling me out of line and pushing me back up the stairs muttering, in English, "No, no, no, no, no."

For a moment, I'm too flustered by the fact that someone has correctly read me as an Anglophone to process what is happening. A strange quirk of traveling in the former Soviet Union is that most people of European and Asian heritage can pass for local. The USSR spanned such a large swath of the world that everyone from fair-skinned redheads to Mediterranean Turkmen to ethnic Koreans can easily be native Russian speakers. Like many Americans, I'm used to traveling to Europe in clothes purchased from Europe, and before I even open my mouth to butcher the local language, the person in the shop says, "How can I help you?" in English. It's refreshing to visit places where locals are surprised when my accent gives me away as an Anglophone, and also as someone with truly horrendous Russian grammar. How has this monk seen through me? Does he have special powers?

Then I remember that I'm being pushed up the stairs by a monk, of whom I'm technically afraid. It's one thing to face your fears, but it's another thing to find them affixed to your shoulders, like you are a horse, and they are the carriage.

We conga-line over to a rack holding the kind of smocks you put on a preschooler who's about to make art. Still murmuring a steady chant of "No, no, no, no, no, no, no," the monk points to a sign with a picture of shapely women's legs in pants, covered by a giant X, beside a picture of the same legs under a floor-length skirt, which does not have an X.

The smocks apparently come in different sizes, and the monk looks me up and down while flipping through the rack to find the one that will best suit me, all the while continuing to mumble, "No." He pulls out a smock and holds it up to me before nodding approvingly and handing it over. Then he turns and walks away before I can thank him, or even make sense of his eye for smock fitting.

I tie the smock around my waist and get back in line, feeling somewhere between shaken and silly. If you've never worn a unisex smock in public, let me assure you: it's not flattering.

I descend into the cramped, candlelit caves. The flickering candlelight makes only a minimal dent in the vast darkness of the caves, which is probably for the best, because they are jammed full of glass coffins. These are not tombstones marking the graves of deceased holy men; these are mummified monks.

This I did not sign up for. I like to think I'm semicomfortable with the idea of death, but I don't particularly enjoy staring it in the face. And I mean that literally: here, inches away from my nose, is the actual face of a person who died four hundred years ago.

After approximately twenty seconds, I'm thoroughly creeped out and ready to leave. But because the caves are arranged in a narrow, winding labyrinth, ducking out early isn't really an option. We all have to file through in a line. To make matters worse, most of the grown men in that line are silently weeping. I remind myself that many of these people are pilgrims who have come to be somber and reverent. I will add to that atmosphere. But I will not kiss the coffins right above the feet.

I shuffle past on the slow conveyor belt of devout believers, trying my best not to gawk at the bodies or ruin the mood for the people to whom this is meaningful. Soft chanting plays in the background.

Suddenly, the chanting cuts out and overhead fluorescent lights flicker on. A group of living monks appear to usher us out of the tombs, like it's long past closing time at a bar and we're the bachelorette party needlessly debating whether to order another round of shots.

The harsh lighting is not doing wonders for the nonliving monks. They look significantly less miraculously preserved than they did in the soft glow of candlelight. Their bodies seem small and shriveled; it's a reminder of my own mortality that I did not exactly go out looking for.

The live monks usher us out of a fire exit that dumps us straight onto the sidewalk, like a secret escape from a mad scientist's castle. If this ruined the experience for any of the pilgrims, they don't let on. The women remove their head scarves. The men wipe tears from the corners of their eyes. We all depart to get on with the rest of our days.

I'm halfway to the metro when I realize I'm still wearing the smock.

By the 1980s, unrest was spreading across the Soviet Union. Growing disillusionment had been spurred at least in part by the economy, which had begun to falter in the previous decade. Wages stagnated; consumer goods were less readily available. The government's efforts to keep out information from the West were increasingly futile. Through radios and smuggled publications, Soviet citizens were catching glimpses of a different way of life, which, to many, looked more appealing.

The Soviet system centered around a planned economy in which the government set everything from the number of employees at a company to the prices people paid at department stores. Each year, the central planning committee handed down production targets and quotas for each farm and factory in the country.

Managers were often expected to exceed these production quotas. In practice, this was almost always impossible. So it had become common for the managers to instead fudge numbers on their own production reports to make it look like they had surpassed the requirements. This behavior wasn't limited to factory managers. Unrealistic targets handed down from Moscow encouraged everyone from elite government ministers to the lowly assembly line workers to lie, cut corners, and cover up mistakes so that everything looked good on paper.

On paper, the Chernobyl Nuclear Power Plant was a model power station. In reality, it blew up twice.

In 1984, the Chernobyl Nuclear Power Plant launched reactor four into operation two months ahead of schedule. This was no small feat for the time and place. In the 1980s, the Soviet Union was experiencing increases in demand for energy and decreases in pretty much everything else—money, available construction materials, morale.

For all of these reasons, Moscow was eager to develop alternative sources of energy. Nuclear energy was particularly attractive, because the Soviet Union was also blessed with vast deposits of uranium.

The Soviet Union was notorious for delays in virtually all construction projects, both because project managers knowingly underestimated the time required to complete a project in order to ensure approval, and because the central planning committee regularly overpromised resources.

Thus, when Chernobyl was able to launch its newest reactor ahead of schedule, it was celebrated as a major victory.

Nuclear reactors launched in two phases. The first phase was a soft launch devoted solely to testing and, if necessary, repairing each of the reactor's complex systems and components. After successful testing, the reactor launched into full commercial operations.

The full battery of inspections and tests usually took at least six months to complete, and even longer if there were problems. But it was here that the Chernobyl team was able to shave two months off the schedule. The way in which it did that may be the reason you've heard of Chernobyl today.

To prep for my visit to the actual power plant, I take the metro from the cave monastery to the Ukrainian National Chernobyl Museum, which is located in Kiev.

The building that houses the museum was originally a fire station. From the outside, it still looks like one. The ground level has a row of polished wooden doors the rough dimensions of something a shiny red fire truck would drive out of to save a burning building. Perhaps to reduce the impact of visual association, the museum had inexplicably parked a tank out front.

Inside, the museum tells the entire story of the Chernobyl accident and its aftermath in incredible detail. Some might argue, too much detail.

Russian museums tend to be very thorough. "I'm not sure visitors need to see this candy wrapper that was made two decades before Lenin was born" is a sentence I doubt any Russian docent has uttered.

The Chernobyl Museum's collection features such objects as spoons similar to those used in the power plant's cafeteria. I have opted for the audio guide, which lists every fact pertinent to all fifty objects in each display case. "The booklet on the bottom right is a ration booklet for a typical family of four. It contains coupons for three kilograms of meat, twelve kilograms of potatoes, one kilogram of flour, seven kilograms of rice, and three oranges, which the family could use at one of seventeen markets operating in the city, which took up seventy-six hectares of land. Beside this, you'll see a photograph of a playground, typical of those found in each of the city's forty-five residential compounds."

I can tell that the voice actor who recorded the English audio guide found this script just as exhausting as I do. As the audio guide goes on, the actor becomes noticeably bored, sighing more frequently, and then flubbing his lines, clearing his throat, and starting over from the beginning. These stumbles are not edited out. "Track twenty-eight," he begins wearily. "There were three men in charge of reactor four that flight. AHEM. Track twenty-eight. There were three men in charge of reactor four that night."

The final exhibit is a large, dimly lit room that the museum would have no trouble renting out as a set for horror movies. Creepy music plays in the background while a seemingly random assortment of objects dangles from the ceiling: a doll, a map of the world, large furniture.

"The floor looks like a chessboard," the audio guide announces, "reminding us of the game of life." The guide moves on, leaving me to wonder if I'm missing a very obvious connection between the Chernobyl disaster and the game of life, and also what, exactly, the game of life is.

But the message behind the Chernobyl museum is clear: the meltdown at reactor four was a freak accident that no one could have seen coming.

"No one believed that the reactor could ever explode" is a line repeated throughout the museum. In an oft-quoted anecdote of questionable veracity, the president of the USSR's Academy of Sciences frequently bragged that the reactor that would go on to melt down at Chernobyl was so safe, authorities could have installed one on Red Square.

This interpretation would have benefited the Soviet authorities under whose watch the accident happened. But I'm surprised that this opinion continues to be popular today, when a new Ukrainian government is in charge.

After the USSR collapsed, files that were sealed under Soviet institutions no longer had agencies to keep them hidden away. When the Soviet Union dissolved, so did the Soviet KGB. The Soviet KGB had conducted its own investigation into the Chernobyl accident, and as the no longer classified files reveal, it reached a conclusion that differed significantly from that of the museum.

By April 26, 1986, reactor four at the Chernobyl Nuclear Power Plant had been operating for two years. In that time, the plant had come to produce about 10 percent of Ukraine's total electricity. But it had yet to verify that one of reactor four's most vital safety features worked.

This was not ideal.

The USSR mainly employed two types of reactors in these plants: a pressurized water reactor, which was popular in Western countries, and the RMBK, which was not.

The Soviets liked the RMBK because the reactor was cheap, quick to build, and easy to repair. It achieved these efficiencies by doing away with frivolous safety features like containment structures, which protect against the release of radioactive material in the event of an accident. This omission was justified using the same logic that led the *Titanic* builders to go easy on the lifeboats: the nuclear reactor was unsinkable, and also, unexplodable.

On April 25, 1986, reactor four at the Chernobyl power plant was scheduled to be shut down for routine maintenance. While it was being shut down, the plant hoped to finally conduct a successful test of the reactor's emergency backup system.

One of the worst things that can go wrong at a nuclear power plant is a sudden loss of power. The systems used to control and regulate the reactors run on electricity, without which operators can quickly lose control of the nuclear reaction taking place in the reactor's core.

The Chernobyl plant was equipped with backup generators that could power the reactor controls in this situation, but there was a lag between the time when the generators were switched on and the time when they reached full power. The reactors were therefore designed to power themselves using the run-down of energy in the turbogenerator. This was the system plant management planned to test on April 25.

Outside observers would later question why this test was taking place in 1986, and not 1984. The official report released by the Soviet government claimed that plant management was testing a new enhanced safety feature, but what they termed a new enhancement was identical to the safety system listed in the reactor's design specifications. In other words, it seemed like they were testing the reactor's original emergency backup system.

This system should have been assessed before the reactor launched into full production. If the Chernobyl plant was testing it now, two years after the reactor started operating, it would seem that this essential safety feature never passed the initial prelaunch inspection. It would be fair to conclude that plant managers may have decided to launch the reactor before ensuring that the safety system was in working order, in order to please their higher-ups.

Not long after the Chernobyl accident, an energy minister named Grigori Medvedev was sent to the plant to conduct an official investigation. The report he went on to publish was scathing. In its official account presented to the International Atomic Energy Agency, the Soviet government blamed the accident entirely on two operators, who had conveniently died of radiation poisoning and thus made excellent scapegoats. Medvedev, in contrast, faulted design flaws and a work culture that put little emphasis on safety.

In his report, Medvedev recounted a meeting he'd attended at the Kremlin two months before the Chernobyl accident. A construction manager at a different nuclear power plant had announced that a reactor's launch would be delayed because the plant hadn't received parts from an outside vendor on time.

The government minister didn't care—he told the construction manager to find a way to launch the reactor by the original deadline. The manager protested that the part he was waiting for would barely be ready by then. The minister repeated his instructions: find a way to make it work. In essence, the minister was telling the plant manager to make sure that he fulfilled the work plan on paper—even if that meant launching the reactor with a piece missing.

"This is our national tragedy," the plant manager lamented to Medvedev afterward. "We ourselves lie and we teach our subordinates to lie. No good will come of this."

All of this created a culture of cutting corners and meaningless stamps of approval in the Soviet nuclear power industry. And in this context, Chernobyl seems like far less of a freak accident.

I meet Igor, the guide who has arranged my trip to Chernobyl, at seven on a cold, gray morning. He's easy to find: he's standing outside a white minibus covered in the black-and-yellow nuclear hazard symbol.

"Good morning!" he says cheerfully. "Can you eat pork?"

The back of the bus displays a split image of a young girl. Half of the frame is a normal photo, but in the other half, she's wearing a gas mask.

I board the bus, already wary of the kitsch, and I find a half-dozen other sleepy tourists. A few minutes later, Igor bounds onto the bus, full of energy, and takes roll.

"Mark Cameron," he calls. "Can you eat pork?"

As we drive out of Kiev and head for the Chernobyl Exclusion Zone, Igor preps us by playing a two-hour video introduction to Chernobyl. This collection of videos can best be described as "Every Video Referencing Chernobyl That Igor Was Able to Find." The log line, if it has one, would be "Some of Which I Suspect He Did Not Fully Understand."

Here is some information you will not glean from Igor's Chernobyl video clips.

The Chernobyl Nuclear Power Plant was staffed in three shifts. The morning crew arrived at eight a.m. and left at four p.m.; their evening replacements clocked in at four and out at midnight. The unlucky night shift worked from midnight to eight a.m.

The test that led to the Chernobyl accident was scheduled to begin at one p.m. on the afternoon of April 25. A special team of outside engineers had been brought in to make sure things ran smoothly, and the day shift had been thoroughly briefed on the plan.

At one p.m., the day shift operators began to power down one of reactor four's turbogenerators, as planned. The reactor would produce only half as much electricity for the duration of the experiment. Following test instructions, the operators disabled the emergency core cooling system.

At two p.m., the manager of the electrical grid serving Kiev called the station to report an unexpected surge in demand for electricity (post-Soviet reports indicate that another plant unexpectedly went off-line) and requested that the test be postponed. The turbogenerator was switched back on, and the test was put on hold. Crucially, the emergency core cooling system was never switched back on.

The test was still on hold at four p.m., when the evening shift arrived at the plant. The day shift passed on the instructions it had received that morning and then packed up to go home.

At 11:10 p.m., just as the evening shift was getting ready to leave, the Kiev grid gave the go-ahead to resume the experiment. The reactor had been operating all afternoon and evening with its emergency core cooling system disengaged, in blatant violation of safety protocol.

This was also an inopportune time to resume a risky test. The day shift that had been briefed on the experiment was gone, and the staff would switch again at midnight, when the night shift arrived.

But, perhaps because most employees on-site didn't understand the dangers the test posed, operators went forward with the experiment and once again commenced powering down the reactor.

At midnight, in the middle of the test, the evening crew was relieved by the night shift. A thirty-three-year-old engineer named Aleksandr Akimov became shift supervisor, while twenty-six-year-old operator Leonid Toptunov took the helm in the control room.

Neither man had particularly expert knowledge of the reactor. Toptunov had been working independently as a senior engineer for only a few months. Akimov was a nuclear engineer, but he had held more of a management role at the plant, and he had never operated the reactor.

The evening shift passed along the instructions, as the day shift had done for them. But by now Akimov and Toptunov were receiving third-hand information—what the evening shift recalled from what the day shift had told them. Later investigations would reveal how haphazard this relay had been. Some of the printed experiment documentation had been annotated with messy handwritten notes that the night shift couldn't read.

Toptunov took over the controls and continued the power-down that the previous operator had started. The Soviet report would later indicate that Toptunov made a small but fatal error: he positioned the reactor's control rods a few centimeters below where he should have, and because of this the power dropped drastically.

Once a reactor falls below a certain power level, it begins emitting particles that inhibit nuclear reactions, making it difficult to bring the power level back up. The test required that the reactor be operating at an output of at least seven hundred megawatts (MW); when Toptunov incorrectly positioned the rods, the power dropped to thirty MW—close to shutdown state.

At this point, Toptunov (correctly) concluded that it would be too dangerous to even try to bring the reactor up to seven hundred MW, and his supervisor, Akimov, agreed. Both believed that the test should be aborted and the reactor should be shut down completely.

But the deputy chief engineer, Anatoly Dyatlov, disagreed.

Dyatlov had come to the plant a decade earlier, after working at a physics lab and at a plant that built nuclear submarines. His colleagues knew him as a man of few social graces whose management style leaned heavily on upbraiding.

Perhaps because he'd been pressured by his superiors, or maybe because he took any opportunity to chastise his subordinates, Dyatlov insisted that the test be completed on his shift. He accused Akimov and Toptunov of incompetence and told them if they didn't raise the power level, he'd put the evening shift supervisor (who had stayed after his shift ended to help) back on duty. This move would have served to humiliate Akimov.

Toptunov reluctantly gave in, removing more rods than was safe to offset the obstructing particles. By one a.m., he'd stabilized power at two hundred MW, an improvement, but still far below what the test called for.

To try to increase power, Toptunov began removing more and more protective rods from the reactor core, which was like taking his foot off the brake pedal of the nuclear reaction. This was in direct violation of safety protocol, because if he were to later try to reinsert the rods, this would cause a surge in power, which could lead to an explosion.

And that, it turns out, is precisely what happened.

Igor's videos include an interview with Mikhail Gorbachev, who was the leader of the Soviet Union at the time of the Chernobyl accident. Gorbachev is often criticized for being slow to inform the Soviet public and the international community about what happened at Chernobyl.

The first hint the world received that it had just experienced its worst nuclear disaster came two days after it happened, from Sweden.

On April 28, a Swedish nuclear power plant detected unusually high levels of radiation, which it traced back to the Soviet Union. Swedish scientists hypothesized that there had been some kind of nuclear accident. Foreign media quickly picked up the story, and the Soviets released a terse statement that evening, confirming that an accident had taken place at the Chernobyl plant and declaring, "The effects of the accident are being remedied. Assistance has been provided for any affected people."

In the film, the interviewer asks Gorbachev, gently, why it took the Soviet Union two days to confirm the accident, and almost three weeks for Gorbachev to discuss it publicly.

"I didn't know about the radiation," Gorbachev replies. He got a call saying there had been a fire at the Chernobyl plant, he claims, but no one told him that the smoke was radioactive.

At a rest stop, I ask Igor if he thinks Gorbachev is telling the truth in the video. I assume he gets this question all the time.

Apparently, he does not. "Why, if the Soviet Union was a closed country, was Pripyat evacuated the next day?" he replies, sounding annoyed. "And why, if Japan is an open country, did they take one week to evacuate after Fukushima? The Japanese government also lied." He shakes his head.

I'm fairly certain Fukushima was evacuated immediately, but I don't get the sense that Igor would welcome this fun fact. Fukushima was featured heavily yesterday at the Chernobyl Museum, where the reaction to Japan's nuclear accident could best be described as giddy. Now Ukraine isn't the only country with a disastrous nuclear meltdown on its record. The museum has set up an entire exhibit dedicated to showing how the Fukushima accident was almost as bad as Chernobyl's.

Igor goes on to reiterate what I'd heard at the museum: that no one believed the reactor could fail, and that news of a fire wouldn't have prompted suspicion of radioactive release as it moved up the chain of command. "To hear that the reactor was leaking radiation—it would be like if I told you that a tree had exploded!" Igor exclaims. "Just, for no reason, a tree exploded!"

He sighs. "Anyway, these questions are not for us, normal people. They are for the government. We are only ants."

But as I get back on the bus, I wonder why no one ever asks him what seems to me like a fairly obvious question. Why, I wonder, is everyone coming to Chernobyl, if not to better understand what happened?

Pripyat, the city Igor mentioned, was not evacuated the day after the accident.

At 1:23 a.m. on April 26, 1986, the control room at the Chernobyl power plant was jolted by two powerful explosions.

The first explosion ruptured the roof of the building that housed the reactor. The second sent burning radioactive debris shooting out through the breach. The buildup of heat before the explosion had evaporated uranium fuel and fission products, which quickly rose into the atmosphere. Cooling water spilled out and air rushed in, igniting graphite material and allowing nuclear reactions to continue unimpeded. Radioactive dust quickly coated equipment, walls, floors—anything and everything. Other particles assembled above the plant in a cloud, ready to disperse wherever the wind led.

But because no one had a bird's-eye view of the plant, the operators and engineers didn't immediately realize that the damage to the reactor had been so severe that the core was exposed. An exposed core is catastrophic, in terms of radiation release, and also fire management. The water firefighters would later aim at the reactor to subdue the flames could actually ignite materials in the core.

At this time, Dyatlov assumed the reactor was still intact. He sent two low-level engineers to manually lower the control rods into the reactor. When they returned, they reported that the reactor had been completely destroyed, leaving the core so exposed they had seen it with their own eyes.

It was so difficult for Dyatlov to believe that the indestructible reactor had been destroyed that he didn't. Despite the fact that the two men had returned with tanned faces that indicated they'd received lethal doses of radiation, Dyatlov dismissed their report. He told himself, along with his superiors, that the explosion had come from some piece of equipment outside the reactor, that the building was structurally in trouble, but that the reactor had suffered no damage.

Meanwhile, everyone could see the fires that had sprouted all around the destroyed reactor and, most critically, were now licking the roof on the adjacent hall containing reactor three. If the fire reached reactor three, it could trigger a second round of equally potent explosions. Putting out the fire on the roof of the reactor three hall became crucial.

The first fire brigade to arrive came from the plant itself. It was followed, soon after, by backup from the nearby city of Pripyat, then the slightly farther town of Chernobyl, and finally, two hours later, reinforcements from far-away Kiev.

Few of the first responders knew that the flames they were battling were radioactive. Fires could occur at nuclear power plants
for many reasons unrelated to the core or uranium fuel. The crews
didn't have equipment to test for radiation levels, and they didn't
have protective equipment to prevent them from receiving dangerous doses of radiation.

Two firefighters died that night of acute radiation poisoning; by
the end of the year, twenty-eight more had been killed by the radiation they'd been exposed to that night.

But the firefighters were unquestionably the first heroes of the
disaster, because by six thirty in the morning on April 26, the fire
on the roof of reactor three had been extinguished, as had all others except the one inside the reactor. Reactor four was still pouring radioactive material into the atmosphere, but there wouldn't
be any further explosions, which would have released even more
radiation.

Meanwhile, a few miles down the road, the city of Pripyat was
waking up to an ordinary Saturday morning. It was a warm spring
day, and the city buzzed in anticipation of the upcoming May Day,
one of the biggest holidays in the Soviet Union.

Children went to Saturday classes and spent the afternoon playing outside, laughing and soaking up the season's first strong dose
of sunshine. Their bodies were also unwittingly soaking up dangerous doses of radiation, as invisible hot particles settled on their
clothes, hair, and skin.

No one in Pripyat was told that there had been a nuclear accident
at the Chernobyl plant or that the air was filled with radioactive iso-
topes. The surrounding area should have been evacuated immediately after the accident, but the people who lived closest to the plant
were not warned of the danger until two p.m. on April 27, almost
thirty-six hours after the first explosion.

A few years ago, Igor helped a musician shoot a music video at Chernobyl. When this video comes on in the bus, I pick up on something

I suspect Igor has not, which is that the music video's star, Crucifix, is a Christian artist.

To a non-native speaker, his religious overtones would be easy to miss.

"We're sleeping in the dirt of Chernobyl still tonight," he rages into the microphone as musicians in gas masks go to town on guitars and drums. "Dying from inside, poisoned by our pride."

The subtle language evangelicals employ can really make it hard to see the Jesus coming. But you only need to have one conversation take a surprise turn toward salvation to forever pick up on references to "free will" and a "fallen man." I wonder if Igor repeatedly heard Crucifix blame the Chernobyl disaster on "pride" and figured it was better than letting the ax fall on the Soviet government.

When things went wrong in the Soviet Union, a significant portion of the response was devoted to covering it up.

The Chernobyl disaster was not the first accident at a Soviet nuclear power station. In fact, it wasn't even the first accident at the Chernobyl Nuclear Power Plant. In 1981, a KGB report that was made public after the collapse of the Soviet Union reported that, in the Chernobyl plant's first four years of operations, there had been twenty-nine emergency shutdowns of reactors, only eight of which were attributed to human error. The rest, it declared, were "for technical reasons." The report goes on to warn that the plant's "control equipment does not meet the requirements for reliability due at the nuclear power plant."

The next year, reactor one at Chernobyl suffered a partial core meltdown.

In 1984, the KGB again recorded safety concerns at the Chernobyl plant. A report noted that "The first and second [reactor] units are less reliable in terms of environmental safety," and "the system of cooling of main circulation pumps is insufficient (lower than norms by approximately 39%)."

This is not to say that the Soviet Union was the only country that struggled to harness nuclear energy safely. In fact, if you tally reported nuclear accidents by country, the United States comes up first.

But the key word is *reported*.

Sweeping things under the rug was the preferred method of problem-solving in the Soviet Union. It wasn't always the highest echelons of government conspiring to deceive the public (though it often was). Sometimes, a cover-up emanated from a lower-level official trying to keep his superiors ignorant of a mistake that would cost him his job.

The pervasiveness of secrecy and lies kept information out of the hands of people who could use it against you, but it also kept it from people who could put it to good use. Case in point: an accident at a nuclear power station in Kursk had put the reactor under the same conditions the operators at Chernobyl were trying to test.

It's possible that the accident at Kursk could have provided insights into potential safety issues in Chernobyl reactor four. But we'll never know, because the accident at Kursk was kept secret, and the operators at Chernobyl were none the wiser.

The final video we have to watch before stepping out into the Exclusion Zone explains radiation and Geiger counters. We watch this while we pass through a series of military checkpoints, where our passports are compared to preapproved lists while we sit on the bus and Igor greets familiar soldiers. I realize this is his regular commute.

The point of the video is that visiting Chernobyl is very safe.

Lots of things you might encounter every day emit small doses of radiation—marble, granite ("check your countertops before you install them," the video advises), televisions, the sun. In small doses, radiation isn't especially harmful. You get exposed to higher levels of radiation when you do things like sit for an X-ray or fly across an ocean, but this is not thought to carry increased health risk. While it's hard to measure how much radiation your body absorbs, a Geiger counter is a small, handheld device that allows you to measure how much radiation something is giving off.

The Geiger counters most tour companies in the Exclusion Zone use are small devices the size of a walkie-talkie and covered in yellow plastic. They emit a high-pitched beeping noise that seems more for effect than functionality, because the beep doesn't change with the radiation reading. In the video, we see a Geiger counter take readings in various locations: downtown Kiev, the entrance to the Exclusion Zone, various points within the Exclusion Zone. The readouts are all more or less the same, which might have reassured us if we had any idea what they meant. Next to the infamous reactor four, the Geiger reading jumps to three. Is three a low reading, or a high one? It doesn't say. Three is a small number if you're talking about slices of pizza, but a big number if you're talking about late-night calls to an ex-boyfriend.

Flying from Kiev to Toronto exposes you to ten times more radiation than a day trip to the Chernobyl Exclusion Zone, the video assures us. This doesn't seem right, but we'll go with it.

Because I had kind of assumed the Chernobyl Nuclear Power Plant was shut down and sealed off shortly after releasing vast quantities of radiation into the atmosphere, I'm somewhat taken aback when Misha casually mentions that we'll be visiting the reactor.

"Like, the . . . bad one?" someone asks.

Misha shrugs. "Why not? People are still working there, you know." We did not know that.

Misha is our guide in the Chernobyl Exclusion Zone (through some murky arrangement, companies like Igor's have to hire guides like Misha once they cross into the Exclusion Zone), and half of Misha's job seems to be responding to our incredulity with practiced nonchalance.

"The Exclusion Zone today is one of the safest places to live," Misha declares, offering no supporting evidence. "You don't believe me?" He reaches up and plucks an apple from a tree growing less than a mile from the nuclear reactor. He takes a bite. "You see?" he continues. "Very safe."

We all stare, unconvinced that he has proven anything, or that he understands how radiation poisoning works.

But this does get to a larger point, which is that the most surprising thing about the Chernobyl Exclusion Zone is the degree to which it is not actually abandoned. This is only surprising because articles about Chernobyl tend to have titles like, "Abandoned: Visiting the Ruins of the World's Worst Nuclear Disaster, Which Is Surrounded by Places That Have Been Completely Abandoned, Which Means the Buildings Are Still There, But the People Aren't," or, if it's a nature magazine, something more fuzzy, like, "The Animals Have Returned to Chernobyl—And They're Looking for Revenge."

On the main street in the city of Chernobyl, it's pretty much business as usual. Cars drive by on the street; in government buildings, public employees still administrate the surrounding region.

I had pictured Chernobyl as a deserted, postapocalyptic wasteland, possibly covered in fog. I did not picture a thriving nightlife scene, which is what Misha misses most while he's gone.

I had also assumed that Chernobyl was one place, and also *the* place where the nuclear meltdown happened, but that, too, is not quite accurate. Chernobyl is the name of the region in which the eponymous power plant is located, and it's also the name of the region's capital city. But the city of Chernobyl is nine miles away from the Chernobyl Nuclear Power Plant, which sits on the outskirts of the former city of Pripyat.

As the settlement closest to the reactor, Pripyat is the place that's been most thoroughly abandoned in the wake of the accident. Many power-plant employees lived in Pripyat, which was a Soviet "model city," constructed for the purpose of housing plant workers and their families. Because the Soviet government took such pride in its nuclear program, it endowed Pripyat with the best amenities. The children of Pripyat studied at gleaming schools and their parents swam laps in one of the city's three swimming pools. A newly constructed amusement park was scheduled to open five days after the accident.

On April 27, 1986, a full day after the accident, the Soviet government finally began evacuating Pripyat and the surrounding areas. At first, residents were told that the evacuation would be temporary—families, thinking they'd be gone for a few weeks at most, didn't bother taking all their belongings with them.

When the extent and severity of contamination became clear, the Exclusion Zone was expanded and rendered something closer to permanent. It was cordoned off and closed to the public.

But it was never really abandoned. Perhaps because a picture of workers swimming in a pool a mile and a half away from the Chernobyl Nuclear Power Plant a handful of years after the accident is less exciting than a photograph of an abandoned amusement park, this detail does not always make it into the aforementioned magazine articles.

The explosion occurred in reactor four, which was connected to reactor three by a vent building. You might expect that, given that the greatest nuclear disaster in the history of mankind occurred mere feet from reactor three, reactor three would have been immediately evacuated and abandoned. But you would be wrong, because reactor three continued operating, which is to say, using nuclear fission to generate electricity, for *fourteen years* after the accident.

The plant didn't enter the decommissioning phase until April of 2015, six months before I arrive. People still go to work every day at the Chernobyl Nuclear Power Plant.

Well, not every day.

If you work in the Exclusion Zone, you pretty much have to live there, too, but safety regulations prohibit employees from living and working in the Zone full-time. Most workers have some setup like two weeks on, two weeks off, and they're supposed to spend the off weeks outside the Zone.

But Misha hates this. His friends are here, his apartment is here, his favorite bar is here.

"Sometimes," he finally admits, after I've asked him five million questions, "I sneak back in early."

We drive to the main square in Chernobyl, where it feels like it could be a slow Tuesday morning anywhere. This seems to disappoint Janice.

At the nearby memorial, Misha makes an offhand comment about how Sweden forced the Soviet Union to admit to the accident. His tone is so different from Igor's defense of Gorbachev at the rest stop that I ask for clarification. Misha explains how the Soviet government didn't want to tell people what happened; Igor jumps in and adamantly disagrees. "No, they plan to say," Igor corrects.

Thus begins a daylong power struggle between Misha and Igor.

The difference between the way Misha and Igor interpret what happened at Chernobyl is this: Misha blames the government; Igor blames the reactor. Misha criticizes the authorities; Igor defends them.

Igor is in his early forties. He grew up in Kiev when it was still the Soviet Union. Misha, in contrast, was born in a town not far from the Chernobyl reactor, two years after the accident. After the collapse of the Soviet Union, the newly independent Ukrainian government expanded the Exclusion Zone to include the town in which Misha and his parents lived, and so they were forced to move. This isn't as bad as what happened to many people in Pripyat, who were evacuated in 1986 to towns that became part of the expanded Exclusion Zone after Ukraine gained independence, which meant those families had to relocate twice.

I wonder if this explains the difference in worldview. Igor was raised under a government that provided; Misha saw the havoc it wreaked.

"I don't believe authorities," Misha says. "They did lie, they lie now, and they will lie in the future." It's half English lesson, half political statement. Janice laughs. "Why are you laughing?" Misha snaps.

Everyone marvels at our good fortune to have been blessed with perfect weather. It's a cold, gray day, the sky a drop cloth of clouds.

The occasional flock of crows rises and scatters. The gloominess is the perfect backdrop for taking photos of derelict structures, which seems to be why everyone is here.

"It would suck to visit on a sunny day," someone muses as we pull up at an abandoned day-care center on the edge of Pripyat.

On the outside, it's not much to look at: a two-story building slowly in the process of becoming a one-story building.

Inside, it's exactly what you'd hope for: peeling walls and a carpet of leaves and shattered glass, a room of rusting cots with grotesque, weathered dolls sitting up on the crumbling mattresses, waving. It's almost like the room has been staged for a horror movie, which, I quickly realize, it has.

It's just a little too perfect: the toys arranged as though a child fled in the middle of playing with them, the books opened to pages with uncanny resonance: emergency instructions for evacuating a school bus, a little boy's handwriting. The group lustily whips out cameras and begins snapping photos of the doll with the face blackened by smoke or the cot that's been overturned in the middle of the room.

I don't even have to ask Misha if recent visitors have rearranged everything to maximize creepiness: I know that they have. Most people come here to take pictures of battered dolls with wild hair and eerie smiles.

Another group joins us at the day-care center: a group of Germans in army fatigues. I ask Misha about them. "Chernobyl freaks," he says. "They've been here fifteen times."

"How do you know that?" I ask.

"Their guide told me."

Why am I here? I wonder as I wander through empty rooms with scattered paper and overturned buckets of blocks. Morbid curiosity? Regular curiosity? Fear of missing out on radioactive waste? Am I just drawn to anything that calls itself "abandoned"? Is there something inherently interesting about a place where people once lived and now do not?

In Igor's Chernobyl videos, one of Crucifix's guides had a moment of pensiveness, overlooking the ruins of Pripyat. "This is what it will look like when there are no people," he mused.

I can't help but think that will only be true if a nonhuman race figures out how to turn the ruins of our civilization into a tourist attraction. Because even if you dismiss all the staging, the improbable dolls sitting up on their cots, there's also a sense that the tragedy is being overshadowed by highlighting only what it left behind.

All the uninhabited structures are being attacked, on all sides, by plants: trees that take root in the middle of lecture halls, vines slowly consuming what were once walls. But somehow this isn't enough for the tourists, which, I presume, is why someone has taken the liberty of firing a rifle into the day-care walls, leaving bullet holes that Misha points out to us. Janice gasps and lunges for her camera.

Before we leave the day-care center, Misha calls us over to an unremarkable patch of grass: he wants to show us a hot spot. He holds the Geiger counter over the spot as the number leaps up, and we all *ohh* and *ahh*, more impressed than concerned for our health. The Geiger counter, I realize, is not to keep us safe. It adds to the ambience. It's what we paid to see.

I ask Misha why he started working as a Chernobyl guide. I expect him to give some pat answer about sharing his culture or meeting people from all over the world, but to my surprise, he gives it to me straight. "It's good money," he says, "and you don't have to work very much."

Because of the regulations forbidding most people from living in the Exclusion Zone, Chernobyl guides get a lot of time off. Their schedules are either four days on, three days off, or fifteen days on, fifteen days off. Most people come Monday morning and leave Thursday night, Misha says, which is why today, Friday, everything feels so deserted. "I work half the time of a normal worker," Misha continues, "plus I must have forty-six days of holiday each year."

"This is for people who come from very far to work here," Igor explains.

"No," Misha snaps, "the authorities don't care about normal people like us."

"How many people died here?" Janice is calling over to us.

The square that we're standing on joins what used to be a hotel, restaurant, and civic center. Trees have pushed up through cracks in the concrete, amassed twenty-nine years of growth, and, because it is late October, exploded in autumnal foliage. If anyone died here, it was from the intersection of communism and capitalism.

"No one," Misha calls back.

Ultimately, the version of Chernobyl I'd heard strikes me as a game of telephone. Many of the most haunting images of "abandoned" Chernobyl lose much of their power when captioned with the real story. There's an indoor swimming pool that has long been drained and now sits, bone-dry, littered with leaves and graffiti and a shopping cart.

"Actually, the workers used this pool for many years after the accident," Misha explains.

There's the shuttered amusement park that makes for great photos, but wan't technically abandoned. "They never opened it," Misha tells us.

There is the high school with hundreds of gas masks covering the floor. Most people would see this and think they were dropped by fleeing students who'd been wearing them to protect against radiation.

"Every school in the Soviet Union must have gas masks," Misha says, shaking his head. "They were just, like, sitting in some box, and somebody put them all over the ground."

"Why?" I ask.

"Some people who want to, you know, undermine the feeling of the Exclusion Zone."

Misha has been saying this all day. The people who wear surplus army uniforms, for example, are undermining the accident. At first I missed the malapropism; later, I realize he means *underline*.

But I don't correct him, because in some ways he's right. Maybe these people aren't *trying* to undermine the Chernobyl disaster. But at the end of the day, that's what they're doing.

The reason tourists can visit Chernobyl and Pripyat today is that these areas were largely decontaminated by liquidators, who spent years collecting and disposing of radioactive material. Some of these men volunteered, seeing their actions as a heroic sacrifice for their motherland. Others were sent involuntarily. Many of these men went on to have health problems as a result of the radiation to which they were exposed.

So where are the victims of Chernobyl, the children who stayed in my neighborhood back in Boston each summer?

Some are those of the liquidators, who are now spread throughout the former Soviet Union, some living, others not. The children we tend to picture when we think of the accident grew up largely in Belarus, which received the majority of the radioactive particles released from the accident. But sometimes it can be hard to pin casualties squarely on the Chernobyl disaster. Some studies suggest that children in Belarus had higher rates of thyroid cancers, others point out that the general population isn't typically screened for thyroid cancers. In the years that followed Chernobyl, Belarus was also afflicted with higher rates of poverty. Sometimes it was hard to say if health problems in children came from Chernobyl or impoverishment.

Despite the manifold caveats and nuances, the most commonly accepted statistic says that four thousand deaths can be attributed to Chernobyl directly. And I think everyone agrees that, given how easily it could have been prevented, that's four thousand too many.

So, Janice, I hope this answers your question.

15

HALLOWEEN IN YOUR LOVER'S HOMELAND (BELARUS)

There's no quick fix for a broken heart, but the badly stricken try to find one anyway. Some turn to tequila, others exercise, ice cream, poetry, a new boyfriend who looks just like the old one. If all else fails, you can always go to Belarus.

Belarus is a country you may not have heard of surrounded by countries you probably have. It snuggles up against Poland to the west, Ukraine to the south, Latvia and Lithuania to the north, and Russia to the east. It's an isolated, authoritarian state said to most closely replicate life behind the iron curtain.

It can be difficult for foreigners to visit Belarus, which I suspect, for some, is part of the appeal. To get a visa, I had to buy Belarusian health insurance. But the country also doesn't present itself as a particularly appealing tourist destination.

Belarus is often referred to as "Europe's last dictatorship." Its President, Alexander Lukashenko, has been in power since 1994.

Whenever Anton's friends from Belarus visit China, they all have the same reaction. Not long after I meet Anton, we're in a taxi with his friend Anya speeding down an elevated highway that passes neon skyscrapers, TV billboards, and sprawling brick colonial buildings. Anya says something to Anton in Russian. I assume she's marveling at the view. But then she switches to English for my benefit. "I was just saying, everyone here is so free!" she exclaims.

"Free?" I don't understand.

"Yes—no one will stop people on the street and ask them for their documents, or tell them, 'No, you can't stand here.' At home, the police are always doing this."

When I get to know him better, Anton rails against this, too: the indignity of being harassed by police officers while walking down the street, the absurdity of a floundering economy burdened by state-owned businesses. Belarus has one of the highest numbers of police per capita in the world. It emerged from the Soviet Union with high standards of living and a highly industrialized economy, which the government has since run into the ground.

The picture Anton paints of his homeland is often bleak. He remembers the chaos that followed the collapse of the Soviet Union and the promise of changes that never materialized. He describes hardship that morphed into desperation and finally settled into a hopeless resignation.

I suppose you could ask, given all this, why I wanted to go.

Anton and I still communicate a few times a year, usually just on special occasions, like when I have the flimsiest excuse to reach out. A few weeks before I leave for this trip, I tell Anton that I'm planning to visit Belarus and ask if he has any recommendations. He helpfully recommends that I not go. "This place can be very unpleasant for foreigners," he explains.

This makes me sad.

It has been two years since Anton and I broke up, and in that time I've missed him in different ways. Sometimes I miss his presence in a way that aches physically; other times I miss the possibilities he represented. I still half expect to bump into him one day, and both go, *Dude, what the fuck, this was so silly,* and laugh like this was all some huge joke. But mostly I just miss him.

The actual breakup happens in an airport Burger King. The split is planned—we had booked a nonrefundable trip to Vietnam for our back-to-back birthdays, then decided we were sick of the logistics our relationship required, then decided to go on the trip anyway.

We get in from Saigon early in the morning, and our plan is to go our separate ways as soon as we land. But we are both hungry, and the only good place to eat at the airport is Burger King, so we decide to postpone the breakup until after breakfast.

"It was still a good trip," I tease, both because I did all the planning and because it doesn't seem real. He is reticent, morose, and, most creepily, he has ordered something off the nonbreakfast menu.

"Whatever." He scowls. His face shouldn't still strike me as remarkable, but it does. He has smooth skin and a smile that the world has to work for; when he does grin, his face melts like you've won some prize. He keeps his hair perfectly coiffed and dresses however he pleases. He looks exactly how I want him to.

"Will you at least kiss me goodbye?" I ask as I stand up to leave.

"No." He shakes his head. "I don't think you understand this is real."

"I do!" I protest. I'm keeping things light. He is a stand-up, too, and my favorite joke of his goes: "My girlfriend is also a comedian, so it's hard to take our relationship seriously. But we're madly in love! People always ask if she writes my jokes, and I say, 'Just that one.'"

"Okay, I gotta go," I say, and I try to kiss him anyway, but he turns his head.

It takes a few days for reality to set in, but when it does, sadness swallows me whole. It feels like this needs to be the end of something bigger, too—this stage of my life, or China, or spending my days tutoring. For reasons that have nothing to do with Anton, what comes next is a question to which I have no answer, or even a gut feeling. Anton had been the one who knew the path forward—without him, I don't know how I will ever be great, or even better. Between the pain of heartbreak and fear of uncertainty, the former is less difficult to dwell in. And so I step into heartbreak with both feet.

Which is not to say I don't miss Anton. I fucking miss him, man. In some ways, it feels like we never broke up, because his physical absence is more than offset by his starring role in my thoughts. My

mind has become a mere venue for The Anton Show, a carefully cu-
rated collection of euphoric moments that have now become excruciating memories, conjectures about his exact whereabouts at any
given moment, and brutal assessments of my own shortcomings
that prove Anton never loved me at all.

In time, The Anton Show subsides, though never completely
fades, along with the pain, but the pull of Belarus doesn't. If anything, it grows in intensity, and with it, my sense that I won't be
able to navigate the country without Anton. When we were in love,
I longed to go to Belarus because I longed to soak up every aspect
of Anton's being—his mere scent triggered intoxication. Now that
we're not, what could his homeland possibly hold for me?

I've always joked that I fall in love with Russians because I want
to go to Russia. But I'm starting to wonder if I have it backward.
Maybe I want to go to Russia because I fell in love with Russians.

This feels, sounds, and is less logical than my first read, but
somehow, it makes more sense to me. Even if I'm wrong, there are
times when I feel like the only way to get Belarus out of my head is
to just go there and get it over with.

In the end, I decide that if something has such a hold on you, you
might as well explore it and try to figure out why.

It's strange both how much and how little distance two years can
create. Even now, Anton still lingers in the back of my thoughts.
And yet in the real world we've grown to be strangers. I know this
because Anton's e-mail is a mark of his forgetting my personality.
Two years ago, he would have known that telling me not to go to
Belarus would be the one thing guaranteed to get me there.

My trepidation is multifold as I wait on the bus to Brest, Belarus.
Which, coincidentally, is the source of trepidation number one: entering Belarus by bus does not exactly feel like the triumphant *I
made it anyway* I'm going for. If a bus is a statement, it's more of a
meek *I didn't plan ahead* or a whispered *The train website wouldn't
take my credit card.*

This bus, by the way, smells *truly* terrible. And I say that as someone well aware that few buses really smell neutral, and that no bus ever smells good.

The larger and more salient causes for trepidation are: Will everything in Belarus remind me of this lost love, the person I once knew and now do not? Will this shroud me in a post-Soviet-style cloak of misery that will prove impossible to shake? Am I willingly walking into more suffering? Is Belarus a dark, cruel country with a population that matches its atmosphere?

When Belarus shows up on the news, it's rarely for something good. It's for protesters being beaten and jailed so readily that they've been forced to come up with new, innovative ways of expressing dissent, promoting the government to retaliate with new, innovative ways of cracking down on dissent.

Take the "clapping protest," in which three thousand people gathered in a square and seemed to give a round of applause to no one in particular, though everyone knew it was a proclamation demanding the resignation of Lukashenko, who, at that point, was seventeen years into what was looking like a lifelong presidential term. Police rounded up clappers, and officials rewrote the constitution, which had previously banned "gatherings for any action," to now ban "gatherings for any action or no action."

Belarus is known for average salaries that hover around a few hundred dollars a month and the second-lowest life expectancy in Europe.

It suddenly seems obvious that everyone on this bus will hate me: the old man in the newsboy cap, the young guys with hands stuffed in pockets, the group of women who seem much younger than me but have children that look incongruously close to adulthood. The fifty-something woman with short hair and penciled-in eyebrows sitting behind me.

I take a seat and do my best to avoid all eye contact.

Sometimes I still replay the past in my head and only remember it's a terrible idea halfway through. *I made it this far,* I think. *Might as well see how it ends.*

Like this: I'm picking Vadik up from his Chinese preschool, at a time when my Chinese is limited to a handful of basically scripted conversations I have every day: "I'm going here," "How much does this cost?" "Do you have Diet Coke?"

I'm here to pick up a five-year-old Belarusian is so beyond my taxi and restaurant vocabulary that by the time I find him, he's one of the last kids left.

"Audrey!" he squeals when he sees me, running over and hugging me so tightly that it suddenly brings back a sensation from my own childhood that I'd forgotten. I know *exactly* what he's feeling: I remember, viscerally, what it was like to wait for my mother to pick me up and take me home, how every second felt like an eternity, the fear that she'd never come, the unrestrained joy that came with the arrival of the expected face.

That night I tell Anton about it and he has no clue what I'm talking about. Vadik's asleep in his room and Elena's in Belarus and Anton's insisting he and I squeeze into one sleeping bag to stay warm. None of our apartments in China have heating. It's so uncomfortable but I'm laughing—I don't remember why.

Sometimes I wonder what I could have done differently or how I can forget Anton or if I'll ever find love again. I like to imagine that he's tortured by my absence, but in terms of thinking about his feelings, that's as far as I'll allow myself to go. It's easier for me to picture him as someone unburdened by complex and contradicting human emotions. That's why I don't wonder why he wouldn't let me kiss him goodbye in the Burger King or what the e-mails and phone calls and messages that have come since mean. I milk them for evidence that he's being punished and discard everything else. I avoid questions of whether stumbling across my name or unexpectedly seeing my face jolts him like it does me, because I've long assumed that it doesn't, that he may have been sad for a brief moment, in the way we mourn the smallest changes, and then he shrugged and moved on. That way, I'm absolved of any wrongs.

Is Belarus all that I didn't understand about Anton, about my relationship with him, about myself? Anton had always represented places I'd never been, and I thought he could show me how to get there. Not just Belarus, but to the other parts of his life that seemed foreign to me: marriage, parenthood, the domestic version of adulthood to which I'd been raised to aspire. Is coming to Belarus my attempt to confront that on my own terms?

Maybe this, too, is why I find myself unexpectedly jumpy on the bus to Brest: it somehow feels like Anton could pop out at any moment and ask me what I'm doing here. But it's a trepidation tempered by equal parts excitement. I made it this far. Might as well see how it ends.

I also worry that Belarus will be a nation filled with people like Anton, people who will hurt you suddenly and decisively, without meaning to, but still.

After we break up, I decide to stop talking to Anton, because I sense that's the post-breakup protocol that my spiritual guru, the book *Why Men Love Bitches*, would recommend. Also, just hearing Russian makes my heart pound—how is our casually texting about TV shows going to make me anything but miserable?

His absence defines my life in ways I didn't know longing could. It always feels like he's not there. Some days, everything I see seems sent to torture me with memories. *That pencil!* I think. *Anton used to use pencils.*

But each time he reaches out, his overtures don't feel like enough. Once, he e-mails me after eating in a restaurant we used to frequent. "Went to DSD tonight, and fucking everything reminded me of you," he writes, "which was difficult, but also nice." *I know exactly what you mean*, I think, but what I say is nothing. I never respond.

He can be cold, too. And this is my new image of everyone else on the bus: cold, and capable of unexpected callousness.

They have been hardened, I imagine, by decades of hardship.

Anton's stories of home were never happy ones. They were of a woman weathered in a way I'd never seen—not even forty, probably, but with skin that had been tanned and cracked and worn until it looked decades older—waiting outside of a wine shop at 8:55 in the morning because it opened at nine. They were of poverty and the things it drove people to, the relatives who couldn't remember his son's name but still hit him up for money. When he came back, he told me, people begged him to marry their daughters and get them out of Belarus.

Belarus was hit hard by the collapse of the Soviet Union, in no small part because of Lukashenko, who bolstered his popularity by maintaining the untenable programs that had bankrupted the USSR. The elderly got the pensions promised by a now-defunct nation. Unprofitable Soviet state-owned enterprises became unprofitable Belarusian state-owned enterprises.

So now I've forgiven both the bus and Belarus in advance for the difficulty and cruelty it's about to inflict on me, because life in this country has been marked by more difficulties and cruelties, and also because, I guess, on some level, I understand that my oceans of pain don't mean I was the only one who ever felt any. That maybe I was hurtful, too. That perhaps in the same way I see Belarus as responsible for all of my tears, it sees me as the cause of Anton's.

The driver starts up the bus and goes outside for one last cigarette, and as he does a lanky kid jumps on and asks us if we can spare a little money. To my surprise, pretty much everyone pulls out their wallets and hands him a few bills. I'm trying to figure out how to square this with my image of an uncaring populace, but then the kid thanks us all and hops off the bus and the driver puts out his cigarette and we pull out into the Ukrainian countryside.

The Ukrainian countryside is so beautiful, it makes me understand why Russian novels digress for a hundred pages to describe farmland. We pass rust-colored fields framed by fresh bales of hay and birch trees with thin white trunks topped with golden crowns of leaves. Grass grows easily, the vibrant green of long-awaited spring.

I go to take a sip of my water and realize the bottle is empty. A moment later, the woman behind me taps me on the shoulder and hands me a plastic cup filled with water.

"Thank you!" I exclaim.

A little while later, there's another tap on my shoulder, and the same woman has now made me a sandwich. She continues feeding me for the duration of the trip.

In keeping with the theme of natural resplendence, the border crossing takes place in a national park. Golden light filters through a thicket of trees. We cross lakes and rivers running with water pure enough to drink. It is the Beyoncé of border crossings.

On the Ukrainian side, we pull over in a clearing and our documents are checked by two soldiers who board our bus. One is a woman with perfectly manicured, bedazzled fingernails. I'm taken aback by the sight of a female soldier—an effect, I realize, of my time in Central Asia. But I was only there for six weeks. I'm surprised by how quickly my expectations adapted to my surroundings.

After driving a few minutes from the Ukrainian checkpoint, but before we reach the Belarusian side, we pull over and let some women out in the middle of the woods. They disappear into the trees as we keep going.

I turn to my new snack friend behind me.

"Are they okay?" I ask, worried that they've unknowingly embarked on some kind of Ukrainian *Survivor* spinoff.

"Of course," she reassures me. "They probably don't have jobs in Ukraine, and they want to sneak into Belarus."

Great. Now I've unwittingly participated in a cross-border smuggling operation. Which reminds me that I still have that Xanax in my suitcase, and that Belarus has harsh drug sentencing laws.

"Open your suitcase," the guard at the Belarusian border orders.

"Sorry, I don't speak Russian," I respond, in English.

Surprisingly, this works. He shrugs and gestures for me to get back on the bus, suitcase uninspected.

I look at the landscape ahead of us. Those green fields are Belarus! Those trees are Belarusian!

As we continue driving through the forest, we start to hear a strange sound that seems to be coming from under the bus. It's faint, but it sounds almost like a child crying. Are we now smuggling a baby into Belarus?

The noise grows louder and louder, and people start to shift uncomfortably. Finally, the driver pulls over and opens the hatch. A kitten darts out and sprints into the underbrush. The whole bus laughs with relief. A stowaway kitten!

I wonder if everything in Belarus that seems terrifying will turn out to be equally innocuous.

When we get to Brest, a tiny old woman tries to give the bus driver money. When he refuses, she becomes more forceful. There's a back-and-forth banter that reminds me of fights that would break out in restaurants in China over who got to pay the bill. I'm beginning to worry that someone needs to step in and save this bus driver from being beaten up by a tiny old lady, but eventually she laughs and concedes defeat. She puts the money back in her purse.

Next, the woman who's been feeding me from behind insists that I let her husband give me a ride to my hotel.

While we're waiting for her husband, she volunteers that some of the countries I've visited have had many presidents. "In Belarus," she says dryly, "we've only had one."

I'm surprised to hear her say this so openly. Even in more open countries, like Kyrgyzstan, people haven't really talked politics much. I'd gone into Turkmenistan without an official tour guide so that I could get the real scoop on dissent, only to find that that wasn't at the forefront of most people's minds. Januzak had had nothing but good things to say about the President of Tajikistan, a man who seems to think one man's human wrong is another man's human right. For the most part, it seemed less like people were turning a blind eye, and more like a symptom of lack of information (courtesy of state-run media) and, in many places, a focus on making ends meet that didn't leave time for luxuries like political debate.

But still, is it safe to speak so openly about Lukashenko in Belarus?

"Belarus is much cleaner than Ukraine," she continues.

I've picked up on a mild rivalry between the two neighboring countries. When Oleg tells his parents that I have a new Belarusian boyfriend, they laugh. "Belarus—our hat!" I tell Anton, who does not find it funny. "Well, you can just say Ukraine is . . . Belarus' sock," I suggest. I ask my bus buddy how Ukraine is dirty.

"There are leaves all over the streets!" she exclaims. She seems astonished that I didn't notice.

The hotel I'm staying in is nicer than what I normally book. At $40 U.S. a night, it's the most expensive lodging I've used so far, but I need to stay in an official hotel so that I can be "registered" with the authorities.

That $40 comes with a Belarusian nod toward top-of-the-line service. In the bathroom, I find proof that my room was cleaned. It's like when an American hotel wraps a toilet in a strip of paper that breaks when you lift the seat. Except here, it's just a card they've placed on the sink and toilet that says, "Cleaned."

Brest used to be called Brest-on-the-Bug, because the city isn't far from the Bug River. The river has also lent its name to some unfortunately christened businesses, my favorite of which is the Bug Hotel.

Brest also used to be part of Poland, then Russia, then Poland again, then a Nazi-occupied territory, then the Soviet Union, and, most recently, Belarus. You don't feel it in the city, but in the countryside, people say, you hear it in the dialects that vary from village to village. Each is a different mixture of Polish, Belarusian, Ukrainian, and Russian.

Brest reminds me of suburbs in China. Historic buildings still stand sentry in the center—improbably, given how many times the city has been forced to host occupying armies—but farther out, new LEGO-block apartment buildings painted muted salmon and olive green sprout from the tops of commercial complexes. One features a spacious, American-style gym, a store selling Columbia sportswear, and a restaurant called Pizza Smile.

I find out the hard way that there are no black markets in Belarus, after I casually ask a waitress where to find one. She looks horrified and promptly tells me not to take any pictures in the restaurant.

Belarus has its own currency quirk: there aren't any coins. Even the smallest denominations are printed notes. The stack of bills that quickly fills my wallet reminds me of Uzbekistan's garbage bags full of cash. I wonder if Belarus requires its own styles of wallet, ones without pockets for change.

I ask the receptionist at my hotel what there is to do in Brest, and she tells me there's a beautiful forested national park just outside of town. "But actually," she reconsiders, "it's probably hard for foreigners to get there."

The next morning, I'm up early to head to the national park, exclusively to prove that it's easy for this foreigner to get there. I've learned that the forest is where children believe Belarusian Santa lives, and that it is Europe's last primeval forest.

I have not, however, learned what a primeval forest is, or how to get to this one. This turns out not to be a huge problem, because Belarus is apparently full of helpful strangers. People keep coming up to me on the street, asking if I'm lost, and offering to help. They explain the bus schedule and walk me to the proper stop. When the bus comes, they tell the driver where I need to get off. And on and on. I think of the woman who kept feeding me on the bus to Belarus and how she and her husband insisted on driving me to my hotel, and I'm not sure what to make of any of this, because this is all so at odds with everything I'd heard from Anton.

On the way to Belarusian Santa's woodland workshop, the bus passes a church made out of old train cars, and then wooden dachas, simple country homes where people in the former Soviet Union keep vegetable gardens and spend summers. The dachas in Belarus seem more rustic than the others I've seen. Many look like they were built using leftover lumber and whatever materials people could find.

But the countryside is again stunning. For a better description, flip open any Russian novel, and look for a really long passage with no dialogue.

By the end of my ride, the handful of remaining passengers have all become invested in my journey, and at my stop, they point out the park entrance and where I can catch the bus back.

It almost feels like the whole country is happy to have me here, which is kind of the opposite of what I expected.

The park is so big that I have to rent a bicycle to get around. The kindly woman running the log cabin bike shop is in the middle of a heated argument with a cat. She delivers long tirades to him in Russian while copying the information from my passport, hotel registration, and visa, which seems like a lot of personal details to keep on file as collateral. If I don't return this bicycle, is she allowed to steal my identity?

I follow a bike trail that runs in a loop back to the bike-rental cabin. The park is mostly empty, and the trail cuts a path through towering firs and patchworks of colored leaves blotting at a clear blue sky. Sunlight seems to drift down and land on autumn-hued leaves; white swans float on the glass surface of a still pond. It's so beautiful that I understand why this part of the world believes in magic. It's also why I'm not at all expecting to stumble upon an outdoor exhibit called Fascists in the Forest.

Unfortunately, only the title has been translated into English, so I can't understand anything beyond the fact that Nazis once lurked in this forest, which is not great, but also not surprising, given that Germany invaded the Soviet Union through Brest.

When I get back to my hotel, I learn that Brest, like many Belarusian cities, had been home to a sizable Jewish population before the Second World War. In 1941, about 40 percent of Brest residents were Jewish, and Jewish people comprised 40 percent of the population of Belarus as a whole. When the Nazis invaded, they forced Belarusian Jews into ghettos and sent many to extermination camps. By the end of the war, a staggering two-thirds of the Jewish population in Belarus had been murdered. In Brest, almost all of the twenty thousand Jews who'd been living there in 1941 were killed. The few who managed to escape sought refuge in the forest.

A random passerby in the train station helps me book my ticket to Minsk, the next stop on my journey. It's an open sleeping compartment, though I'll only be on it for a few hours in the afternoon. I'm not sure what the protocol is in this situation—should I pretend to sleep, just to be polite? The woman across the aisle from me pulls a plastic bag full of clean bedding out from under her berth and makes up her bed, then gets on top of it and reads a comic book with a magnifying glass.

The train passes through birch forests topped with buttery leaves and crosses over water with surfaces that reflect the clear blue sky. I'm starting to understand why the woman from the bus considered leaves to be litter.

So far Belarus has been stunningly beautiful, and the people have been almost comically helpful. Why had Anton warned me that visiting would be unpleasant?

The answer, of course, is obvious. The real question is: why has it been so important to me to believe that I was the only one who was heartbroken?

As we near Minsk, we pass a giant industrial development with a smokestack on which the year it opened is proudly displayed: 1990. Looking at it in 2015, I can only see the year that will follow, and the future that the people who built that smokestack might not have seen coming. Because, of course, the Soviet Union operated the factory for one year, and then had to hand the reins over to newly minted Belarus.

Minsk is enormous.

The city unfurls along wide boulevards stacked with imposing Stalinist buildings whose façades seem to say, *Keep moving.*

It is therefore strange to find that McDonald's is a major landmark.

"Oh, perfect," Ilya says when I tell him where I'm staying. "You're near the McDonald's."

I assume he means *a* McDonald's, or *the* McDonald's on Lenin Street (an address so incongruous it almost feels like corporate America extending a middle finger to communism), but no, he means *the* McDonald's.

The city now has three places to buy Big Macs, but the original location is still enough of a novelty that it's an ideal landmark for directions and meeting locations.

"This neighborhood seems kind of quiet at night," I tell Ilya cautiously, over lunch at a Belarusian restaurant across from the McDonald's.

Ilya is Anton's childhood friend; we met when Ilya and his wife came to China to visit Anton. I hesitated before reaching out to Ilya when I arrived in Belarus: it felt like getting too close to something I wasn't sure I could handle. But in the end, curiosity won out.

Like all of Anton's friends from school, Ilya speaks English, a skill that helped him land a good job with an airline in its nearby offices. He's surprised that I think this part of town is quiet.

"This is probably the top neighborhood in Minsk," he tells me.

It does have a few notable residents. The next block houses the headquarters for the Belarusian KGB, famous for being the only post-Soviet security agency not to stop calling itself the KGB. (The Russian successor, for example, is called the FSB.) Across the river, you can visit Minsk's only historic neighborhood left after the city was flattened in World War II. All the big companies in Minsk have offices nearby, and it's within walking distance of the circus. (Circuses apparently being something Soviets saw as basic human rights, and every Soviet city has one.)

"So people work here, and then they go out in the neighborhoods they live in?" I ask.

Ilya considers. "Well, we don't really go out to restaurants."

At the time of my visit, the Belarusian economy is going through a particularly rough patch. Like other post-Soviet states tied to the Russian economy, Belarus has seen its currency plummet as its northern neighbor struggles with declining oil prices. People have stopped thinking in Belarusian rubles, Ilya says. "If you're buying a TV, a car, anything, you have to think in U.S. dollars." Which makes sense from a math perspective, because 1 U.S. dollar is currently worth 20,000 Belarusian rubles.

Young, educated people like Ilya are frustrated. Domestically, Lukashenko likes to brand his policies as playing Russia and the EU against each other, but the reality is that he's alienating all potential trading partners. Integration with the European market would give Belarusian companies a much-needed expanded customer base, but the EU won't accept Lukashenko's habits of doing things like rigging elections and grooming his eleven-year-old son to be his successor.

Right now, Belarus is helping Russia skirt harsh EU sanctions that prevent European products from being exported to Russia. But there's nothing stopping companies from exporting to Belarus, repacking their products, and reexporting to Russia with a Belarusian label, which is why Russian consumers can now dine on "mussels from Belarus," a country that does not touch the ocean.

Still, I press Ilya about what he means by "going out."

"I got in last night at eight p.m.," I say, "and there was *nothing* open. Like, not even a shop to buy water." I don't say this, but as I paced the streets looking for water, I also noticed that there wasn't much that could have been closed, either. Minsk has fewer stores than any capital city I've seen. The street levels are neat lines of uncommercialized ground floors. I think about another joke Anton used to tell. "When I was a kid, I opened a lemonade stand. I'm just kidding: private enterprise is illegal in Belarus."

Not only does there seem to be a dearth of businesses, Minsk also has almost no billboards. I try to recall another capital city with a lack of outdoor advertisements. I guess Ashgabat.

Belarus was the only country to emerge from the Soviet Union without a strong ethnic identity. Like Brest, Belarus as a whole had always shifted between surrounding regional powers. The borders of present-day Belarus have no historical precedent, and the Belarusian ethnicity was murky prior to 1991. Language is an important component of ethnic identity, but by the twentieth century, Russian had largely replaced Belarusian as the language spoken at home.

The Belarusian government is often seen as promoting the Belarusian identity in order to strengthen its own legitimacy. At the time Belarus declared independence in 1991, most of its citizens spoke Russian and would have identified more strongly as Soviet or with their language than as Belarusian. This can create challenges for nation-building, as Ukraine would prove three decades later.

While countries like Kazakhstan and Kyrgyzstan could remind themselves that they were gaining independence and self-determination while they weathered the transition to nationhood, on the whole Belarusians didn't have the same unifying desire for a homeland.

Ilya very much supports the movement to build a stronger sense of national identity, which at first surprises me, because he's so liberal. "I hate the government," he proclaims whenever he has the chance.

But the point of many who support a stronger sense of national identity is that people "feeling" Belarusian is essential to the country's longevity. Russia is bigger, militarily more powerful, and just across the border. As in eastern Ukraine, Belarusians look, speak, and behave much like their Russian neighbors. If Belarusians don't feel particularly different from Russians, they might not be opposed to erasing that border and becoming part of Russia, especially if they thought it would bring better standards of living.

Belarus has been one of the slowest post-Soviet states to privatize its economy, which has prevented growth.

In other former republics in the 1990s, the sudden removal of price controls generally caused staggering inflation, and unemployment rose as newly privatized companies cut staff that had been bloated under state ownership. The Belarusian government sought to prevent these hardships with much more gradual reforms. Large enterprises remained in state hands and continued to staff and produce as they had under the Soviet system, while the government preserved the USSR's generous but costly social safety net. But without Soviet state-mandated demand, which had ensured that Lithuania and Uzbekistan would purchase the tractors Belarus produced, by the late 1990s the economy was in crisis.

Little has changed since then. Lukashenko continues to be popular among large segments of the population that might otherwise lose their jobs or pensions. Its economy continues to carry a lot of dead weight.

So it surprises me, given how much Ilya loathes economic propaganda, that he supports its nationalist iteration.

When the Germans invaded the Soviet Union in the Second World War, they came in through Belarus. It's estimated that between one-quarter and one-third of the population of Belarus was killed. In Minsk, 85 percent of all structures are said to have been destroyed.

Modern-day Minsk is thus an architectural Stalinist dreamland. The city was rebuilt right after the war, at a time when Stalin was experiencing a shift in aesthetic taste. He wanted everything to be big, the buildings a bold declaration of the Soviet's victory in war. I get the impression that the instructions he gave to the Minsk city planners were something along the lines of, "Let's still do those beautiful neoclassical buildings, but let's make them a little terrifying."

Structures dating back to before the 1940s are rare, so when I catch a glimpse of one that afternoon, I head for a closer inspection. But when I get to the street, I realize it's the Belarusian equivalent of a maximum security prison. It's the only prison in Europe to carry out the death penalty.

It seems odd to keep a prison in the city center, but I also get the sense that the government might not mind having the prominent visual reminder that actions have consequences.

To add to its superlatives, Minsk is also the most orderly major city I've visited.

"Minsk is the only city in the world where you'll never see anyone jaywalk," a friend tells me, laughing.

"Yeah, why is that?" I ask.

"Because they don't want to get a ticket."

The police ticket effectively for jaywalking in Minsk, but the fine isn't always the biggest deterrent. Most Belarusians are eager to avoid any interaction with police, who have a reputation for causing more trouble whenever the mood strikes them.

No one litters, either. The streets are free not only of garbage, but also of cigarette butts—surprising, given how many people smoke. But over the course of my stay in Minsk, I watch countless people stub out their cigarettes on the sides of buildings or the metal coverings on trashcans and properly dispose of the butts.

When Anton saw that, against his advice, I went ahead with my plan to come to Belarus, he offered to put me in touch with some more of his friends in an uncharacteristically generous gesture. They're all young, like twenty, which is kind of weird, but I also can see why Anton gravitates toward people whose lives pick up where his youth ended. When he was their age, he was about to get married.

Anton's friends call themselves *apolitical*, a term that seems to mean that they refuse to engage with the economic or political systems. Hence, the no jobs. Also hence why I rarely see them eat.

They take me out to clubs improbably located in what look like former gymnasiums and old factories. We spend all night dancing to music that is 90 percent bass, and when the night turns to morning, we walk home, because there's no question of taking a cab.

The guy at the center of it all, for me anyway, is Anton's friend Daniil, a handsome, rail-thin twenty-three-year-old who chooses each word he says very carefully, a habit that lends his speech a staccato cadence. Daniil seems to have aspirations of breaking into "art installations," but for now, he spends most of the day sleeping in an undisclosed location, and he spends his nights in Minsk's nightlife scene.

"It's very small," he tells me. "I can go to any party, and probably, I will know almost everyone there."

It's hard to picture Anton in these scenes, because I felt like I didn't know his Belarusian side. I heard him speak Russian, but I could never understand it enough to know who he was in Russian. I still can't speak well enough to know that.

Still, I know he would blend in more fluidly than I do. Not just linguistically: he would understand these small gestures that I don't, these weird laughs, the awkward game of hot potato when the group has to make a decision. This would all be familiar to him; perhaps sometimes he would find himself slipping into mannerisms he'd long forgotten. He wouldn't instinctively step into a crosswalk against the light on an empty street.

The one thing I definitely can't picture is Anton and me here together. It wouldn't have worked, I realize. I'd be the odd one out: they'd all be speaking Russian, Anton would have to translate, and this would annoy him. If he were here, I'd never be able to communicate with his friends. Without him, we're forced to make it work. It's a weird moment when you realize the thing you think you want doesn't actually exist.

One night, I'm walking with Daniil and his friend Anya when we bump into Daniil's friend Zhenya, who is not apolitical, though he is "hardcore," in the sense of completely abstaining from alcohol and substances of any kind. He also loves meeting foreigners, which is why he accompanies us to a nearby coffee shop.

"Anton says that the culture of Minsk is more like a small suburb than a big city," Daniil says. "Do you agree?"

I am instantly irrationally angry because I can hear Anton saying it, and it brings me back to a thousand fights I had forgotten. *That's ridiculous*, I want to snap. But instead I ask, "Do you agree with Anton?"

"Not at all," he says. The city is changing quickly, he explains. It used to be taboo to not eat meat, for example. "But now, almost everyone is a vegetarian."

Anya and Zhenya pounce on him: that's not true, they protest.

"Okay," Daniil concedes. "But, for example, these two waitresses." He lowers his voice to a conspiratorial whisper. "One is a vegetarian, and the other is a vegan."

The next day Zhenya wants to take me on a tour of Minsk. There are a few options, he tells me. I can either have the historic tour or the political tour.

I opt for the political tour.

Zhenya is wonderful. He's friendly and curious and eager to share what he knows about Belarus with others. He has strong ties to Minsk: his grandfather was an architect who designed many of the city's buildings. Zhenya lives with his girlfriend in an apartment a few metro stops from the McDonald's. This kind of cohabitation is unusual.

People marry young in Belarus, and they live with their parents until they marry, though in most cases, a young couple has to keep shacking up with a set of parents for a few years until they can save up for their own house.

The apartment Zhenya lives in was his grandfather's, a stroke of luck that allows him more autonomy than most people his age. He works in technology and takes free English lessons from evangelical missionaries at night.

I ask Zhenya about something I've noticed, which is that Belarus is the first republic I've been to that seems not only to have preserved its Soviet monuments, but also to have built more of them. Buildings that could only have gone up a few years ago still say "USSR."

Zhenya tells me that Lukashenko was one of the few politicians not to turn in his communist party card after the Soviet Union dissolved. I take this to be metaphorical at first, but no: it's literal. Lukashenko still has the card, and he uses it as a campaign rallying point.

This seems like the main problem that Belarus faces: it can't accept that the Soviet Union is over, that it's no longer a thing. And it's sad, because as long as Lukashenko keeps trying to bring back the past, people like Zhenya won't have a future.

One night, Ilya invites me to dinner at his house. He picks me up after work and we drive to the new supermarket that opened in the recently built mega-shopping complex near Ilya's house.

Ilya shakes his head as he shops for flour. "Who would have thought we needed many choices?" he laughs. "Why must we have four different kinds of flour?"

Ilya's apartment is small but comfortable: it's a one-bedroom in a new high-rise a short drive from the city center, and inside, I re-meet his wife and meet his dog, cat, and one-year-old daughter. Anton had mentioned this to me the last time I saw him.

"Ilya has a daughter now," he told me. Anton happened to be home when she was born. "We were all waiting on the street outside the hospital, drinking and celebrating."

This suddenly feels too weird: like, I am here, eating dinner at my ex-boyfriend's friend's house in Belarus. I'm doing something that feels as though it's against the laws of nature, and it's like my lizard brain is waking up from a nap and going, *Whoa, I would not have signed off on this.*

His wife has been home all day taking care of their daughter, labor whose difficulty Ilya appreciates. "Sometimes, I'll come home and the baby's so easy," Ilya told me on the ride over. "But my wife says, 'Today was such a nightmare—you have no idea.'"

The Belarusian government gives three years of paid maternity leave, but the salary is less than $100 U.S. per month. Ilya's wife is staying home for now because it's more economical than paying for child care.

Ilya tells me he and his wife gave their daughter a Belarusian name. "I hate Russians," he says bitterly, "and I don't want my child to have a Russian name."

At first I'm not sure what to make of this comment—I know Anton is half Russian, and I suspect many Belarusians have at least some Russian ancestry.

But so far in Ukraine and Belarus, the term *Russian* has been far from straightforward. It's sometimes a stand-in for the Soviets, other times a reference to the Russian government. It's rarely used positively, but it even more rarely refers to ethnic Russians.

I wonder if *Russian*, in this context, means people who show up from somewhere else and impose their own system of government. And maybe in this context, Belarusian nationalism seems more appealing to Ilya—if only as an antidote to that.

"Do you see Anton often?" Ilya asks carefully as he prepares dinner.

"Sometimes," I say. "You know, we're rarely in China at the same time, so . . ." I keep it light, because it seems Ilya has no idea Anton and I are on terrible terms. Or maybe I can't read him, because it's all too close to home. But if he has no idea, that hurts, too, that Anton hasn't told him. Also, this is all just so fucking weird. Most of all because I asked for it. I could have easily gone to Belarus without looking up Ilya, could have gotten out of dinner at his house even more easily. And yet I think the discomfort is part of what appealed to me. I'm eating dinner at Ilya's house because it's hard and uncomfortable and I'm showing myself that I can get through it.

Later, when we're eating, Ilya's daughter keeps wandering over to me, gesturing that I should pick her up, and I do, gingerly. Ilya laughs. "You don't have to be so careful," he tells me. "You won't break her."

My last night in Belarus is Halloween, and Zhenya wants to take me on another walk, this time near the McDonald's. I'm surprised to find people on the street in costume. Zhenya tells me Halloween is becoming more and more popular each year.

It seems like every third person is dressed up as a member of the Illuminati, which feels incredibly random, until I realize it's an easy costume to make. We also find a Grim Reaper with a to-die list, which sadly has only two targets on it: "not you," which has been crossed out, presumably upon completion, and "you."

I've realized that Ilya was right about this neighborhood: it is one of Minsk's most happening, and it's quiet at night, not because everyone goes out closer to home, but because there's not much business to justify keeping things open. I've never seen a capital city with fewer private businesses. It's incredible to find yourself in the center of a country's biggest financial city, at eight p.m. on a Friday, and have no place to buy a bottle of water. And by *incredible*, I mean awful and hard to believe.

People say, "Meet me at the McDonald's," because they can't say, "Meet me at the coffee shop on the corner of Lenin and October Revolution." This won't stop me, when I return home, from complaining about a Starbucks opening directly across the street from another Starbucks. But it has left me with this odd appreciation sometimes when I walk past a McDonald's. It always takes me a second to place where it's coming from, and then I remember.

COUCHSURF THE BALTICS
(LITHUANIA)

To outsiders, the three Baltic countries of Lithuania, Latvia, and Estonia can seem very similar. The three small nations are located, geographically and culturally, between Eastern Europe and Scandinavia. They share strong cultural affinities, and, in the case of Lithuania and Latvia, speak closely related languages.

But the Lithuanians, Latvians, and Estonians have retained distinct identities, and current borders have been drawn in such a way as to more or less give each ethnic group its own country. Latvians are quick to tell you that they are known for being musical (though they warn that Estonians will claim *they* are the musical ones). Everyone agrees that the Lithuanians are known for dancing, except for the Lithuanians themselves, who believe their reputation is for basketball.

The Baltic countries are the only ones I know to have overthrown a colonial regime and gained independence by holding hands and singing, which is why it seems like the perfect place to finally try Couchsurfing.

Crossing from Belarus into Lithuania feels like leaving the Soviet Union and entering Europe, which it sort of is. While Lukashenko was reminding the world that he never gave up his communist card, the Baltics were busy trying to join the European Union, which they did in 2004.

If you can tell a lot about a country by the bathrooms on its trains,

Lithuania is off to a good start. In Belarus, the train toilets provided a peek at the track beneath. On the Lithuanian train, I push a button and a space-agey door slides open to reveal a previously hidden bathroom.

Even passport control seems more European. We don't stop at the border and wait hours for a full-train inspection. I'm not even sure we actually come to a complete stop; it feels more like we slow down enough for a Lithuanian border guard to hop on, and then we speed up again.

When the squat, stern woman steps into our car, I momentarily panic. For the first time in ages, I don't have a visa. Then I remember I don't need one. This is the EU.

The border guard wears something that looks like a necklace, but where the pendant would be there's instead a tiny computer that also doubles as a makeshift work table. Or maybe it's more accurate to say she's wearing both her desk and her work PC around her neck. Either way, she pulls out a spyglass that fits over her eye and carefully examines my passport. It's momentarily unclear if I'm crossing into Lithuania or a Wes Anderson film.

But no, when she stamps it, the stamp says I'm in the EU, which is a strange place to find myself in after all this, and also, in Lithuania.

One of the first things you notice about Lithuania is that the mullet is in. Because everyone is doing it, it starts to look cool. How have I never noticed that a mullet is the perfect haircut in which to smoke a cigarette, aggressively drink a soda, or wait for a bus at night outside of a train station, as everyone around me is doing?

I too am waiting for the bus. Thanks to the train station's free Wi-Fi, I've learned that I need to take the 42 bus to the 72 bus to the top of a quiet country lane where Aiste, a recent architecture graduate and my Couchsurfing host, lives with her mother.

I've wanted to try Couchsurfing because I've heard so many rave reviews of it on this trip, and also because it's good to try things that scare you. For those unaware, Couchsurfing is a website and online community where people offer to put up strangers in their homes free of charge. The potential drawbacks to this arrangement are both obvious and numerous.

But travelers I've met on the road have described Couchsurfing as a unique opportunity for cultural exchange, given that the community self-selects for those looking to meet people from different countries and backgrounds. This particular selling point has piqued my interest—I'm hoping that in staying with my hosts, I'll learn more about Lithuania.

I picked Aiste and her mother for the reason I'm sure many first-time Couchsurfers pick their hosts, which is that they seemed least likely to murder me. A twenty-something woman living with her mother is about as nonthreatening as a random person on the Internet goes. Though I'm still nervous about showing up at a stranger's house for a sleepover.

The 42 bus is a smooth ride. We take what I assume is the scenic route through Vilnius, but I can't confirm because it's extremely dark outside. All of the lights have been put to work illuminating statues. So I don't get much of a sense of the city, besides that there are a lot of marble horses.

I applaud myself for knowing where to get off the bus. I don't yet have cell phone service in Lithuania, but I have a preloaded map and the cleverness to trace my progress via a blue dot. The place where I'm supposed to switch buses appears to be an empty bus terminus with not much around. For a moment, things don't look promising. I'm not sure where to catch the 72. But then I see the 72 bus pulling up beside a sign, and I race over to catch it. The driver looks perplexed but collects my fare. Well done, Audrey. [10]/10.

The 72 bus pulls directly into the same terminus I'd just gotten off at. The driver is now ushering us all off with a broom. There may not be a literal broom, but emotionally, that's what it feels like.

In broken Russian, the driver and I come to an understanding that he will take a break for twenty minutes, and then drive the 72 bus to my Couchsurfers' surf shack. I'm starving and see a pizza shop catty-corner to the bus stop. But because all the streets are thruways, it takes four minutes of walking and six minutes of trying to cross a highway to get there. I'm so worried about missing the bus that I just buy a bottle of water and head back.

When I get back on the 72 bus, the driver kindly refuses to let me pay again. From here, the bus ride quickly goes south. Or maybe north: it's hard to tell, because it's pitch-dark outside, there are no streetlights, we've gone outside the zone of my Google Maps, and we appear to be driving through a forest. The bus has somehow emptied of passengers, except for the couple in front of me, who seem to have used the twenty-minute rest break to drink a liter of vodka. They are loudly, drunkenly, and aggressively making out. *Thanks for rubbing it in*, I think.

There are times to put on a brave face, and there are times to admit that you're lost on a bus in the middle of the night in Lithuania.

I opt for the former.

I set my face into an expression that I hope reads, *No, I am not wondering whether I passed my stop thirty minutes ago*, when we pull over by an unmarked tree at what appears to be the edge of a ravine, and a normal-looking blonde woman my age gets on.

I wait approximately ten seconds before pouncing. I get up and beeline for the back of the bus, where she's taken a seat, and ask her, desperately, if she speaks Russian.

She takes off her headphones.

"Do you speak English?" she asks.

Twenty minutes later, I'm standing outside her parents' house while she goes inside to borrow her mother's phone. We use it to call my Couchsurfers. They live, miraculously, two streets over. The Couchsurfer is coming to get me; the blonde girl is waiting with me outside.

"There are a lot of nice people in the world," the mystery blonde says as we see a hazy outline—my Couchsurfer?—emerge from the murky fog at the top of the dark lane.

Maybe I *am* in a Wes Anderson film, because I find myself reply-
ing, "Thank you for being one of them."

Aiste recently graduated from university in England, where she
earned both her undergraduate and master's degrees in architecture. She speaks English without hesitation and in the charming,
lilting way of someone who attained the final flourishes of fluency
surrounded by Brits terrified that their country was becoming "less
British."

Her mother speaks Russian, a language Aiste claims to understand not a word of. This claim will be repeated by young people
throughout the Baltics, particularly by those who, like Aiste, were
born after the Baltics won a hard-fought struggle for independence.
Of the fifteen Soviet republics, the Baltics were perhaps the least enthusiastic participants. Latvia, Lithuania, and Estonia had all been
forcibly incorporated into the Russian Empire, and when the end of
World War I provided an opening for independence, the Baltic states
jumped at it. A few decades later, Stalin and Hitler signed a secret
pact that divided up Eastern European territories that neither leader
controlled, and Germany "gave" the Baltics to the Soviet Union in
the same way that the Native Americans "welcomed" the Europeans.

Latvia, Lithuania, and Estonia were too small and nascent to do
much about this, and after the war, the three states were folded into
the Soviet Union.

Today, Aiste and her mother, Victoria, live in a sleek, modern
house in the suburbs of Vilnius, the capital of Lithuania. They grow
vegetables in a backyard greenhouse, bake their own bread, and
compost food scraps. Their neighbors seem to do the same. Every
backyard has a greenhouse, a charming quirk I attribute to a Baltic
affinity for gardening.

"Oh, no," Aiste corrects me cheerfully. "It's a habit from Soviet
times, when there wasn't enough food."

Victoria has cooked us a hearty breakfast from locally sourced
ingredients—an omelet made from a neighbor's eggs, bread she

bakes fresh every morning, jam from last summer's garden. We're all enjoying these labors in the kitchen, or I'm trying to, but I feel so awkward.

I have spent the night on a couch that was made up into a comfortable bed in the living room, while Aiste and Victoria slept in their bedrooms upstairs. With the exception of a few fish, who kept to themselves in a tank by my bed, I had the whole downstairs to myself. I took advantage of this cozy setup by staying up half the night fretfully tossing and turning.

Despite the terms of our arrangement, I can't help feeling like I'm imposing on these two lovely Lithuanian women, and that makes me feel truly terrible. I'm worried I'm a burden or a nuisance, which, of course, is ridiculous. People sign up to host on Couchsurfing.com because they want to have guests.

Prior to my arrival, my main concern about Couchsurfing had been safety, but as with everything in life, the actual problem ends up being something else entirely. I feel like I'm taking advantage of someone else's generosity, the way I did with Sayed when I thought he was Jafar.

I find myself thinking that I would be so much more comfortable if I could just give them money! But that goes against the whole premise of Couchsurfing, which one person explained to me as, "giving without worrying about what you'll get back." I know that actually we would *all* be happier if I could just relax and appreciate their hospitality, but I can't. Maybe this is something I need to learn how to do.

I have brought Aiste and Victoria a small gift of Belarusian chocolate. But maybe in Couchsurfing, the best thing a guest can bring is the gift of not feeling weird about showering in a stranger's bathroom. And that, it seems, I forgot to pack.

Victoria is a trim, stylish woman with two grown daughters, whom she raised on her own after being widowed when the girls were young. She works part-time in an office downtown and, at her daughter's urging, has recently started Couchsurfing.

Victoria is probably the last person I'd expect to find Couchsurfing. She lives in a wooded, suburban home whose minimalist decor suggests an understated affluence. She seems more suburban mom than intrepid backpacker, maybe because she is.

Victoria first tried Couchsurfing about a year ago, on a trip to Italy with Aiste and Aiste's sister. This summer, Victoria and Aiste traveled to Georgia (the country, not the state), and again arranged lodging through the site.

Victoria enjoyed both experiences, though they were clearly Aiste's idea. I also have to take Aiste's word for her mother's positive review, because Victoria doesn't speak English. Aiste is translating from Lithuanian.

Aiste started Couchsurfing back in university when she was sharing an apartment with a group of friends. A few of her housemates were into Couchsurfing, and Aiste got hooked. She used it to meet people and find lodging all over the world, and when the job market for architects forced her to move back into her mother's house after finishing her master's degree, Aiste begged her mother to let her keep hosting. At first, Victoria was understandably uncomfortable with the idea of travelers on a shoestring budget lounging on her couch, but she eventually warmed to the idea, and here we are. There were some Germans here last week. There always are. Every Couchsurfing stay, it seems, is preceded or followed by Germans.

In Lithuania, it's rude to put your hands in your pockets. Days of the weeks are abbreviated with Roman numerals—I for Monday, VII for Sunday, and so on. People, I think, take apples everywhere. Or maybe just Aiste and her mom. That's the thing about being a tourist constantly scanning for cultural cues—you're never sure if *we* refers to the whole country or just the people talking. Before I go sightseeing this morning, Aiste hands me a few apples, and when I look confused, she laughs and tells me to take them in case I get hungry. "We usually take apples everywhere," she adds.

Lithuanians are apparently famous for being good at basketball, which I did not know, but quickly pretend to, because this seems to be what the people of Lithuania think is their claim to fame outside of Lithuania. "I think many people know Lithuania because there are many Lithuanians in the NBA," someone tells me, and I do not have the heart to inform her that, strong as the Lithuanian contingent may be, they do not quite have the starpower of a LeBron or a Steph Curry.

Folklore and fairies still reign in the Baltic countries, which converted to Christianity belatedly, begrudgingly, and, one senses, half-heartedly. The Lithuanians, Latvians, and Estonians are apparently known as the last pagans of Europe.

Aiste is telling me that, in Lithuanian folklore, an unmarried woman is supposed to put a glass of water beside her bed before she goes to sleep on Christmas Eve, because Christmas Eve makes you very thirsty (in the sense of craving water) (also, what?), and then at night, she might dream of walking over a bridge(??), and if she does, and if there's a man walking toward her, the man will have her future husband's face. "It's silly." She laughs, and then she grows serious. "Or, who knows, maybe it's true."

I file this away, because I am unmarried, though I do have trouble remembering my dreams. What if I forgot what my future husband's face looked like? Even if I remember, now what? Do I go around searching for that face? And when I find it say, *You were on the bridge in my thirsty Christmas dream! Let's get married?*

We're sitting around their wooden kitchen table, eating a stew Victoria made fresh for dinner, which, good lord, is just making me feel even more terrible. Aiste spent the day looking for a job, and Victoria spent it working one, while I explored some of Vilnius' medieval old town and some of its 65 churches. And now they've cooked me dinner?

I can understand why the unmarried women of Lithuania might find comfort in folk remedies for identifying your future husband. Unless she consciously avoids it, the quest for a husband can easily consume the first years of a woman's adult life.

Aiste is twenty-five; already, most of her friends are married. She delivers this news with a sigh. She tells me about a close friend with a boyfriend with a sexual habit of forgetting he has a girlfriend. They just got engaged, and her friend is thrilled. "For her, the most important thing is just to be married."

This is one reason Aiste isn't eager to stay in Lithuania. Right now, she's focused on building her career, and she worries about fitting in socially in a country where a gender imbalance has created pressure for young women to prioritize finding a spouse.

A combination of migration and shorter life expectancies for men has left Lithuania with a population in which women generally outnumber men. Among twenty-five- to fifty-four-year-olds, there are 0.97 men for every woman in Lithuania. Between the ages of fifty-five and sixty-four, that ratio drops to 0.79 men for every woman, and for the population above age sixty-five, it's just .51 men for every woman, or two women for every man. This, of course, isn't a perfect picture of the marriage market—some of those men and women will partner with members of their own gender, while others might choose not to pair off at all—but for women who wish to marry men in Lithuania, the general perception is that there aren't enough spouses to go around.

Women tend to outlive men all over the world, but in Lithuania, the difference in longevity is particularly pronounced. Sociologists tend to attribute this to higher rates of work, car, and alcohol-related accidents for men, along with early deaths caused by alcohol.

Though women don't dramatically outnumber men at the age of most first marriages, many say that the gender ratio has been exacerbated by economic migration facilitated by the Baltic nations' EU membership. Men make up a higher percentage of migrants in all three countries, and data suggests that male migrants are less likely to return to their home countries than their female counterparts.

Still, the perception that women have to compete for a smaller pool of eligible men has taken hold in the Lithuanian ethos. And as I've learned from personal experience, cultural expectations and perceived pressures can be hard to shake. If the whole country believes that educated, ambitious, and attractive women are fighting over a small cohort of potential matches, it can become a self-fulfilling prophecy—both on the national and individual levels.

It probably doesn't help that, in Lithuania, a woman's marital status is announced every time she writes her last name. As in most Balto-Slavic languages, Lithuanian surnames take different forms for men and women. A woman's last name further indicates whether or not she is married. (A man's does not.) Let's say, for example, that I were to marry my Lithuanian crush Juozas Glinskis, or as I like to call him, 'Zas, who pioneered a little something called the Lithuanian "theater of cruelty." (Yes, he DOES sound irresistibly dangerous/emotionally unavailable, and yes I DO think we will triumph over the fifty-five year age gap.)

Glinskis, like most male Lithuanian last names, ends in a/y/i + s. So, after I promise to have and to hold, I would become Mrs. Glinskienė, -ienė being the most common ending for a married woman's surname. Our son, if we had one, would be named Barack Obama Glinskis, because men's last names don't change with marriage. Our daughter, however, would be Ruth Bader Ginsberg Glinskyte, the -yte/-aitė/-iūtė/-utė suffixes serving as the standard heads-up that a woman is a free agent.

When people in Central Asia had been surprised to learn that I was twenty-eight and unmarried, I invariably responded by explaining that in the U.S., women don't think about getting married until they're in their thirties.

I'm about to deliver this familiar speech to Aiste when I realize how insincere it is.

In truth, I know these fears. Well-meaning elders have given me the same horrible advice dispensed to young women the world over: that if I wait too long, all the good husbands will be taken, and that the ones who aren't might, and may prefer to, marry younger women.

I want to give Aiste advice first imparted to me by my personal

Bible, the dating self-help book *Why Men Love Bitches*. I want to tell her that your best chance for success in anything is to follow your passion and not worry about things other people want you to be afraid of. I want to say that as someone who has stopped letting those fears dictate my decisions, but it feels hypocritical, because I haven't stopped fearing them.

So instead, I ask her what she wants to do.

"Live abroad again," she says.

She's been applying for jobs ever since she graduated, but Aiste studied architecture, a field almost as famous for its high rates of unemployment as it is for the buildings it has given us. This is months before Brexit, but she's already warning me about the rising British nationalism and xenophobia—especially against Eastern Europeans from EU countries, who are now free to live in any other member state, and, Aiste says, have overwhelmingly settled in the UK, where wages are highest.

"There are really so many people from Poland, Lithuania, Latvia," she says. "I really understand why people are so afraid."

This myth, of course, will be dismantled during Brexit debates, when data will show that far more migrants come from outside the EU than inside, and that immigrants make up less than 10 percent of the UK's population and workforce. The fact that Aiste repeats this rhetoric, when she presumably had five years of firsthand evidence that the population of the United Kingdom is predominately British, provides some insight into what it can feel like to make a home in a place where other people see you as a threat.

Luckily, I have an entire anxious, sleepless night ahead to mull this all over. My own fears about the increasingly prolonged period of time I've spent single change shape. It's not that the tragic plight of the poor, pitiable Baltic women has made my own anxieties seem moot, but more that I see them in a new context. Particularly the context of: how is every country in the world terrifying women into marrying?

I wonder if my urge to pair off comes from a genuine desire for romantic partnership or fear of not finding that. Are my motivations so different from those of Aiste's friend?

Most of all, I think about women's fashion trends in Eastern Europe, and what outsiders think and assume when they see them, and while I'm not here to defend the tube top or lip injections or boots that come up to the inner thigh, I'll never again look at them and not see the weight of scarcity and the pressure these women face in their sultry clothing.

Aiste and Victoria had vastly different childhoods. Aiste grew up in the first years of Lithuania's independence, Victoria in the first years of its forced integration into the Soviet Union. When Victoria was young, her family was sent to Siberia, along with 130,000 other Lithuanians.

Depending on who you ask, either the Soviet Union forcibly took over Lithuania at the end of the Second World War, or the Lithuanians begged the Soviets to let them in. One of these narratives is at odds with the unassailable fact that there was massive Lithuanian resistance to joining the Soviet Union.

To prevent the resistance from growing into a powerful, organized movement and, as an added bonus, to get rid of the farmers who didn't want to turn their land and livestock over to collectivized farms, the Soviets sent thousands of Baltic families to remote, desolate parts of the country. They were given housing that could be bleak, sometimes providing little protection from the harsh Russian winters. In some places, food and medical treatment was scarce. The men were forced to work physically demanding jobs, often in logging or timber. Their wives and children were "encouraged" to Sovietize, using the classic carrot-and-stick method of implying that if they thought things were bad now, they should see how much worse they could get.

Children were punished for speaking Lithuanian in school. Fearing that their children might get confused and accidentally speak the wrong language in public, Victoria's parents switched to Russian at home.

After Stalin's death, many of the Lithuanian deportees were allowed to return. Victoria had left Lithuania as a young child and returned as a teenager. She'd forgotten how to speak Lithuanian. Coming back to her homeland was as much of a cultural shock and transition as it must have been for her parents to land in Siberia.

Victoria and Aiste tell me this story as we're walking on the grounds of a castle. I'm not sure what to say. I think back to the manhole covers I saw in Vilnius, where the Soviet insignia had been scratched out. I say that that's terrible and they nod.

"Anyway," Aiste continues, gesturing to the wide river below us, "isn't this a nice view?"

Before arriving in the Baltics, I'd never heard of the Grand Duchy of Lithuania, and I am dedicated to avoiding ever trying to pronounce its name. I'm surprised to learn it was the largest state in fifteenth-century Europe. Perhaps my ignorance comes from having grown up in the suburbs of Boston, an area that derives potentially excessive pride from its geographic contributions to the Revolutionary War. You know what they say the three most important factors in a revolution are: location, location, location.

The Grand Duchy united the territories of present-day Lithuania, Belarus, and Ukraine, with slivers of Russia and Poland. It was a popular destination for crusaders, who had a cure for the region's pagan traditions, and that cure was Jesus.

For this and other reasons, the Grand Duchy built castles. When you visit them, you realize they were more designed to ward off armed missionaries than to provide luxurious accommodations. Trakai Island Castle feels like a military fortress, not a five-star hotel. If the eponymous royal from *The Princess and the Pea* had been forced to spend the night here, she would have died of low back pain.

The castle is made of red bricks and accessed by a long bridge leading up to its gates. At Lithuanian weddings, Aiste tells me, it's tradition for the groom to carry his new wife over a bridge, and newlyweds from in and around Vilnius like to use this bridge because it's so long. I shudder at the image of the Lithuanian diaspora of New York forcing its young men to haul their brides across the Verrazano-Narrows.

"Did your mom come here on her wedding day?" I ask.

"I don't think so," Aiste says.

Victoria giggles and says something to Aiste.

"Never mind, she says she did."

As they drive me to the bus to Latvia, I wonder what made Victoria agree to let strangers from the Internet stay in her home.

Aiste wanted to give her sister something special for her upcoming twentieth birthday, so she posted a message on Couchsurfing asking people to send videos with birthday greetings. Responses poured in from all over the world—Pakistan, Guatemala, Tunisia ("don't be afraid to enjoy your party and do something stupid"), Cuba, Saudi Arabia, Greece—and when she shows me a cut of the compilation, I find myself fighting back tears. A group of friends in Turkey baked a cake that said, "Happy Birthday Indre!" (because of differences in time/location, they ate the cake for her). Lots of people made signs, bought balloons, picked up flowers. A family in Nepal sang her a song; a man in the United Arab Emirates offered sage advice to Indre and to all of his friends: "Love what you do and do what you love; just make sure it keeps you out of prison." A man from Qatar shares similarly uplifting advice-turned-joke. ("My advice for your birthday is: don't worry about the past, you can't change it; don't worry about the future, you can't predict it; don't worry about the present, I haven't got you one.") A party in Latvia drank a champagne toast in her honor. A couple wrapped in towels wishes her happy birthday from a sauna; a Moroccan doctor in Senegal examines "her" X-ray (doctor-patient confidentiality?) and muses that "everything is normal here, except for the fact that it's your birthday!" A guy from Mexico appears to send birthday wishes from a funeral.

A few videos were made by hosts and guests who were currently Couchsurfing, and some of the pairings made me wish I could send them a list of questions for my own video. How did the young Chinese guy end up in Transnistria, a thin strip of land that claims it broke away from Moldova (though no sovereign nation, including Moldova, recognizes its independence) and outdoes even Belarus in terms of preserving the Soviet Union? Are the gorgeous Swiss woman and the hunky Brazilian man hooking up? What did the Chinese student discuss with his host in Alexandria, Virginia?

I wonder if Victoria was convinced to try Couchsurfing by the community, or the spirit of generosity that seems to drive it, or the chance to try to understand and be understood by people she'd only know for a few hours.

I can't honestly say that I find Couchsurfing easy. I've felt less anxious about some job interviews. But if my goal has been to get a better grasp on Lithuania, I think Couchsurfing has done the trick, and, if not, I'll go to bed beside a glass of water on Christmas Eve and get all my answers.

As I board the bus to leave Lithuania, I think about the story Aiste and Victoria told me, about how the Baltics sang their way to freedom.

By the late 1980s, the Soviet Union was collapsing under the weight of its own bloat, corruption, and repression. All of the purges, lies, and shoddy policy had taken their toll, politically, psychically, economically. Wages stalled, the black market swelled, and people agitated for change.

To ease some of this pressure, in the mid-'80s Soviet leader Mikhail Gorbachev pursued a policy of glasnost, which strived for more transparency and openness in government, and instituted a series of political and economic reforms known as perestroika.

Soviet citizens suddenly had access to information the government had previously kept secret and the freedom to express discontent. Dissent was on the rise all over the USSR, particularly in the Baltic states, which had never really been willing members of the Union.

Newly permitted protests and demonstrations popped up in each republic, and maybe it was inevitable that the Baltic people, with their long history of singing and dancing, would voice their grievances through song.

One night, after a music festival in Tallinn, a group of attendees migrated to a hill in the center of the city and began singing patriotic Estonian songs that had been banned in the Soviet Union. Over the next three years, all the Baltic countries held similar rallies in which they sang national songs to agitate for freedom.

This story I'd known, in broad strokes, when I'd asked Victoria and Aiste for details, but the next part I hadn't.

I'd seen a monument to something called the Baltic Way in Vilnius that day. I asked my hosts about it.

"You don't know?" Aiste asks, surprised. "It's really incredible. People stood in the streets, and they held hands across the whole Baltics."

On August 23, 1989, more than two million Baltic citizens created a human chain that spanned more than four thousand miles, from Vilnius in southern Lithuanian to Tallinn in northern Estonia, and linked the three capital cities. I ask Victoria if she went. "Oh, yes!" she exclaims.

I keep thinking about this story for weeks after. I obsessively search for images and sometimes get choked up when I see them.

I think what moves me most about that story is not the knee-jerk American misty-eyed view of freedom, because what is freedom, really? Even the most liberal among us would probably say that we stand for it, would fight for it if necessary and not terribly inconvenient. When we use *freedom* in those contexts, we have some vague idea of what we're referring to—maybe elections, or the right to show up at a protest with a witty poster. But I don't think two million people line up on highways because they're so excited to vote or publish an opinion in a newspaper. Most protesters agitating for revolution aren't there because they have a few points of constructive criticism; they're there because a system seems broken beyond repair.

What makes two million people hold hands on the highway, I think, is hope, and hope in the face of a system as powerful and flawed as the Soviet Union's, a system that has been the only way of life most people remember, is a powerful thing.

"Back then, people did it because they hadn't been free for fifty years," Victoria tells me, through Aiste. "But I'm not sure they'd do it now."

The conversation moves on, but then a few minutes later, Victoria says something to Aiste. They have a brief but impassioned exchange.

"My mom says, maybe today, people would still do it."

17

ALL TRAINS LEAD TO RUSSIA

The journey to a place you've long dreamed about can seem filled with signs that everything you've hoped for is about to come true. On my train to Russia, for example, I'm sitting across from a woman wearing a T-shirt with a picture of Freud in neon sunglasses that is captioned, in English, with a Spice Girls lyric: "I'll tell you want, what I really really want."

Oleg's mother once told me that it would have been social suicide for a Soviet teenager to admit to not having read Camus and Derrida. Ever since then, I've imagined the Soviet Union as a place that, in its better moments, fostered a culture of intellectualism (as long as no one was intellectually debating the legitimacy of the Soviet government) and celebrated literature (as long as it was written by people who were dead or loved shock workers). And lo and behold: this T-shirt! *Of course* "Wannabe" has been about latent desires all along! And the neon sunglasses . . . well, that one has me stumped, but I'm ready to be enlightened.

"Hello," I say, in Russian, opening what I hope will be a robust, probing conversation about the influence of nineteenth century psychoanalysis on recent pop culture that will perhaps venture on to the topic of how I can purchase a SIM card when we arrive in St. Petersburg.

"Hello," she replies, and then immediately turns to the window.

A few hours into our trip, the train stops, and a border guard with flowers carefully stenciled onto her fingernails checks our passports and stamps us in, and with this, I have made it, in so many ways.

I shake my head. Almost three months ago, I flew to Kazakhstan with a few half-baked plans and the hopes of making it to Russia. At so many points along the way, that outcome seemed uncertain. There were moments, when I was bombarding strangers on message boards or walking the streets with garbage bags full of cash, where I questioned if I'd make it.

But still: all of the hand-wringing, visa-blundering, and yurt-insomnia was building toward something that was at times clouded by the minutia. Each excursion had been a step toward this triumphant culmination. I didn't give up halfway through or curtail my ambition when the reality of it proved tedious. I set out to do something that I wasn't sure I could, and I did it.

It really hits me when I step off the platform in St. Petersburg and the cold jolts me like an energy drink that's been recalled for causing heart palpitations. I'm in Russia.

It's late. The sky is black and the air is tinged with the familiar scent of burning charcoal. Above the roof of the station, smoke from unseen smokestacks curls up into the heavens. I made it to Russia.

I start laughing at the sheer improbability of this all. I think back to the darkest hours post-Anton, when it had seemed as if pain would forever permeate every aspect of my life. It's both easy and misleading, in moments of exultation, to look back on periods of despair and remember the former self who would have never believed this jubilant reality possible. Though I felt that way at the time, it was a mood, not a prior and different me. But that mood lasted a long time, and so I allow myself this moment of fallacy.

Parents kneel to zip jackets and foist hats upon the unwilling heads of sleepy children, and across the platform men in long coats and women wheeling suitcases exchange the winter night for a cozy berth in an old-fashioned train, bound for Moscow in their sleep. I know this, because I can read the Russian scrolling past on the board above. I think back to those first helpless days in Kazakhstan, when I stood at a pharmacy and said, "Hello, I am inside a car, I am vomiting," and now I'm laughing and crying, but mostly crying.

Well, I do cry easily.

Still, the sense of accomplishment I feel is overwhelming. It feels like for the first time in a long time, I embarked on something ambitious and entirely of my own making, and I saw it through to the end.

These tears feel so different from the ones I've spilled over the past years when I couldn't talk to Anton and when I missed his family and when I thought that my dreams were dead and my life was over and I'd never be happy again. That I would never love something or someone as much as this person whose absence defined every moment.

For a long time, I felt like I needed Anton, or someone, to show me what to do next. But it turns out, in spite of all the doubts and missteps, I was capable of guiding myself. The part I'm most proud of is that leap of faith—that I thought I could make this trip and it could lead to something bigger, even if I couldn't say what shape that would take.

The horse treks and black markets and taxi rides: even if I sense that most people would have made it just as far, it still feels, not like everything, but like something.

St. Petersburg stuns you, first with its beauty and then with its sprawl. It's like Paris, but with more stamina. The City of Love eventually peters out into the City of Look, a Lot of People Showed Up, and We Had to House Them Somewhere.

St. Petersburg keeps going. I should know: I'm staying on its farthest edges.

To be fair, the newly built complex where I'm staying is not technically in St. Petersburg. It's at the end of a subway line in the first suburb over the city limits. It's a new development, and because the roads won't be paved until construction finishes, it's a reminder that St. Petersburg was built on top of a swamp. What I mean is: it's very muddy.

The development has the feel of a stop along a larger journey. In addition to the above-mentioned subway stop, there's a long-distance train station and a bus terminus, surrounded by high-rise apartments that shot up in the late 2000s. But construction stalled, they didn't build schools, and now the place has a half-finished vibe. In between the apartments and the transport is a caravan-esque enclave of makeshift shops and bakeries, many on wheels or built out of mismatching material that looks like it was left over from the nearby construction site. Most of the vendors are Azerbaijani, and I find myself buying deep-fried pastries and cups of coffee so hot they burn through the plastic cups they're served in, just to sit in their cafes and listen to their music. It makes me miss Central Asia. It's EDM meets accordion—not a sound I ever expected to trigger nostalgia.

I'm determined to get over my discomfort of storing my snacks in a stranger's refrigerator, which is why I'm here, Couchsurfing again. Though I am already regretting this, because it's requiring me to barge in on this sweet young family well after midnight on a weekday.

Natalia doesn't seem annoyed, which says far more about her than it does about the situation. I've been wandering around her apartment complex for close to an hour in a state that is close to full-blown panic. I have only her address, written in too many dashes and slashes for me to decipher, directions that rely on colors that I can't make out in the dark, and her phone number. Having just arrived, I have no functioning SIM card. The darkness is also impeding my ability to make out building numbers, which are, helpfully, written on doors that are, unhelpfully, located too far behind gates for me to see clearly. Once again, my Couchsurfing has left me stranded on the distant outskirts of a city in a country I've only just arrived in with nothing to help me find my way but the kindness of strangers, which arrives, this time, in the form of teenagers who help me call Natalia and wake her up just before one a.m.

Natalia lives in one of the brand-new apartments with her new husband and an eleven-year-old daughter from a previous relationship.

"Sorry," I whisper repeatedly, excessively, as she shows me to a room she's set up with a cot and leaves me to make myself at home in her bathroom.

I'm soon able to fall asleep, thanks to some potent sleeping pills that are sold over the counter in Ukraine, but should not be.

The nice thing about St. Petersburg in November is that it's easy to catch the sunrise. In the morning, I lie in bed and try to will myself to get up. Outside of my window, the first blushes of sunrise are starting to stain the horizon. It's eight forty-five.

The not-nice thing is that the sun starts to set in the middle of the afternoon, leaving only a few hours of daylight, which generally has to work its way through a thick blanket of gray clouds, because, according to my meteorological calculations, in winter St. Petersburg is overcast approximately all of the time. I have seasonal depression just checking the times for sunrise and sunset.

Speaking of, I force myself to kick back the covers. The other downside of living in extended night punctuated by brief periods of lackluster daylight is that I start to crave eleven to twelve hours of sleep. I'm tempted to Google "symptoms of body going into hibernation."

I hear someone else in the apartment open a door.

The incomparable allure of bunking with strangers is that it dangles the prospect of a direct hit of the thing I came here for, which is a deeper understanding of these places. Aiste and Victoria gave me a taste, and now I'm hooked.

In the kitchen, I meet Dima, Natalia's husband, who is home sick with a cold that seems worrisome. I'm not a doctor, but I do spend a lot of time on WebMD. His sinuses are so swollen that it looks like he has two black eyes.

"Are you okay?" I ask nervously.

He shrugs. "Maybe, if it will be really bad still tonight, I will go to hospital."

I'm concerned about Dima's health, but I'm also not sure, as a Couchsurfer, how much of a say I get in his medical decisions.

A polite houseguest, I think, would say something flattering. "You don't look sick at all," I tease. "In fact, maybe you should be at work."

As soon as I leave the house, these barbs seem irresponsible.

Dima is a scientist, I remind myself. I'm actually not sure why I think this is his job—did Natalia say this on their Couchsurfing profile? Or did Dima tell me this morning? Maybe he's not a scientist at all, and took that as medical advice?

How's Dima doing? I text Natalia later in the afternoon, because if I can't be chill about searching for cups in a stranger's kitchen, at least I can dive right in and start getting involved in the family issues.

He's in the hospital, she writes back. He might have to stay overnight.

I'm freaking out but trying to stay cool. It's okay, she finally reassures me. This is normal. And I am again struck by the unique opportunities Couchsurfing offers, because by butting into a family's medical emergency, I've learned about the Russian health-care system.

Russian culture strikes me as both deeply superstitious and, incongruously, deeply enamored with exhaustive medical testing.

In China, some of my Russian friends would return home in summer for a full month of medical tests that they would often translate as "full-body check." Doctors would test their blood, monitor vital organs, poke and prod and sample, and then provide suspiciously precise predictions for future health outcomes. "My doctor says I have a forty-two percent chance of getting Alzheimer's when I am older," a language partner once told me.

This seemed at odds with how Anton would sometimes run back across the street to redo our goodbye because I'd accidentally kissed him three times (three being an unlucky number because of the holy trinity), and, though he wanted to be rational, he couldn't get his day off to such an inauspicious start.

I often wondered if, no matter what the battery of routine annual physical tests revealed, the treatment would just be tossing salt over your shoulder.

But these are also impressions I've picked up from Russians abroad, or, in the cases of Oleg and Anton and Anton's family—from people who weren't even Russian at all, just Russian-speaking—and it's so strange, and borderline unbelievable, that I'm finally *here* in Russia.

My first impressions of St. Petersburg are of the ubiquitous underground pedestrian walkways, which provide safe passage at almost every intersection. In St. Petersburg, you rarely cross a major avenue; instead, you descend the set of stairs found on each corner and instantly lose all sense of direction.

At first, the subterranean network of pedestrian tunnels seemed like a stroke of city-planning genius. It means never having to wait for the light at a crosswalk! Never being goaded by impatience into precarious jaywalking! But I soon conclude it would be much faster to just cross the street.

In the cold winter months, the tunnels let people move through the city without battling the elements. The underground walkways have bakeries, fur stores, hair salons blasting techno music. You can buy a wedding dress or take English lessons while crossing Nevsky Prospect. Sometimes people refer to this as an underground city.

Many extend off of exits for the St. Petersburg metro, which is an upgrade that reveals what the others have been striving for. Like the station that reduced me to tears in Tashkent, the stops are all relics of an earlier era filled with details that feel like antiques. The escalators with giant teeth, the brass lamps on the railings, the '60s clocks that hang from the ceiling—they all feel like collectors' items. But no one seems to pay much attention to the marble hallways making me misty-eyed. The strangest part of being a tourist is how normal everyone around you seems to find the things that stop you mid-commute and overwhelm you with awe.

"Don't cry," I whisper to myself. "They'll know you're a tourist."

———————

One peculiarity of the St. Petersburg metro is that a lot of the platforms have doors that only open when the trains' do, which means that you wait in relative blindness. You can't lean over the edge and crane your neck to see if a train's coming around a bend in the track. You can't see the track at all, because your view is blocked by solid walls and metal doors. There's a Soviet vibe to the whole thing: you feel powerless standing in front of imposing doors that open and close at an unseen overlord's command, and you realize, of course, that you never have any control over the whimsy of a metropolitan transit authority. It's like riding an elevator without buttons.

I pace the platform. Finally, I hear a train arrive, and the doors open, and I take the metro to the first of many museums.

To Americans, Carlo Rossi is the name of a wine you can buy by the jug.

To Petersburgians, it's the name of one of the Italian architects responsible for the city's resplendent buildings.

Each building in downtown St. Petersburg feels like a unique work of art. The avenues are lined with miles of incredible architecture, stunning churches, homes, structures brightly painted and enlivened with lavish façades. Spires of gold and green copper poke out over the skyline.

Petersburgian buildings also feature a unique architectural support I can only describe as "hunky naked men holding up buildings." In the place where traditional neoclassical buildings would have columns, the façades of St. Petersburg's finest instead have statues of Adonis-like figures, with long, flowing hair, and extremely chiseled abs, who are posed to look like they're bearing the weight of the building. It's . . . original.

To walk down the street in St. Petersburg is to consistently gasp at architecture. Even the Burger King is in an elegant yellow building with a row of sculpted flowers planted below its eaves.

St. Petersburg was built by Peter the Great, who had the temerity to both build the Russian Empire a new capital from scratch and, one assumes, figure the Russian Orthodox Church would eventually get around to canonizing him.

Peter the Great is best remembered for modernizing the empire over which he presided. Depending on who you ask, he either brought contemporary European ideas to his subjects, or he dragged them out of their old ways kicking and screaming.

Before gaining full control of the throne in 1696, Peter developed a fascination with Europe, a place seen as very different and separate from Russia. Ideas from the nascent Enlightenment had spread through Western Europe, which was connected by a unifying Catholic religion. Russia, as an Eastern Orthodox empire, missed out on this shift in philosophy. At the end of the seventeenth century, Russia was seen by its European neighbors as a backward, old-fashioned country still stuck in the Dark Ages. While Europe was pumping out symphonies and the *Mona Lisa*, Russia was giving the world more wooden paintings of Jesus with weirdly proportioned limbs, along with monk chantings. It was still wildly enamored with the feudal system. It did not see much value in idle pastimes like science, technology, and education. Also, Russian men wore really long, unflattering beards.

Peter was determined to change all this. Early in his reign, legend has it, he traveled to Holland in disguise and took an undercover apprenticeship in a shipyard. He returned to Russia and declared that Russians would shave their beards and become more like their European neighbors.

To kick off this campaign, Peter needed a new European-style capital. He'd recently relieved the Swedes of a swampy parcel of land near the banks of the Neva River, and this, he decided, would be his new metropolis. Since no one was particularly lining up to work construction in a bog that spent most of its year in winter, Peter conscripted tens of thousands of serfs, many of whom died while building his gleaming new seat of government.

The finished product thus has the unifying architectural themes associated with Haussmann's Paris. There are wide boulevards with elegant buildings that seem to stretch along the entire block. There are triumphant arches and exquisite churches and towering monuments just because.

There are also a lot of museums.

I start off at the Hermitage, the vast art collection displayed in the former Winter Palace. There's a throne hall with red velvet walls, a gold-plated room filled with jewels, and the tsar's two-story library made of carved wood. There are fourteen da Vincis. There's an audioguide with a distinctly Russian sensibility. "Raphael lived the life span of a true genius," the narrator declares gravely. "He died on his thirty-seventh birthday."

I stroll along the canals that connect the city. The brightly colored buildings stand out against the gray sky and murky water. It's cold, but not as bad as I was expecting.

The Yusupov Palace is described, in all the guidebooks, as the place where Rasputin was assassinated. To attract visitors, the museum that now operates and manages the eighteenth-century mansion, which makes the couple that tried to recreate Versailles look restrained, plays up this connection. There's a tour of the basement that details the particulars of the grisly execution, which took numerous tries to get right, though the tour is unfortunately not offered on the day I visit.

At first, I am disappointed. Rasputin is one of maybe three Russian historical figures most Americans can name. The reasons for this are unclear and possibly heavily influenced, at least for the generation born after the 1980s, by the Disney movie *Anastasia*.

But his outsized reputation is at odds with his modest historical impact, which falls somewhere along the spectrum between slight and negligible. He's known for having the ear of the final tsarina, a skill for manipulation that often gives him a reputation for something like evil incarnate, and, as a teenager who's been bored in a history class can tell you, a giant penis.

In reality, Rasputin was more like a shady religious leader with a penchant for mysticism and a talent for making the best friends and the worst enemies. He won the Romanov family's trust by seeming to heal Alexei, the tsar's youngest child, only son, and heir to the throne. He also, some argue, assured the downfall of the Romanov family simply by being so divisive and disliked. In 1916, he was lured to the Yusupov Palace by a group of noblemen, and over the course of a dinner, he was poisoned, poisoned again, shot, left for dead, discovered to still be alive, shot again, and finally dumped in a nearby river.

I have arrived at the Yusupov Palace shortly before closing, and whatever pains the institution as a whole may have taken to draw visitors to the palace, this philosophy has not extended to the staff, who follow me, hover, remind me that the museum is closing soon, and turn off the lights in each room once I leave. The Rasputin story, I realize, is not half as interesting as the mansions Russian nobility built for themselves. The Yusupov Palace, for example, belonged to your average, run-of-the-mill Russian princelings, and includes a gold-leaf theater and a gold-leaf Turkish bath.

In the Turkish bath, I strike up a conversation with two French girls who are also being rushed through the Yusupov Palace by docents eager to go home. We speed through a sumptuous mahogany library, and I learn that one of the two is studying here; the other is visiting.

The girls are friendly, and we bond in the way that foreigners even from different countries can, because they're instantly in the same boat. We laugh over the impossibility of the Russian language and the women shooing us out of the palace.

In the Turkish bath, I overheard the girls discussing finding a sauna to go to next, and I sense that I might be invited. We're hitting it off; they're probably picking up on my *unlike most Americans, I've gotten comfortable with public nudity* vibe.

We find ourselves back outside on the dark cobblestone streets. The reflection of the palace lights floats on the surface of the dark canal below us.

"So pretty," one of the girls says, and we admire the row of illuminated buildings across the water.

This is just like Camilla, I remind myself, *only this time I've learned my lesson.* I won't let fear of rejection thwart a budding friendship; I won't keep passing their building while I work up the courage to ask them to lunch.

"Which way are you going?" one asks, gesturing up the road. "We will maybe find a sauna, or . . ."

"North!" I exclaim, loudly, immediately, and untruthfully. North leads directly into the canal, and, more problematically, away from where they're pointing.

There's still time to correct myself or ask if I can join them at the sauna, but instead I find myself saying goodbye and heading toward a bridge that will take me north, so that I can at least make good on my word.

Stupid, stupid! I admonish myself as I walk away.

I shiver on the sidewalk, imagining the sisterhood that could have been. I picture us sitting in the sauna, laughing, joking, improbably sipping champagne. Meeting up for reunions thirty years later, and somehow we haven't aged a day.

But instead I'm back on the subway platform with nothing to do but stare at the metal doors until they open.

That night, I make pizza with Natalia and her daughter. Her daughter seems sweet but shy. I ask her about school and how she likes St. Petersburg. (She grew up with her grandparents and only moved here a few months ago; she misses her friends but likes that she can walk to her new school.) I wonder what it would be like to grow up with parents who Couchsurf, with strangers periodically arriving at your home in the middle of the night.

I decide that a good Couchsurfer would try to share her culture with Natalia's daughter. I start by describing New York.

"It's really big," I tell her. "And there are many tall buildings." I'm off to a terrible start.

"One thing I noticed about America," Natalia chimes in helpfully, "is that, in some places, maybe Wyoming, you have a house, and then no other houses around it for one hundred kilometers."

I nod, and Natalia sees that I'm missing something. "In other countries, China and Russia for example, yes, we have villages in the countryside, but it's a small community, and then no one around for one hundred kilometers. And in that small community, all the houses are close together, like in a city."

This strikes me as a very good point, and very illustrative of American culture. I try to explain to Natalia's daughter how most Americans would rather build big houses in the suburbs than buy an apartment in the city, and how we all have cars, but it suddenly strikes me as strange how we almost seek out privacy that borders on isolation, and that maybe that's why I'm so bad at Couchsurfing.

"Also," Natalia explains to her daughter, "the big difference between the Russian countryside and the American countryside is that in America, there isn't trash everywhere."

I take a bullet train to Moscow four days before the end of my trip. I'm speeding both to another city and away from the knowledge that I'll soon have to return to China. There, I'll have to make another decision: After my next stretch of work, do I return to New York, my curiosity somewhat satiated, or keep traveling through this part of the world?

Much as I'll be glad to be back with friends in familiar places, I don't quite feel ready to leave the former Soviet Union.

My trip started out at the edges of the Russian Empire and inched closer to its center. Each capital I visited, no matter how glorious, was still in some ways looking to Moscow. No matter that Moscow was now a different country or that now there were resentments about Moscow's imperial rule, people still gestured around at their trendy cafes and proudly declared it to be like Moscow or pointed to a beloved building and sighed, "Yes, but in Moscow . . ." You could hate the people it had sent you, but you couldn't hate *Moscow*; it charmed people from afar, seduced them up close. The way New York City swallows even the most worldly, jaded European tourists and spits them out as children, starstruck by billboards and babbling about buildings, Moscow mesmerized the masses. In some countries, it feels like the young and ambitious are still looking to Moscow, because if you want to make it big, that's where you go.

Any great city seems to embody the dreams of its countrymen. St. Petersburg may be Russia's most beautiful city, but Moscow is more glamorous.

Also colder.

Here the buildings soar into the sky in wedding-cake tiers for whom we also have Stalin to thank. After the war, Stalin commissioned the seven iconic skyscrapers, known in English as the Seven Sisters, that still captivate visitors today. They're massive, truly gargantuan Gothic towers topped with spires and finally a five-pointed star. Unlike most skyscrapers I know, their bases are wide and support secondary smaller towers on each side. The aesthetic was applied to Soviet-financed buildings all over the world, and I recognize it from a structure across from my office in Shanghai: the Sino-Soviet Friendship Building.

Looking out at the elegant and foreboding church-like spires from the steps of the train station in Moscow, I have the same sensation as when I arrived in St. Petersburg.

I'm in Moscow.

Also it's freezing.

I'm Couchsurfing again. This time, I'm staying with a young couple: Anna and Kolya. They host so many Couchsurfers that they've set up a Google calendar to track requests, and their profile is filled with glowing reviews.

Anna gives me precise, step-by-step directions to her apartment. "Walk out of exit number three and turn right." While I'm doing that, an older man in a dapper winter hat wordlessly picks up my suitcase and carries it up the stairs. For all the glory of the Soviet Metros—and Moscow's by the way puts all others to shame—they rarely have escalators leading up to the street.

Outside, the man asks where I'm headed, and when he hears my accent he switches to English.

"I STUDY ENGLISH IN UNIVERSITY," he explains, speaking in the vocal equivalent of all caps. I smile. It's a universal impulse, I suppose, to speak loudly and overenunciate through a language barrier.

He insists on carrying my suitcase to Anna's apartment. "EX-CUSE ME, CAN I ASK YOU, WHY YOU ARE ONE PERSON TRAVEL AND CARRY SUCH HEAVY BAGGAGE?"

"I NEED MANY CLOTHES," I explain, and we both laugh. I stare enviously at his thick leather gloves. It's so cold here that I feel like stepping into a walk-in freezer would warm me up.

Anna's apartment is on the sixth floor, and miraculously, she has an elevator. It's tiny and one of the old-fashioned caged cars where you pull the door closed and watch yourself ascend.

As soon as Anna opens the door, I can tell something is not quite right. She has two fresh scars on her face. Her kitchen window is open, and one of the gas burners on her stove is turned up all the way. I offer her the bottle of wine I've brought to say thank you.

"I've already had one"—she shrugs—"but let's drink this, too."

In an earlier message, she'd told me that her husband would be away while I visited, but I now notice that she wears no ring. She begins telling me stories about an older pilot, whose relevance I can't understand until she finally tells me, "We are together, in a way." She pulls up photos. He's divorced and in his sixties. His ex-wife and teenage daughter know about Anna and aren't happy. "I know what you mean," I say, thinking of Anton and Vadik and Elena.

She shows me pictures of a recent vacation she took with the pilot to Rhode Island. "We saw all of the lighthouses!" she exclaims.

I try to take this all in. She sounds happy with the pilot. Though she doesn't mention her husband, I assume they're in the process of separating. This, too, is a familiar pain. But so many of Anna's stories take a dark turn. "I fell down, but I don't remember" is a common refrain. While we're halfway through splitting a bottle of wine, she starts rolling a joint. "If I get arrested, I just need to pay someone not to go to jail." She shrugs.

Anna hates Russia. She hates the government, the corruption, the mentality the post-Soviet system has forced upon the people who've endured it. She tells me about her semi-estranged brother, who lives in the U.S. "When the Soviet Union collapsed, my mom got us all visas," she explains. "Because, you know, we are Jewish."

"Why didn't you go?" I ask.

She shrugs. "My life is here. Why would I go?"

By this point, I'm drunk, too, and I want to say something, make a suggestion, but I have no right. Like with Dima and his sinus infection. Besides, what do I say? Would someone look at my life and say, *I'm worried*, too?

The next morning, it's snowing. It's the first snow I've seen all year, and I'm giddy. Anna rolls her eyes. "So now, there will be snow until May."

Anna sees what I'm trying to wear and insists on bundling me up in a scarf and fur hat. I'm glad she does: as soon as I step outside, my eyes tear up from the cold.

The snow makes Red Square look like it's been sprinkled with powdered sugar: the iconic Kremlin clock towers, the gumdrop onion domes of St. Basil's Cathedral, the spired redbrick State Historical Museum. I feel like I've walked into a postcard.

The western edge of the square is dominated by the imposing Kremlin walls, which circle the perimeter of the government headquarters. I hadn't expected the Kremlin to feel so much like a fortress. But that's what it is. The Kremlin is one of the oldest parts of the city. It's an ancient walled citadel from which eleventh-century princes administered the expanding city-state of Muscovy.

The creepiest part of Red Square is Lenin's mausoleum. Conscious of the ease with which leaders could be elevated to the level of a deity, Lenin was adamant about not being turned into the patron saint of the Soviet Union when he died. To him, this was no different from the way people worshipped the tsar he'd worked to overthrow.

Lenin spent the last years of his life warning other Soviet higher-ups about Joseph Stalin, a man he thought had the potential for ruthless abuse of power. As soon as Lenin died, Stalin set about pursuing just that. He started by embalming Lenin, putting his body in a glass casket on Red Square, and erecting Lenin statues all over the country. Even today, people wait in line for hours to file past Lenin's casket.

Actually, I take it back: the creepiest thing about Red Square isn't the Lenin mausoleum, it's the Stalin impersonators roaming around, hoping to pose for photos with tourists in exchange for tips.

I shudder when I see the first, a stout man with a thick mustache and a long gray overcoat.

Stalin is thought to be responsible for more human deaths than almost anyone else in history. Historians place his death toll between 20 and 50 million. And yet here he is, smiling and waving across Red Square, ducking into the nearby mall when he needs to use the bathroom.

Few of the Russians around me seem troubled by this. Stalin's grave still sits beside those of venerated Soviet leaders outside the gates of the Kremlin, and though his body has been moved to another location, on the day that I visit, someone has left roses at his marker. Though few families in Russia today would be completely untouched by Stalin's waves of repression and terror, neither the Soviet nor Russian government felt it could afford to sacrifice the political capital of his victory in the Second World War. So they left Stalin hovering in the awkward space between international tribunal criminal and war hero. The problem with not taking your despots out back and shooting them, however, is that time erases the memories of their worst crimes, and today, it's not hard to find young Russians who admire Stalin.

As I always do to cope with things that enrage me, I log this detail for a future joke. Something about Stalin impersonators trolling for tips, or no, that's too easy. Maybe something about what jobs a person goes out for before they try Stalin impersonating, or how they know they'd be good at the job. Maybe there's a job interview. "What would you say is your greatest weakness?" "Trusting Adolf Hitler." I wonder how this material would play here.

On my third day in Moscow, I take the metro to a famous park, and when I get out, I find a long line of people holding flowers for no discernible reason. I pull out my phone and Google "flowers Russia line." I Google the date—maybe today is some kind of holiday? I find nothing. The line is *long*, easily a thirty-minute wait, but people keep arriving on the metro from different parts of the city and joining the end of it, by themselves or in groups. No one seems in much of a hurry.

I walk all the way down to the front of the line, and I realize that it's stretching to the gates of the French embassy. People are waiting to add to what's already easily a four-foot mountain of flowers and candles and teddy bears. Then I remember: there has been a terrorist attack at a nightclub in Paris. It seemed so sad and distant when I read about it on the news this morning; now, all at once, it's real.

I'm again sobbing. (Potential tourism slogan for the former Soviet Union: "Come for a few good cries!")

I never make it to the park. Instead, I spend the whole day outside the French embassy, watching the line of people grow, watching the other tourists gape, as stunned and spellbound as I am. "No one would ever do this back home," I hear an Australian man tell his companions. People hold signs that say NO HATE. An old man with a look of profound sadness wears a beret and carries flowers arranged to look like the French flag.

I strike up a conversation with two high school students, Dima and Andre, who thankfully speak English, and I ask them the questions that have been burning in my mind all day: What made you come here? How did you know to do this?

They looked shocked by the question. "It is a pity," Andre says, shaking his head. "Only in such moments like this we remember that we're mostly the same, our nation and France, and only in such moments we remember that there is something like humanity in us. That's why I'm here—it's my duty as a human."

Dima looks upset. He tells me he couldn't sleep last night when he heard the news, and he stayed up all night watching videos of the concert, trying to help the police by identifying the terrorists in the video, which, okay, Interpol might have better resources, but still.

I think about what the Australian said, and what Natalia said about the difference between America and Russia, and I think, yeah, there's no way this scene would happen in New York. I can't picture ordinary people taking a few hours out of their day to show up and make a gesture. And maybe that's all it is: a gesture.

But I think about the way even the most worldly Americans I know have a tendency to see Russians as cartoonish villains, how they almost imagine that the country is full of people who think and speak like Vladimir Putin, and I think about all the people who saw my heavy suitcase and, without saying a word, picked it up and carried it, and the people who offered me rides and put me up in their homes, and I think about Andre and his duty as a human.

"Little Joseph was born in Georgia," Pavel is telling us. "As a child, he was very poor. He often played in the streams and forests."

Little Joseph is perhaps better known by his adult name, which is Joseph Stalin, and we're talking about him because we're poking around in his former secret underground bunker, which is no longer secret, but still very much underground, to the tune of twenty stories below street level, and accessible only by stairs or a single, overworked elevator, which Pavel repeatedly reminded us we could not take down unless we were "quite old" or "having a very big illness."

Built at the height of Cold War tensions, the seventy-five-thousand-square-foot complex was meant to serve as a secure command center in the event of nuclear war. It was designed to withstand a nuclear blast and provide enough clean air, water, and food to sustain staff for up to three months without outside intervention.

Today, it's a Cold War museum, set up to look like an active Soviet bunker and displaying artifacts from that era, like radio equipment and military maps, and things that should never be displayed, like a life-sized, lifelike Stalin mannequin, which is casually seated behind a stately wooden desk.

Pavel is leading the one English-language bunker tour of the day.

"I can do the Russian tour," I said when the woman at the front desk informed me of this.

Upon hearing my accent, she'd narrowed her eyes and replied, "No, you can't."

At first, I'm impressed by Pavel's English, but after a while, I start to suspect he has simply memorized the entire tour, perhaps even phonetically. When I ask him questions, his answers alternate between scripted and nonsensical.

"So did people ever live in the bunker?" I ask him.

He asks me to repeat myself and I do, slowly, and afterward he shakes his head. "Sorry, I do not understand your question."

In addition to Russian and English tours, the bunker offers laser tag, and can be rented out for children's birthday parties.

I start feeling bad for Pavel after a mishap in one of the final rooms. "So now we will do a live demonstration of launching a nuclear missile," he announces. "Who would like to volunteer?"

I'm somewhat of a tour fanatic. I take tours whenever I travel, and I scope out the offerings on my home turf. I'd probably take a guided tour of my own apartment, if it were offered. I can therefore say fairly confidently that if a tour guide asks for volunteers on an excursion where the median age is higher than twelve, he's going to get a bunch of adults staring at one another, waiting for someone else to raise her hand first.

This is exactly what happens to Pavel: we all kind of look at each other. I think everyone, at this point, feels a little sorry for him—I doubt any of us would be surprised if he told us, at the end of it, that this was his first day on the job.

Pavel seems to take our reluctance to volunteer immediately as a denunciation of his skill as a tour guide. "Okay," he says quietly. "So the demonstration is canceled."

I spend my last night in Russia on an overnight train from Moscow to St. Petersburg, where I'll catch a connecting flight back to Moscow, and then on to China. This the end of the first leg of my trip. I'm heading back to China for a planned work break that will also allow me to save money for the next leg of my trip—if I decide to go.

If I'd looked at a map before planning my trip, I would have flown home from Moscow, not St. Petersburg. But because I think geography is best intuited, I paid extra to fly out of St. Petersburg, which I knew was farther north than Moscow, and therefore assumed would be farther away from Europe.

Already, I can feel the things I will miss about the former Soviet Union while I'm gone. I'll miss getting a torn receipt for every purchase, even trips to the bathroom. I'll miss how, at restaurants, you sign your bill, and then the server witnesses it by adding her own signature. I'll miss the cozy beds on trains and the awkward cots in Couchsurfing stays.

The train I book to St. Petersburg is accidentally top-of-the-line—the bathrooms are automated and clean and each carriage has an upper and lower deck. There's real coffee, instead of a cup full of instant grounds and directions to the closest samovar.

In the morning, the train wakes us with music that slowly grows louder. A soothing female voice comes over the loudspeaker to welcome us to St. Petersburg. "We hope it was a pleasant journey," she purrs, "and that your trip in the city will be useful."

Wet, heavy snow falls from the sky. I climb to a rooftop and look out over the city at dawn (which, lucky for me, is still going strong at nine a.m.). I feel so many things, but above all, I'm smiling, almost laughing, because even if this trip never turns into a book or part of a college's core curriculum, I'm so proud of what I've done, that I did this, that I made it, that I did what I set out to.

The signs at the airport are wonderfully mistranslated. FOR YOUR SAFETY, one warns, PLEASE DON'T TOUCH ANYTHING ONEROUS.

I don't know what flight path the plane follows, but I like to imagine it goes due east from Moscow, undoing all of the travel I just finished. Though I don't feel it happen, at some point on the plane my trip slips from present tense to past. "I'm traveling through the former Soviet Union" becomes "I traveled through the former Soviet Union."

Even now, I know I'm not finished. I feel there's more Russian to be learned and more Russia to see, and I also have a vague sense that I need to cross a continent by train.

I think about how Moscow seemed to symbolize the ambitions of the Soviet Union, and I contemplate my own aspirations. *What would it be like*, I wonder as the plane speeds through the clouds, *to do a stand-up gig in Moscow?*

THREE
THE TRANS-SIBERIAN
RAILWAY

18

TRANS-SIBERIAN PRELUDE: A
BRIEF STOPOVER IN CHINA

"Come on, dude, you should have known I grew up in Brest," Anton says, smiling. It's a familiar smile, one that conjures up the past without warning.

I've been back in Shanghai two weeks, and already my life is returning to well-worn rhythms: work, comedy, dinner with friends, trips to the grocery store that don't end, as they once did in Uzbekistan, with my accidentally buying pinecone-flavored mouthwash. Also, because I'm an idiot, I'm having beers with Anton.

"Whatever," I say, biting my lip to fight back my own grin, "Belarus is a small country."

To be fair, Anton and I probably couldn't have avoided each other if we wanted to, but we're 100 percent not trying. Since we broke up, Anton has started performing at the comedy club I started in Shanghai. This bothered me at first. He doesn't live in Shanghai and when we were together, this was unquestionably my turf. When we first broke up, I didn't have to see him if I didn't want to. Now I have no choice. But it's been two years, and I'm trying to be a better person.

Anton and I were on the same show tonight and coincidentally ended up at the same bar after. We're in a group but keep catching each other's eyes, slipping in words that carry coded meanings only the other will understand, referencing the private language we once shared.

In Turkmenistan, I went out of my way to camp beside a crater filled with fire. Now it seems I have returned to Shanghai to play with it.

To return to a place you know after being somewhere else is to see the familiar with fresh eyes. By this point I've lived in Shanghai, on and off, for almost six years and know the city like my childhood bedroom, but for my first few days back, everything seems foreign and new. For me, half the magic of travel is returning to some version of home and noticing all the odd details rendered invisible by familiarity.

The air is warm and smells faintly of cigarettes. I'm shocked by the sight of two men walking down the street hand in hand and then saddened by the implications of my reaction. I hadn't even noticed how hidden queerness had been in the places I just visited. It seems strange that the Internet is censored here and not in Belarus.

I realize I'd grown used to certain quirks of the former Soviet Union—the sticks of gum delivered with each restaurant bill, the way that metro stations that connected two lines assigned two different names to the same station, one for each line. Mostly, I marvel at how easy it is to buy things. Grocery stores sell all different kinds of cereal and produce that's not in season—a luxury I hadn't realized I'd taken for granted, until I watched the produce sections grow smaller and more paltry as autumn wore on in the former USSR.

At first, I have the impulse to purchase everything I could conceivably someday need. I pick up tape at convenience stores and buy three different types of shampoo. I quickly amass a collection of batteries and umbrellas.

In the former Soviet Union, shopping was a struggle. Some of the smaller cities still felt like they were running on the Soviet system of commerce, with a few enormous department stores that sold everything, instead of many small stores that sold some things.

I assumed that my Russophilia would take a hiatus while I was back in Shanghai. I am, after all, in a Chinese city, surrounded by

Mandarin speakers and fed daily reminders of the one undeniable realm in which China had achieved cultural superiority over the Russians: the food. Russian cuisine is a valiant attempt to do one's best with root vegetables. Chinese dishes, in contrast, burst with flavor and abound in variety. There's a reason you can find Chinese food almost anywhere you go and would be hard-pressed to name two Russian restaurants in your city.

Plus, there was the fact that I had already done the thing my Russian obsession had pushed me to do: I had gone and seen these places with my own eyes, built a foundation in the language, celebrated a wedding, and visited Lenin's embalmed remains.

But in the months I spend in Shanghai, I somehow manage, in the middle of a Chinese city, to surround myself with Russians.

My first lead comes from my friend Olga, who has recently hired a personal trainer. "He's Russian," she tells me, "and very good."

I had never considered hiring a personal trainer. I prefer exercise that feels like napping, like yoga and promising myself I'll do the seven-minute workout tomorrow.

But I'm intrigued by the fact that he's Russian. "Do you feel like you've gotten in better shape?" I ask.

"Oh, yes!" she exclaims. And then, sensing where this is going, she adds, "But I don't think he speaks English."

This sells me on it. I imagine myself killing two birds with one stone: developing a six-pack while also keeping up my Russian.

"Can I have his number?" I ask.

Olga frowns. "I think . . . it will be very hard for you to communicate."

Her trainer's name is Sergey, and I message him with some help from Google Translate. He sends me an address that sounds familiar; when I arrive, I realize why. His gym is in an office building that happens to house the first company I worked for in Shanghai.

I take the elevator up to the fifth floor, hoping I don't bump into any former colleagues on the floor below. *I didn't know this place had a gym,* I muse.

It didn't, I realize when I get off the elevator. Sergey's gym has simply taken the office space directly above my old company and converted it into a gym. Across the hall, white-collar workers in business casual manage accounting books and prepare visa applications. The bathrooms near the elevators are used by gym patrons and middle managers alike. It doesn't feel like a gym; it feels like an office space that was turned into a gym in the middle of the night and without proper permits.

Sergey greets me with a firm handshake and no smile. He's serious, solidly built, and extremely hot.

He nods that I should get on the treadmill.

It quickly becomes apparent that Sergey's English is better than my Russian, but he's much shyer to speak in a second language than I am.

"What you eat?" he asks as I walk on the treadmill.

"Like, today?" I reply.

He shakes his head. "Every day, what you eat?"

"Umm . . ." I struggle to think of all the foods I eat on a daily basis. I begin to list them, leaving off the things I sense he wouldn't approve of. "Quinoa, kale, cereal, yogurt, dumplings, sushi . . ."

From the look in his eyes, I can tell he understood none of this. "Eggs?" he asks.

I nod. "Sometimes."

He shakes his head. "Always."

"Always?" I ask.

"Me, every day, twenty eggs. Each time, ten eggs."

"Umm . . ." I am not going to eat twenty eggs a day. "Isn't that bad for your cholesterol?"

He doesn't understand cholesterol.

I try pronouncing it in a Russian accent. *"Kolestrol?"*

He shakes his head, not understanding. "You eat carbs?"

"Good carbs," I say. "Quinoa, oats, fruit."

He grows angry. "You must never eat carbs!" he shouts. I'm glad there's no table nearby for him to overturn.

I had pictured our sessions as half workout, half language lesson, but our first is a struggle against what seems like an insurmountable language barrier. Sergey attempts to communicate the complexities of nutrition and proper form, mostly via pantomime.

The one thing we have going for us is that many of the Russian words for muscle groups sound similar to their English equivalents. *Bee-tseps*, I realize, is bicep. *Tree-tseps*, tricep.

Some are different.

"This exercise," Sergey declares, "for ass muscle."

"Glutes?" I try.

He shakes his head. "Ass muscle."

At the end of the session, we're both exhausted. I sense that Sergey is surprised when I text him later that evening and tell him I'd like to see him three times a week.

I'm torn. After this round of work, I want to go back to Russia and cross the country on the Trans-Siberian Railway, but the doubts that preceded my first trip have resurfaced. All around me in Shanghai, friends are following the same path out of their twenties. They're settling in their careers, taking next steps in relationships, starting to plan for a more grounded future. When I Skype with friends in the States, it's the same.

It's not that I don't see the appeal. The sense of limitless possibility I have felt in my first decade of adulthood has also come with a great deal of uncertainty. Maybe it would be easier to settle in to something more rooted than continue to chase dreams across the steppes of Central Asia.

Besides, I've already done that. What would a few more months give me that the first leg of my trip hasn't?

But to not return for the final stretch feels like backing out. My dream was to spend the whole year exploring the Soviet Union; my fears said stay at home and grow up. Going back to the U.S.

without seeing it all the way through feels like trying to have it both ways.

Which would be nice. Who said there was anything wrong with having your cake and eating it too? Well, Sergey. Cake has carbs.

"I speak Russian now," I tell Anton the next time I see him. We're at an open mic; we keep finding excuses to touch, hug, get closer. When he gets offstage, he kisses my hand. It's sweet but I'm unsure how to respond.

Anton shakes his head; he's not smiling anymore. "Listen, I don't know how to tell you this, but you really don't," he says. We're both nervous and jumpy around each other. We drink too quickly and then keep an eye out for the smallest slight.

"Yes, I do," I assure him.

"Honestly, those e-mails you sent me from Belarus . . . Your Russian is really terrible."

"*Nyet.*"

"Oh, really?" He raises his eyebrows and then switches to his native language; I don't understand a word.

"Well, whatever," I say. "You were speaking too quickly."

I want to tell Anton all that I've seen, but he doesn't want to hear. He can't seem to decide whether to be thrilled or outraged by my new adventure. Sometimes I overhear him tell people that I've been to Belarus and I hear the pride in his voice, but when I speak to him in Russian, he gets angry. We've spent years hurting each other since our Burger King breakup: one reaching out and the other never answering, one offering an olive branch and the other snapping it in two, the rare moments of tenderness ruined by an explosive fight. We both light the fuse, because whatever it is that we're grasping toward, we both want, above all, to feel like the one walking away with dignity intact.

While we were together, I think we each represented access to a world the other wanted. Anton's was Russian, and maybe he's angry because I decided he wasn't the gatekeeper. In a way, I understand, because I've felt the same wrong before. For me, it came after we broke up, when Anton decided to get serious about comedy.

Sergey and I are making progress. Before I met him, I had never lifted weights, both because I didn't know how to, and because I was afraid that the second I touched a squat rack, muscles would burst my clothes at the seams and I'd have to go shopping. Now I'm wearing weighted belts and doing push-ups on bars. Sergey promises me I will develop an "ass like spider."

We communicate in our own language. Officially, we're supposed to alternate languages: one session in Russian, the next in English, but we come up with our own way of speaking. He teaches me to say *pussy* in Russian when an exercise is difficult, and I tell him it's better to say goodbye at five p.m. with "Have a good night" instead of "Good night!" We call lunges *zombies*. Each time he divides our sessions into "leg day," "arm day," and "ass muscle day," I want to correct him, but can't.

Each day I come in and he asks me the same question. "Did you eat carbs today?"

I list all my meals but skip the foods that I know will make him mad, a list that includes apples, brown rice, and everything that's not salad with cucumbers. His feedback is always the same: "Eat eggs."

Sergey's other clients are all from the Russian diaspora, and they are all extremely perplexed by the redheaded American who constantly mixes up twelve and twenty and frequently pouts when the exercises are too hard. Most have a Russian sense of discipline: they follow Sergey's rigid dietary guidelines without wavering and look horrified when I admit I eat fruit. When Sergey tells them to do too many push-ups, they say nothing until they collapse; I whine constantly that "It's not fair!"

I chat up Sergey and his other clients to try to get out of the leg workouts I hate. I invite them to my shows and out for drinks after.

One day, he pulls me aside for what I assume will be an assessment of my progress.

"You've been exercising for a few months now," he says. "And in that time, you have made many friends."

It's strange to see Anton, now that I know I don't need him for the thing I once thought only he could deliver. It would be easy to look at him now and see only how quickly he gets fucked up after shows or the false bravado with which he swaggers around the club before he goes onstage, but when he squinches his face to itch his nose in a way I'd forgotten but instantly remember, the air disappears from the room.

I see him almost weekly, and our interactions develop a predictable pattern. Sometimes I ignore him; other times I let him give me lingering hugs, inch too close on the bench where the comics watch the show. We stand in a group and he references a past only he and I share, as though everyone else were back there with us, following along.

"You're on this poster twice," he'll say, gesturing to his head shot, which has been cropped, but not close enough to remove the hand on his shoulder. "That's your hand," he reminds me, as if I had forgotten. The other comics awkwardly fidget.

"I feel very zen toward you," Anton tells me another night. "I've moved on; I have a new life now."

He does. Elena and Vadik have moved back to Belarus. Elena has remarried and will soon have a new baby with her new husband. Anton visits twice a year.

The nights often end in massive, dramatic fights. We never play out this part in front of people we know; the only witnesses are strangers and cabdrivers.

"I've only gotten better since we broke up," he spits bitterly one night. "And you've gotten worse."

"We used to be in love!" I cry. "What happened to that?"

The cab pulls up to my office where I left my bicycle. He jumps out and runs away.

It's hard to say what either of us wants out of these interactions. Maybe that's the problem: neither of us has figured out an agenda. I go home and furiously journal about how much I never want to see him again, come up with elaborate plans for him to leave me alone. I'm so angry that I can't read myself, much less him.

In an alternate universe, maybe, we're both performing in Moscow together. But at the shows in Shanghai, it just feels like we're trapped in the past.

Sergey figures out that the best way to motivate me is not to assure me that I can do something, but rather to insist that I can't.

"That's too much weight," I protest as he pulls out a ten-kilogram dumbbell.

"Yes," he nods. "You are weak American girl."

Each time he says this, I correct him. "American *woman.*" Then I finish the set.

We still struggle to make small talk in between sets.

"You know *Rocky?*" he asks me one day.

"Like the movie?" I say.

"Yes."

"I've heard of it, but never seen it."

He nods. "You eat eggs every day?"

Sometimes I can't tell if he's giving me advice on form or life.

"You control mind," he reminds me whenever my right shoulder raises higher than my left. "Mind control body."

Slowly, I develop a new reputation around the gym.

"Sergey told me you squatted with fifty kilograms!" Tatiana whispers the first time I meet her.

"Good night!" Sergey calls as I walk out at five p.m. "Do not eat carbs!"

Sometimes my interactions with Anton leave me with days of simmering anger. Other times he's wearing a sweatshirt I remember and I just want to curl up with him in a corner, whisper everything, the whole truth, without posturing.

I tell Sergey I'm going to visit his hometown in the Russian Far East. He stares at me for a long time and then says, "Why?"

I start questioning the prudence of taking the Trans-Siberian. Pros: I'm dying to do it, I have the time and money, it's a chance to improve my Russian, I can see more of Russia, I can write about it. Cons: may not help quest to avoid dying alone. I'm reliving the debate I had before setting off on my journey in the first place, and the doubts are doubling in strength. Seeing Anton reminds me both of what I could maybe have and how far I am from it, and this only increases my anxiety.

There's a tiny park around the corner from my old apartment in Shanghai. I used to go there when I first broke up with Anton, because everything in my apartment was something he had once touched, but the park is a place where I'd never seen him. The park has some kind of musical theme—it's filled with statues of instruments—but it's mostly used by the old men in the neighborhood as a place to gather and play chess. The crew hasn't changed much since I started coming here. The man with an ambitious comb-over who, in summer, goes outside in boxers is still here, now in real pants and a coat. So is the man with yellowed teeth who chain-smokes from a red box of cigarettes, though they all do that when they're losing. Two men play, and a dozen others crowd around them, shouting advice and commentary like it's a football game.

I ride my bike here and sit on a bench when I need to be alone and think. One night I stop by on my way home from a show, and I ask myself what I want.

I keep coming back to that line that slipped out in the taxi with Anton. "We used to be in love!" Maybe the problem isn't that *we* used to be in love, but that I did. And I'm putting my life on hold out of fear of not finding that again.

One day I come into the gym and Sergey looks upset.

"Someone say me, it's bad to say 'ass muscle,'" he tells me.

I hesitate. "Well, technically, yes," I reply. "But for you, it's part of your charm."

The Trans-Siberian is just a two-month trip, but in my head it has become a decision between rootlessness and stability. My personal life has become so confusing I can see it only in extremes. If I go, I'm choosing a life of travel but also loneliness. If I go back to New York like my parents want me to, I'm signing up for safety but a life I don't want.

It never occurs to me that I have neither a job offer nor marriage proposal waiting in New York.

I buy a ticket to Siberia. The first person I tell is Sergey.

"What will I do without you?" I ask.

"Whatever you do, do not eat carbs after sunset."

A MONTH ON THE TRANS-SIBERIAN

First Leg: Shanghai to Ulaanbaatar (Three Hours and Thirty Minutes)
The Trans-Siberian starts in Russia's Far East and runs clear across the country to Moscow. My journey on it, however, begins the night before I fly to Mongolia, when I throw myself an unnecessarily raucous going-away party. I wake up the next morning exhausted and profoundly hungover. This is bad, because I have an afternoon flight for which I haven't even started packing, and an apartment I need to move out of before I leave for the airport, and also because, what?!?! I'm about to turn twenty-nine—how am I such a hot mess?

I somehow make my flight and immediately pass out on the plane. A few hours later, a flight attendant shakes me awake to ask if I want lunch.

"No!" I shriek.

He flinches. "Maybe some water?" he suggests.

I recover from being jolted awake. "Okay," I acquiesce. "Also, I changed my mind, and I'd like lunch."

I'm starting the Trans-Siberian in Mongolia because I've heard that route offers the most stunning views from the windows. But first, I have a layover in Beijing, China's famously polluted capital.

Surprisingly, the skies today are clear, a stretch of blue with no smog in sight. It could be an auspicious start to my journey, minus the whole hangover.

I have hours to kill at Beijing's Capital Airport, which is perfect, because the airport is a wonderful environment in which to enjoy the exhaustion and nausea of a hangover. I lie comatose in an up-scale McDonald's. It strikes me that my life has reached a new low.

My first trip through the former Soviet Union was many things I hoped it would be. I saw some places I'd dreamed about for years and gained the tiniest glimmerings of understanding of others that had long seemed unknowable. I reawakened some of the insatiable curiosity and sense of direction that had characterized my time in China—even if that direction was sending me aboard a train for the next month.

Maybe it's because of this that I still feel torn, besieged by an off-brand version of late-twenties malaise. This feels like the period in my life where I should be reading a lot of memoirs and worrying that what I'm doing isn't what I want to be doing for the rest of my life. The frightening thing is, I'm already doing what I want—I'm just so afraid that I want the wrong thing that I can't commit to it whole-heartedly. Maybe I should be back home, trying to settle down.

Did I expect that learning Russian and discovering a new corner of the world would kick-start the solving of all my problems? And if so, why hasn't it?

As I check in for my flight to Ulaanbaatar, I realize that my shirt is on inside out and sporting a sizable wine stain. To compensate for this, I go to duty-free and douse myself in free samples of perfume. Now I have a headache. I get on the plane and again fall directly to sleep.

This time, I wake up of my own volition. The Mongolian woman next to me smiles and tells me she saved me the dinner that was passed out while I was also passed out. An unsupervised baby climbs into my lap. It's a gentler reacquainting with the world of the living, one I'm not quite sure I'm ready to reenter.

When a plane lands in Ulaanbaatar, it lands at Genghis Khan International Airport. The winds blowing in from the Mongolian steppe are so strong, only Mongolian pilots are allowed to land there.

A recent boom in the Mongolian mining industry has brought an influx of foreigners to the country. Many of my friends and acquaintances from China have visited over the years, and few had anything positive to say about the experience.

"I was punched in the face" is a common story brought back, usually followed up with "in broad daylight." Stories of street brawls, public drunkenness, and general pugnacity had painted a fairly terrifying picture of Mongolia in my mind, and landing at an airport named for one of the most feared warriors of all time is more or less confirming this. Before we get off the plane, we're asked to give a round of applause for the Mongolian National Boxing Team. It's not clear if they're on our flight, or if we're just proud (or afraid) of them.

A driver from the hostel I've booked meets me at the airport and leads me to the parking lot. I'm so hungover and sleep-deprived that I barely register the Mongolian winter that hits me like a steel door. The air is thick and dark with night, and the cold is instantly everywhere. My head spins on the long drive through dark streets.

At the hostel, I curl up in the bed and take a well-deserved Xanax and collapse into the kind of sleep that feels like a new lease on life.

I've arrived in Mongolia in April, which I thought would be spring, but is not. I've also arrived in a country that I thought was once part of the Soviet Union, but I quickly learn was not.

"You don't speak Russian?" I ask the woman making breakfast, after she gave me a confused look when I asked for coffee.

She shakes her head. She's in her forties, old enough to have been educated in the Soviet system—if that's the system that was in charge.

It slowly dawns on me. "Was Mongolia . . . not part of the Soviet Union?" I ask.

Mongolians will often tell you that their country was the sixteenth Soviet republic, a nickname that comes from their close ties to the USSR. But while the Soviets helped overthrow the Mongolian monarchy and installed a communist government that answered to Moscow, they never formally annexed Genghis Khan's homeland.

This feels like something I should have researched before coming here.

Julia, my friend from Sergey's gym, puts me in touch with her childhood friend Darima, who was born in Russia but now lives in Ulaanbaatar. She moved here a few years ago with her Mongolian husband, whom she'd met in New York, married in Vegas, followed to Australia, and finally settled with in Mongolia. But in some ways, moving to Ulaanbaatar felt like a homecoming.

Darima grew up in post–Soviet Russia, in a Siberian city not far from the Mongolian border. "Not far" means something different in this part of the world, where two cities separated by "only" a two-day train journey are "close," but Darima's hometown is only about 150 miles from Mongolia.

Darima is Buryat, an ethnic subgroup of Mongols indigenous to Siberia. Buryats share many cultural and linguistic similarities with Mongolians, and when their homeland, Buryatia, was incorporated into the Soviet Union, it was done so under the name Buryat-Mongolian Autonomous SSR. Few Buryats were excited about joining the USSR, and even fewer were on board with Soviet-imposed collectivization, which forced people to give up their livestock and land to form collectivized state farms. Many Buryats still lived as nomadic herders, as their ancestors had for centuries, and when the state ordered them to turn in their animals, thousands rebelled. Fearing that further Buryat rebellions could achieve their intended effect, Moscow quickly redrew borders so that Buryats would be spread out across multiple SSRs (which would make it difficult for a rebellion to organize or nationalize using state infrastructure) and removed Mongolian from the name. It's in the Russian Federation's interest to continue to downplay the ties between Buryatis and Mongolians, because Buryatis could start wondering if they might prefer to be part of Mongolia.

The first place Darima takes me is a war memorial up on a hill on the outskirts of town. In the taxi there, she points to all of the development that's taken place in the last five years. Shopping malls, apartment buildings, entire neighborhoods—all of this, she says, was empty land a decade ago.

The money came from the mining boom, which brought foreign money in as coal, copper, and gold flowed out. For a while, Mongolia was the hot new thing—its economy grew 17 percent in 2011—but then commodities prices fell, followed by demand from China, which purchased three-quarters of Mongolia's exports. Now the currency is plummeting, and Darima says many of the brand-new apartments we pass sit empty.

I like Darima immediately. She's warm, curious, and interesting, and most important, she likes comedy.

"My husband and I went to a show a few months ago!" she exclaims when I mention stand-up. She insists that I bring a group of Shanghai comedians up to Ulaanbaatar for a show. "It's so easy to get here—only two days on the train!"

Though Darima speaks basic Mongolian, we're both technically foreigners. We notice similar things.

"It's crazy that everyone here speaks English!" I exclaim. Because Mongolia is surrounded by Russia and China, I expected those languages, and not English, to be prevalent. But when I had to communicate while wandering around this morning, Russian and Chinese did me no good. If waiters and taxi drivers had to use a second language, it seemed most preferred English.

"I know," Darima replies. "When I first got here, it was strange for me, too."

She, too, notes the casual ease with which Mongolians seem to live abroad. The woman running my hostel has a sister living in

Chicago—everyone, it seems, has a relative in the U.S., and they've lived in Asia, Australia, the Middle East.

"Some people say it's because Mongolians are nomads," Darima tells me as we hike up the path to the hilltop. "So they're used to moving around, and they adapt to new places."

Around us, brown hills gently rise and fall in waves that remind me of Central Asia. In New England, our prominences are covered with trees, and even in winter, topography is obscured by bare trunks and branches. Here, with nothing to block the view, every dip and boulder is exposed.

"That was strange about Americans, too," Darima is saying. "How much you move around."

"What do you mean?" I ask.

"For example, you grow up in one city, and then you go to university in another city, and then you move to another city just because you want to live there. And so the city your parents live in is not the city your grandparents live in, and the city you live in is new, too." She shakes her head. "In Russia, it's not like that."

We reach the top of the hill, where a mural memorializing the victims of the Second World War wraps around an eternal flame (encased in glass because of the wind). It's *so* Soviet. All the major laborers are represented—soldiers, doctors, astronauts. (Ah yes— who can forget the brave astronauts of the Eastern Front?) Members of different ethnic groups hold hands. It's a reminder of how close the two countries were, and also maybe reassurance that my *Whoops, I thought Mongolia was part of the Soviet Union* snafu was an honest mistake.

The memorial provides a panoramic view of Ulaanbaatar, and I notice that at the bottom of the hill we just climbed, someone has erected a ninety-foot gold statue of Buddha. That's so strange, I tell her. I never thought there would be Buddhism in Mongolia.

Darima stares at me. "You didn't know that Mongolians are Buddhist?" she asks.

My knowledge of Mongolian history pretty much begins and ends with Genghis Khan, which is probably why I pictured modern-day Mongolians as possessing more of a warrior spirit than a penchant for mindfulness. I try to delicately explain this to Darima.

It turns out that after Mongolia finished conquering the world, the country got really into spirituality. Before World War II, Darima tells me, half of the men in Mongolia were monks. This just does not square with any of my preconceived notions, which is maybe the point of travel, but anyway, tomorrow, Darima is taking me to a Buddhist temple.

Much of travel can be tedious and unpleasant in the moment: you're tired, you're lost, you're cranky, you're hungry. You're alone and you can't find your brand of granola. And as evangelists throughout the ages have found, spirituality shines brightest in times of suffering.

I often find myself killing an afternoon in a foreign country in a church, which feels like a betrayal of my lifelong distrust of religion. But when you're worn down from a day of decision-making and navigating an unfamiliar place, you can warm to the idea of a way of outsourcing your problems.

The Gandantegchinlen Monastery, in downtown Ulaanbaatar, is the only Buddhist temple to have made it through the communist years as an active temple and monastery.

The Soviet Union helped install a communist government in Mongolia in the 1920s and, as it did in many satellite states, provided Soviet "advisors" who "encouraged" the nominally independent leaders to do Moscow's bidding. The Mongolian People's Party quickly set about murdering monks and burning temples, but the Gandantegchinlen Monastery was, bizarrely, kept open as a kind of tourist attraction.

Inside is the world's tallest indoor statue, an oddly specific record that reminds me a little of Ashgabat's record for highest concentration of marble buildings. But it's dark and quiet. In the distance, we can hear bells ringing and faint chanting. The air is perfumed with incense.

A maze of prayer wheels—large, brass cylinders inscribed with Mongolian script—leads you through the temple, and Darima whispers for me to wish for something and spin them as we pass. Something about the whole thing clicks. While I'd normally roll my eyes but also cover my bases with shallow wishes for things like astounding financial success derived from minimal effort and a metabolism that allows me to maintain a hot bod while eating mostly ice cream, I'm swept up in a wave of sincerity. I find myself playing the best version of myself, wishing for things that seem simple and honorable and true. I wish for love and happiness, whatever shape that takes. I wish that I might do good work.

Maybe I'm a Buddhist, I think.

Outside of the temple is a stake where monks were supposedly burned alive in communist times. Today, it's a sacred talisman. Babies are brought here to touch the splinters for good luck; adults whisper their wishes into the wood. There's a crowd gathered around it, but Darima decides we should wait in line and ask for the things we want. There's something humbling about watching young men in trendy sneakers display such naked vulnerability as they lean in to whisper their desires, about realizing that everyone has wishes. "It feels like ancient times," Darima murmurs, and I know what she means. I'm all in; I'm ready to convert.

As we leave, Darima buys a bag of bird feed from people selling them outside the gate. Everything attached to the temple is auspicious, even the pigeons who land here, and Darima tells me to feed them for good luck. The pigeons swarm and I squeal, but Darima laughs.

"It's good!" she says. "They can tell you're a good person."

That feeling stays with me for the rest of the day. Maybe the pigeons are right, and I am a good person, deep down. Sure, I have some issues to work through. But maybe there's hope?

Later in the afternoon, as Darima takes me on a tour of old busts of Lenin that remain from the communist period, I mention something about the pigeons knowing I was a good person.

"Oh, that!" She laughs. "No, I was just joking—I don't really know everything about Buddhism." She sees my face and quickly changes her tune. "But maybe it's true!"

That night, Darima wants to take me to Ulaanbaatar's North Korean restaurant.

Many large cities in countries that have diplomatic relations with North Korea have restaurants run by the North Korean government. They're staffed by North Korean citizens and serve traditional dishes with heavily inflated prices and tend to be frequented by members of the Hermit Kingdom's diplomatic missions.

The restaurant is difficult to find, so Julia's brother, Arthur, agrees to take us, along with his wife, Sasha, and their young daughter. We walk into a nondescript office building and ride the elevator up to the third floor.

The restaurant is dark and empty, and the staff is practicing karaoke. When they see us, they calmly turn off the karaoke machine, turn on the lights, and seat us.

"That was interesting," I say nervously.

"Very interesting," Darima agrees.

There's a stage at the front of the restaurant with equipment set up for a full band. Neon Christmas lights trace flowers on the backdrop.

The waitresses all wear the same black dress and keep their hair pulled back in identical buns. My head spins each time they hand us menus or take our orders. I can't imagine the world they come from. I'm brimming with questions I want to ask about their lives—what did you study in school, what does your house look like, what do you do for fun—but I also realize that they're people, not a fascinating museum exhibit, and, anyway, I get the sense that personal conversation would be a terrible idea. The strangest part is their mannerisms. They're all are eerily quiet and their faces make no expressions. But in some sense, they're just people working in a restaurant. I have been a person working in a restaurant.

Three hundred North Koreans work in Ulaanbaatar, Arthur and Darima tell me.

Muzak covers of Simon & Garfunkel play softly from hidden speakers. I notice that all the potted trees are plastic. A few tables over, a waiter silently studies an English textbook I've used with my students in China.

The restaurant has a gift shop that sells flowers, pins, and embroidered paintings. All of the prices are exorbitant and listed in U.S. dollars. The profits are likely funneled directly back to the regime, and the choice of paintings is odd. Some are copies of well-known works like da Vinci's *Last Supper*, while others appear to be original compositions. There's one of two lions licking each other like cats, and I'm floored by the symbolism. Was this composed by a North Korean artist, trying to encode some message of peace? Like, this animal we normally think of as ferocious can also express affection? And is that maybe the lesson of my trip to Mongolia, too? That this country that terrified me in theory ended up being something else?

Or maybe that's just the pattern they had?

I join Darima next to an innocuous, though, admittedly not great, embroidered painting of clams. Darima shakes her head. "It must have taken years to finish this," she says. I'm about to object when I realize she's right. I had imagined these canvases coming out of a factory of sewing machines, but I realize it's far more likely they were hand-stitched. I flip through translated books of Kim Jong-Un's sayings. The English is terrifyingly flawless and natural. The North Korean who translated this knew what he was doing.

After dinner, the room goes dark, except for spotlights on the stage. Our waitresses appear and perform a highly choreographed song and dance, complete with costume changes and live accompaniment. Throughout the performance, their faces are frozen in plastic smiles.

We stay late, and when we go to leave, the doors to get out of the restaurant are locked. For a moment, my blood runs cold—are we about to be taken hostage? But then a man appears and calmly opens the door. He shakes our hands as we leave.

"Where are you from?" he asks in English with barely a trace of an accent.

"Russia," Darima says.

"Russia," Arthur says.

"Russia," Sasha says.

I swallow. "America."

He nods and thanks us for coming.

I keep saying I want to make changes in my life, but I keep going on horse treks and waking up in yurts.

Actually, this isn't a yurt; it's a *ger*, which is the Mongolian word for yurt. The Mongolians, like their southern Central Asian brethren, were traditionally nomadic herders who hunkered down in the winter and in warmer months moved to pastures for grazing. Today, many continue this practice, both in the cities and out in the countryside, where I am.

The *gers* are most striking in the cities, where they often form districts around the edge of town. The fact that homes can be disassembled and easily moved once allowed herders to head off in search of greener pastures, and today allows similar movement for employment prospects.

Urban *ger* districts aren't always filled exclusively with *gers*—some families erect more permanent structures—but they generally don't have heat or running water. It's hard to tell much of this, walking through them, because the homes are surrounded by tall wooden fences. The districts themselves are further concealed by strategically placed billboards the government "happened to" erect in a path that directly blocks views of the settlements, which the government, eager to attract foreign investment and rebrand Mongolia as a modern country, sees as an unsightly embarrassment.

The *gers* shape life in Ulaanbaatar in more ways than one. In addition to allowing newly minted urbanites—many of whom moved to the city after a devastating cold snap killed ten million animals—to retain their traditional ways of living, the *ger* districts also shape the environment in winter. Lacking gas or indoor heating, *ger* residents burn coal for cooking and warmth, which contributes to Ulaanbaatar's notoriously noxious winter pollution. The city sits in a bowl, and in winter, a layer of thick smog hangs over it, blocking the view and leaving a sharp taste in your mouth, even if the scent can be oddly homey.

While the city is crowded and bustling, the countryside is a blank, empty slate of barren grassland beneath an endless blue sky, and the weather changes quickly. In my first thirty minutes in Gorkhi-Terelj National Park, it snowed, hailed, and then cleared into a blue sky with blinding sunlight, and if the takeaway is anything, it's that life out here must be hard.

The *gers*, are therefore, similarly versatile. We pass a *ger* that offers karaoke and stop in another that serves as a restaurant. As we eat a mercifully warm stew, a television plays a music video in which a man in traditional Mongolian dress gets drunk and goes hunting with automatic weapons. If the takeaway is anything here, it's that hunting is more efficient when you're emotional.

My guide is a perpetually smiling woman named Mogi who has given us a few colorful interpretations of Mongolian history.

"You know, Mongolia is trapped between the two most powerful countries on Earth," Mogi says, echoing a sentiment I hear multiple times a day in Mongolia. "In the 1960s, Mongolia gave Lake Baikal to Russia as a gift," Mogi continues. The Dutch couple I'm traveling with and I exchange glances. "But it was like, you know, a gift you always give back." More exchanged glances. "So actually," Mogi continues, her voice rising with emotion, "Russia stole Lake Baikal from Mongolia!"

We're on a two-day trip through the park that includes a horse trek and a *ger* stay with a nomadic family, but so far we have primarily visited rocks.

"This cave, yeah, the monks are hiding here," Mogi says, after making us climb a slippery pile of rocks and wedge ourselves into a crevice between them. "But the army found them," she continues, "and they are all dead."

After this unexpected dark turn in the story, she is quiet, leaving us to picture the horrible deaths that must have befallen people in the exact place we're crouching.

The next rock looks like a turtle. "You see?" Mogi says, pointing out the shell and head that do kind of resemble a turtle, though to me, it primarily looks like a rock. Does it have any religious significance? No, it looks like a turtle. Do I want to climb it? After the dead monk rock, I'm good.

In the afternoon, we ride horses up to a Buddhist temple high in the mountains. As we cross icy streams and circle up the hillsides, it starts to snow. Wet, heavy flakes drop from the sky and drift through the pine trees, and although it is freezing, it's also stunningly quiet and beautiful. The temple complex, too, is dreamy: a series of red pagodas and statues of Buddhas overlooking the valley below. We cross a rickety wooden bridge to reach the highest building, a brightly painted wooden pagoda with intricate carvings and a sloping roof made of tiles. Mogi doesn't tell us to make a wish, but I close my eyes and do anyway.

In early evening we arrive at the camp of a goat-herding family, with whom we'll be spending the night. Their *gers* are located beside a dry riverbed that will fill with water in a few weeks when the snow begins to melt.

The women are inside making fried dough while the men finish their afternoon chores. As we warm up with tea, the father pops into the *ger* and asks Mogi a question; she looks uncertain but asks us if we want to help him feed the baby goats.

Do we ever! The Dutch couple and I are outside before she's finished asking the question. The new goats are only a few weeks old, and they range in size from adorably tiny to adorably miniscule. Some can't really open their eyes yet, most stagger around their pen on shaky legs, and I want to adopt all of them.

Our task is simple: each baby has a tag affixed to its ear that matches a tag on its mother's ear. The tags are resourceful: a bottle cap, a torn label with a brand logo, the occasional piece of paper with a number scribbled on it. When it's time for the goats to nurse, each baby is placed directly beneath its mother; otherwise, the strongest kids would starve the smallest runts.

The babies are kept in a separate pen while their mothers spend the day grazing. On horseback, the men have rounded up the mothers and cornered them in an adjacent pen. Our job is to scoop up the babies and hand them over the pen to the herders, who use the tags to match them with their mothers.

We gingerly cradle the goats like babies; the herders, in contrast, don't see them as fragile. They carry the kids by their legs and fling them around with a less-than-delicate touch.

"I see why they asked us to help," the Dutch guy muses as we hand the last of them over. "Can you imagine how long it would have taken them without us?"

With more than double the manpower, I realize, it still took over an hour. I go to bed that night with more understanding of what it takes to get a herd through winter.

Second Leg: Ulaanbaatar to Irkutsk (Twenty-Three Hours and Fifty-Five Minutes)

If you're in a hurry, you can make it from Mongolia to Moscow in four days, three hours, and thirty-six minutes; because I'm not, I decide to take a month.

When you try to picture the Trans-Siberian Railway you might be, as I was, a little unsure where to start. Most of us are vaguely aware that it's a long train line crossing Siberia to link Asia and Europe. But I'd always thought of the Trans-Siberian as a kind of express train that started on one end and shot through to the other without stopping.

In actuality, the Trans-Siberian Railway is a network of railways that runs from Moscow to the Pacific Ocean on 5,772 miles of track. A lot of times, when people say "the Trans-Siberian," they're referring to connections on both ends that would allow you to go from London to Beijing without stepping off a train.

All kinds of trains run along these routes, from luxe carriages with TVs and showers to low-budget basics that feel like one step up from a boxcar. You can book private compartments in first-class cabins or single bunks in open carriages. Some trains have restaurants that serve freshly made borscht and blinis, but even the least peckish travelers need to pack additional provisions, a feat made trickier by the fact that you won't have access to refrigeration or anything to heat things up. You will, however, have unlimited access to boiling water. Your staple foods become ramen, instant oatmeal, and bread, a diet you so quickly tire of that you soon start to question whether items like cheese really require refrigeration, which becomes a gateway to convincing yourself that pasteurization is a sham we've been sold by Louis Pasteur, or that occasionally pressing perishable foods against the cold window while your compartment-mate goes to the bathroom is adequate refrigeration.

I think a lot about what kind of ticket to purchase before booking my journey. My main concern is safety. I grumble about the special sections for solo female travelers at the back of each guidebook, resenting the way they make women traveling alone sound as fragile as glass figurines being shipped via zip line.

Still, it is impossible to ignore the fact that women almost never travel alone in the former Soviet Union, and that falling asleep on a moving vehicle open to the public is not without its risks. There are a few schools of thought. For an average trip of, say, just over a day, a first-class ticket would cost around $120 U.S., which by my standards is a fortune, but more reasonable when you consider that it includes transport, lodging, a few meals, a modest toiletry kit, and, of course, unlimited boiling water. (In a nod to Soviet ideals of equality, it's not called "first class" but instead "SV," which stands for *spalny vagon*, or sleeping train, but which I prefer to think of as shaggon vagon.) SV carriages are blinged out, with luxuries like throw pillows, fresh flowers, and generic art. There are also, occasionally, en suite bathrooms and showers. Most notably, SV compartments are built for two, meaning you only share a room with, at maximum, one stranger.

The next step down from SV is *kupe*, or second class, where a ticket for the same train runs closer to $50 U.S., if you're okay with top bunk, or $60 U.S., if you aren't. *Kupe* compartments accommodate four, which translates to you plus up to three strangers, but there's still a door that can be locked, which provides a greater or lesser degree of safety, depending on whether you're more afraid of the people outside your room or the passengers in it.

The cheapest option is third class, known as *platskart*, an open carriage with about fifty bunks, where tickets for the same ride start at less than $25 U.S. While the main cabin is likely to be clean, the bathrooms, it is rumored, can quickly descend into anarchy.

I initially assume SV is the safest bet, because it comes with the lowest potential for being locked in a room with a serial killer. But travel books and people chiming in on message boards disagree.

There's safety in numbers, many argue. If things get sketchy in a *platskart*, forty-nine other people will hear you scream. "SV can be nice if you're traveling with one other person," one travel book wrote. "But it can be more awkward to be in a room with one stranger than with three."

After much consulting and discussing and falling into unrelated Wikipedia holes, I decide to travel in second class.

In some ways, I luck out on my first train, because though the cabin sleeps four, there are only two of us in it. In other ways, I'm less lucky.

My roommate's name is Oorma, and she immediately gives off the vibes of the freshman-year roommate who inspires you to start researching medical conditions that warrant a single. As she unpacks her bags to settle in for the trip, she begins throwing her belongings on my bed, and, when that space runs out, on me. Then she sighs, sits down, and starts snacking, a pursuit she will continue, loudly, for the duration of our journey.

"So . . . Audrey," she begins, in the kind of slow, singsongy Russian you'd use with a child or someone recovering from a traumatic brain injury. "Where . . . are . . . YOU . . . from?"

We talk about where we're from and the countries we've traveled to, and she suggests we show each other our passports, which doesn't strike me as a terrible idea until she starts taking pictures of mine. I freeze. Is she a thief? Or is this part of train etiquette? Should I take out my phone and photograph hers just to be polite?

"I'll show my friends," she announces as she hands me back the proof of citizenship that could also double as a how-to guide for stealing my identity.

People advocate traveling by rail for the same reason they say you should bike or hitchhike: so that you can see the country. Airplanes take you from one city to the next without giving you any sense of the distance you've traveled or the land in between. Which is mostly fine by me. "Land" has struck me as something that comes with drawbacks, including bugs, cold weather, and lack of trendy restaurants. But I have to admit, the Mongolian countryside is pretty. Very brown, but pretty. It's all grassland, and grass, notoriously, spends the winter dead. You wouldn't think dead grass would look nice (especially if you were raised by my father), but it's more golden than I remember the patches of lawn we left our toys out on being. It's empty, rugged, bare, as though an overzealous bikini waxer yanked off all the people and plants, leaving only the mountains and the wide spaces in between.

Russian trains all run on Moscow time, which is meant to prevent confusion but instead creates chaos. Outside your window, it's eight p.m. in Mongolia, but the clock on the wall and the time on your ticket insists that it's three in the afternoon. This eliminates the need to reset the clock as the train crosses each of Russia's eleven time zones, but also induces panic at the checkout counter.

"I wanted the train that left at nine a.m.!" you exclaim, after handing over piles of cash for a ticket that is probably technically refundable in the same way that waffle fries are technically vegetables.

"Yes," the woman behind the glass window mumbles through a garbled microphone. "Two a.m."

"No!" you exclaim, close to tears. "Nine a.m.!"

"Nine a.m. here is two a.m. in Moscow."

Each car is ruled by a *provodnitsa*, a word often translated as "carriage attendant," but might be better thought of as "drill sergeant who occasionally serves you meals." The *provodnitsi* run a tight ship; ours already poked her head into our cabin, for no discernible reason, and barked at us to straighten out our rug.

Oorma is telling me about her career, which seems to have taken a series of extremely implausible twists.

"First," she tells me, "I was training to be a gynecologist. But then I discovered that I am allergic to blood."

"You mean, you realized you don't like blood?"

"No, I am allergic to it."

After this unfortunate setback, Oorma became a mechanical engineer, and then a genetic engineer, before finishing her career working in the "auto service."

"Auto service?" I ask.

"You know," she clarifies. "Like cars."

"Fixing them?"

"No."

Now Oorma is retired. Her daughter is a schoolteacher in Irkutsk, a Siberian city not far from the Mongolian border.

As the Soviet Union was beginning to come apart at the seams, Mongolians, too, began agitating for democracy. After a series of hunger strikes and peaceful protests, the Soviet-backed communist ruling party resigned in 1990, and Mongolia held free, democratic elections.

In the communist period, the most elite schools operated in Russian, which is presumably how Oorma and her daughter came to speak it well enough for her daughter to teach in Russia, and for Oorma to read the original edition of Putin's biography, which she's doing right now, for the third time.

"You know, Putin published a list of books that every schoolchild must read," she tells me.

Oorma is educated and well traveled, and I assume that, like me, she has generally unfavorable opinions of Putin and the idea of him handing schoolchildren a list of must-read books, and so I sympathetically roll my eyes while shaking my head, because I lack the vocabulary to say anything other than *wow* in English, a language Oorma does not understand.

Luckily, Oorma also does not seem to understand what rolling your eyes while shaking your head means, because it quickly becomes apparent that she loves Putin.

As part of their indoctrination, I guess, Russian schoolteachers are encouraged to write an essay that I first assume is original, but then Oorma indicates that they are just supposed to copy an essay Putin wrote. ("My daughter has very good handwriting!" Oorma informs me with pride.) Either way, Oorma's daughter's essay/recitation was so good that she was selected to speak to the president for one minute, by teleconference.

"That's . . ." I can't remember how to say something like *That's terrible*, which is lucky, because Oorma is telling me how proud she is, and that she immediately went out and bought this very biography she's holding. Great: I'm traveling with a Putin fan.

Outside, the golden grasslands dimple as they stretch out and rise suddenly into hills on the horizon, like a sheet unfurled with a snap. In some places, the ground has been sliced open to reveal veiny rivers colored a crisp blue, but the land seems, above all, empty.

As afternoon fades, the hills draw closer, revealing crumbling, graveled slopes. Mongolia is dusty, which is not something I thought a place could be, until I spent a week shaking and swatting all of my outerwear, eventually beating it against walls and heavy furniture, in an attempt to remove the fine layer of earth that caked everything. Where American homes would have welcome mats to shake the mud from your boots, Mongolian thresholds have wet towels, which you step on to catch the dust. Outside my window, it's like I'm watching the earth fracturing into smaller and smaller particles that will eventually become the outer coating of my backpack.

This is when Oorma casually suggests that I might help her smuggle Adidas tracksuits and sausages over the border.

Oorma is carrying about three dozen packages of sausages, a quantity that strikes me as excessive but unlikely to arouse suspicion, and ten identical men's tracksuits, which might require an explanation. She's thinking that if we each take half of her load, it'll make things easier.

I'm not really feeling this plan, mostly because I hate Oorma. In the past half hour, she opened a container of extremely pungent cabbage, which she's eating far too slowly, and, unforgivably, asked to borrow my pen and then *placed it in her purse* when she was finished.

I tell Oorma that I do not want to help her smuggle sausages and men's tracksuits over the Russian border.

Undeterred, Oorma proceeds to rip all of the price tags off of the tracksuits and stash half of them, along with two dozen sausages, in compartments on my side of the cabin. I'm too fed up with her to even protest, and so I stare out the window, fuming.

"If the police ask, it's better to say that the tracksuits are yours," Oorma helpfully suggests, and for a moment, I'm charmed by the idea of my declaring, *Yes, these five identical size-large men's tracksuits are mine.*

I didn't take the Trans-Siberian to make friends, but I wasn't expecting to garner a mortal enemy, as I have with Oorma. As the train hurdles over the tracks, I vow to avenge my pen.

At the border, a tall, lanky officer enters our cabin. Like a ninja, he scales the ladders to the cabin's upper berths in three nimble steps and then perches on the lip of the cubby where the train staff stores bedding. He proceeds to fling all of the spare blankets, comforters, pillows, and sheets over his shoulder, instantly making a huge mess of our compartment. Unsurprisingly, he finds no contraband. Rather than peek in the obvious place for smuggling—the closed cabinets where Oorma has actually stuffed the good stuff—he jumps down and rips all the sheets off our beds, tossing these, too, in an unwieldy pile on the floor. Then he pats down the cushions, as though feeling for the telltale lump of drugs? Finding none, he nods and departs our cabin, having not so much as glanced at our luggage or personal belongings.

Oorma starts putting our compartment back together, as though it weren't just ransacked by a shockingly incompetent border guard. Though I don't want to root for Oorma, I find myself feeling oddly violated by the search. Oorma doesn't seem to be. I wonder if that's because, where she's from, this kind of thing is normal.

The next morning, I wake up in Siberia.

Gone are the brown grasslands, and in their place is a frozen landscape of snow and birch trees. Every once in a while, we pass a village of clapboard houses painted bright colors and trimmed with fairy-tale eaves.

Lake Baikal makes a sudden, dramatic entrance. One minute, we see nothing but trees, and then the next, the frozen expanse of the world's largest freshwater lake. It contains almost a quarter of the world's freshwater, and it spends the winter completely frozen. It's also the world's deepest lake, and, in the winter, its surface becomes a road. You may hear this and assume, as I did, that this is a metaphor, like a path to serenity. But no, no, it's a literal, government-maintained, police-monitored, speed-limit-restricted road.

When the temperatures drop, the lake's surface turns to ice that can be up to six feet thick. At this point, the government jumps in and maintains the roads, adding signs, flooding the surface with more water to thicken the ice, providing insulation, and building on- and off-ramps if needed. Tractor trailers drive over them.

Where we are, the surface of the lake is buried under drifts of snow, but when the tracks edge closer to the shore, I see that the water at the edges is frozen midwave. It looks so strange and unnatural, almost like we're seeing the waves through a strobe light.

I keep thinking about Oorma and the photos she took of my passport. I have two competing fears as I glower at her. One, that she is a spy. Two, that she has been sent specifically to spy on me, and that she will report back that she found nothing interesting.

What is it like to spend almost twenty-four hours on a train?

It is somewhat like passing through the five stages of grief, out of order, and with the most intense stage being hunger.

The first stage is acceptance. *With the right clothes and snacks, trains are perfect,* you think. Haute train couture involves layers, bike shorts, sports bras, and a change of clothes, because, although it's below freezing outside, inside, the train is heated to approximately four billion degrees Fahrenheit. Because there is little privacy inside a four-person compartment the size of an average American refrigerator, bike shorts and sports bras allow you to change with relative modesty, which is not something Oorma seems overly concerned about.

The next stage is hunger. Somehow you had imagined twenty-four hours of moderate lounging would create minimal caloric demands, but you were very wrong. A day full of sleeping and reading has left you starving. You are not alone in this. Oorma is also hungry, and when you both confess this to each other, she comes up with a plan by which she will go to the restaurant in the dining car first while you watch over both of your belongings, and then she will do the same for you. Oorma is gone for what feels like two hours. You actually begin to worry that someone has pushed her off the train, and then you wonder if this should be a cause for concern or joy, but then she saunters back with an air that suggests she took her goddamn time, and when you finally reach the restaurant car, you realize a person would have to work to kill time in here, because the restaurant is empty and the food comes quickly, and also, though this has nothing to do with Oorma idling while your body began to consume itself, the waitress is growing flowers in window pots, which, well, that's not something you see every day: green sprouts in window boxes on the Trans-Siberian.

This is followed by the reading stage, or possibly the journaling stage, or maybe, if you're lucky, the napping stage. The nice thing about a train, you realize, is that there's nowhere to be, and no one to bother you, except your enemy/roommate, Oorma. A plane, of course, also cuts you off from the outside world and pleasantly unburdens you of responsibility and agency. You're not steering the plane and you can't make it get you there faster. A train goes two steps further, by also giving you a view, and removing the seat belt sign.

In truth, this is the real pleasure of the train: the sense of being somewhere with nothing to do and no one to answer to, but still on your way to something. It's travel without a to-do list. You can't tick certain monuments off your list, but you can watch the countryside roll by.

In the afternoon, the sun finally breaches the barrier of gray clouds and paints the sky blue. Light barrages the trees—naked white birch trunks with errant fir tops poking up.

Five minutes later, it's all fir, thick boughs clinging to rocky landscape with only a few dots of snow visible when the train crests a hill. Bright evergreen shrubbery covers ground; it could almost be summer, but then the snow pokes back into view.

Before we get into Irkutsk, Oorma helpfully points out a nervous habit I have of fiddling with the ends of my hair.

"I know," I say, because I do not know how to say, *Boy, do you get extra points for personality*, in Russian.

But then she surprises me. "I do this," she says, showing me how she smacks her lips when she's anxious. "I think we all have something."

I nod, but she's not done.

She can tell by the way I nervously finger my hair while writing, she says, that my book will be a huge success. And with this, she is no longer my enemy, but in the running for future maid of honor.

Once we're out of the train, and I've replaced my stolen pen, Oorma starts to look a little less one-dimensional. I can see hints of a crisis of identity. I remember little things that suggested she was seen as too Russian in Mongolia, and too Mongolian in Russia. It's the lesson of the Kazakh cowboy, with the added reminder that not everyone will tell you up front that he cried and cried.

Stopover: Irkutsk

Irkutsk has twenty-four-hour flower shops, twenty-four-hour Subway sandwich shops, and a dental clinic that claims to be open twenty-four hours, but looks dark and closed when I walk by at nine p.m.

Grocery stores devote half of their shelf space to alcohol of an unimaginable quantity and variety. Beer is sold, by default, in one-liter bottles. The conveyor belts beside cash registers don't move, and, as if in testament to their permanent stationary positions, the checkout aisle displays have encroached onto them.

But there's more to Irkutsk than round-the-clock bouquets and enabling grocery stores. There's also a rich history, historic architecture, and a giant lake.

Siberia is known for the wooden houses you probably picture if you close your eyes and imagine a Russian village. The windows are surrounded with intricately carved wooden frames, and the houses are painted different shades of pastel.

Historically, Siberia is where the Russian Empire and Soviet government sent the people they wanted to get rid of. Its name is synonymous with gulags and prison camps, and Irkutsk, in particular, was where the Decembrist revolutionaries were exiled. Their wives followed them here, and Anton used to ask me, if he were sent to

Siberia, if I would follow him, and I would always say yes, because I figured it would help me learn Russian.

Siberia is also synonymous with wild landscapes perpetually covered in winter, which is why today, I'm going to see frozen Lake Baikal up close.

At breakfast, I'm seated one table over from a handsome European man in horn-rimmed glasses. We both give each other the once-over that indicates that we both recognize each other as foreigners in a strange land. It's his neatly pressed pants and discreetly expensive watch that give him away. I wonder what tipped him off in my case—the fact that I'm not wearing a bra or makeup?

I direct my attention to the inane music videos playing on TV in the hotel dining room. They all seem to follow the same basic plot: guy raps in front of late-'90s-model car while carrying machine guns, eventually robs bank, beautiful woman dies in process.

After breakfast, the receptionist gives me directions to a minibus that will take me to the lake. I take a long, snowy walk through town to the bus stop.

Inside the minibus, I find the most unpleasant odor one can find inside a panel van, and also the handsome European guy from breakfast.

Quel surprise! Except, he's Spanish, not French. Still, very handsome.

The minibus starts driving with just me and the Spanish man, and I ask the driver how much it'll cost to get to Lake Baikal. Oh, he's not going to take us to the lake, he's going to take us to his friend's minibus, which will take us to the lake.

The Spanish man and I are now seated backward on a minibus whose windows quickly become fogged. Here is a list of things that make me nauseated to the point of vomiting: 1) minibuses, 2) sitting backward, 3) moisture inside moving vehicles.

To make matters worse, I'm down a Sea-Band, a medicinal wristband that harnesses the healing powers of the placebo effect, and my one proven method for preventing motion sickness. The Spanish guy, who I learn is named Jorge, is also taking the Trans-Siberian alone, and he's eager to swap stories, but now is not the time.

I could see frozen Baikal from the train, but up close, it's even more incredible. An expanse of ice extending from here to the horizon. What's more, people are out there walking on it.

"Do you think it's safe?" I ask Jorge, and before he can answer, I'm jumping down an embankment toward the ice.

At the shoreline, it cracks under my feet, and I jump back. Below, I see water gently sloshing under the frozen surface. But there are people so far out!

I take a deep breath and try a few tentative steps on a different path that looks more sturdy. The ice creaks under my feet but doesn't give way.

On the ice, I spot two women taking pictures.

"Is it safe?" I ask.

"Oh, yeah," one says, brushing away the snow on top of the ice to reveal a blue glass floor that's easily inches thick.

She's taking a photo of her friend, who wears trendy winter boots that seem ill-suited for stomping around on a frozen lake. "Do you want me to take a picture of the two of you?" I ask.

They'd love that, and then I ask them to take a picture of me, and then they ask to take a picture of me, and suddenly there's a German couple, who also need someone to snap a photo, and then a Chinese guy named Max, and his Russian girlfriend, Nadia, and soon we're all chatting, and Max suggests we all go back up to dry land and get lunch.

Inside a cozy wooden restaurant, I gravitate toward Max because he's studying Russian and speaks almost fluently. I ask him how long he's been studying, and he tells me two years.

"Wow, if you've only been studying for two years, and you speak so well, it gives me hope," I say. "How many hours a day do you study?"

He shakes his head. "All the time. I'm studying all hours, every day." Okay, so our results may differ. Max lives with Nadia, who doesn't really speak English, and he goes to a local university. "You know, I get up in the morning, and it's *'Chto ti hochesh yest,'* "—what do you want to eat?

Max's mother is ethnically Korean, and he grew up speaking Chinese and Korean. He learned English in school and came here two years ago for a graduate degree. He shakes his head. "You know, sometimes, I have things that I want to say, but I don't even know which language to say them in. I don't even know how to say them in any language. Before I came here, I used to think Chinese and Korean are my mother languages, English is my third language. But now I think Russian becomes my third language, English fourth."

Max speaks English better than I speak Chinese or Russian, but we switch between the three because he's kind and humors me. He's tall and gregarious, and in him I see the kind of person I want to be. He's taken it upon himself to be our group tour guide. "Come on!" he announces, when he sees we're finishing our food. "It's time to climb a mountain."

He takes us to a hiking path that promises a panoramic view of the lake, and I chat with the German couple on the way up. They're doing the Trans-Siberian, too, as are the women I first spoke with, who have come here from Thailand. So that explains the boots.

From the top, the lake expands to fill more of the space below. The ice still stretches out to the horizon, but it's starting to melt at the hilly shoreline to our right. We can see open water there.

We all ride the bus back to Irkutsk together and get dinner, and afterward the German couple takes me to the grocery store and helps me meal-prep for my next train.

That night, I marvel at the world. I have many stories of meeting strangers while traveling. One of my closest friends in China was an Israeli woman my sister started talking to as we boarded a flight from Yunnan to Beijing.

But I've never had a group of people from all over the world spontaneously come together on a frozen lake. I think about what would have happened if I'd caught a later bus, or an earlier one, or if I hadn't offered to take the Thai women's picture.

So much of life is like that, I guess. Anton used to say that everything you could imagine had a 50 percent chance of happening. "Either it'll happen," he would say, grinning, "or it won't." This drove me crazy, but now I kind of see what he means. Sometimes a group of strangers from all walks of life converges on a frozen lake in Siberia, and sometimes it doesn't.

Third Leg: Irkutsk to Novosibirsk (One Day, Seven Hours, and Twenty-Five Minutes)
Unbeknownst to me, the train I shared with Oorma was the nicest that runs on the Trans-Siberian.

As soon as I board the train to Novosibirsk, I realize how good Oorma and I had it. This carriage is older, darker, still spotless, but more worn. The *kupes* are dark, cramped faux-wood-paneled compartments with sailors' netting for stowing belongings and pilled bedding that looks like it survived all of the twentieth-century wars. A cheesecloth has been placed over the small fold-out table. Most notably, my room doesn't have an outlet, which I guess is good, but I didn't sign up for a digital detox. I think back on the liberties I'd taken on my first train. I'd left my computer open! Used my data on my cell phone!

Last night at dinner, the German man from the lake group giggled feverishly when he heard the route the Thai women and I were taking. "It's so strange," he says, between gasps, "that you would start your trip in Asia and not Europe."

The Thai women and I exchange glances. "But we live in Asia," we explain. "It's the same as you starting your trip in Europe."

"Besides," I say, "I have this romantic vision of starting in this far-flung, backwater outpost, and then arriving in"—I pause for dramatic effect—"Moscow."

I'm now seeing the flaw in this logic. Perhaps I should have saved the nicest train for last.

Luckily, as we pull out of Irkutsk, I'm alone in my compartment. I giddily, greedily study my guidebook. Just seven more stops to make it through with no one getting on, and then I'm guaranteed to have my cabin to myself for a few hours.

Fifteen minutes later, the train stops at a platform crowded with people, and my heart sinks. Sure enough, a quiet, meticulous man in his fifties enters my compartment with a single briefcase. He nods at me and says hello.

I'm immediately uncomfortable, for all the reasons a woman traveling alone would be nervous, though he's quiet and respectful as he takes his seat across from me. I notice he's wearing a jacket emblazoned with the railroad company's logo. I avoid eye contact.

But then I notice a younger man hovering outside in the hallway, wearing the same uniform. I make room for him on my seat, and he comes in, also avoiding eye contact. This emboldens me, and I try to ask the younger guy if he works for the railway company. I speak softly, and he looks confused. I wonder if it's his first time speaking to a foreigner.

The older man carefully spreads a newspaper over our tiny table and unloads a lunch that he and his younger friend share: noodles with bread and coffee sipped from a tin can, eaten with real silverware. They eat in silence. Not a word passes between them, and they don't try to talk to me. I'm very weirded out. Then the older man climbs into the top bunk, lays out the bedding, and goes to sleep.

I ask the younger man if they're riding to Novosibirsk. He shakes his head. Taking that as a sign that he doesn't want to talk, I stare out the window. We pass freight cars full of lumber, more villages, a graveyard.

I become aware that the young man is trying to get my attention. "Do you speak English?" he asks, in Russian.

"Yes," I tell him.

He nods.

That's it? I think. So bizarre.

But after a moment, he hands me a tablet computer, open to Google Translate. A single question has been written in Russian, translated into English. "I'm Alexandr. What is your name?"

I smile. "My name is Audrey," I say out loud, in Russian.

He takes the tablet from my hands, and when he hands it back, it says, "We're going to Zima."

Our conversation proceeds like this. For reasons I don't fully understand, he types his questions into the tablet, hands it to me, and I respond out loud in mangled Russian. Sometimes, though not often, I have to type back. I begin to wonder if he's mute, but then he asks me if I like politics, and then he starts speaking out loud, and I can't understand, so we switch back to typing.

Alexandr went to university in Irkutsk and now works on short-haul electric trains.

"Is this train electric?" I ask.

"No."

He tells me that world oil prices are down, but in Russia, they're up. I ask why.

"Corruption in government levels," he says. "How is the political situation in America?"

I try to explain that a reality television star named Donald Trump and a politician named Hillary Clinton are running for president, and I think I do a not great but okay job of conveying the basics. I ask him how the political situation is in Russia.

"Terrible," he says.

Why?

He gets a mischievous look in his eyes, and then writes, "Official explanation is economic crisis. Unofficial? Corruption at government levels."

Alexandr hates corruption, and I realize I have strong views on this. It takes me so long to type the following message that he falls asleep before I'm finished: "I think corruption is the most important problem, because if there's corruption, you can't fix other problems like health, education, job, food supply."

When he wakes up, he reads my message and smiles. Then he changes the subject.

"Do you have a boyfriend?" he writes.

We talk about our families, and he asks me what my sign is. I say I don't know, although I do, I just don't know how to say it in Russian. He asks my birthday, and my answer excites him: it's the same as his mother's. He tells me that the man sleeping above us is his colleague.

Then he types a bolder question. "What life goals haunt you?"

I give an answer that's part of the truth, but not the whole truth. "To publish a book," I tell him. "What about you?"

He types. "Raise a son, buy a house, plant a tree."

"Why plant a tree?" I ask.

"Outside of a house it's nice to have trees," he types. "Also nice for nature."

I wonder why I can't admit that I am also haunted by the life goals of raising a son, buying a house, and planting a tree.

Alexandr is four years younger than me, though he looks much older. His face is deeply lined. He smokes, he says, because it gives him confidence.

I get up to walk around and find the hallway filled with tipsy men who stare at me for a little too long. I'm suddenly glad for Alexandr and his quiet companion.

Alexandr and I pass the tablet back and forth for a little longer, and then I fall asleep while reading a book, and when I wake up, they're getting ready to get off the train.

Alexandr's older colleague closes the door to our compartment and gently combs his thinning hair with his fingers until it's neat. He pulls up his pants to make sure he looks presentable. Alexander comes back in, and they grab their belongings and start leaving.

"*Do svidaniya,*" the older colleague says, using the formal good-bye.

Alexandr smiles. "*Poka*," he says, using the more casual form that melts my heart whenever a Russian man says it.

After Zima, brown fields rise and fall outside my window like dolphins playing in a ship's breakwater. I know it's cold when a thin layer of snow covers to the hills and warmer when bogs form beneath us.

It's quiet without Alexandr and his colleague in my compartment. I close the door behind them and watch the fields reflect the early-evening light. Occasionally, we pass houses that look like they've long ceased to be homes: sad, sagging buildings with broken windows and overgrown yards. Other times smoke billows from narrow chimneys.

I have the compartment to myself for a few blissful hours, and then another Alexandr gets on. He's an older man with a large belly who smiles at me before methodically unpacking his belongings and making his bed. I've realized that Russians are very neat, which is why it must horrify them the way I strew my belongings all over my bed and leave crumbs after I eat.

I go to the bathroom, and when I return, I notice that Alexandr II has spread candies out on the shared table for anyone to take. It's a sweet, touching gesture. He's splayed out in his bed, and in my terrible Russian I tell him that, if he wants to go to sleep, I can turn out the overhead light. He shakes his head. He sees that I've been reading a book, and he's worried that the small lamp on my berth doesn't give enough light for reading. We begin chatting— he's disembarking in the morning, at Khojasomething. We chat briefly about my trip, but my Russian has long since faded, and I'm fading with it.

When I wake up in the morning, Alexandr II is gone, and the compartment is filled with three strangers, one of whom is snoring so loudly I can't sleep.

I go out into the corridor, where I find a few older travelers in matching short-sleeved white button-downs emblazoned with the

Russian national railway logo on one arm. They stare out at the scenery. The layer of snow on the ground has grown thicker.

For no logical reason, I resent the other people in my compartment. I feel like the space belongs to me and the first two Alexandrs. There's a younger guy in a neat sweater and Hugo Boss shoes who sees that my phone is dying and lends me his portable battery-pack charger. We're joined by two older men, who put on railway uniforms as soon as they wake up.

It's strange how the cast of characters in the entire carriage keeps changing. I feel like I'm in this for the long haul; the only other person in my car who's been here since the beginning is a guy with long blond hair who constantly makes phone calls.

Everyone gets off at the first big stop of the morning, and once again, I have the compartment to myself. I've been on the train since lunchtime yesterday, but I somehow have another eleven mind-boggling hours to go.

I read. I sleep. I snack. I think. I remember my first overnight train, with the identical twins preparing for the IELTS, and their chaperone, who poured me Pepsi instead of beer. My awful guide in Samarkand, who thought it was high time I fill myself with babies. The taxi driver in Turkmenistan who tried to explain sex. The university students who helped me find the secret police hotel in Ashgabat. Really, all of the people who helped me, for no reason other than to be kind: the women in Kyrgyzstan who gave me their phone numbers, the Belarusian consular staff who arranged my $5 health insurance, Anton's friends in Minsk, my Couchsurfing hosts in Lithuania. Rain gently taps at my window, then stops, and then the sun plays hide-and-seek behind a blanket of clouds.

I unscrew the lid of my jar of instant coffee and pour the last of the grounds into the dirty paper cup I've been reusing. I walk out into the hall and past the men staring out of the window and reeking of alcohol to the samovar at the end of the carriage. As I fill my cup with hot water, I think about the candies Alexandr II left on the table, and how satisfying it would be to remove one from its crinkly wrapper and let it melt slowly in my mouth. But then I think of Sergey and how the least I can do if I'm going to his hometown is to not eat too many carbs.

I pass the final few hours torturing myself with a task I have single-handedly brought upon myself: writing about this trip.

In my sophomore year of college, I declared a creative writing major after accepting the fact that the economics classes I'd been taking to rebel against my parents' expectations were not really going well. I begrudgingly enrolled in classes like Narrative Voice while still secretly clinging to dreams of becoming an investment banker.

I spent my childhood scribbling bizarre stories into free notepads that drug companies give to the elderly. TRY LIPITOR! each story began.

The thing about writing that no one explained to me as I was dictating confusing narratives about all twenty-four of my kindergarten classmates to my grandmother, or while I was preparing passionate love scenes for a college short-story workshop, is that it's incredibly hard and boring. If someone had told me I'd spend most of my time forcing myself to write while I was feeling about as creative and articulate as a meat cleaver, I would have begged my way back into Econometrics.

Writing is the least enjoyable way in which I could choose to spend my time, and the worst part is that I'm *constantly* forgetting this.

Each time I close my computer at the end of a day, the memory of the hour I spent trying to remember a naggingly specific word and then rage-scrolling through Facebook immediately vanishes.

I return to my romantic notions of writing as a noble, not particularly labor-intensive pursuit. I imagine myself getting up around ten the next morning, going to an elaborate brunch, returning to my office in a sprawling castle, and then sitting down at my computer, where words, worlds, stories, and characters flow onto the page as effortlessly as if I were reciting the alphabet. After about an hour, I print out ten single-spaced pages, which I'm shocked and delighted to find are roughly on par in quality and substance with *Lolita*. I then spend the rest of the day drinking cocktails with Russians.

Imagine the shock and horror when the next day arrives and I'm confronted with reality. Rather than writing on the balcony of my stone manor that somehow overlooks both the Swiss Alps and the East Village, I'm writing on a five-year-old laptop ruled by an evil, spinning rainbow wheel, while an angelic child who is somehow able to go three hours with zero entertainment mocks me with her tranquility. At the end, when I look down to read what I wrote, I find not *Lolita*, but an exact replica of the novel Jack Nicholson's character was working on in *The Shining*.

Stopover: Novosibirsk
Novosibirsk is the third-biggest city in Russia and the largest in Siberia, and it's famous for having a well-known secret scientific institute hidden in the woods.

"Maybe you've heard of it?" John asks.

I haven't, which I guess means the "secret" part is working.

John is a friend of a friend who graciously dropped whatever he was doing and agreed to spend two days showing me around his city. His job has been made more tedious by the fact his English is about as good as my Russian, which means we spend a lot of time pantomiming, or in silence.

Novosibirsk is a huge, sprawling city that has, for reasons that are not apparent, earned the nickname "the Chicago of Siberia." I've never been to Chicago, but I'm relatively sure its driving industries are not weapons factories and power plants, as they are here. Novosibirsk is proud of its heavy industry. It even built a park with models of the tanks and armored vehicles its factories have produced.

It was snowing when John picked me up this morning, but a few hours later the weather has shifted suddenly and dramatically to bright sun. I know, I know: everyone is convinced that the weather in their region is crazy and rapidly changing, but in Siberia, it does seem like the strong winds flip the forecast like a light switch.

The parks in Novosibirsk all seem to have mismatched, home-made bird feeders. Some are more elaborate, with felt attached to the exterior for insulation, or colorful designs stenciled onto the side, while others seem motivated by the desire to reuse milk jugs. But still I've never seen anything like it: a bunch of people building bird feeders, just because, and in the end you have a sanctuary.

"Who made these?" I ask.

John pauses. He's never thought about this before. "Maybe some schoolchildren? Or . . . people who like birds?"

The things that surround us so quickly become normal that they're hard to notice, much less describe. Maybe that's why when you ask someone on Couchsurfing to describe Lithuania, they don't know where to begin. We all walk around assuming the whole world does things exactly as we do, which is why the strangest parts of traveling are the little things, like the three-som coins, that seem so normal to people around you and so utterly foreign to you.

My first impression of Novosibirsk is that it is somehow both the muddiest and dustiest city I've ever visited.

The ground is starting to thaw with the first signs of spring, and mud oozes everywhere. At the same time, you come in from the street, and find your jeans and shoes coated in a thin layer of dust.

This is not the only dichotomy.

Novosibirsk is, oddly, known for both heavy industry and theater. A city in which weapons manufacturing and the performing arts not only coexist, but thrive, creates a beautiful image in my head of burly men clocking out of a munitions factory and heading straight to the ballet. This image, of course, was pretty much the Soviet so-cialist dream, and perhaps why Novosibirsk cultivated such dispa-rate industries.

I must see the ballet in Novosibirsk; on this, everyone is in agreement. Each Russian friend who learns about my trip to Novosibirsk frowns and tells me there's not much to do in Novosibirsk. "Maybe see the ballet?" they offer.

The Novosibirsk Opera and Ballet Theatre is the largest in Russia. It's located directly behind a giant statue of Lenin wearing a cape. I feel for him. I, too, have walked into Urban Outfitters and overestimated my ability to pull off a trendy accessory.

Russian ballets are rumored to be the best in the world. Though ballet first developed in France, the Russians took it over from them in the mid-1800s, and many of the shows and composers best known today come from Russia. *The Nutcracker, Sleeping Beauty, Swan Lake.* Tchaikovsky. Stravinsky. And let's not forget Aleksandr from *Sex and the City.*

I see my first Russian ballet in Novosibirsk. It's *Don Quixote,* which I've never seen before, and it's so dreamy and lovely that I go to the ballet at each subsequent city I stop in.

My mother took me to the Boston Ballet when I was young, and my main memories of the performances is that they took three hours to tell a story that could have been over in twenty minutes if the performers had talked instead of dancing around.

What makes the Russian ballets somewhat more enjoyable is that they each have approximately fourteen thousand intermissions. Just as you've settled into your seat, scanned the program to figure out what's going on plot-wise, passed the ten-minute threshold where the novelty of watching masterful ballet starts to wear off, the curtains drop and the lights come on for yet another intermission. In the lobby, you can buy coffee, cake, and hard alcohol.

I'm surprised by how full the performances are. I'd been concerned that on a Wednesday evening, the performers might outnumber the audience. But the entire floor is full, and though I can't see the balconies, they don't seem empty, either. And because some of these intermissions are, like, twenty, thirty minutes long, I have a lot of time to people-watch (and, presumably, the performers can watch an episode of a sitcom). I try to figure out who comes to the ballet in Siberia. It's not an easily qualifiable demographic. There are parents with children, twenty-something couples on dates, old people, young people, some wearing jeans, others in formal wear. Is the answer just, everyone? Is the ballet just a normal outing in Siberia? Tickets are certainly more affordable than I was expecting: they start at $10 U.S.

Most surprising of all, for me anyway, is the way Russian theaters see *The Nutcracker*, or more specifically, the way they don't see it as a holiday-season show.

The Nutcracker plays in March, July, November—whenever. I will see it in April in Yekaterinburg, a city famous for being the place where the Romanov family was murdered. In the Russian staging of *The Nutcracker*, Christmas plays a minor role. I think there's maybe a tree. But if you didn't know the story, you'd think the ballet was taking place at a birthday party. Also, in the Russian version, the leads are played by children, which makes me wonder about my own deficiencies in discipline. Let me repeat: a three-hour, complex ballet, starring children. On second thought, is that legal?

The next afternoon, John is taking me to an English class, because he worries that his English is so bad that I need someone else to talk to.

The school is called Business Class, and it provides group English lessons for children and adults. The center is decorated to look like all of London crammed into one small office: there are tiny red phone booths and tube signs and pictures of double-decker buses, plus a giant cutout of Big Ben. There is also, for no apparent reason, a fake fireplace, and a few American flags scattered throughout. I guess the message is: we're here to speak English.

The administrator is a retired teacher named Bella; she taught elementary school for forty years, she says, and she loved her job.

Marina, the teacher who has invited me to join her class, has different feelings about the municipal schools.

"I hated it," she tells me in crisp English. Marina is sipping tea from a personalized mug with her name on it, and she tells me she's much happier here.

In the municipal school, she says, classes were divided into groups where the same fifteen students studied together all eleven years. It wasn't good. She felt micromanaged by the administration, and she didn't have the freedom to do what she loved, what had driven her to language teaching in the first place, which is: to help her students improve their English.

"It was just, 'You must teach this, you must do that,'" she says. "Even if I say, 'But this book is wrong! The grammar, look, it is wrong!'"

Her teenage students arrive slowly and sleepily. They've sat through a long day at school, and they slump down onto their desks. Only four have shown up: two boys, Denis and Grigor, and two girls, Liza and Anna.

"Well, okay, I told you I think it would be a small class today," Marina announces, mostly to me, before beginning. Because I'm here, she scraps the lesson plan for today and instead has the students practice speaking with me.

"What do you think of our city?" they want to know.

I tell them I like it. I tell them about the ballet and the monuments John showed me. Marina has a soothing, encouraging patience in the classroom, and when she notices that Grigor, a tall, quiet boy who says he doesn't like learning English, hasn't said anything, she makes him ask me a question.

He hesitates, then asks, "What else have you visited here in our city?"

I'm kind of out of Novosibirsk landmarks, so I bring up the World War II memorial again. The names of each person from Novosibirsk who'd been killed in the fighting were inscribed on the walls of the monuments, and I'd been shocked by the length of the list. "The number dead, it was . . . unreal."

"Yes," Marina says, shaking her head. "During the war, we say every family lost at least one person." But then she brightens. "You know, in Germany now, they're saying that Russia tried to occupy Germany by staying too long after the war." She laughs and shakes her head. "And now they're saying Russia is trying to occupy Ukraine."

The kids join in her laughter. "So stupid," Denis echoes.

I have to stop my jaw from hitting the floor. Marina once took a road trip from New York to Florida; Liza has lived in Japan, and the other three have at least traveled abroad. I had assumed that they would have been exposed to foreign media sources that would be more critical of Putin. Undoubtedly they had been, but I'd overestimated how well those ideas would stick.

"I hadn't heard people saying Russia tried to occupy Germany after the war," I say, cautiously. But still—can they all really support Putin?

Luckily, Marina moves on.

"What would you recommend Audrey to do before she leaves our city?" Marina asks.

Their answer is unanimous: I must go to the zoo.

"The zoo?" I ask.

They tell me their zoo is the most humane zoo in all of Russia. "It's like the animals are actually in nature," Anna says.

"And also," Denis chimes in, "you must see the liger."

"Oh, yes!" they all exclaim. "The liger is so cute." But I'm like, "Wait, a liger?"

"Yes," Denis continues. "It's a cross between a lion and a tiger."

This has to be fake; I'm picturing a lion spray-painted with zebra stripes. I haven't been to a zoo in years and don't have any particular desire to break that streak, but I have to see whatever this liger thing is.

The class decides Liza will walk me there after the lesson finishes because it's on her way home, and they assure me that the zoo is not far.

Liza has striking red hair, deep blue eyes, and a smattering of freckles across the bridge of her nose, so I'm not totally shocked, on our walk, to learn that she is a model.

Her English is by far the best in the class, because she mostly works in Japan.

"I love Japan," she gushes. She tells me about Tokyo, and the apartment she stayed in, and how much she loved her life there, because she and the other models would go to clubs and dance all night.

"How old are you?" I ask.

"Fourteen," she tells me.

We reach the gates of the zoo, and I offer to buy her a ticket, but she has to go home and do her homework.

I do find the liger. He's nibbling on a raw carcass of meat that's been left in the center of his cage. The kids were right, it turns out. I'd half come to the zoo just to prove them wrong, but ligers are a real thing.

Also, this zoo may be the most humane in Russia, but that says more about the state of zoological practices in Russia than it does about the Novosibirsk Zoo.

All Russian women seem to have perfectly sculpted eyebrows and lacquered fingernails adorned with delicate nail art. This, perhaps, explains why I'm having trouble getting into a beauty salon.

I check out of my hotel in the morning, but my train isn't until after midnight, and I've tapped out most of Novosibirsk's main tourist attractions. Novosibirsk has a USSR museum, and a handful of churches and the standard Soviet halls of knowledge and culture: history and art museums.

The best and worst part of traveling alone is the quantity of quality time you get with yourself. When you're centered and secure, these moments are blissful pockets of self-discovery, but if your mind even veers toward the rabbit holes of self-doubt and insecurity, it's hard to derail that train.

Daily routines provide ample opportunity to get out of your head. Joking with colleagues or blowing a red light on your bicycle force you out of your thoughts and into the present. I have none of that, so

I decide to get a manicure. Except every store I enter is only booking for appointments next week.

As I wander through churches and along random streets, I start to feel very lonely. Like, why am I trying to take a train by myself across Russia, why do I think something interesting will happen, how will I remember everything I want to write? And then, even if I can do that, how will I edit it? Print it? What if my computer crashes while printing? What if I can't find a printer? Am I getting a little ahead of myself? Maybe. Am I making a huge mistake? Definitely. What mistake am I even talking about? Honestly, I've kind of lost track of that, but the point is, everything is terrible and hopeless.

Out in the bright sunshine, people unzip winter coats, and every other person I pass seems to be eating ice cream. I check the temperature. It's fifty-seven degrees. Balmy for Siberia. I stop at a hipster coffee shop, which reminds me that I'll never find love. I ride the subway back and forth, which I have to admit is extremely fun, but when I'm done, I'm still swimming in anxiety.

Some shops on the main street seem more Brooklyn than Siberia. There's a drybar and a bougie appliance store selling retro-style refrigerators and coffee makers. The window display is full of chrome and muted colors.

I stand there for a long time trying to assign meaning to what I see. The aesthetic these blenders and dishwasher are going for is 1950s America—in other words, a nostalgia for something that never existed here.

Really, though, what I'm struggling with is myself: I'm growing weary of my own compulsion to unpack this image or contradiction or whatever it is, line the pieces up in a way that makes sense, and extract some larger point or conclusion from it. I need my findings to make sense but also be slightly profound.

I feel this way not just about the appliance store, but also about this trip, and my life in general. I want it all to make sense, want to see a clear picture in my head of what this all means and where it's going.

Future Audrey has the distinct advantage of knowing this all works out. But in this moment, I genuinely don't know if everything will be fine. I have no idea that this is all going to turn into a book, that I won't still be wandering the streets of Siberia a year from now, that my instincts were right, or that I'm more in control than I realize. Right now, I feel like I have no idea what I'm doing, and no clue what this is all building toward. It feels like so much is riding on this trip, because my parents, friends, and Russian strangers on the street don't think I should be taking it. I'm eager for concrete, tangible proof that I have been right to pursue this, because absent that, all I can point at to prove I'm not crazy is trust in myself. Which, at this moment, I don't have.

I'm slowly building it, though. Of course, I can't see this now, but I've been building it ever since I left for Kazakhstan against the advice of my parents and medical providers. (Well, technically, they would have only disapproved of the Kyrgyz horse trek.) I have no idea that ultimately it will be this trust, and not a book, that will validate my decision to take this trip, that by choosing to listen to myself and pursue this, I have already given myself the sincerest validation of all.

On my way back into the main city square, which I'm honestly returning to out of habit more than anything else, a few elementary school kids come up to me and ask for 5 rubles.

I can't be bothered. "Sorry," I say in English, "I don't speak Russian."

Their eyes light up. "English!" I hear one of them whisper.

I keep walking, but I hear the patter of footsteps, and I turn to see that they've caught up with me.

"Hello!" one exclaims. He hands me his phone, which, like Alexandr I's, is open to Google Translate behind its cracked screen.

"Where are you going?" it says.

I look at their eager, smiling faces, and I realize, *Awww, they want to help me!*

I go to type in "Lenin Square" to humor them, but their last search pops up.

"Smoke weed every day?!" I exclaim. They shriek, and everyone runs away laughing, except the kid whose phone I must be holding, so I hand it back to him, and he, too, escapes.

By now it's almost night, and, okay, I need to stop feeling sorry for myself.

The winter sun in Siberia is bright and glaring. People wear sunglasses until the sun is safely below the horizon at eight p.m. because a low light sometimes comes slanting in over the horizon and blinds you.

I finally find a salon with an opening, although it feels less like a beauty parlor and more like a dentist's office. My manicure takes place in a private room with lots of high-tech equipment that moves on retractable arms, and the chair that I'm using was definitely intended for use by a dental practitioner. It fully reclines, and not in the *kick back and relax!* sense, but in a way that says, *I need to get at your back molars.* The machine the manicurist uses to remove my chipping nail polish looks like it could easily drill a cavity.

I study the Russian women's magazines fanned out on the table beside me. I suppose I shouldn't be surprised that the headlines are identical to those back home.

Russian *Cosmo* promises to explain, "Why he: isn't married, doesn't want children."

"Bad girl, good sex!" another reads.

"Do you need to give birth before thirty?" one asks.

When the manicurist hears my accent, she asks me where I'm from, and then asks me what I'm doing here. I tell her about my trip.

"You must be very brave," she says, shaking her head.

I laugh. "It's not brave to sit on a train and read," I tell her. And that breaks the spell. Somehow, by the time I walk out of the salon, I feel fine.

"Hey, hey, hey," I find myself singing on the walk to the train station. "Smoke weed every day."

Fourth Leg: Novosibirsk to Tobolsk (Twenty-One Hours, Thirty-Two Minutes)

There comes a moment in any great train journey, I think, when one is consumed by a desire to get off the train. This moment, I've found, arrives more quickly when one is trapped in a compartment with a two-year-old.

I wake up in the morning to find that I've had the compartment to myself all night. I eat breakfast and start to work, but then we pull up to a packed platform, and my heart sinks. Sure enough, a mother and her son appear in the cabin.

"You're American," the mother says when she hears my Russian.

I'm impressed; she's the first person to guess correctly. It seems like we're about to be friends, but then the *provodnitsa* comes in to check our tickets and to see if we'd like to buy anything, and I hear the mother tell the *provodnitsa* that my Russian is very bad.

This seems like welcome news to the *provodnitsa*, who returns with a stack of commemorative magnets. "Maybe you'd like to buy one?" she asks.

The tracks have taken a southward bend, and the snow has been replaced with swamplands. When I think of swamps, I always pictured some unsightly combination of mud and alligators, but this is clear blue water pierced with yellow brush and white birch trees.

The *provodnitsa* is back. "Maybe you'd like to buy a postcard?" she asks.

The two-year-old, Ilyusha, is doing his best, but it's a long train ride. I hear his mother telling him stories about Yuri Gagarin, the Soviet cosmonaut who was the first man in space. I want to tell the mother that, actually, I can understand Russian perfectly when it's being spoken to a two-year-old, but then I realize Ilyusha can conjugate verbs, nouns, and adjectives better than I can, and I'd probably make a stronger argument by staying silent.

The weather changes quickly on a train. A swollen black cloud hangs, pregnant-like, over the scraggly swamps, and I realize my main source of entertainment today has been watching for the rain to start. I begin to wonder if it's healthy to spend so much time on a train. As we pass through a town, I see an old man in a newsboy cap and a heavy coat standing beside a little girl on a pink bicycle. His hand rests on her shoulder as they watch the train go by.

Ilyusha starts to cry, and for no reason at all, I do, too. I can't stop thinking about what feels like the central crisis of my life: this pull between settling down and chasing adventure, and this question of how I can do both. If I could just, like, find some speed-marrying app, it feels like all of my problems would be solved. Maybe Ilyusha and his mom symbolize an alternate unrealized view of myself.

Now the *provodnista* is back with, and I'm not making this up, a GoPro around her neck. I want to explain to her that she's negating her camera's main feature by putting it on a conventional camera strap, but I don't get the chance, because she wants to take a picture of me sitting in my seat and sell me the print.

On the platform at Tobolsk, the moon hides behind a thin layer of gauzy clouds, and though it is freezing and pitch-black, and I'm slightly concerned because this train station is in the middle of the woods, I am so, so happy to be off the train.

I do not tear up when saying goodbye to Ilyusha, who spent the last six hours screaming, or his mother, who has told me, multiple times, how well Ilyusha speaks for a two-year-old, which, to be fair, is true, but also feels like a dig at how bad my Russian is, and I am not sorry to leave the *provodnitsa*, whose parting gift is an attempt to sell me a model of the train I'd just spent almost twenty-two hours on, in case I want to, I guess, remember it forever.

Outside the station, I find one taxi driver. He's a sweet guy from

Azerbaijan, and when his sons calls him, to my delight, his ringtone is Mariah Carey's "I'd Give My All."

Stopover: Tobolsk

I'm awoken in the morning by chirping birds. The sun is shining, and spring has arrived in Siberia!

I walk to the nearest railway office to buy my next ticket onward.

"You've come so far!" the woman exclaims when I tell her about my trip. "Also, all the trains you want are sold out."

Tobolsk is not exactly a city you want to get stuck in for a few extra days. For starters, the fact that it's even designated a city really feels like someone pulled a few strings. It's a tiny, sleepy town with only a handful of restaurants. Most intersections don't have stoplights.

It's famous for its picturesque Kremlin, a charming, walled old town that dates back to the 1500s. (Not to be confused with the Moscow Kremlin—kremlins are fortified complexes containing administrative and religious buildings that are found in many Russian cities.) The buildings have been painted a gleaming white, and the skyline is made up of gold-topped bell towers and onion domes.

Like many other Siberian cities, Tobolsk's main historical claim to fame is as a stop on the road to exile. There's a statue commemorating Dostoevsky's sojourn, which would seem like a strange thing to celebrate if every other city didn't do the same. I'm also starting to realize the reason most Siberian cities can claim that famous exiles stopped in them is that there's really only one main road through Siberia.

Tobolsk, however, is so Siberian that it even has a bell that was exiled east. It does not explain who exiled a bell, or why it was exiled, but does give a sense of how little it took to get sent to Siberia.

The local history museum offers tours guided by historical reenactors in costume, which I'm dying to do, but I know the language barrier would prove tortuous for everyone. The museum also offers free entry for heroes of the Soviet Union. Victims of Chernobyl only get reduced entry.

The top floor is devoted to the brief period the Romanov family spent here as political prisoners, and there's a whole room about how much the final tsar and tsarina were in love. Russians are obsessed with the love story of their final monarchs—if Romanovs are mentioned, there's always a quote about how, even if they were murdered, they never lost their love! There's also a room with traditional costumes for the region's original inhabitants, the Tatars.

Outside people walk around in T-shirts and sun themselves on the lawn outside the Kremlin, where the last piles of snow are still melting.

Because there's nothing else to do, I spend the next few days walking around and thinking. When I leave Tobolsk, I'll also be leaving Siberia, and I decide to make a kind of Ural resolution, which is like a New Year's resolution, except one that you make when you're crossing the Ural Mountains instead of the timeshold of a new year. I decide I want to be more honest and less afraid of making myself vulnerable. I want to trust myself and my decisions. Would like, but not a necessity: to meet a smoking-hot boyfriend on the train. Also, I want to eat fewer carbs.

Fifth Leg: Tobolsk to Yekaterinburg (Eleven Hours, Fifty-Four Minutes)
Only twelve hours on a train almost feels like not enough time, until I meet my companions. They're three men: one kind, middle-aged Muslim Tatar, and two oil workers returning from the fields in Siberia. One of the oil workers is very drunk.

The oil workers spend a month in the field, and then return home for a month, alternating all year. The drunk man is carrying most of his wages on him. I know this, because first he shows them to me, and then tries to hand me thousands of rubles. He wears torn, dirty clothes, and he smells like he hasn't bathed recently.

"He drank too much," the Muslim Tatar tells me.

The drunk man is probably too incapacitated to be dangerous, but I'm still on alert. He's trying to speak to me; I don't understand.

"He's speaking Tatar," the Muslim man tells me gently.

The drunk man wanders off for a while, and I must look scared, because the Muslim Tatar looks up from his book and starts talking to me about hockey. He keeps talking to me, about how most Tatars, like the three men in this car, speak Tatar poorly—we're all Russians, he explains—until the drunk man returns, and he's inexplicably bought us all coffees.

"Go to sleep," the Muslim Tatar pleads softly.

I barely sleep that night; it's the first time on the whole trip I've felt really afraid.

In the morning, I can tell the drunk man is sober and extremely embarrassed—he doesn't make eye contact with any of us. He's a different person from the man who was yelling and breaking things the night before.

I'm surprised by how little everyone else reacted to him. No one yells at him, throws him off the train, or even raises a voice. It's hard to tell if people have written him off, or they just shrug and accept that some people can't handle their drink.

I'm so shaken by the whole thing that I have to stop and eat something. At the nearest cafe, I order a Caesar salad, mostly because it's listed on the menu as "Roman Emperor Salad."

Stopover: Yekaterinburg

Yekaterinburg is famous for being the site where the Romanov family was murdered, but I will forever remember it as the site of Roman's Airbnb.

I've rented a small but extremely reasonably priced apartment not far from the train station, and Roman calls to tell me, in shaky English, that his daughter, Olga, will let me in. She's giving me the grand tour, which is kind of self-explanatory, given that from the bed, you can reach out and touch the stove.

Olga has braces and a sharp outfit: she wears a red silk scarf, a studded Hermès belt, and nude stockings she keeps brushing like I'm getting dust on her. To be fair, I am very dusty.

Still, I'm really impressed with the apartment. There's a hotel-room level to detail: hair dryer, Q-tips, toothbrush. No other Airbnb I've stayed in in the former Soviet Union has been so meticulous. Whoever this Roman guy is, he knows what he's doing.

He also doesn't seem to be Olga's father, because when she calls him, she addresses him as "Roman." She's calling because she has just learned that I don't have a Russian passport, and she's fairly certain I can't stay here.

"What?!" I exclaim when she casually informs me I am no longer welcome.

"Wait," she says, holding up a finger. "I'll call Roman."

The problem is just that Olga doesn't know how to input my information into the form Roman had given her, which is purely for his records and set up for a Russian passport. Roman explains this to me and apologizes while Olga composes herself.

Back to business, she copies out the information on my passport and hands me the keys. "Any questions?" she asks.

"Do you have a favorite restaurant in Yekaterinburg?" I ask.

She pauses for a long time, and then replies honestly, "No."

Luckily, a friend from my Russian gym has tipped me off to a pie shop, where I plop down with a book and struggle to order a pre-lunch dessert. The problem is that I don't know the names of any of the fruits the pies are made from, and eventually I settle for just pointing.

My waitress, whose name tag says OLYA, is sweet: she asks me where I'm from, and I try to ask her about Yekaterinburg, but I've realized, while I've really nailed the conversations I have every day, I haven't really moved beyond them. I can buy train tickets, check into a hotel, order dinner, but I can't really ask someone about her life. I know how to explain that I'm a writer from America, but I

don't always understand the follow-up questions. Olya is beyond pa-
tient, but we don't make much progress.

It's frustrating, the ways in which I can almost predict how my
conversations will stall out each time. The other person will ask
what I do, and I'll explain, and then I'll say, "What do you do?" and
they'll use a word I don't know, so I'll have to say, "What's that?"
and they'll say, "You know, a smhemeh," and I'll say, "No, what's a
smhemeh?" and they'll say, "You know, when a person is sick and
they go to a premeheh," and I say, "Oh, like a nurse," and they'll say,
"No, a nurse is someone who does memehe or gives temehe. I'm a
person who does gamehe," and I'll say, "A doctor?" and they'll say,
"Oh, yes, *doctor* is another word for smhemeh."

At the table beside me, a group of older women are wearing paper
hats and reading a script. They've brought their own flowers to the
restaurant. I try to ask Olya about it, she tries to explain, and we
both seem to agree that the best option is for me to order more pie.

When I go to leave the pie shop, I stop to thank Olya for being so
kind, and I say I'm sorry that we couldn't communicate. "I speak
English"—I laugh—"but not really Russian."

"I speak Chinese," she replies, smiling, "but not Russian."

"WHAT??!?!?!" I exclaim in Chinese.

"You speak Chinese, too?!" she squeals.

We go back and explain everything we'd failed to convey the first
time. She tells me the women beside me were doing a play, and I
have to admit that I kind of like the mystery better, and she tells me
about where she's studying, and I fill her in on my trip.

It's an amazing feeling, to have struggled so hard to communicate, and then to figure out an even better work-around. I'm so excited I have to tell someone. I message my sister to ask if she can
talk, and by a miracle she can (it's eight a.m. her time), and I call
home from the Urals.

"Um, why are you talking so weirdly?" she asks when I've finished the story.

"I am?" I ask.

"Yeah," she says, "you're speaking sooo slowly, and you're like using all these weird phrases."

"Oh my God," I realize. "This is the first real conversation I've had in . . . days."

It's been so long since I've spoken to someone who speaks English fluently, I realize, that it's become more natural for me to pidgin my English so that it mimics Russian grammar, and the mistakes native Russian speakers would make. Rather than saying, "Olya worked in the restaurant," I might say, "Olya: woman who worked in restaurant."

I burst into tears. "But, Ang!" I exclaim. "What if I've permanently ruined my English?"

"Well," she says, "then I guess you'd have to stay in Russia."

The next morning, I'm awoken by a fierce knock on my door. I don't move. Did Roman's daughter, Olga, call the police because of my passport?

The knocking grows louder, and I reach for my phone and start Googling "American embassy, Yekaterinburg." The knocking finally subsides, and I lie in my bed, my heart still pounding. Then I hear someone outside my window. My curtains are drawn, and the lights are off, but now I'm terrified. I think back to a nightmare I had on one of the endless train rides, in which I'd been sentenced to a gulag, and my punishment was, somehow, to clean the bathrooms on the Trans-Siberian train cars.

Suddenly, Roman starts calling me. I don't pick up, and he texts me.

"Olga say you want restaurant," he says. "I send Dima."

Dima is the muscle behind Roman's Airbnb operation. Roman bought the basement of an apartment building, and Dima is renovating it into a suite of Airbnb units. Dima wears overalls covered in flecks of paint, and he chain-smokes as he leads me to the restaurant Roman sent him to show me, which is actually a grocery store.

It's not open yet, so we wait outside with a crowd of people that feels like a holdover from Soviet days of shortages. When the gates finally open, everyone rushes inside.

It's my last day in Yekaterinburg, so I set out to see the city's main museum, a kind of Russian version of a presidential library. It's dedicated to the nation's first leader, Boris Yeltsin. It heavily emphasizes Yeltsin's commitment to freedom.

"He cared so much about democracy," one placard reads, "that he thought long and hard about who to choose as his successor." At the end, there's an exhibition dedicated to freedom, where visitors can record messages of what freedom truly means to them, which I presume will be sent directly to the police.

The museum's main selling point is its sweeping view of the river that runs through Yekaterinburg. Across the water is a huge church that was erected on the spot where the Romanov family was murdered in a basement. The Romanovs have since been sainted, in a move that seems to emblemize so perfectly the complicated relationship Russia has to its history, how it picks and chooses the parts of the twentieth century to celebrate while glossing over the lessons that each could have taught.

I head back to the Airbnb, where Roman has told me to find Dima, and then they're all going to give me a ride to the train station.

I knock on Dima's door, and he invites me in. His clothes are still flecked with white paint, and I see that the room he sleeps in is dusty and piled with boxes. The air is heavy with cigarette smoke.

Dima is on the phone with his wife, whom he insists I say hello to.

"Hello," I say in Russian.

"Hello," she replies in English.

Dima shows me a picture of his son, a smiling, chubby toddler.

"So cute!" I exclaim.

"He's fourteen," Dima tells me. I guess it's an old picture. "I have five children," he continues.

"Five children?" I exclaim.

"It will be six," he tells me. "In July?" He checks with his wife. "Oh, in August," he corrects himself.

He shows me photos of his daughter, a smiling girl who looks like she's five or six. "And now she is sixteen?" He checks with his wife. "No, seventeen," he tells me.

This is a lot to process. I don't know what to make of it. There's so much unsaid in all of this, and I think of my own parents, and how they may have given me terrible advice, and how they drive me crazy, but how I can't picture my father having to call my mother to double-check how old I am.

Roman appears in the doorway. It's our first time meeting face-to-face. He's a polite, handsome guy in a suit who has kindly offered to drive me to the train station. Dima, it turns out, is just for muscle: he carries my suitcase to the trunk and then disappears inside.

"How did you meet Olga and Dima?" I ask Roman on the drive to the train station.

"Olga worked in a cafe."

Here, Olga jumps in. "I saw him," she says emphatically.

"Oh, Roman is your boyfriend?" I ask, surprised and not. I'm not surprised, because they both seem young and ambitious, but I am surprised, because when Roman called the first day, he told me Olga was his daughter, which I now realize was likely a word he mixed up with *girlfriend*.

"Yes, we're a couple," Roman says proudly.

He says a word in Russian, which, when we look it up in my dictionary, has three translations: chance, luck, and accident. "Luck is good," I explain in English. "Chance is . . . not bad, not good. Accident is bad."

"Then I meet Dima by luck," he tells me.

"Dima has six children!" I exclaim.

"Yes"—Roman shakes his head—"by two women." As though this is a shock to him. "Two women!"

Olga asks for clarification, and he repeats what he's said. "Olga hears with a machine," he explains, "and she reads lips."

Dima's procreational habits don't seem unusual for Russia, but I also get the sense that Roman will not be having six children, and when I leave, I offer to help them translate their Airbnb listings into English.

I board the final train of this trip, ready for luck, chance, or accident.

Final Leg: Yekaterinburg to Moscow (One Day, Three Hours, and Thirty-Four Minutes)

The final train ride runs through western Russia, and we pass the remains of hulking Soviet industrial projects. Sunlight filters through trees that turn into houses and back into forests. I fall asleep with one set of roommates and wake up with another, but there's become a predictable pattern and flow.

I stare out at the landscape that has become familiar and think about what this whole trip has been about. A person I realize I have to thank for it.

Maybe he was all three, Anton. Luck, chance and accident.

We're on an overnight flight to a tiny island in Vietnam. It's ten days before the end, but it doesn't feel like it. We have the row to ourselves, and he insists that I be the one to lie across it while he sleeps upright. At midnight, he shakes me awake. "It's my birthday."

On the island, nothing works—cell phones, Internet, roads—except our relationship, which becomes seamless. We ride bikes to a white sand beach and wade out into the water, where we take turns holding the other's body up so we can close our eyes and float. When we get hungry, we stop for mangos or bowls of noodles covered in spicy broth. "If it could just be us like this all the time, we wouldn't have to break up," Anton muses.

And he's right. It's the real world, where the past can't be changed and petty grievances can grow to fill the space left by distance, that has come between us.

One night we're walking along the beach and Anton pulls me toward a row of lounge chairs deserted for the evening. I sit down on the one next to him but he tugs me on to his. He does this sometimes, insist that we squeeze both of our bodies into things that were built for one—both of us sleeping on one twin bed instead of pushing two together. Waves crash onto the beach as we hold each other and stare up at the stars.

"If we could have just been friends, it would have been this pure, beautiful thing that lasted forever," he says. "We wouldn't have ruined everything."

Months earlier he has free tickets to a concert, and I take the train out for the weekend. The first moment I see him each week, I still marvel at the fact that the world could have produced such a beautiful person who fits me so perfectly, and that we found each other. I spend the days we're apart half in the real world, half eyeing the countdown clock in my head that ticks down the seconds until his fingers are wrapped around my arm. And maybe that's the problem. You can't live when you're busy loving someone so fully and without restraint.

The concert is perfect because when we're not fighting, everything with Anton is perfect. Although, if he were not there, I might notice that a nightclub with fog machines and a catwalk is an odd venue for a funk band. Toward the end, the lead singer says he wants to get someone onstage dancing with him, and suddenly he's tugging on my arm, pulling me up to the catwalk.

I know why he picked me—I've spent the night dancing the way the happy and deliriously in love can—but I shriek in protest. Although I'll stand on stage talking into a microphone for as long as people will have me, I can think of few things more mortifying than dancing onstage at a concert.

I look back at Anton for help, but he's laughing and he helps the singer pull me up. I look out at the crowd in panic, and then at Anton, and I watch his face mirror my own mere seconds ago as the lead singer grabs his arm and yanks him on-stage with me.

I look at Anton like, "Well, we're stuck in this now," and then he grins and I do too and we dance until the song's over.

Another time I'm biting my lip and fidgeting with my hair because the shower in my apartment has been leaking raw sewage and my landlord won't fix it. I've asked him to come over because I'm telling him that I want to break my lease and get all my money back. I've done a free consultation with a lawyer whose role in my life I'm planning on greatly exaggerating during this exchange. And Anton's here because he can always appeal to the humanity in people. Maybe because he always sees it.

The landlord wears blue suede shoes and smokes in the apartment. He finally agrees to what we're asking and sits down to sketch out a written agreement. My eyes meet Anton's above the landlord's head and Anton mouths, "I love you" just as I was about to do the same.

There was something rare in our connection, or in Anton, that I didn't recognize at the time, because I didn't think I'd ever not have it. I wish I'd told him that. Sometimes I pull up old e-mails, either as proof or penitence.

Like this one, which I revive as I catch sight of the switches that say we're pulling into the train yard in Moscow. He's telling me about a night he spent playing music with acquaintances. "And this couple played this song and the girl had her head on his shoulder and they both sang so beautifully. And it reminded me of you and us, and like we are exactly like that only in other things, you know, and it's just beautiful. Or just being together, you know, in a peaceful moment, just kinda having each other. I'm listening to the song right now."

A few days later. "Are you also getting this new way of looking at us, almost like, we should be together, like it doesn't make sense not to be together—it would be dumb not to be together—because we'd miss out on so much awesomeness? Do you get that feeling? And like it's scary 'cause maybe it's not good to be so attached because you get so vulnerable? But you want to be even more attached? Is that how you feel? That's how I feel."

The woman in my compartment is trying to get my attention. I look up from my phone and swipe my fingers under my eyes in a covert gesture I've perfected over the years.

"Audrey," she says, "I have something to tell you." We talked earlier about our jobs and lives and she told me about the sensations she has when we pass certain churches. "I have a strong sense about these things. And I feel that you are very . . . mystical."

I look back down at my screen. "I love you, Aud. I'm sorry we don't talk on the phone all the time. I think we're still great though."

OPEN MIC NIGHT IN MOSCOW

Moscow in summer is a different city from the one I saw last winter. The air is warm, and night is a brief blip between twenty-hour spans of daylight.

I'm awoken one morning by the soft chirping of birds and the sounds of my hostel roommate clamoring down our metal bed frame to use the bathroom. Sun filters in through gauzy curtains. *I'll just lie here for a few more minutes and then get up*, I think.

I lean over to check the time on my iPad: 3:54 a.m.

Good lord.

The city feels familiar. I revisit Red Square and the candy-colored St. Basil's Cathedral, this time with no jacket. I make it to places that were too cold to bother with in November: Gorky Park, which is helpful because one series of audiotapes I listened to taught me all about how to ask for directions, but only in relation to Gorky Park. For a few weeks, the only directions I understood were "to the left of Gorky Park," "to the right of Gorky Park," "near Gorky Park," and "very far from Gorky Park."

Inside Gorky Park is a contemporary art museum called Garage. It's extremely cutting-edge. The exhibit in the foyer is a live group of regular people stretching and massaging one another; a nearby placard identifies the work as *Untitled* and the materials as "objects," "the audience's attention," and "people passing by."

Yevgeniy tells me to meet him on the platform at the metro station where Stalin announced the start of the Second World War, and it's only when I get there that I realize I have no idea what he looks like.

Yevgeniy is a friend of a manager at my hostel; the manager put us in touch because we're both stand-ups. I've booked spots in all of the English-language shows in Moscow, while Yevgeniy is starting to break out in the Russian-language scene. I'm curious what Russian stand-up is like in Moscow, but mostly, I'm curious how Yevgeniy and I will recognize each other.

The former Soviet republics are the first places I've visited where I effortlessly blend in. This constantly catches me off guard: the surprised looks on people's faces when I open my mouth and they hear my accent, the strangers who address me in Russian, the way I can slip onto a subway car without arousing suspicion. No matter how good my spoken Chinese got, my red hair made me stick out like a sore thumb in Shanghai.

I scan the passengers disembarking from the train in both directions, looking for someone who is similarly searching for eye contact.

The station, like all on the Moscow metro, looks less like a public transportation depot and more like the lobby of a five-star hotel. The walls and floors are patterned marble; elegant art deco arches line the platform and form a vaulted ceiling. If you look up, you can see one of thirty-four ceiling mosaics that depict various Soviet skyscapes.

Stalin is once again to thank for this architectural flourish. He envisioned metro stations as "palaces of the people," and commuters in Moscow pass chandeliers, mosaics, painted ceilings, and statues.

A guy with short red hair walks toward me with a smile.

"Audrey?" he asks. Then he hugs me. I'm flustered: Russians don't smile, and they definitely don't hug.

Even stranger: Yevgeniy is wearing a Red Sox hat.

"I used to live in Brighton Beach," Yevgeniy tells me as we walk toward the venue where tonight's Russian-language open mic will be held. He enrolled in the work-travel program and then lived in New York and Canada.

"I miss America and Canada," he says. "Everyone is so nice, happy, friendly. Here . . ." He trails off.

Stand-up is still new in Russia, but it's growing. There's now a stand-up show on one of the biggest TV channels, and audiences are growing in the big cities. Yevgeniy tells me there are ten main comedians who run the show, which has the original name *Stand-Up*. He's trying to get on the show, and he will, a few weeks after I leave, but right now they're making him rewrite all his jokes. He's paying his dues.

The open mic is at a bar called Stalingrad, and it does not feel like an open mic.

"There are like, a hundred people here," I say.

"Yeah," Yevgeniy says. "They don't want too many people to come, because they'll do these sets again on TV."

I explain that, to me, one hundred people is an insanely huge audience for an open mic.

"They're very popular," Yevgeniy explains. "So many people know them from TV, so they just post on Instagram, 'open mic at Stalingrad tonight,' and all these people come."

This is something else I find funny: the comics make all of their announcements through Instagram. When I meet them, they ask how many Instagram followers I have. I try to explain that American comedians build followings on Twitter, because you can post jokes, but this logic does not compute.

The show is two hours long, and much of it goes over my head. Sometimes I can follow the setup, but not the punch line; other times I understand only the punch line, and therefore don't get why it's funny. I understand how my audience in Kazakhstan must have felt.

There are only two women on the show. One is the host, who does well. When the second woman comes on later, the laughter becomes softer and higher-pitched. It takes me a while to realize that it's because only the women are laughing.

But they're *really* laughing. The men, in contrast, sit stone-faced. One of her few jokes I could follow in its entirety goes like this:

"When you're younger, you think, *I want a guy who's handsome, rich, and intelligent*. When you're thirty-three and still single, you think, *I want a guy who can read. And eat food with a fork.*"

I ask Yevgeniy about this after. "Unfortunately, I think, for a lot of Russian men—and I was this way before I went to the U.S. and Canada—it's difficult to laugh at a woman."

"What about the host?" I ask.

Yevgeniy shakes his head. "She's been on TV for five years," he explains. "Everyone knows her."

Stand-up might be new to Russia, but comedy is not. Ex-Soviet universities all participate in something called KVN, which is a hybrid of sketch comedy and improv and functions as more or less the cultural equivalent of American college football. KVN is *huge* in the former USSR. University teams sell out theaters, and the best go on to TV deals after college.

Bizarrely, much of the English-language stand-up available in Russian is dubbed, not subtitled. The Russian comics show me this the next day—hanging out with them again thanks to Yevgeniy. They pull up a Hannibal Buress special, and it's a video of Hannibal Buress, with what sounds like a Russian movie announcer delivering translations of his jokes. The timing is all off; sometimes, Russian-voice-over Hannibal is still speaking after actual Hannibal has hit his punch line and the audience is laughing.

"It's so bad!" they tell me, and I agree, but it's also funny. Just not in the way that it was intended to be.

I ask them about their favorite act from last night, and it's nearly unanimous: the final performer. I didn't understand much of his set, but he got one of the most tepid responses from the crowd.

"No, no," one tells me. "It's not that. Everyone liked him because he really makes you think."

The next night, I'm bored and wander to a nearby bar for a drink, which is promptly ruined by a drunk man who keeps trying to hug me. A German guy steps in to help, and I end up chatting with his colleagues, one of whom is a Muscovite named Alex who speaks perfect English. We never manage to fully shake the drunk man, and when everyone goes outside to smoke, he starts punching the German. I freak out, but Alex reassures me.

"No, no, they're not fighting," he explains. "They're just making friends."

Alex is unfailingly polite. He wears a tucked-in button-down shirt and initially speaks to me only in French. He and the German work for a European electronics company. The German has been visiting Moscow for work but has an early flight home tomorrow. After he leaves, the drunk man is still hovering; Alex has been pretending not to know Russian in order to get rid of him.

"I. Am. Moscow," the drunk guy is saying.

"Ah, okay, yes," Alex replies, and then, under his breath, he asks me, "Do you have your things near?"

"Yes," I whisper.

"MOOOOOS. COOOOW," the drunk man yells.

"Yes, it is a wonderful city," Alex says, and then to me, "Good. Have you paid for your beer?"

I nod.

"Good."

"I. HOCKEY!" the drunk guy shouts.

"Truly a wonderful sport," Alex agrees. To me, "Do you have everything?"

"My phone is charging at the bar," I whisper.

"Go get it."

I feel like I'm in some sort of KGB operation. I return and find Alex inspecting the drunk man's scars.

"Oh, wow, yes, that looks very painful." To me: "This is about to be a fight." To the drunk man: "Ah, okay, did someone hit you very hard?"

"HOCKEY!" the drunk man screams.

"Now you have everything?" Alex whispers.

I nod.

"That is your jacket?"

Nod.

"Good, put it on."

"YOU LOVE RUSSIA. HOCKEY?" the drunk man wants to know.

"I'm afraid I have never seen such things," Alex replies patiently. "But perhaps I will love it if I have the chance." Alex leans over. "When I give the signal, you will be ready to leave?"

I nod.

"You know, I think my friend and I would love to watch a Russian hockey game with you," Alex continues, so smoothly and full of charm that I'm worried he might actually be ex-KGB, except he's my age, and the KGB dissolved when we were four.

"*Ne ponimayu*," the drunk man slurs.

"I'm terribly sorry," Alex says, "but I'm afraid we do not speak Russian." He laughs, and I take his cue and join him. Alex leans in. "Now."

I freeze. I feel like I'm missing a lot of spy training.

Alex sees this and doesn't miss a beat. "Pretend to go have a cigarette. I will join you."

Alex spends the next few days showing me around Moscow. We visit museums, go for walks. One night, we take a taxi to Moscow State University, which sits on top of a huge hill overlooking the city. It's two a.m., but the hillside is packed with people hanging out in their cars, drinking beers, and cooking on portable grills. Alex checks his watch. "Soon it will be sunrise!" he announces.

I invite him to my biggest stand-up show, which takes place at a bar called Lucky Jack's. I'm surprised that most of the performers are Russians who prefer performing in English. There's a dedicated DJ to play stingers between acts. He sits onstage for the entire show, facing the audience and never laughing.

This time, I don't have to start off by asking if everyone knows what comedy is, because four other people have done it before me.

There's no meditative drum circle waiting to go on. There's also no bongo player, which I find myself missing. The crowd responds to each joke, and also each segue and throwaway comment, with long, reasoned reactions. Though this is actually a legitimate stand-up show, it feels more like Socratic dialogues. We get slightly side-tracked by a discussion on LGBT rights. It's so easy to imagine Russia as a country where everyone buys into homophobic propaganda and to forget that whenever you place people in urban environments, they tend to think more liberally and progressively.

Afterward, Alex and I celebrate in a bar that is trying to be a nightclub.

"You know," Alex shouts over the aggressively loud music, "I was so shocked, because the first night, we exchanged numbers, and then, the next, you texted *me*."

"Yeah," I say. "I wanted to invite you to the museum."

He shakes his head. "In Russia, a woman will never text first."

I wake up the next morning with a sense of completeness. It's difficult to place. This trip has been filled with milestones and mini-endings. Leaving Central Asia; arriving in Russia; finishing the Trans-Siberian. Why is this any different?

Outside, it's warm, and I walk to a nearby art museum with an outdoor Georgian restaurant.

It hits me that maybe what I'm feeling is a sense of having come, seen, and comedied. Everything I've done in the former Soviet Union has seemed as inconsequential and simple as putting one foot in front of the other, but I realize that someone who would not see it that way is me, three years ago.

The version of me that thought breaking up with Anton meant I would never learn to count to ten in Russian and only ever stop in Moscow on the way to somewhere else. Or twenty-year-old Audrey who thought Prague was the most exotic place she'd ever been and that languages were things you were forced to learn in school and comedy was something you watched on TV. She would never have believed that one day she'd perform stand-up in Russia.

The strangest part is, I had seen so much of this trip as choosing between two diverging paths: one that circled around New York, and another that left and never came back. But even though I felt like I'd signed up for the latter, I now see that isn't true. I have my story. I can go back with it. And then it will continue.

I think back to my pre-Trans-Siberian hangover in a Beijing McDonald's, and how I worried that this Soviet thing wasn't kick-starting the solving of my problems. But it was. I had just forgotten the definition of kick-starting something is to start it, not finish.

ACKNOWLEDGMENTS

First of all, thank you, dear reader, for reading this book all the way through, and then sticking around for the acknowledgments section. This was a long book to get through, and you could have been on Instagram. From the bottom of my heart, I appreciate your time, attention, and (in advance) nomination for a MacArthur Genius Grant.

Though I'm not the first person to say this, the fantastic Stephanie Delman is an agent extraordinaire and a maker of dreams come true. She was instrumental in conceiving this book and encouraging me to follow my voice, and she has supported me in so many ways for so many years. (I hereby officially bestow upon her the world record for most Greenpoint Comedy Night attendances.) I am so, so grateful for everything she did and does.

I will forever be indebted to my brilliant editor Emma Brodie, who took a lot of unbridled passion for the former Soviet Union and shaped it into a narrative. This book would not have been possible without her generous guidance, patience, kindness, and vision, and throughout this process, she has been a snake charmer coaxing out the best that I'm capable of. Thank you for pushing me to take risks that created a book I'm so proud of and helping me do something I wasn't sure I could.

Thank you to my wonderfully talented team at William Morrow: Liate Stehlik, Lynn Grady, Cassie Jones, Susan Kosko, Leah Carlson-Stanisic, Jeanne Reina, Serena Wang, Lauren Lauzon, and Kaitlyn Kennedy.

I'm grateful to friends who read early draft chapters: Allison

Khederian, Christie Volden, Clare Richardson, Danny Kaplan, DTF, Gus Tate, Jamie Blume, Joe Schaefer, Kristen Van Nest, Lizzy Hussey, Melissa Brzycki, Mike Zaccardo, Reyhaneh Rajabzadeh, Sophie Friedman, Tom Caya, and Topher Brantley. I'm also thankful for two friends who did not read draft chapters, but who have always been there: Alex Folkenflik and Michael Tanenbaum. A huge je t'aime to Laura Gordon, who read whatever I sent her approximately 30 seconds after I hit send and provided so much feedback and encouragement.

This trip would not have been possible without Vicky Zhang, who asked me to come back to China, and whose passion and determination I miss dearly. Thank you to everyone who helped me plan my trip, gave me information, put me in touch with friends, and provided encouragement when I was brooding over my sixth straight meal of instant oatmeal on a train. A special thank you to Sarah Reeve, who provided invaluable information on Central Asia.

I met countless wonderful, generous, inspiring people on this trip—too many to name, and some of whose names I never learned. They provided much-needed company, illegal visa application translations, rides, yurts, and friendship, and they taught me so much and helped me grow as a person. Thank you.

Thank you to Mom, Dad, Andrew, Aunt Pat, and the rest of my family, who also read drafts, fielded many a late-night phone call, and kept me alive by doing things like helping me decide what kind of takeout to order. Angela probably read this entire book at least seven times and caught approximately twelve billion typos, and I'm so lucky she is my sister.

Finally, thank you Oleg Shik, the source of my love for the former Soviet Union, and the best thing it ever created.